CONTENTS ✔ KT-225-034

Fodor's 98

Arizona

The complete guide, thoroughly up-to-date

Packed with details that will make your trip

The must-see sights, off and on the beaten path

What to see, what to skip

Vacation itineraries, walking tours, day trips

Smart lodging and dining options

Essential local do's and taboos

Transportation tips

Key contacts, savvy travel advice

When to go, what to pack

Clear, accurate, easy-to-use maps

Books to read, videos to watch, background essays

Fodor's Travel Publications, Inc.
New York • Toronto • London • Sydney • Auckland
www.fodors.com/

Fodor's Arizona

EDITOR: Rebecca Miller

Editorial Contributors: Robert Andrews, Jenner Bishop, David Brown, Mark Hein, Edie Jarolim, Daniel Mangin, Gregory McNamee, Heidi Sarna, Helayne Schiff, M. T. Schwartzman (Gold Guide editor), Howard Seftel, Dinah A. Spritzer.

Editorial Production: Stacey Kulig

Maps: David Lindroth Inc., Mapping Specialists, *cartographers*; Robert Blake, *map editor*

Design: Fabrizio La Rocca, *creative director*; Guido Caroti, *associate art director*; Jolie Novak, *photo editor*

Production/Manufacturing: Mike Costa

Cover Photograph: Rob Boudreau/TSW

Copyright

Special Sales

ON THE ROAD WITH FODOR'S

WE'RE ALWAYS THRILLED to get letters from readers, especially one like this:

It took us an hour to decide what book to buy and we now know we picked the best one. Your book was wonderful, easy to follow, very accurate, and good on pointing out eating places, informal as well as formal. When we saw other people using your book, we would look at each other and smile.

Our editors and writers are deeply committed to making every Fodor's guide "the best one"—not only accurate but always charming, brimming with sound recommendations and solid ideas, right on the mark in describing restaurants and hotels, and full of fascinating facts that make you view what you've traveled to see in a rich new light.

About Our Writers

Jenner Bishop is an L.A.–based freelance writer whose months in Phoenix have convinced her that Arizona may be her spiritual home. This year she has written a brand-new chapter, "Eastern Arizona," on areas east of Phoenix including the White Mountains, Petrified Forest National Park, and the Painted Desert. Jenner has written for several publications including *Fodor's Great American Vacations*.

Edie Jarolim, who wrote the "North-Central Arizona," "Tucson," and "Southern Arizona" chapters, abandoned her senior editor's desk at Fodor's in 1992 to settle among the saguaros in Tucson. Her articles about Arizona have appeared in *Arizona Highways, Bride's,* and *The Wall Street Journal*.

Restaurant critic **Howard Seftel** has added an entirely new Phoenix dining section to this edition; not only is the section larger, but the coverage wider, from Mexican taquerias to eclectic international bistros. Howard is popular in Phoenix for his weekly restaurant column in the *New Times*.

New This Year

This year, Fodor's joins Rand McNally, the world's largest commercial mapmaker, to bring you a detailed color map of Arizona. Just detach it along the perforation and drop it in your tote bag.

We're also proud to announce that the American Society of Travel Agents has endorsed Fodor's as its guidebook of choice. ASTA is the world's largest and most influential travel trade association, operating in more than 170 countries, with 27,000 members pledged to adhere to a strict code of ethics reflecting the Society's motto, "Integrity in Travel." ASTA shares Fodor's devotion to providing smart, honest travel information and advice to travelers, and we've long recommended that our readers consult ASTA member agents for the experience and professionalism they bring to the table.

On the Web, check out Fodor's site (www.fodors.com/) for information on major destinations around the world and travel-savvy interactive features. The Web site also lists the 85-plus stations nationwide that carry the Fodor's Travel Show, a live call-in program that airs every weekend. Tune in to hear guests discuss their adventures—or call in to get answers for your most pressing travel questions.

How to Use This Book

Organization

Up front is the Gold Guide, an easy-to-use section divided alphabetically by topic. Under each listing you'll find tips and information that will help you accomplish what you need to in Arizona. You'll also find addresses and telephone numbers of organizations and companies that offer destination-related services.

The first chapter in the guide, Destination: Arizona, helps get you in the mood for your trip. What's Where gets you oriented, New and Noteworthy cues you in on trends and happenings, Pleasures and Pastimes describes the activities and sights that really make Arizona unique, Fodor's Choice showcases our top picks, and Festivals and Seasonal Events alerts you to special events.

Chapters in *Arizona '98* are arranged geographically, from north to south. Each city chapter begins with an Exploring section subdivided by neighborhood; each subsection recommends a walking or driving tour and lists sights in alphabetical order. Each regional chapter is divided by geographical area; within each area, towns are covered in logical geographical order, and attractive stretches of road and minor points of interest between them are indicated by the designation *En Route*. Throughout, Off the Beaten Path sights appear after the places from which they are most easily accessible. And within town sections, all restaurants and lodgings are grouped together.

To help you decide what to visit in the time you have, all chapters begin with recommended itineraries. The A-to-Z section that ends all chapters covers getting there and getting around. It also provides helpful contacts and resources.

At the end of the book you'll find Portraits, wonderful essays about Native American history and desert geography, followed by suggestions for recommended reading and movies on tape with Arizona as a backdrop.

Icons and Symbols

★ Our special recommendations
✕ Restaurant
🏠 Lodging establishment
✕🏠 Lodging establishment whose restaurant warrants a special trip
⚠ Campgrounds
☺ Good for kids (rubber duckie)
☞ Sends you to another section of the guide for more information
✉ Address
☎ Telephone number
☉ Opening and closing times
💰 Admission prices (those we give apply to adults; substantially reduced fees are almost always available for children, students, and senior citizens)

Numbers in white and black circles that appear on the maps, in the margins, and within the tours correspond to one another.

Dining and Lodging

The restaurants and lodgings we list are the best in each price range. Price charts appear in the Pleasures and Pastimes section that follows each chapter introduction.

Hotel Facilities

We always list the facilities that are available—but we don't specify whether they cost extra: When pricing accommodations, always ask what's included. In addition, assume that all rooms have private baths unless otherwise noted.

Restaurant Reservations and Dress Codes

Reservations are always a good idea; we note only when they're essential or when they are not accepted. Book as far ahead as you can, and reconfirm when you get to town. Unless otherwise noted, the restaurants listed are open daily for lunch and dinner. We mention dress only when men are required to wear a jacket and tie.

Credit Cards

The following abbreviations are used: **AE**, American Express; **D**, Discover; **DC**, Diners Club; **MC**, MasterCard; and **V**, Visa.

Don't Forget to Write

You can use this book in the confidence that all prices and opening times are based on information supplied to us at press time; Fodor's cannot accept responsibility for any errors. Time inevitably brings changes, so always confirm information when it matters—especially if you're making a detour to visit a specific place. In addition, when making reservations be sure to mention if you have a disability or are traveling with children, if you prefer a private bath or a certain type of bed, or if you have specific dietary needs or other concerns.

Were the restaurants we recommended as described? Did our hotel picks exceed your expectations? Did you find a museum we recommended a waste of time? If you have complaints, we'll look into them and revise our entries when the facts warrant it. If you've discovered a special place that we haven't included, we'll pass the information along to our correspondents and have them check it out. So send us your feedback, positive *and* negative: e-mail us at editors @ fodors.com (specifying the name of the book on the subject line) or write the Arizona editor at Fodor's, 201 East 50th Street, New York, NY 10022. Have a wonderful trip!

Karen Cure
Editorial Director

The Western United States

Arizona

NEW MEXICO

UTAH

NEVADA

CALIFORNIA

Gallup

St. Johns

Sanders

Round Rock

Mexican Water

Canyon de Chelly National Monument

Window Rock

Greasewood

Concho

Show Low

Petrified Forest National Park

Chinle

Many Farms

160

191

191

191

40

666

60

77

Monument Valley

NAVAJO INDIAN RESERVATION

Dilkon

Holbrook

Heber

Kayenta

Polacca

Hotevilla

HOPI INDIAN RESERVATION

Winslow

Forest Lakes

Lake Powell

Page

Cow Springs

Little Colorado River

87

Caconino National Forest

Payson

Tuba City

Cameron

Strawberry

160

40

Flagstaff

89

Sedona

89

Camp Verde

Cordes

Jacob Lake

Grand Canyon National Park

Kaibab National Forest

17

180

Williams

Clarkdale

Prescott

89

Fredonia

Grand Canyon Village

Valle

Jerome

Ash Fork

89A

Colorado River

Seligman

Prescott National Forest

15

66

93

Littlefield

Grand Canyon National Park

HUALAPAI INDIAN RESERVATION

40

Meadview

Kingman

Bill Williams River

Temple Bar

Lake Mead

Lake Havasu City

93

Bullhead City

Lake Mohave

Needles

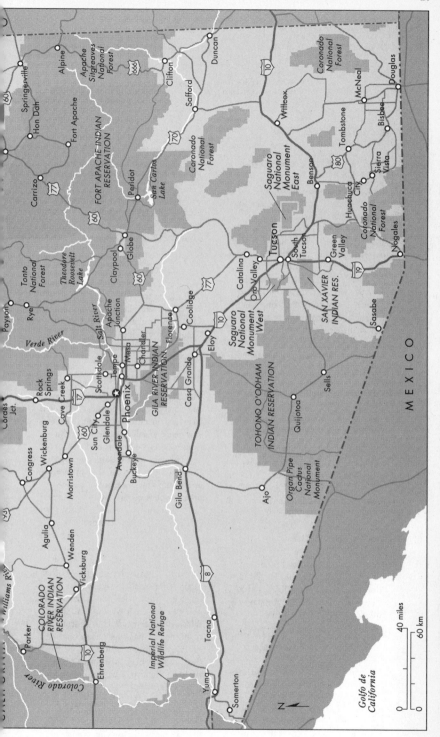

SMART TRAVEL TIPS A TO Z

Basic Information on Traveling in Arizona, Savvy Tips to Make Your Trip a Breeze, and Companies and Organizations to Contact

A

AIR TRAVEL

MAJOR AIRLINE OR LOW-COST CARRIER?

Most people choose a flight based on price. Yet there are other issues to consider. Major airlines offer the greatest number of departures; smaller airlines—including regional, low-cost and no-frill carriers—usually have a more limited number of flights daily. Major airlines have frequent-flyer partners, which allow you to credit mileage earned on one airline to your account with another. Low-cost airlines offer a definite price advantage and fewer restrictions, such as advance-purchase requirements. Safety-wise, low-cost carriers as a group have a good history, but **check the safety record before booking** any low-cost carrier; call the Federal Aviation Administration's Consumer Hotline (☞ Airline Complaints, *below*).

➤ MAJOR AIRLINES: **American** (☎ 800/433–7300) to Phoenix, Tucson. **America West** (☎ 800/235–9292) to Phoenix, Tucson. **Alaska Airlines** (☎ 800/426–0333) to Phoenix. **Continental** (☎ 800/525–0280) to Phoenix, Tucson. **Delta** (☎ 800/221–1212) to Phoenix, Tucson. **Northwest** (☎ 800/225–2525) to Phoenix, Tucson. **TWA** (☎ 800/221–2000) to Phoenix. **United** (☎ 800/241–6522) to Phoenix, Tucson. **US Airways** (☎ 800/428–4322) to Phoenix.

➤ SMALLER AIRLINES: **Aero California** (☎ 800/237–6225) to Tucson. **America Trans Air** (☎ 800/225–2995) to Phoenix. **Frontier Airlines** (☎ 800/432–1359) to Phoenix. **Great Lakes Airlines** (☎ 800/274–0662) to Phoenix, Tucson. **Midwest Express** (☎ 800/452–2022) to Phoenix. **Reno Air** (☎ 800/736–6247) to Tucson. **Southwest** (☎ 800/435–9792) to Phoenix, Tucson. **Western Pacific** (☎ 800/930–3030) to Phoenix.

➤ FROM THE U.K.: **Delta** (☎ 0800/414–767) flies from London's Gatwick Airport to Phoenix via Atlanta or Cincinnati. **Continental Airlines** (☎ 0800/776–464 or 01293/776–464) from Gatwick to Houston and from Manchester via Newark. **American Airlines** (☎ 0345/789–789) from Heathrow via Chicago or from Gatwick via Dallas.

➤ WITHIN ARIZONA: Within the state, **America West Express/Mesa** (☎ 800/235–9292) operates regularly scheduled flights from Phoenix to Flagstaff, Prescott, Lake Havasu, Laughlin, Kingman, Sierra Vista, and Yuma. **Great Lakes Aviation** (☎ 800/274–0662) flies from Phoenix to Show Low and Page.

GET THE LOWEST FARE

The least-expensive airfares to Arizona are priced for round-trip travel. Major airlines usually require that you **book in advance and buy the ticket within 24 hours,** and you may have to **stay over a Saturday night.** It's smart to **call a number of airlines, and when you are quoted a good price, book it on the spot**—the same fare may not be available on the same flight the next day. Airlines generally allow you to change your return date for a fee of $25–$50. If you don't use your ticket you can apply the cost toward the purchase of a new ticket, again for a small charge. However, most low-fare tickets are nonrefundable. To get the lowest airfare, **check different routings.** If your destination or home city has more than one gateway, compare prices to and from different airports. Also price off-peak flights, which may be significantly less expensive.

DON'T STOP UNLESS YOU MUST

When you book, **look for nonstop flights** and **remember that "direct" flights stop at least once.** Try to **avoid connecting flights,** which require a change of plane. Two airlines may jointly operate a connecting flight, so ask if your airline operates every segment—you may find that your preferred carrier flies you only part of the way.

USE AN AGENT

Travel agents and ticketing services, especially those who specialize in finding the lowest fares (☞ Discounts & Deals, *below*), can be especially helpful when booking a plane ticket. When you're quoted a price, **ask your agent if the price is likely to get any lower.** Good agents know the seasonal fluctuations of airfares and can usually anticipate a sale or fare war. However, waiting can be risky: The fare could go *up* as seats become scarce, and you may wait so long that your preferred flight sells out. A wait-and-see strategy works best if your plans are flexible, but if you must arrive and depart on certain dates, don't delay.

AVOID GETTING BUMPED

Airlines routinely overbook planes, knowing that not everyone with a ticket will show up, but sometimes everyone does. When that happens, airlines ask for volunteers to give up their seats. In return these volunteers usually get a certificate for a free flight and are rebooked on the next flight out. If there are not enough volunteers the airline must choose who will be denied boarding. The first to get bumped are passengers who checked in late and those flying on discounted tickets, **so get to the gate and check in as early as possible,** especially during peak periods.

Always **bring a photo ID to the airport.** You may be asked to show it before you are allowed to check in.

ENJOY THE FLIGHT

For better service, **fly smaller or regional carriers,** which often have higher passenger-satisfaction ratings. Sometimes you'll find leather seats, more legroom, and better food.

For more legroom, **request an emergency-aisle seat;** don't however, sit in the row in front of the emergency aisle or in front of a bulkhead, where seats may not recline.

If you don't like airline food, **ask for special meals when booking.** These can be vegetarian, low-cholesterol, or kosher, for example.

COMPLAIN IF NECESSARY

If your baggage goes astray or your flight goes awry, complain right away. Most carriers require that you file a claim immediately.

➤ AIRLINE COMPLAINTS: U.S. Department of Transportation **Aviation Consumer Protection Division** (✉ C–75, Washington, DC 20590, ☎ 202/366–2220). **Federal Aviation Administration (FAA) Consumer Hotline** (☎ 800/322–7873).

AIRPORTS

Major gateways to Arizona include **Phoenix Sky Harbor International,** about 3 mi east of Phoenix city center, and **Tucson International Air Terminal,** about 8½ mi south of the central business area. Flying time is 5½ hours from New York, 3½ hours from Chicago, and 1¼ hours from Los Angeles.

➤ AIRPORT INFORMATION: **Phoenix Sky Harbor International** (☎ 602/273–3300). **Tucson International Air Terminal** (☎ 520/573–8000).

B

BUS TRAVEL

Greyhound (☎ 800/231–2222) provides service to many Arizona destinations from most parts of the United States.

C

CAMERAS, CAMCORDERS, & COMPUTERS

Always **keep your film, tape, or computer disks out of the sun.** Carry an extra supply of batteries, and **be prepared to turn on your camera, camcorder, or laptop** to prove to security personnel that the device is real. Always **ask for hand inspection of film,** which becomes clouded after successive exposure to airport X-ray machines, and **keep videotapes and computer disks away from metal detectors.**

➤ PHOTO HELP: **Kodak Information Center** (☎ 800/242–2424). *Kodak Guide to Shooting Great Travel Pictures,* available in bookstores or from Fodor's Travel Publications (☎ 800/533–6478; $16.50 plus $4 shipping).

CAR RENTAL

Rates in Phoenix begin at $34 a day and $140 a week for an economy car with air-conditioning, an automatic transmission, and unlimited mileage. This does not include tax on car rentals, which is 9.5%.

➤ MAJOR AGENCIES: **Alamo** (☎ 800/327–9633, 0800/272–2000 in the U.K.). **Avis** (☎ 800/331–1212, 800/879–2847 in Canada). **Budget** (☎ 800/527–0700, 0800/181181 in the U.K.). **Dollar** (☎ 800/800–4000; 0990/565656 in the U.K., where it is known as Eurodollar). **Hertz** (☎ 800/654–3131, 800/263–0600 in Canada, 0345/555888 in the U.K.). **National InterRent** (☎ 800/227–7368; 0345/222525 in the U.K., where it is known as Europcar Inter-Rent).

CUT COSTS

To get the best deal, **book through a travel agent who is willing to shop around.** When pricing cars, **ask about the location of the rental lot.** Some off-airport locations offer lower rates, and their lots are only minutes from the terminal via complimentary shuttle. You also may want to **price local car-rental companies,** whose rates may be lower still, although their service and maintenance may not be as good as those of a name-brand agency. Remember to ask about required deposits, cancellation penalties, and drop-off charges if you're planning to pick up the car in one city and leave it in another.

Also **ask your travel agent about a company's customer-service record.** How has it responded to late plane arrivals and vehicle mishaps? Are there often lines at the rental counter, and, if you're traveling during a holiday period, does a confirmed reservation guarantee you a car?

NEED INSURANCE?

When driving a rented car you are generally responsible for any damage to or loss of the vehicle. You also are liable for any property damage or personal injury that you may cause while driving. Before you rent, **see what coverage you already have** under the terms of your personal auto-insurance policy and credit cards.

For about $14 a day, rental companies sell protection, known as a collision- or loss-damage waiver (CDW or LDW) that eliminates your liability for damage to the car; it's always optional and should never be automatically added to your bill.

In Arizona, the car-rental company must pay for damage to third parties up to a preset legal limit. Once that limit is reached your personal auto or other liability insurance kicks in. However, **make sure you have enough coverage to pay for the car.** If you do not have auto insurance or an umbrella policy that covers damage to third parties, purchasing CDW or LDW is highly recommended.

BEWARE SURCHARGES

Before you pick up a car in one city and leave it in another, **ask about drop-off charges or one-way service fees,** which can be substantial. Note, too, that some rental agencies charge extra if you return the car before the time specified on your contract. To avoid a hefty refueling fee, **fill the tank just before you turn in the car,** but be aware that gas stations near the rental outlet may overcharge.

MEET THE REQUIREMENTS

In the United States you must be 21 to rent a car, and rates may be higher if you're under 25. You'll pay extra for child seats (about $3 per day), which are compulsory for children under five, and for additional drivers (about $2 per day). Residents of the U.K. will need a reservation voucher, a passport, a U.K. driver's license, and a travel policy that covers each driver in order to pick up a car.

CHILDREN & TRAVEL

CHILDREN IN ARIZONA

Many large resorts and dude ranches have special activities for children, and many offer baby-sitting services. Children of all ages are enthralled by the Wild West flavor around Tucson and the southeastern part of the state, with Tombstone ranking as a particular favorite. If you're driving on long desert stretches, take along plenty of games and snacks.

Be sure to plan ahead and **involve your youngsters** as you outline your trip. When packing, include things to keep them busy en route. On sightseeing days try to schedule activities of special interest to your children. If you are renting a car don't forget to **arrange for a car seat** when you reserve.

➤ LOCAL INFORMATION: The monthly magazine **Raising Arizona Kids** focuses on Phoenix happenings, but also includes a calendar of children-friendly events around the state. You can buy single copies for $1.95 each at Borders, L'il Things, and Smith stores in Tucson and Phoenix, or send $24.95 for a year's subscription (✉ 2445 E. Shea Blvd., Suite 201, Phoenix 85028, ☎ 602/953–KIDS or in Arizona 888/RAISING, FAX 602/953–3305).

FLYING

As a general rule, infants under two not occupying a seat fly free. If your children are two or older **ask about children's airfares.** In general the adult baggage allowance applies to children paying half or more of the adult fare.

According to the FAA it's a good idea to use safety seats aloft for children weighing less than 40 pounds. Airlines, however, can set their own policies: U.S. carriers allow FAA-approved models but usually require that you buy a ticket, even if your child would otherwise ride free, since the seats must be strapped into regular seats. Airline rules vary regarding their use, so it's important to **check your airline's policy about using safety seats during takeoff and landing.** Safety seats cannot obstruct any of the other passengers in the row, so get an appropriate seat assignment as early as possible.

When making your reservation, **request children's meals or a free-standing bassinet** if you need them; the latter are available only to those seated at the bulkhead, where there's enough legroom. Remember, however, that bulkhead seats may not have their own overhead bins, and there's no storage space in front of you—a major inconvenience.

FAMILY GROUP TRAVEL

If you're planning to take your kids on a tour, look for companies that specialize in family travel.

➤ FAMILY-FRIENDLY TOUR OPERATORS: **Grandtravel** (✉ 6900 Wisconsin Ave., Suite 706, Chevy Chase, MD 20815, ☎ 301/986–0790 or 800/247–7651), for people traveling with grandchildren ages 7–17. **Families Welcome!** (✉ 92 N. Main St., Ashland, OR 97520, ☎ 541/482–6121 or 800/326–0724, FAX 541/482–0660). **Rascals in Paradise** (✉ 650 5th St., Suite 505, San Francisco, CA 94107, ☎ 415/978–9800 or 800/872–7225, FAX 415/442–0289).

LODGING

All **Holiday Inns** allow children under age 19 to stay free when sharing a room with an adult. **Westin La Paloma Hotel** in Tucson has supervised activities year-round for children ages 6 months–12 years, as well as junior tennis camps for kids 5–14 years old in summer. From Thanksgiving through April, the **Tanque Verde Guest Ranch**, also in Tucson, offers activities for children 4–11. In the Phoenix area, the **Pointe Hilton Resort at Squaw Peak** runs its Coyote Camp for children ages 4–12 year-round. The **Phoenician Resort** in Scottsdale has junior golf and tennis clinics for kids 5–14 throughout the year; Scottsdale's **Hyatt Regency** also offers a full range of supervised daytime activities geared for kids 3–12. All of the above resorts also have baby-sitting services.

➤ HOTEL RESERVATIONS: **Holiday Inns** (☎ 800/465–4329). **Westin La Paloma Hotel** (☎ 800/228–3000). **Tanque Verde Guest Ranch** (☎ 800/234–3833). **Pointe Hilton Resort at Squaw Peak** (☎ 800/934–1000). **Phoenician Resort** (☎ 800/888–8234). **Hyatt Regency** (☎ 800/233–1234).

CONSUMER PROTECTION

Whenever possible, **pay with a major credit card** so you can cancel payment if there's a problem, provided that you can provide documentation. This is a good practice whether you're buying travel arrangements before your trip or shopping at your destination.

If you're doing business with a particular company for the first time, **contact your local Better Business Bureau and the attorney general's offices** in your state and the company's home state, as well. Have any complaints been filed?

Finally, if you're buying a package or tour, always **consider travel insurance** that includes default coverage (☞ Insurance, *below*).

➤ LOCAL BBBs: **Council of Better Business Bureaus** (⊠ 4200 Wilson Blvd., Suite 800, Arlington, VA 22203, ☎ 703/276–0100, FAX 703/525–8277).

CUSTOMS & DUTIES

ENTERING THE U.S.

Visitors age 21 and over may import the following into the United States: 200 cigarettes or 50 cigars or 2 kilograms of tobacco, 1 liter of alcohol, and gifts worth $100. Prohibited items include meat products, seeds, plants, and fruits.

ENTERING CANADA

If you've been out of Canada for at least seven days you may bring in C$500 worth of goods duty-free. If you've been away for fewer than seven days but more than 48 hours, the duty-free allowance drops to C$200; if your trip lasts 24–48 hours, the allowance is C$50. You may not pool allowances with family members. Goods claimed under the C$500 exemption may follow you by mail; those claimed under the lesser exemptions must accompany you.

Alcohol and tobacco products may be included in the seven-day and 48-hour exemptions but not in the 24-hour exemption. If you meet the age requirements of the province or territory through which you reenter Canada you may bring in, duty-free, 1.14 liters (40 imperial ounces) of wine or liquor *or* 24 12-ounce cans or bottles of beer or ale. If you are 16 or older you may bring in, duty-free, 200 cigarettes and 50 cigars; these items must accompany you.

You may send an unlimited number of gifts worth up to C$60 each duty-free to Canada. Label the package UNSOLICITED GIFT—VALUE UNDER $60. Alcohol and tobacco are excluded.

➤ INFORMATION: **Revenue Canada** (⊠ 2265 St. Laurent Blvd. S, Ottawa, Ontario K1G 4K3, ☎ 613/993–0534, 800/461–9999 in Canada).

ENTERING THE U.K.

From countries outside the EU, including the United States, you may import, duty-free, 200 cigarettes or 50 cigars; 1 liter of spirits or 2 liters of fortified or sparkling wine or liqueurs; 2 liters of still table wine; 60 milliliters of perfume; 250 milliliters of toilet water; plus £136 worth of other goods, including gifts and souvenirs.

➤ INFORMATION: **HM Customs and Excise** (⊠ Dorset House, Stamford St., London SE1 9NG, ☎ 0171/202–4227).

D

DISABILITIES & ACCESSIBILITY

ACCESS IN ARIZONA

➤ LOCAL RESOURCES: **Southern Arizona Group Office** (☎ 602/640–5250) for information on accessible facilities at specific parks and sites in Arizona.

GETTING AROUND

➤ BY BUS: **Greyhound** (☎ 800/752–4841; 800/345–3109 TTY), which provides service to many destinations in Arizona, will carry a person with disabilities and a companion for the price of a single fare.

➤ BY TRAIN: **Amtrak** (⊠ National Railroad Passenger Corp., 60 Massachusetts Ave. NE, Washington, DC 20002, ☎ 800/872–7245) advises that you request redcap service, special seats, or wheelchair assistance when you make reservations. Also note that not all stations are equipped to provide these services. All passengers with disabilities are entitled to a 15% discount on the lowest fare, and there are special fares for children with disabilities as well. Contact Amtrak for a free brochure that outlines services for older travelers and people with disabilities.

➤ BY CAR: **Avis** (☎ 800/331–1212), **Hertz** (☎ 800/654–3131), and **National** (☎ 800/328–4567) can provide hand controls on some rental cars with advance notice.

TIPS AND HINTS

Most of the region's national parks and recreation areas have wheelchair-accessible visitor centers, rest rooms, campsites, and trails, and more are being added every year. Even so, when discussing accessibility with an operator or reservationist, **ask hard questions.** Are there any stairs, inside *or* out? Are there grab bars next to the toilet *and* in the shower/tub? How wide is the doorway to the room? To the bathroom? For the most extensive facilities meeting the latest legal specifications, **opt for newer accommodations,** which are more likely to have been designed with access in mind. Older buildings may offer more limited facilities. Be sure to **discuss your needs before booking.**

➤ COMPLAINTS: **Disability Rights Section** (✉ U.S. Department of Justice, Box 66738, Washington, DC 20035–6738, ☎ 202/514–0301 or 800/514–0301; FAX 202/307–1198; TTY 202/514–0383 or 800/514–0383) for general complaints. **Aviation Consumer Protection Division** (☞ Air Travel, *above*) for airline-related problems. **Civil Rights Office** (✉ U.S. Department of Transportation, Departmental Office of Civil Rights, S–30, 400 7th St. SW, Room 10215, Washington, DC 20590, ☎ 202/366–4648) for problems with surface transportation.

TRAVEL AGENCIES & TOUR OPERATORS

The Americans with Disabilities Act requires that travel firms serve the needs of all travelers. That said, you should note that some agencies and operators specialize in making travel arrangements for individuals and groups with disabilities.

➤ TRAVELERS WITH MOBILITY PROBLEMS: **Access Adventures** (✉ 206 Chestnut Ridge Rd., Rochester, NY 14624, ☎ 716/889–9096), run by a former physical-rehabilitation counselor. **Hinsdale Travel Service** (✉ 201 E. Ogden Ave., Suite 100, Hinsdale, IL 60521, ☎ 630/325–1335), a travel agency that benefits from the advice of wheelchair traveler Janice Perkins. **Wheelchair Journeys** (✉ 16979 Redmond Way, Redmond, WA 98052, ☎ 206/885–2210 or 800/313–4751), for general travel arrangements.

➤ TRAVELERS WITH DEVELOPMENTAL DISABILITIES: **Sprout** (✉ 893 Amsterdam Ave., New York, NY 10025, ☎

212/222–9575 or 888/222–9575, FAX 212/222–9768).

Be a smart shopper and **compare all your options before making a choice.** A plane ticket bought with a promotional coupon may not be cheaper than the least expensive fare from a discount ticket agency. For high-price travel purchases, such as packages or tours, keep in mind that what you get is just as important as what you save. Just because something is cheap doesn't mean it's a bargain.

LOOK IN YOUR WALLET

When you use your credit card to make travel purchases you may get free travel-accident insurance, collision-damage insurance, and medical or legal assistance, depending on the card and the bank that issued it. American Express, MasterCard, and Visa provide one or more of these services, so **get a copy of your credit card's travel-benefits policy.** If you are a member of the American Automobile Association (AAA) or an oil-company-sponsored road-assistance plan, always **ask hotel or car-rental reservationists about auto-club discounts.** Some clubs offer additional discounts on tours, cruises, or admission to attractions. And don't forget that auto-club membership entitles you to free maps and trip-planning services.

DIAL FOR DOLLARS

To save money, **look into "1-800" discount reservations services,** which use their buying power to get a better price on hotels, airline tickets, even car rentals. When booking a room, always **call the hotel's local toll-free number** (if one is available) rather than the central reservations number—you'll often get a better price. Always ask about special packages or corporate rates.

➤ AIRLINE TICKETS: ☎ **A Better Airfare** (☎ 800/359–2727).

➤ HOTEL ROOMS: **Central Reservation Service (CRS)** (☎ 800/548–3311). **RMC Travel** (☎ 800/245–5738).

SAVE ON COMBOS

Packages and guided tours can both save you money, but don't confuse the two. When you buy a package your travel remains independent, just as though you had planned and booked the trip yourself. Fly/drive packages, which combine airfare and car rental, are often a good deal.

JOIN A CLUB?

Many companies sell discounts in the form of travel clubs and coupon books, but these cost money. You must use participating advertisers to get a deal, and only after you recoup the initial membership cost or book price do you begin to save. If you plan to use the club or coupons frequently you may save considerably. Before signing up, find out what discounts you get for free.

➤ DISCOUNT CLUBS: **Entertainment Travel Editions** (✉ Box 1068, Trumbull, CT 06611, ☎ 800/445–4137); $28–$53, depending on destination. **Great American Traveler** (✉ Box 27965, Salt Lake City, UT 84127, ☎ 800/548–2812); $49.95 per year. **Moment's Notice Discount Travel Club** (✉ 7301 New Utrecht Ave., Brooklyn, NY 11204, ☎ 718/234–6295); $25 per year, single or family. **Privilege Card International** (✉ 201 E. Commerce St., Suite 198, Youngstown, OH 44503, ☎ 330/746–5211 or 800/236–9732); $74.95 per year. **Sears's Mature Outlook** (✉ Box 9390, Des Moines, IA 50306, ☎ 800/336–6330); $14.95 per year. **Travelers Advantage** (✉ CUC Travel Service, 3033 S. Parker Rd., Suite 1000, Aurora, CO 80014, ☎ 800/548–1116 or 800/648–4037); $49 per year, single or family. **Worldwide Discount Travel Club** (✉ 1674 Meridian Ave., Miami Beach, FL 33139, ☎ 305/534–2082); $50 per year family, $40 single.

DRIVING

Major approaches from the east and west are I–40, I–10, I–8, and U.S. 60. Main north–south routes are I–17, I–10 (from Phoenix to Tucson), and U.S. 89. Other artery roads are U.S. 70 and U.S. 64 (U.S. 160 in Arizona) from the east.

Most highways into the state are good to excellent, with easy access, roadside facilities, rest stops, and scenic views. The speed limit on the freeways is now 75 mph, but **don't drive much faster than the limit—** police use sophisticated detection systems to catch violators.

At some point you will probably pass through one or more of the state's 23 Native American reservations. Roads and other areas within reservation boundaries are under the jurisdiction of reservation police and governed by separate rules and regulations. **Observe all signs and respect Native Americans' privacy.** Be careful not to hit any animals, which often wander onto the roads; the penalties can be very high.

➤ AUTO CLUBS: In the U.S., **American Automobile Association** (☎ 800/564–6222). In the U.K., **Automobile Association** (AA, ☎ 0990/500–600), **Royal Automobile Club** (RAC, ☎ 0990/722–722 membership; 0345/121–345 insurance).

PRECAUTIONS

DUST STORMS. These usually occur mid-July to mid-September (the monsoon months), just before thunderstorms hit, causing extremely low visibility. If you're on the highway, **pull as far off the road as possible, turn on your headlights, and wait for the storm to subside.**

FLASH FLOODS. They may sound apocalyptic or overly cautious, but warnings about flash floods should not be taken lightly. Sudden downpours send torrents of water racing into low-lying areas so dry that they are unable to absorb such a huge quantity of water so quickly. The result is powerful walls of water suddenly descending upon these low-lying areas, devastating anything in their paths. If you see rain clouds or thunderstorms in the area, stay away from dry riverbeds (also called arroyos or washes). If you find yourself in one, get out quickly. If you're with a car in a long gully, leave your car and climb out of the gully. You simply won't be able to outdrive a speeding wave. The idea is to **get to higher ground immediately when it rains.** Major highways are mostly flood-proof, but some smaller roads dip through washes. If showers are nearby, look before you cross. Washes filled with water should not be crossed until you can see the bottom. By all means, don't camp in these areas at any time, interesting as they may seem.

DESERT HEAT. Vehicles and passengers should be well equipped for searing summer heat in the low desert. If you're planning to drive through the desert, **carry plenty of water, a good spare tire, a jack, and emergency supplies.** If you get stranded, stay with your vehicle and wait for help to arrive.

FRAGILE DESERT LIFE. The dry and easily desecrated desert floor takes centuries to overcome human damage. Consequently, it is illegal for four-wheel-drive and all-terrain vehicles and motorcycles to travel off established roadways.

G
GAY & LESBIAN TRAVEL

➤ GAY- AND LESBIAN-FRIENDLY TRAVEL AGENCIES: **Advance Damron** (✉ 1 Greenway Plaza, Suite 800, Houston, TX 77046, ☎ 713/682–2002 or 800/695–0880, FAX 713/888–1010). **Club Travel** (✉ 8739 Santa Monica Blvd., West Hollywood, CA 90069, ☎ 310/358–2200 or 800/429–8747, FAX 310/358–2222). **Islanders/Kennedy Travel** (✉ 183 W. 10th St., New York, NY 10014, ☎ 212/242–3222 or 800/988–1181, FAX 212/929–8530). **Now Voyager** (✉ 4406 18th St., San Francisco, CA 94114, ☎ 415/626–1169 or 800/255–6951, FAX 415/626–8626). **Yellowbrick Road** (✉ 1500 W. Balmoral Ave., Chicago, IL 60640, ☎ 773/561–1800 or 800/642–2488, FAX 773/561–4497). **Skylink Women's Travel** (✉ 3577 Moorland Ave., Santa Rosa, CA 95407, ☎ 707/585–8355 or 800/225–5759, FAX 707/584–5637), serving lesbian travelers.

H
HIKING

Be sure to take the following precautions when you go for a hike of any length.

SUN PROTECTION

Wear a hat and sunglasses and put on sunblock to protect against the burning Arizona sun. And **watch out for heatstroke.** Symptoms include headache, dizziness, and fatigue, which can turn into convulsions and unconsciousness and can lead to death. If someone in your party develops any of these conditions, have one person seek emergency help while others move the victim into the shade, wrap him or her in wet clothing (is a stream nearby?) to cool him or her down.

DEHYDRATION

This underestimated danger can be very serious, especially considering that one of the first major symptoms is the inability to swallow. It may be the easiest hazard to avoid, however; simply **drink every 10–15 minutes,** up to a gallon of water per day in summer.

ANIMAL BITES

Wherever you're hiking, particularly between April and October, **keep a lookout for rattlesnakes.** You're likely not to have any problems if you maintain distance from snakes that you see—they can strike only half of their length, so a 6-ft clearance should allow you to stay unharmed, especially if you **don't provoke them.** If you are bitten by a rattler, don't panic. Just get to a hospital within two–three hours of the bite. Keep in mind that 30%–40% of bites are dry bites, where the snake uses no venom (still, get thee to a hospital). **Avoid night hikes without rangers,** when snakes are on the prowl and less visible. You may want to pick up a kit called the Extractor for use if bitten; they're sold in major sporting goods stores in Phoenix and Tucson.

Scorpions and Gila monsters are really less of a concern, since they strike only when provoked. To avoid scorpion encounters, **don't put your hands where you can't see with your eyes:** under rocks and in holes. Likewise, if you move a rock to sit down, make sure that scorpions haven't been exposed. Campers should shake out shoes in the morning, since scorpions like warm, moist places. If you are bitten, see a ranger about symptoms that may develop. Chances are good that you won't need to go to a hospital. Children are a different case, however: Scorpion stings can be fatal for them. Always try to keep an eye on what they may be getting their hands into to avoid the scorpion's sting. Gila monsters are relatively rare, but they are most active between April and June, when they do most of their hunting.

THE GOLD GUIDE / SMART TRAVEL TIPS

HYPOTHERMIA

Temperatures in Arizona can vary widely from day to night—as much as 40°F. Be sure to **bring enough warm clothing for hiking and camping, along with wet weather gear.** Exposure to the degree that body temperature dips below 95°F produces the following symptoms: chills, tiredness, then uncontrollable shivering and irrational behavior, with the victim not always recognizing that he or she is cold. If someone in your party is suffering from any of this, wrap him or her in blankets and/or a warm sleeping bag immediately and try to keep him or her awake. The fastest way to raise body temperature is through skin-to-skin contact in a sleeping bag. Drinking warm liquids also helps.

POTABLE WATER

Never drink from any stream, no matter how clear it may be. Giardia organisms can turn your stomach inside out. The easiest way to purify water is to **dissolve a water purification tablet** in it. Camping-equipment stores also carry purification pumps. **Boil water for 15 minutes,** a reliable method, if time- and fuel-consuming.

I
INSURANCE

Travel insurance is the best way to **protect yourself against financial loss.** The most useful policies are trip-cancellation-and-interruption, default, medical, and comprehensive insurance.

Without insurance you will lose all or most of your money if you cancel your trip, regardless of the reason. It's essential that you **buy trip-cancellation-and-interruption insurance,** particularly if your airline ticket, cruise, or package tour is nonrefundable and cannot be changed. When considering how much coverage you need, look for a policy that will cover the cost of your trip plus the nondiscounted price of a one-way airline ticket, should you need to return home early. Also **consider default or bankruptcy insurance,** which protects you against a supplier's failure to deliver.

Citizens of the United Kingdom can buy an annual travel-insurance policy valid for most vacations during the year in which it's purchased. If you are pregnant or have a preexisting medical condition, make sure you're covered. According to the Association of British Insurers, a trade association representing 450 insurance companies, it's wise to buy extra medical coverage when you visit the United States.

If you have purchased an expensive vacation, comprehensive insurance is a must. **Look for comprehensive policies that include trip-delay insurance,** which will protect you in the event that weather problems cause you to miss your flight, tour, or cruise. A few insurers sell waivers for preexisting medical conditions. Companies that offer both features include Access America, Carefree Travel, and Travel Insured International (☞ *below*).

Always **buy travel insurance directly from the insurance company;** if you buy it from a travel agency or tour operator that goes out of business you probably will not be covered for the agency or operator's default, a major risk. Before you make any purchase, **review your existing health and home-owner's policies** to find out whether they cover expenses incurred while traveling.

➤ TRAVEL INSURERS: In the U.S., **Access America** (⊠ 6600 W. Broad St., Richmond, VA 23230, ☎ 804/285–3300 or 800/284–8300), **Carefree Travel Insurance** (⊠ Box 9366, 100 Garden City Plaza, Garden City, NY 11530, ☎ 516/294–0220 or 800/323–3149), **Near Travel Services** (⊠ Box 1339, Calumet City, IL 60409, ☎ 708/868–6700 or 800/654–6700), **Travel Guard International** (⊠ 1145 Clark St., Stevens Point, WI 54481, ☎ 715/345–0505 or 800/826–1300), **Travel Insured International** (⊠ Box 280568, East Hartford, CT 06128–0568, ☎ 860/528–7663 or 800/243–3174), **Travelex Insurance Services** (⊠ 11717 Burt St., Suite 202, Omaha, NE 68154-1500, ☎ 402/445–8637 or 800/228–9792, FAX 800/867–9531), **Wallach & Company** (⊠ 107 W. Federal St., Box 480, Middleburg, VA 20118, ☎ 540/687–3166 or 800/237–6615). In Canada, **Mutual of Omaha** (⊠ Travel Division, 500

University Ave., Toronto, Ontario M5G 1V8, ☎ 416/598–4083, 800/ 268–8825 in Canada). In the U.K., **Association of British Insurers** (✉ 51 Gresham St., London EC2V 7HQ, ☎ 0171/600–3333).

LODGING

Arizona's hotels and motels run the gamut—from world-class resorts to budget chains, and from historic inns, bed-and-breakfasts, and mountain lodges to dude ranches, campgrounds, and RV parks. **Make reservations well in advance for the high season**— winter in the desert south and summer in the high country. Tremendous bargains can be found off-season, when even the most exclusive establishments cut their rates by half.

APARTMENT AND HOUSE RENTALS

If you want a home base that's roomy enough for a family and comes with cooking facilities, **consider a furnished rental.** These can save you money, however some rentals are luxury properties, economical only when your party is large. Home-exchange directories list rentals (often second homes owned by prospective house swappers), and some services search for a house or apartment for you (even a castle if that's your fancy) and handle the paperwork.

➤ RENTAL AGENTS: **Property Rentals International** (✉ 1008 Mansfield Crossing Rd., Richmond, VA 23236, ☎ 804/378–6054 or 800/220–3332, ℻ 804/379–2073). **Rent-a-Home International** (✉ 7200 34th Ave. NW, Seattle, WA 98117, ☎ 206/789–9377 or 800/488–7368, ℻ 206/789– 9379). **Hideaways International** (✉ 767 Islington St., Portsmouth, NH 03801, ☎ 603/430–4433 or 800/ 843–4433, ℻ 603/430–4444) is a travel club whose members arrange rentals among themselves; yearly membership is $99.

BED-AND-BREAKFASTS

➤ ORGANIZATIONS: **Mi Casa Su Casa** (✉ Box 950, Tempe 85280, ☎ 602/ 990–0682 or 800/456–0682, ℻ 602/990–3390). **Bed & Breakfast Southwest** (✉ 2916 N. 70th St., Scottsdale 85251, ☎ 602/995–2831 or 800/762–9704, ☎ 602/874–

1316). **Arizona Association of Bed and Breakfast Inns** (✉ Box 7186, Phoenix 85012, ☎ 602/277–0775). The Arizona Office of Tourism (☞ Visitor Information, *below*) has a statewide list of bed-and-breakfasts.

CAMPING

You can choose from a feast of federal, state, Native American, and private campgrounds in virtually all parts of the state. Facilities range from deluxe parks with swimming pools and recreation rooms to primitive backcountry wilderness sites. Most campgrounds provide toilets, drinking water, showers, and hookups. Camping is also permitted in Arizona's seven national forests, but be forewarned that they have no facilities whatsoever.

Pack according to season, region, and length of trip. Basics include a sleeping bag, a tent (optional, and forbidden in some RV parks), a camp stove, cooking utensils, food and water supplies, a first-aid kit, insect repellent, sunscreen, a lantern, trash bags, a rope, and a tarp. In case you forget something, almost every camping item is available for sale or rent at one of Arizona's many sporting-goods shops.

Individual campgrounds should be contacted before travel for suggestions as to specific equipment to bring, as well as necessary reservations, advance deposits, and permits. Most state parks have a 15-day maximum-stay limit.

➤ INFORMATION: **National Park Service** (✉ 3121 North 3rd Ave., Suite 142, Phoenix 85013, ☎ 602/ 640–5250), **Bureau of Land Management** (✉ 222 N. Central Ave., Phoenix 85014, ☎ 602/417–9528), **Arizona State Parks Department** (☞ National & State Parks, *below*), **Apache Sitgreaves National Forest** (✉ 309 S. Mountain Ave., Springerville 85938, ☎ 520/333–4301), **Coconino National Forest** (✉ 2323 E. Greenlaw La., Flagstaff 86004, ☎ 520/527– 3600), **Coronado National Forest** (✉ Federal Bldg., 300 W. Congress St., Tucson 85701, ☎ 520/670–4552), **Williams-Forest Service Visitor Center** (✉ 200 W. Railroad Ave., Williams 86046, ☎ 520/635–4061), **Prescott National Forest** (✉ 344 S. Cortez St., Prescott 86303, ☎ 520/771–4700,

TTY 520/771–4792), or **Tonto National Forest** (✉ 2324 E. McDowell Rd., Phoenix 85006, ☎ 602/225–5200).

DUDE RANCHES

Down-home western lifestyle, cooking, and activities are the focus of guest ranches, situated primarily in Tucson and southern Arizona and Wickenburg. Some are resortlike properties where guests are pampered, whereas smaller family-run ranches expect *everyone* to join in the chores. Horseback riding and other outdoor recreational activities are emphasized. Most dude ranches are closed in summer.

➤ INFORMATION: Contact the Arizona Office of Tourism (☞ Visitor Information, *below*) for the names and addresses of dude ranches throughout the state.

HOME EXCHANGES

If you would like to exchange your home for someone else's, **join a home-exchange organization,** which will send you its updated listings of available exchanges for a year and will include your own listing in at least one of them. Making the arrangements is up to you.

➤ EXCHANGE CLUBS: **HomeLink International** (✉ Box 650, Key West, FL 33041, ☎ 305/294–7766 or 800/638–3841, FAX 305/294–1148) charges $83 per year.

M

MONEY MATTERS

ATMS

Before leaving home, **make sure that your credit cards have been programmed for ATM use.**

➤ ATM LOCATIONS: **Cirrus** (☎ 800/424–7787). **Plus** (☎ 800/843–7587).

N

NATIONAL & STATE PARKS

You may be able to **save money on park entrance fees** by getting a discount pass. The Golden Eagle Pass ($50) gets you and your companions free admission to all parks for one year. (Camping and parking are extra.) Both the Golden Age Passport, for U.S. citizens or permanent residents age 62 and older, and the Golden Access Passport, for travelers with disabilities, entitle holders to free entry to all national parks plus 50% off fees for the use of many park facilities and services. Both passports are free; you must show proof of age and U.S. citizenship or permanent residency (such as a U.S. passport, driver's license, or birth certificate) or proof of disability. All three passes are available at all national park entrances. Golden Eagle and Golden Access passes are also available by mail.

➤ PASSES BY MAIL: **National Park Service** (✉ Department of the Interior, Washington, DC 20240).

➤ STATE PARKS: **Arizona State Parks Department** (✉ 1300 W. Washington St., Phoenix 85007, ☎ 602/542–4174) for a complete listing of all state parks and their facilities.

P

PACKING FOR ARIZONA

Wear casual clothing and resort wear in Arizona. When in more elegant restaurants in larger cities, as well as in dining rooms of some resorts, most men wear jackets and appropriate pants (few places require ties). Dressy casual wear is appropriate for women even in the nicest places—take along a silky blouse and chunky silver jewelry and you'll fit in almost anywhere.

Stay cool in cotton fabrics and light colors. T-shirts, polo shirts, sundresses, and lightweight shorts, trousers, skirts, and blouses are useful year-round in the south. **Bring sun hats, swimsuits, sandals, and sunscreen**—mandatory warm-weather items. **Bring a sweater and a warm jacket in winter,** particularly for high-country travel—anywhere around Flagstaff and north of it. And **don't forget jeans and sneakers or sturdy walking shoes;** they're important year-round.

Take along appropriate sports gear, although tennis, golf, ski, and horseback-riding equipment is readily available for rental.

Bring an extra pair of eyeglasses or contact lenses in your carry-on luggage, and if you have a health problem, **pack enough medication** to last the entire trip. It's important that you **don't put prescription drugs or valuables in luggage to be checked**: It might go astray.

LUGGAGE

In general you are entitled to check two bags on flights within the United States. A third piece may be brought on board, but it must fit easily under the seat in front of you or in the overhead compartment.

Airline liability for baggage is limited to $1,250 per person on flights within the United States. On international flights it amounts to $9.07 per pound or $20 per kilogram for checked baggage (roughly $640 per 70-pound bag) and $400 per passenger for unchecked baggage. Insurance for losses exceeding these amounts can be bought from the airline at check-in for about $10 per $1,000 of coverage; note that this coverage excludes a rather extensive list of items, which is shown on your airline ticket.

Before departure, **itemize your bags' contents** and their worth, and label the bags with your name, address, and phone number. (If you use your home address, cover it so that potential thieves can't see it readily.) Inside each bag, **pack a copy of your itinerary.** At check-in, **make sure that each bag is correctly tagged** with the destination airport's three-letter code. If your bags arrive damaged or fail to arrive at all, file a written report with the airline before leaving the airport.

PASSPORTS & VISAS

CANADIANS

A passport is not required to enter the United States.

U.K. CITIZENS

British citizens need a valid passport to enter the United States. If you are staying for fewer than 90 days on vacation, with a return or onward ticket, you probably will not need a visa. However, you will need to fill out the Visa Waiver Form, 1-94W, supplied by the airline.

➤ INFORMATION: **London Passport Office** (☎ 0990/21010) for fees and documentation requirements and to request an emergency passport. **U.S. Embassy Visa Information Line** (☎ 01891/200–290) for U.S. visa information; calls cost 49p per minute or 39p per minute cheap rate. **U.S. Embassy Visa Branch** (✉ 5 Upper Grosvenor St., London W1A 2JB) for U.S. visa information; send a self-addressed, stamped envelope. Write the **U.S. Consulate General** (✉ Queen's House, Queen St., Belfast BTI 6EO) if you live in Northern Ireland.

R

ROCKHOUNDING

The **Department of Mines and Mineral Resources** (✉ 1502 W. Washington St., Phoenix 85007, ☎ 602/255–3795) is an excellent source of information about specimens that can be found in each part of the state.

S

SENIOR-CITIZEN TRAVEL

To qualify for age-related discounts, **mention your senior-citizen status up front** when booking hotel reservations (not when checking out) and before you're seated in restaurants (not when paying the bill). Note that discounts may be limited to certain menus, days, or hours. When renting a car, **ask about promotional car-rental discounts,** which can be cheaper than senior-citizen rates.

➤ EDUCATIONAL TRAVEL PROGRAMS: **Elderhostel** (✉ 75 Federal St., 3rd floor, Boston, MA 02110, ☎ 617/426–7788).

SHOPPING

Keep in mind that the high quality of Native American arts and crafts is reflected in the prices they fetch. Bargaining is the exception, not the rule. In general, the best buys are to be had in the fall, after most of the tourists have gone home. Many uniquely southwestern products—chili pepper strings or locally produced salsas—make inexpensive souvenirs.

SPORTS

BASEBALL

During spring training, the **Chicago Cubs** play at Hohokam Park in Mesa (☎ 602/964–4467), the **Oakland Athletics** at Phoenix Municipal Stadium (☎ 602/392–0217), the **San**

Francisco Giants at Scottsdale Stadium (☎ 602/990–7972), the Anaheim Angels at Diablo Stadium in Tempe (☎ 602/438–9300), and the Milwaukee Brewers at the Compadre Stadium in Chandler (☎ 602/895–1200). Both the San Diego Padres and the Seattle Mariners train at Peoria Stadium (☎ 602/878–4337) in another Phoenix suburb. The Colorado Rockies play at Tucson's Hi-Corbett Field (☎ 520/327–9467). For current information on all aspects of Cactus League baseball, contact the Mesa Convention and Visitor's Bureau (⌧ 120 North Center St., Mesa 85201, ☎ 602/827–4700 or 800/283–6372).

In April 1998, the major league Arizona Diamondbacks will begin playing at the Bank One Ballpark. Call 602/379-7900 for information.

BASKETBALL

The NBA's Phoenix Suns strut their stuff at the America West Arena (⌧ One Phoenix Suns Plaza, 201 E. Jefferson St., ☎ 602/379–7900).

BICYCLING

Call the county Parks and Recreation Department in the area you're visiting for information on nearby bike paths. The Arizona Bicycle Club, Inc. (⌧ Box 7191, Phoenix, AZ 85011, ☎ 602/264–5478 or 602/279–6674) publishes a schedule of the many bicycle races and tours that take place throughout the state.

FISHING

Fishing licenses are required and can be obtained from the Arizona Game and Fish Department (⌧ 2222 W. Greenway Rd., Phoenix 85023, ☎ 602/942–3000). For permission to fish San Carlos Lake on the San Carlos Indian reservation call 520/475–2343.

FOOTBALL

The NFL's Arizona Cardinals have flown from St. Louis to Phoenix, where they play at Sun Devil Stadium (⌧ 5th St. and College Ave., Tempe, ☎ 602/379–0102).

GOLF

For a list of Arizona's golfing facilities, contact the Arizona Golf Association (⌧ 7226 N. 16th St., Suite 200, Phoenix 85020, ☎ 602/944–3035; 800/458–8484 in AZ).

HIKING

The Backcountry Office (☎ 520/638–7888) provides hikers with trail details, weather conditions, and packing suggestions for the Grand Canyon. For hikers who prefer to travel with a group, the Sierra Club (☎ 602/253–8633) leads a variety of wilderness treks. Contact the local chapters in Phoenix, Tucson, Kingman, Prescott, Sedona, and Flagstaff for information on guided hikes in these areas.

RIVER RAFTING

Contact the Arizona Office of Tourism (☞ Visitor Information, below) for an extensive list of rafting outfits, or see Tour Operators, below.

SKIING

For cross-country skiing, Arizona Snowbowl & Flagstaff Nordic Center (☎ 520/779–1951), North Rim Nordic Center (☎ 520/526–0924; 800/525–0924 outside AZ), Williams Ski Area (☎ 520/635–9330), and miles of crisscrossing trails around Alpine (⌧ Alpine Ranger District, ☎ 520/339–4384) are recommended. Equipment and instruction are readily available. We advise making reservations in the busy season.

For downhill skiing, Sunrise Park Resort (☎ 520/735–7600) in McNary, owned and operated by the White Mountain Apache Indians, encompasses three mountain peaks and is the state's largest ski area. Arizona Snowbowl (☞ above), and Mt. Lemmon Ski Valley (☎ 520/576–1321), near Tucson, are also popular. Though they aren't as impressive as those in the Rockies, ski resorts cater to all levels and provide instruction and equipment rental.

TENNIS

Arizona offers a multitude of tennis opportunities, from hard courts at city parks and university campuses to full-scale programs at ultraposh tennis-oriented resorts, such as Gardiner's Resort on Camelback (⌧ 5700 E. McDonald Dr., Scottsdale 85253, ☎ 602/948–2100 or 800/245–2051), one of the country's best. Most hotels either have their own courts or are affiliated with a private or municipal facility.

➤ STUDENT IDs AND SERVICES: **Council on International Educational Exchange** (✉ CIEE, 205 E. 42nd St., 14th floor, New York, NY 10017, ☎ 212/822–2600 or 888/268–6245, FAX 212/822–2699), for mail orders only, in the United States. **Travel Cuts** (✉ 187 College St., Toronto, Ontario M5T 1P7, ☎ 416/979–2406 or 800/667–2887) in Canada.

➤ HOSTELING: **Hostelling International—American Youth Hostels** (✉ 733 15th St. NW, Suite 840, Washington, DC 20005, ☎ 202/783–6161, FAX 202/783–6171). **Hostelling International—Canada** (✉ 400-205 Catherine St., Ottawa, Ontario K2P 1C3, ☎ 613/237–7884, FAX 613/237–7868). **Youth Hostel Association of England and Wales** (✉ Trevelyan House, 8 St. Stephen's Hill, St. Albans, Hertfordshire AL1 2DY, ☎ 01727/855215 or 01727/845047, FAX 01727/844126). Membership in the U.S., $25; in Canada, C$26.75; in the U.K., £9.30).

➤ STUDENT TOURS: **Contiki Holidays** (✉ 300 Plaza Alicante, Suite 900, Garden Grove, CA 92840, ☎ 714/740–0808 or 800/266–8454, FAX 714/740–0818).

T

CALLING HOME

AT&T, MCI, and Sprint long-distance services make calling home relatively convenient and let you avoid hotel surcharges. Typically you dial an 800 number in the United States.

➤ TO OBTAIN ACCESS CODES: **AT&T USADirect** (☎ 800/874–4000). **MCI Call USA** (☎ 800/444–4444). **Sprint Express** (☎ 800/793–1153).

Arizona sets its clocks to mountain standard time—two hours earlier than eastern standard, one hour later than Pacific standard. However, from April to October, when other states switch to daylight saving time, Arizona does *not* change its clocks; during this portion of the year, the mountain standard hour in Arizona is

the same as the Pacific daylight hour in California. To complicate matters, the vast Navajo reservation in the northeastern section of the state *does* observe daylight saving time, so that from April to October it's an hour later on the reservation than it is in the rest of the state. Finally, the Hopi reservation, whose borders fall within those of the Navajo reservation, stays on the same non-Navajo, non–daylight saving clock as the remainder of the state.

Buying a prepackaged tour or independent vacation can make your trip to Arizona less expensive and more hassle-free. Because everything is prearranged you'll spend less time planning.

Operators that handle several hundred thousand travelers per year can use their purchasing power to give you a good price. Their high volume may also indicate financial stability. But some small companies provide more personalized service; because they tend to specialize, they may also be more knowledgeable about a given area.

A GOOD DEAL?

The more your package or tour includes, the better you can predict the ultimate cost of your vacation. Make sure you know exactly what is covered, and **beware of hidden costs.** Are taxes, tips, and service charges included? Transfers and baggage handling? Entertainment and excursions? These can add up.

If the package or tour you are considering is priced lower than in your wildest dreams, **be skeptical.** Also, **make sure your travel agent knows the accommodations** and other services. Ask about the hotel's location, room size, beds, and whether it has a pool, room service, or programs for children, if you care about these. Has your agent been there in person or sent others you can contact?

BUYER BEWARE

Each year consumers are stranded or lose their money when tour operators—even very large ones with excellent reputations—go out of business. So **check out the operator.** Find out how long the company has been in business, and ask several agents about its reputation. **Don't book unless the firm has a consumer-protection program.**

Members of the National Tour Association and United States Tour Operators Association are required to set aside funds to cover your payments and travel arrangements in case the company defaults. Nonmembers may carry insurance instead. Look for the details, and for the name of an underwriter with a solid reputation, in the operator's brochure. Note: When it comes to tour operators, **don't trust escrow accounts.** Although there are laws governing charter-flight operators, no governmental body prevents tour operators from raiding the till. For more information, *see* Consumer Protection, *above*.

➤ TOUR-OPERATOR RECOMMENDATIONS: **National Tour Association** (⊠ NTA, 546 E. Main St., Lexington, KY 40508, ☎ 606/226–4444 or 800/ 755–8687). **United States Tour Operators Association** (⊠ USTOA, 342 Madison Ave., Suite 1522, New York, NY 10173, ☎ 212/599–6599, FAX 212/599–6744).

USING AN AGENT

Travel agents are excellent resources. When shopping for an agent, however, you should **collect brochures from several sources**; some agents' suggestions may be skewed by promotional relationships with tour and package firms that reward them for volume sales. If you have a special interest, **find an agent with expertise in that area** (☞ Travel Agencies, *below*). Don't rely solely on your agent, who may be unaware of small-niche operators. Note that some special-interest travel companies only sell directly to the public and that some large operators only accept bookings made through travel agents.

GROUP TOURS

Among companies that sell tours to Arizona, the following are nationally known, have a proven reputation, and offer plenty of options. The classifications used below represent different price categories, and you'll probably encounter these terms when talking to a travel agent or tour operator. The key difference is usually in accommodations, which run from

budget to better, and better-yet to best.

➤ DELUXE: **Globus** (⊠ 5301 S. Federal Circle, Littleton, CO 80123-2980, ☎ 303/797–2800 or 800/ 221–0090, FAX 303/795–0962). **Maupintour** (⊠ Box 807, Lawrence, KS 66047, ☎ 913/843–1211 or 800/ 255–4266, FAX 913/843–8351). **Tauck Tours** (⊠ Box 5027, 276 Post Rd. W, Westport, CT 06881, ☎ 203/ 226–6911 or 800/468–2825, FAX 203/221–6828).

➤ FIRST-CLASS: **Brendan Tours** (⊠ 15137 Califa St., Van Nuys, CA 91411, ☎ 818/785–9696 or 800/ 421–8446, FAX 818/902–9876). **Caravan Tours** (⊠ 401 N. Michigan Ave., Chicago, IL 60611, ☎ 312/ 321–9800 or 800/227–2826). **Collette Tours** (⊠ 162 Middle St., Pawtucket, RI 02860, ☎ 401/728–3805 or 800/832–4656, FAX 401/728–1380). **Gadabout Tours** (⊠ 700 E. Tahquitz Canyon Way, Palm Springs, CA 92262, ☎ 619/325–5556 or 800/ 952–5068). **Mayflower Tours** (⊠ Box 490, 1225 Warren Ave., Downers Grove, IL 60515, ☎ 708/960–3793 or 800/323–7604, FAX 708/ 960–3575).

➤ BUDGET: **Cosmos** (☞ Globus, *above*).

PACKAGES

Like group tours, independent vacation packages are available from major tour operators and airlines. The companies listed below offer vacation packages in a broad price range.

➤ AIR/HOTEL/CAR: **Certified Vacations** (⊠ Box 1525, Fort Lauderdale, FL 33302, ☎ 305/522–1414 or 800/ 233–7260). **Continental Vacations** (☎ 800/634–5555). **Delta Dream Vacations** (☎ 800/872–7786). **SuperCities** (⊠ 139 Main St., Cambridge, MA 02142, ☎ 617/621–0099 or 800/333–1234). **TWA Getaway Vacations** (☎ 800/438–2929). **United Vacations** (☎ 800/328–6877). **US Airways Vacations** (☎ 800/455–0123).

➤ CUSTOM PACKAGES: **Amtrak's Great American Vacations** (☎ 800/321–8684).

➤ FROM THE U.K.: **British Airways Holidays** (⊠ Astral Towers, Betts

Way, London Rd., Crawley, West Sussex RH10 2XA, ☎ 01293/723–121). **Jetsave Travel Ltd.** (✉ Sussex House, London Rd., East Grinstead, West Sussex RH19 1LD, ☎ 01342/312–033). **Key to America** (✉ 1–3 Station Rd., Ashford, Middlesex TW15 2UW, ☎ 01784/248–777). **Kuoni Travel** (✉ Kuoni House, Dorking, Surrey RH5 4AZ, ☎ 01306/742–222). **Premier Holidays** (✉ Premier Travel Centre, Westbrook, Milton Rd., Cambridge CB4 1YG, ☎ 01223/516–688).

THEME TRIPS

➤ ADVENTURE: **American Southwest Tours** (✉ Box 4300, Durango, CO 81302, ☎ 970/247–2955 or 800/644–5755). **American Wilderness Experience** (✉ Box 1486, Boulder, CO 80306, ☎ 303/444–2622 or 800/444–3833, FAX 303/444–3999). **Smithsonian Study Tours and Seminars** (✉ 1100 Jefferson Dr. SW, Room 3045, MRC 702, Washington, DC 20560, ☎ 202/357–4700, FAX 202/633–9250). **Trek America** (✉ Box 189, Rockaway, NJ 07866, ☎ 201/983–1144 or 800/221–0596, FAX 201/983–8551) specializes in trip for ages 18–38. **World Wide River Expeditions** (✉ 153 E. 7200 S, Midvale, Utah 84047, ☎ 801/566–2662 or 800/231–2769, FAX 801/566–2722).

➤ ARCHAEOLOGY: **American Southwest Tours** (☞ Adventure, *above*). **Archaeological Conservancy** (✉ 5301 Central Ave. NE, #1218, Albuquerque, NM 87108-1517, ☎ 505/266–1540). **Crow Canyon Archaeological Center** (✉ 23390 Country Rd. K, Cortez, CO 81321, ☎ 970/565–8975 or 800/422–8975, FAX 970/565–4859). **Earthwatch** (✉ Box 403, 680 Mount Auburn St., Watertown, MA 02272, ☎ 617/926–8200 or 800/776–0188, FAX 617/926–8532. **Nature Expeditions International** (✉ Box 11496, Eugene, OR 97440, ☎ 503/484–6529 or 800/869–0639, FAX 503/484–6531). **Southwest Ed-Ventures** (✉ Four Corners School of Outdoor Education, Box 1029, Monticello, UT 84535, ☎ 800/525–4456 or 801/587–2156, FAX 801/587–2193).

➤ BICYCLING: **Backroads** (✉ 1516 5th St., Berkeley, CA 94710-1740, ☎ 510/527–1555 or 800/462–2848, FAX 510/527–1444). **Timberline** (✉ 7975 E. Harvard, #J, Denver, CO 80231, ☎ 303/759–3804 or 800/417–2453, FAX 303/368–1651). **Cycle America** (✉ Box 485, Cannon Falls, MN 55009, ☎ 507/263–2665 or 800/245–3263).

➤ CULTURAL: **Southwest Ed-Ventures** (☞ Archaeology, *above*). **American Southwest Tours** (☞ Adventure, *above*).

➤ DUDE RANCHES: **American Wilderness Experience** (☞ Adventure, *above*). **Off The Beaten Path** (☞ Self-Drive, *below*).

➤ GOLF: Packages including accommodations, confirmed tee times, and golfing fees are sold by **Golfpac** (✉ Box 162366, Altamonte Springs, FL 32716-2366, ☎ 407/260–2288 or 800/327–0878, FAX 407/260–8989) and **Stine's Golftrips** (✉ Box 2314, Winter Haven, FL 33883-2314, ☎ 941/324–1300 or 800/428–1940, FAX 941/325–0384).

➤ HEALTH: **Spa-Finders** (✉ 91 5th Ave., #301, New York, NY 10003-3039, ☎ 212/924–6800 or 800/255–7727) represents several spas in Arizona.

➤ HIKING: **Backroads** (☞ Bicycling, *above*). **Timberline** (☞ Bicycling, *above*).

➤ HORSEBACK RIDING: **FITS Equestrian** (✉ 685 Lateen Rd., Solvang, CA 93463, ☎ 805/688–9494 or 800/666–3487, FAX 805/688–2943). **American Wilderness Experience** (☞ Adventure, *above*).

➤ KAYAKING: **Orange Torpedo Trips** (✉ Box 1111, Grants Pass, OR 97526-0294, ☎ 541/479–5061 or 800/635–2925, FAX 541/471–0995).

➤ MOTORCYCLING: **Western States Motorcycle Tours** (✉ 1823 W. Seldon La., Phoenix, AZ 85021, ☎ FAX 602/943–9030).

➤ MUSIC: **Dailey-Thorp Travel** (✉ 330 W. 58th St., #610, New York, NY 10019-1817, ☎ 212/307–1555 or 800/998–4677, FAX 212/974–1420).

➤ NATIVE AMERICAN HISTORY: **American Southwest Tours** (☞ Adventure, *above*). **Crow Canyon Archaeological Center** (☞ Archaeology, *above*). **Southwest Ed-Ventures** (☞ Archaeology, *above*).

► RIVER RAFTING: For trips on the Colorado River: **Action Whitewater Adventures** (✉ Box 1634, Provo UT 84603, ☎ 800/453–1482, FAX 801/375–4175). **Canyoneers** (✉ Box 2997, Flagstaff, AZ 86003, ☎ 602/526–0924 or 800/525–0924). **Grand Canyon Dories** (✉ Box 67, Angels Camp, CA 95222, ☎ 209/736–0811 or 800/877–3679, FAX 209/736–2902). **OARS** (✉ Box 67, Angels Camp, CA 95222, ☎ 209/736–4677 or 800/346–6277, FAX 209/736–2902). Rafting on the Salt River Canyons: **Far Flung Adventures** (✉ Box 377, Terlingua, TX 79852, ☎ 915/371–2489 or 800/359–4138, FAX 915/371–2325).

► SELF-DRIVE: **Off the Beaten Path** (✉ 109 E. Main St., Bozeman, MT 59715, ☎ 406/586–1311 or 800/445–2995, FAX 406/587–4147).

► WALKING: Country Walkers (✉ Box 180, Waterbury, VT 05676-0180, ☎ 802/244–1387 or 800/464–9255, FAX 802/244–5661).

TRAIN TRAVEL

The *Southwest Chief* operates daily between Los Angeles and Chicago, stopping in Kingman, Flagstaff, and Winslow. The *Sunset Limited* travels three times each week between Los Angeles and Miami, with stops at Yuma, Phoenix, Tempe, Coolidge, Tucson, and Benson. For details, contact **Amtrak** (☎ 800/872–7245).

TRAVEL AGENCIES

A good travel agent puts your needs first. **Look for an agency that specializes in your destination, has been in business at least five years, and emphasizes customer service.** If you're looking for an agency-organized package or tour, your best bet is to choose an agency that's a member of the National Tour Association or the United States Tour Operator's Association (☞ Tour-Operator Recommendations, *above*).

► LOCAL AGENT REFERRALS: American Society of Travel Agents (✉ ASTA, 1101 King St., Suite 200, Alexandria, VA 22314, ☎ 703/739–2782, FAX 703/684–8319). **Alliance of Canadian Travel Associations** (✉ Suite 201, 1729 Bank St., Ottawa, Ontario K1V 7Z5, ☎ 613/521–0474, FAX 613/521–0805). **Association of British Travel Agents** (✉

55–57 Newman St., London W1P 4AH, ☎ 0171/637–2444, FAX 0171/637–0713).

TRAVEL GEAR

Travel catalogs specialize in useful items, such as compact alarm clocks and travel irons, that can **save space when packing.**

► MAIL-ORDER CATALOGS: **Magellan's** (☎ 800/962–4943, FAX 805/568–5406). **Orvis Travel** (☎ 800/541–3541, FAX 540/343–7053). **TravelSmith** (☎ 800/950–1600, FAX 800/950–1656).

U

U.S. GOVERNMENT

The U.S. government can be an excellent source of inexpensive travel information. When planning your trip, **find out what government materials are available.**

► ADVISORIES: **U.S. Department of State American Citizens Services Office** (✉ Room 4811, Washington, DC 20520); enclose a self-addressed, stamped envelope. **Interactive hot line** (☎ 202/647–5225, FAX 202/647–3000). **Computer bulletin board** (☎ 202/647–9225).

► PAMPHLETS: **Consumer Information Center** (✉ Consumer Information Catalogue, Pueblo, CO 81009, ☎ 719/948–3334) for a free catalog that includes travel titles.

VISITOR INFORMATION

For general information and brochures contact the Arizona Office of Tourism; for specific information on the state's indigenous culture, contact the Native American attractions.

► STATEWIDE INFORMATION: **Arizona Office of Tourism** (✉ 2702 N. Third St., Ste. 4015, Phoenix 85004, ☎ 602/230–7733 or 800/842–8257, FAX 602/240–5475).

► NATIVE AMERICAN ATTRACTIONS: **Hopi Tribe Office of the Chairman** (✉ Box 123, Kykotsmovi 86039, ☎ 520/734–2441, FAX 520/734–2435). **Navajo Tourism Development Department** (✉ Box 663, Window Rock 86515, ☎ 520/871–6436 or 871–7371 or 871–6659, FAX 520/871–7381).

W
WHEN TO GO

When you travel to Arizona depends on whether you prefer scorching desert or snowy slopes, elbow-to-elbow resorts, or wide-open territory. Our advice: **Visit during spring and autumn,** when the temperatures are milder and the crowds have thinned out.

Winter is prime time in the central and southern parts of the state. The weather is sunny and mild, and the cities bustle with travelers escaping the cold. Conversely, northern Arizona—including the Grand Canyon—can be wintry, with snow, freezing rain, and subzero temperatures; the road to the Grand Canyon's North Rim is closed during this time.

Arizona's desert regions sizzle in summer, and travelers and their vehicles should be adequately prepared. Practically every restaurant and accommodation is air-conditioned, though, and you can get great deals on tony southern Arizona resorts you might not be able to afford in high season. Summer is also a delightful time to visit northern Arizona's high country, when temperatures are 18°F–20°F lower than they are down south —but hotel prices are commensurately high.

CLIMATE

Phoenix averages 300 sunny days and 7 inches of precipitation annually. Tucson gets all of 11 inches of rain each year, and the high mountains see about 25 inches. The Grand Canyon is usually cool on the rim and about 20°F warmer on the floor. During winter months, approximately 6–12 inches of snow falls on the North Rim; the South Rim receives half that amount.

The following average daily maximum and minimum temperatures for two major cities in Arizona offer a representative range of temperatures in the state.

➤ FORECASTS: **Weather Channel Connection** (☎ 900/932–8437), 95¢ per minute from a Touch-Tone phone.

Climate in Arizona

TUCSON

Jan.	64F	18C	May	89F	32C	Sept.	96F	36C
	37	3		57	14		68	20
Feb.	68F	20C	June	98F	37C	Oct.	84F	29C
	39	4		66	19		57	14
Mar.	73F	23C	July	101F	38C	Nov.	73F	23C
	44	7		73	23		44	7
Apr.	82F	28C	Aug.	96F	36C	Dec.	66F	19C
	51	11		71	22		39	4

FLAGSTAFF

Jan.	41F	5C	May	66F	19C	Sept.	71F	22C
	14	−10		33	1		41	5
Feb.	44F	7C	June	77F	25C	Oct.	62F	17C
	17	− 8		41	5		30	− 1
Mar.	48F	9C	July	80F	27C	Nov.	51F	11C
	23	− 5		50	10		21	− 6
Apr.	57F	14C	Aug.	78F	26C	Dec.	42F	6C
	28	− 2		48	9		15	− 9

1 Destination: Arizona

THE GRAND CANYON STATE

ARIZONA IS an ancient land, visibly etched by the passage of the earth and the human race through time. Aeons of our planet's story are written in the deep, multicolored walls of the Grand Canyon and the cathedral-like stone spires of Monument Valley. Ages of human history echo in the hidden grandeur of Canyon de Chelly, the "sky villages" perched atop Hopi reservation mesas, and the prehistoric ruins of Montezuma Castle and Casa Grande.

At the same time, Arizona is a lively hub of modern life, a quickening center in the emerging web of communications and trade, travel, and recreation that links western North America with the Pacific Rim. Phoenix, the state capital and the metropolitan center of the Southwest, is America's seventh-largest city.

Visitors usually wonder about the desert: How hot is it? What should we wear? Is it safe? These are intelligent questions about a place where summer daytime temperatures often exceed 100°F (38°C), major rivers run underground, and the native flora are spiny cactus and thorny scrub.

What few people realize is that Arizona has two deserts. The low desert (roughly the southwestern third of the state) is indeed arid and dotted with tall saguaro cacti, but the high desert—the northeastern tier, with the Grand Canyon and Navajo and Hopi lands—is a savanna-like plain, thousands of feet above sea level and mantled in snow all winter. The White Mountains of Arizona aren't desert at all but rather lush, rugged terrain of cool, alpine lakes, burbling streams, and the world's largest ponderosa pine forest.

Even with—and partly because of—its low-desert climate, Arizona has an irresistible draw. Long one of the nation's prime tourist destinations, visited annually by millions from around the world, in the past two decades Arizona has been one of America's fastest-growing states, with tens of thousands of immigrants arriving each year. After Las Vegas, Phoenix is the most rapidly expanding city in the United States.

That growth transformed Phoenix from a farming town of 60,000 in 1940 to an urban center of 1 million by 1990. It also doubled and redoubled the population of Tucson, the "Old Pueblo" in the southern part of the state. Yet Arizona remains a place of boundless vistas, with more than 80% of its land in U.S. and state parks and preserves or Native American reservations. Whether they are in the deserts or the mountains, Arizona's small towns still have vast spaces between them.

The state has also retained much of its rich Native American and Spanish colonial heritage. More Native Americans live here than in any other state, and the Hopi village of Oraibi is the oldest continuously inhabited community in North America. Mexican and Central American families continue to immigrate, many following routes opened by Spanish explorers a century before the Pilgrims landed. Numerous Tucson families trace their lineage to Mexican pioneers who arrived in the days of the American Revolution.

Visitors can readily see some of the gifts modern Arizona has received from these ancient cultures: the Native American and Spanish names of most of its mountains and rivers, plants, and animals, even its streets and the pervasive influence of Hopi and Mexican architecture in homes and public buildings. Other aspects of this heritage appear only after some study: in the canals that carry Arizona's mountain streams into the low desert and the legal system that gives husband and wife equal shares in their "community property."

One part of Arizona's cultural heritage that almost everyone gets to share is the relaxed pace and style of living: In almost everything, from clothing to art, from home decor to meals, the desert dwellers of each era have learned to prize the unhurried and the informal, to accept the calming lessons of the heat and the majestic landscape. Leave your tie and tails at home and, even if you're on business, plan to take time out: Lean back for a leisurely late lunch during the hottest part of the day; stretch out under a patio awning beside a pool or fountain during the long, cool evenings.

And wherever you take your siesta, cast your eye toward the horizon: You'll see deep skies and luminous, gold-edged sunsets; the towering silhouettes of buttes and mountain ranges, their rugged surfaces subtly alive with shifting shadows and pastel colors; a forest of widely spaced saguaro cacti, standing firm like many-armed sentinels amid sketchy creosote and ocotillo bushes while birds and lizards dart from one spiny haven to the next; or the long, green bowl of a mountain meadow, dusted with poppy clusters and blue lupine beds, edged with shimmering aspens. Arizonans and visitors alike never tire of watching the play of sun and shadows on some corner of this magnificent land.

–Mark Hein

NEW AND NOTEWORTHY

The new $47 million **Arizona Science Center** opened in Phoenix in 1997. The 40,000-square-ft indoor/outdoor exhibit space is a delight for kids of all ages. Lively "please touch" exhibits explain the physics of making gigantic soap bubbles, the technology of satellite weather systems, and more. Check out dazzling simulated orbits and eclipses under the 60-ft dome of the planetarium.

Phoenix's **Heard Museum,** internationally recognized for its exhibits on Native American history, culture, and art, broke ground in April 1997 for a $13.6 million, 50,000-square-ft expansion project. A new educational facility is going up on the lot north of the museum's 1929 main building and a 400-seat auditorium, new galleries, and a snack area are being added. The museum's archives and library will not only double in size, but they will also be linked by computer to research centers around the world.

The biggest news in Arizona is the long-awaited opening of **Kartchner Caverns**

State Park in the Whetstone mountain foothills near the southeast Arizona town of Benson, scheduled for November 1997. It is predicted that the caverns, said to rival those in Carlsbad for size and splendor of formations, will be the crown jewel of the state park system and draw some 150,000 visitors a year. Benson is banking on the lure of the underground, and is planning to add more tourist facilities. Widening Highway 90, which leads to the caves from the south, is also on the drawing board.

WHAT'S WHERE

The Grand Canyon and Northwest Arizona

In the face of this vast marvel, words can be hard to come by—except on the subject of recommendations: Go to the North Rim. It may take longer to get there, and it is closed in winter to all but cross-country skiers, but you will be rewarded by having a Wonder of the World more to yourself. In and around the state's northwest corner, Lake Mead, the Hoover Dam, and the gambling halls of Laughlin, Nevada, have their appeals, too.

The Northeast

This sprawling corner of the state is the home of the Navajo Nation and Hopi Reservation. Native American crafts draw some visitors, as does interest in gaining an understanding of the lives, past and present, of some of our land's true founding mothers and fathers. Along with the living Navajo and Hopi reservations, ancient Pueblo ruins at Betatakin, Keet Seel, and Canyon de Chelly are haunting, unforgettable sights. And don't forget about Monument Valley, and activities at another man-made lake, Lake Powell, when planning your trip.

North-Central Arizona

Jerome and Prescott are two of the state's most popular towns for their Wild West history, some of it bawdy and outrageous, all of it interesting, and for their place in yet another wondrous, beautiful locale. Sedona's red rocks, recognizable for the roles that they played in numerous Hollywood westerns, are as captivating as they are easy to hike. Flagstaff has become more of a destination in its own right, with historic buildings, an increasing number of good restaurants, and nightlife. Outside of the city, ancient Native American dwellings at Wupatki and Walnut Canyon national monuments and Sunset Crater are windows onto the world of a thousand years past.

Phoenix

The ever-widening Phoenix metropolitan area provides a tremendous variety of activities for almost all interests. Hike in the Valley of the Sun's superb desert parks, golf on championship courses, dine at the restaurants where Southwestern cuisine was born, or experience the last word in pampering at world-class spas and resorts.

Eastern Arizona

The White Mountains of Eastern Arizona are a sportsman's paradise. Hundreds of thousands of acres of virgin pine forest are crisscrossed by hiking and skiing trails of rugged beauty. Anglers delight in over 65 lakes and reservoirs well-stocked with bluegill, bass, and multiple varieties of trout. Even golfers should be pleased with the spruce-lined fairways, crisp air, and temperatures in the mid-eighties in the middle of the summer. To the north, Eastern Arizona's desert flatlands are home to one of the nation's natural wonders, the Petrified Forest National Park and the Painted Desert.

Tucson

Tucson's Spanish roots are still evident in the adobe buildings in the El Presidio neighborhood, the red-tile roof houses seen all around town, and the many great Mexican restaurants. The city's Native American heritage is evident not only in the crafts sold in many local shops, but also on the nearby Tohono O'odham Reservation, where you can visit Mission San Xavier del Bac, an architectural and art-historical masterpiece. But most people come here to enjoy nature: Tucson is flanked on its east and west sides by Saguaro National Park, and Sabino Canyon and Mt. Lemmon offer delightful respites from the summer heat.

Southern Arizona

Tombstone may be the best known of the mining boomtowns that dot Southern Arizona, but others such as Ajo and Bisbee also draw those interested in Wild West lore. For nature and bird lovers, Ramsey Canyon, Organ Pipe National Monument, and Chiricahua National Monument have fascinating flora and fauna and great hiking. Chiricahua is a particularly unique zone where species from the Southwest, the Chiricahua Mountains, and Mexico all live amid forests and volcanic rock formations.

PLEASURES AND PASTIMES

Ballooning

If you're so inclined, floating in a balloon can be a delight. In both Phoenix and Tucson pilots will take you up over metropolitan areas as well as the Sonoran Desert.

Baseball

Baseball fans visiting Arizona in March have a chance to watch major-league teams during spring training. Exhibition games, most of them held in the Phoenix area, begin in early March, but the eight Cactus League teams start practice at training camps as much as three weeks earlier. Their free drills—held in the morning before an exhibition game—are fun to watch, and there's a good chance you might be able to chat with the players before or after these sessions. In some cases, reserved seats sell out the fall before an upcoming season, but you can almost always get general admission seats on the day of the games.

Boating and Lake Activities

You may be surprised to find so many lakes in what most consider a desert state. In fact, Arizonans own more boats per capita than residents of any other state. The two national recreational areas, Glen Canyon (Lake Powell) in north-central Arizona and Lake Mead (including Lake Mohave) in the northwest, have marinas, launching ramps, and boat and ski rentals. At both lakes you can take a paddle-wheeler tour or take the wheel yourself in a fully equipped houseboat. Lake Havasu, fed by the Colorado River in the western part of the state, is another favored site for boating, waterskiing, windsurfing, and jetskiing. London Bridge, which was moved block by block from England and re-assembled here, is a surreal vision at this lakeside resort. Saguaro and Canyon lakes, just east of Scottsdale, offer good boating and waterskiing for those based in the Phoenix area who are looking for a convenient day trip.

Fishing

Fish virtually jump out of Arizona's cool mountain streams, major rivers, and man-made lakes and are especially plentiful at Colorado River resorts. Rainbow, brown, brook, and cutthroat trout, as well as catfish, crappie, bass, pike, and bluegill, are the primary game. Trout are plentiful at Lees Ferry, and in lakes and streams throughout the White Mountains. Fishing licenses *are* required.

Golf

Your clubs certainly won't gather dust in Arizona. Aside from the big-draw Phoenix and Tucson opens (☞ Festivals and Seasonal Events, *below*), golfers flock to this state to tee off at the myriad top-ranked private and municipal courses. Year-round desert courses offer cheaper greens fees during the summer, and those in the northern part of the state usually shut down for winter. Just about every resort has its own course or is affiliated with a private club.

Hiking

Throughout the state, hikers can choose from trails that wind through the desert, climb mountains, meander past supernal rock formations, delve deep into forests, or circumnavigate cities.

Horseback Riding

Traveling by horseback through the somewhat wild West or the scenic high country is perhaps the most appropriate way to explore Arizona. Stables offer a selection of mountain or desert trail rides lasting a half day, two days, or as long as two weeks. In northern regions the season is from May through October. If riding is the focus of your Arizona holiday, you might consider staying at a dude ranch, where you can saddle up every day.

Native American Culture

Watching Native American festivals and exploring the remains of earlier settlements can be a rewarding part of a trip to Arizona—we recommend any effort to enhance your understanding of aspects of Native American culture on your trip.

Rockhounding

Arizona is rock-hound heaven, its deserts and mountains laden with a dazzling variety of rocks and minerals: agate, jasper, tourmaline, petrified wood, quartz, turquoise, amethyst, precious opal, fire agate, and more. The Department of Mines and Mineral Resources has a fine Mining and Mineral Museum as well as a rockhounding reference library. Remember, however, to inquire about restrictions before you fill your pockets. Taking rocks is illegal on the Navajo and Hopi reservations, for example.

You can purchase rocks and minerals at specialty shops or at one of the state's year-round rock and gem shows. The largest shows are held in Quartzsite, about 19 mi from the California border, and in Tucson, generally from late January to mid-February.

Shopping

Many tourists come to Arizona for no other reason than to purchase fine Native American jewelry and crafts. Collectibles include Navajo rugs and sand paintings, Hopi kachina dolls (intricately carved and colorful representations of Hopi spiritual beings) and pottery, Tohono O'odham (Papago) basketry, and Apache beadwork, as well as the highly prized silver and turquoise jewelry produced by several different tribes.

Skiing

Cross-country and downhill skiing are winter pastimes in Arizona, even if the mountains in the state don't quite match the scale of the Rockies. Flagstaff Nordic Center, Mormon Lake Ski Touring Center southeast of Flagstaff, the North Rim Nordic Center, and miles of crisscrossing trails around Alpine are good places for cross-country skiing. The three peaks of Sunrise Park Resort in the White Mountains are owned and operated by the White Mountain Apache Indians and constitute the state's largest ski area. Other popular areas are Arizona Snowbowl near Flagstaff and Mount Lemmon Ski Valley near Tucson, the continent's southernmost ski slope.

FODOR'S CHOICE

Natural Wonders

★ **Grand Canyon, North Rim.** The only way to get to know the canyon is to hike or ride a mule down through all of those geological years to the bottom of the great chasm.

★ **Canyon de Chelly National Monument, Navajo Nation, the Northeast.** The silence and harmony with which these ancient cliff dwellings exist in their surroundings are truly profound—as they must have been for the canyon's inhabitants 700 and more years past.

★ **Sedona's red rocks.** Picnic or hike among Sedona's natural monuments and just feel the wonder of the place—it's the real reason to visit here.

★ **Desert Botanical Gardens, Phoenix.** An early morning walk through the desert gives perhaps the best, and most pleasant, view of the lives of its flora and fauna.

★ **Saguaro National Park, Tucson.** You'll see the world's largest stand of the towering saguaro cactus here, as well as fascinating petroglyphs (rock art) made by the Hohokam people at sites such as Signal Hill, on the park's west side.

★ **Taliesin West, Phoenix.** Architect Frank Lloyd Wright's winter residence is an ingenious integration of indoor and outdoor space.

Scenic Drives

★ **Coronado Trail.** The 123-mi stretch of steep highway from Springerville to Clifton is renowned for the dramatic transitions of its 5,000-ft elevation change—winding from verdant meadows down into the Sonoran Desert's piñon pine and cacti.

★ **Point Sublime, North Rim, Grand Canyon.** The dirt road out to the point provides one of the most awe-inspiring panoramic views you'll have from a car, anywhere.

★ **U.S. 163 from Kayenta, Arizona, to the Goosenecks of the San Juan River in southern Utah.** This drive through the archetypal Wild West landscape of Monument Valley ends in a winding, water-carved canyon of the San Juan River, a unique counterpart to the Grand Canyon.

★ **Flagstaff to Sedona via Oak Creek Canyon, North-Central Arizona.** Another stunning canyon, this one quiet and tree-lined on its low end, towering and majestic as it looks toward Sedona, marks the transition from northern Arizona's Colorado Plateau to the southern desert landscape.

★ **Jerome to Prescott, North-Central Arizona.** The winding road through Prescott National Forest is one of Arizona's most breathtaking mountain drives—precipitous at times, but beautiful.

★ **Texas Canyon, Southern Arizona.** Does one ever tire of canyons? We don't think so, especially when they are hung with giant boulders apparently defying their great mass in astonishing formations, as in this one, east of Tucson.

★ **Tucson to Kitt Peak, Tucson and Southern Arizona.** About 20 mi southwest of Tucson, upon entering the Tohono O'odham reservation, you enter the heart of the desert and climb the mountain that's home to a world-renowned astronomical observatory.

Restaurants

★ **Chistopher's, Phoenix.** Christopher Gross offers the Valley's finest French cuisine. His flawlessly prepared and sauced creations are worthy of the Champs-Elysées. *$$$–$$$$*

★ **Heartline Café, Sedona, North-Central Arizona.** What some might call hippie haute cuisine—because they love it, of course—includes tasty grilled food, inventive pizza, and southwestern dishes in a pleasant, friendly atmosphere. *$$–$$$*

★ **Such Is Life, Phoenix.** Come to Moises Treves's corner of Phoenix to taste cactus, chicken Maya, garlic shrimp—yes, delicious regional Mexican food. *$$*

★ **Café Poca Cosa, Tucson.** Ooh, those tropical colors, and ooh, what fantastic regional Mexican cooking—especially if you like chicken mole. You won't find any excesses of cheese here. *$–$$*

★ **Los Dos Molinos, Phoenix.** Pure, hot New Mexico–style cooking graces colorful tile tables in this bustling, white-adobe cantina. Be careful: The fresh, homemade green- and red-chili salsas can rip your lips off. *$*

★ **Prescott Brewing Company, Prescott, North-Central Arizona.** The name doesn't lie: Four draughts are brewed on the premises and are served up along with a menu of good pub fare—even vegetarians will be pleasantly surprised. *$*

Hotels and B&Bs

★ **The Boulders, Phoenix.** The Valley's most serene and secluded luxury resort hides among the hill-size granite boulders in the foothills town of Carefree. *$$$$*

★ **The Phoenician, Phoenix.** French-provincial decor, fine European paintings, gleaming marble, and spacious rooms make this the swankiest joint in town. A 2-acre desert garden shelters hundreds of cacti and succulents, and Windows on the Green offers some of the best Southwest cuisine in the city. *$$$$*

★ **Arizona Inn, Tucson.** With almost all that you would want from a landmark inn—period furnishings, fireplaces, quiet and friendly service, even a downtown location on property of its own—you won't be disappointed with a stay here. *$$$–$$$$*

★ **Briar Patch Inn, Sedona, North-Central Arizona.** It may not be in the heart of Sedona's red rocks, but its lovely Oak Creek Canyon location alongside the laughing water, and so many touches, sets the Briar Patch apart. *$$$–$$$$*

★ **Wahweap Lodge at Lake Powell, the Northeast.** A central and well-equipped location for Lake Powell recreation, Wahweap has cruises; river excursions; boat, ski, and tackle rentals; and a restaurant that make for a nearly all-in-one resort. *$$$*

★ **Grand Canyon Lodge, North Rim, Grand Canyon.** We've said it once, and we'll say it again—come to the North Rim to avoid the crowds and *enjoy* the mighty abyss. While you're here, why not stay in the historic, rustic Grand Canyon Lodge, with spectacular views of you-know-what. *$–$$$*

★ **Casa Tierra Bed & Breakfast, Tucson.** In an adobe brick building, this friendly bed-and-breakfast outside of town is a great desert getaway, highly recommended. *$$*

★ **Cameron Trading Post at Cameron, Grand Canyon.** This may well be the best base, or even jumping-off point, for both the Grand Canyon, North and South rims, and Navajo-Hopi country, all with its own trading-post–style charm. *$–$$*

FESTIVALS AND SEASONAL EVENTS

JAN. 1➤ Tempe's nationally televised **Fiesta Bowl Footbowl Classic** (☎ 602/350–2900) kicks off the year with a match between the nation's top two college teams.

JAN.➤ At the **Phoenix Open Golf Tournament** (☎ 602/870–4431) in Scottsdale, top players compete at the Tournament Players Club.

JAN.➤ The **Dixieland Jazz Festival** (☎ 800/624–7939) at Lake Havasu City uses London Bridge as the backdrop to traditional Dixieland sounds and more, including a parade, dancing on a riverboat, and Sunday-morning gospel.

JAN.–FEB.➤ **Parada del Sol Rodeo and Parade** (☎ 602/990–3179), a popular state attraction on Scottsdale Road, features lots of dressed-up cowboys and cowgirls, plus horses and floats.

EARLY FEB.➤ The **Quartzsite Pow Wow Gem and Mineral Show** (☎ 520/927–6325) is a gigantic flea market, held the first Wednesday through Sunday of the month in Quartzsite, about 19 mi from the California border (take I–10 west of Phoenix and then turn north on AZ 95).

FEB.➤ At **O'odham Tash** (☎ 520/836–4723) in Casa Grande, Native American tribes from around the country host parades, native dances, a rodeo, costume displays, and food stands.

FEB.➤ History comes to life during **Wickenburg Gold Rush Days** (☎ 520/684–5479) when the Old West town puts on a rodeo, dances, gold-panning demonstrations, a mineral show, and other activities.

FEB.➤ **La Fiesta de los Vaqueros** (☎ 520/741–2233) features the world's longest "nonmechanized" parade—horses pull floats and carry dignitaries—launching a four-day rodeo at the Tucson Rodeo Grounds.

FEB.➤ The huge **Tucson Gem and Mineral Show** (☎ 520/322–5773) attracts rock hounds—amateur and professional—from all over the world who come to buy, sell, and display their geological treasures and to attend lectures and competitive exhibits.

MAR.➤ In Phoenix, the **Heard Museum Guild Indian Fair and Market** (☎ 602/252–8840) is a prestigious juried show of Native American arts and crafts. Visitors can also enjoy Native American foods, music, and dance.

MAR.➤ The highlight of the **Ostrich Festival** (☎ 602/963–4571) in Chandler is a race of the big birds; it also features a parade, live entertainment, and crafts and food.

MAR.➤ For the **Lost Dutchman Gold Mine Superstition Mountain Trek** (☎ 602/258–6016) in Apache Junction, the Dons of Arizona search for the legendary lost mine, pan for gold, and eat lots of barbecue to keep up their strength. There are crafts demonstrations and fireworks, too.

APR.➤ Tucson hosts the **International Mariachi Conference** (☎ 520/884–9920), four days of mariachi music, along with cultural and educational exhibits.

APR.➤ During the **Route 66 Fun Run Weekend** (☎ 520/753–5001) from Seligman to Topock, the historic road between Chicago and Los Angeles is feted with classic car rallies, hot-rod and antique-car shows, and various other events—including a 1950s hop.

APR.➤ **Yaqui Easter** (☎ 520/791–4609) is celebrated in old Pasqua Village (Tucson) on the Saturday nights preceding Palm Sunday and Easter Sunday. Visitors are welcome to watch traditional Yaqui dances and ceremonies.

APR.➤ Bisbee's **La Vuelta de Bisbee** (☎ 520/432–4271) is Arizona's largest bicycle race and attracts top racers from around the country to the hills of the historic mining town.

MAY➤ During the **Bill Williams Rendezvous** (☎ 520/635–4061), the townspeople of Williams reenact the annual trek to town by 1800s mountain traders. Events include a steak fry and a

Buckskinners black powder shoot.

MAY–JUNE➤ At Flagstaff's **Trappings of the American West Festival** (☎ 520/779–6921), the featured attraction is cowboy art—everything from painting and sculpture to cowboy poetry readings.

SUMMER

JUNE➤ Festivities of **Old West Day/Bucket of Blood Races** (☎ 520/524–6558), in Holbrook, include arts and crafts, western dress, and Native American song and dance, in addition to the 10-km (2-mi) fun run and 20-mi bike ride from Petrified Forest National Park to Holbrook.

JULY➤ **Prescott Frontier Days and Rodeo,** billed as the world's oldest rodeo, finds big crowds and an equally big party on downtown Whiskey Row.

JULY➤ The **Native American Arts & Crafts Festival** (☎ 520/367–4290) in Pinetop-Lakeside brings storytellers, dancers, musicians, and artists together for two days in a beautiful mountain setting.

AUG.➤ The **Payson Rodeo** (☎ 520/474–4515) draws top cowboys from around the country to compete for top prizes in calf- and steer-roping contests at what they call the world's oldest continuous rodeo.

AUG.➤ Flagstaff's **SummerFest** (☎ 520/774–5130) is a gathering of painters, potters, musicians, and other artists from around the United States. They vie with carnival rides and food vendors for the crowd's attention.

AUG.➤ The **Southwest Wings Birding Festival** (☎ 520/378–0233), held in Sierra Vista, the self-proclaimed Hummingbird Capital of the United States, includes field trips, lectures by recognized Audubon authorities, and other avian-oriented events.

AUTUMN

SEPT.➤ At the **Jazz on the Rocks Festival** (☎ 520/282–1985) in Sedona, six or seven ensembles perform in a spectacular red-rock setting.

SEPT.➤ The **Navajo Nation Annual Tribal Fair** (☎ 520/871–6702) is the world's largest Native American fair. Held in Window Rock, it includes a rodeo, traditional Navajo music and dances, food booths, and an intertribal powwow.

OCT.➤ **Rex Allen Days** in Willcox honors the local cowboy film star and narrator for Walt Disney productions with a parade, country fair, rodeo, dances, and more.

OCT.➤ Spicy food lovers revel at **La Fiesta de Los Chiles** (☎ 520/326–9686), Tucson's two-day salute to the chili, which is cooked, hung, made into art, and otherwise celebrated.

OCT.➤ At **Tombstone's Helldorado Days,** the town relives the spirited Wyatt Earp era and the shoot-out at the OK Corral.

OCT.➤ A weeklong event, **London Bridge Days** (☎ 520/453–3444) includes a triathlon, a parade, and a variety of British-themed contests in Lake Havasu City.

NOV.➤ At 110 mi, **El Tour De Tucson** (☎ 520/745–2033) is the largest perimeter bicycling event in the world, attracting international celebrity cyclists.

NOV.➤ During the **Thunderbird Balloon Classic & Air Show** (☎ 602/978–7208), 150 or more balloons participate in Scottsdale's colorful race.

DEC.➤ The **Arizona Temple Gardens & Visitors Center Christmas Lighting** (☎ 602/964–7164) in Mesa finds more than 300,000 lights illuminating the walkways, reflection pool, trees, and plants at the Arizona Temple Gardens and Visitors Center.

DEC.➤ The waters of Lake Powell alight with the **Festival of Lights Boat Parade** (☎ 520/645–1001) as dozens of illuminated boats glide from Wahweap Lodge to Glen Canyon Dam and back.

DEC.➤ For the three days of **Old Town Tempe Fall Festival of the Arts** (☎ 602/967–4877), the downtown area closes to traffic for art exhibits, food booths, music, and other entertainment.

2 The Grand Canyon and Northwest Arizona

To appreciate the Grand Canyon, you must see it for yourself. Even the finest photographs fail to deliver a fraction of the impact of a personal glimpse into this vast, beautiful scar on the surface of our planet—277 mi long, 18 mi across at its widest spot, and more than a mile below the rim at its deepest point. The Grand Canyon is the quintessence of the high drama of the American western landscape. In and around the state's northwest corner, Lake Mead, the Hoover Dam, and the gambling halls of Laughlin, Nevada, have their appeals, too.

By William E.
Hafford and
Edie Jarolim

Updated by
Gregory
McNamee

ALTHOUGH MILLIONS of words have been devoted to describing the Grand Canyon, writers generally have conceded that the earth's greatest gorge is beyond the scope of language. Southwestern author Frank Waters has come closer than most to capturing its power. "It is the sum total," he writes, "of all the aspects of nature combined in one integrated whole. It is at once the smile and frown upon the face of nature. In its heart is the savage, uncontrollable fury of all the inanimate Universe, and at the same time the immeasurable serenity that succeeds it. It is Creation." Less eloquently, but no less spiritedly, an 1892 visitor remarked, "By Joe! This canyon takes the whole shooting-match!"

More than 65 million years ago, a long series of violent geological upheavals created a domed tableland, today called the Colorado Plateau. Then the Colorado River, racing south through present-day Utah, began chewing at the uplifted region. The river is responsible for much of the erosion, but many side gullies and canyons were formed by melting snow and fierce rainstorms that sent water rushing into the gorge through smaller tributaries. Softer rock formations were washed away by the Colorado and carried to the distant sea; the harder formations remained as great cliffs and buttes. Above the twisting line of river are otherworldly stone monuments with colors that range from muted pastels to deep purples, vibrant yellows, fiery reds, and soft blues. This palette shifts with the hours: What you see at mid-morning is repainted by the setting sun, and each scene is just a little different from the one that preceded it.

This is also a land of ancient peoples. In some of the deepest, most inaccessible reaches of the Grand Canyon, evidence of early human habitation exists. Stone ruins high in the cliffs reveal the archaeological secrets of cultures 8,000 to 10,000 years old. In higher country, above both the North and South rims, are the remains of prehistoric Pueblo settlements that were active until about AD 1350. A period of harsh and sustained drought, climatic change, soil erosion, and heavy use of local resources is thought to have caused the people to seek more favorable lands. Today's Hopi Indians, along with New Mexican Pueblo people, view themselves as descendants of the earlier inhabitants, whose former dwellings, they believe, hold ancestral spirits.

In the year 1540 a band of Spanish soldiers under the command of Captain García López de Cárdenas became the first white men to look into the canyon. The members of the expedition, dispatched by Francisco Coronado to find the fabled golden cities of Cibola, found the Grand Canyon instead. Spanish Franciscan missionary and explorer Francisco Tomás Garcés visited a Havasupai Indian village in the canyon in 1776, and Lieutenant Joseph Ives went on an official mission for the U.S. government to explore the area in 1857–58. Ives did not like the region much, writing in his report to Congress that "it seems intended by nature that the Colorado River, along the greater portion of its lonely and majestic way, shall be forever unvisited and undisturbed." That was indeed the case until 1869, when John Wesley Powell, a one-armed Civil War hero, adventurer, and scholar, put rough-hewn boats into the Colorado and let the swirling white water of the mighty river take him along its length. After Powell came countless other explorers, fortune hunters, and visitors to prove Ives wrong.

During the last years of the 19th century, almost all development at or near the canyon was related to mining. The earliest trails down into the canyon were built by miners searching for precious minerals.

Shortly after the beginning of the 20th century, the Santa Fe Railroad completed a line to the canyon's South Rim. This and Theodore Roosevelt's 1903 visit drew public interest to the site, which was declared a national park in 1919. Today close to 5 million visitors come each year from around the world to peer into the gorge.

Your first view of the Grand Canyon will last a lifetime. After a half dozen lookouts, however, your sense of wonder will begin to diminish—it's difficult to establish a personal relationship with so much grandeur. Traveling along the rim, you will soon tire of putting your nose up against all this beauty, safely, almost antiseptically. But take the plunge: Even a short hike down any of the trails will open up a totally new perspective on the incredible scale of this massive abyss.

Pleasures and Pastimes

Cross-Country Skiing

The North Rim Nordic Center at Kaibab Lodge (☞ Outdoor Activities and Sports *in* The North Rim, *below*) contains the largest groomed-trail wilderness skiing system in the United States: 52 mi of regularly groomed trails and 21½ mi of marked backcountry trails within the 1.6-million-acre Kaibab National Forest. The center's challenging trails, including the 8½-mi Tater Ridge Trail and the appropriately named Adrenaline Alley, a mile-long screamer that gauges one's talent for dodging tree trunks.

Dining

Throughout Grand Canyon country and northwestern Arizona, restaurants cater to tourists who generally move from one place to another at a good clip. Most establishments serve standard American fare, prepared quickly and offered at reasonable prices. An exception to this general rule is the world-class restaurant and service at El Tovar, the oldest hotel in the canyon. Restaurants are open daily unless otherwise noted, and dress throughout this recreational area is casual (though you may want to don your hole-free jeans for the El Tovar dining room).

CATEGORY	COST*
$$$$	over $25
$$$	$17–$25
$$	$10–$17
$	under $10

per person, excluding drinks, service, and 5% sales tax

Hiking

Hiking opportunities range from leisurely walks on well-defined paths through easy-rolling country to arduous multiday treks to the bottom of the canyon—and across to the other rim if you'd like. Some of the more popular trails are outlined in this chapter; park rangers or visitor-center personnel can provide you with information about other routes.

Lodging

The Fred Harvey Company opened the El Tovar Hotel on the South Rim in 1905, heralding the development of Grand Canyon Village. Now there are more than 900 motel and hotel rooms in the Village, but even that number of accommodations is insufficient in summer. The North Rim is less crowded but has limited lodging facilities. Make reservations as soon as your itinerary has been decided, even as early as a year in advance. The South Rim's National Park Service Visitor Center, just outside Grand Canyon Village, posts the availability of hotel rooms inside the park and in the nearby town of Tusayan. If you can't find accommodations in the immediate area of the South Rim, you'll probably find something in the nearby communities of Williams or Flagstaff (☞ Flagstaff *in* Chapter 4). Prices at many of the hotels and motels in Grand Canyon country are lower in spring, fall, and winter.

CATEGORY	COST*
$$$$	over $110
$$$	$85–$110
$$	$60–$85
$	under $60

All prices are for a standard double room, excluding 5.5%–6.7% tax.

Mountain Biking

Mountain-bike enthusiasts revel in the network of dirt access roads that lace the North Rim, among them a 17-mi muscle tester that leads to Point Sublime, overlooking the inner canyon's Granite Gorge and its fierce rapids. A network of Jeep trails fans out north of Point Sublime, leading to other vistas to the west; mountain bikers who follow those trails are likely to have the place to themselves during most of the year.

Rafting

Many people who have made the white-water trip down the Colorado River through the Grand Canyon say it is the adventure of a lifetime. Trips embark from Lees Ferry, below Glen Canyon Dam near Page, Arizona. Those that run the length of the canyon can last from three days to three weeks. Shorter treks, also starting at Lees Ferry, let passengers off at Phantom Ranch at the bottom of the Grand Canyon (about 100 mi). These pass through a great amount of white water, including Lava Falls rapids (on longer trips), considered the wildest navigable rapids in North America. For those who would like a more tranquil turn on the Colorado, there are also one-day, quiet-water raft excursions that begin below Glen Canyon Dam near Page.

Exploring the Grand Canyon and Northwest Arizona

The Grand Canyon stretches across northwest Arizona. Its popular South Rim includes the Village Rim, East Rim Drive, and West Rim Drive. The drive to the less-visited North Rim, in the Arizona Strip—a 12,000-square-mi tract of land isolated from the rest of the state by the Colorado River—takes in views of the Painted Desert to the east. Havasu Canyon, south of the middle part of the national park, provides another respite from the crowds. To the northwest is Lake Mead, the largest man-made body of water in the United States, formed by the construction of giant Hoover Dam.

Numbers in the text correspond to numbers in the margin and on the South Rim and East Rim Drive, South Rim and West Rim Drive, North Rim, and Northwest Arizona and Lake Mead maps.

Great Itineraries

A visit of three days will make hurried travelers feel they have "done" the Grand Canyon; a lengthier stay of 10 days or so is enough to make most visitors feel like old hands—particularly if they've been able to experience some white-water rafting on the Colorado River. Budgeting a few extra days will allow for a trip to the Lake Mead area.

IF YOU HAVE 2 OR 3 DAYS

Spend the first night in 🏨 **Williams** ㉓. The next morning, board the historic **Grand Canyon Railway,** which takes you to the South Rim of the canyon. Spend the afternoon visiting **Grand Canyon Village** and then perhaps take in the informative IMAX film in nearby **Tusayan** (taxis or a shuttle bus will take you there). Spend the night at 🏨 **Grand Canyon Village** and the next morning take a tour of the **Village Rim** ⑨–⑭ or

Grand Canyon National Park

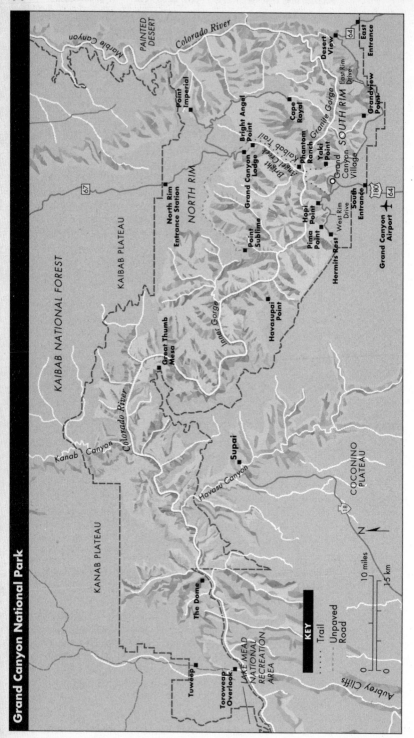

KEY

Trail

Unpaved Road

build up an appetite with a short hike before lunch, then take the 3:15 train back to Williams.

If you don't want to be at the Grand Canyon itself, try hiking in the less-frequented **Havasu Canyon.** Hike 8 mi down into the canyon to the small village of Supai and the Havasupai Lodge. You'll want to spend at least two days in this hiker's heaven. On the morning of the third day, give yourself plenty of time and water to climb back out of the canyon, or consider riding up by mule.

IF YOU HAVE 4 OR 5 DAYS

You will have time to ponder the marvels of the Grand Canyon, both from above as well as from below. After a night at the **Grand Canyon Village,** take the mule-pack expedition down the **Bright Angel Trailhead** ⑬, stopping along the way for a picnic lunch on a plateau with breathtaking views. Arrive at **Phantom Ranch** for dinner and a night's sleep, then return by mule pack to the **South Rim** and another night or two in the Grand Canyon area.

IF YOU HAVE 7 TO 10 DAYS

You will have time for a memorable expedition that includes hiking the canyon as well as experiencing the thrill of white-water rafting along the Colorado River. If time allows, drive through the Arizona Strip to the North Rim. Alternatively, head to the northwest to visit **Lake Mead** ㊲ and view **Hoover Dam** ㉟.

When to Tour the Grand Canyon and Northwest Arizona

If you can arrange it, try to visit the Grand Canyon in the fall or spring. You might encounter cold weather during those periods, but chances are good that most days will be clear and pleasantly cool or even warm. In autumn and spring, when the crowds have thinned, reservations are much easier to arrange, and in some cases prices drop. Or consider a winter visit to the South Rim. Snow on the ground only enhances the site's sublime beauty. Note: The North Rim is closed from mid-October to mid-May, when heavy snows close the area's highways and facilities.

THE SOUTH RIM AND ENVIRONS

The approach to the South Rim of the Grand Canyon is across the relatively level surface of the 7,000-ft Coconino Plateau, so you won't see the great gorge until you're past Tusayan, practically at its edge. Truth be told, the South Rim is a bit of a circus in summer. Most of Grand Canyon Village was laid out before the park service existed; the area is not well equipped to accommodate the crowds that converge on the area every summer (and increasingly throughout the spring and fall). It's hard to commune with one of nature's great spectacles when you've just spent two hours looking for a parking spot (there are only 1,400 spaces for the approximately 6,000 cars that enter each day) and are now being asked to step out of the range of someone's video camera. Not even a descent into the canyon itself guarantees a getaway at this time of year. For your sake as well as that of the canyon, it's best to avoid the South Rim in its busiest season.

Tusayan and Environs

81 mi northwest of Flagstaff on U.S. 180.

The town of Tusayan, 2 mi south of Grand Canyon National Park's south entrance has dining, lodging, and other facilities. Its main attraction is an IMAX theater that screens an exciting 34-minute film, *Grand*

Canyon—The Hidden Secrets, shown on a 70-ft-high screen. The script is informative, and some of the shots—especially those of boats running the rapids—are positively dizzying. ✉ *AZ 64/U.S. 180*, ☎ *520/638–2203.* ☞ *$7.* ☉ *Mar. 1–Oct. 31, daily 8:30–8:30; Nov.–Feb., daily 10:30–6:30; shows every hr on the ½ hr.*

Lodging

$$$–$$$$ 🏨 **Best Western Grand Canyon Squire Inn.** About 2 mi south of the park entrance, this motel lacks some of the historic charm of the older lodges at the canyon rim, but it has more amenities—including a bowling alley, a small cowboy museum in the stylish lobby, and an upscale gift shop. Spacious rooms have southwestern-style furnishings. Ask for one with a view of the woods; others face the highway. ✉ *AZ 64/U.S. 180, Box 130, Grand Canyon 86023,* ☎ *520/638–2681 or 800/622–6966,* ℻ *520/638–2782. 250 rooms, 4 rooms accessible to people with disabilities. Coffee shop, dining room, lounge, pool, beauty salon, sauna, 2 tennis courts, bowling, exercise room, billiards, video games, travel services. AE, D, DC, MC, V.*

$$$ 🏨 **Quality Inn.** First-floor rooms can be entered either from a drive-up door or from an atrium featuring a spa and lounge. Accommodations, done in soothing shades of light blue, peach, or tan, have coffeemakers and two sinks. An all-you-can-eat buffet breakfast at the full-service restaurant is a good way to fortify yourself for a day at the canyon. ✉ *AZ 64/U.S. 180, Box 520, Grand Canyon 86023,* ☎ *520/638–2673 or 800/221–2222,* ℻ *520/638–9537. 176 rooms. Restaurant, lounge, minibars, pool. AE, D, DC, MC, V.*

🔥 **Flintstones Bedrock City.** You'll find 28 tent sites and 32 partial RV hookups in a cartoon-kitsch setting here. Basic rates are $12 per site for two people; add $2 for electricity hookup, $2 for water hookup, and $1.50 for each additional person. Facilities include a gift shop full of Flintstones memorabilia, a diner, and pay showers. ✉ *Grand Canyon Hwy. (30 mi south of Grand Canyon National Park at U.S. 180/AZ 64 junction), HC 34, Box A, Williams 86046,* ☎ *520/635–2600.* ☉ *Apr.–Oct. (may open earlier or close later, depending on weather).*

🔥 **Grand Canyon Camper Village.** The village has 250 RV hookups, some partial, some full ($23 for two people, plus $2 for each additional person over the age of 12), and 100 tent sites ($15 for two people). ✉ *Off AZ 64/U.S. 180, Box 490, Grand Canyon 86023,* ☎ *520/638–2887.* ☉ *Year-round.*

🔥 **Ten X Campground.** This campground has 70 family sites, water, and pit toilets for $10 per day but no hookups or showers. No reservations are accepted. ✉ *Kaibab National Forest, 9 mi south of Grand Canyon National Park east of AZ 64/U.S. 180. Tusayan Ranger District:* ✉ *Box 3088, Grand Canyon 86023,* ☎ *520/638–2443.* ☉ *May 1–Sept. 30.*

Outdoor Activities and Sports

HORSEBACK RIDING

You can rent extremely gentle horses at the **Apache Stables** at Moqui Lodge (✉ *U.S. 180,* ☎ *520/638–2891 or 520/638–2424).* The cost is $22 an hour, $36 for two hours. A four-hour East Rim ride goes for $57.50, a campfire horse and hay-wagon ride for $27 ($7.50 if you ride in the wagon rather than on your own horse). The stables open in March, and rides are offered, weather permitting, through the end of November.

Approaching the South Rim

❶ **Mather Point,** approximately 4 mi north of the south entrance, gives you the first glimpse of the canyon from one of the most impressive and accessible vista points on the rim; from it, you can see nearly one quarter of Grand Canyon. This overlook, named for the National Park Service's first director, Stephen Mather, yields extraordinary views of the Inner Gorge and the numerous buttes that rise out of the eroded chasm: Wotan's Throne, Brahma Temple, Zoroaster Temple, and many others. The Grand Canyon Lodge, on the North Rim, is almost directly north from Mather Point and only 10 mi away—yet you have to drive nearly 210 mi to get from one spot to the other.

★ ❷ The **National Park Service's Visitor Center,** in Grand Canyon Village just west of Yavapai Point, is an excellent place for gathering information, whether you're interested in escapist treks or group tours. Park rangers are on hand to answer questions and aid in planning Grand Canyon excursions; short movies and slide shows on the canyon are presented regularly; and there's a bookstore. A daily schedule for ranger-led hikes and evening lectures is also posted. Buses and taxis leave from here for the IMAX theater in Tusayan (☞ *above*).

A separate exhibit area profiles the area's natural and human history. The first inhabitants were probably nomadic Paleo-Indians, arriving more than 10,000 years ago. Artifacts that were found in caves deep in the canyon were left by a later Archaic culture. They are perfectly preserved figurines of animals, made from willow twigs more than 4,000 years ago—thus predating Homeric Greece by 1,000 years. About 2,200 years ago, ancestral Pueblo culture began to develop around the canyon. The museum also traces the arrival of explorers Captain García López de Cárdenas, John Wesley Powell, and others. ⊠ *East side of Grand Canyon Village, about 1 mi east of El Tovar Hotel,* ☎ *520/ 638–7888.* ▨ *Free.* ☉ *Memorial Day–Labor Day, daily 8–6; rest of yr, daily 8–5.*

Outdoor Activities and Sports

If you'd like a little exercise and great overlooks of the canyon, it's an easy hike from the back of the visitor center to the El Tovar Hotel (☞ The Village Rim, *below*). Walk through a pretty wooded area for about ½ mi, where the path then runs along the rim for another ½ mi or so.

East Rim Drive

The breathtaking East Rim Drive proceeds east for about 25 mi along the South Rim from Grand Canyon Village to Desert View. Before beginning the drive, consider stopping to see the exhibits and attend the free lectures offered by park naturalists at Yavapai Observation Station, ¾ mi east of the visitor center. There are four posted picnic areas along the route and rest rooms at Tusayan Museum and Desert View.

❸ **Yaki Point,** east of Grand Canyon Village on AZ 64, provides an exceptional view of Wotan's Throne, a majestic flat-top butte named by François Matthes, a U.S. Geological Survey scientist who developed the first topographical map of the Grand Canyon. Due north is Buddha Temple, capped by limestone; Newton Butte, with its flat top of red sandstone, lies to the east. At Yaki Point the popular **Kaibab Trail** starts the descent to the Inner Gorge, crosses the Colorado over a steel suspension bridge, and wends its way to rustic Phantom Ranch (☞ Dining and Lodging, *below*), the only lodging facility at the bottom of the Grand Canyon. A short hike down the Kaibab Trail will give you a feel for a descent into the canyon. If you plan to go more than a mile, carry water with you (☞ Hiking *in* Outdoor Activities and Sports, *below*). If you encounter a mule train, the animals have the right-of-way. Move to the inside of the trail and wait as they pass.

The South Rim and East Rim Drive

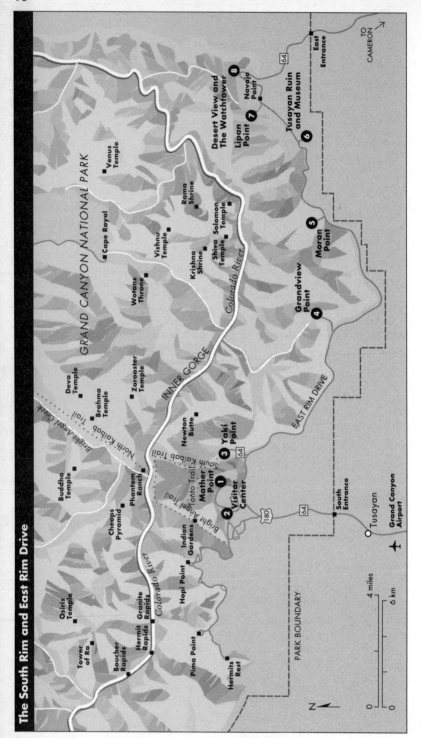

❹ About 7 mi east of Yaki Point, **Grandview Point,** at an altitude of 7,496 ft, has large stands of ponderosa pine, piñon pine, oak, and juniper. The view from here is one of the finest in the canyon. To the northeast is a group of dominant buttes, including Krishna Shrine, Vishnu Temple, Rama Shrine, and Shiva Temple. A short stretch of the Colorado River is also visible. Directly below the point and accessible by the Grandview Trail is Horseshoe Mesa, where you can see ruins of the Last Chance Copper Mine. Grandview Point was also the site of the Grandview Hotel, constructed in the late 1890s but closed in 1908; logs salvaged from the hotel were used for the Kiva Room of the Desert View Watchtower (☞ *below*).

❺ **Moran Point,** about 5 mi east of Grandview Point, was named for American landscape artist Thomas Moran, who painted Grand Canyon scenes from many points on the rim but was especially fond of the play of light and shadows from this location. He first visited the canyon with John Wesley Powell in 1873, and his vivid canvases helped persuade Congress to create a national park at the Grand Canyon. "Thomas Moran's name, more than any other, with the possible exception of Major Powell's, is to be associated with the Grand Canyon," wrote the noted canyon photographer Ellsworth Kolb, and it is fitting that Moran Point is a favorite spot for photographers and painters.

Three miles east of Moran Point on the south side of the highway is ❻ the entrance to the **Tusayan Ruin and Museum,** which contains evidence of early habitation in the Grand Canyon and information about the lifestyles of ancestral Pueblo people. *Tusayan* comes from a Hopi phrase meaning "country of isolated buttes," which certainly fits the scenery. The partially intact rock dwellings here were occupied for roughly 20 years around AD 1200 by 30 or so Indian hunters, farmers, and gatherers. They moved elsewhere, like so many others, pressured by drought and depletion of natural resources to find better settlements. A museum and a bookstore display artifacts, models of the dwellings, and exhibits on modern tribes of the region. Free 30-minute guided tours—as many as five during the summer, fewer in winter—are given daily. ⊠ *East Rim Dr., 3 mi east of Moran Point,* ☎ *520/638–2305.* ☜ *Free.* ☉ *Daily 9–5.*

❼ **Lipan Point,** 1 mi northeast of Tusayan Ruin, is the canyon's widest point. From here you can get an astonishing visual profile of the gorge's geologic history, with a view of every eroded layer of the canyon. You can also see Unkar Delta, where a wide creek joins the Colorado to form powerful rapids and a broad beach. Anasazi farmers worked the Unkar Delta for hundreds of years, growing corn, beans, and melons.

Just over 1 mi east of Lipan Point lies 7,461-ft **Navajo Point,** the probable site of the first Spanish descent into the Canyon, in 1540. Just west of Navajo Point is the head of the unmaintained Tanner Trail, a rugged route historically favored by gold prospectors, rustlers (it is also called Horsethief Trail), and bootleggers. Navajo Point is the highest elevation on the South Rim.

❽ **Desert View** and **The Watchtower** make for a climactic final stop. From the top of the 70-ft stone-and-mortar watchtower, built in 1932 by the Fred Harvey Company and the Santa Fe Railroad in the style of Native American structures, even the muted pastel hues of the distant Painted Desert to the east and the 3,000-ft-high Vermilion Cliffs rising from a high plateau near the Utah border are visible. In the chasm below, angling to the north toward Marble Canyon, an imposing stretch of the Colorado River reveals itself. The Watchtower houses a glass-enclosed observatory with powerful telescopes. ⊠ *The Watch-tower,* ☎ *520/638–2736; 520/638–2360 trading post.* 🖾 *Free; 25¢ to climb Watchtower.* ☼ *Daily 8–7 or 8–8 in summer, daily 9–6 in winter.*

Dining and Lodging

$ ✕🖾 **Phantom Ranch.** Built in 1932 on the site of an earlier hunting camp, this group of wood-and-stone buildings is set among a grove of cottonwood trees at the bottom of the canyon. For hikers (who need a backcountry permit to come down here), dormitory accommodations—20 beds for men and 20 for women—are available, as are two cabins (one sleeps four people, the other 10). Seven additional cabins are re-served exclusively for mule riders; lodging, meals, and mule rides are offered as a package (☞ Guided Tours *in* The Grand Canyon and North-west Arizona A to Z, *below*). The restaurant at Phantom Ranch, prob-ably the most remote eating establishment in the United States, has a limited menu. All meals are served family style, with breakfast, din-ner, and box lunches available. Arrangements—and payment—for food and lodging should be made 9 to 11 months in advance. ⊠ *Amfac Parks and Resorts, 14001 E. Iliff, Suite 600, Aurora, CO 80014,* ☎ *303/297–2757,* 🖾 *303/297–3175. 4 dormitories with shared bath and 2 cabins for hikers, 7 cabins with shower outside for mule riders. Dining room. AE, D, DC, MC, V.*

⚠ **Bright Angel.** This free campground is en route to Phantom Ranch, close to the bottom of the canyon. There are toilet facilities and run-ning water but no showers. A backcountry permit is required to stay here. ⊠ *Backcountry Office, Box 129, Grand Canyon 86023,* ☎ *520/ 638–7875.* ☼ *Year-round.*

⚠ **Desert View Campground.** RV and tent sites, flush toilets, and water but no hookups are available here for $10 per night, with no reservations. ⊠ *23 mi east of Grand Canyon Village off AZ 64; Box 129, Grand Canyon 86023,* ☎ *520/638–7888. Reservations: Destinet,* ⊠ *Box 85705, San Diego, CA 92186–5705,* ☎ *800/365–2267.* ☼ *May–Sept.*

⚠ **Indian Garden.** About halfway down the canyon is this free camp-ground, located en route to Phantom Ranch. Running water and toi-let facilities are available, but there are no showers. A backcountry permit, which serves as a reservation, is required. ⊠ *Box 129, Grand Canyon 86023,* ☎ *520/638–7875.* ☼ *Year-round.*

Outdoor Activities and Sports

HIKING

South Kaibab Trail, starting near Yaki Point on East Rim Drive near Grand Canyon Village, connects at the bottom of the canyon (after the Kaibab Bridge across the Colorado) with the North Kaibab Trail. Plan on two to three days if you want to hike the gorge from rim to rim (if you do this, we recommend that you descend from the North Rim, as it is more than 1,000 ft higher than the South Rim). South Kaibab Trail is steep, descending 4,800 ft in just 7 mi, with no water or campgrounds (there are portable toilets at Cedar Ridge, 2¼ mi from the trailhead) and very little shade. The trail corkscrews down through some spectacular geology, closely following the 300-million-year-old Supai and Redwall formations; look for (but don't remove) fossils in the limestone when you take your frequent water breaks. If you're going back up to the South Rim, ascend Bright Angel Trail. Accommoda-tions for hikers along the way include the campgrounds at Indian Gar-den and Bright Angel, or Phantom Ranch (☞ Dining and Lodging, *above*).

Shopping
Desert View Trading Post (✉ East Rim Dr., near the Watchtower at Desert View, ☎ 520/638–2360) sells a mix of traditional southwestern souvenirs and authentic Native American pottery.

The Village Rim

The Village Rim can be explored on foot (about 1 mi round-trip); a paved pathway over level ground runs along the rim. Cars can be left at the nearby El Tovar parking lot.

⑨ Hopi House, a multistoried structure of rock and mortar, was modeled after buildings found in the Hopi village of Oraibi, Arizona, the oldest continuously inhabited community in the United States (☞ The Hopi Mesas *in* Chapter 3). Part of an attempt by the Fred Harvey Company to encourage Southwest Indian crafts at the turn of the century, Hopi House was established as one of the first curio stores in the Grand Canyon. It has the air of a museum, with some artifacts too priceless to sell today, but it remains one of the best-stocked gift shops in the vicinity.

★ **⑩** A few yards to the west of Hopi House is the historic **El Tovar Hotel.** Built in 1905 to resemble the great hunting lodges of Europe, this log structure underwent a major renovation in 1991 yet retains the ambience of its early days. If the weather is cool, stop in front of the stone fireplace to warm your hands. The rustic lobby, with its numerous stuffed and mounted animal heads, is a great place for people-watching, and the back porch provides a front-row seat for viewing the canyon.

★ **⑪** A trail at the rim leads west toward **Lookout Studio.** Built in 1914 to compete with the Kolbs' photographic studio (☞ *below*), the building was designed by architect Mary Jane Colter to resemble a Hopi pueblo. The combination lookout point, museum, and gift shop has an extensive collection of geologic samples from around the world and many fossil specimens. An upstairs loft provides another excellent overlook into the mighty gorge below.

⑫ A half dozen yards west of Lookout Studio are a few steps that descend to the **Kolb Studio,** built in 1904 by the Kolb brothers as a photographic workshop. If you look out the window, you can see Indian Gardens, where, in the days before a pipeline was installed, Emery Kolb descended 3,300 ft each day to get the water he needed to develop his prints. Perhaps the exercise was beneficial: He operated the studio until he died in 1976 at age 95. The gallery here is worth checking out— painting, photography, and crafts exhibits are presented from mid-April through November 30. There's also a bookstore.

★ **⑬** **Bright Angel Trailhead,** a few feet from Kolb Studio, is the starting point for perhaps the best known of all the trails that descend to the bottom of the canyon. Originally a bighorn sheep path that was later used by the Havasupai Indians, it was widened in 1890–91 for prospectors trying to reach mining claims in the canyon. Bright Angel Trail is a well-maintained avenue for mule and foot traffic. If you intend to go very far—the trail descends 5,510 ft to the Colorado River—you should be prepared with proper shoes, clothing, equipment, and water; discuss your intentions with the park-service representatives at the visitor center before you go.

⑭ Directly east of Bright Angel Trailhead are railroad tracks over which the Santa Fe trains once passed. Here you'll see the barn that houses some of the tour mules; it's worth a brief stop, especially if children are along. Farther east, **Bright Angel Lodge** was built in 1935 of Oregon pine logs and native stone; rustic cabins are set off from the main

The South Rim and West Rim Drive

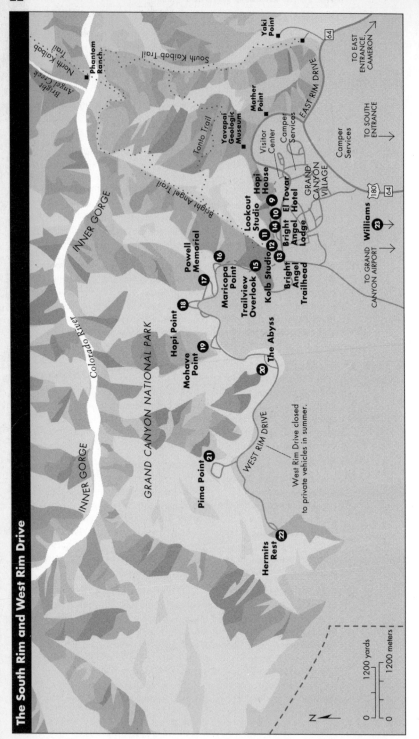

Yaki Point

Phantom Ranch

North Kaibob Trail

Bright Angel Creek

South Kaibab Trail

Tonto Trail

Mather Point

Yavapai Geologic Museum

Visitor Center

Camper Services

EAST RIM DRIVE

TO EAST ENTRANCE, CAMERON

TO SOUTH ENTRANCE

Camper Services

INNER GORGE

Bright Angel Trail

Hopi House

Lookout Studio

El Tovar Hotel

GRAND CANYON VILLAGE

9

14 10

11

12

13

Bright Angel Lodge

Kolb Studio

Bright Angel Trailhead

15

Trailview Overlook

Maricopa Point

17

16

Powell Memorial

180

64

64

Williams

23

TO GRAND CANYON AIRPORT

Colorado River

INNER GORGE

18 Hopi Point

19

Mohave Point

20 The Abyss

GRAND CANYON NATIONAL PARK

WEST RIM DRIVE

West Rim Drive closed to private vehicles in summer.

21 Pima Point

22 Hermits Rest

N

0   1200 yards

0   1200 meters

building. The lodge's "geologic" fireplace was constructed of regional rocks arranged in the order in which they are layered in the Grand Canyon. A history room displays memorabilia from the South Rim's early years. For light snacks and espressos, cappuccinos, and soft drinks, try the soda fountain in the Bright Angel Lodge. It has the distinction of selling the most Breyer's ice cream in the United States.

Dining and Lodging

$$$$ ✕🏨 **El Tovar Hotel.** Built in 1905 of native stone and heavy pine logs,
★ El Tovar is reminiscent of a grand European hunting lodge. As when it first opened, the hotel is operated by the Fred Harvey Company. It still maintains its excellent reputation for service, though at a time when indoor plumbing is no longer a luxury, rooms don't seem as posh as they might have in the past. Some are small, but all are nicely appointed, and a number have canyon views. For decades the hotel's restaurant has enjoyed a reputation for fine food served in a classic 19th-century room of hand-hewn logs and beamed ceilings. The Southwest-inspired menu changes seasonally but includes a daily vegetarian special along with innovative fish, poultry, and meat dishes: Free-range chicken breast with smoked tomato pine-nut sauce or grilled salmon with tomatillo salsa are possible dinner options. ✉ *Amfac Parks and Resorts, 14001 E. Iliff, Suite 600, Aurora, CO 80014,* ☎ *303/297–2757,* 𝔽𝔸𝕏 *303/297–3175. 70 rooms, 10 suites. Bar, dining room, room service. AE, D, DC, MC, V.*

$–$$$$ ✕🏨 **Bright Angel Lodge.** Mary Jane Colter designed this 1935 log-and-
★ native-stone structure that sits within a few yards of the canyon rim. Most rooms in the main lodge share baths; cabins, some with fireplaces and/or canyon views, are scattered among the pines. Don't come for luxury but for a historic building that blends superbly with the natural environment, and for bargain prices. The Bright Angel coffee shop is open for breakfast, lunch, and dinner; the more upscale but still casual Arizona Steak House serves dinner only. ✉ *Amfac Parks and Resorts, 14001 E. Iliff, Suite 600, Aurora, CO 80014,* ☎ *303/297–2757,* 𝔽𝔸𝕏 *303/297–3175. 11 rooms with bath, 13 rooms with ½ bath, 6 rooms with shared bath, 42 cabins with bath. Restaurant, bar, coffee shop, beauty salon. AE, D, DC, MC, V.*

$$–$$$ 🏨 **Grand Canyon National Park Lodges.** The Fred Harvey Company has seven lodges on the South Rim. El Tovar and Bright Angel (☞ *above*) are outstanding, but Maswik Lodge, Yavapai Lodge, Moqui Lodge, Kachina Lodge, and Thunderbird Lodge are all comfortable, if not luxurious. The setting, rather than the amenities, is the draw here. It's a good idea to bring a flashlight; the dimly lit, wooded grounds can be rather difficult to negotiate in the evening. In addition to lodge rooms, Maswik has rustic cabins ($). Moqui, which is only open from March through November, is on U.S. 180, just outside the national park; the others are in Grand Canyon Village. ✉ *Amfac Parks and Resorts, 14001 E. Iliff, Suite 600, Aurora, CO 80014,* ☎ *303/297–2757,* 𝔽𝔸𝕏 *303/297–3175. 855 rooms with bath. Restaurant, 2 cafeterias (at Yavapai Lodge and Maswik Lodge). AE, D, DC, MC, V.*

⚠ **Mather Campground.** There are 97 RV and 190 tent sites (no hookups), flush toilets, water, showers, and a laundromat at Mather; the cost is $10 per site. No reservations are accepted from December to March. ✉ *Grand Canyon Village; reservations through Destinet, Box 85705, San Diego, CA 92138,* ☎ *800/365–2267; 619/452–0150 outside the U.S.* ☉ *Year-round.*

⚠ **Trailer Village.** This campground has 78 RV sites with full hookups for $18 per site. ✉ *Grand Canyon Village; reservations through Amfac*

Parks and Resorts, ✉ *14001 E. Iliff, Suite 600, Aurora, CO 80014,* ☎ *303/297–2757,* FAX *303/297–3175.* ⊙ *Year-round.*

Nightlife and the Arts

Nightlife in these parts consists of watching a full moon above the soaring buttes of the Grand Canyon, roasting marshmallows over a crackling fire, crawling into your bedroll beside some lonely canyon trail, or attending a free evening program on area history. The following Grand Canyon properties have cocktail lounges: **El Tovar Hotel** (piano bar), **Bright Angel Lodge** (live entertainment), **Maswik Lodge** (sports bar), and **Moqui Lodge** (live entertainment).

Every September the **Grand Canyon Chamber Music Festival** (✉ Box 1332, Grand Canyon 86023, ☎ 520/638–9215) is held in the Shrine of the Ages auditorium at the South Rim visitor center. Call or write for schedule information and advance tickets. A lecture series on scientific topics, cosponsored by the National Park Service and the Grand Canyon Association, coincides with the chamber-music festival; ask for details at the area lodges or the visitor center.

Outdoor Activities and Sports

HIKING

The well-maintained Bright Angel Trailhead (☞ *above*) is one of the most popular and scenic hiking paths from the South Rim to the bottom of the canyon (9 mi). Rest houses are equipped with water at the 1½- and 3-mi points from May through September and at Indian Gardens year-round. Water is also available at Bright Angel Campground, 9¼ mi below the trailhead. Plateau Point, about 1.5 mi below Indian Gardens, is as far as you should go on a day hike. Bright Angel Trail is the easiest of all the footpaths into the canyon, but because the climb out from the bottom is an ascent of 5,510 ft, the trip should be attempted only by those in good physical condition and should be avoided in midsummer due to extreme temperatures. The top of the trail, a tight set of switchbacks called Jacobs Ladder, can be icy in winter. Note that you will be sharing the trail with mule trains, which have the right-of-way.

Shopping

Nearly every lodging facility and retail store at the South Rim stocks Native American artifacts and Grand Canyon souvenirs. After a while, all the merchandise begins to look alike, but most of the items sold here are authentic. The **El Tovar Hotel Gift Shop** (✉ Grand Canyon Village, ☎ 520/638–2631) carries Native American jewelry, rather expensive casual wear, and souvenir gifts. **Hopi House** (✉ East of El Tovar Hotel, ☎ 520/638–2631), which opened in 1905, still has one of the widest selections of Native American artifacts—some of museum quality and not for sale—in the vicinity of the Grand Canyon. **Verkamp's** (✉ Across from El Tovar Hotel, ☎ 520/638–2242) is in a historic (1906) building where a huge buffalo head surveys those browsing the fine artwork and crafts.

West Rim Drive

Originally called Hermit Rim Road, West Rim Drive was constructed by the Santa Fe Company in 1912 as a scenic tour route. Ten overlooks spread out over an 8-mi leg, and each of them is worth a visit. Since you have to return on the same road, consider stopping at half of the overlooks on the way out and the others on the way back; access to the lookout points is easy from both sides of the road. West Rim Drive has many hairpin turns, so be sure to observe the posted speed limits. In the summer months West Rim Drive is closed to auto traffic because of congestion. From Memorial Day weekend to October 1, a free shuttle bus (☞ Getting Around *in* The Grand Canyon and Northwest Arizona A to Z, *below*) makes most of the stops described below.

⑮ Trailview Overlook provides a dramatic view of the Bright Angel and Plateau Point trails as they zigzag down the canyon. In the deep gorge to the north flows Bright Angel Creek, one of the few permanent tributary streams of the Colorado River in the region. If you turn and look away from the canyon toward the south, you'll have an unobstructed view of the distant San Francisco Peaks, Arizona's highest mountains (the tallest is 12,633 ft), as well as of Bill Williams Mountain (on the horizon) and Red Butte (about 15 mi south of the canyon rim).

⑯ Less than a mile from Trailview Overlook, **Maricopa Point** merits a stop not only for the arresting scenery, which includes the Colorado River below, but also for its towering opening and mining operation. On your left as you face the canyon are the Orphan Mine and (below) a mine shaft and cable lines leading up to the rim. The copper ore in the mine, which started operations in 1893, was of excellent quality, but the cost of removing it finally brought the venture to a halt. The Battleship, the red butte directly ahead of you in the canyon, was named at the time of the Spanish–American War, when battleships were much in the news.

★ **⑰** About ½ mi beyond Maricopa Point, the large granite **Powell Memorial** stands as a tribute to the first man to ride the wild rapids of the Colorado River through the canyon in 1869. John Wesley Powell measured, charted, and named many of the canyons and creeks of the river. It was here that the dedication ceremony for Grand Canyon National Park took place on April 3, 1920.

⑱ From **Hopi Point** (elevation 7,071 ft) you can see a large section of the Colorado River; although it appears as a thin line, the river is nearly 350 ft wide below this overlook. Across the canyon to the north is Shiva Temple, which, until 1937, remained an isolated section of the Kaibab Plateau. In that year, Harold Anthony of the American Museum of Natural History led an expedition to the rock formation in the belief that it supported life that had been cut off from the rest of the canyon. Imagine the expedition members' surprise when they found an empty Kodak film box on top of the temple. Directly below Hopi Point lies Dana Butte, named for a prominent 19th-century geologist. In 1919, an entrepreneur proposed connecting Hopi Point, Dana Butte, and the Tower of Set across the river with an aerial tramway, a technically feasible plan that fortunately has not been realized.

⑲ Four-fifths of a mile to the west of Hopi Point, **Mohave Point** also has striking views of the Colorado River and of 5,401-ft Cheops Pyramid, the grayish rock formation behind Dana Butte. Granite and Salt Creek rapids can also be seen from this spot.

⑳ The Abyss (elevation 6,720 ft) is one of the most awesome stops on West Rim Drive, revealing a sheer drop of 3,000 ft to the Tonto Platform. From the Abyss you'll also see several isolated sandstone columns, the largest of which is called the Monument.

㉑ Pima Point provides a bird's-eye view of the Tonto Platform and the Tonto Trail, which wends its way through the canyon for more than 70 mi. Also to the west, two dark, cone-shape mountains—Mt. Trumbull and Mt. Logan—are visible on clear days. They rise in stark contrast to the surrounding flat-top mesas and buttes.

★ **㉒ Hermits Rest,** the westernmost viewpoint, and the Hermit Trail that descends from it (☞ *below*) were named for the "hermit" Louis Boucher, a 19th-century French-Canadian prospector who had a number of mining claims and a roughly built home down in the canyon. Canyon views from here include Hermit Rapids and the towering cliffs of the Supai and Redwall formations. The stone building at Hermits Rest sells curios and refreshments and has the only rest rooms on West Rim Drive.

Outdoor Activities and Sports

HIKING

The steep, 9-mi Hermit Trail beginning at Hermits Rest (⊠ 8 mi west of Grand Canyon Village) is suitable only for experienced long-distance hikers. The trail is in generally good condition, but there is a tricky spot—a short section damaged by rock slides in 1993. For much of the year, no water is available along the way; ask a park ranger about water supplies at Santa Maria Springs and Hermit Creek to determine how much water you'll need to bring. The route leads down to the Colorado River and has inspiring views of Hermit Gorge and the Redwall and Supai formations. Six miles from the trailhead you'll come across the scattered ruins of Hermit Camp, which the Santa Fe Railroad ran as a tourist camp from 1911 until 1930.

Williams

❷ *55 mi south of Grand Canyon Village, 30 mi west of Flagstaff on I–40 and AZ 64. Use I–40 exits 161, 163, or 165.*

Once a tough turn-of-the-century town of saloons, bordellos, and opium dens, Williams gained some respectability with the construction of one of the first Harvey Houses, the original Fray Marcos, completed in 1908. It is said to be the first poured-concrete building in Arizona. The bordello is now a bed-and-breakfast, the saloon and opium den are a Mexican restaurant, and the Fray Marcos is a luxury hotel.

Often considered just a jumping-off point for the Grand Canyon (it's only an hour away from the South Rim by car and a little over two hours by train), Williams retains its own funky frontier charm despite a proliferation of motels and fast-food restaurants on its main street (named, like the town itself, after mountain man "Crazy Bill" Williams). The wooded area (elevation 6,700 ft) is temperate in summer, and in winter a small ski center operates (☞ Outdoor Activities and Sports, *below*). Many of the neon signs on Bill Williams Avenue hark back to the days when it was known as Route 66. Indeed, Williams was not bypassed by I–40 until 1984. Antiques shops with reasonable prices and retailers selling Native American crafts and jewelry line this main drag, where a number of historic buildings have been restored and period lampposts installed.

The **Williams Visitor Center,** which also houses the Chamber of Commerce and Forest Service office, is a good resource for information about the area. It's an interesting structure in its own right. Built in 1901, it was the original passenger-train depot, and its brick walls still show graffiti scrawled by early railroad workers and hoboes. ⊠ *200 W. Railroad Ave., at Grand Canyon Blvd.,* ☎ *520/635–1418 or 520/635–4061.* ☉ *Daily 8–5.*

The **Grand Canyon Railway** began running from Williams Depot to the South Rim in 1989 on a modern 65-mi version (2½ hours each way) of a route that was first established in 1901. The train chugs through prairie, ranch, and national park land to the South Rim's log-cabin Grand Canyon Railway Depot. The ride includes refreshments, commentary, and corny but fun onboard entertainment. Club Class, with its fully stocked mahogany bar and complimentary morning pastries and coffee, costs an additional $12. Chief Class, for an additional $50, gets you complimentary snacks, cocktails, and beverages, served in an elegant parlor car with overstuffed seats and a small open-air platform. The company also offers a number of good tour and lodging packages.

Even if you don't take the train, it's worth visiting the **Williams Depot,** built in 1908 to replace the terminal where the visitor center now resides. Attractions here include a passenger car and the locomotive of a turn-of-the-century steam train, a gift shop where you can find kitschy souvenirs like a tie that plays "I've Been Working on the Railroad," and a café, open for breakfast only. The small **Railroad Museum** is next to the depot in the original dining room of the old Harvey House. The museum holds an interesting collection of old railroad and Harvey-girl photographs and is a good place to learn about the history of the Grand Canyon Railway, which once carried American presidents, Franklin D. Roosevelt among them, on their whistle-stop campaigns through the West. ⊠ *Williams Depot: N. Grand Canyon Blvd., at Fray Marcos Blvd.,* ☎ *800/843–8724 for railway reservations and information.* 🎫 *Round-trip fare $49.50 plus 8½% tax and $6 national park entrance fee.* ⊙ *Departures from Williams daily 9:30, returns to Williams at 5:30.*

🅲 Children enjoy the **Grand Canyon Deer Farm,** where visitors can pet pygmy goats, llamas, and other animals and can pet and feed the deer, including the tiny fawns born every June and July. ⊠ *100 Deer Farm Rd., 8 mi east of Williams off I–40's Exit 171,* ☎ *520/635–4073.* 🎫 *$5.* ⊙ *Mar.–May, daily 9–dusk; June–Aug., daily 8–dusk; Sept.–Oct., daily 9–dusk; Nov.–Feb., daily 10–5 in good weather.*

Dining and Lodging

$–$$ ✕ **Pancho McGillicuddy's.** Originally the Cabinet Saloon, this restaurant is on the National Register of Historic Places. Gone are the spittoons and pipes—the smoke-free dining area now has a Mexican decor, which sets the scene for such specialties as armadillo eggs, the local name for deep-fried jalapeños stuffed with cheese. ⊠ *141 Railroad Ave.,* ☎ *520/635–4150. MC, V.*

$–$$ ✕ **Rod's Steak House.** You can't miss this steak house with the plastic Angus cow out front. Obviously the emphasis here is on meat—sizzling mesquite-broiled steaks, prime rib, and the like. A children's menu is available. Smoking is not allowed in the dining area. ⊠ *301 E. Rte. 66,* ☎ *520/635–2671 or 800/562–5545. D, MC, V.*

$ ✕ **Tiffany's Restaurant and Lube Lounge.** Route 66 icons fill this old gas station–turned–restaurant: 1950s gas pumps, hubcaps, neon signs, and black-and-white photos of "the way it used to be." The fun spot draws all ages, who come for the Italian specials, including pizza. The bar-lounge is open until 1 AM. ⊠ *233 W. Rte. 66,* ☎ *520/635–2445. AE, DC, MC, V.*

$$$$ 🛏 **Fray Marcos Hotel.** This hotel across from the train station has been designed to resemble the depot's original Fray Marcos lodge. Neoclassic Greek columns flank the grand entrance, which leads into a lobby with a 35-ft-high ceiling, maple balustrades, an enormous flagstone fireplace, and gigantic oil paintings of the Grand Canyon, beautifully rendered by local artist Kenneth McKenna. Bronzes by Frederic Remington, from the private collection of hotel owners Max and Thelma Biegert, also adorn the lobby. The southwestern-style rooms have large bathrooms. Adjacent to the lobby is Spenser's, a pub with an ornate hand-carved bar from England; light meals are served here after 4 PM. ⊠ *235 N. Grand Canyon Blvd., 86046,* ☎ *520/635–4010 or 800/843–8724. 89 rooms. Bar. AE, DC, MC, V.*

$$$ 🏨 **Ramada Inn, "Canyon Gateway."** At the east entrance to town, this member of the Ramada chain has comfortable rooms, a good restaurant, and live country-and-western bands in summer. ✉ *642 E. Rte. 66, Williams 86046,* ☎ *520/635–4431 or 800/462–9381. 96 rooms. Restaurant, pool, hot tub. AE, D, DC, MC, V.*

$$ 🏨 **Red Garter.** A restored bordello dating from 1897 now houses a small bed-and-breakfast. Ask for one of the "Best Girl" rooms, which have their own sitting rooms overlooking the train tracks. Included in the room rate is a Continental breakfast at the on-site bakery. Even if you don't stay here, the bakery's fresh goodies are worth a stop. ✉ *137 W. Railroad Ave., 86046,* ☎ *520/635–1484 or 800/328–1484. 4 rooms with private bath. AE, D, MC, V. Closed Jan.–mid-Feb.*

Outdoor Activities and Sports

FISHING

Fishing for trout, crappie, catfish, and smallmouth bass is popular at a number of lakes surrounding Williams. For information on obtaining a fishing license, contact the **Arizona Game and Fish Department** (☞ Fishing *in* The Grand Canyon and Northwest Arizona A to Z, *below*).

SKIING

The **Williams Ski Area** (✉ Box 953, Williams 86046, ☎ 520/635–9330) is usually open mid-December through March; take South 4th Street for 2 mi, and then turn right at the sign and go another 1½ mi. There are four groomed runs (including one for beginners) and other downhill trails as well as areas suitable for cross-country enthusiasts.

Havasu Canyon

141 mi from Williams (to head of the Hualapai Trail), west on I–40 (to Seligman) and AZ 66, north on Indian Hwy. 18. Note: Last gas is at the junction of AZ 16 and Hwy. 18.

Havasu Canyon, south of the middle part of the national park and away from the crowds, possesses a Shangri-la–like beauty. It is the home of approximately 500 Havasupai, a tribe that has populated this isolated country for centuries. Their name means "people of the blue water," and you'll know why when you see the canyon's waterfalls, as high as 200 ft, cascading over red cliffs into travertine pools surrounded by thick foliage and sheltering trees. Eight-mile-long **Hualapai Trail** twists into the canyon along the edges of sheer rock walls. Be sure to call ahead if you plan to hike the trail—or ride a horse or mule down for about $70. You'll definitely want to spend the night if you're hiking or riding (☞ Dining and Lodging, *below*). The hurried can take a helicopter: **Papillon Helicopters** (☎ 800/528–2418) operates an excursion from Tusayan to Supai for $440 per person, which includes the ground and landing fee, as well as the horseback and guide fee. All visitors are charged a $12 fee to enter the Havasupai tribal lands. ✉ *Contact Havasupai Tourist Enterprise, Supai 86435,* ☎ *520/448–2141 for general information; 520/448–2111 for lodging reservations.*

Dining and Lodging

$$$ ✕🏨 **Havasupai Lodge.** The lodge and restaurant at the bottom of Havasu Canyon, operated by the Havasupai tribe, has rooms at about $80 for a double (this rate is in addition to the $12 per-person fee to enter the Havasupai tribal lands). The restaurant serves three meals a day, generally sandwiches and fast-food-type fare, and a special daily meal; dinner prices are about $8–$10. ✉ *Supai 86435,* ☎ *520/448–2111. 24 rooms. Restaurant. No credit cards; call for payment guidelines and restrictions.*

CAMPING

For information about camping in Havasu Canyon, call the **Havasu-pai Tourist Enterprise** (☎ 520/448–2121).

THE NORTH RIM AND ENVIRONS

The North Rim, within the 12,000-square-mi Arizona Strip, draws only about 10% of the Grand Canyon's visitors but is, many believe, even more gorgeous than the South Rim. There's plenty to see on the long drive to the rim, which is about 210 mi whether you start out from the South Rim of the canyon or from Flagstaff. This trip is not an option during the winter, when heavy snows block highway access and facilities are closed.

Cameron Trading Post

㉔ *53 mi north of Flagstaff on U.S. 89; 57 mi east of Grand Canyon Village on AZ 64.*

Most of the jewelry, rugs, baskets, and pottery sold at the historic **Cameron Trading Post** (☎ 520/679–2231 or 800/338–7385) are made by Navajo and Hopi artisans, but some are created by New Mexico's Zuni and Pueblo Indians. The goods and prices will satisfy everyone's taste and purse, but it helps to come armed with knowledge of Native American artisanship if you're looking at high-ticket items, some of which are sold at a gallery separate from the main building. Also on the post are a restaurant, a cafeteria, a grocery store, a butcher shop, and a post office. An outlet of the **Navajo Arts and Crafts Enterprises** (⊠ AZ 64/U.S. 89, ☎ 520/679–2244) stocks authentic Navajo products.

Dining and Lodging

$–$$ **✕☑ Cameron Trading Post.** Southwestern-style rooms at this modern
★ (mid-1990s) two-story complex have carved-oak furniture, tile baths, and balconies overlooking the Colorado River. The original native-stone landscaping—including fossilized dinosaur tracks—of the 1930s inn previously on this site was retained, as was the small, well-kept garden with lilacs, roses, and crab-apple trees. Be sure to call ahead for reservations; the motel is usually booked solid throughout the high tourist season. A cafeteria—hot and cold sandwiches and other buffet-style fare—is unusually well fitted, with an antique back bar and light fixtures. Service here is faster than at the older dining room, which has original tinwork ceilings, a kiva fireplace, and oak sideboards. The restaurant's hearty menu includes huge Navajo tacos on fry bread, heaped with cheese, chopped meat, guacamole, and salad. The trading post is on the Navajo reservation, so no alcohol is served here. ⊠ *Box 339, Cameron 86020,* ☎ *520/679–2231 or 800/338–7385, ext. 414;* ☎ *520/679–2350. 62 rooms, 4 suites. Restaurant, cafeteria, grocery. AE, DC, MC, V.*

⚠ Cameron RV Park. This park, open year-round, is adjacent to the Cameron Trading Post. The fee with hookup is $15 per day. There are no public rest rooms or showers. ⊠ *U.S. 89,* ☎ *520/679–2231 or 800/338–7385,* ☎ *520/679–2350.*

En Route The route north from Cameron Trading Post on U.S. 89 affords a wide and unobstructed view of the **Painted Desert** off to the right. The desert, which covers thousands of square miles and extends far to the south and east, is a vision of harsh beauty, with windswept plains and mesas, isolated buttes, and barren valleys in delicate patterns of soft pastels. The sparse vegetation is mostly desert scrub, which provides

The North Rim

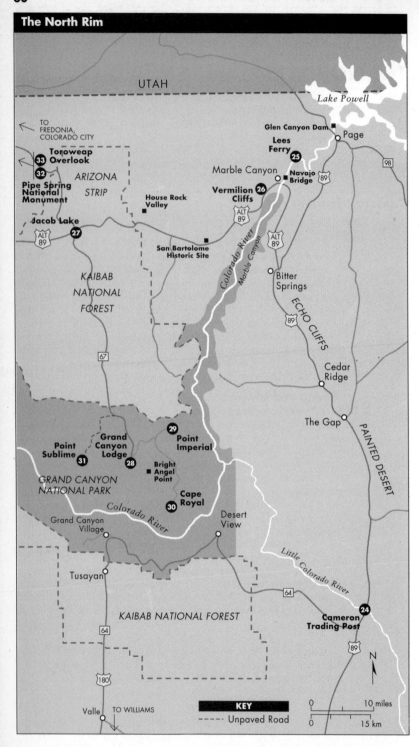

UTAH

Lake Powell

TO
FREDONIA,
COLORADO CITY

**Toroweap
Overlook** 33

32

ARIZONA

**Pipe Spring
National
Monument**

STRIP

**House Rock
Valley**

Jacob Lake

ALT
89   27

Glen Canyon Dam

**Lees
Ferry** 25

Page

98

Marble Canyon

**Navajo
Bridge**

89

**Vermilion
Cliffs** 26

ALT
89

KAIBAB

NATIONAL

FOREST

**San Bartolome
Historic Site**

Colorado River

Marble Canyon

ALT
89

Bitter
Springs

ECHO CLIFFS

89

67

Cedar
Ridge

The Gap

PAINTED DESERT

**Point
Sublime** 31

**Grand
Canyon
Lodge** 28

29 **Point
Imperial**

**Bright
Angel
Point**

**GRAND CANYON
NATIONAL PARK**

**Cape
Royal**
30

Colorado River

Grand Canyon
Village

Desert
View

Little Colorado River

Tusayan

KAIBAB NATIONAL FOREST

64

**Cameron
Trading Post** 24

89

N

64

180

Valle   TO WILLIAMS

KEY

- - - - Unpaved Road

0   10 miles

0   15 km

sustenance for only the hardiest wildlife. Most of the undulating hills belong to the Chinle formation, deposited more than 200 million years ago and containing countless fossil records of ancient plants and animals.

About 30 mi north of Cameron Trading Post, the Painted Desert country gives way to sandstone cliffs that run for many miles off to the right. Brilliantly hued, and ranging in color from light pink to deep orange, the **Echo Cliffs** rise to well over 1,000 ft in many places. They are also essentially devoid of vegetation, but in a few places high up you'll spot thick patches of tall cottonwood and poplar trees, nurtured by springs and water seepage from the rock escarpments.

At Bitter Springs, 60 mi north of Cameron, U.S. 89A branches off from U.S. 89, running north and providing views of **Marble Canyon,** the geographical beginning of the Grand Canyon but outside the national park. Like the rest of the Grand Canyon, Marble Canyon has been carved by the force of the Colorado River. Traversing a gorge nearly 500 ft deep is **Navajo Bridge,** a narrow steel span built in 1929. Formerly used for car traffic, it now functions only as a pedestrian overpass; a newer, wider bridge, built 120 ft downriver, was dedicated in 1995. An interpretive area and rest rooms are being designed for a former parking lot near the old bridge, which is listed on the National Register of Historic Places.

Lees Ferry Area

76 mi north of Cameron Trading Post, U.S. 89 to U.S. 89A.

★ ㉕ A turnoff at Marble Canyon Lodge, about 1 mi past Navajo Bridge in the small town of Marble Canyon, leads to historic **Lees Ferry,** 3 mi away. On a sharp bend in the Colorado River at a break in the Echo Cliffs, Lees Ferry is considered mile zero of the river, the point from which all distances on the river system are measured. This spot, one of the last areas in the mainland United States to be completely charted, was first visited by non–Native Americans in 1776, when Spanish priests Fray Francisco Atanasio Domínguez and Fray Silvestre Velez de Escalante tried but failed to cross the Colorado. Explorer John Wesley Powell also visited in 1870 on an expedition with Mormon leaders. After the ferry was established, it became part of the Honeymoon Trail, a gateway to Utah for young couples who wanted their civil marriages in Arizona sanctified at the Latter-Day Saints temple in St. George. It also became a crossing and a supply point for miners and other pioneers who shaped much of the American West.

Lees Ferry retains a number of vestiges of the mining era, but it's now primarily known as the spot where most of the Grand Canyon river rafts put into the water. In addition, huge trout lurk in the river near here, so there are several places to pick up angling gear and/or a guide (☞ Fishing *in* Outdoor Activities and Sports, *below*).

★ ㉖ West from the town of Marble Canyon, rising to the right of the highway, are the sheer, spectacular **Vermilion Cliffs,** in many places more than 3,000 ft high. Keep an eye out for condors, giant birds reintroduced into the area in the winter of 1996–97.

Dining and Lodging

$–$$ ✕🏨 **Marble Canyon Lodge.** This Arizona Strip lodge opened in 1929 ★ on the same day the Navajo Bridge was dedicated. Three types of accommodations are available: rooms with lace curtains, brass beds, and hardwood floors in the original building; standard motel rooms in the newer building across the street; and two-bedroom apartments, each bedroom containing a queen and a single bed, in a small, recently built complex. Guests can sit on the porch swing of the native-rock lodge building and look out on the Vermilion Cliffs and the desert, or they can play the piano that was brought over from Lees Ferry in the 1920s. Zane Grey and Gary Cooper are among the well-known guests who have stayed here. The restaurant serves plenty of beef (steaks, burgers, prime rib), plus seafood, pasta and other dishes. ⊠ *¼ mi west of Navajo Bridge on U.S. 89A, Marble Canyon 86036,* ☎ *520/355–2225 or 800/726–1789,* FAX *520/355–2227. 52 units. Restaurant, coin laundry, private airstrip. D, MC, V.*

$ ✕⌶ **Lees Ferry Lodge.** Geared toward the Lees Ferry trout-fishing trade, this lodge will outfit you, guide you, and freeze your catch (if it's legal size). At the end of the day you can sit out on one of the garden patios of this rustic building, constructed of native stone and rough-hewn beams in 1929. Rooms are charming, if a bit quirky in their plumbing. The hotel's Vermilion Cliffs Bar and Grill is a popular gathering spot for the men and women who pilot and guide the river rafts through the Grand Canyon, and it serves good American fare—especially the steaks and seafood—in an authentic western setting. ⊠ *4 mi west of Navajo Bridge on U.S. 89A, HC 67, Box 1, Marble Canyon 86036,* ☎ *520/355–2231. 9 rooms with shower, 5-person trailer with shower. Restaurant. MC, V.*

$$ ⌶ **Cliff Dwellers Lodge.** Built in 1949 in the Marble Canyon area of the Arizona Strip, this dining and lodging complex sits at the foot of the Vermilion Cliffs. Rooms in the modern motel building are attractive and clean. ⊠ *U.S. 89A, 9 mi west of Navajo Bridge, HC 67–30, Marble Canyon 86036,* ☎ *520/355–2228 or 800/433–2543,* FAX *520/ 355–2229. 21 rooms. Restaurant, bar, grocery. D, MC, V.*

Outdoor Activities and Sports

FISHING

The Colorado River in the Lees Ferry area is known for good-size German brown and rainbow trout. Marble Canyon Lodge (☞ Dining and Lodging, *above*), sells Arizona fishing licenses. **Lees Ferry Anglers** (⊠ HC 67, Box 2, Marble Canyon 86036, ☎ 520/355–2261; 800/962–9755 outside AZ) operates guided fishing trips, starting from $225 per day; it practices year-round catch and release.

En Route   As you continue the journey to the North Rim, the immense blue-green bulk of the Kaibab Plateau stretches out before you. About 18 mi past Navajo Bridge, a sign directs you to the **San Bartolome Historic Site,** an overlook with plaques that tell the story of the Domínguez-Escalante expedition of 1776. At **House Rock Valley,** a large road sign announces the House Rock Buffalo Ranch, operated by the Arizona Division of Wildlife. A 23-mi dirt road leads to the home of one of the largest herds of American bison in the Southwest. You may drive out to the ranch, but be aware that you may not see any buffalo—the expanse of their range is so great that they frequently cannot be spotted from a car.

As it nears its junction with AZ 67, U.S. 89A starts climbing to the top of the **Kaibab Plateau,** heavily forested, rife with animals and birds, and more than 9,000 ft at its highest point. The rapid change from barren desert to lush forest is dramatic.

Jacob Lake

㉗ *25 mi west of town of Marble Canyon on U.S. 89A, at AZ 67.*

Jacob Lake junction is a good place to stop for groceries and gas. The forest service's **Kaibab Plateau Visitor's Center** (P 520/643–7298) here is open from May 1 through mid-October.

Dining and Lodging

$$ ✕🏠 **Jacob Lake Inn.** Basic cabins and standard units are available at this modest 5-acre complex in Kaibab National Forest. All rooms overlook the highways. The bustling lodge center, a popular stop for those heading to the North Rim, has a grocery, a coffee shop, a restaurant, and a large gift shop. ⊠ *AZ 67/U.S. 89A, 86022,* ☎ *520/643–7232. 11 motel units, 3 family units, 22 cabins. Restaurant, café, grocery. AE, D, DC, MC, V.*

🏕 **Demotte Campground.** This forest-service campground 29 mi south of Jacob Lake is open from late-May or early June into October. It has 22 single-unit RV and tent sites, but no hookups, for $10 per day. There are interpretive campfire programs in summer. No reservations are accepted. ⊠ *Off AZ 67. Business Address:* ⊠ *Southwest Natural and Cultural Heritage Association, Box 620, Fredonia 86022,* ☎ *520/643–7395 off-season; 520/643–7633 in season.*

🏕 **Jacob Lake Campground.** Family and group RV and tent sites (no hookups) are available for $10 per vehicle per day here. On summer evenings, rangers present interpretive programs. No reservations are accepted (except for groups of 10 or more). It's open year-round, but there are no facilities or running water in winter; fees are only charged from mid-April through October. ⊠ *U.S. 89A/AZ 67. Business address:* ⊠ *Southwest Natural and Cultural Heritage Association, Box 620, Fredonia 86022,* ☎ *520/643–7395 off-season; 520/643–7633 in season.*

🏕 **Kaibab Lodge Camper Village.** This campground has 50 tent sites ($10 for two people) and 80 RV and trailer sites ($20 for a pull-through with full hookups, $10 without hookups). Fire pits and more than 70 picnic tables are available in this wooded spot, located near a gas station, store, and restaurant. Reservations are accepted. Camper Village is open mid-May to November, weather permitting. ⊠ *AZ 67, ¼ mi south of U.S. 89A. Reservations:* ⊠ *Box 3331, Flagstaff 86003,* ☎ *520/643–7804 in season; 520/526–0924 or 800/525–0924 (outside AZ) in winter;* 📠 *520/527–9398.*

En Route   AZ 67 runs south from U.S. 89A to the North Rim; the route passes through one of the thickest stands of ponderosa pine in the United States. Visitors frequently see mule deer and Kaibab squirrels, which live only on the plateau; you can recognize them by their all-white tails and the long tufts of white hair on their ears. Keep an eye out for mountain lions, elk, and black bears, too.

The North Rim

44 mi south of Jacob Lake on AZ 67.

★ ㉘   The historic **Grand Canyon Lodge** is, literally, at the end of the road (AZ 67). Built in 1928 by the Union Pacific Railroad, the massive stone structure is listed on the National Register of Historic Places. Its huge lounge area has hardwood floors, high-beam ceilings, and a marvelous view of the canyon through plate-glass windows. Don't forget to pay your respects to Brighty, the faithful burro of children's-book fame, honored by a near-life-size bronze sculpture near the lounge's west entrance. On warm days visitors sit in the sun and drink in the surrounding beauty at an equally spacious outdoor viewing deck, where park-service employees deliver free lectures on geology and history. Lunch, dinner, or a snack in the lodge's rock-and-log dining room is an integral part of the North Rim experience; the food is good and reasonably priced. If you don't want a full meal, just buy a drink at Pizza Place, sit out on the viewing deck, and watch the sun set over the canyon.

★ The trail to **Bright Angel Point,** one of the most awe-inspiring overlooks on either rim, starts on the grounds of the Grand Canyon Lodge and proceeds along the crest of a point of rocks that juts into the canyon for several hundred yards. The walk is only 1 mi round-trip, but it's an exciting trek because there are sheer drops just a few feet away on each side of the trail. In a few spots where the route is extremely narrow, metal railings along the path ensure visitors' safety. The temptation to clamber out to precarious perches to have your picture taken is great, but be very careful: Every year several people die from falls at the Grand Canyon.

The **Transept Trail** begins near the corner of the lodge's east patio. This 3-mi (round-trip) trail stays near the rim for part of the distance before it plunges into the forest, ending at the North Rim Campground and General Store, 1½ mi from the lodge.

Eleven miles northeast of Grand Canyon Lodge is one of the North
㉙ Rim's most popular lookouts, **Point Imperial,** the highest vista point (elevation 8,803 ft) at either rim, offering magnificent views of both the canyon and the distant country for many miles around: the Vermilion Cliffs to the north, the 10,000-ft Navajo Mountain to the northeast in Utah, the Painted Desert to the east, and the Little Colorado River canyon to the southeast.

★ ㉚ **Cape Royal,** another popular lookout, is about 23 mi southeast of Grand Canyon Lodge. A short walk on a paved road from the parking lot leads to this southernmost viewpoint on the North Rim. In addition to a large slice of the Grand Canyon, Angel's Window, a giant, erosion-formed hole, can be seen through the projecting ridge of Cape Royal. At Angel's Window Overlook, ⅓ mi north of here, **Cliff Springs Trail** starts its 1-mi route (round-trip) through a forested ravine. The trail, narrow and precarious in spots, passes ancient dwellings, winds beneath a limestone overhang, and terminates at Cliff Springs, where the forest opens on another impressive view of the canyon walls.

An excellent option for those who want to get off the beaten path, the
㉛ trip to **Point Sublime** is intended only for visitors driving vehicles with high-road clearance (pickups and four-wheel-drive vehicles). It is also necessary to be properly equipped for wilderness road travel: Check with a park ranger or at the information desk at Grand Canyon Lodge before taking this journey. The road winds for 17 mi through gorgeous high country to Point Sublime, an overlook that lives up to its name. You may camp here, but only after obtaining a permit from the Backcountry Office at the park ranger station (☞ Hiking *in* The Grand Canyon and Northwest Arizona A to Z, *below*).

Dining and Lodging

$–$$$ ✕🏨 **Grand Canyon Lodge.** This historic property, constructed mainly
★ in the 1920s and '30s, is the premier lodging facility in the North Rim area. The main building has limestone walls and timbered ceilings. Additional lodging options include small, very rustic cabins; larger cabins (some with a canyon view and some with two bedrooms); and traditional motel rooms in newer units. You might find marinated pork kebabs, grilled swordfish, or linguine with cilantro on the dining room's surprisingly sophisticated dinner menu. ⊠ *Amfac Parks and Resorts, 14001 E. Iliff, Suite 600, Aurora, CO 80014,* ☎ *303/297–2757,* ℻ *303/297–3175. 44 rooms, 157 cabins. Bar, dining room, cafeteria. AE, D, MC, V.*

$$ 🏨 **Kaibab Lodge.** In a wooded setting just 5 mi from the North Rim entrance, this 1920s property contains rustic cabins with simple furnishings. When they're not out gazing into the abyss, guests can sit around

a stone fireplace (it can be chilly up here in spring and early fall). The lodge is open mid-May to early November for the summer season and early December to early April for the skiing season. ⊠ *AZ 67, HC 64, Box 30, Fredonia 86022,* ☎ *520/638–2389; 800/525–0924 for reservations in winter. 24 cabins with shower. Restaurant. D, MC, V.*

🏕 **North Rim Campground.** The only designated campground inside Grand Canyon National Park, 3 mi north of the rim, has 83 RV and tent sites (no hookups) for $10 per day. It's open mid-May to the end of October. ⊠ *Reservations through Destinet, Box 85705, San Diego, CA 92138,* ☎ *800/365–2267 or 619/452–0150 outside the U.S.*

Outdoor Activities and Sports

CROSS-COUNTRY SKIING

In season, when the road to the national park is closed, the **North Rim Nordic Center at Kaibab Lodge** (⊠ c/o Canyoneers, Inc., Box 2997, Flagstaff 86003, ☎ 520/526–0924; 800/525–0924 outside AZ; FAX 520/527–9398) transports visitors via a SnoVan—a contraption made up of the battered shell of a van perched atop an ungainly half-track fitted with skis where the front tires would be—from Jacob Lake to the Kaibab Lodge, a 20-mi trip. It takes 1½ hours. The center's Point Imperial guided tour, for guests who stay at the lodge for three nights or longer, leads skiers across unmarked open country and over steep hills to the very edge of the Grand Canyon. A half-day ski-and-snowshoe trip, offered each weekend, takes adventuresome travelers to Saxophone Point on the east rim, with views of Marble Canyon and the Vermilion Cliffs. Several other ski packages are offered, including one that involves an overnight at a remote yurt (a heated dome-shape cabin).

MULE RIDES

Canyon Trail Rides (☎ 801/679–8665 preseason; 520/638–2292 after May 15 at Grand Canyon Lodge) conducts short mule rides suitable for children on the easier trails along the North Rim. A one-hour ride, available to those six and older, runs about $12. Half-day trips on the rim or into the canyon (minimum age eight) cost $35; full-day trips (minimum age 12), which include lunch and water, go for $85. These excursions are very popular, so try to make reservations in advance. Rides are available daily from May 15 to October 15.

Elsewhere in the Arizona Strip

The Arizona Strip, sometimes called the American Tibet because it's so isolated, holds only two small towns: Fredonia, known for farming and lumbering, and Colorado City, home to a polygamous Mormon sect that has lived there for more than a century. The combined population of these two towns is less than 7,000; fewer than 700 permanent residents—including 150 members of the Kaibab-Paiute tribe—live in the rest of the strip. Services in this part of the state are extremely limited; top off your tank when you find a gas station, and keep an ample supply of drinking water in your car.

❸❷ **Pipe Spring National Monument,** 90 mi from the North Rim and 14 mi from Fredonia, is one of the few reliable sources of water in the Arizona Strip. The park contains a restored rock fort and ranch, with exhibits of southwestern frontier life; in summer there are living-history demonstrations that focus on such things as ranching operations or weaving. The fort was intended to fend off Indian attacks (which never came because a peace treaty was signed before it was finished). It ended up functioning mainly as headquarters for a dairy operation and in 1871 became the first telegraph station in the Arizona territory. About ½ mi north of the monument is a campground, a picnic area, and a casino run by the Kaibab-Paiute tribe. The slots draw busloads of people to this remote spot. ⊠ *HC 65, Box 5, Fredonia 86022,* ☎ *520/643–7105.* 🖼 *$2.* ☉ *Historic structures daily 8–4:30; visitor center/museum daily 8–5.*

Six miles back toward Fredonia from Pipe Spring on AZ 389, a dirt road leads 50 mi south through starkly beautiful uninhabited country
③③ to **Toroweap Overlook,** a lonely and awesome overlook that is one of the narrowest stretches of the canyon (less than 1 mi across). The overlook also contains the deepest sheer cliff (more than 3,000 ft straight down). From this vantage point, you can see upstream to sedimentary ledges, cliffs, and talus slopes. Looking downstream, you can see miles of the lava flow that forms steep deltas, some of which look like black waterfalls frozen on the cliff. Be sure you have plenty of gas, drinking water, good tires, and a reliable car; a high-clearance vehicle (one that sits high up off the ground, like a pickup truck) is best for this trip. Don't try to go in wet weather, when the dirt road is likely to be washed out. There's a ranger station near the rim as well as a primitive campground. If you plan to return the same day, you should make motel reservations in advance at one of the Arizona Strip motels (☞ Dining and Lodging *in* The North Rim and Environs, *above*).

NORTHWEST ARIZONA, LAKE MEAD, AND LAUGHLIN

If the Grand Canyon is the most dramatic natural attraction in northwest Arizona, it is by no means all there is to see. Towns like Kingman hark back to the glory days of the old Route 66, while the ghost towns of Chloride and Oatman bear testament to the mining madness that once reigned in the region. Water-sports fans, or those who just want to laze on a houseboat, will enjoy Lake Mead, just across the Nevada border, or Lake Havasu, over which London Bridge surrealistically presides. Another bridge across the Colorado leads to Nevada and the casinos of Laughlin. And if you need an antidote to the Grand Canyon, visit Hoover Dam, the towering monument to that age-old human endeavor: the control of nature.

Kingman

③④ *112 mi west of Williams via I–40 or Rte. 66.*

Route 66 cuts through the town of Kingman (population 13,000), which is surrounded on three sides by rugged hills. The neon-lined roadway here is named for native son Andy Devine, the gravelly voiced actor who played sidekick in innumerable westerns. Because I–40, U.S. 93, AZ 68, and Route 66 all converge in Kingman, which is also served by Amtrak, Greyhound, and America West airlines (offering three flights a day from Phoenix), it is a hub for local attractions like Hoover Dam, Laughlin, and Lake Havasu.

The **Kingman Area Chamber of Commerce** (⊠ 333 W. Andy Devine Ave., ☎ 520/753–6106) carries T-shirts, postcards, and the usual brochures to acquaint you with local attractions. The **Mohave Museum of History and Arts** (⊠ 400 W. Beale St., ☎ 520/753–3195) includes an Andy Devine Room with memorabilia from Devine's Hollywood years, an exhibit of carved Kingman turquoise, and a diorama depicting the expedition of Lt. Edward Beale, who led his ill-fated camel-cavalry unit to the area in search of a wagon road along the 35th parallel. Follow the White Cliffs Trail from downtown, and you'll see the deep ruts cut into the desert floor by the wagons that eventually came to Kingman after Beale's time.

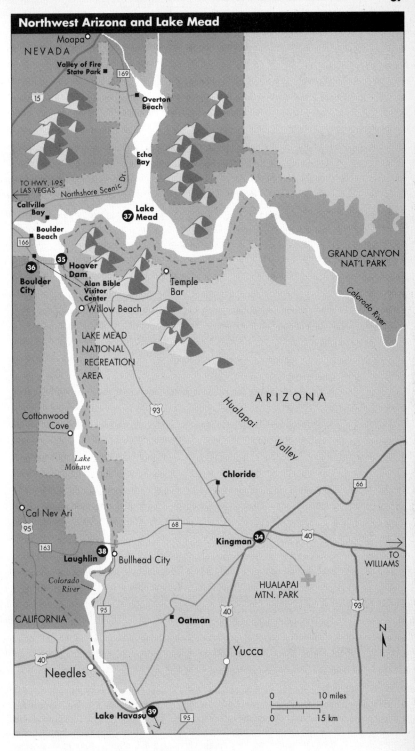

Northwest Arizona and Lake Mead

The **Bonelli House** (✉ 430 E. Spring St., ☎ 520/753–3195), an excellent example of the Anglo-Territorial architecture popular in the early 1900s, is one of 62 buildings in the business district listed on the National Register of Historic Places. A 15-mi drive from town up Hualapai Mountain Road will take you to **Hualapai Mountain Park** (☎ 520/753–0739) where more than 2,200 wooded acres at elevations ranging from 6,000 to 8,400 ft hold 6 mi of hiking trails as well as picnic areas, rustic cabins, and RV and tenting areas.

OFF THE BEATEN PATH

OATMAN – A worthwhile detour from Kingman, the ghost town of Oatman is reached via old Route 66 (now 68). It's a straight shot across the Mohave Desert valley for a while, but then the road narrows and winds precipitously for about 15 mi through the Black Mountains. (This road is public, but beyond a narrow shoulder the land is privately owned and heavily patrolled, thanks to still-active gold mines throughout these low but rugged hills.) Oatman's main street is right out of the Old West; scenes from a number of films, including *How the West Was Won,* were shot here. It still has a remote, old-time feel: Many of the natives carry sidearms, and they're not acting. You can wander into one of the three saloons or visit the Oatman Hotel, where Clark Gable and Carole Lombard honeymooned in 1939 after they were secretly married in Kingman, but the burros that often come in from nearby hills and meander down the street are the town's real draw. A couple of stores sell hay to folks who want to feed these "wild" beasts, which at last count numbered about a dozen and which leave plenty of evidence of their visits in the form of "burro apples"—so watch your step.

Lodging

Kingman has about three dozen motels, most of them along Andy Devine Avenue.

🏨 **Quality Inn.** This chain member has comfortable rooms and a spiffy coffee shop stocked with Route 66 memorabilia. ✉ *1400 E. Andy Devine Ave., 86401,* ☎ *520/753–4747 or 800/221–2222. 98 rooms. Coffee shop. AE, D, DC, MC, V.*

En Route   If you're heading on to Hoover Dam and Lake Mead, take U.S. 93 north; you'll come to a marked turnoff for the ghost town of **Chloride,** which takes its name from a type of silver ore mined in the area. Many buildings were lost to fires that ravaged the town in its heyday, but some historic treasures still stand, including the old bank vault, now a museum; the 1890 Jim Fritz house; and the Tennessee Saloon, now a general store and dance hall. Don't miss the huge murals painted on the rocks at the outskirts of town by western artist Roy Purcell, who worked the mines here in his youth. One copper mine, owned by the Duval Corporation, is still in operation at Chloride; their huge ore trucks often barrel down the road.

Lake Mead and Hoover Dam

67 mi northwest of Kingman on U.S. 93.

㉟ The visual impact of **Hoover Dam**'s incredible mass and height makes it a popular stop on a visit to the Lake Mead area. Created to control floods and generate electricity, the dam is 727 ft high (the equivalent of a 70-story building) and 660 ft thick (more than the length of two football fields). Its construction required 4.4 million cubic yards of concrete, enough to build a two-lane highway from San Francisco to New York. Every year more than 700,000 people take the Bureau of Reclamation's guided tour, which heads deep inside the structure for a look at its inner workings. Tours leave every few minutes from the exhibit building at the top of the dam; the guides are well-informed and entertaining. A visitor center built on the Nevada side in June 1995 contains a theater with three revolving sections, an exhibition gallery, an observation tower, and a five-story parking garage. ⊠ *Lake Mead,* ☎ *702/294–3523.* 🖾 *$6 entrance fee and guided tour.* ☉ *Daily 8:30–6:30 (last tour at 5:45). Hrs may change; call ahead.*

㊱ About 8 mi west of Hoover Dam on U.S. 93, **Boulder City,** Nevada, is a small town with a movie theater, numerous gift shops and eateries, and several hotels and motels. Developed in the early 1930s to house the 4,000 Hoover Dam workers and to deter them from spending their hard-earned dollars on wine, women, and Las Vegas, Boulder City is the only community in Nevada where gambling is illegal. There are, however, several roadside casinos just outside the town limits. When the dam was completed, the city served as a center for the management and maintenance of the site.

The **Alan Bible Visitor Center** (⊠ 601 Nevada Hwy., Boulder City, NV 89005, ☎ 702/293–8990), just northeast of Boulder City at the intersection of U.S. 93 (also called Nevada Highway here) and Lakeshore Scenic Drive (NV 166), is a good place to become acquainted with the Lake Mead area. The center is open daily 8:30 to 4:30.

Lakeshore Scenic Drive (NV 166) wends its way along the shore of
㊲ **Lake Mead,** the largest man-made body of water in the United States, with a surface covering 229 square mi and an irregular shoreline extending for 550 mi. It was formed when Hoover Dam was built in 1935 to hold back the Colorado River. Recreation areas with marinas include Boulder Beach, Callville Bay, Echo Bay, and Overton Beach.

Dining and Lodging
Facilities in the Lake Mead area are limited. **Seven Crown Resorts** (⊠ Box 16247, Irvine, CA 92623–9801, ☎ 800/752–9669) operates the Echo Bay Resort, the Temple Bar Resort, and the Lake Mead Resort, with room rates at $43–$89; each motel has a modest restaurant, laundry facilities, and other amenities. The Lake Mead and Temple Bar resorts have rooms with kitchen units. The Echo Bay and Lake Mead resorts have full RV hookups for $18 per day.

The **National Park Service** (☎ 520/767–3401) maintains a campground at Temple Bar. Space is available on a first-come, first-served basis, but there are usually plenty of unoccupied sites on all but the busiest holiday weekends. The nightly fee is $6.

Outdoor Activities and Sports
BOATING
Rental options include houseboats, patio boats, fishing boats, and ski boats—pick up a list of marinas at the Alan Bible Visitor Center (☞ *above*). Houseboat rentals are available at **Callville Bay Resort and Marina** (☎ 800/255–5561) or at **Echo Bay Resort** (☎ 702/394–4000 or 800/752–9669). Smaller boats are available at these locations and at **Lake Mead Resort** (⊠ Boulder Beach, ☎ 702/293–3484), in addition to other marinas.

CRUISES
A 1½-hour cruise of the Hoover Dam area on a 250-passenger sternwheeler is available through **Lake Mead Cruises** (⊠ Lake Mead Marina, near Boulder Beach, ☎ 702/293–6180). A 15-mi motorized raft trip on the Colorado from the base of Hoover Dam down Black Canyon to Willow Beach is offered by **Gray Line Tours** (☎ 702/384–1234 or 800/634–6579).

Laughlin

❸❽ *32 mi west of Kingman on U.S. 93 to AZ 68 into Nevada.*

Don Laughlin opened the first casino here in 1966, but the town didn't really take off until the early 1980s. Though often considered just a smaller version of Las Vegas, Laughlin has a character of its own: Wayne Newton may play Vegas, but Laughlin is Waylon Jennings territory. It generally attracts older, retired travelers who spend at least part of the winter in Arizona—the sandstone bluffs above Laughlin are lined with their RVs, bearing license plates from all over the United States and Canada—and other folks who prefer the low-pressure, low-minimum tables, the cheap food, the low-cost rooms, and the slots galore. The dealers are generally friendlier, the bettors more relaxed, and, especially compared to the shuttered rooms in Las Vegas, Laughlin casinos have an airy feeling, lent by large picture windows that overlook the Colorado. Laughlin's outdoor activities include water sports, golf, tennis, and strolls along the tree-lined River Walk.

The gambling halls lining Casino Drive include **Riverside Resort** (✉ 1650 S. Casino Dr., ☎ 702/298–2535 or 800/227–3849), **Flamingo Hilton** (✉ 1900 S. Casino Dr., ☎ 702/298–5111 or 800/352–6464), **Regency Casino** (✉ 1950 S. Casino Dr., ☎ 702/298–2439), **Edgewater** (✉ 2020 S. Casino Dr., ☎ 702/298–2453 or 800/677–4837), **Colorado Belle** (✉ 2100 S. Casino Dr., ☎ 702/298–4000 or 800/458–9500), **Pioneer Hotel** (✉ 2200 S. Casino Dr., ☎ 702/298–2442 or 800/634–3469), **Ramada Express** (✉ 2121 S. Casino Dr., ☎ 702/298–4200 or 800/272–6232), **Golden Nugget** (✉ 2300 S. Casino Dr., ☎ 702/298–7111 or 800/237–1739), **Gold River** (✉ 2700 S. Casino Dr., ☎ 702/298–2242 or 800/835–7903), and **Harrah's** (✉ 2900 S. Casino Dr., ☎ 702/298–4600 or 800/447–8700).

Lake Havasu

❸❾ *19 mi south of Laughlin.*

Lake Havasu is renowned for hosting London Bridge—not the London Bridge of the nursery rhyme, but London Bridge all the same. A brilliant stroke of entrepreneurship turned what might have been just another desert town on the Colorado into a crowd-drawing curiosity: When the City of London put the sinking bridge, erected in 1831, up for sale in 1967, developer Robert McCulloch decided it would make the perfect centerpiece for the community he had planned on the shores of the 46-mi-long lake formed by the construction of Parker Dam in 1938. He bought the historic bridge for nearly $2.5 million, had it dismantled stone by stone, shipped to the U.S., and reassembled (all 10,000 tons of it) to span a narrow arm of Lake Havasu.

An Olde English theme is played to the hilt here: A Tudor-style village replete with pub, red London telephone booths, Beefeaters, and other Britobilia abuts the base of the bridge. But Havasu City is on a lake, and in Arizona after all, so the sunshine, water sports, and fishing can amuse visitors after they've seen the surprising span. The weather is wonderful in spring, fall, and winter, but summers see temperatures that exceed 100°F for weeks at a time. Among the recreational opportunities in and around Lake Havasu are houseboat, ski-boat, Jet Ski, and sailboat rentals; marinas, RV parks, and campgrounds; and golf, tennis, and guided fishing expeditions. Those interested in exploring the desert—including old mines and a wildlife refuge—might consider booking a four-wheel-drive tour with **Outback Off-Road Adventures** (✉ 1350 McCulloch Blvd., ☎ 520/680–6151).

Dining and Lodging

The area has several RV parks and campgrounds, more than 25 lodging establishments—from inexpensive roadside motels to posh resorts—and more than 45 restaurants, from fast-food emporiums to fine-dining establishments.

THE GRAND CANYON AND NORTHWEST ARIZONA A TO Z

Arriving and Departing

By Bus

Greyhound Lines (☎ 800/231–2222) provides bus service to Flagstaff and Williams. **Nava-Hopi Tours** (☎ 520/774–5003 or 800/892–8687) operates buses from Flagstaff to service to the South Rim of the Grand Canyon from early April to late October.

By Car

If you are driving to Arizona from the east, or coming up from the southern part of the state, the best access to the Grand Canyon is from Flagstaff. You can take U.S. 180 northwest (81 mi) to Grand Canyon Village on the South Rim. Or, for a scenic route with stopping points along the canyon rim, drive north on U.S. 89 from Flagstaff, turn left at the junction of AZ 64 (52 mi north of Flagstaff), and proceed north and west for an additional 57 mi.

To visit the North Rim of the canyon, proceed north from Flagstaff on U.S. 89 to Bitter Springs. Then take U.S. 89A to the junction of AZ 67, which leads to the North Rim, a distance of approximately 210 mi from Flagstaff.

If you are crossing Arizona on I–40 from the west, your most direct route to the South Rim is on AZ 64 (U.S. 180), which runs north from Williams for 58 mi to Grand Canyon Village.

By Plane

AIRLINES

The many carriers that fly to the Grand Canyon from Las Vegas include **Air Nevada** (☎ 800/634–6377), **Air Vegas** (☎ 800/255–7474), **Las Vegas Airlines** (☎ 800/634–6851), and **Scenic Airlines** (☎ 800/ 634–6801). **Scenic Airlines** (☎ 800/445–8738 from Phoenix) operates two daily flights from Phoenix to Grand Canyon Airport.

Laughlin is served by **Reno Air** (☎ 800/736–6247). **America West** (☎ 800/235–9292) flies to Bullhead City and Lake Havasu. **Laughlin Air Vacations** (☎ 888/528–4454) provides visitor packages from dozens of U.S. cities.

AIRPORTS

McCarran International Airport (☎ 702/261–5743) in Las Vegas is the primary air hub for flights to **Grand Canyon National Park Airport** (☎ 520/638–2446). You can also make connections into the Grand Canyon from **Sky Harbor International Airport** (☎ 602/273–3300) in Phoenix.

FROM THE AIRPORT

The **Tusayan/Canyon Airport Shuttle** (☎ 520/638–0821) operates between Grand Canyon Airport and the nearby towns of Tusayan and Grand Canyon Village; it makes hourly runs daily between 8:15 AM and 5:15 PM, with additional trips in the summer months.

Fred Harvey Transportation Company (☎ 520/638–2822 or 520/638–2631) offers 24-hour taxi service at Grand Canyon Airport, Grand

Canyon Village, and the nearby village of Tusayan; taxis also make trips to other destinations in and around Grand Canyon National Park.

By Train
Amtrak (☎ 800/872–7245) provides daily service to Arizona from both the east and west, with its most convenient stop (for Grand Canyon access) at Flagstaff. From Flagstaff, bus connections can be made for the final leg of the trip to the South Rim through **Nava-Hopi Tours** (☞ By Bus, *above*).

Getting Around

By Car
Most of Arizona's scenic highlights are many miles apart, and an automobile is the most practical mode of transportation for touring the state. However, you won't really need a car if you're planning to visit only the Grand Canyon's most popular area, the South Rim. Many people choose to fly to the Grand Canyon and then hike, catch a shuttle or taxi, or sign on for bus tours or mule rides in Grand Canyon Village. Caution: When driving off major highways in low-lying areas, watch for rain clouds. Flash floods from sudden summer rains can be deadly.

Summer car traffic leading to the South Rim is badly congested in the vicinity of Grand Canyon Village and the parking areas along the rim. If you visit from October through April, you should experience only light to moderate traffic. The more remote North Rim has no services available from late October through mid-May. Reaching elevations of more than 8,000 ft, the road is open for day use only until the first heavy snowfall of the year (generally in November or December), at which point roads close until spring. The South Rim stays open to auto traffic all year, though access to the West Rim is restricted in summer because of overcrowded roads.

By Shuttle Bus
In the South Rim area, free summer shuttle buses operate between Grand Canyon Village and the West Rim approximately every 15 minutes from 6:30 AM to 6:45 PM, late May through September. In addition, during these months free shuttles go to Yaki Point on a more limited basis. **Mayflower** runs a year-round shuttle taking hikers from the South Rim's Backcountry Office (across from the visitor center), Maswik Lodge, and Bright Angel Lodge to South Kaibab Trailhead at Yaki Point; there are two departures every morning. Check for times upon arrival. From May 15 through the end of October, **Trans Canyon Van Service** (☎ 520/638–2820), a South Rim to North Rim shuttle, leaves from Bright Angel Lodge at 1:30 PM and arrives at the North Rim at about 6 PM; the return from Grand Canyon Lodge is at 7 AM, with arrival at the South Rim at about noon. The fare is $60 each way ($100 round-trip), and a 50% deposit is required two weeks in advance.

Contacts and Resources

Banks
There is a 24-hour teller machine at the **Bank One** (☎ 520/638–2437) South Rim office, across from the visitor center in Grand Canyon Village. No banking facilities are located within Grand Canyon National Park at the North Rim.

Bicycling
Bicycles are not permitted on any of the Grand Canyon's designated trails, but there are miles of scenic paved thoroughfares in the national park. The park roads have narrow shoulders and are heavily trafficked;

use extreme caution. There are no rentals or tours available at either North or South Rim.

Car Rentals

Major companies serving Phoenix and Flagstaff include **Avis** (☎ 800/331–1212), **Budget** (☎ 800/527–0700), and **Hertz** (☎ 800/654–3131).

Emergencies

Ambulance (☎ 911). **Fire** (☎ 911). **Police** (☎ 911).

SOUTH RIM

Grand Canyon Health Center (⌧ Grand Canyon Village, ☎ 520/638–2551 or 520/638–2469) offers physician services and receives patients weekdays 8–5:30, Saturday 9–noon. After-hours care and 24-hour emergency services are also available. Dental care (☎ 520/638–2395) is offered by appointment only.

NORTH RIM

The **North Rim Clinic** (⌧ Grand Canyon Lodge, Cabin 1, ☎ 520/638–2611, ext. 222) is staffed by a nurse practitioner. The clinic is open for walk-ins and appointments Friday through Monday 9–noon and 3–6, and Tuesday 9–noon.

PHARMACIES

At the South Rim, the well-stocked **Grand Canyon Clinic Pharmacy** (☎ 520/638–2460) in Grand Canyon Village is open weekdays 8:30–5 year-round and also Saturday morning in the summer; it's generally closed for an hour at lunchtime during the week. There is no pharmacy at the North Rim.

Entrance Fees

Fees levied by the National Park Service vary depending on your method of entering Grand Canyon National Park. If you arrive by automobile, the fee is $20, regardless of the number of passengers. Individuals arriving by bicycle or on foot pay $10. The entrance gates are open 24 hours but are generally supervised from about 7 AM until 6:30 or 7 PM. If you arrive when there's no one at the gate, you may enter legally without paying.

Fishing

Contact the **Arizona Game and Fish Department** (⌧ 2222 W. Greenway Rd., Phoenix 85023, ☎ 602/942–3000) to apply for a fishing license.

Food and Camping Supplies

SOUTH RIM

Babbitt's General Store has three locations in the South Rim area: at Grand Canyon Village (☎ 520/638–2262), in the nearby village of Tusayan (☎ 520/638–2854), and at Desert View (☎ 520/638–2393) near the east park entrance. The main store, in Grand Canyon Village, is a department store that has a deli and sells a full line of camping, hiking, and backpacking supplies in addition to groceries.

NORTH RIM

The **North Rim General Store** (☎ 520/638–2611), inside the park across from the North Rim Campground, carries groceries, some clothing, and travelers' supplies.

Guided Tours

BY BOAT

Wilderness River Adventures (☎ 800/992–8022) offers a seven-day excursion that includes hiking and white-water rafting along the Colorado River.

BY BUS

From late May to late September, a free **shuttle bus service** is offered by the National Park Service (☞ Getting Around by Shuttle Bus, *above*) in the South Rim area. This does not provide a guided tour, but you can get a good feel for the region by taking advantage of trips through Grand Canyon Village, to Yavapai Museum, and to Hermits Rest on the West Rim. The **Fred Harvey Transportation Company** (☎ 520/638–2822 or 520/638–2631) in Grand Canyon Village operates daily motor-coach sightseeing trips along the South Rim and to destinations as far away as Monument Valley on the Navajo reservation. Prices range from $12 for short trips to $80 for all-day tours. Children's half-price fares apply to those under 16 for in-park tours, under 12 on the longer out-of-park tours. For schedules, call the South Rim Reservations number (☎ 520/638–2401) or inquire at any Grand Canyon Lodge transportation desk (☞ Visitor Information, *below*). **TW Recreational Services, Inc.** (☎ 801/586–7686) offers an interpretive van tour of the North Rim for $20; schedules and other details are available in the lobby of the Grand Canyon Lodge.

BY MULE

Mule trips down the precipitous trails to the Inner Gorge of the Grand Canyon are nearly as well known as the canyon itself. But, especially for the summer season, it's very hard to get reservations unless you make them months in advance; write to the **Reservations Department** (✉ Amfac Parks and Resorts, 14001 E. Iliff, Suite 600, Aurora, CO 80014, ☎ 303/297–2757, ᶠᴬˣ 303/297–3175). These trips have been conducted since the early 1900s, and no one has ever been killed by a mule falling off a cliff. Nevertheless, the treks are not for the faint of heart or people in questionable health. Riders must be at least 4 ft 7 inches tall, weigh less than 200 pounds, and understand English. Pregnant women are not allowed to ride, and children under 15 must be accompanied by an adult. The all-day ride to Plateau Point costs $102 (lunch included). An overnight with a stay at Phantom Ranch at the bottom of the canyon (☞ East Rim Drive, *above*) is $250.25 ($447.50 for two) for one night, $347.50 ($589 for two) for two nights; meals are included in these prices.

BY PLANE

Flights over the Grand Canyon by airplane or helicopter are offered by a number of companies operating either from Grand Canyon Airport or from heliports in Tusayan. **Air Grand Canyon** (☎ 520/638–2618 or 800/247–4726) and **Grand Canyon Airlines** (☎ 520/638–2407 or 800/528–2413) fly small planes; **AirStar Helicopters** (☎ 520/638–2622 or 800/962–3869), **Papillon Helicopters** (☎ 520/638–2419 or 800/528–2418), and **Kenai Helicopters** (☎ 520/638–2412 or 800/541–4537) operate whirlybirds. Prices and length of flights vary greatly with tours, but they start at about $55 per person for short airplane flights and $90 per person for short helicopter runs. Inquiries and reservations can also be made at any Grand Canyon Lodge transportation desk (☞ Visitor Information, *below*).

BY TRAIN

See Grand Canyon Railway *in* Williams, *above*.

ON FOOT

The **Grand Canyon Field Institute** (✉ Box 399, Grand Canyon 86023, ☎ 520/638–2485) leads educational guided hikes around the canyon from April through October. Tour topics include everything from archaeology and backcountry medicine to photography and landscape painting.

For a very personalized tour of the Grand Canyon and surrounding sacred sites, contact **Marvelous Marv** (✉ Box 544, Williams 86046, ☎ 520/635–4948), the Indiana Jones of Williams, whose knowledge of the area is as extensive as his repertoire of local legends.

Hiking

Overnight hikes in the Grand Canyon require a permit that can be obtained only by written—and, new as of 1997, faxed—request to the **Backcountry Office** (✉ Box 129, Grand Canyon 86023, ☎ 520/638–7875, FAX 520/638–2125). Permits are extremely limited—only 1,600 are issued each year—and the office strongly recommends that reservations be made a full year in advance due to the ever-growing number of visitors to the park. The cost is $20 per permit plus $4 per night for each member of your party. If you arrive without a permit, go to the Backcountry Office at either rim: South Rim near the entrance to Mather Campground, North Rim at the ranger station. There is a slim chance that a cancellation will leave a space available.

SAFETY TIPS

Carry water on hikes to the Inner Canyon—at least 1–1½ gallons per day. To avoid dehydration, drink frequently, about every 10 minutes, especially during summer months. Likewise, take food—preferably salty energy snacks such as trail mix and pretzels, along with bananas, fig bars, and other fructose-rich foods. Do not drink alcohol or caffeine, which accelerate dehydration; for the same reason, avoid processed sugar. Wear hiking boots that have been broken in and proven on previous hikes. Carry a first-aid kit. In case of a medical emergency, stay with the distressed person and ask the next hiker to go for help. Do not attempt to make the round-trip to the Colorado River in one day. The trek down is deceptively easy; the route back up is much longer than most other mountain day-hikes and very fatiguing. The Grand Canyon is unforgiving, and it claims several lives each year. Most of those deaths are avoidable.

Rafting

Although more than 25 companies currently offer excursions, reservations for raft trips (excluding smooth-water, one-day cruises) often need to be made more than six months in advance. For a complete list of river-raft companies, call 520/638–7888 from a touch-tone telephone and press 1-3-71, or write to request a *Trip Planner* (☞ Visitor Information, *below*). National Park Service white-water concessionaires include **Canyoneers, Inc.** (☎ 520/526–0924; 800/525–0924 outside AZ); **Diamond River Adventures, Inc.** (☎ 520/645–8866 or 800/343–3121); **Expeditions, Inc.** (☎ 520/779–3769 or 520/774–8176); and **Outdoors Unlimited** (☎ 520/526–4546 or 800/637–7238). Smooth-water, one-day-trip companies include **Fred Harvey Transportation Company** (☎ 520/638–2822 or 502/638–2631) and **Wilderness River Adventures** (☎ 520/645–32796 or 800/992–8022). Prices for river-raft trips vary greatly, depending on type and length. Half-day trips on smooth water run as low as $40 per person; trips that negotiate the entire length of the canyon and take as long as 12 days can cost close to $2,000.

Road Service

SOUTH RIM

At Grand Canyon Village, the **Fred Harvey Public Garage** (☎ 520/638–2631) is a fully equipped AAA garage that provides auto and RV repair from 8 to 5 daily (closed 12–1 for lunch) as well as 24-hour emergency service. About ¾ mi down the road, across from the visitor center, **Fred Harvey Chevron** (☎ 520/638–2631) does minor repairs, oil and tire changes, and carries propane and diesel fuel.

NORTH RIM

The **Chevron** service station (☎ 520/638–2611), which repairs autos, is located inside the park on the access road leading to the North Rim Campground. No diesel fuel is available at the North Rim.

Safety Tips

Be careful when you or your children are near the edge of the canyon or walking any of the trails that descend into it. Guardrails exist only on portions of the rims. Tragically, a few visitors are killed each year in falls from viewing points. Before engaging in any strenuous exercise, be aware that the canyon rims are more than 7,000 ft in altitude. Being at this height can cause some people—even those in good shape—to become dizzy, faint, or nauseated. Before hiking into the canyon, assess the distance of the proposed hike against your physical condition. Although the descent may not be especially difficult, coming back up can be very strenuous. Take sufficient water and food on hikes into the canyon (☞ Hiking, *above*). During summer months, temperatures in the Inner Gorge can climb above 105°F.

Skiing

Though you can't schuss down into the Grand Canyon, you can cross-country ski in the woods near the rim when there's enough snow. **Babbitts General Store** in the South Rim's Grand Canyon Village (☎ 520/638–2234 or 520/638–2262) rents equipment and can guide you to the best trails.

For downhill skiing, you may wish to visit the **Arizona Snowbowl** (☞ Flagstaff *in* Chapter 4), northwest of Flagstaff. It's larger than the Williams Ski Area (☞ Outdoor Activities and Sports *in* Williams, *above*), though still small by Rocky Mountain standards; it tends to be very crowded in season.

Telephones

You're likely to have a hard time getting through to the Grand Canyon: Trunk lines into the area are limited and often overloaded with people calling this most popular of Arizona's attractions. You'll get a fast busy signal if this is the case. In addition, when you do get through to the National Park Service or South Rim Reservations numbers—which handle many of the services listed in this chapter—you'll have to punch a lot of numbers on a computer-voice system before you reach the service you want. Be patient; it's possible to get through to a human being eventually. Writing ahead for the information-packed *Trip Planner* (☞ Visitor Information, *below*) is likely to save you a phone call. Remember, too, that the park does not accept reservations for backcountry permits by phone; they must be made in writing.

Traveling with Children

The Grand Canyon is family vacation country, and most activities can be enjoyed by all ages. However, many of the daily activities at both the North and South rims, detailed in the free Grand Canyon newspaper, *The Guide,* will appeal especially to children. In addition, the Junior Ranger program, geared toward those ages four through 12, introduces kids to the concept of caring for the national parks via an activities checklist found in *Young Adventurer,* a publication available at the South Rim Visitor Center and the Tusayan and Yavapai museums.

Visitor Information

Every arriving visitor at the South or North Rim is given a detailed map of the area. Both rims also publish a free newspaper, *The Guide,* which contains a detailed area map; it is available at the visitor center and many of the lodging facilities and stores. The park also distributes

"Accessibility Guide," a free newsletter that details the facilities accessible to travelers with disabilities.

In summer, transportation-services desks are maintained at **Bright Angel Lodge, Maswik Lodge,** and **Yavapai Lodge** in Grand Canyon Village; in winter, the one at Yavapai is closed. The desks provide information and handle bookings, sightseeing tours, taxi and bus services, mule and horseback rides, and accommodations at Phantom Ranch (at the bottom of the Grand Canyon). The concierge at **El Tovar** can also arrange most tours, with the exception of mule rides and lodging at Phantom Ranch.

Grand Canyon Lodge (✉ TW Recreational Services, Inc., Box 400, Cedar City, UT 84720, ☎ 801/586–7686, FAX 801/586–3157; ✉ Amfac Parks and Resorts, 14001 E. Iliff, Suite 600, Aurora, CO 80014, ☎ 303/297–2757, FAX 303/297–3175) has lodging and general information about the North Rim year-round. For information on local services during the season in which the North Rim is open, generally mid-May through late October, depending on the weather, you can phone the lodge directly (☎ 520/638–2611).

Grand Canyon National Park Lodges (✉ Amfac Parks and Resorts, 14001 E. Iliff, Suite 600, Aurora, CO 80014, ☎ 303/297–2757, FAX 303/297–3175) can provide information on lodging, tours, and all other recreation inside the park at the South Rim.

Grand Canyon National Park (✉ Box 129, Grand Canyon 86023, ☎ 520/638–7888) is the contact for general information. Write ahead for a complimentary *Trip Planner,* updated regularly by the National Park Service.

Williams and Forest Service Visitor Center (✉ 200 W. Railroad Ave., at Grand Canyon Blvd., Williams 86046, ☎ 520/635–4061), run jointly by the National Forest Service, the city of Williams, and the Williams Chamber of Commerce, has information on Williams, Kaibab Forest, and the entire Grand Canyon area.

North and South Rim Camping (✉ Destinet, Box 85705, San Diego, CA 92138, ☎ 800/365–2267; 619/452–0150 outside the U.S.) provides information on camping in the park. When you call this computer-operated system, have the exact dates you'd like to camp on hand.

Some other resources: **Boulder City Chamber of Commerce** (✉ 1497 Nevada Hwy., Boulder City, NV 89005, ☎ 702/293–2034). **Kingman Area Chamber of Commerce** (✉ 333 W. Andy Devine Ave., ☎ 520/753–6106). **Lake Havasu Visitor and Convention Bureau** (✉ 314 London Bridge Rd, Lake Havasu City 86403, ☎ 520/453–3444 or 800/242–8278). **Laughlin Chamber of Commerce** (✉ 1725 Casino Dr., Box 77777, Laughlin, NV 89028, ☎ 702/298–2214 or 800/227–5245).

Weather

Weather information and road conditions for both the North and South rims, updated at 7 AM daily, can be obtained by calling 520/638–7888.

In general, the South Rim has summer temperatures that range from lows in the 50s to highs in the upper 80s. There are frequent afternoon thunderstorms. The area cools off quickly when the sun goes down, so bring a sweater or light jacket for the evening. Winter temperatures average lows around 20°F and highs near 50°F, with the mercury occasionally dropping below zero. In spring and fall, temperatures generally stay above 32°F and often climb into the 70s. The North Rim gets heavy winter snow and is thus open to the public only from mid-

May through October. Temperatures during this open season range from lows in the 30s to highs in the 70s. As in the South Rim, afternoon rain is common; in May and October, it occasionally snows as well. As you proceed down either rim toward the canyon's Inner Gorge, temperatures rise. In summer along the Colorado River—at an elevation of about 2,400 ft—temperatures range from lows in the 70s to highs above 100°F. Winter sees lows in the 30s, highs around 50°F. It rarely snows at the bottom of the Grand Canyon, even in winter; snow on the rims usually turns to rain as it falls into the Inner Gorge.

3 The Northeast

To the Navajo and Hopi people who inhabit northeastern Arizona, the land is their spiritual guide and history book. From the echoing ancestral red canyons to the windswept desert and mountains of towering ponderosa pine, the land is full of sacred symbols, legends, and memories. Visitors to the area are enchanted by the ancient Pueblo ruins at the Navajo National Monument and Canyon de Chelly, the sculpted rock formations of Monument Valley, the brilliant hues of the Bisti Badlands, and the jade-green waters of rugged Lake Powell.

By William E.
Hafford

Updated by
Gregory
McNamee

AVAST AND LONELY LAND of shifting red dunes, soaring buttes, and turquoise skies so clear that horizons are almost always 100 mi or more away, northeastern Arizona covers more than 30,000 square mi. Most of the northeast belongs to the Navajo and Hopi peoples, who have held on to ancient cultural traditions that are based on strong spiritual values, close kinship ties, and an affinity for nature. Excellent Native American arts and crafts can be found in shops, galleries, and trading posts throughout the region. Visiting here is like crossing into a foreign country—one that is, sadly, less prosperous than much of the rest of the United States. In some respects, life on the Hopi Mesas seems to resemble what it must have been in the last century. In towns like Tuba City and Window Rock it's not uncommon to hear Navajo—a beautiful language full of gliding vowels and soft consonants, as different from Hopi as English is from Chinese.

The Navajo reservation, known to its people as the Navajo Nation, spreads across some 25,000 square mi of the northeastern corner of Arizona. In its approximate center lie 4,000 square mi of Hopi reservation, a series of stone and adobe villages built on high mesas overlooking cultivated land. And on Arizona's northern and eastern borders, where the Navajo Nation continues into Utah, Colorado, and New Mexico, the Navajo National Monument and Canyon de Chelly contain haunting cliff dwellings of ancient Pueblo people who lived in the four-corners area.

Glen Canyon Dam abuts the far northwestern corner of the reservation on U.S. 89. Behind that, more than 120 mi of the emerald waters of Lake Powell are held in precipitous canyons of erosion-carved stone.

Most of the northeast is arid land, with soil and rock formations in astonishing colors from delicate salmon pink to rusty orange and even red. Immense mesas, rock spires, canyons, cliffs, and some impressive mountain ranges make up the landscape. Inviting stands of ponderosa pine cover the Chuska Mountains to the north and east of Canyon de Chelly. Navajo Mountain to the north and west in Utah soars above 10,000 ft.

Pleasures and Pastimes

Camping

Although Navajo–Hopi country stretches thousands of square miles across an open and sparsely populated region, visitors are allowed to camp only in posted authorized areas. Most campgrounds are primitive, in many cases nothing more than open, level areas where sleeping bags can be laid out or RVs can be parked; outside the Lake Powell area, only Monument Valley has developed camping facilities.

Dining

Because northeastern Arizona is a vast area and few communities have eating establishments, visitors should keep in mind that the following major locations have restaurants: Cameron, Tuba City, Page, Kayenta, Goulding's Trading Post–Monument Valley, Hopi Second Mesa, Keams Canyon, Chinle, Ganado, St. Michael's, Tsaile, Window Rock, and Fort Defiance. Fine dining is scarce, but you'll find very good Native American food. Some eateries serve Mexican dishes; most serve standard American fare. In the smaller reservation communities, only fast food may be available. Only in the Page–Lake Powell area at the height of the summer season are reservations advisable.

CATEGORY	COST*
$$$$	over $25
$$$	$15–$25
$$	$10–$15
$	under $10

per person, excluding drinks, service, and sales tax (9.5% in Page), except on the Hopi and Navajo reservations, where no tax is charged

Fishing

Lake Powell and the area below Glen Canyon Dam are excellent fishing sites. Lake Powell holds largemouth bass, black crappie, striped bass, bluegill, green sunfish, carp, smallmouth bass, threadfin, shad, walleye, rainbow trout, channel catfish, brown trout, and northern pike. The Colorado River below Glen Canyon Dam is known for its large trout. Keep in mind that Lake Powell stretches into Utah; an appropriate permit is required for each locale. The eastern region of the Navajo reservation has scattered lakes, most of them remote and small, that contain game fish. Two of the more popular and accessible lakes are in the vicinity of Canyon de Chelly: Wheatfields Lake, on Indian Highway 12 about 11 mi south of the community of Tsaile, and Many Farms Lake, near the community of Many Farms, on U.S. 191. Permits are always required for fishing on the reservation. *See* Fishing *in* The Northeast A to Z for information about permits.

Hiking

Some of the best hikes in this region are in Canyon de Chelly, up the streambed between the soaring orange-and-white sandstone cliffs, with the remains of the old Pueblo communities frequently in view. Mummy Cave is especially worth a look: The ancient apartment house lies atop the remains of even earlier structures that are at least 2,000 years old, and its three-story watchtower is nearly perfectly preserved. The more weathered Antelope House and White House stand against the sweeping canyon cliffs—impressive reminders of a bygone era.

Hopi Ceremonies

The Hopi are well known for colorful ceremonial dances, many of which are supplications for rain, fertile crops, and harmony with nature. Most of these ceremonies take place in village plazas and kivas (underground ceremonial chambers) and last two days or longer; outsiders are permitted to watch only certain segments of a few ceremonies and are never allowed into kivas. Dancers may wear masks and beaded costumes, beat drums, and chant. The best known is the snake dance, in which participants carry live snakes, including poisonous rattlers. However, this ceremony has not been open to the public in recent years. Seasonal kachina dances have also been restricted: Now only those in Moenkopi, Old Oraibi, Hotevilla, and Kykotsmovi may be observed by those who are not Native American. Dances that visitors are allowed to watch usually take place on weekends, extending through the day until dusk. Each clan has its own sacred rituals, starting times, and dates, which are determined by tribal elders. Visitors should be respectful and adhere to the proper etiquette while observing dances.

Lodging

When you travel in northeastern Arizona, a top priority should be making sure that you have a place to lay your head at the end of the day. Half the battle is knowing which of the scattered communities have motels. During summer months, it is especially wise to make reservations. Most motels throughout the northeast are clean, comfortable, and well maintained.

Bed-and-breakfasts have begun to proliferate in Page. Zoning restrictions currently prevent them from being anything other than informal homestays, but that is likely to change soon. Contact the Page–Lake Powell Chamber of Commerce (☞ Visitor Information *in* The Northeast A to Z, *below*) for a list of area B&Bs.

Unless otherwise indicated, all the establishments listed have air-conditioning, private baths, telephones, and TVs in their rooms.

CATEGORY	COST*
$$$	over $80
$$	$50–$80
$	under $50

All prices are for a standard double room at summer rates (rates may be lower at other times), excluding hotel tax: 10.5% in the Page area, 8% on the Navajo reservation. No hotel tax is charged on the Hopi reservation.

Native American Reservations

Visitors to the Navajo Nation and Hopi reservation have the opportunity to gain an understanding of the lives, past and present, of some of our land's true founding mothers and fathers. Both the Hopi and Navajo peoples are friendly to tourists. Their privacy, customs, and laws should be respected:

- Do not wander across residential areas or disturb property.

- Always ask permission before taking photographs of the locals; you may have to pay to take the picture, and even if no money is requested, consider offering a dollar or two to the person whose photograph you have taken.

- Do not litter.

- No open fires are allowed; fires are permitted only in grills and fireplaces. Bring your own wood or charcoal.

- Observe quiet hours from 11 PM until 6 AM at all camping areas.

- Do not disturb or remove animals, plants, rocks, or artifacts. They are protected by Tribal Antiquity and federal laws, which are strictly enforced.

- The possession and consumption of alcoholic beverages or drugs is illegal. Do not bring them onto reservation lands.

- No off-trail hiking or rock climbing is allowed.

- A tribal permit is required for fishing in lakes or streams or for hunting game; the use of firearms is otherwise prohibited. Violations of fish and game laws are punishable by heavy fines, imprisonment, or both.

- Off-road travel by four-wheel-drive vehicles, dune buggies, Jeeps, and motorcycles is not allowed.

- Do not wear bikinis or similar scanty clothing in public.

- Pets should be kept on a leash or in a confined area.

- On the Hopi reservation, taking photographs or making videos, tape recordings, and sketches of villages and ceremonies is strictly prohibited. At all sacred events, neat attire and a respectful demeanor are requested; women should not expose their thighs or midriffs. Camping is permitted for a maximum of two nights, but only in designated areas. All Hopi villages have separate rules about visitors; check with the individual village Community Development Offices or call the Hopi Tribe Office of Public Relations (☞ Visitor Information *in* The Northeast A to Z, *below*) in advance for information.

- Be aware that relations between the Navajo and Hopi peoples are sometimes tense, owing to long-standing property disputes that have engaged the federal courts for years. It's best not to ask Navajos about Hopi matters, and vice versa.

Shopping

Most visitors to the area are tempted by pottery, turquoise and sterling-silver jewelry, handwoven baskets, Navajo wool rugs, and other examples of Native American crafts. In addition to the work of Hopi and Navajo artisans, many trading posts also carry the work of New Mexico's tribes, including exquisite inlaid Zuni jewelry and the world-acclaimed pottery of the Pueblo people. Many vendors have roadside stands that resemble Navajo shade arbors. Most products offered on the Hopi and Navajo reservations are authentic, but the possibility of imitations exists. The trading posts are usually reliable.

Exploring the Northeast

The Navajo Nation, which encircles the Hopi reservation, occupies most of northeastern Arizona. The Canyon de Chelly is in the eastern part of the reservation. In the northwestern corner of the Arizona portion of the reservation are Lake Powell and Glen Canyon Dam.

Numbers in the text correspond to numbers in the margin and on the Northeast Arizona map.

Great Itineraries

IF YOU HAVE 2–3 DAYS

If you're based in ☒ **Holbrook** or ☒ **Winslow,** you'll have an easy drive to some of the most interesting sights in northeastern Arizona. On your first day, visit **Canyon de Chelly** ③. On the second, set out for the **Hopi Mesas** ⑥–⑧, stopping at the **Hubbell Trading Post National Historic Site** ④ along the way.

An alternative would be to head from Flagstaff or Holbrook to ☒ **Window Rock** ①. The next day head west on State Highway 264 (AZ 264) for about 70 mi to **Keams Canyon Trading Post** ⑤, where you can have lunch and do some exploring before pushing on to the **Hopi Mesas** ⑥–⑧. Spend the night on ☒ **Second Mesa** ⑦. If you don't want to spend the night in Hopi country, move on to ☒ **Tuba City** ⑨ or the ☒ **Cameron Trading Post.**

IF YOU HAVE 5 DAYS

On your first day drive to ☒ **Cameron Trading Post,** explore the area, and spend the night at the motel there. The next morning, make your way north on U.S. 89 to **Tuba City** ⑨, the last stop for gas before heading east at Moenkopi on State Highway 264 for the **Hopi Mesas** ⑥–⑧. Have lunch at the **Hopi Cultural Center.** Returning to Tuba City, head north on U.S. 160 toward ☒ **Kayenta** ⑩, where you can spend your second night. Get up early the next day to visit the **Navajo National Monument** ⑭ and hike to Betatakin or Keet Seel pueblo (if you have made reservations in advance). Spend your third night at the lodge at ☒ **Goulding's Trading Post** ⑬ in Monument Valley. The next day, visit **Monument Valley Navajo Tribal Park** ⑪, and then take U.S. 160 north to where it connects with U.S. 191 near the town of Mexican Water. Head south for **Chinle,** a good base for touring ☒ **Canyon de Chelly** ③.

When to Tour the Northeast

Summer is a busy time in the Lake Powell area, and reservations for accommodations are essential. Travelers seeking a quieter vacation should plan a visit during late October through early May, when there are fewer people and lower prices. The first weekend of September after Labor Day is a good time to be at Window Rock, when the Navajo Nation Annual Tribal Fair takes place. It's the world's largest Native Ameri-

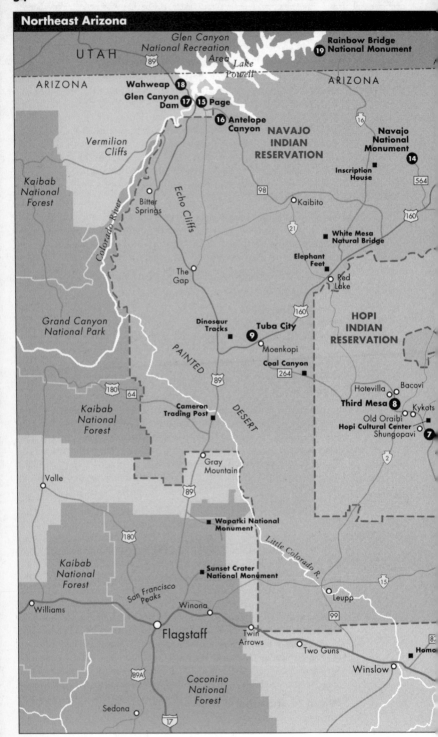

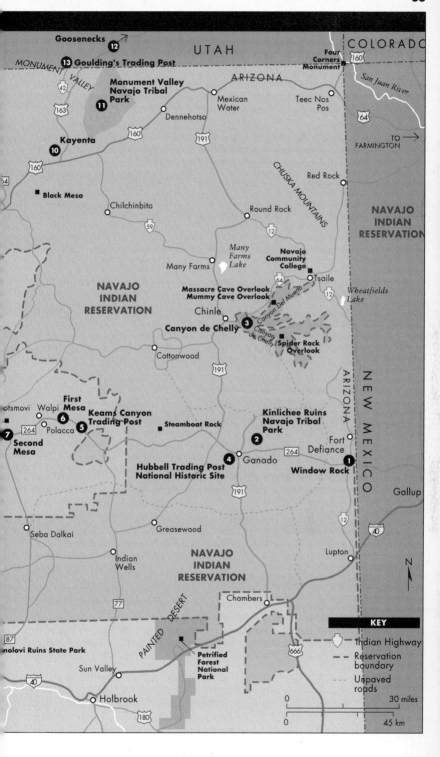

Goosenecks
Goulding's Trading Post
Monument Valley Navajo Tribal Park
UTAH
COLORADO
Four Corners Monument
San Juan River
MONUMENT VALLEY
ARIZONA
Mexican Water
Teec Nos Pos
Dennehotso
TO FARMINGTON
Kayenta
Red Rock
CHUSKA MOUNTAINS
Black Mesa
Chilchinbito
Round Rock
NAVAJO INDIAN RESERVATION
Many Farms Lake
Navajo Community College
Tsaile
Many Farms
NAVAJO INDIAN RESERVATION
Massacre Cave Overlook
Mummy Cave Overlook
Chinle
Wheatfields Lake
Canyon de Chelly
Canyon Del Muerto
Spider Rock Overlook
Cottonwood
Canyon de Chelly
First Mesa
otsmovi Walpi
Keams Canyon Trading Post
Polacca
Steamboat Rock
Kinlichee Ruins Navajo Tribal Park
Fort Defiance
Second Mesa
Hubbell Trading Post National Historic Site
Ganado
Window Rock
ARIZONA
NEW MEXICO
Gallup
Greasewood
Seba Dalkai
Lupton
Indian Wells
NAVAJO INDIAN RESERVATION
N
Chambers
PAINTED DESERT
KEY
nolovi Ruins State Park
Petrified Forest National Park
Indian Highway
Reservation boundary
Sun Valley
Unpaved roads
Holbrook
0   30 miles
0   45 km

can fair, and includes a rodeo, traditional Navajo music and dances, food booths, and an intertribal powwow.

NAVAJO NATION EAST

The eastern portion of the Arizona Navajo Nation (in Navajo, *diné bikéyah*) is a dry but often surprisingly green land, especially in the vicinity of the aptly named Beautiful Valley, south of Canyon de Chelly along U.S. 191. A landscape of rolling hills, wide arroyos, and small canyons, the area is dotted with traditional Navajo hogans (eight-sided domed houses), sheepfolds, and cattletanks. The region's easternmost portion is marked by tall mountains and towering sandstone cliffs cut by primitive roads that are generally accessible only by four-wheel-drive vehicles.

Window Rock

❶ *192 mi from Flagstaff, east on I–40 and north on Indian Hwy. 12; 26 mi from Gallup, New Mexico north on U.S. 666 and west on NM and AZ 264.*

Named for an immense hole in a massive sandstone ridge nearby, Window Rock is the capital of the Navajo Nation. With a population of fewer than 5,000, this community serves as the business and social center for countless Navajo families from the surrounding areas. It is also the home of the **Navajo Nation Council Chambers** (⊠ Turn east off Indian Hwy. 12, about ½ mi from AZ 264), a handsome structure that resembles a large hogan. Visitors can observe sessions of the council, where 88 delegates representing 100 reservation communities meet on the third Monday of January, April, July, and October. Sessions are conducted mostly in the Navajo language. When the council is not being held, you can walk around the chamber, where colorful murals decorate the walls. **Window Rock Navajo Tribal Park** is near the Council Chambers. The Tribal Park is used in several Navajo religious ceremonies, most of them closed to outsiders.

The **Navajo Nation Museum,** a small space devoted to the art and culture of the region and the history of the Navajo people, has an excellent selection of books on the Navajo Nation here. In the same building, the **Navajo Arts and Crafts Enterprise** (☞ Shopping, *below*) displays local artwork, including pottery, jewelry, and blankets. ⊠ *AZ 264, next to Navajo Nation Inn. Museum:* ☎ *520/871–6673.* ☞ *Free.* ☉ *Weekdays 1–5. Enterprise:* ☎ *520/871–4095.* ☞ *Free.* ☉ *Apr.–Oct., Mon.–Sat. 8–6; Nov.–Mar., weekdays 8–5 (often later during busy season, from Thanksgiving to Jan. 1).*

If you're curious about wildlife in northeastern Arizona, stop at the **Navajo Nation Zoological Park.** Set amid sandstone monoliths are indigenous birds and animals that figure in Navajo legends—golden eagles, elk, and coyotes, among others. ⊠ *East of Navajo Nation Inn and north of AZ 264,* ☎ *520/871–6573.* ☞ *Free.* ☉ *Daily 8–5.*

Window Rock is a good place to stop for food, supplies, and gas. Near the center of downtown, the **Navajo Tribal Fairgrounds** is the site of many all-Indian rodeos (in the Navajo Nation, many Indians are cowboys). The community hosts the annual July 4 Powwow, with a major rodeo, ceremonial dances, and a parade, and the Navajo Nation Tribal Fair, much like a traditional state fair, in early September. Contact the Navajo Nation Fair Office (⊠ Box 2370, Window Rock 86515, ☎ 520/871–6478) for information about both events.

Dining and Lodging

$$ ✕🏠 **Navajo Nation Inn.** Native American officials in town on government business frequently stay in this motel. The exterior is typical of contemporary roadside motels, but the rooms have been decorated with Spanish colonial furniture and Navajo art. The inexpensive restaurant serves standard American and Navajo entrées; the mutton stew is hearty, and the tasty fry-bread taco could easily feed two. ✉ *W. Hwy 264 and Hwy. 12, Box 2340, 86515,* ☎ *520/871–4108 or, for reservations only, 800/662–6189,* ⅋ *520/871–5466. 56 rooms. Restaurant, meeting rooms. AE, DC, MC, V.*

🏕 **Summit Campground.** The campground is open year-round and charges a fee of $1 per person. There are picnic tables but no water. ✉ *Off AZ 264, 9 mi west of Window Rock,* ☎ *520/871–6645.*

🏕 **Tse Bonito Tribal Park.** Set among sandstone monoliths—the name is a combination of the Navajo and Spanish words meaning "beautiful rock"—this area has shaded picnic tables and nearby rest rooms but no water. A fee of $2 per person may be charged. ✉ *Near AZ 264, Window Rock,* ☎ *520/871–6645.*

Shopping

An outlet of the **Navajo Arts and Crafts Enterprises** (✉ Off AZ 264, next to Navajo Nation Inn, ☎ 520/871–4090 or 520/871–4095) stocks authentic tribal products.

Kinlichee Ruins Navajo Tribal Park

② *22 mi west of Window Rock off AZ 264.*

A marked road leads to this 640-acre park, where you'll see dwellings built by the Anasazi, an ancestral Pueblo people. The park, which is always open, has a self-guided trail that takes you past the ruins and trailside exhibits (you are not permitted to descend into the kiva pit). There are also picnic areas and a primitive campground. A camping fee of $1 per person may be collected.

Canyon de Chelly

★ **③** *40 mi from Kinlichee Ruins Navajo Tribal Park, west on AZ 264 and north on U.S. 191.*

The nearly 84,000-acre Canyon de Chelly (pronounced duh-*shay*) is one of the most spectacular national monuments in the Southwest. Its main gorges—the 26-mi-long Canyon de Chelly and the adjoining 35-mi Canyon del Muerto—have sheer, heavily eroded sandstone walls that reach up to 1,000 ft. Ancient pictographs decorate some of the cliffs, and within the canyon complex lie some 7,000 archaeological sites. Gigantic stone formations rise hundreds of feet above small streams, hogans, tilled fields, peach orchards, and grazing lands. Although the monument is administered by the National Park Service, the land itself belongs to the Navajo.

The first inhabitants of the canyons, ancestral Pueblo people, arrived more than 2,000 years ago and constructed stone cliff dwellings. Their departure around AD 1300 is widely believed to have resulted from changing climatic conditions, soil erosion, and dwindling local resources. Present-day Hopis see these people as their ancestors, who quite simply moved to find a better place to live. Beginning around AD 780, Hopi farmers settled here, followed by the Navajo around 1300. (There is much learned controversy about when the early Navajo, who migrated from the Canadian subarctic over many generations, arrived in the Southwest. Most Navajos hold that their people have always lived here.) Centuries-old traditions have been passed down to the Navajo families who now live, farm, and raise sheep in the area.

Both Canyon de Chelly and Canyon del Muerto have a paved rim drive (each takes about two hours) with views of the great canyon. Prehistoric ruins can be found near the base of cliffs or perched on high, sheltering ledges. The dwellings and cultivated fields of the present-day Navajo lie in the flatlands between the cliffs. The Navajo who inhabit the canyon today farm much the way their ancestors did.

The **South Rim Drive** (36 mi round-trip) of Canyon de Chelly starts at the visitor center and ends at **Spider Rock Overlook,** where cliffs plunge 1,000 ft. Here you'll have a view of two pinnacles, Speaking Rock and Spider Rock; the latter rises about 800 ft from the canyon floor. Other highlights on the South Rim Drive are **Junction Overlook,** where Canyon del Muerto joins Canyon de Chelly; **White House Overlook,** from which a trail leads to the **White House Ruin,** with dwelling remains of nearly 60 rooms and several kivas; and **Sliding House Overlook,** where you can see ruins on a narrow, sloped ledge across the canyon.

The **visitor center** has exhibits on the history of the cliff dwellers and provides information on scheduled hikes, tours, and other programs within the national monument. ⊠ *AZ 7, 3 mi east of U.S. 191,* ☎ *520/ 674–5500.* ☞ *Free.* ☉ *Memorial Day–Labor Day, daily 8–6; Labor Day–Memorial Day, daily 8–5.*

The **North Rim Drive** (34 mi round-trip) of Canyon del Muerto also begins at the visitor center and continues northeast on Indian Highway 64 toward the town of Tsaile. Major stops include **Antelope House Overlook,** the site of a large ruin named for the animals painted on an adjacent cliff; the **Mummy Cave Overlook,** where two mummies were found inside a remarkably unspoiled pueblo dwelling, the monument's largest; and **Massacre Cave Overlook,** the last stop, which marks the spot where an estimated 115 Navajo were killed by the Spanish in 1805. (The rock walls of the cave are still pockmarked from the Spaniards' ricocheting bullets.) In Tsaile, Navajo medicine men worked in conjunction with architects to design the town's six-story **Navajo Community College.** Because all important Navajo activities traditionally take place in a circle (a hogan is essentially circular), the campus was laid out in the round, with all of the buildings within its perimeter. The college's **Hatathli Museum** is devoted to Native American culture. To the north of Tsaile are the impressive **Chuska Mountains,** covered with sprawling stands of ponderosa pine. Although there are no established hiking trails in the mountains, logging roads provide good access. A backcountry-use permit can be obtained at the **Parks and Recreation Department** (⊠ Box 9000, 86515, ☎ 520/871–6647 or 520/871–6636), next to the Navajo Nation Zoo in Window Rock. ⊠ *Navajo Community College and Hatathli Museum, Tsaile,* ☎ *520/724–3311.* ☞ *Donations accepted.* ☉ *Weekdays 8:30–noon and 1–4; groups by appointment.*

Chinle is the closest town to Canyon de Chelly. There are three good lodgings with restaurants here (☞ Dining and Lodging, *below*), as well as a large supermarket and a campground.

Dining and Lodging

$$$ ✕⊡ **Holiday Inn Canyon de Chelly.** This name-brand property near Canyon de Chelly is less generic than you might expect: The territorial-style, Navajo-staffed complex stands on the site of a former trading post and incorporates part of the historic structure. Rooms, on the other hand, are predictably pastel and contemporary. The lobby restaurant, low-key by most standards, is the most upscale eatery in town, serving well-prepared specialties like fresh Navajo mountain trout dusted in blue cornmeal and sautéed with piñon nuts. Closed at lunchtime, the hotel restaurant offers to pack a box picnic for its guests. ✉ *BIA Rte. 7, Box 1889, Chinle 86503,* ☎ *520/674–5000 or 800/234–6835,* FAX *520/674–8264. 108 rooms. Restaurant, pool. AE, D, DC, MC, V.*

$$$ 🏨 **Coyote Pass Hospitality.** You're not likely to encounter a more unusual lodging than this roving B&B run by the Coyote Pass clan of the Navajo Nation. It's not for everyone: You sleep on bedding on the dirt floor of a hogan (its location depends on the season, but most are near Canyon de Chelly), use an outhouse, and eat a Navajo-style breakfast—blue-corn pancakes and herbal tea, for instance—prepared on a wood-burning stove. If you don't mind roughing it a bit, this is a rare opportunity to immerse yourself in Native American culture in beautiful surroundings. Guided hikes, nature programs, and other meals are optional extras. ✉ *Contact Will Tsosie Jr., Box 91–B, Tsaile 86556,* ☎ *520/724–3383 or 520/724–3258.*

$$$ 🏨 **Thunderbird Lodge.** Set in an ideal spot at the mouth of Canyon de Chelly, this pleasant establishment has stone and adobe units that match the architecture of the site's original 1896 trading post. Some rooms have roughly hewn beam ceilings, rustic wooden furniture, and Navajo decor. The staff is friendly and knowledgeable about the locale. The manicured lawns and large, sheltering cottonwood trees help create a resortlike atmosphere. A cafeteria offers an inexpensive American menu of soups, salads, sandwiches, and complete meals, including charbroiled steaks, prepared by an all-Navajo staff. ✉ *Box 548 (½ mi south of Canyon de Chelly visitor center), Chinle 86503,* ☎ *520/ 674–5841. 72 rooms. Cafeteria. AE, D, DC, MC, V.*

$$ 🏨 **Best Western Canyon de Chelly Inn.** This two-story motel about 3 mi from Canyon de Chelly has cheerful rooms with modern oak furnishings and Native American–print bedspreads and drapes. All rooms have cable TV and coffeemakers. ✉ *Box 295, Rte. 7 (¼ mi east of U.S. 191), Chinle 86503,* ☎ *520/674–5875, 520/674–5288, or 800/ 327–0354. 102 rooms. Restaurant, indoor pool, shop. AE, D, DC, MC, V.*

🏕 **Cottonwood Campground.** Free first-come, first-served camping is offered at 52 RV sites (maximum length 35 ft; no hookups) and 95 tent sites on grounds with cottonwood trees and a picnic area. The campground is open all year, with water and flush toilets available April–September. ✉ *Canyon de Chelly National Monument, near visitor center, Chinle 86503,* ☎ *520/674–5500.*

Outdoor Activities and Sports

HIKING

Only one hike within Canyon de Chelly National Monument—the **White House Ruin Trail** on the South Rim Drive—can be done without an authorized guide. The easy-to-negotiate trail starts near White House Overlook and runs along sheer walls that drop about 550 ft. The trail leads to the White House Ruin (☞ *above*). Bring your own water for this 2½-mi hike (round-trip).

Other hikes are led by rangers and paid guides who charge about $10 per hour with a three-hour minimum for groups of up to four people for day hikes. (Do not venture into the canyon without a guide, or you'll face a stiff fine.) For overnights, there's a $20 surcharge for the guide and usually a $30 charge for permission to stay on private land; groups of up to 15 people can be accommodated. From Memorial Day through Labor Day, free three-hour ranger-led hikes leave from the visitor center at 9 AM. Also during the summer, four-hour hikes costing $10 per person leave from the visitor center in the morning and afternoon; rates for two-hour evening hikes are $5 per person. Some of the hikes are strenuous and precipitous, without clearly defined or gently graded trails. Visitors with health problems or a fear of heights should ask guides about the difficulty of the hike they're considering.

HORSEBACK RIDING

Justin's Horse Rental (⊠ Box 881, Chinle 86503, ☎ 520/674–5678), near the South Rim Drive entrance of Canyon de Chelly, conducts trips into the canyon for $8 per hour for each horse plus $8 per hour for a guide. The owner, Justin Tso, is well-informed about the area.

Hubbell Trading Post National Historic Site

❹ *32 mi south of Canyon de Chelly.*

This trading post was established in 1878 by John Lorenzo Hubbell, who was born in Pajarito, New Mexico. To the Navajo, Hubbell was not only a merchant but also a good friend and teacher who translated letters, settled family quarrels, explained government policy, and helped the sick. During an 1886 smallpox epidemic, he turned his home into a hospital and personally ministered to the sick and dying. Hubbell died in 1930 and is buried not far from the trading post.

Today the Hubbell Trading Post operates much as it did more than a century ago. At the **visitor center,** National Park Service exhibits illustrate the post's history, and Navajo men and women frequently demonstrate jewelry and rug making. You may also take a guided tour of Hubbell's house, which contains one of the finest personal collections of Native American artistry anywhere, including rugs and paintings. Tours are given six times daily in summer, four in winter. ⊠ *AZ 264, 1 mi west of Ganado,* ☎ *520/755–3475.* ⊡ *Free.* ☉ *June–Sept., daily 8–6; Oct.–May, daily 8–5.*

Shopping

Hubbell Trading Post (⊠ Off AZ 264, 1 mi west of Ganado, ☎ 520/755–3254) is famous for its "Ganado red" Navajo rugs; the quality is outstanding but prices are accordingly high. Still, it's hard to resist these beautiful designs and colors. The Hubbell staff is fond of staging unannounced one-day sales, so you may get an unexpected bargain. Navajo artists frequently show their work here, too.

En Route   About 20 mi west of the trading post, on AZ 264, you'll reach **Steamboat Rock,** an immense, jutting peninsula of stone that resembles an early steamboat, complete with a geologically formed waterline. At Steamboat Rock you are only 5 mi from the eastern boundary line of the Hopi reservation.

THE HOPI MESAS

The Hopi Mesas and the small villages that line their tops have a feel of nearly fathomless antiquity. Generation after generation of Hopitu, "the peaceful people," much like their Anasazi ancestors, have lived in these settlements of stone and adobe houses, which blend in with the dun-color rocky earth so well that they appear to be a natural part of the land. Even today, their rooftops studded with television aerials and satellite dishes, their narrow streets lined with cars, the Hopi villages impart the air of another time.

First Mesa, Second Mesa, and Third Mesa—the tall escarpments that form the center of the Hopi universe—have been overrun with so many non-Hopi visitors over the years that tourist access to many villages is now limited and advance permission is necessary to view them. For information, call the **Hopi Tribe Office of Public Relations** (☞ Visitor Information *in* The Northeast A to Z, *below*), which also provides phone numbers for village leaders or community development offices.

To see the Hopi Mesas at a reasonable pace, it's a good idea to take at least one overnight on this tour, either at the Hopi Cultural Center on Second Mesa in the heart of the reservation or, if you're planning to head north into Navajo country, at a lodging in Tuba City (☞ *below*).

Keams Canyon Trading Post

❺ *48 mi west of Hubbell Trading Post.*

The Keams Canyon Trading Post is the main tourist attraction in the Keams Canyon area, established by Thomas Keam in 1875. Originally, it served only Native Americans, but today the trading post also includes a motel, a primitive campground, a restaurant, a service station, and a shopping center. An administrative center for the Bureau of Indian Affairs, Keams Canyon also has a number of government buildings.

The first 3 mi of the 8-mi wooded canyon running toward the northeast can be seen by car. At **Inscription Rock,** about 2 mi down the road, early frontiersman Kit Carson engraved his name in stone. There are several picnic spots in the canyon.

Dining

$ ✕ **Keams Canyon Restaurant.** At this typical roadside dining spot with Formica tabletops, you can choose from American dishes and a few Native American items, including Navajo tacos, made with Indian fry bread (not unlike a soft pizza crust) heaped with ground beef, chili, beans, lettuce, and grated cheese. It's open weekdays from 7 AM to 8 PM, weekends until 6 PM. (Note: The inexpensive motel in the same complex cannot be recommended.) ✉ *Keams Canyon Shopping Center (near AZ 264),* ☎ *520/738–2296 and 520/738–2297. MC, V.*

Shopping

Keams Canyon Arts and Crafts (✉ Keams Canyon, ☎ 520/738–2295) sells Hopi wares.

First Mesa

❻ *15 mi west of Keams Canyon.*

On First Mesa you will initially approach Polacca; the older and more impressive villages of Hano, Sichomovi, and Walpi are at the top of the mesa. From Polacca, a paved road (off AZ 264) angles up to a parking lot near the village of Sichomovi. For permission to visit Hano, Sichomovi, and Walpi, or for information on the guided walking tours of these villages, call the **First Mesa Visitor's Center at Ponsli Hall.** ☎ *520/737–2262.* 🎫 *Tours free; contribution suggested.* ☼ *Guided tours can be arranged 9 AM–4 PM daily, except when ceremonies are being held.*

All the older Hopi villages have structures built of rock and adobe mortar in a simple architectural style. **Hano** actually belongs to the Tewa, a Pueblo tribe that fled from the Spanish in 1696 and secured permission from the Hopi to build a new home on First Mesa. **Sichomovi** is built so close to Hano that only the residents know the actual boundary line. Constructed in the mid-1600s, this village is believed to have been built to ease overcrowding at Walpi, the highest point on the mesa.

★ **Walpi** can be visited only if you are accompanied by a Hopi guide. Built on solid rock and surrounded by steep cliffs, Walpi stands against an expanse of distant earth and sky. At its narrowest point, the mesa measures only 15 ft across. Inhabited for more than 500 years, Walpi's cliff-edge houses seem to grow out of the nearby terrain. Today, only about 30 residents occupy this settlement, which has neither electricity nor running water. Important ceremonial dances frequently take place here.

Second Mesa

❼ *12 mi southwest of First Mesa.*

One of the livelier spots on Second Mesa is the **Hopi Cultural Center,** a good place to stop for information about the reservation. Shops here carry the work of Hopi artisans; the selection is very good and the prices are reasonable. In addition, the center, which hails itself to be "at the Center of the Universe," includes a pueblo-style museum, a good restaurant that serves American and Native American dishes, and a decent motel. ✉ *On the north side of AZ 264, west of the junction at AZ 87. Restaurant and motel,* ☎ *520/734–2401; 520/734–6650 museum.* 🎟 *Museum $3.* ☉ *Mid-May–Oct., weekdays 8–5, weekends 9–4; rest of yr, weekdays 8–5.*

Shungopavi, the largest and oldest village on Second Mesa, may be reached by a paved road angling south off AZ 264, between the junction of AZ 87 and the Hopi Cultural Center. The famous Hopi snake dances (now closed to the public) are held here in August during even-numbered years.

The small villages of Sipaulovi and Mishongnovi are off a paved road that runs north from AZ 264, about ⅓ mi east of the Hopi Cultural Center. **Mishongnovi,** the easternmost settlement, was built in the late 1600s. If you'd like to visit **Sipaulovi,** the most recently established village, call the Sipaulovi Village Community Center (☎ 520/737–2570).

Dining and Lodging

$ ✕ **Tunosvongya Restaurant.** Also known as the Hopi Cultural Center Restaurant, this establishment operated by Native Americans is one of the only places to eat in the area. It serves traditional dishes, including Indian tacos, Hopi blue-corn pancakes, fry bread (delicious with honey and salsa), and *nok qui vi* (a tasty Hopi lamb stew made with tender bits of lamb, hominy, and mild-green chilies). ✉ *AZ 264,* ☎ *520/734–2401. DC, MC, V.*

   ⛺ **Hopi Cultural Center Campground.** There's no charge to stay at the modest camping and picnic area on the west side of the Hopi Cultural Center. There are no water hookups, but campers can use the rest rooms in the cultural center. ✉ *AZ 264, Second Mesa 86043.*

Shopping

Shops at the **Hopi Cultural Center** (✉ AZ 264, Second Mesa 86043, ☎ 520/734–2463) carry the works of local artists and artisans. The **Hopi Arts and Crafts/Silvercrafts Cooperative Guild** (✉ Just west of the Hopi Cultural Center, no phone) hosts many craftspeople selling their wares; you might even see some silversmiths at work here. **Tsakurshovi** (✉ 1½ mi east of the Hopi Cultural Center, Second Mesa 86043, ☎ 520/734–2478) is a small shop brimming with everything you'd expect and more. The Hopi sometimes come here to buy kachina dolls and other ceremonial objects, such as bundles of sweetgrass and sage, rustling baskets of deer hooves to make rattles with, and ceremonial belts adorned with seashells.

Third Mesa

8 *8 mi northwest of Second Mesa.*

At the eastern base of Third Mesa is the village of **Kykotsmovi.** Hopi from Old Oraibi descended from the mesa and built this village in a canyon with a perennial spring; the community is known for its greenery and its peach orchards. The town also serves as the home of the **Hopi Tribal Headquarters Chairman's Office** and the **Office of Public Relations** (☞ Visitor Information *in* The Northeast A to Z, *below*), good sources of information regarding ceremonies and dances. Along AZ 264 are crafts shops and art galleries, as well as occasional roadside vendors. The Third Mesa villages are known for their baskets, kachina dolls, weaving, and jewelry.

Old Oraibi, a few miles west and on top of Third Mesa, is widely believed to be the oldest continuously inhabited community in the United States, dating from around AD 1150. It was also the site of a rare, bloodless conflict between two groups of the Hopi people; in 1906, a dispute, settled uniquely by a "push of war," a pushing contest, sent the losers off to establish the town of Hotevilla. Oraibi is a dusty spot, and as an act of courtesy, tourists are asked to park their cars outside and approach the village on foot.

Hotevilla and Bacavi are about 4 mi west of Oraibi, and their inhabitants are descended from the former residents of that village. The men of Hotevilla continue to plant crops along the mesa slopes, and in warmer months these gardens on the cliffs are lovely to behold.

En Route Beyond Hotevilla, AZ 264 descends from Third Mesa, exits the Hopi reservation, and crosses into Navajo land, running by **Coal Canyon,** where Indians have long mined coal from the dark seam just below the rim. This canyon of colorful mudstone, dark lines of coal, and bleached white rock has an eerie appearance, especially by the light of the moon. Twenty miles west of Coal Canyon, at the junction of AZ 264 and U.S. 160, is the town of Moenkopi, the last Hopi outpost. Established as a farming community, it was settled by the descendants of former Oraibi residents.

Tuba City

9 *50 mi northwest of Third Mesa on AZ 264.*

Tuba City, with about 12,000 permanent residents, is the administrative center for the western portion of the Navajo Nation. In addition to a motel, hostel, and a few restaurants, this small town has a hospital, a bank, and a historic trading post. The octagonal **Tuba City Trading Post** (⊠ Main St., ☎ 520/283–5441), founded in the early 1880s, carries authentic Indian rugs, pottery, baskets, and jewelry; it also sells groceries.

About 5½ mi west of Tuba City, between mileposts 316 and 317 on U.S. 160, is a small sign for the **Dinosaur Tracks.** More than 200 million years ago, dilophosaurus, carnivorous bipedal reptiles more than 10 ft tall, left their imprints in soft mud that subsequently turned to sandstone. There's no charge for a look. Four miles west of here on U.S. 160 is the junction with U.S. 89. This is one of the most colorful regions of the **Painted Desert,** with amphitheaters of maroon, orange, and red rocks facing west; it's especially glorious at sunset.

Dining and Lodging

$ ✕ **Pancho's Family Restaurant.** The main fare here is Mexican, but the menu also lists American and Navajo dishes. The chicken enchiladas and beef tamales are as good as any you'll find south of the border. The large dining room looks like a western coffee shop but incorporates such Native American touches as handmade pottery chandeliers. ⊠ *Main St., adjacent to Tuba City Motel and Trading Post,* ☎ *520/283–5260. AE, D, DC, MC, V.*

$ ✕ **Tuba City Truck Stop Cafe.** Home cooking is what you'll get at this small, conveniently located fast-service restaurant. Try the delicious Navajo vegetarian tacos. ⊠ *AZ 264/U.S. 160,* ☎ *520/283–4975. No credit cards.*

$$ ⊞ **Tuba City Motel.** This property is conveniently situated near Pancho's Family Restaurant, a trading post, and shops for essentials, gifts, and souvenirs. The spacious, well-maintained rooms are fine for an overnight stop before or after a visit to the Hopi Mesas. ⊠ *Box 247 (at AZ 264/U.S. 160 junction), 86045,* ☎ *520/283–4545 or 800/ 644–8383,* ⨏ *520/283–4144. 80 rooms. AE, D, DC, MC, V.*

$–$$ ⊞ **Grey Hills Inn.** Students at Grey Hills High School run this unusual lodging, a former dorm with large, clean accommodations. The beds are comfortable, and eclectic decor and kitschy paintings add character to the otherwise plain rooms. Bathrooms and showers are down the hall, and it's hard to find your way to the inn's entrance in the large high school complex at night, but the rates are reasonable, especially for Youth Hostel members. ⊠ *Box 160 (off U.S. 160, ½ mi north of junction with AZ 264), 86045,* ☎ *520/283–6271, ext. 141; 520/283– 6273 weekends or after school hrs. 32 rooms. No credit cards.*

Nightlife

There's an inexpensive first-run movie theater in Tuba City.

Shopping

The **swap meet** (⊠ Main St., behind the community center and next to the baseball field), held every Friday from 8 AM on, has good prices on jewelry, rugs, pottery, and other arts and crafts; there are also food concessions and booths selling herbs.

OFF THE BEATEN PATH
CAMERON TRADING POST – Established in 1916, the Cameron Trading Post is one of the few remaining authentic trading posts in the Southwest. A good place to stop if you're driving from the Hopi Mesas to the Grand Canyon (☞ Chapter 2), it has dining, lodging, camping, and shopping. Fine authentic Navajo products are sold at an outlet of the Navajo Arts and Crafts Enterprises (⊠ U.S. 89, at junction with AZ 64, ☎ 520/679–2244). ⊠ *25 mi from Tuba City, west on U.S. 160 and south on U.S. 89.*

En Route   Twenty-two miles northeast of Tuba City on U.S. 160 is the tiny community of Red Lake. Off to the left of the highway is a geologic phenomenon known as **Elephant Feet.** These massive eroded sandstone buttes make a good photo stop. Northwest of here, in real Navajo backcountry, is **White Mesa Natural Bridge,** reached via a graded dirt road. The payoff is a view of a massive arch of white sandstone that extends from the edge of White Mesa. The long **Black Mesa** plateau runs for about 15 mi along U.S. 160. Above the prominent escarpments of this land formation, mining operations—a major source of revenue for the Navajo Nation—delve into the more than 20 billion tons of coal deposited there.

NAVAJO NATION NORTH

The magnificent Monument Valley stretches to the northeast of Kayenta into Utah. At a base altitude of approximately 5,500 ft, this sprawling, arid expanse was populated by the ancestral Pueblo people and has been home to generations of Navajo who have farmed and herded livestock. The soaring red buttes, eroded mesas, deep canyons, and naturally sculpted rock formations of Monument Valley are easy to enjoy by driving through and pausing from time to time at roadside stops. Scenes from many movies—among them *She Wore a Yellow Ribbon, Waiting to Exhale, How the West Was Won, Forrest Gump, Stagecoach,* and *2001: A Space Odyssey*—have been filmed here, and Monument Valley is the setting of more television commercials than any other single location in the world.

Kayenta

⑩ *80 mi northeast of Tuba City.*

Kayenta, a small town with a few grocery stores, two motels, and a hospital, is a good base for exploring nearby Monument Valley Navajo Tribal Park (☞ *below*).

Dining and Lodging

$ ✕ **Golden Sands Restaurant.** Fill up on Navajo tacos and other regional specialties at this local favorite next door to the Wetherill Inn Motel. It's a good place to learn about the area from residents who stop by for coffee. ⊠ *U.S. 163,* ☎ *520/697–3684. No credit cards.*

$$ ✕🏨 **Anasazi Inn at Tsegi.** This unpretentious roadside motel, convenient to the Navajo National Monument and Monument Valley, offers striking views of Tsegi Canyon from its rear-facing rooms. Its restaurant, which features tasty Navajo fry-bread sandwiches and tacos. ⊠ *Box 1543 (on U.S. 160, 10 mi west of Kayenta), 86033,* ☎ 🖷 *520/697–3793. 59 rooms. Restaurant. AE, D, DC, MC, V.*

$$ 🏨 **Holiday Inn.** Except for the contemporary southwestern-style decor, this accommodation about ½ mi from Monument Valley provides what you would expect from the Holiday Inn chain. It has one of the few swimming pools in the western section of the region. ⊠ *Box 307 (south of junction of U.S. 160 and U.S. 163), 86033,* ☎ *520/697–3221 or 800/465–4329,* 🖷 *520/697–3349. 164 rooms. Restaurant, pool, travel services. AE, D, DC, MC, V.*

$$ 🏨 **Wetherill Inn Motel.** Named for John Wetherill, a frontier rancher, trader, and explorer who discovered many of the major prehistoric Native American ruins in Arizona, this clean two-story motel with no frills has southwestern decor and a well-stocked gift shop. ⊠ *Box 175 (on U.S. 163), 86033,* ☎ *520/697–3231. 54 rooms. AE, D, DC, MC, V.*

OFF THE **FOUR CORNERS MONUMENT** – A concrete slab inlaid into the ground
BEATEN PATH marks the only point in the United States where four states meet: Arizona, New Mexico, Colorado, and Utah. Most visitors—in summer, nearly 2,000 a day—stay only a few minutes to record the spot on film; you'll see many people posed awkwardly, with an arm or a leg in each state. The monument, a 75 mi-drive from Kayenta, is administered by the Navajo Nation Parks and Recreation Department. ⊠ *Off U.S. 160, 7 mi northwest of the U.S. 160 and NM 502 junction (near Teec Nos Pos),* ☎ *520/871-6647.*

Monument Valley Navajo Tribal Park

⑪ *24 mi northeast of Kayenta.*

Within Monument Valley lies the 30,000-acre Monument Valley Navajo Tribal Park. A 17-mi self-guided tour on a rough dirt road passes the memorable **Mittens and Totem Pole formations,** among others. Drive slowly, and be sure to walk (15 minutes round-trip) from North Window around the end of Cly Butte for the views. The park has a 100-site campground, which closes from early October through April. If you are visiting the area in winter, the rocks may have a beautiful covering of snow. Be sure to call ahead for road conditions.

The Monument Valley **visitor center** holds a crafts shop and exhibits devoted to ancient and modern Native American history. Most of the guided tours offered by operators in and around the center drive visitors in enclosed vans and charge about $15 for 2½ hours. ⊠ *Visitor center: 3½ mi off U.S. 163,* ☎ *801/727–3287.* ☞ *Park $2.50.* ☉ *Visitor center May–Sept., daily 7–7; Oct.–Apr., daily 8–5.*

Outdoor Activities and Sports

HORSEBACK RIDING

If you've always wanted to ride off into the sunset at Monument Valley, get in touch with **Ed Black's Horseback Riding Tours** (⊠ Box 155, Mexican Hat, UT 84531, ☎ 800/551–4039).

Goosenecks

⑫ *33 mi north of Monument Valley Navajo Tribal Park.*

Monument Valley's scenic route, U.S. 163, continues from Arizona into Utah, where the land is crossed, east to west, by a stretch of the San Juan River known as the Goosenecks—so named for the type of twists and curves it takes at the bottom of a wildly carved canyon. Set in a lonely, untrafficked domain, this barren, erosion-blasted gorge has a stark beauty that is nearly as awesome as that of the Grand Canyon. The scenic overlook for the Goosenecks is reached by turning west from U.S. 163 onto UT 261, 4 mi north of the small community of **Mexican Hat** (named for the sombrero-like rock formation you'll see on the hills to your right as you drive north), then proceeding on UT 261 for 1 mi to a directional sign at the road's junction with UT 316. Turn left onto UT 316 and proceed 4 mi to the vista-point parking lot. If you visit during the week, you're likely to find yourself alone there, or perhaps joined by one or two Navajo women selling crafts.

Goulding's Trading Post

⑬ *8 mi northwest of Monument Valley Navajo Tribal Park.*

Established in 1924 by Harry Goulding and his wife, this remote outlet was used as a headquarters by director John Ford when he filmed the western classic *Stagecoach.* Because of the numerous westerns that have been shot in the area, the trading post, motel, and restaurant have gained a measure of international fame. In the old trading-post building, a museum displays prehistoric and modern Indian artifacts as well as memorabilia of the Goulding family. The lodge here is an ideal place for an overnight stay, but call in advance for reservations. You can also rest overnight in or near Kayenta (☞ *above*), where there are three motels.

Dining and Lodging

$$$ ✕⌂ **Goulding's Lodge.** Built near the base of an immense red sandstone butte with spectacular views of Monument Valley from all the rooms, this comfortable motel often serves as headquarters for the lo-

cation crews of filmmakers. The lodge has handsome pueblo-style buildings stuccoed in a deep reddish brown that makes them appear to be a part of the surrounding red-rock formations. The cozy rooms are furnished in contemporary style, with southwestern colors and Navajo-design bedspreads. The on-premises Stagecoach restaurant, serving good American fare, is decorated with memorabilia from movies shot in the area; the service is excellent, and large windows provide a splendid view across the valley. ✉ *Box 360001 (2 mi west of U.S. 163, just north of Utah border), Monument Valley, UT 84536,* ☎ *801/727–3231 or 800/874–0902. 62 rooms. Restaurant, pool, shop, travel services. AE, D, DC, MC, V.*

⚠ **Goulding's Good Sam Campground.** This campground with tents and RV sites is open from mid-March to mid-October. The fee is $14 with no hookups, $22 with hookups (plus tax). ✉ *Off U.S. 163, near Goulding's Trading Post, 27 mi north of Kayenta,* ☎ *801/727–3231, ext. 425.*

⚠ **Mitten View Campground.** Here you'll find sites with a table, a grill, and a deck. Water is available, but there are no hookups; the fee is $5 per site, with hot showers extra. More sites are open in summer, but 10 or 15 are open year-round. ✉ *Monument Valley Navajo Tribal Park, near visitor center, off U.S. 163, 25 mi north of Kayenta,* ☎ *801/727–3287.*

Navajo National Monument

⑭ *53 mi southwest of Goulding's Trading Post.*

At the Navajo National Monument, two unoccupied 13th-century cliff pueblos, Keet Seel and Betatakin, stand under the overhang of orange and ocher cliffs. The largest ancient dwellings in Arizona, these stone-and-mortar complexes were also built by ancestral Pueblo peoples obviously for permanent occupancy, though they were abandoned in less than half a century.

The well-preserved, 135-room **Betatakin** (Navajo for "ledge house") seems almost to hang in midair before a sheer sandstone wall. When the complex was discovered in 1907 by a passing American rancher, the apartments were full of baskets, pottery, and preserved grains and ears of corn—as if the occupants had been chased away in the middle of a meal. For an impressive view of Betatakin, walk to the rim overlook about ½ mi from the visitor center. You can also hike to Betatakin on ranger-led tours, 5 mi round-trip from the visitor center, that leave once a day in early May, most of September, and early October, and twice a day from Memorial Day to Labor Day (weather permitting) at 9 and noon. They are limited to groups of 25. No reservations are accepted; groups form on a first-come, first-served basis.

Keet Seel (Navajo for "broken pottery") is also in good condition in a serene setting, with 160 rooms and five kivas. Explorations of Keet Seel, which lies at an elevation of 7,000 ft and is 17 mi (round-trip) from the visitor center, are restricted: Only 20 people are allowed to visit per day, and only between Memorial Day and Labor Day, when a ranger is present at the site. A permit—which also allows campers to stay overnight near the ruins—is required. Those interested in horseback trips can make arrangements at the visitor center to rent horses and guides from a Navajo family. Trips to Keet Seel are very popular, and places can be reserved up to (but not beyond) two months in advance. Anyone who suffers from vertigo might want to avoid this trip: The trail leads down a 1,100-ft near-vertical rock face.

The **visitor center** houses a small museum, exhibits of prehistoric pottery, and a crafts shop. Free campground and picnic areas are nearby, and rangers sometimes present campfire programs in summer. No food, gasoline, or lodging is available at the monument. ⊠ *Navajo National Monument, HC 71, Box 3, Tonalea 86044,* ☎ *520/672–2366.* ⌨ *Free.* ⊙ *Memorial Day–Labor Day, daily 8–6; Dec.–Feb., daily 8–4:30; rest of yr, daily 8–5.*

Lodging

⚲ **Navajo National Monument.** The free campground here has RV and tent sites, water, and rest rooms, but no hookups. Camping is available May–October. ⊠ *Reached by turnoff on U.S. 160, 21 mi south of Kayenta,* ☎ *520/672–2366.*

Outdoor Activities and Sports

HORSEBACK RIDING

Native American guides conduct daily **horseback tours** to Keet Seel at Navajo National Monument from Memorial Day weekend through Labor Day weekend; rates are approximately $65 per day. Contact Virginia Austin (c/o ⊠ *Navajo National Monument, HC 71, Box 3, Tonalea, AZ 86044,* ☎ *520/672–2366 or 520/672–2367). Reservations should be made two months in advance; there's often a waiting list.*

Shopping

The gift shop at **Navajo National Monument** (☎ 520/672–2366) has an excellent selection of Native American jewelry.

GLEN CANYON DAM AND LAKE POWELL

Lake Powell, with more than 1,900 mi of shoreline, is the heart of the huge 1,255,400-acre **Glen Canyon National Recreation Area.** Created by the barrier of Glen Canyon Dam and fed by the mighty Colorado and five other rivers, the lake extends through eroded canyon country that is nearly devoid of vegetation and so rugged that it was the last major area of the United States to be mapped. The green waters of Lake Powell are confined by red cliffs that twist off from the main body of the lake into 96 major canyons and countless inlets and coves—so many, in fact, that no single person claims to have explored all of them. In a number of places, huge sandstone buttes jut from the water. Seeing the stark geography of Lake Powell often makes tourists feel as if they are visiting another planet.

Skies in the Lake Powell area are blue nearly all year, and only about 8 inches of rain falls annually. Summer temperatures range from the 60s to the 90s (sometimes they rise to more than 100°F). Many fall and spring days are balmy, with daytime temperatures often in the 70s and 80s, but it is possible for chilly weather to set in. In winter, the risk of a cold spell increases, but all-weather houseboats and tour boats make year-round cruising possible.

South of Lake Powell the landscape gives way to the **Echo Cliffs,** orange sandstone formations rising 1,000 ft and more above the highway in places. At **Bitter Springs,** the road ascends the cliffs and provides a spectacular view of the 9,000-square-mi Arizona Strip to the west and the 3,000-ft Vermilion Cliffs to the northwest.

The entry fee at Glen Canyon National Recreation Area and Lake Powell is $5 per vehicle; for hikers, motorcyclists, and bicyclists, the fee is $3. Marinas charge a $5 launching fee; a one-week pass costs $10.

Annual passes are also available: The fees are $15 per car; $10 per hiker, motorcyclist, or bicyclist; and $25 per boat.

Page

⑮ *96 mi west of the Navajo National Monument, 136 mi north of Flagstaff.*

Page was born out of the construction of Glen Canyon Dam in 1957. Prior to that, the broad mesa on which it lies was essentially barren. Initially a construction camp, Page became a tourist stop after Lake Powell formed behind the dam. The town has gradually grown to its present population of about 7,000—the largest community in far-northern Arizona. Most of the motels, restaurants, and strip shopping centers in Page can be found along **Lake Powell Boulevard,** the name given to U.S. 89 as it loops through the town's business district in a roughly northwest direction.

At the corner of Navajo Drive is the **John Wesley Powell Memorial Museum,** a small building honoring the work of explorer John Wesley Powell, who between 1869 and 1872 led the first expeditions down the Green River and the rapids-choked Colorado through the Grand Canyon. Powell mapped and kept detailed records of his trips, naming the Grand Canyon and many other geographic points of interest in northern Arizona. The displays—drawings and photographs of the expedition, area fossils, minerals, and Native American crafts—are rather unimpressive, but the museum serves as an information center for the area and a place to book river and lake trips and scenic flights. It also has a good selection of regional books and maps. ⊠ *6 N. Lake Powell Blvd.,* ☎ *520/645–9496.* ☞ *Requested donation $1.* ☉ *May–Oct., Mon.–Sat. 8–6:30, Sun. 10–6:30; Nov. and Mar., weekdays 9–5; Apr., weekdays 8–6.*

Dining and Lodging

$$ ✕ **Salsa Brava.** This cheerful Mexican restaurant with upholstered booths, lots of windows, and beamed ceilings, emphasizes charbroiled preparations and uses vegetable oil instead of lard. Good versions of the standard burritos, tamales, and enchiladas are available, along with more unusual fare—*carnitas* (slow-cooked pork), chicken with mole, and fish tacos. There's an outdoor patio and a dark and clubby bar. ⊠ *635 Elm St.,* ☎ *520/645–9058. MC, V.*

$$–$$$ 🏨 **Best Western Arizona Inn.** This modern, well-run motel on a high bluff at the northern end of Page has large rooms with queen-size beds and southwestern-print bedspreads. ⊠ *Box C (716 Rim View Dr.), 86040,* ☎ *520/645–2466 or 800/826–2718. 103 rooms. Restaurant, bar, pool, hot tub, meeting rooms. AE, D, DC, MC, V.*

$$ 🏨 **Weston's Empire House.** This classic 1950s-style motel on Page's main street has comfortable rooms with individual air-conditioning and heating units. The smoky bar has a huge jukebox and a big-screen TV. ⊠ *107 S. Lake Powell Blvd., 86040,* ☎ *520/645–2406 or 800/551–9005,* 🆔 *520/645–2647. 69 rooms. Restaurant, bar, lounge, shop, pool. MC, V.*

⚑ **Page–Lake Powell Campground.** More than 70 full-hookup RV sites ($18 per night, $2 extra for cable-TV hookup), and 15 tent sites ($15) are open year-round; reservations are accepted. A coin laundry, an indoor swimming pool, and two sets of men's and women's bathrooms and showers are available for no extra charge to both tenters and RVers. ⊠ *849 Hwy. 98,* ☎ *520/645–3374.*

Nightlife

Canyon Bowl (⊠ 24 N. Lake Powell Blvd., ☎ 520/645–2682) is a combination bowling alley, off-track-betting parlor, comedy club, and bistro. **Ken's Old West** (⊠ 718 Vista Rd., ☎ 520/645–5160) has country-and-western music and dancing; you can also get a pretty good steak or barbecued-chicken dinner. **Mesa Theater** (⊠ 42 S. Lake Powell Blvd., ☎ 520/645–9565) is Page's movie house.

Outdoor Activities and Sports

CRUISES

Guided, piloted, 4½-hour rafting excursions cover a portion of the Colorado River that is relatively calm, with no white-water rapids. The scenery through Glen Canyon Dam is spectacular as the rafts glide beneath multicolored sandstone cliffs that are frequently adorned with Indian petroglyphs. The point of departure is the **Wilderness River Adventures office** (⊠ 50 S. Lake Powell Blvd., ☎ 520/645–3279 or 800/528–6154) in Page; transportation is furnished to the launch site and back from Lees Ferry, where the raft trip ends. The cost is $42.75.

GOLF

Lake Powell National Golf Course (⊠ 400 Clubhouse Dr., ☎ 520/645–2023), a 27-hole, par-72 municipal course that overlooks Glen Canyon Dam and Lake Powell, has wide fairways, tiered greens, and a generous lack of hazards.

HORSEBACK RIDING

Trail rides in the Lake Powell area are available from **Rope & Saddle Promotions** (⊠ Vermilion Downs on Haul Rd., ☎ 520/645–2752 or 520/645–2077); the fee is $20 for the first hour for adults and $10 for each additional hour.

Shopping

Corral West Ranchwear (⊠ Gateway Park Mall, S. Lake Powell Blvd., east of U.S. 89, ☎ 520/645–9391) carries cowboy and cowgirl duds. **Page Factory Stores** (⊠ 644 N. Navajo Dr., at Lake Powell Blvd., ☎ 520/645–5975) has discount outlets for London Fog, Benetton, and Polo Ralph Lauren.

Antelope Canyon

16 *4 mi east of Page.*

You'll probably recognize Antelope Canyon from one of many photographs: Red sandstone rising majestically in a corkscrew formation, dramatically illuminated by a chink of light streaming in from above. And you're likely to see assorted shutterbugs standing patiently next to tripods, waiting hours for just the right shot. A highlight of any trip to the Lake Powell area, Antelope Canyon is on the Navajo reservation, about 3 mi from Page. If you don't have a four-wheel-drive vehicle (or the time to wait for the rather erratic—and limited—hours that the gate to the site is open), book a tour from Page (☞ Guided Tours *in* The Northeast A to Z, *below*).

Glen Canyon Dam

17 *2 mi west of Page.*

Once you leave the Page business district, the Glen Canyon Dam and Lake Powell behind it immediately become visible. This concrete-arch dam was completed in September 1963, its power plant an engineering feat that rivaled the building of Hoover Dam. Nearly 5 million cubic ft of concrete were required. The dam's crest is 1,560 ft across and rises 710 ft from bedrock and 583 ft above the waters of the Colorado River. Lake Powell is 560 ft deep at the dam at full pool elevation.

Just off the highway at the north end of the bridge is the **Carl Hayden Visitor Center,** a museumlike facility dedicated to telling the story of the creation of Glen Canyon Dam and Lake Powell. Among the several exhibits is a giant three-dimensional topographic map of Lake Powell country. The center's huge reception and observation room, with floor-to-ceiling glass, provides panoramic views of the dam, the wildly sculpted cliffs that border Lake Powell, and the sandstone buttes that protrude, islandlike, from the lake. Between May and October, free guided tours of the dam are offered daily between 8 and 4, every hour on the half hour. The rest of the year, visitors can take a 40-minute self-guided tour through the complex. ⊠ *Glen Canyon Dam,* ☎ *520/ 645–2511.* ☜ *Free.* ☉ *Memorial Day–Labor Day, daily 7–7; Labor Day–Memorial Day, daily 8–5.*

Wahweap

18 *5 mi north of Glen Canyon Dam.*

The most popular destination on Lake Powell, which stretches 180 mi through northern Arizona and southern Utah, is the vacation village of Wahweap. Most recreational activity in the region takes place around here, where everything needed for a lakeside holiday is available: fishing, boat rentals, dinner cruises, and much more. Stop at **Wahweap Lodge** (☞ Dining and Lodging, *below*) for an excellent view of the lake area.

★
19 The best way to appreciate the beauty of Lake Powell is by boat. If you don't have access to one, the five-hour excursion cruise to **Rainbow Bridge National Monument** is the way to go. Along the 52-mi route (one-way from Wahweap Marina), you're treated to ever-changing, beautiful, and bizarre scenery, including huge monoliths that look like people turned into stone and a butte that resembles a dinosaur. You might also see eagles perched on ragged outcrops of rock. Finally, after gliding through a deep and twisting canyon waterway, the boat docks near Rainbow Bridge, the 290-ft red sandstone arch that straddles a cove of the lake. The world's largest natural stone bridge, it can be reached only by water or an arduous hike from a remote point on the Navajo reservation (☞ Cruises *and* Hiking *in* Outdoor Activities and Sports, *below*).

The excursion boats, which leave Wahweap daily, are two-tier craft with sundecks upstairs and interior seating with windows downstairs. Experienced pilots provide commentary throughout the trip. Pack a lunch or take snacks; no food is sold on the boats, though coffee and water are provided. Other cruises are offered at the Wahweap Marina, including an all-day trip that stops at Rainbow Bridge and then proceeds farther into the Utah portion of the lake (☞ Boating *and* Cruises *in* Outdoor Activities and Sports, *below*).

Dining and Lodging

$$–$$$ ✕ **Rainbow Room in Wahweap Lodge.** You can't beat the beautiful setting of this semicircular restaurant with panoramic views of Lake Powell and a colony of houseboats bobbing offshore. An extensive menu features southwestern, standard American, and some Continental fare, accompanied by a good wine selection. Specialties include Southwest chicken breast marinated in a honey-and-jalapeño-pepper sauce, and coho salmon with a Dijon-mustard cream sauce. ⊠ *Wahweap Lodge*

(on U.S. 89, 5 mi north of Page), ☎ *520/645–2433 or 800/528–6154. AE, D, DC, MC, V.*

\$\$\$ ❏ **Wahweap Lodge.** The lodge, on a promontory above Lake Powell,
★   serves as the center for recreational activities in the area. This land-scaped property offers accommodations with oak furnishings and bal-conies or patios; many of the rooms have a lake view (rates are a bit higher for these). The brightly colored, southwestern-style suites in the newest building are particularly attractive. Guests can enjoy two pools, a cocktail lounge, a marina, and the Rainbow Room (☞ *above*) for dining. Off-season rates are very reasonable. ✉ *Box 1597 (on U.S. 89, 5 mi north of Page), Page 86040,* ☎ *520/645–2433 or 800/528–6154. 350 rooms. Restaurant, bar, boating, waterskiing, fishing, travel ser-vices. AE, D, DC, MC, V.*

⚠ **Wahweap Campground.** This campground has 180 sites, some near the marina. The fee for campsites with drinking water is $8.50; campers can use the coin-op laundry and showers ($2 extra) at the ad-jacent RV park (☞ *below*). Open from April 1 to October 31, the camp-ground operates on a first-come, first-served basis. ✉ *5 mi north of Page on U.S. 89 near shore of Lake Powell,* ☎ *520/645–1059.*

⚠ **Wahweap RV Park.** This RV park has 120 full-service sites with full hookups, showers, and a laundromat; the fee is $22.50. It's open year-round and reservations are accepted. ✉ *5 mi north of Page on U.S. 89 near shore of Lake Powell,* ☎ *520/645–1004 or 800/528–6154.*

Nightlife

Nightlife in Wahweap revolves around **Wahweap Lodge** (☞ Dining and Lodging, *above*), which has a cocktail lounge and offers a sunset dinner cruise.

Outdoor Activities and Sports

BOATING

Docks and launching ramps are available at **State Line Marina,** 1½ mi north of Wahweap Lodge. **Wahweap Marina** (☎ 520/645–2433) is the largest of the four full-service marinas on Lake Powell (☞ Boat-ing *in* The Northeast A to Z, *below*), with 850 slips and the most facilities, including a reasonably good diner.

CRUISES

Excursions on double-decker scenic cruisers piloted by experienced guides leave from the dock of Lake Powell's Wahweap Lodge (☞ Din-ing and Lodging, *above*). The most popular is the one to Rainbow Bridge National Monument; half-day cruises cost $62, full days $82. A 2½-hour sunset dinner cruise also departs from Wahweap Lodge: A buffet-style dinner is served on the fully glassed lower deck of the 95-ft *Canyon King* paddlewheeler, an 1800s riverboat. The meal in-cludes prime rib with fresh garden vegetables and a baked potato, a salad, and dessert; cocktails are available at an extra charge. The cost of the dinner cruise is $48.50; those who wish to take the cruise with-out eating pay $22.

HIKING

Seasoned hikers in good physical condition might want to try either of the two trails leading to Rainbow Bridge; both trails are about 26–28 mi round-trip. Take Indian Highway 16 north toward the Utah state border. When you come to a fork in the road, take either direction for about 5 mi and you'll come to a trailhead leading to Rainbow Bridge. Excursion boats pull in at the dock at the arch, but no supplies are sold there.

THE NORTHEAST A TO Z

Arriving and Departing

By Bus

Greyhound Lines (☎ 800/231–2222) has numerous Arizona destinations, but there is no service into the reservations. If you're coming from out of state and wish to tour northeastern Arizona, take a bus to Phoenix or Flagstaff and then rent a car.

By Car

If you are arriving from southern California or southern Arizona, Flagstaff is the best jumping-off point into northeastern Arizona (☞ Flagstaff *in* Chapter 4). If you are traveling from Utah or Nevada, you might choose to come in from Utah on U.S. 89, starting your tour at Page, Arizona. For those driving south from Colorado, logical entry points are Farmington and Shiprock, New Mexico, via U.S. 64 (what looks like a more direct route to Canyon de Chelly through Red Rock ends up crossing an unimproved road). Gallup, New Mexico, to the east, is also a convenient starting point for exploring the area.

By Plane

No major airlines fly directly into the reservations. To get closer to the northeastern part of the state, travelers will need to fly to **Sky Harbor International Airport** (☎ 520/273–3300) in Phoenix, the primary hub for air travel coming into Arizona from points out of state, and make connections for either the **Flagstaff Pullium Airport** (☎ 520/556–1234) or the **Page Municipal Airport** (☎ 520/645–2494). **Skywest** (☎ 800/453–9417) has daily flights from Phoenix to Page.

By Train

Amtrak (☎ 800/872–7245) provides daily service into Arizona from both the east and the west. It makes scheduled stops in Flagstaff. No passenger train enters the interior of the Navajo or Hopi reservation.

Getting Around

By Bus

The **Navajo Transit System** (✉ Drawer 1330, Window Rock 86515, ☎ 520/729–5449 or 520/729–5457; 520/871–4108 at Navajo Nation Inn) offers regular service on fixed routes throughout the Navajo reservation as well as charter service; write ahead for schedules. The buses are modern, in good condition, and generally on time, but this method of travel may be too slow for some visitors.

By Car

Because a tour of Navajo–Hopi country involves driving long distances among widely scattered communities, a detailed, recently published road map is absolutely essential. A wrong turn in this lonely country could send you many miles out of your way. Gas stations carry adequate state maps, but two other maps are particularly recommended: the Automobile Association of America's guide to Navajo–Hopi country and the excellent map of the northeastern region prepared by the **Navajo Tourism Department** (☞ Visitor Information *in* Contacts and Resources, *below*).

Most of the 25,000 square mi of the Navajo reservation and other areas of northeastern Arizona are off the beaten track. It isn't easy to find a place to service your car here, so have your car inspected and serviced before your trip. Many visitors to the northeast generally stay on the well-maintained paved thoroughfares, which are patrolled by police officers. If you don't have the equipment for wilderness travel—including a four-wheel-drive vehicle, water, food, tools, and bedrolls—and do not have backcountry experience, stay off the dirt roads that crisscross the region unless they are signed and graded, and the skies are clear. Seek weather information if you see ominous rain clouds in summer or signs of snow in winter. Never drive into dips or low-lying road areas during a heavy rainstorm; they could be flooded or could flood suddenly. If you heed these simple precautions (☞ Road Service *and* Weather, *below,* for more tips and information), car travel through the region will be as safe as anywhere else.

Contacts and Resources

Banks

Norwest has branch offices with automated-teller machines (ATMs) in Window Rock and Tuba City on the Navajo reservation. Adjacent to the reservation, Flagstaff, Page, Winslow, and Holbrook have banks and ATMs.

Bicycling

Biking enthusiasts will find endless miles of paved roads and light traffic. But the mostly two-lane highways do not have paved shoulders, and motorists are unaccustomed to encountering cyclists. As a result, you should practice extreme caution when riding. The roads at Canyon de Chelly National Monument, Navajo National Monument, Monument Valley Navajo Tribal Park, and Kinlichee Navajo Tribal Park are your best bets. There are no bicycle-rental companies in Navajo–Hopi country. Be sure to carry spare tires and repair materials.

Boating

There are four full-service marinas at Lake Powell where you can rent small or excursion boats, including houseboats, and water-sports equipment, water sleds, and motorized wave cutters: **Wahweap** (☎ 520/278–8888), **Bullfrog** (☎ 801/684–2233), **Halls Crossing** (☎ 801/684–2261), and **Hite Marina** (☎ 801/684–2278). Houseboats—which should be reserved well in advance—range widely in size and price; one that sleeps six (in three double beds) may cost $675 for three nights. Some have air-conditioning, TVs, VCRs, microwaves, and other amenities. Small boats, too, vary in size and price. An 18-ft powerboat for eight passengers runs about $185 per day. Most of these prices drop after the summer months. Boat-tour and lodging packages are also available. For detailed information on all the Lake Powell options and prices, contact **ARA Leisure Services** (✉ Box 56909, Phoenix 85079, ☎ 800/528–6154, FAX 520/331–5258).

Camping and RV Parks

If you plan to stay in national monument and park areas, camping permission can be obtained on-site; for other camping situations, contact the **Navajo Nation Parks and Recreation Department** (☞ Hiking, *below*) to find out whether you need a permit. Be careful not to camp in low-lying areas, which are subject to extremely dangerous flash floods during sudden summer rains.

Car Rentals

Major companies serving Phoenix and Flagstaff include **Avis** (☎ 800/331–1212), **Budget** (☎ 800/527–0700), **Hertz** (☎ 800/654–3131), and **National** (☎ 800/227–7368). Avis and Budget also offer rentals at the Page Municipal Airport.

Emergencies

POLICE

Canyon de Chelly police (☎ 520/674–5500). **Hopi tribal police: Hopi Mesas** (☎ 520/738–2233). **Navajo tribal police: Chinle** (☎ 520/674–

5291), **Tuba City** (☎ 520/283–5242), **Window Rock** (☎ 520/871–6113 or 520/871–6116).

Medical care in Navajo–Hopi country is not easily accessible: People with chronic medical conditions or those in frail health may wish to avoid a trip into Arizona's sparsely populated northeast. Hospital emergency care is generally not more than 60 minutes' driving time from any location on a paved highway.

Monument Valley Hospital (⌧ Near Goulding's Trading Post off U.S. 163 at the Arizona-Utah border, ☎ 801/727–3241) in Utah has medical and dental services. **Page Hospital** (⌧ N. Navajo and Vista Aves., ☎ 520/645–2424) has emergency-room service. **Sage Memorial Hospital** (⌧ Ganado, on the Navajo reservation, ☎ 520/755–3411), a public hospital, offers medical and dental services. Emergency care through the **U.S. Public Health Service Indian Hospitals** is available in the reservation communities of Fort Defiance (☎ 520/729–5741), Chinle (☎ 520/674–5281), Tuba City (☎ 520/283–6211), and Keams Canyon (☎ 520/738–2211).

There are no pharmacies on the Navajo or Hopi reservation. For emergency medical supplies, *see* the private or public hospitals noted in the Hospital/Medical Clinics section, *above*. In Chinle, **Basha's** (⌧ U.S. 191, across from the Canyon de Chelly National Monument entrance, ☎ 520/674–3464) is open Monday–Saturday 8 AM–10 PM, Sunday 8–8. In Page, **Safeway** (⌧ Page Plaza, ☎ 520/645–5714 or 520/645–5068) is open weekdays 9–9, Saturday 9–6, and Sunday 10–4.

Fishing

Contact the **Navajo Nation Fish and Wildlife Office** (⌧ Box 1480, Window Rock 86515, ☎ 520/871–6451 or 520/871–6452) for permits to fish anywhere on the reservation. For the Lake Powell region, fishing licenses are available at the **Wahweap Marina** (⌧ U.S. 89, 5 mi north of Page, ☎ 520/278–8888) and at **Stix Market** (⌧ 5 S. Lake Powell Blvd., Page, ☎ 520/645–2891). If you want a fishing guide for Lake Powell or the Colorado River at Lees Ferry, about 15 mi below the Glen Canyon Dam en route to the North Rim of the Grand Canyon, contact **Ed Strasburg** (⌧ Box 2699, Page 86040, ☎ 520/645–9489). *See also* Sports *in* The Gold Guide.

Guided Tours

Except during winter months, the **Navajo Transit System** (☞ Getting Around By Bus, *above*) operates tours departing from Window Rock. Destinations include Canyon de Chelly and the Painted Desert. **Nava-Hopi Tours, Inc.** (☎ 520/774–5003 or 800/892–8687) schedules tours into the Navajo and Hopi reservations from Flagstaff. **Crawley's Monument Valley Tours** (☎ 520/697–3463) leaves from the small town of Kayenta. **Goulding's Monument Valley Tours** (☎ 801/727–3231) departs from Goulding's Lodge (☞ Dining and Lodging *in* Goulding's Trading Post, *above*). Half- and full-day truck and Jeep tours into Canyon de Chelly on the Navajo reservation depart from nearby **Thunderbird Lodge** (☎ 520/674–5841). The half-day tours leave twice daily (when there is a minimum of six passengers) throughout the year. Full-day tours are available only from April to October. The newspaper published by the **Navajo Tourism Department** (☞ Visitor Information, *below*) has a listing of operators offering Jeep and horseback tours on the Navajo reservation. Unless you have a four-wheel-drive vehicle or don't mind hiking 8 mi (round-trip) through sand, you'll want to take a guided tour to Antelope Canyon (☞ Antelope Canyon, *above*), one

of the most arresting sights in the Page–Lake Powell area. If Lee
Woods, the owner of **Duck Tours** (☎ 520/645–8581; tickets also available at the Page Chamber of Commerce, ☎ 520/645–2741, and the
John Wesley Powell Museum, ☎ 520/645–9496), is your guide, you're
in for a fascinating introduction to the area.

Hiking

For a backcountry hiking permit, contact the **Navajo Nation Parks and
Recreation Department** (⊠ Box 9000, Window Rock 86515, ☎ 520/
871–6647). Trails are often poorly marked and for the most part not
maintained in this wilderness area. The **Glen Canyon Natural History
Association** (⊠ Box 581, Page 86040, ☎ 520/645–3532) sells good
topographical maps of the region as well as useful hiking publications.
Be sure to bring plenty of water and electrolyte-rich beverages such as
Gatorade when hiking, and drink often.

Road Service

Auto Service Center (⊠ U.S. 191, near Basha's grocery store, Chinle,
☎ 520/674–3240). **Fed Mart Automotive** (⊠ AZ 264, near Window
Rock, ☎ 520/871–4764). **Kayenta Discount Auto Parts** (⊠ U.S. 160,
☎ 520/697–3200). **Onsae Auto Repair** (⊠ Second Mesa, across from
the Hopi Cultural Center, Hopi Mesas, ☎ 520/734–2211). **Tuba City
Motors** (⊠ Corner of Birch and Oak Sts., ☎ 520/283–5315 during
the day; 520/283–5300 at night).

Shopping

Although you may feel more comfortable shopping at an established
store, you may find exactly what you want, at a good price, at a reservation roadside vendor. If you would like some tips on quality, the **Navajo
Tourism Department** (☞ Visitor Information, *below*) has printed material on the subject.

Groceries, over-the-counter medicine, gasoline, and other supplies can
be purchased in all of the major communities and trading posts on the
Navajo and Hopi reservations, including Page, Window Rock, Fort Defiance, Ganado, Chinle, Hopi Second Mesa, Keams Canyon, Tuba
City, Kayenta, Goulding's Trading Post, and Cameron Trading Post.
Some of the smaller communities offer limited supplies; in general, don't
count on a wide selection. Plan your gas stops for the locations cited.

Telephone lines—and thus connections with credit-card verification
sources—are often iffy at the Hopi Mesas. It's a good idea to carry cash
or traveler's checks to make purchases here or anywhere else outside
of the trading posts.

Time

Unlike the rest of Arizona (including the Hopi reservation), the Navajo
reservation observes daylight saving time. Thus for half the year—April
to October—it's an hour later on the Navajo reservation than everywhere else in the state.

Weather

Summer temperatures in northeastern Arizona average about 87°F
but can climb beyond 100°F. Winter daytime temperatures range from
the 30s to the 60s but can drop to zero or below at night, especially
in mountainous areas. Although the region gets less than 10 inches of
rainfall in an average year, fierce summer thunderstorms can instantly
flood low-lying areas. Heavy snows sometimes stop all traffic on dirt
back roads, and it is not uncommon for remote villages to be snowed
in for weeks at a time, particularly in the higher elevations.

KTNN radio (AM 660) provides periodic weather information. This station serves the Hopi and Navajo reservations from studios in Window

Rock. Some programming is in Navajo, but there are news and weather reports in English. You might also telephone Canyon de Chelly police or the Navajo or Hopi tribal police (☞ Emergencies, *above*) for weather updates.

Visitor Information

For more information regarding Navajo–Hopi country, contact the **Navajo Tourism Department** (Box 663, Window Rock 86515, ☎ 520/871–6436, 520/871–7371, or 520/871–7381) and the **Hopi Tribe Office of Public Relations** (✉ Box 123, Kykotsmovi 86039, ☎ 520/734–2441). The **Native American Tourism Center** (✉ 4130 N. Goldwater Blvd., Scottsdale 85251, ☎ 602/945–0771) sells a map of Arizona reservations including a list of annual festivals. The center can help you contact any of the 14 tribal councils in the state. Also contact the **National Park Service/Glen Canyon Recreation Area** (✉ Box 1507, Page 86040, ☎ 520/608–6200 or 520/608–6405) and the **Page/Lake Powell Chamber of Commerce** (✉ Box 727, 106 S. Lake Powell Blvd., Page 86040, ☎ 520/645–2741) for area information.

4 North-Central Arizona

Antiquity, the Wild West—the real one and Hollywood's version—and the New Age all converge (harmonically, of course) in north-central Arizona. Flagstaff, the largest city here, has many historic buildings, an active nightlife, and winter sports in the dramatic San Francisco Peaks. Beyond the city, small towns and desert settings provide glimpses into generations past.

By Edie Jarolim

RICH IN NATURAL attractions, north-central Arizona is also rich in artifacts from its earliest inhabitants: Several national and state parks—among them Walnut Canyon, Wupatki, Montezuma Castle, and Tuzigoot national monuments—hold well-preserved evidence of the architectural accomplishments of Native American Sinagua and other ancestral Puebloans who made their homes in the Verde Valley and the region near the San Francisco Peaks. Flagstaff, the largest city in north-central Arizona and home to two important observatories, is a convenient jumping-off point for tours.

Those interested in exploring the West's wild and woolly days will enjoy a visit to the preserved fort at Camp Verde, which gives an excellent feel for frontier life, and the funky former mining town Jerome. The many Victorian houses in temperate Prescott attest to the attempt to bring "civilization" to Arizona's territorial capital.

The Verde Valley towns of Cornville, Clarkdale, and Cottonwood are as sleepy as their names suggest. Sedona couldn't provide a greater contrast, with its sophisticated restaurants, upscale shops and accommodations, and New Age entrepreneurs. Drive just a few miles, though, and you're among soaring red rocks. U.S. 89A, which heads north out of Sedona through wooded Oak Creek Canyon en route to Flagstaff, is one of the most scenic drives in the state.

Pleasures and Pastimes

Camping

The Prescott and Coconino national forests cover a large part of north-central Arizona. Campgrounds close to Sedona often fill up in summer, especially those along Oak Creek in Oak Creek Canyon; if you want to camp near the red rocks, two good places to try are Manzanita and Banjo Bill. In Coconino National Forest near Flagstaff, the campgrounds near Mormon Lake and Lake Mary—including Pinegrove, Lakeview, Forked Pine, Double Springs, and Dairy Springs—are popular to the point of overcrowding in summer. Sites near Prescott and Jerome in the Prescott National Forest are generally less visited; Potato Patch and Granite Basin are both scenic, and sleeping out on top of Mingus Mountain is unforgettable.

Dining

Sedona remains at the front guard of north-central Arizona's haute-cuisine incursion, but Jerome, Flagstaff, and Prescott have interesting new dining rooms as well. Elsewhere, the fare runs more toward meat and potatoes.

CATEGORY	COST*
$$$$	over $35
$$$	$25–$35
$$	$15–$25
$	under $15

*per person, excluding drinks, service, and sales tax

Hiking

You can hike through thickly wooded areas in the Verde Valley and the Prescott National Forest in the state's highest alpine region (and even ascend a volcano), and among the rock formations around Sedona. National Forest Service offices in Camp Verde, Prescott, Sedona, and Flagstaff direct trekkers to the best trails.

Lodging

Flagstaff has many comfortable motels (all the familiar U.S. chains are represented) and pleasant bed-and-breakfasts but no real luxury. You'll find stunning settings and outstanding amenities in Sedona, but few bargains. Many of Prescott's hotels have fabled pasts. Little Jerome has one historic hotel, along with a few reliable B&Bs, but it's smart to call ahead if you think you might want to spend the night there.

CATEGORY	COST*
$$$$	over $150
$$$	$110–$150
$$	$60–$110
$	under $60

All prices are for a standard double room in high (summer) season, excluding room tax.

Native American Culture

The achievements of the Sinagua people, who lived in north-central Arizona from the 8th through the 15th centuries, reached their height in the 12th and 13th centuries, when various related groups occupied most of the San Francisco Volcanic Field and a large portion of the upper and middle Verde Valley. The Sinagua sites around modern-day Camp Verde, Clarkdale, and Flagstaff provide a window onto this venerable culture.

Exploring North-Central Arizona

The Verde Valley, in the southern part of the area covered in this chapter, is under-visited, but nearby Prescott, which has always been a Phoenician beat-the-heat getaway, is becoming popular among out-of-towners. It's hard to believe that Sedona, which is adding movie screens, chic restaurants, and B&Bs at an alarming rate, was fairly sedate just 10 years ago. Flagstaff has long been the population hub for north-central Arizona.

Numbers in the text correspond to numbers in the margin and on the North-Central Arizona, Prescott, and Flagstaff maps.

Great Itineraries

A short stay can give you a little taste of this rich part of the state, but at least five days are necessary for the full flavor. Linger longer if you want to savor the region's history and landscape or enjoy some outdoor activities. The following itineraries assume you'll start out in Phoenix, as most visitors do, and head north.

IF YOU HAVE 3 DAYS

Spend the first two nights in 🖼 **Sedona** ⑬. Take a Jeep tour or a hike in **Red Rock State Park,** and then explore the town's shops, especially those in the chic Tlaquepaque complex, and sights. On the next day, visit the ghost town of **Jerome** ⑥. On your third day, drive through scenic **Oak Creek Canyon** to 🖼 **Flagstaff** ⑭–㉒, where you can visit the **Riordon Historic State Park** or the **Museum of Northern Arizona** in the afternoon and the **Lowell Observatory** at night.

IF YOU HAVE 5 DAYS

Expand your time in 🖼 **Sedona** ⑬ by exploring Oak Creek Canyon and Red Rock State Park on the first day and shopping or exploring the town on the second. Enjoy a good part of the third day in **Jerome** ⑥ then continue on to 🖼 **Prescott** ⑦–⑫, where you can spend the night in one of the many Victorian-era lodgings. Next day, poke around the town's antiques shops and **Sharlot Hall Museum,** and in the late afternoon drive up to 🖼 **Flagstaff** ⑭–㉒. History lovers and hikers will enjoy an

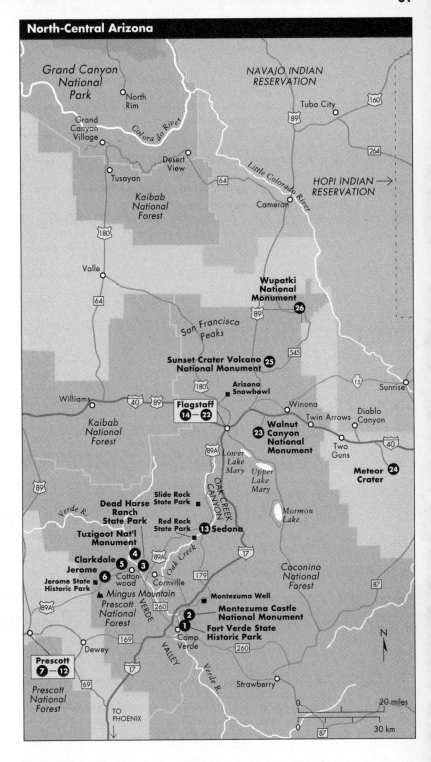

North-Central Arizona

Grand Canyon National Park

NAVAJO INDIAN RESERVATION

North Rim

Tuba City

160

89

Colorado River

Grand Canyon Village

264

Desert View

64

Little Colorado River

Tusayan

HOPI INDIAN → RESERVATION

Kaibab National Forest

Cameron

180

Valle

64

Wupatki National Monument 26

San Francisco peaks

89

545

Sunset Crater Volcano National Monument 25

15

Sunrise

180

Arizona Snowbowl

Williams

40 89

Flagstaff 14 — 22

Winona

Twin Arrows

Diablo Canyon

Kaibab National Forest

89A

Walnut Canyon National Monument 23

Two Guns

40

Meteor Crater 24

Lower Lake Mary

Upper Lake Mary

89

Verde R.

Dead Horse Ranch State Park

Slide Rock State Park

Mormon Lake

Tuzigoot Nat'l Monument

Red Rock State Park

13 **Sedona**

OAK CREEK CANYON

Clarkdale

5 4

3

Jerome

6

17

Coconino National Forest

87

Jerome State Historic Park

Cotton-wood

89A

Oak Creek

Cornville

179

▲ Mingus Mountain

Prescott National Forest

260

■ **Montezuma Well**

VERDE

2 **Montezuma Castle National Monument**

89

1

169

Dewey

Fort Verde State Historic Park

Camp Verde

260

N

Prescott 7 — 12

17

Verde R.

Prescott National Forest

69

VALLEY

Strawberry

0   20 miles

TO PHOENIX ↓

87

0   30 km

excursion to the adjacent **Sunset Crater** ㉕ and **Wupatki** ㉖ national monuments, where Native American artifacts may be explored in an inactive volcanic field.

IF YOU HAVE 7 OR MORE DAYS

Take your time driving up from Phoenix to Sedona, spending the morning of the first day exploring **Fort Verde State Historic Park** ① and **Montezuma Castle National Monument** ②. In the afternoon, ride the **Verde River Canyon Excursion Train** and spend the night in 🔛 **Jerome** ⑥. Continue on to 🔛 **Prescott** ⑦–⑫ for a day or two before heading over to 🔛 **Flagstaff** ⑭–㉒, where you can ski in the winter or view the entire San Francisco Peaks region from the Agassi ski lift in summer. If you conclude your trip in 🔛 **Sedona** ⑬, you'll have made a very satisfying circle of the area.

When to Tour North-Central Arizona

If you're not committed to warm weather, winter is an excellent time to visit: It's often easier to find a hotel (except in Sedona around Christmas), and, in Flagstaff and Prescott, rooms are less expensive. Prescott and Flagstaff hold most of their festivals and cultural events in summer. Sedona's biggest event, the Jazz on the Rocks Festival, takes place in September.

THE VERDE VALLEY, JEROME, PRESCOTT, AND SEDONA

About 90 mi north of Phoenix, as you round a curve approaching Exit 285 of I–17, the valley of the Verde River suddenly unfolds in a panorama of grayish-white cliffs, tinted red in the distance and dotted with desert scrub, cottonwood, and pine. For hundreds of years many Native American communities, especially those of the southern Sinagua people, lined the Verde River. Rumors of great mineral deposits brought Europeans to the Verde Valley as early as 1583, when Hopi Indians guided Antonio de Espejo here, but it wasn't until the second half of the 19th century that this wealth was commercially exploited. The discovery of silver and gold in the Black Hills, which border the valley on the southwest, gave rise to such boomtowns as Jerome—and to military installations such as Fort Verde, set up to protect the white settlers and wealth seekers from the Native American tribes they displaced. Mineral wealth was also the impetus behind the establishment of Prescott, across the Mingus Mountains from Verde Valley, as a territorial capital by President Lincoln and other Unionists who wanted to keep the riches out of Confederate hands.

Camp Verde

94 mi north of Phoenix on I–17.

❶ The military post for which **Fort Verde State Historic Park** is named was established in 1871–73 as the third of three fortifications in this part of the Arizona Territory. To protect the Verde Valley's farmers and miners from Tonto Apache and Yavapai raids, the fort's administrators oversaw the movement of nearly 1,500 Indians to the San Carlos and Fort Apache reservations. A museum details the history of the area's military installations, and three furnished officers' quarters show the day-to-day living conditions of the top brass; even on the frontier, the married men lived far more comfortably than their bachelor counterparts. Signs from any of I–17's three Camp Verde exits will direct you to the 10-acre park. ⊠ *125 Hollamon St., Camp Verde,* ☎ *520/567–3275.* 💺 *$2.* ☉ *Daily 8–4:30.*

② The five-story 20-room cliff dwelling at **Montezuma Castle National Monument** was named by explorers who believed it had been erected by the Aztecs. Southern Sinagua Indians actually built the structure, one of the best-preserved prehistoric ruins in North America—and one of the most accessible. An easy paved trail (⅓ mi round-trip) leads to the dwelling and to adjacent Castle A, a badly deteriorated six-story living space with about 45 rooms. Visitors are not permitted to enter the ruins, but the viewing area is very close by.

Somewhat less accessible but equally striking is the **Montezuma Well** (☎ 520/567–4521) unit of the national monument. Although there are some Sinagua and Hohokam ruins here, the limestone sinkhole with a limpid blue-green pool lying in the middle of the desert is the site's main attraction. This cavity—55 ft deep and 365 ft across—is all that's left of an ancient subterranean cavern; the water remains at a constant 76°F year-round. It's a short hike up here, but the serene setting and the views of the Verde Valley reward the effort. To reach Montezuma Well from Montezuma Castle, return to I–17 and go north one exit; you'll see the signs for the well, which is 4 mi east of the freeway. The drive includes a short section of dirt road. ⊠ *From Camp Verde, take Main St. to Montezuma Castle Rd.,* ☎ *520/567–3322, ext. 12 (ranger) or ext. 15 (bookstore).* ⊠ *$2.* ⊙ *8–5 (hrs sometimes longer in spring and summer).*

Outdoor Activities and Sports

The **Verde Ranger District** office of the **Prescott National Forest** (⊠ 300 E. Hwy. 260, Camp Verde, ☎ 520/567–4121, TTY 520/567–1119) is a good resource for places to hike—as well as to fish and boat—along the Verde River.

Dead Horse Ranch State Park

③ *20 mi northwest of Montezuma Castle National Monument, 1 mi north of Cottonwood, off Main St.*

In the late 1940s, when Calvin "Cap" Ireys asked his family to help him choose among the ranches he was thinking about buying in the Verde Valley, his son immediately picked "the one with the dead horse on it." Ireys sold the land to the state in 1973 at one-third of its value, with the stipulation that the park into which it was to be converted retain the ranch's colorful name.

The 325-acre spread, which combines high-desert and wetlands habitats, is a pleasant place to while away the day. You can fish in the Verde River or the Park Lagoon (it's stocked with panfish, catfish, bass, and, in winter, trout) or hike on some 6 mi of trails that begin in a shaded picnic area and wind along the banks of the river; adjoining forest-service and multiuse agency pathways are available for those who enjoy longer treks. Birders can check off more than 100 species from the Arizona Audubon Society lists provided by the rangers. Many visitors are especially eager to see the bald eagles that perch along the Verde River in winter and the common black hawks—a misnomer for these threatened avians—that nest here in summer. ⊠ *675 Dead Horse Ranch Rd., Cottonwood 86236,* ☎ *520/634–5283.* ⊠ *$4 per car for day use, $10 for camping without electricity, $15 with electricity.* ⊙ *Daily 8–7.*

Dining

$$ ✕ **Manzanita Restaurant & Lounge.** You wouldn't expect to find
★ sophisticated cooking in Cornville, 6 mi west of Cottonwood, but a European-born chef who came to the Verde Valley via Los Angeles prepares Continental fare using organic produce and locally raised meat whenever possible. Roast duckling in orange sauce and rack of lamb

are presented with style; try the venison if it's available. The hours here are not as cosmopolitan as the food: Dinner ends at 8 Wednesday through Saturday and 7 on Sunday. ⊠ *11425 E. Cornville Rd., Cornville,* ☎ *520/634–8851. MC, V. Closed Mon. and Tues.*

$–$$ ✕ **Page Springs Bar & Restaurant.** Come to these two rustic wood-panel rooms on the loop to the town of Page Springs off U.S. 89A for down-home western chow: great chili, burgers, and steaks. You'll get a bosky setting and an Oak Creek view for a lot less money than you'd pay in or closer to Sedona. ⊠ *1975 N. Page Springs Rd., Page Springs,* ☎ *520/634–9954. No credit cards.*

Tuzigoot National Monument

❹ *3 mi north of Cottonwood.*

Not as well preserved as Montezuma Castle (☞ *above*) but more impressive in scope, Tuzigoot is another complex of ruins of the Sinagua people, who lived on this land overlooking the Verde Valley from about AD 1000 to AD 1400. Items used for food preparation, as well as jewelry, weapons, and farming tools excavated from the site, are displayed in the visitor center, where there is also a reconstructed room from the pueblo. ⊠ *Broadway Rd., between Cottonwood's Old Town and Clarkdale, Clarkdale 86324,* ☎ *520/634–5564.* ▣ *$2.* ☉ *Daily 8–5, extended summer hrs.*

Clarkdale

❺ *19 mi northwest of Camp Verde, AZ 260 to U.S. 89A, 23 mi southwest of Sedona on U.S. 89A, 2 mi southwest of Tuzigoot National Monument.*

There's little to see in Clarkdale itself, but the town was once home to the smelter for the copper mines in nearby Jerome. The original settlement is said to have arisen from an encampment of prostitutes and hard-core gamblers who were tossed out of a rowdy mining camp in one of its periodic purges of sinners, but it soon became known as a mellow company town.

★ ☙ Train buffs come to catch the 22-mi **Verde River Canyon Excursion Train** (⊠ Arizona Central Railroad, 300 N. Broadway, Clarkdale 86324, ☎ 800/293–7245), whose knowledgeable announcers regale riders with the area's colorful history and point out natural attractions along the way—in winter, you're likely to see bald eagles. This trip, which takes about four hours, is especially popular in fall-foliage season and in the spring, when the desert wildflowers bloom; make reservations well in advance. Round-trip rides cost $34.95. For $52.95 you can ride the living-room-like first-class cars, where hot hors d'oeuvres, coffee, and a cocktail are included in the price.

Jerome

★ ❻ *3½ mi southwest of Clarkdale, 20 mi northwest of Camp Verde, 33 mi northeast of Prescott, 25 mi southwest of Sedona on U.S. 89A.*

Jerome was once known as the Billion Dollar Copper Camp, but after the last mines closed in 1953, the booming population of 15,000 dwindled to 50 determined souls, earning Jerome the "ghost town" designation it still holds, though its population has risen back to almost 500. It's hard to imagine that this town, which doesn't have a single convenience store, once was home to Arizona's largest JCPenney department store and one of the state's first Safeway supermarkets. Jerome saw its first revival during the mid-1960s, when hippies moved in and turned it into an art colony of sorts, and it's now becoming a tourist attraction. In addition to its shops and historic sites, Jerome is worth visiting for its scenery: It's built into the side of Cleopatra Hill, and from here you can see Sedona's red rocks, Flagstaff's San Francisco Peaks, and even eastern Arizona's Mogollon Rim country.

Jerome is about a mile above sea level, but structures within town sit at elevations that vary by as much as 1,500 ft, depending on whether they're on Cleopatra Hill or at its foot. Blasting at the United Verde (later Phelps Dodge) mine regularly shook buildings off their foundations—the town's jail slid across a road and down a hillside, where it can still be seen today. That's not all that was unsteady about Jerome. In 1903 a reporter from a New York newspaper called Jerome "the wickedest town in America" because of its abundance of drinking and gaming establishments; town records from 1880 list 24 saloons. Whether due to divine retribution or to drunken accidents, the town was burned down several times—some historians say five, others two or three. The mine's financial backers were a bit more respectable: Eugene Jerome, for whom the town was named, was first cousin to Jenny Jerome, Winston Churchill's mother.

Jerome has 50 retail establishments (that's more than one for every 10 residents). You can get a map of the town's shops and its attractions at the visitor-information trailer on U.S. 89A. Except for the state-run historic park, attractions and business don't always stay open as long as their stated hours when things are slow.

Of the three mining museums in town, the most inclusive is part of **Jerome State Historic Park.** Just outside town, signs on U.S. 89A will direct you to the turnoff for the park, reached by a short, precipitous road. The museum occupies the mansion of Jerome's mining king, Dr. James "Rawhide Jimmy" Douglas Jr., who purchased Little Daisy Mine in 1912; the house was built in 1917 at the height of Little Daisy's success. Take a look at some of the tools and heavy equipment once used to grind ore. The bawdy parts—relating, for example, to the onetime brothel, the House of Joy—have been left out, but you can read between the lines for some sense of the town's wild mining days. ⊠ *State Park Rd.,* ☎ *520/634–5381.* 🖾 *$2.* ☉ *Daily 8–5.*

The **Mine Museum** in downtown Jerome is staffed by the Jerome Historical Society. The museum's collection of mining stock certificates alone is worth the (small) price of admission—the amount of money that changed hands in this town 100 years ago boggles the mind. ⊠ *200 Main St.,* ☎ *520/634–5477.* 🖾 *$1.* ☉ *Daily 9–4:30.*

One of the most unusual testaments to Jerome's days of mineral acquisition is the **Gold King Mine and Ghost Town.** This mélange of rusting and refurbished antique trucks and mining artifacts, roamed by sheep, goats, and a donkey, lies 1 mi northeast of town on the site of Haynes, a suburb of Jerome where gold was struck. Remnants of the mining operation include an old shaft, a former miner's hut, a workers' baseball field, and a boardinghouse. It's hard to sort the history from the junk; take a tour with owner Don Robertson for the full-on experience. ⊠ *Perkinsville Rd.,* ☎ *520/624–0053.* 🖾 *$3.* ☉ *Daily 9–5.*

Dining and Lodging

$$$ ✕ **House of Joy.** The two dimly lit dining rooms at this restaurant in a former bordello are strung with red lights, but the stuffed animals and dolls on display offset the lurid tinge. Book a table several weeks in advance—this popular restaurant is open only on Saturday and Sunday and only for dinner. Classic Continental dishes such as chicken Kiev and veal cordon bleu are well prepared. Sample the tasty hot

muffins, home-baked breads, and desserts. ⊠ *Hull Ave., just off Main St.,* ☎ *520/634–5339. No credit cards; personal checks accepted. Closed weekdays. No lunch weekends.*

$–$$ ✕ **Haunted Hamburger/Jerome Palace.** After the climb up the stairs from Main Street to this former boardinghouse, you'll be ready for the hearty burgers, chili, cheese steaks, and ribs that dominate the menu. Lighter fare, including meatless selections like the guacamole quesadilla, is also available. An outdoor deck overlooks Verde Valley. ⊠ *410 Clark St.,* ☎ *520/634–0554. MC, V.*

$ ✕ **Flatiron Cafe.** Ask where to have lunch or a late-afternoon snack and nearly every Main Street shop owner will direct you to a tiny eatery at the fork in the road. The menu includes sophisticated sandwiches, such as black-bean hummus with feta cheese, and many coffee drinks. Breakfast is also served here. ⊠ *416 Main St.,* ☎ *520/634–2733. Reservations not accepted. No credit cards. Closed Wed. No dinner.*

$$–$$$ 🏨 **Surgeon's House.** Abundant plants, knickknacks, bright colors, and
   ★   plenty of sunlight make this Mediterranean-style home that once belonged to Jerome's sawbones a most welcoming place to stay. The friendly ministrations of innkeeper Andrea Prince enhance the experience. Her multicourse gourmet breakfasts might include potato sour-cream soup, overstuffed burritos, or a marinated fruit compote. There are two suites here, plus the former chauffeur's quarters, a separate cottage with a skylight and private patio. You'll enjoy knockout vistas from almost everywhere in the house. ⊠ *101 Hill St., 86331,* ☎ *520/639–1452 or 800/639–1452. 2 suites, 1 cottage. AE, MC, V.*

$$ 🏨 **Ghost City Inn.** The outdoor veranda at this B&B in a converted 1898 home affords sweeping views of the Verde Valley and Sedona. Most rooms are decorated in Victorian style, but two have contemporary western touches. Such luxuries as afternoon tea and turndown with chocolates are especially surprising in a formerly rough-and-ready town. A full breakfast is included. ⊠ *541 N. Main St., 86331,* ☎ FAX *520/634–4678 or 888/634–4678. 4 rooms with 2 shared baths, 1 room with private bath. AE, D, MC, V.*

$–$$ 🏨 **Jerome Grand Hotel.** A welcome event in room-short Jerome was the opening in 1996 of a full-service hotel—the first one in more than 40 years—in the town's former hospital, built by the United Verde Mine Company in 1927. Some accommodations are still being converted and the restaurant had not yet been completed when we visited, but the finished portions—including a handsome lounge with an oak bar and an antique nickelodeon—show promise. The hotel is on Cleopatra Hill, so many rooms have splendid views. All rooms have TVs with VCRs. ⊠ *200 Hill St., 86331,* ☎ *520/634–8200,* FAX *520/639–0299. 27 rooms, including 5 suites. Restaurant, lounge, shop. MC, V.*

Nightlife

Paul & Jerry's Saloon (⊠ Main St., ☎ 520/634–2603) attracts a rowdy crowd to its two pool tables and old wooden bar. On weekends and some Thursday nights, there's live music and a lively scene at the **Spirit Room** (⊠ Main St. and U.S. 89, ☎ 520/634–8809); the mural over the bar harks back to the days when it was a dining spot for the "ladies" of the red-light district.

Outdoor Activities and Sports

CAMPING

For information about camping near Jerome at Mingus Mountain, Playground, or Potato Patch—all open May–October—contact the Prescott National Forest's **Verde Ranger District** (⊠ 300 E. Hwy. 260, Camp Verde, ☎ 520/567–4121, TTY 520/567–1119).

Shopping

Jerome has its share of art galleries (some perched precariously on Cleopatra Hill along with boutiques), but they're more funky than the ones in Sedona. An exception is the **Anderson-Mandette Art Studios** (✉ Old Mingus High School, Bldg. C, ☎ 520/634–3438). Robin Anderson and Margo Mandette made the building their workplace in 1978; at almost 20,000 square ft, it is considered by many to be the largest private art studio and gallery in the United States.

Main Street and Hull Avenue, just around the bend from Main, are Jerome's two main shopping streets. Your eyes may begin to glaze over after browsing through one boutique after another, most offering tasteful southwestern paraphernalia.

Aurum (✉ 369 Main St., ☎ 520/634–3330) focuses on contemporary art jewelry in silver and gold; about 30 artists are represented. **Designs on You** (✉ 233 Main St., ☎ 520/634–7879) carries attractively styled women's clothing. **The Jewel** (✉ 420 Hull Ave., ☎ 520/639–0259) specializes in Australian opals. **Nellie Bly** (✉ 136 Main St., ☎ 520/634–0255) stocks walking sticks, perfume bottles, jewelry, and outstanding kaleidoscopes. **Sky Fire** (✉ 140 Main St., ☎ 520/634–8081) has two floors of items to adorn your person and your house, from Native American pattern dishes to handcrafted mission-style hutches.

En Route   The drive down a mountainous section of U.S. 89A from Jerome to Prescott is gorgeous (if somewhat harrowing in bad weather), filled with twists and turns through Prescott National Forest. If you're coming from Phoenix, the route crosses the Mogollon Rim, overlooking the Verde Valley, is scenic but less precipitous.

Prescott

33 mi southwest of Jerome on U.S. 89A to U.S. 89, 100 mi northwest of Phoenix I–17 to AZ69.

In a forested bowl 5,300 ft above sea level, Prescott is a prime summer refuge for Phoenix-area dwellers. It was proclaimed the first capital of the Arizona Territory in 1864 and settled by Yankees to ensure that gold-rich northern Arizona would remain a Union resource. (Tucson and southern Arizona were strongly pro-Confederacy.) It is believed that ancestors of the Yavapai Indians, whose reservation is today on the outskirts of town, were the area's original inhabitants, but early territorial settlers thought that ruins in the area were of Aztec origin. You can see the results of this notion—inspired by *The History and Conquest of Mexico,* a popular book by historian William Hickling Prescott, for whom the town was named—in such street names as Montezuma, Cortez, and Alarcon.

Despite a devastating downtown fire in 1900, Prescott remains the Southwest's richest store of late-19th-century New England–style architecture (some have called it the "West's most Eastern town"). With two institutions of higher education, Yavapai College and Prescott College, Prescott could be called a college town, but it doesn't really feel like one, perhaps because so many retirees also reside here, drawn by the temperate climate and low cost of living.

The city's main drag is Gurley Street, named after John Addison Gurley, who was slated to be the first governor; he died days before he was ➐ to move to the Arizona Territory. **Courthouse Plaza,** bounded by Gurley and Goodwin streets to the north and south and by Cortez and Montezuma streets to the west and east, is the heart of the city: Here the 1916 Yavapai County Courthouse stands, guarded by an equestrian

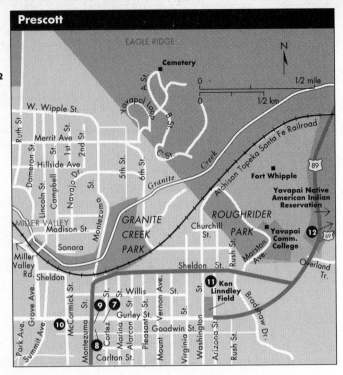

bronze of turn-of-the-century journalist and lawmaker Bucky O'Neill, who died while charging San Juan Hill in Cuba with Teddy Roosevelt during the Spanish–American War. At the south end of the plaza, across from the courthouse's main entrance, the **Chamber of Commerce** is a good place to get your bearings; those interested in architecture should be sure to get a map of the town's Victorian neighborhoods. Most are within walking distance of the chamber office. Many Queen Anne–style houses have been beautifully restored, and a number of them are now bed-and-breakfasts. Antiques and collectibles shops line both sides of Cortez Street just to the north of the courthouse.

8 **Whiskey Row,** named for a string of brawling pioneer taverns, runs along Montezuma Street, flanking Courthouse Plaza's west side; it once held 20 saloons and houses of pleasure. Social activity is more subdued these days, and the historic bars provide an escape from the street's many boutiques.

9 The little **Bead Museum,** which sits demurely on Whiskey Row, tells an intriguing story of international trade and intricate bead craft from 3000 BC through today. ⊠ *140 S. Montezuma St.,* ☎ *520/445–2431.* ☞ *Free.* ◷ *Mon.–Sat. 9:30–4:30, Sun. by appointment.*

★ **10** The remarkable **Sharlot Hall Museum** documents the Prescott area's history. Along with the original ponderosa-pine log cabin that housed the territorial governor and the museum named for pioneering historian and poet Sharlot Hall, the parklike setting contains three fully restored period homes and a transportation museum. Territorial times are the focus, but natural history and artifacts of the area's prehistoric peoples are on display. ⊠ *415 W. Gurley St., 2 blocks west of Courthouse Plaza,* ☎ *520/445–3122.* ☞ *$5 donation requested per family.*

⊘ *Apr.–Oct., Mon.–Sat. 10–5, Sun. 1–5; Nov.–Mar., Mon.–Sat. 10–4, Sun. 1–5.*

⑪ The stone-and-log structure built in 1935 to house the **Smoki Museum** is almost as interesting as the Native American artifacts inside. Priceless baskets and kachinas, as well as pottery, rugs, and beadwork, highlight this fine collection that dates from the Pre-Columbian period to the present. ⊠ *147 N. Arizona St.,* ☎ *520/445–1230.* ⊡ *$2.* ⊘ *May–Sept., Mon., Tues., Thurs.–Sat. 10–4, Sun. 1–4; Oct., Fri.–Sun. 10–4; Nov.–Apr. phone for appointment.*

⑫ Included in the permanent collection of the respected **Phippen Museum of Western Art,** about 5 mi north of downtown, is work by many prominent artists of the West, along with the paintings and bronze sculptures of George Phippen. ⊠ *4701 Hwy. 89 N,* ☎ *520/778–1385.* ⊡ *$3.* ⊘ *Mon. and Wed.–Sat. 10–4, Sun. 1–4.*

Dining and Lodging

$$ ✕ **Nolaz.** Come here for tasty New Orleans–style fare—jambalaya,
★   Creole shrimp, fried oysters, hushpuppies, or blackened salmon—and a friendly down-home atmosphere to match. The recipes are as spicy as you might expect from a chef whose name is Curry, and the creatures contained therein are often exotic (alligator, for example, or frogs' legs), but you can also walk on the mild side. The small dining room, sandwiched between the owner's seafood market and popular bar, really packs them in; call ahead for reservations on the weekends if you don't want to wait. ⊠ *216 W. Gurley St.,* ☎ *520/445–3765. AE, MC, V. Closed Sun. No lunch Sat.*

$$ ✕ **The Palace.** Legend has it that the patrons who saved the Palace's ornately carved 1880s Brunswick bar from a Whiskey Row fire in 1900 continued drinking at it while the rest of the row burned across the street. Whatever the case, the bar remains the centerpiece of the beautifully restored turn-of-the-century structure with a high tin-embossed ceiling. Steaks and chops are the stars here, but the grilled fish and hearty corn chowder are fine, too. ⊠ *120 S. Montezuma St.,* ☎ *520/541–1996. AE, MC, V.*

$ ✕ **Genovese.** Low-price classic southern Italian fare made this restaurant near Courthouse Plaza an instant local favorite. Try the cannelloni stuffed with shrimp, crab, ricotta cheese, and spinach. The cheese-and-sauce-laden lasagna will satisfy the largest appetite. Toppings on the crispy thin-crust pizza include Gorgonzola, artichokes, and ham along with the standards. ⊠ *217 W. Gurley St.,* ☎ *520/541–9089. AE, MC, V.*

$ ✕ **Prescott Brewing Company.** Good beer, good food, good service, and good prices—for a casual meal, it's hard to beat this cheerful, multilevel restaurant. In addition to the pub fare you'd expect, including chili, fish-and-chips, and British-style bangers (sausage) and mash, you'll also find such vegetarian selections as enchiladas made with tofu and a pasta salad with sun-dried tomatoes, avocado, broccoli, and two types of cheese. Fresh-baked beer bread comes with many of the entrées. ⊠ *130 W. Gurley St.,* ☎ *520/771–2795. AE, D, DC, MC, V.*

$$–$$$ ✕⊞ **Hassayampa Inn.** Built in 1927 for early automobile travelers,
★   the Hassayampa Inn oozes character (be sure to look up at the hand-painted ceiling in the lobby). Rooms are individually decorated, a number with original furnishings. A complimentary cocktail at the lounge and free breakfast—anything you want from the restaurant's extensive morning menu—gild the lily of reasonable rates. The Peacock Room, the hotel's pretty art nouveau–style dining room, has tapestried booths, dim lighting, and impressive Continental cuisine. Two drawbacks: The

inn's location, just off the town's main plaza, and sometimes noisy old pipes. ⊠ *122 E. Gurley St., 86301,* ☎ *520/778–9434; 800/322–1927 in AZ;* FAX *520/445–8590. 58 rooms, 10 suites. Restaurant, bar. AE, D, DC, MC, V.*

$ ✕🏨 **Hotel St. Michael.** Don't expect serenity—this place is, after all, on the busiest corner of Courthouse Plaza—but for low rates and historic atmosphere, it's hard to beat the St. Michael. In operation since 1900, the hotel has continually been refurbished, sometimes tastefully, other times not (the red shag carpeting that lined the hallway should be replaced by a Victorian floral pattern by the time you read this). Most rooms have 1920s wallpaper and furnishings; some face the plaza and others look out on Thumb Butte. The first-floor Caffé St. Michael serves great coffee and croissants. ⊠ *205 W. Gurley St.,* ☎ *520/776–1999 or 800/678–3757,* FAX *520/776–7318. 71 rooms. Coffee shop, shops. AE, D, MC, V.*

$$$ 🏨 **Prescott Resort Conference Center and Casino.** On a hill on the outskirts of town, this upscale property has views of the mountain ranges surrounding Prescott or the valley. Many guests hardly notice, so riveted are they by the poker machines and slots in Arizona's only hotel casino. There are plenty of recreational facilities to occupy those able to resist the one-armed bandits. ⊠ *1500 AZ 69, 86301,* ☎ *520/776–1666 or 800/967–4637,* FAX *520/776–8544. 161 rooms and suites. Restaurant, coffee shop, piano bar, indoor-outdoor pool, hot tub, sauna, 4 tennis courts, exercise room, racquetball, casino. AE, D, DC, MC, V.*

$$ 🏨 **Hotel Vendome.** This intimate hostelry, built during World War I and completely overhauled in the mid-1990s, has seen miners, health seekers, and celebrities such as cowboy star Tom Mix walk through its doors. Old-fashioned touches such as the original claw-foot tubs remain. Like many other historic properties, the Vendome has its obligatory resident ghost (her room costs slightly more). Continental breakfast is included in the room rate. Only a block from Courthouse Plaza, this is a good choice for those who want to combine sightseeing, modern comforts, and good value. ⊠ *230 Cortez St., 86303,* ☎ *520/776–0900,* FAX *520/771–0395. 17 rooms, 4 suites. Wine bar. AE, D, DC, MC, V.*

$ 🏨 **Marks House.** Victoria still reigns at this bed-and-breakfast, once owned by the mayor of territorial Prescott. It now belongs to Beth Maitland, star of the daytime soap *The Young and the Restless,* and is ably managed by her parents. Rooms are impeccably furnished with period antiques: The suite in the circular turret, overlooking Thumb Butte, is particularly impressive. A full breakfast is served in the formal dining room, at an hour that guests agree upon in advance. ⊠ *203 E. Union St., 86303,* ☎ *520/778–4632. 2 rooms with private bath, 2 suites. D, MC, V.*

Nightlife and the Arts

Montezuma Street's Whiskey Row, just off the central Courthouse Plaza, is nowhere near as wild as it was in its historic heyday, but most bars have live music—and a lively collegiate crowd—on the weekends. For a more refined atmosphere, head over to the art nouveau piano bar at the **Hassayampa Inn** (⊠ 122 E. Gurley St., ☎ 520/778–9434); there's always someone tickling the ivories on the weekend. The bar at **Lizzard's Lounge** (⊠ 120 N. Cortez St., ☎ 520/778–2244) was shipped from overseas via the Colorado River. **Nolaz** (⊠ 216 W. Gurley St., ☎ 520/445–3765) often features good blues and jazz bands. The main source of entertainment at the **Prescott Resort** (⊠ 1500 AZ 69, ☎ 520/776–1666) is Bucky's Casino, but the mellow tunes of a piano are an alternative to the clank of the slots on Friday and Saturday nights.

The **Prescott Fine Arts Association** (✉ 208 N. Marina St., ☎ 520/445–3286) sponsors musicals and dramas, a series of plays for children, and a variety of concerts. The association's gallery also presents rotating exhibits by local, regional, and national artists. The **Prescott Jazz Society** (✉ 129½ N. Cortez St., ☎ 520/445–0000) has an intimate storefront lounge. The **Satisfied Mind Bookstore** (✉ 113 W. Goodwin St., ☎ 520/776–9766) next door to the Chamber of Commerce is a good place to find out about poetry readings and other literary goings-on about town. The **Yavapai Symphony Association** (✉ 107 N. Cortez St., Suite 105B, ☎ 520/776–4255) hosts performances by the Phoenix and Flagstaff symphonies; call ahead for schedules and venues.

Prescott's popular **Bluegrass Festival on the Square** takes place in June. The town, which had its first organized cowboy competition in 1888, lays claim to having the world's oldest rodeo: the annual **Frontier Days** roundup, held on the Fourth of July weekend at the Yavapai County Fairgrounds. In August, the **Cowboy Poets Gathering** brings together campfire bards from around the country. The major event in December is the **Christmas Parade and Courthouse Lighting.** Call the Chamber of Commerce (☎ 800/266–7534) for contact phone numbers and other details on all these events.

Outdoor Activities and Sports

CAMPING

Campgrounds near Prescott in the Prescott National Forest are generally not crowded. Contact the **Bradshaw Ranger District** (✉ 2230 E. Hwy. 69, Prescott 86301, ☎ 520/445–7253) for information about the section of the forest south of town and extending down to Horse Thief Basin.

GOLF

The city-owned **Antelope Hills** (✉ 1 Perkins Dr., ☎ 520/445–0583; 800/972–6818 in AZ), just outside Prescott, offers 36 holes on two courses, one of them a Gary Panks creation. The 18-hole **Prescott Country Club Golf Course** (✉ AZ 69, 14 mi east of Prescott, ☎ 520/772–8984) is set in the foothills of Bradshaw Mountain.

HIKING

More than a million acres of national forest land surround Prescott. Thumb Butte is a popular hiking spot, but there are lots of other trekking and overnighting options. Contact the **Bradshaw Ranger District** (☞ Camping, *above*) of the **Prescott National Forest** for information on campsites and trails.

HORSEBACK RIDING

Granite Mountain Stables (✉ 2400 W. Shane Dr., 7 mi northeast of Prescott, ☎ 520/771–9551) has daily guided rides as well as group specials, such as hay-wagon outings.

Shopping

Shops selling antiques and collectibles line Cortez Street, just north of Courthouse Plaza. You'll find fun stuff—especially western kitsch—and some good buys on valuable pieces. Many of the stores gather together groups of retailers; at 14,000 square ft, the **Merchandise Mart Antique Mall** (✉ 205 N. Cortez St., ☎ 520/776–1728) is the largest of these collections of collectors. When your eyes glaze over, stop in at **Déjà Vu Antiques** (✉ 134 N. Cortez St., ☎ 520/445–6732) for a bit of refreshment at an old-time soda fountain.

Courthouse Plaza, especially along Montezuma Street, is lined with specialty and gift shops. Many match those in Sedona for quality—and prices. Be sure to check out **Arts Prescott** (✉ 134 S. Montezuma St.,

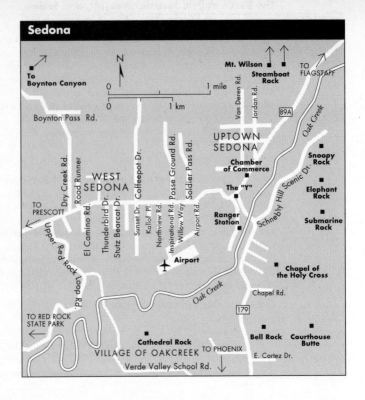

Sedona

☎ 520/776–7717), a cooperative gallery of talented local craftspeople and artists. **Bashford Courts** (✉ 130 Gurley St., ☎ 520/445–9798), has three floors of artsy stores. **St. Michael's Alley,** adjoining the Montezuma Street hotel of the same name, is home to interesting retailers, including Robert Shields Design (don't miss his wonderful ceramic snakes) and Desparado General Store where the displays are almost as imaginative as the local arts and crafts sold.

Sedona and Environs

⑬ *119 mi north of Phoenix, I–17 to AZ 17 to U.S. 89A; 60 mi northeast of Prescott, U.S. 89 to U.S. 89A; 27 mi south of Flagstaff on U.S. 89A.*

It's easy to see what draws so many visitors to Sedona. Red-rock buttes—Cathedral Rock, Bear Mountain, Courthouse Rock, and Bell Rock, among others— reach up into an almost always clear blue sky, both colors intensified by dark-green pine forests. The rugged landscape, at the north rim of the Verde Valley, once attracted surrealist Max Ernst, writer Zane Grey, and many filmmakers (more than 80 westerns were shot in the area in the 1940s and '50s alone).

These days, Sedona lures enterprising restaurateurs and gallery owners from the East and West coasts. New Age followers, who believe that the area contains some of the earth's more important vortices (energy centers), also come in great numbers in the belief that the area's "vibe" confers a sense of balance and well-being and enhances creativity. Several entrepreneurs have set up crystal shops and New Age bookshops that cater to the curious and true devotees.

Expansion since the early 1980s has been rapid, and lack of planning has taken its toll in unattractive strip malls, developments, and increased traffic and congestion, especially on weekends and during busy summer months, when Phoenix residents, overcome by heat, flee north to higher elevations. Still, the future is looking more promising. In 1996, the town was chosen to take part in the federally sponsored Main Street program, which means, among other things, that a number of Red Rock Territorial–style buildings in the Uptown section will be preserved and that a separate parking district will be built. A proposed bridge over Oak Creek should help alleviate some of the traffic, though at a price— it will also impinge on the natural glory of Red Rock Crossing, one of the town's most photographed vistas.

Canyons, creeks, Indian ruins, and the red rocks are readily accessible on foot; the area is thrilling and easy to hike (☞ Hiking *in* Outdoor Activities and Sports, *below*). Another option is to take one of the ubiquitous Jeep tours (☞ Special-Interest Tours *in* North-Central Arizona A to Z, *below*). Those with their own wheels might want to take the drive out to **Boynton Canyon,** sacred to the Yavapai Apache, who believe it was their ancient birthplace. These days, it's home to the Enchantment Resort; even if you're not staying there, you can hike the canyon and stop in for a scenic lunch or late-afternoon drink. Weather permitting, the **Schnebly Hill Scenic Drive** is another ooh-and-ah– inspiring option (though it's a bit rough on a car's suspension system), and the vistas of Sedona from **Airport Mesa** at sunset can't be beat. The **Upper Red Rock Loop** will likely consume a roll or two of film. Many of the most picturesque spots in Sedona are considered energy centers; vortex maps of the area are available at most of Sedona's New Age stores.

You needn't be religious to be inspired by the setting and the architecture of the **Chapel of the Holy Cross.** Built by Marguerite Brunwige Staude, a disciple of Frank Lloyd Wright, this modern landmark, with a huge cross on the facade, rises between two red-rock peaks. Vistas of the town and the surrounding area are spectacular. There are no regular services, but visitors are welcome for quiet meditation. A small gift shop sells religious articles and books. A trail east of the chapel leads you—after a 20-minute walk over occasional loose-rock surfaces— to a seat surrounded by voluptuous red-limestone walls, worlds away from the bustle and commerce around the chapel. ⊠ *Chapel Rd. (off AZ 179),* ☎ *520/282–4069.* ☜ *Free.* ☉ *Daily 9–5.*

Although it's set in an area that was inhabited by Native Americans for centuries, the town of Sedona itself is very new—it wasn't incorporated until 1988—so there are few historical sights. The main activity in the town proper is shopping, mostly for southwestern-style paintings, clothing, rugs, jewelry, and Native American artifacts (☞ Shopping, *below*). During warmer months it makes sense to visit air-conditioned shops at midday and save hiking and Jeep tours for the early morning or late afternoon, when the light is softer and the heat less oppressive.

Two miles west of Sedona on Highway 89A is the turnoff for the 286-acre **Red Rock State Park,** an ideal place to enjoy both the red-rock formations of the Sedona area and Oak Creek; it's also a less crowded (though nonswimming) alternative to the popular Slide Rock State Park (☞ *below*). The 5 mi of interconnected park trails are well marked and provide beautiful vistas. There are bird-watching excursions on Wednesday, Thursday, and Saturday and a guided hike to Eagle's Nest scenic overlook—the highest point in the park—every Saturday. Nature walks are given daily, weather permitting. Call ahead for times, which change with the season. ⊠ *4050 Red Rock Loop Rd., Sedona 86336,* ☎ *520/ 282–6907.* ☜ *$5 per car.* ☉ *Daily 8–5, 8–6 summer.*

Whether you want to swim, hike, picnic, or enjoy beautiful scenery framed through a car window, head north on Highway 89A through
★ the wooded **Oak Creek Canyon,** which begins about 1 mi north of Sedona. It's the most attractive route to Flagstaff and the Grand Canyon and worth a drive-through even if you're not heading north. Although the forest is primarily evergreen, the fall brings enough changing colors to make the view especially glorious then. The road winds through a steep-walled canyon, and visitors crane their necks for views of the dramatic rock formations above. Oak Creek, which runs along the bottom of the canyon, is lined with tent campgrounds, fishing camps, cabins, motels, and restaurants.

☺ Anglers young and old will enjoy the sure catch at the **Rainbow Trout Farm.** For $1 you'll get a cane pole with a hook and bait. There's no charge if your catch is under 8 inches; above that it's $2.85 to $5.85, depending on the length. The real bargain is that the staff will clean your fish for 50¢ each and pack them in ice for you. ⊠ *3500 N. Hwy. 89A, 3 mi north of Sedona,* ☎ *520/282–3379.* ⌨ *$1.* ☉ *Daily 9–5; summer, daily 8–6, weather permitting.*

☺ **Slide Rock State Park,** 7 mi north of Sedona, is a good place for a picnic. On a hot day, you can plunge down a natural rock slide into a swimming hole—a delightful experience. (Bring an extra pair of jeans to wear on the slide.) The only downside to this trip is the traffic, particularly on summer weekends; you might have to wait to get in. ⊠ *6871 N. Hwy. 89A,* ☎ *520/282–3034.* ⌨ *$5 per car.* ☉ *Daily 8–5 winter, 8–6 spring, 8–7 summer.*

Dining and Lodging

Some Sedona restaurants close for stretches in January and February. Call to make sure that a restaurant will be open before you go. In high season (April to October), it's always best to make reservations; the lines can be long.

$$$ ✕ **Pietro's.** Good northern Italian cuisine, a friendly and attentive
★ staff, and a lively yet casual atmosphere have made this one of Sedona's most popular dining spots. Try *gamberi giardinieri* (grilled shrimp with shiitake mushrooms in white wine) for a starter, followed by fettuccine with duck, cabbage, and figs, or a veal piccata entrée. ⊠ *2445 W. Hwy. 89A,* ☎ *520/282–2525. AE, D, DC, MC, V. No lunch.*

$$$ ✕ **Rene's.** Ease into the plush banquettes of this pretty lace-curtained restaurant for classic Continental dishes. Recommended starters include a delicate French onion soup and the salade Walter—baby spinach leaves and sautéed mushrooms in a hazelnut vinaigrette. Rack of lamb is the house specialty, but the tender antelope in juniper sauce is a worthy competitor. The three-course prix-fixe dinner is a good buy at just under $30. Service is formal, as befits the room and menu, but you won't feel uncomfortable if you come in your shopping duds. ⊠ *Tlaquepaque, B-117, Hwy. 179,* ☎ *520/282–9225. AE, MC, V.*

$$–$$$ ✕ **Dahl & Di Luca.** The skills and enthusiasm of a Rome-born chef (Andrea Di Luca) and his partner (Lisa Dahl) have made a success of this relative newcomer that serves updated versions of traditional Italian dishes. The cheerful Tuscan yellow dining room has terra-cotta tile floors, painted ivy on the walls, and modern art—unfortunately, the room is too dim after dark to see many of these lovely details (or the menu). Try the *aglio al forno* (roasted head of garlic with chèvre), followed by linguine and shrimp in a spicy vodka pomodoro sauce or maybe osso buco. And if you can't handle a rich dessert, linger over a nice grappa. ⊠ *2321 W. Hwy. 89A,* ☎ *520/282–5219. AE, D, DC, MC, V. No lunch except weekdays during high season.*

$$–$$$ ✕ **Heartline Café.** Fresh flowers on the tables and innovative south-
  ★   western cuisine are this attractive café's hallmarks. The oak-grilled salmon
         marinated in tequila and lime and the chicken breast with prickly-pear
         sauce are two options. Appealing vegetarian plates are also on the menu.
         On nice days grab a seat on the rosebush-lined terrace. ⊠ *1610 W. Hwy.
         89A,* ☎ *520/282–0785. AE, D, MC, V. No lunch Sun.*

$$–$$$ ✕ **Sedona Swiss.** It's hard to go wrong with a chef who's used to pleas-
         ing Swiss embassy diplomats in Washington—and this European-style
         restaurant doesn't make any mistakes. Breakfast pastry in the adjoin-
         ing café is light and buttery, and such classic dinner entrées as veal ten-
         derloin Zurichoise, with a sauce containing mushrooms, cream, and
         cognac, are delicately seasoned. Lighter alternatives like pasta with fresh
         salmon are also available. A low-price buffet lunch draws in the tour-
         bus crowd, but in the evening the chalet-style dining room is suitably
         sedate and romantic. ⊠ *350 Jordan Rd.,* ☎ *520/282–7959. MC, V.
         Closed Sun.*

$$–$$$ ✕ **Shugrue's West.** At lunch you can get your basic omelets, burgers,
         and Mexican fare, but more sophisticated risottos and salads are avail-
         able. At dinner, surf and turf has taken on a new dimension: The New
         York strip steak has a five-peppercorn coating and a bourbon and
         pancetta demi-glace; while roasted Icelandic cod comes wrapped with
         Parma ham and is served over red cabbage. The light-wood dining rooms
         are still almost coffee-shop casual, but a redesign is in the works. ⊠
         2250 W. Hwy. 89A, ☎ *520/282–2943. AE, MC, V.*

$$ ✕ **Takashi.** Those seeking some serenity and a respite from heavy
         meals will enjoy this Japanese restaurant, which provides aesthetic plea-
         sure in everything from tea (with little bits of floating popcorn and brown
         rice) to dessert (sweet ginger or red-bean ice cream). Salads include a
         spicy sushi tuna with Japanese mayonnaise on a bed of cabbage and
         other fresh vegetables. Combination dinners such as sashimi and tem-
         pura or teriyaki let you sample a little bit of everything. ⊠ *465 Jor-
         dan Rd.,* ☎ *520/282–2334. AE, DC, MC, V. Closed Mon. No lunch
         Sun.*

$$ ✕ **Top of Sedona.** Don't be put off by the Quality Inn location and non-
         descript dining room. This restaurant has some of the best red-rock
         views in town, especially from its outdoor deck, and owners Matt and
         Corey Erwin have toiled in some of Arizona's finest resort kitchens.
         Try a grilled polenta appetizer with Gorgonzola and mushrooms, an
         eggplant Napoleon entrée layered with ratatouille, vegetables, and
         rice, or well-prepared grilled lamb chops. The chef prides herself on
         fulfilling special orders (it's best to phone these ahead). Prices here are
         much lower than those at many comparable Sedona eateries. ⊠ *771
         Hwy. 179,* ☎ *520/282–1662. AE, MC, V.*

$–$$ ✕ **The Hideaway.** There's nothing pretentious about this southern
         Italian restaurant and pizzeria with a wood-beam ceiling and red-and-
         white-check tablecloths. But what a setting: Every one of the many decks
         (upstairs, downstairs, indoors, outdoors, smoking, no-smoking) has eye-
         popping vistas of Oak Creek and the towering buttes. Go for one of
         the large antipasto salads at lunch and the hearty lasagna or manicotti
         at dinner. This is a place that visitors stumble upon and locals tend to
         keep to themselves. ⊠ *Country Square, AZ 179 (just south of the "Y"),*
         ☎ *520/282–4204. AE, D, DC, MC, V.*

$ ✕ **Mandarin House.** Its name notwithstanding, the Mandarin House
         serves everything from standard Cantonese to Szechuan and Hunan
         fare, with dishes ranging from the exotic (shark-fin salad) to the old
         standbys (egg foo yong). The lemon chicken is particularly recom-
         mended. Everything is fresh—even the noodles and egg rolls are made
         on the premises. ⊠ *6486 AZ 179, Suite 114,* ☎ *520/284–9088. AE,
         D, MC, V.*

$$$$ ✕🏨 **Enchantment Resort.** Designed as a tennis resort, Enchantment has
★ excellent sports facilities, but it's the setting of Boynton Canyon that
makes it unique. Southwest-pattern rooms are set in 71 pueblo-style
casitas (15 of these scheduled to be completed by mid-1998). Many
have beehive fireplaces and kitchenettes, and all have superb views. Fresh-
squeezed orange juice and a newspaper are delivered to rooms each
morning. The Yavapai Room has more vistas and good Continental
cuisine. Uqualla, the resort's Havasupai Indian concierge, can direct
you to the best places in the canyon to hike or bicycle (mountain-bike
rentals are available). ⊠ *525 Boynton Canyon Rd., 86336,* ☎ *520/
282–2900 or 800/826–4180,* ℻ *520/282–9249. 222 rooms. Restaurant, bar, kitchenettes, 4 outdoor pools, 12 tennis courts, aerobics, croquet, health club, hiking, mountain bikes, pro shop, children's programs.
AE, D, MC, V.*

$$$$ ✕🏨 **Garland's Oak Creek Lodge.** In the heart of Oak Creek Canyon,
this lodge was built in the 1930s and bought by its current owners,
Gary and Mary Garland, in 1972. Sixteen comfortably furnished cabins, some including fireplaces and pullout beds for extra guests, share
17 acres of beautiful land (at an elevation of 5,000 ft) with an organic
apple orchard. Accommodations look out over the rugged cliffs of the
canyon or the creek. The lodge is operated on a Modified American
Plan, with excellent breakfasts and dinners included in the room price,
along with afternoon tea. Garland's is often booked solid a year in advance—it's open only from April 1 to November 15—but it's worth a
phone call to check. ⊠ *Hwy. 89A, 8 mi north of Sedona, Box 152,
86339,* ☎ *520/282–3343. 16 cabins with bath. Restaurant, tennis court,
croquet, volleyball, fishing. MC, V.*

$$$$ ✕🏨 **L'Auberge de Sedona Resort.** This tri-level resort consists of a
central lodge building; a motel-style structure called The Orchards
abutting Uptown Sedona and reachable from the rest of the property by a "hillovator"; and—the major attraction—cabins in a wooded
setting along Oak Creek. Phoenix couples flock to these country-French
hideaways and dine in the hotel's French restaurant, one of the most
romantic eateries in Arizona. The six-course prix-fixe dinner runs
$60—a bit steep even for Sedona—but it comes with a view of
Oak Creek; jacket and reservations are required. ⊠ *L'Auberge La.,
Box B, 86336,* ☎ *520/282–1661 or 800/272–6777,* ℻ *520/282–
2885. 69 rooms, 30 cottages. 2 restaurants, pool, hot tub. AE, D,
DC, MC, V.*

$$$$ ✕🏨 **Los Abrigados.** This place really sparkles at Christmas, when
★ more than a million tiny lights illuminate the grounds, but it's a daz-
zler year-round. All the suites, attractively decorated in earth tones, have
microwaves, refrigerators, coffeemakers, and two TVs; some have private whirlpool tubs and fireplaces. A state-of-the-art health club, including a luxurious spa, will help you burn off any calories picked up
at Joey Bistro, the resort's southern Italian restaurant. Another eatery,
Steak & Sticks, has an adjoining billiards lounge and humidor for sophisticated cigar smokers. The shops of Tlaquepaque are right next door.
If you're interested in something more rustic (and less expensive) ask
about the affiliated Lomacasi Cottages, arrayed along the banks of Oak
Creek. ⊠ *160 Portal La., 86336,* ☎ *520/282–1777 or 800/521–
3131,* ℻ *520/282–2614. 175 suites. 3 restaurants, bar, grill, 2 pools,
2 tennis courts, basketball, health club, volleyball, baby-sitting, children's programs. AE, D, DC, MC, V.*

$$$–$$$$ 🏨 **Briar Patch Inn.** Set in a verdant canyon with a rushing creek, this
★ bed-and-breakfast has hewn-wood cabins (in Native American and Mex-
ican styles), some with decks overlooking Oak Creek and many with

fireplaces. On summer mornings you can sit outside and enjoy home-baked breads and fresh egg dishes while listening to classical music performed live. New Age and crafts workshops are sometimes held on the premises. ⊠ *3190 N. Hwy. 89A, 86336,* ☎ *520/282–2342,* ℻ *520/282–2399. 13 2-person cabins, 4 4-person cabins. Kitchenettes, massage, fishing, library, meeting room. MC, V.*

$$$–$$$$ 🍽 **Casa Sedona.** You can have all the modern amenities—whirlpool bathtubs for two, air-conditioning and heating units—and still be able to commune with nature at this appealing bed-and-breakfast in a building, designed by a protégé of Frank Lloyd Wright. A large redwood deck, where a full breakfast is served when the weather is fine, has stunning red-rock views, also enjoyed by all of the rooms. The accommodations have a Southwest-oriented decor (including a wheelchair-accessible one with cowboy decor), but there's also a safari-style room with a ceiling-height palm tree in the corner. All have refrigerators and gas fireplaces, and the newest suite has a full kitchen. ⊠ *55 Hozoni Dr., 86336,* ☎ *520/282–2938 or 800/525–3756,* ℻ *520/282–2259. 16 rooms. Outdoor hot tub. MC, V.*

$$$–$$$$ 🍽 **Graham Inn.** The attractive rooms at this inn south of Sedona in the village of Oak Creek have TVs with VCRs (there's a good video library) and some have Jacuzzi tubs and balconies that look out onto the red rocks. On the lot next door are four large (900-square-ft) casitas. One is done in vibrant Taos style and another resembles a log cabin; all have two fireplaces and two-person Jacuzzi tubs. Room rates for all accommodations include a copious breakfast prepared in the main house. ⊠ *150 Canyon Circle Dr., Oak Creek 86351,* ☎ *520/884–1425 or 800/228–1425,* ℻ *520/284–0767. 4 rooms with bath, 2 suites, 4 casitas. Kitchenettes, outdoor pool, hot tub, library. D, MC, V.*

$$$–$$$$ 🍽 **Lodge at Sedona.** A first-class operation—including a professional
★   chef who prepares breakfast and afternoon hors d'oeuvres—the Lodge still manages to feel intimate and friendly. Rooms in this rambling wood-and-stone house are decorated in every style from romantic Renaissance to cowboy kitsch; some have fireplaces, redwood decks, or hot tubs, and one has a gentle resident ghost. Of the five public areas where guests can mingle, perhaps the best is the lace-curtained breakfast nook, shaded by trees and looking out onto the red rocks in the distance. ⊠ *125 Kallof Pl., 86336,* ☎ *520/204–1942 or 800/619–4467,* ℻ *520/204–2128. 10 rooms with bath, 3 suites. Shop, library, meeting room. D, MC, V.*

$$$–$$$$ 🍽 **Wishing Well.** Although it's less than a mile from Uptown Sedona,
★   this bed-and-breakfast on a plateau at the mouth of Oak Creek Canyon will make you forget there's a town nearby. All the rooms are ultra-romantic, with views of Cathedral Rock; one has a private outdoor hot tub. A hiking trail behind the house once served as a cattle route for the area's Native American inhabitants. Hosts Valda and Esper Esau make you feel welcome while respecting your privacy. Room rates include Continental breakfast, served on fine china in your room. ⊠ *995 N. Hwy. 89A, 86336,* ☎ *520/282–4914 or 800/728–9474,* ℻ *520/204–9766. 4 rooms. MC, V.*

$$ 🍽 **Sky Ranch Lodge.** There may be no better vantage point in town
★   from which to view Sedona's red-rock canyons than the private patios or balconies at Sky Ranch Lodge, near the top of Airport Mesa. Some rooms have stone fireplaces, and some have kitchenettes; all are well decorated in dark blues and beiges with ceramic tile trim. Paths on the grounds wind around fountains and, in summer, through colorful flower gardens. This is an excellent value. ⊠ *Airport Rd., 86339,* ☎ *520/282–6400,* ℻ *520/282–7682. 92 rooms, 2 cottages. Pool. MC, V.*

Nightlife and the Arts

Nightlife in Sedona tends to be fairly sedate. On high-season weekends, there's usually live music at **Dahl & Di Luca,** the **Enchantment Resort,** and **Shugrue's West** (☞ Dining and Lodging, *above*). You can find someone playing year-round in nearby Oak Creek at **Irene's** (✉ 6466 AZ 179, ☎ 520/284–2240) and the **Bell Rock Inn** (✉ 6246 AZ 179, ☎ 520/282–4161). The offerings vary from jazz to rock and pop; in all cases, call ahead. The closest you'll come to a rollicking cowboy bar is **Rainbow's End** (✉ 3235 W. Hwy. 89A, ☎ 520/282–1593), a steak house with a large dance floor and live country-and-western bands on weekends.

Find out about cultural events in Sedona at the **Book Loft** (✉ 175 AZ 179, just south of the "Y," ☎ 520/282–5173), which often hosts poetry readings, theatrical readings, book signings, and lectures. The Sedona **Jazz on the Rocks Festival** (☎ 520/282–1985), held every September, always attracts a sellout crowd that fills the town to capacity. The **Sedona Arts Center** (✉ N. Hwy. 89A and Art Barn Rd., ☎ 520/282–3809) sponsors events ranging from classical concerts to plays. The **Sedona Heritage Day Festival** (☎ 520/282–7038), a family-oriented event in early October, includes pioneer storytellers, square-dance exhibitions, music, and a barbecue.

Outdoor Activities and Sports

CAMPING

For information on the six **forest-service campgrounds** in the Sedona–Oak Creek Canyon area, call 520/282–4119.

GOLF

The **Beaver Creek Golf Resort** (✉ Montezuma Ave. and Lakeshore Dr., 20 mi from Sedona off I–17, ☎ 520/567–4487) is a championship par-71 course. The **Oak Creek Country Club** (✉ 690 Bell Rock Blvd., ☎ 520/284–1660) is a good semiprivate option. The 18-hole **Sedona Golf Resort** (✉ 7260 AZ 179, Oak Creek, ☎ 520/284–9355) was designed by Gary Panks to take advantage of the many changes in elevation and scenery. The 10th hole, said to be the most photographed hole in all of Arizona, takes in a sweeping view of the Sedona Valley's red rocks.

HIKING

For free detailed maps and hiking advice, contact the rangers at the **Sedona Ranger District Office** (✉ 250 Brewer Rd., 86339, ☎ 520/282–4119), which is open Monday through Saturday from 7:30 to 4:30. Ask here or at your hotel for directions to trailheads for Doe's Mountain (an easy ascent, with many switchbacks), Loy Canyon, Devil's Kitchen, and Long Canyon.

Among the forest-service paths you can hike in the Oak Creek Canyon is the popular **West Fork Trail.** A walk through the woods and a dip in the stream make a great summer combination. You'll find the trailhead about 3 mi north of Slide Rock State Park.

HORSEBACK RIDING

El Rojo Grande Ranch & Stables (✉ 7 mi west of Uptown Sedona on Hwy. 89A, ☎ 520/282–1898 or 800/362–2692), a 143-acre equestrian center, offers stagecoach excursions, trail rides, and lessons. Among the equine tour options at **Kachina Stables of Sedona** (✉ 5 J La., Lower Red Rock Loop Rd., West Sedona, ☎ 520/282–7252) are a midday picnic and an Oak Creek swim and a full-moon ride with a campfire cookout.

Shopping

Many stores in what is known as the Uptown area, running along U.S. 89A to the east of its intersection with AZ 179, cater to the tour-bus trade. Exceptions include **Native & Nature** (✉ 248 N. Hwy. 89A, ☎ 520/282–7870), outstanding for its regional books and Southwest artifacts. **Looking West** (✉ 242 N. Hwy. 89A, ☎ 520/282–4877) sells the spiffiest cowgirl-style getups in town. Check out **Robert Shields Design** (✉ Sacajawea Plaza, 301 N. Hwy 89A, 520/284–1393) for colorful clay snakes and unusual silver jewelry (and yes, it's the same Shields who used to perform with Yarnell).

For upscale shopping, **Tlaquepaque** (✉ AZ 179, just south of the "Y," ☎ 520/282–4838) gathers together more than 100 artisans, many of them painters and sculptors. The complex of red-tile-roof buildings arranged around a series of courtyards shares its name and architectural style with a crafts village just outside Guadalajara. It's a lovely place to browse, but prices tend to be high; when asked how to pronounce the name of this shopping complex, locals joke that it's "to-lock-your-pocket." A good bet for southwestern art is **El Prado Gallery by the Creek** (✉ No. 101, Bldg. E, ☎ 520/282–7390). **Estebans** (✉ No. 103, Bldg. B, ☎ 520/282–4686) focuses on ceramics and Native American crafts. **Isadora** (✉ No. 120, Bldg. A, ☎ 520/282–6232) has beautiful handwoven jackets and shawls. **Kuivato** (✉ No. 122, Bldg. B, ☎ 520/282–1212) carries gorgeous glassware.

At the junction of AZ 179 and Schnebly Hill Road, a small strip of shops includes **Garland's Navajo Rugs** (✉ 411 AZ 179, ☎ 520/282–4070), with its dazzling collection of new and antique carpets, as well as Native American kachina dolls, pottery, and baskets. In the same building as Garland's Navajo Rugs, **Sedona Pottery** (✉ 411 AZ 179, ☎ 520/282–1192) sells unusual pieces, including flower-arranging bowls, egg separators, and life-size ceramic statues by shop owner Mary Margaret Sather.

The **Hozho Center** (✉ 431 AZ 179, ☎ 520/282–1038) is a small, upscale complex in a beige Santa Fe–style building. **Lanning Gallery** (☎ 520/282–6865) sells attractive southwestern art and jewelry. **James Ratliff Gallery** (☎ 520/282–1404) has fun and functional pieces by not-yet-established artists. Drive a minute or two south of the Hozho Center on AZ 179 and you'll come to the **Hillside Courtyard & Marketplace** (✉ 671 AZ 179, ☎ 520/282–4500). Among Hillside's 23 shops and galleries, the **Clay Pigeon** (☎ 520/282–2845) carries boldly designed dishes and sculptures with a Western accent.

West Sedona, the more residential area that stretches west of the "Y" along U.S. 89A, doesn't have such concentrated areas of shops as Uptown and AZ 179, but it's worth a trip over to **Artisans Galleria** (✉ 1420 W. Hwy. 89A, ☎ 520/282–2300), which showcases the output of more than 100 artists and craftspeople.

Inveterate bargain hunters will want to head south on AZ 179 2 mi past Chapel of the Holy Cross to the village of Oak Creek. At the **Oak Creek Factory Outlets** (✉ 6601 S. AZ 179, ☎ 520/284–2150) are such stores as Corning/Revere, Mikasa, Anne Klein, Bass, Jones New York, and Van Heusen.

FLAGSTAFF

146 mi northwest of Phoenix, 27 mi north of Sedona via Oak Creek Canyon.

Few visitors slow down long enough to explore Flagstaff, a town of 54,000, known locally as "Flag." Most stop only to spend the night at one of the town's many motels before making the last leg of the trip to the Grand Canyon, 80 mi north. But the city, set against a lovely backdrop of pine forests and the snowcapped San Francisco Peaks, retains a frontier flavor downtown. Flag makes a good base for day-trips to Native American ruins and the Navajo and Hopi reservations, as well as to the Petrified Forest National Park and the Painted Desert (☞ Chapter 3).

Flagstaff has more fast-food outlets per permanent resident than most cities do, no doubt because of the incredible demand for it: Two major interstate highways crisscross the town; thousands of tourists drive through; thousands of students attending Northern Arizona University reside here; and many Native Americans come in from nearby reservations. During the summer, Phoenix residents head here, seeking relief from the desert heat. At any time of the year, temperatures in Flagstaff are approximately 20°F cooler than in Phoenix.

Phoenicians also come to Flagstaff in winter to ski at the small Arizona Snowbowl, about 15 mi northeast of town among the San Francisco Peaks. Accommodation rates are low at this time of year, making winter visits an excellent option for downhill and cross-country enthusiasts. Flagstaff has many accommodations (though no major hotels or resorts), but it's wise to reserve a room anytime during the year. During the summer months it's essential.

Exploring Flagstaff

A Good Tour

Start your exploration of Flagstaff at the restored **Santa Fe Depot** on Route 66, still a functioning train station and also a visitor center. Drive east (right) from here to reach the raucous **Museum Club** ⑭; head west and you'll be going in the direction of the **Lowell Observatory** ⑮. To the southwest, Route 66 branches off into Milton Road, which will take you to a turnoff for **Riordon State Historic Park** ⑯ and, a little farther to the south, one for the **Northern Arizona University Observatory** ⑰. Directly across Route 66 to the north is the **Historic Railroad District** ⑱. After walking around here, get back into your car and head north on Humphreys Street, a major downtown thoroughfare; about a mile after it transforms itself into Fort Valley Road, you'll reach Fort Valley Park, home to the **Pioneer Museum** ⑲ and the **Coconino Center for the Arts** ⑳. Continue north for just a few minutes on Fort Valley Road to reach the **Museum of Northern Arizona** ㉑. Five miles farther along the same road is the turnoff for **Arizona Snowbowl** ㉒.

TIMING

You can see almost all of Flagstaff's attractions in a single day if you're lucky enough to come at a time when you can visit the Lowell Observatory or the Northern Arizona University Observatory in the evening—which is also when the Museum Club is best experienced. You'll need to consult the schedule of tour times if you want to visit the Riordon State Historic Park. Plan on devoting at least an hour to the excellent Museum of Northern Arizona. The Historic Railroad District is a good place to find yourself at lunchtime. If you're a skier, you might be spending a good part of a winter's day at Arizona Snowbowl; in summer, be sure to allot a couple of hours to taking the skyride and walking around on some of the scenic trails at the top.

Sights to See

㉒ **Arizona Snowbowl.** One of Flagstaff's most popular winter attractions (☞ Skiing *and* Snowboarding *in* Outdoor Activities and Sports, *below*) also lures patrons in the summer, when the Agassi ski lift, which climbs to a height of 11,500 ft in 25 minutes, doubles as a skyride through the Coconino National Forest. From this vantage point, you can see

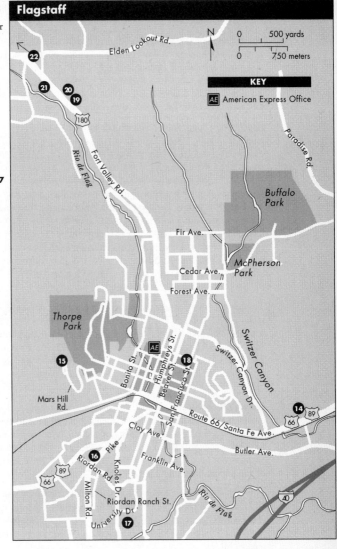

up to 70 mi; views include the North Rim of the Grand Canyon. There's a lodge nearby with a restaurant and bar. ⊠ *U.S. 180 to Snowbowl Rd., then 7 mi to skyride entrance,* ☎ *520/779–1951.* ☞ *$9.* ☼ *Skyride operates mid-June–Labor Day daily, Labor Day–mid-Oct. Fri.–Sun. only (weather permitting) 10–4.*

⓴ Coconino Center for the Arts. The nonprofit community center puts on two major annual arts-and-crafts festivals (☞ Nightlife and the Arts, *below*) and hosts performing-arts events and educational programs throughout the year. A gallery exhibits the works of regionally and nationally known artists, from photographers to sculptors and lithographers. The gift shop, filled with jewelry, pottery, and posters, can be detrimental to your pocketbook. All proceeds go to the center, though, so you're shopping for a worthy cause—and there's no tax on your purchases. The center is a few hundred feet up a gentle hill from the Pioneer Museum. ⊠ *2300 N. Fort Valley Rd., 86002,* ☎ *520/779–*

6921. ✉ *Free.* ☉ *May–Labor Day, Tues.–Sun. 10–5; Labor Day–Apr., Tues.–Sat. 10–5. Closed Dec. 24–early Jan.*

⑱ Historic Railroad District. Flagstaff downtown recently underwent a major restoration. Some excellent examples of late Victorian, Tudor Revival, and early art deco architecture in this district give a feel for life in this former logging and railroad town. A walking-tour map of the area is available at the visitor center, now in the Tudor Revival–style **Santa Fe Depot** (✉ 1 E. Rte. 66), an excellent place to begin sightseeing.

Highlights include the 1927 **Hotel Monte Vista** (✉ 100 N. San Francisco St.), built after a community drive raised $200,000 in 60 days. The 1888 **Babbitt Brothers Building** (✉ 12 E. Aspen Ave.) was constructed as a building-supply store and then turned into a department store by David Babbitt, the mastermind of the Babbitt empire (many structures around town bear the name Babbitt, after one of Flagstaff's wealthiest founding families; former Arizona governor and current Secretary of the Interior Bruce Babbitt is the latest member of the family to wield power and influence). Most of the area's first businesses were saloons catering to railroad construction workers, which was the case with the 1888 **Vail Building** (✉ 1 & 5 N. San Francisco St.), a brick art deco–influenced structure covered with stucco in 1939. It now houses the Sweet Life ice-cream parlor.

The town's most interesting shops are concentrated here, and there are spots where you can grab a quick bite. Students, skiers, new and aging hippies, and just about everyone else who likes good coffee jams into **Macy's** (✉ 14 S. Beaver St., ☎ 520/774–2243) for the best cup in town. The **Black Bean** (✉ 12 E. Rte. 66, ☎ 520/779–9905) is the place for do-it-yourself burritos, as healthy or as guacamole-smothered as you like.

⑮ Lowell Observatory. Boston businessman, author, and scientist Percival Lowell founded the observatory in 1894 and studied the planet Mars from here. His predictions of the existence of a ninth planet led to the discovery of Pluto at Lowell in 1930 by Clyde Tombaugh. V. M. Slipher's observations here between 1912 and 1920 led to the theory of the expanding universe.

The 6,500-square-ft Steele Visitor Center hosts exhibits and lectures and has a gift shop; a "Tools of the Astronomer" display explains what professional stargazers do. Several interactive exhibits—among them the Pluto Walk, a scaled-down version of our solar system—will interest children.

On some evenings throughout the year, weather permitting, the public is invited to peer through the 24-inch Clark telescope, which celebrated its 100th anniversary in 1996, or through a more up-to-date 16-inch reflecting telescope. The greatest number of viewings (four a week) are offered from June through August; call ahead for a schedule. The observatory dome is open and unheated—any change in temperature would affect the telescope lens—so dress for the outdoors. To reach the observatory, which is less than 2 mi from downtown, drive west on Route 66, which resumes its former name, Santa Fe Avenue, before it merges into Mars Hill Road. ✉ *1400 W. Mars Hill Rd.,* ☎ *520/774–2096.* ✉ *$3.* ☉ *Visitor center and night viewing hrs change seasonally; call ahead.*

⑭ Museum Club. For real Route 66 color, don't miss this local institution, fondly known as the Zoo because the building housed an extensive taxidermy collection in the 1930s. Most of the stuffed animals—including such bizarre specimens as a one-eyed sheep—are mercifully gone, but some owls still perch above the dance floor of what is now a popular country-and-western club. Even if you don't like crowds or country music, it's worth coming to see the building, a gigantic log cabin constructed around five trees; the entryway consists of a huge forked pine in the shape of a wishbone. ⊠ *3404 E. Rte. 66,* ☎ *520/ 526–9434.* 🖃 *Free.* ☉ *Sun.–Thurs. noon–1 AM, Fri. and Sat. noon– 3 AM.*

★ ㉑ **Museum of Northern Arizona.** It's worth visiting the museum for its setting alone, a striking native-stone building shaded with trees. But the institution, founded in 1928, is also respected worldwide for its research and its collections centering on the natural and cultural history of the Colorado Plateau; only 1% of its vast holdings on the archaeology, ethnology, geology, biology, and fine arts of the region is on display at any given time. Among the permanent exhibitions are an extensive collection of Navajo rugs as well as an authentic Hopi kiva (men's ceremonial chamber).

A gallery devoted to area geology is usually a hit with children: It includes a life-size model dilophosaurus, a carnivorous dinosaur that once roamed northern Arizona. The Harvey W. Branigar Hall hosts a fascinating 27-minute film, *Sacred Lands of the Southwest,* and the Babbitt Gallery will eventually display the museum's extensive ceramics collection.

Outdoors, a life-zone exhibit shows the changing vegetation from the bottom of the Grand Canyon to the highest peak in Flagstaff. A nature trail, open only in summer, heads down across a small stream into a canyon and up into an aspen grove.

Every summer, the museum hosts exhibits and sales by Native American artists (☞ Nightlife and the Arts, *below*), whose wares are also sold in the museum gift shop. The museum's education department sponsors excellent tours of the area and as far away as New Mexico and Utah (☞ Guided Tours *in* North-Central Arizona A to Z, *below*). ⊠ *3101 N. Fort Valley Rd.,* ☎ *520/774–5213.* 🖃 *$5.* ☉ *Daily 9–5.*

⑰ **Northern Arizona University Observatory.** Along with a 24-inch telescope, the observatory was built in 1952 by Dr. Arthur Adel, who had been a scientist at Lowell Observatory until he joined the college faculty as a professor of mathematics. His work on infrared astronomy pioneered research into molecules that absorb light passing through the earth's atmosphere. Today's studies of our planet's shrinking ozone layer rely on some of Dr. Adel's early work. Visitors to the observatory—which houses one of the largest telescopes that the public is allowed to move and manipulate—are usually hosted by friendly students and faculty members of the university's Department of Physics and Astronomy.

Public viewings take place every clear Friday night from 7 to 10. Tours for individuals and small groups can be arranged any day except Friday by calling at least one week in advance. ⊠ *Bldg. 47, Northern Arizona Campus Observatory, Dept. of Physics and Astronomy, S. San Francisco St.,* ☎ *520/523–7170.* 🖃 *Free (except private tours).*

⑲ **Pioneer Museum.** Operated by the Arizona Historical Society in a volcanic-rock building constructed in 1908—Coconino County's first hospital for the poor—the museum includes among its displays one of the depressingly small nurses' rooms, an old iron lung, and a reconstructed doctor's office. But most of the exhibits touch on more cheerful aspects of Flagstaff history—for example, road signs and children's toys. The museum hosts a folk-crafts festival on the Fourth of July, where you can watch traditional tradespeople, such as blacksmiths, weavers, spinners, quilters, and candle makers, at work. Their crafts, and those of other local artisans, are sold in the museum's gift shop, a tiny space filled with teddy bears, dolls, hand-dipped candles, and the like. The museum is part of the Fort Valley Park complex, in a wooded residential section at the northwest end of town. ⊠ *2340 N. Fort Valley Rd.,* ☎ *520/774–6272.* ☞ *$1 suggested donation per individual, $3 per family.* ⊙ *Mon.–Sat. 9–5.*

★ ⑯ **Riordan State Historic Park.** This must-see artifact of Flagstaff's logging heyday is near Northern Arizona University. Its centerpiece is a mansion built in 1904 for Michael and Timothy Riordan, lumber-baron brothers who married two sisters. The 13,300-square-ft, 40-room log-and-stone structure—designed by Charles Whittlesley, who was also responsible for the El Tovar Hotel at the Grand Canyon—contains a good deal of furniture by Gustav Stickley, father of the American Arts and Crafts design movement. Fascinating details abound; one room holds "Paul Bunyan's shoes," a 2-ft-long pair of boots made by Timothy in his workshop. Everything on display—from books to family photos and clothes—is original to the house, half of which was occupied by members of the family until 1986. The mansion may be explored on a guided tour only. ⊠ *1300 Riordan Ranch St.,* ☎ *520/ 779–4395.* ☞ *$4.* ⊙ *May–Sept. daily 8–5, with tours on the hr 9– 4; Oct.–Apr. daily 11–5, with tours noon–4.*

Dining and Lodging

By city ordinance, all restaurants in Flagstaff forbid smoking. Some eateries stay open longer in summer, the time of year when lodging prices are also at their highest.

$$–$$$ ✕ **Cottage Place.** An unexpectedly elegant spot in a town known for
★ heavy food and drive-through service, this cozy restaurant in a 50-year-old cottage has intimate dining rooms decorated in traditional style, with fresh flowers and candles. The menu strays only slightly from Continental to include some classic American dishes, such as charbroiled lamb chops. Try the artichoke chicken breast or chateaubriand for two carved tableside. Dinner includes soup and salad, but save room for Chocolate Decadence and other desserts. In 1996, the restaurant won the Wine Spectator's Award of Excellence for its wine list. ⊠ *126 W. Cottage Ave.,* ☎ *520/774–8431. AE, MC, V. Closed Mon. No lunch.*

$$–$$$ ✕ **Down Under New Zealand Restaurant.** Started as a tearoom and now a full-service restaurant, Down Under has gained a loyal local following. At midday, businesspeople flock to the green-and-white dining room or onto an outdoor terrace for potato-leek soup with sherry and copious Greek salads. In the evening, when the lights are dim, couples dine on such dishes as grilled rack of lamb and Cornish game hen with sun-dried cherry stuffing. The emphasis on New Zealand fish and meat and the availability of good Australian wines by the glass attest to the friendly owner's far-flung origins. ⊠ *413 N. San Francisco St.,* ☎ *520/774–6677. AE, MC, V. Closed Sun. No lunch weekends.*

$$ ✕ **Black Bart's Steakhouse Saloon & Old West Theater.** Fans of the Wild West—or a sanitized version thereof—will enjoy the atmosphere in this rustic barnlike structure, complete with beamed ceilings and hanging-lantern light fixtures. Aged prime beef is grilled over an open oak fire, and the barbecued chicken is tender and flavorful. Don't be surprised if your server suddenly jumps onstage to belt out a couple of show tunes. ⊠ *2760 E. Butler Ave.,* ☎ *520/779–3142. Reservations not accepted in summer. AE, MC, V. No lunch.*

$$ ✕ **Sakura Restaurant.** The excellent fish at this Japanese restaurant is flown in every other day from the West Coast, but if sushi doesn't

entice you, dine at a large table accompanied by a grill chef's pyrotechnics, and choose from grilled entrées; even if you haven't set foot in a Benihana in years, you'll probably enjoy well-seasoned, large portions of steak or seafood with vegetables being flipped in front of you. ⊠ *1175 Rte. 66,* ☎ *520/773–9118. AE, D, DC, MC, V. No lunch Sun.*

$–$$ ✕ **Beaver Street Brewery.** Most everyone enjoys the wood-fired pizzas that this bustling restaurant's open kitchen turns out. Standouts include the Enchanted Forest, with Brie, artichoke pesto, Portobello mushrooms, roasted red pepper, and spinach. Whichever pie you order, expect serious amounts of garlic to be involved. Sandwiches, such as the southwestern chicken with three types of cheese, come with a hefty portion of tasty fries. You won't regret ordering one of the down-home desserts, like the supergooey chocolate bread pudding. Among the excellent microbrews, the raspberry ale is a local favorite. An outdoor beer garden opens up in summer. ⊠ *11 S. Beaver St.,* ☎ *520/779–0079. AE, D, DC, MC, V.*

$–$$ ✕ **Buster's Restaurant.** At lunchtime, families and students from nearby Northern Arizona University settle into the comfortable booths and tables at Buster's. The menu includes fresh seafood, homemade soups, salads, giant burgers, and mesquite-grilled steaks. Try the *lahvosh* appetizer—a giant cracker heaped with toppings ranging from smoked salmon to mushrooms—or the Caesar salad with grilled Cajun chicken. At night, upscale single professionals and skiers crowd the bar and work through its impressive beer selection. ⊠ *1800 S. Milton Rd.,* ☎ *520/774–5155. AE, D, DC, MC, V.*

$–$$ ✕ **Pasto.** This downtown Italian restaurant, comprising two intimate dining rooms in adjacent historic buildings, is extremely popular with a young crowd for its good and plentiful food at reasonable prices. Such southern Italian standards as lasagna and spaghetti with meatballs appear on the menu along with more innovative fare, like artichoke orzo and salmon Caesar salad. A courtyard in the back, tucked away among higher buildings, has a romantic urban feel. ⊠ *19 E. Aspen St.,* ☎ *520/ 779–1937. MC, V. No lunch except in high season.*

$ ✕ **Café Espress.** The menu is largely vegetarian at this wholesome
★ all-day (7 AM–10 PM Monday–Thursday and 7 AM–11 PM Friday–Saturday) natural-food restaurant. Stir-fried vegetables, pasta dishes, Mediterranean salads, tempeh burgers, pita pizzas, fish or chicken specials, and wonderful baked goods made on the premises all come at prices that will make you feel good, too. The atmosphere is gallery hip (the work of local artists hangs on the walls) but friendly. ⊠ *16 N. San Francisco St.,* ☎ *520/774–0541. MC, V.*

$ ✕ **Café Olé.** Chili-pepper strings, a neon cactus, and a pastel mural make for an upbeat atmosphere at this little family-run restaurant, popular with local politicos and university professors. Vegetarian green-chili-and-cheese tamales and the best guacamole in town are among the specialties here, and you can sample freshly prepared Mexican dishes in well-priced combination plates. ⊠ *119 San Francisco St. ,* ☎ *520/774– 8272. Reservations not accepted. No credit cards. Closed weekends in winter, Sun. in summer.*

$ ✕ **Dara Thai.** East meets West at this unusual Route 66 eatery, where one dining area is done up in semiformal Asian style and the other resembles a cowboy diner. But the food in both is consistently Thai—and consistently good. Many dishes are prepared with tofu instead of meat or poultry, but strict vegetarians should be aware that fish oil is often used as a base. Don't pass up the coconut ice cream, made on the premises and served with chopped peanuts. ⊠ *Western Hills Motel, 1580 Rte. 66,* ☎ *520/774–8390 or 520/774–0047. AE, D, DC, MC, V. No lunch Sun.*

$ ✕ **Hunan West Restaurant.** The hands-down local favorite for Chinese food, this west-side restaurant has far more atmosphere than its strip-mall setting would suggest: An imposing dragon decorates the back wall, and white cloths dress the tables. The friendly staff will guide you through a menu that includes many Hunan specialties along with familiar Cantonese fare. The hot-and-sour soup is super, as is the "eight-treasure" shrimp and chicken. You can order anything in a "spicy," "not spicy," or reduced-fat version. ⊠ *University Plaza Shopping Center, 1302 S. Plaza Way,* ☎ *520/779–2229. AE, D, DC, MC, V. Closed Mon.*

$ ✕ **Salsa Brava.** This cheerful Mexican restaurant, with light-wood booths and colorful designs, eschews heavy Sonoran-style fare in favor of the grilled dishes found in Guadalajara (determined artery-cloggers will still find enough cheese-smothered items on the menu). The fish tacos are particularly tasty, and this place has the only salsa bar in town. On weekends, come for a huevos rancheros breakfast. ⊠ *1800 S. Milton Rd.,* ☎ *520/774–1083. AE, MC, V.*

$ ✕ **Strombolli's.** Nicer-than-average decor raises Strombolli's above pizza-joint status, but the pies are still the biggest draw. Many come for the huge calzones, which, as with pizza, you can have with any of 25 fresh ingredients. Of course, you may prefer pasta, like linguine with basil pesto cream sauce. If you're very hungry, consider the spinach-dip appetizer, which comes with tortilla chips, odd as that may seem in an Italian place. Reservations aren't accepted, but you can call ahead to get yourself put on the waiting list. ⊠ *1435 S. Milton,* ☎ *520/773–1960. Reservations not accepted. AE, D, MC, V.*

$ ✕ **Tea and Sympathy.** How civilized. Flagstaff now has a shop where you can sink down in an overstuffed chair and enjoy an assortment of tea services—a breakfast tea with granola and fruit, or a Sand and Sea tea, with smoked salmon pâté, fruit, and dessert. There's a huge assortment of tea from which to chose. If you like what you've tried, you can buy it loose. Tea and Sympathy is open Monday–Saturday 9–6; Sunday 10–6. ⊠ *409 N. Humphreys St.,* ☎ *520/779–2171. AE, D, MC, V.*

$$$ ⊞ **Best Western Woodlands Plaza Hotel.** This is the glitziest accommodation in town—which isn't saying much in Flagstaff. The hotel is near downtown and major outbound roads; rooms are large, comfortable, and furnished in southwestern pastels. Sakura (☞ *above*) is one of the two good restaurants on the premises. ⊠ *1175 W. Rte. 66, 86001,* ☎ *520/773–8888 or 800/528–1234,* ℻ *520/773–0597. 183 rooms. Bar, pool, sauna, spa, steam room, exercise room. AE, D, DC, MC, V.*

$$$ ⊞ **Inn at Four Ten.** A good alternative to the chain motels in Flagstaff,
★ this bed-and-breakfast has a quiet but convenient downtown setting. All the accommodations in this beautifully restored 1907 residence are suites with private baths. Some have private entrances, fireplaces, or hot tubs; all have refrigerators and coffeemakers. The full breakfasts are delicious and health-conscious; in the afternoon, the hosts bring out fresh-baked cookies. There's no smoking allowed. ⊠ *410 N. Leroux St., 86001,* ☎ *520/774–0088 or 800/774–2008,* ℻ *520/774–6354. 9 suites (1 accessible to travelers with disabilities). Refrigerators. MC, V.*

$$ ⊞ **Birch Tree Inn.** This historic home in a tree-filled neighborhood near downtown is nicely appointed with antiques. The atmosphere here is relaxed, in part because the hosts (two friendly couples who trade off innkeeping stints) enjoy chatting with their guests; they even sit down with them during breakfast. The billiard table adjoining the living room gets visitors talking to each other, too. You'll start your day well

fueled for sightseeing: The morning meal might consist of a cheese, sausage, and potato casserole accompanied by fresh fruit and banana bread made on the premises. ⊠ *824 W. Birch Ave., 86001,* ☎ *520/ 774–1042 or 800/645–5805. 3 rooms with private bath, 2 rooms with shared bath. Outdoor hot tub. AE, MC, V.*

$$ 🏨 **Comfi Cottages of Flagstaff.** Ideal for people who dislike the cold-
★ ness of motels but don't enjoy breakfasting with strangers in a tradi-
tional bed-and-breakfast environment, these appealing individual
cottages come stocked with breakfast fixings. They provide most of
the conveniences of home (only one doesn't have a washer-dryer), plus
such extras as picnic tables, bicycles, and barbecue grills. You can choose
from a variety of styles (English country or southwestern, for exam-
ple) and sizes; all are located in a residential neighborhood less than
½ mi from downtown. If you're traveling with family or with a group
of friends, you can't beat the convenience and price. ⊠ *1612 N. Aztec,
86001,* ☎ *520/774–0731 or 888/774–0731. 1 1-bedroom cottage, 3
2-bedroom cottages, 2 3-bedroom cottages. Bicycles. D, MC, V.*

$$ 🏨 **Jeanette's.** A stylish new addition to the Flagstaff B&B scene,
Jeanette's will appeal to those who prefer the clean lines of the 1920s
to Victorian froufrou. Rooms in this residence on the city's east side
are all beautifully appointed with art deco pieces; one room has a private porch, another a fireplace. Details such as handmade soap and
fine china at breakfast enhance the time-travel experience, as does owner
Jeanette's devotion to antique clothing, which she often dons. ⊠ *3380
E. Lockett Rd., 86004,* ☎ *520/752–1912 or 520/527–1912. 4 rooms.
MC, V.*

$$ 🏨 **Little America of Flagstaff.** The biggest motel in town is a deservedly
★ popular place. It's far enough from the tracks to allow visitors to sleep
undisturbed as trains roar through town, the grounds are surrounded
by evergreen forests, and it's one of the few places in Flagstaff with
room service. Plush rooms have brass chandeliers, comfortable sitting
areas with French provincial–style furniture, phones in bathrooms, large
stereo TVs, and small refrigerators. Other pluses are courtesy van ser-
vice to the airport and Amtrak station and a 24-hour gift shop with
great southwestern stuff. ⊠ *2515 E. Butler Ave., 86004,* ☎ *520/779–
2741 or 800/352–4386,* 📠 *520/779–7983. 248 rooms. Restaurant,
bar, coffee shop, kitchenettes, refrigerators, room service, outdoor
pool, exercise room, hiking, playground, coin laundry, airport shut-
tle. AE, D, DC, MC, V.*

$–$$ 🏨 **Hotel Monte Vista.** Over the years many Hollywood stars have
stayed at this historic downtown hotel built in 1926—so the guest rooms
come by the glamorous names attached to them honestly. The restored
southwestern-deco lobby, with its shoe-shine stand and curved arch-
ways, is appealing, and rates are low, but rooms and hallways are somewhat dark, and the men buying racing forms who hang out at the front
desk make this an iffy choice for female travelers. Bunk-bed rooms at
less than $15 per person are available. ⊠ *100 N. San Francisco St.,
86001,* ☎ *520/779–6971 or 800/545–3068,* 📠 *520/779–2904. 48
rooms. Restaurant, 2 bars. AE, D, DC, MC, V.*

Nightlife and the Arts

For current information on what's going on in town, pick up the free
Flagstaff Live.

Flagstaff's large college contingent has plenty of places to gather after
dark, most of them in the historic downtown district and most of them
charging little or no cover. It's easy to walk from one rowdy spot to
the next.

Club Depot (⊠ 26 S. San Francisco St., ☎ 520/773–9550) inspires dancing fools to move to either live or DJ sounds. For live entertainment

nightly—everything from bluegrass to jazz and rock—in a low-key atmosphere, try the **Main Street Bar and Grill** (⊠ 14 S. San Francisco St., ☎ 520/774–1519); the food's good, too, so come early for dinner. **The Monsoons** (⊠ 22 E. Rte. 66, ☎ 520/774–7929) books live music, from alternative to world beat. The **Monte Vista Lounge** (⊠ 100 N. San Francisco St., ☎ 520/774–2403) packs them in with nightly live blues, jazz, classic rock, punk, and an open mike on Wednesday. The ground floor of the **Weatherford Hotel** (⊠ 23 N. Leroux St., ☎ 520/779–1919) is home to both **Charly's,** featuring late-night jazz and blues bands, and the **Exchange Pub,** which tends to attract folksy ensembles.

On the east side, the **Museum Club** (⊠ 3404 E. Rte. 66, ☎ 520/526–9434) is the town's cowboy honky-tonk, offering free dance lessons on Thursday night and good country-and-western bands like Mogollon on the weekends.

Between the **Flagstaff Symphony Orchestra** (☎ 520/774–5107), **Theatrikos** (⊠ 11 W. Cherry Ave., ☎ 520/774–1662), and Northern Arizona University's **College of Creative and Performing Arts** (⊠ Ardrey Auditorium, Knoles and Riordon Rds., ☎ 520/523–5661), there's bound to be something cultural going on in Flagstaff when you visit. This is especially true in summer: During the month of August, the **Flagstaff Festival of the Arts** (☎ 520/774–7750 or 800/266–7740) fills the air with the sounds of classical-music and pops performances, many by world-renowned artists.

Flagstaff SummerFest, held the first weekend in August (⊠ Fort Tuthill Coconino County Park, S. Hwy. 89A, ☎ 520/774–5130), includes an arts-and-crafts fair. The **Coconino Center for the Arts** (⊠ 2300 N. Fort Valley Rd., ☎ 520/779–6921) hosts a **Festival of Native American Arts** each July and August and also sponsors the **Trappings of the American West** from mid-May to early June; the latter focuses on cowboy art—everything from paintings and sculpture to cowboy poetry readings. **A Celebration of Native American Art,** featuring exhibits of work by Zuni, Hopi, and Navajo artists, is held at the Museum of Northern Arizona (⊠ 3101 N. Fort Valley Rd., ☎ 520/774–5211) from late May through September. Flagstaff's observatories help make September's **Festival of Science** (☎ 800/842–7293 for information) a stellar attraction.

Outdoor Activities and Sports

BIKING

A map of the **Urban Trails System,** available at the Flagstaff Visitors Center (⊠ 1 E. Rte. 66, ☎ 520/774–9541 or 800/842–7293), details biking options in the area. From mid-June through mid-October, the **Flagstaff Nordic Center** (☎ 520/779–1951) opens its cross-country trails to mountain bikers, gratis if you bring your own wheels; rentals are also available.

In town you can rent mountain bikes at **Absolute Bikes** (⊠ 18 N. San Francisco St., 520/779–5969) or **Mountain Sports** (⊠ 1800 S. Milton Rd., ☎ 520/779–5156 or 800/286–5156). **Arizona Mountain Bike Tours** (⊠ Box 816, Flagstaff 86002, ☎ 520/779–4161; 800/277–7985 in Arizona) can guide you along the Colorado Plateau or the volcanic craters near Flagstaff.

CAMPING

Contact the **Coconino National Forest** (⊠ 2323 Greenlaw La., ☎ 520/527–3600) for information on camping in the area.

GOLF

In addition to many private clubs in the area, golfers will find semi-private courses, which accept a limited number of nonmembers, as well as public courses. The best club open to the public in the Flagstaff vicinity is the **Elden Hill Golf Course** (✉ 2380 N. Oakmont Dr., ☎ 520/527–7999 for tee times; 520/527–7997 for the pro shop).

HIKING

You can explore Arizona's alpine tundra in the San Francisco Peaks, where more than 80 species of plants grow on the upper elevations. The habitat is fragile, so hikers are asked to stay on established trails (and there are lots of them). The altitude here will make even the hardiest hikers breathe a little harder, so individuals with cardiac or respiratory problems should be cautious of overexertion. The **Humphreys Peak Trail** is 9 mi round-trip, with a vertical climb of 3,843 ft to the summit of Arizona's highest mountain (12,643 ft). Those who don't want a long hike will be well rewarded if they do just the first mile of the 5-mi-long **Kachina Trail;** completely flat, this route is surrounded by huge stands of aspen and offers fantastic vistas. It's particularly worthwhile in fall, when changing leaves paint the landscape shades of yellow, russet, and amber. You'll find the Humphreys Peak and Kachina trailheads at the Arizona Snowbowl (☞ Skiing, *below*). Others, such as the short but rewarding **Fatmans Loop** on Mt. Eldin, can be accessed in town.

Contact the **Coconino National Forest** (✉ 2323 Greenlaw La., ☎ 520/527–3600), which maintains these and other trails, for details on hiking in the area; it's open Monday–Friday 7:30–4:30. The **Peaks Ranger Station** (✉ 5075 N. U.S. 89, ☎ 520/527–3630) also has excellent hiking and recreational guides.

HORSEBACK RIDING

The wranglers at **Hitchin' Post Stables** (✉ 4848 Lake Mary Rd., ☎ 520/774–1719) lead rides into Walnut Canyon and operate horseback or horse-drawn wagon rides with sunset barbecues. In winter, they'll take you through Coconino National Forest on a sleigh—bells and all.

ROCK CLIMBING

Flagstaff Mountain Guides (✉ Box 2383, Flagstaff 86003, ☎ 520/635–0145) facilitates peak experiences around town or as far away as Sedona. If you'd prefer to hone your skills first, **Vertical Relief Rock Gym** (✉ 205 S. San Francisco St., ☎ 520/556–9909) provides the tallest indoor walls in the Southwest.

SKIING

CROSS-COUNTRY: The **Flagstaff Nordic Center,** owned and operated by Arizona Snowbowl (☞ Downhill, *below*) is 9 mi north of Snowbowl Rd. on U.S. 180. There are 25 mi of well-groomed trails here. Instruction packages and rental combinations are available. The **Mormon Lake Ski Center** (✉ 28 mi southeast of Flagstaff by way of Lake Mary Rd., Mormon Lake, ☎ 520/354–2240), with trails in the Coconino National Forest, is another option. Instruction, equipment rentals, and moonlight tours on full-moon weekends are available.

DOWNHILL: The ski season usually starts in mid-December and ends in mid-April. **Arizona Snowbowl** (✉ 7 mi north of Flagstaff on U.S. 180, ☎ 520/779–1951) has 30 runs (37% beginner, 42% intermediate, and 21% advanced), four chairlifts, and a vertical drop of 2,300 ft. Those who have skied Colorado's Rockies might find Snowbowl disappointing—there are a couple of good bump runs, but it's better for skiers of beginning or moderate ability. Still, it's a fun place to spend the day. The Hart Prairie Lodge has an equipment-rental shop and a SKIwee center for ages four–eight.

All-day adult lift tickets are $31. Half-day discounts are available, and group-lesson packages (including two hours of instruction, an all-day lift ticket, and equipment rental) are a good buy at $47. A kids' program (which includes lunch, progress card, and full supervision 9–3:30) runs $50. Many Flagstaff motels offer ski packages, including transportation to Snowbowl; call 800/828–7285 for details. For the current snow report, call 520/779–4577.

SNOWBOARDING

Snowboarders share trails with downhill skiers at the **Arizona Snowbowl** (☞ Skiing, *above*) and can rent equipment there; an all-day Snowboard Package (board, boots, all-day lift ticket, and two-hour lesson) runs $60.

SNOWMOBILING

Adult Toyz Center (☎ 520/522–0018) rents snowmobiles and conducts guided tours (including ones by moonlight).

Shopping

Flagstaff's prime shopping area is downtown. Even if you're not looking for anything in particular, it's fun to stroll along San Francisco Street and Route 66.

For fine arts and crafts—everything from ceramics and stained glass to weaving and painting—visit the **Artists Gallery** (⌧ 17 N. San Francisco St., ☎ 520/773–0958), a local artists' cooperative. You can pick up any sporting-goods items you might be missing at **Babbitt's Backcountry Outfitters** (⌧ 12 E. Aspen Ave., ☎ 520/774–4775). The 20-odd vendors at **Carriage House Antique and Gift Mall** (⌧ 413 N. San Francisco St., ☎ 520/774–1337) sell vintage clothing and jewelry, furniture, fine china, and other collectibles. **Four Winds Traders** (⌧ 118 W. Rte. 66, ☎ 520/774–1067) has good buys on pawned and new Native American jewelry. The **Kitchen Source** (⌧ 112 E. Rte. 66, ☎ 520/779–2302) sells every cooking implement imaginable and has courses to help you figure out how to use them. Come to **McGaugh's Newsstand** (⌧ 24 N. San Francisco St., ☎ 520/774–2131) for international newspapers and books; even some nonsmokers enjoy the aroma of the pipe tobacco sold in back. **Winter Sun Trading Company** (⌧ 107 N. San Francisco St., ☎ 520/774–2884) carries medicinal herbs, jewelry, and crafts in a soothing New Age atmosphere. **Zani** (⌧ 111-C S. San Francisco St., ☎ 520/774–9409) stocks hip home furnishings and greeting cards in addition to futons.

The gift shops at the **Coconino Center for the Arts** and the **Museum of Northern Arizona** (☞ Sights to See, *above*) carry high-quality jewelry and crafts.

The **Flagstaff Mall** (⌧ 4650 N. U.S. 89, ☎ 520/526–4827) is just east of town off I–40's Exit 201. This mall has the greatest number of department and specialty stores in the area, including Dillards, Sears, and JCPenney. There's also a food court and a two-screen cinema.

Side Trip East of Flagstaff

Visitors who head straight out of town for the Grand Canyon often neglect the area east of Flagstaff. But traveling east has its rewards. If you don't have enough time to do everything, take a quick drive to Walnut Canyon—only about 15 minutes out of town—and linger here for as long as you can.

★ ㉓ **Walnut Canyon National Monument** consists of a group of cliff-dwelling homes constructed by the Sinagua people, who lived and farmed in and around the canyon starting around ad 700. The more than 300 dwellings here were built between 1080 and 1250 and abandoned, like those at so many other settlements in Arizona and New Mexico, around 1300.

The Sinagua traded far and wide with other Native Americans, including people at Wupatki (☞ San Francisco Volcanic Field, below). Even macaw feathers, which would have come from tribes in what is now Mexico, have been excavated in the canyon. The area wasn't explored by Europeans until 1883, when early Flagstaff settlers shamelessly looted the site for pots and "treasure." Woodrow Wilson declared the site a national monument in 1915, which began a 30-year process of stabilizing the ruins.

Walnut Canyon is fascinating, in part because of the opportunity to enter the dwellings and feel ancient life at close range. Some of the Sinagua homes are in near-perfect condition, in spite of all the looting, because of the dry, hot climate and the protection of overhanging cliffs. You can reach them by descending 185 ft on the 1-mi stepped Island Trail, which starts at the visitor center. As you follow the trail, stop occasionally to look across the canyon for other dwellings not accessible on the path.

Island Trail takes about an hour to complete at a normal pace. The entrance to the trail closes one hour before the park does. Those with health concerns should opt for the easier Rim Trail (a ½-mi route that most people complete in about a half hour), which has overlooks from which dwellings can be viewed, as well as an excavated, reconstructed pit house. Attractive picnic areas dot the grounds and line the roads leading to the park. Guides conduct tours on Wednesday, Saturday, and Sunday from Memorial Day through Labor Day. Visitors are permitted to enter about two dozen ruins. ⊠ *Walnut Canyon Rd., 3 mi south of I–40 Exit 204,* ☎ *520/526–3367.* ➁ *$2 per person entering on foot or bicycle, $4 per vehicle.* ☉ *Daily 9–5; hrs extended during summer.*

🖐 ㉔ **Meteor Crater,** a natural phenomenon set in a privately owned park 43 mi east of Flagstaff, is impressive if for no other reason than its sheer size. A hole in the ground 600 ft deep, nearly 1 mi across, and more than 3 mi in circumference, Meteor Crater is large enough to accommodate the Washington Monument or 20 football fields. It was created when a meteorite came hurtling through space at a speed of 43,000 mi per hour and crashed here 49,000 years ago. The area looks so much like the surface of the moon that NASA made it one of the official training sites for the Project Apollo astronauts.

Visitors can't descend into the crater because of the efforts of its owners to maintain its condition—scientists consider this to be the best-preserved crater on earth—but guided rim tours, given every hour on the hour from 9 to 3, weather permitting, give visitors a bird's-eye view of the hole. A small snack bar sells soft drinks, coffee, and sandwiches. Rock hounds will enjoy the Rock Shop, filled with raw specimens from the area as well as with jewelry made from native stones. ⊠ *I–40 east of Flagstaff to Exit 233, then 6 mi south on Meteor Crater Rd.,* ☎ *520/ 289–2362.* ➁ *$8.* ☉ *May 16–Sept. 14, daily 6–6; Sept. 15–May 15, daily 8–5.*

Side Trip to the San Francisco Volcanic Field

The San Francisco Volcanic Field north of Flagstaff encompasses 2,000 square mi of fascinating geological phenomena—ancient volcanoes, cinder cones, and valleys carved by water and ice, and the San Francisco Peaks themselves, some of which soar to almost 13,000 ft—as well as some of the most extensive Native American ruins in the Southwest. If you have any time at all, don't miss Sunset Crater and Wupatki. These national monuments can be explored in relative solitude during much of the year. The area is short on services, so fill up on gas and consider taking along a picnic and have lunch along the way. A good source for hiking and camping information in this area is the **Peaks Ranger Station** (⊠ 5075 N. U.S. 89, ☎ 520/526–0866). If you camp, do not pitch your tent in a low-lying area, where dangerous flash floods can literally wipe you out.

★ ㉕   **Sunset Crater Volcano National Monument** lies 19 mi northeast of Flagstaff off U.S. 89. Sunset Crater, a cinder cone that rises 1,000 ft into the air, was an active volcano 900 years ago. The final eruption contained iron and sulfur, which gives the rim of the crater its glow and thus its name, Sunset. You can walk around the base, but you can't descend into the huge, fragile cone. If you take the Lava Flow Trail, a half-hour, mile-long, self-guided walk, you'll have a good view of the evidence of the volcano's fiery power: lava formations and holes in the rock where volcanic gases vented to the surface. Three smaller cones to the southeast were formed at the same time and along the same fissure.

If you're interested in hiking a volcano, head to **Lenox Crater,** about 1 mi east of the visitor center, and climb the 280 ft to the top of the cinder cone. Wear closed, sturdy shoes; the cinder is soft and crumbly. From **O'Leary Peak,** 5 mi from the visitor center on Forest Route 545A, great views can be had of the San Francisco Peaks, the Painted Desert, and beyond; the road is unpaved and rutted, however, so it's advisable to take only high-clearance vehicles, especially in winter. In addition, there's a gate, about halfway along the route, that's usually closed—in which case, it's a steep 2½-mi hike to the top. ⊠ *From Flagstaff, take Santa Fe Ave. east to U.S. 89, head north for 17 mi; turn right onto the road marked Sunset Crater and go another 2 mi to the visitor center,* ☎ *520/556–7042.* ⊡ *$4 per car, $2 to enter on foot or by nonmotorized vehicle; admission includes Wupatki National Monument (☞ below).* ⊙ *Daily 8–5; hrs may be extended in summer.*

★ ㉖   Families from the Sinagua and other ancestral Puebloans are believed to have lived together in harmony on the site that is now **Wupatki National Monument,** farming and trading with one another and with those who passed through their "city." The eruption of Sunset Crater may have caused migration to this area—and may have disrupted the settlement more than once around AD 1064. Although there is evidence of earlier habitation, most of the settlers moved here around 1100 and left the pueblo by about 1250. The 2,700 identified sites contain archaeological evidence of Native American settlement.

The site for which the national monument was named, the **Wupatki** (meaning "tall house" in Hopi), was originally three stories high, built above an unexplored system of underground fissures. The structure had almost 100 rooms and an open ball court—evidence in itself of southwestern trade with Mesoamerican tribes for whom ball games were a central ritual. Next to the ball court is a blowhole, a geologic phenomenon in which air is forced upward by underground pressure; scientists speculate that early inhabitants may have attached some spiritual significance to the region's many blowholes.

Other ruins to visit are **Wukoki, Lomaki,** and the **Citadel,** a pueblo on a knoll above a limestone sink. Although the largest remnants of Native American settlements at Wupatki National Monument are open to the public, other sites are off-limits to casual visitors. Rules regarding entering closed sites are strictly enforced. If you are interested in an in-depth tour, consider taking a ranger-led overnight hike to the **Crack-in-Rock Ruin.** The 14-mi (round-trip) trek covers areas marked by ancient petroglyphs and dotted with well-preserved ruins. There are a limited number of trips, conducted in April and October; it's best to call by February or August if you'd like to take part in the lottery for one of the 100 available places on these hikes. The cost is $25.

Between the Wupatki and Citadel ruins, the **Doney Mountain** affords 360-degree views of the Painted Desert and the San Francisco Volcanic Field. It's a perfect spot for a sunset picnic. In summer, rangers give interpretive lectures. ⊠ *Wupatki National Monument: 20 mi north of the Sunset Crater visitor center along the unmarked Sunset Loop Rd. (☞ above for directions from Flagstaff to Sunset Crater; HC 33, Box 444A, Flagstaff 86004, ☎ 520/556–7040. ᠗ $4 per vehicle (collected at Sunset Crater); $2 to enter on foot, bicycle, motorcycle, or nonmotorized vehicle. ☉ Daily 8–5; hrs may be extended in summer.*

NORTH-CENTRAL ARIZONA A TO Z

Arriving and Departing

By Air
America West (☎ 800/235–9292) has daily flights from Phoenix to **Flagstaff Pullium Airport** (☎ 520/556–1234), 3 mi south of town off I–17 at exit 337. A taxi ride from the airport to the downtown area should cost about $9 to $11. Cabs are not regulated; some, but not all, have meters. It's wise to agree on a rate before you leave with a driver for your destination. **A Friendly Cab** (☎ 520/774–4444) and **Sun Taxi** (☎ 520/774–7400) are two reliable options.

If you've rented a car in the Flagstaff airport and want to get downtown, follow signs to I–17 (the airport is just off the highway). Turn right (north) on I–17, and in about 3 mi exit at the downtown turnoff.

America West (☎ 800/235–9292) flies frequently from Phoenix into **Prescott Municipal Airport** (☎ 520/445–7860), 8 mi north of town on U.S. 89.

By Bus
Greyhound (⊠ 399 S. Malpais La., Flagstaff, ☎ 520/774–4573 or 800/231–2222) has daily connections from throughout the west to Flagstaff, but none to Sedona. Buses also run between Prescott (⊠ 820 E. Sheldon Ave., ☎ 520/445–5470) and Phoenix Sky Harbor airport. **Nava-Hopi** buses depart daily to the Grand Canyon. See Special-Interest Tours, *below*, for information about Nava-Hopi sightseeing trips to Sedona.

The **Sedona/Phoenix Shuttle Service** (⊠ Box 3342, West Sedona 86340, ☎ 520/282–2066; 800/448–7988 in AZ) makes six trips daily between those cities; the fare is $30 one-way, $55 round-trip. The bus leaves from three terminals of Sky Harbor International Airport in Phoenix. Reservations are required.

By Car
The most direct route to Prescott from Phoenix is to take I–17 north for 60 mi to Cordes Junction, and then drive northwest on AZ 69 for 36 mi into town. A four-lane divided highway, I–17 has several steep inclines and descents (you'll see a number of runaway-truck ramps). However, it's generally an easy and scenic thoroughfare. If you want to take the more leisurely route through Verde Valley to Prescott, continue north on I-17 another 25 mi past Cordes Junction until you see

the turnoff for AZ 260, which will take you to Cottonwood in 12 mi. Here you can pick up U.S. 89A, which leads southwest to Prescott (41 mi) or northeast to Sedona (19 mi).

To reach Sedona more directly from Phoenix, take I–17 north for 113 mi until you come to AZ 179; it's another 15 mi on that road into town. The trip should take about 2½ hours. The 27-mi drive from Sedona to Flagstaff on U.S. 89A, which winds its way through Oak Creek Canyon, is breathtaking.

Flagstaff lies at the intersection of I–40 (east–west) and I–17 (running south from Flagstaff), 134 mi north of Phoenix via I–17.

By Train
Amtrak (⊠ 1 E. Rte. 66, ☎ 520/774–8679 or 800/872–7245) comes into the downtown Flagstaff station twice daily. There is no rail service into Prescott or Sedona.

Getting Around

Flagstaff
Flagstaff is a compact town, much of it along the railroad tracks. Just north of, and roughly parallel to, the tracks is the busy street that was called Santa Fe Avenue for many years. In 1992 it officially resumed its famous original name, Route 66. I–40 lies south of the tracks and also runs east–west. The main north–south thoroughfare is I–17, which turns into Milton Road, Humphreys Street, and then U.S. 180 as you drive north through town.

Because Flagstaff is the gateway to the Grand Canyon, most people on the road here are from out of town; keep that in mind when you ask for directions.

BY BUS

Pine Country Transit (☎ 520/779–6624) provides clean and reliable service throughout Flagstaff for 75¢. Three bus lines run weekdays from 6:15 AM to 7:10 PM; only one bus line, on a more limited schedule, operates Saturday and holidays, and there is no service on Sunday. Passengers with disabilities should check with the office to find out which buses can accommodate wheelchairs.

BY CAR

It makes sense to rent a car at the airport if you fly into Flagstaff (☞ Car and Jeep Rentals, *below*), and there are some rental agencies near the Amtrak station.

Prescott
In Prescott, U.S. 89 turns into Gurley Street, the main drag, lined with motels and businesses. Gurley leads into Courthouse Square, the heart of town. The most interesting shops, restaurants, and historic hotels are located within a 10-block radius, and you'll be able to do most of your sightseeing on foot. The local bus service is not very regular; call **Ace City Cab** (☎ 520/445–1616) or **Reliable Cab** (☎ 520/772–6618) if you don't have a car.

Sedona
Sedona stretches along U.S. 89A (also called Highway 89A), its main thoroughfare, which runs roughly east–west through town. U.S. 89A is bisected by AZ 179. The more commercial section of U.S. 89A east of AZ 179 is known as Uptown; locals tend to frequent the shops on the other side, called West Sedona. To the south of U.S. 89A, AZ 179 is lined with upscale retailers for a couple of miles. There is no public transportation in Sedona; if you don't have your own wheels, you'll need to rent some (☞ Car and Jeep Rentals, *below*) or rely on the ser-

vices of Bob's Sedona Taxi (☎ 520/282–1234) or Bell Rock Taxi (☎ 520/282–4222).

Contacts and Resources

Camping and Hiking

For a full listing of campgrounds, in the Sedona, Prescott, and Jerome area, consult the *Arizona Camping and Campgrounds Guide,* available from the **Arizona Office of Tourism** (☞ Visitor Information *in* The Gold Guide). Reservations for many campgrounds are handled by **Destinet** (☎ 800/280–2267), but you'll need to choose one before you call in order to make the most of the automated phone system—it's nearly impossible to get hold of a human being.

If you're staying outside in winter, remember that this area gets quite cold, with frequent snowstorms. In summer, night temperatures can dip to 40°F, whereas daytime temperatures can reach 90°F. Be sure to bring plenty of water with you when hiking and drink often. Dehydration can become a life-threatening condition. Be careful not to camp in low-lying areas, which are subject to extremely dangerous flash flooding during sudden summer rains.

Car and Jeep Rentals

FLAGSTAFF

Agencies represented at the Flagstaff Pullium Airport include Avis (☎ 520/774–8421), **Budget** (☎ 520/779–0306), and **Hertz** (☎ 520/774–4452). Budget also has a downtown office, as do Sears (✉ 100 N. Humphreys St., ☎ 520/774–1879 or 800/527–0770), **National** (✉ Holiday Inn, 2320 E. Lucky La., ☎ 520/779–1975), and **Enterprise** (✉ 800 W. Rte. 66, ☎ 520/774–9407).

PRESCOTT

Budget (✉ 1031 Commerce Dr., ☎ 520/778–3806), **Enterprise** (✉ 202 S. Montezuma, ☎ 520/778–6506), and **Hertz** (✉ Airport, ☎ 520/776–1399) all have offices in Prescott.

SEDONA

Budget (☎ 520/282–4602) has an office at the Sedona Airport. If you want to explore the back roads of Sedona's red rocks on your own, you can rent a four-wheel-drive vehicle from **Sedona Jeep Rentals** (✉ Sedona Airport, ☎ 520/282–2227 or 800/879–5337) or **Canyon Jeep Rentals** (✉ Oak Creek Terrace Resort, 4548 Hwy. 89A, ☎ 520/282–6061 or 800/224–2229).

Emergencies

Ambulance (☎ 911). **Fire** (☎ 911). **Police** (☎ 911).

FLAGSTAFF

At an altitude of nearly 7,000 ft, Flagstaff has "thin" air; heart and respiratory patients may experience difficulty here, particularly upon exertion.

Flagstaff Medical Center (✉ 1200 N. Beaver St., ☎ 520/779–3366), a full-service hospital, has a 24-hour emergency room downtown, about nine blocks north of Route 66. The facility also provides referrals to local doctors and dentists.

The pharmacy at the **Flagstaff Medical Center** (☞ *above*) is open 24 hours. The pharmacy at **Smith's Food and Drug** (✉ 201 N. Switzer Canyon Dr., at Rte. 66, ☎ 520/774–3389) is open Monday through Saturday 9–9, Sunday 10–4. **Walgreen's** (✉ 1500 E. Cedar Ave., ☎ 520/773–1011), a few blocks north of downtown, is open Monday through Saturday 9 AM–10 PM, Sunday 10–6.

Yavapai Regional Medical Center (⊠ 1003 Willow Creek Rd., ☎ 520/445–2700).

The Goodwin Street Pharmacy (⊠ 406 W. Goodwin St., ☎ 520/776–9939) has a 24-hour prescription service.

The Sedona Medical Center (⊠ 3700 W. Hwy. 89A, ☎ 520/204–4900) has a doctor on call 24 hours. Walk-in hours are weekdays 8–5, most Saturdays 9–2.

The pharmacy at **Payless** (⊠ 2350 W. Hwy. 89A, ☎ 520/282–9577) closes at 8 PM on weekdays, 6 on Saturday, and 5 on Sunday. **Walgreen's** (⊠ 180 Coffee Pot Dr., ☎ 520/282–2528) stays open until 9 PM Monday–Saturday, until 8 on Sunday.

Guided Tours

Gray Line of Flagstaff, operated by **Nava-Hopi Tours** (⊠ Box 339, 114 W. Rte. 66, Flagstaff 86002, ☎ 520/774–5003 or 800/892–8687), runs bus trips from its downtown bus station to the Grand Canyon; $38 round-trip, not including park entry fee. A tour of Sedona costs $36 per person plus a $2 entry fee for Montezuma Castle; there are no drop-offs—that is, all passengers must return to Flagstaff on the same bus that evening. The company has other package tours, such as the one to the Hopi Indian Reservation for $62 round-trip. All require reservations, which are taken until two hours before departure.

The Ventures program, run by the education department of the **Museum of Northern Arizona** (⊠ 3101 N. Fort Valley Rd., Flagstaff 86001, ☎ 520/774–5213), offers tours of the area led by local scientists, artists, and historians. Trips might include rafting excursions down the San Juan River, treks into the Grand Canyon or Colorado Plateau backcountry, or bus tours into the Navajo reservation to visit with Native American artists. Prices start at about $400 and go up to $1,200, with most tours in the $500–$600 range.

Plane tours of the area's attractions run by the **Flagstaff Safe Fliers, Inc.** (⊠ Flagstaff Pullium Airport, 6200 S. Pullium Dr., Suite 104, 86001, ☎ 520/774–7858 or 800/438–6359) range from 20-minute Red Rock Quick Tours ($28) to Nelson's Ultimate Two-Day Adventure ($679), which includes a bird's-eye view of the Grand Canyon and London Bridge at Lake Havasu, with an overnight at Las Vegas, lunch in Jerome, and dinner in Sedona.

On Monday and Friday at 10 AM from Memorial Day through Labor Day, volunteer guides offer free orientation tours of Prescott that leave from the **Chamber of Commerce** (⊠ 1 E. Rte. 66). The rest of the year, tours can be booked with **Melissa Roughner** (☎ 520/445–4567), who'll be wearing territorial garb when she guides you around town.

Orientation: Sedona Trolley (☎ 520/282–6826 or 282–5400) offers two types of daily orientation tours, both departing from the main bus stop in Uptown and lasting less than an hour. One goes along AZ 179 to the Chapel of the Holy Cross, with stops at Tlaquepaque and some galleries; the other passes through West Sedona to Boynton Canyon (Enchantment Resort). Rates are $7 each or $11 for both.

Special-Interest Tours: One of the most popular things to do in the Sedona area is to take a Jeep tour; several operators headquartered along Sedona's main Uptown drag conduct various excursions, some focusing on geology, some on astronomy, some on vortices, some on all three. You can even find a combination Jeep tour and horseback ride. The ubiquitous **Pink Jeep Tours** (✉ 204 N. Hwy. 89A, Box 1447, Sedona 86339, ☎ 520/282–5000 or 800/873–3662), as well as Sedona Adventures (✉ 276 N. Hwy. 89A, Suite A, Box 1476, Sedona 86339, ☎ 520/282–3500 or 800/888–9494) and **Sedona Red Rock Jeep Tours** (✉ 270 N. Hwy. 89A, Box 10305, Sedona 86339, ☎ 520/282–6826 or 800/848–7728), are all reliable operators. Prices start at about $22 per person for one hour and go up to $65 per person for four hours. Although all the excursions are safe, those who dislike heights or bumps should choose one that's easy on the nerves and spine. It's also advisable to inquire if the stops involve any physical activity; some excursions are not for the out-of-shape or infirm.

Prices for hot-air-balloon tours generally start at $135 per person for a one- to two-hour tour. The only two companies with permits to fly over Sedona are **Northern Light Balloon Expeditions** (✉ Box 1695, Sedona 86339, ☎ 520/282–2274 or 800/230–6222), open since 1974 and the longest-operating in Northern Arizona, and **Red Rock Balloon Adventures** (✉ Box 2759, Sedona 86339, ☎ 520/284–0040 or 800/258–3754).

Sedona Art Tours (✉ Box 10578, Sedona 86339, ☎ 520/282–0788) guides visitors through the town's art galleries.

Sedona Photo Tours (✉ 252 N. Hwy. 89A, Box 1650, 86339, ☎ 520/282–4320 or 800/973–3662) will take you to all the prime spots and help you take your best (photographic) shot. Rates are $35 per person for a basic two-hour tour.

Visitor Information

Camp Verde Chamber of Commerce (✉ 435 S. Main St., 86322, ☎ 520/567–9294). **Clarkdale Chamber of Commerce** (✉ Box 161, 86324, ☎ 520/634–3382). **Cottonwood/Verde Valley Chamber of Commerce** (✉ 1010 S. Main St., Cottonwood 86326, ☎ 520/634–7593). **Flagstaff Visitors Center** (✉ 1 E. Rte. 66, 86001, ☎ 520/774–9541 or 800/842–7293) is open Monday–Saturday 9–6 and Sunday 8–5. **Jerome Chamber of Commerce** (✉ Box K, 86331, ☎ 520/634–2900). **Prescott Chamber of Commerce** (✉ 117 W. Goodwin St., 86303, ☎ 520/445–2000 or 800/266–7534) is open weekdays 9–5, weekends 10–2. The **Sedona–Oak Creek Canyon Chamber of Commerce** (✉ 331 Forest Rd., at the corner of N. Hwy. 89A, Sedona 86339, ☎ 520/282–7722 or 800/288–7336) is open Monday–Saturday 9–5, Sunday 9–3.

5 Phoenix and Central Arizona

The ever-widening Phoenix metropolitan area provides a tremendous variety of activities—from golfing on championship courses and hiking on some of the country's most-traveled (and appreciated) trails to dining at the restaurants where southwestern cuisine was born and experiencing the last word in pampering at world-class resorts. Scottsdale and the college town of Tempe are packed with great boutiques and art galleries. Outside of metropolitan Phoenix, Wickenburg is an authentic Old West town, and the Apache Trail drive is one of the most scenic routes in America.

Updated by
Jenner Bishop

N CENTRAL ARIZONA, one of the world's great deserts meets one of its great mountain ranges, providing a stunning variety of natural environments for visitors to enjoy in a relatively small area. Central Arizona also combines some of the oldest human dwellings in the western hemisphere with the homes of contemporary Native American tribes and America's fastest-growing major urban center: metropolitan Phoenix, a melding of 22 communities and, with a population of over a million people, the seventh-largest city in the United States.

At the heart of central Arizona lies the Valley of the Sun—which gives its name to the common nickname of metro Phoenix, the Valley—named for its 330-plus days of sunshine each year. This 1,000-square-mi valley is the northern tip of the Sonoran Desert, a surprisingly fertile, rolling expanse of prehistoric seabed that stretches from central Arizona deep into northwestern Mexico. The valley is studded with cacti and creosote bushes, crusted with hard-baked clay and rock, and scorched by summer temperatures that can stay above 100°F for weeks at a time. But its dry skin responds magically to the touch of rainwater. Spring is a miracle of poppies strewn among the flower-crowned saguaro cacti, of ruby, ivory, and golden blossoms bursting from the dry spikes of the ocotillo and the thorny beaver-tail pads of the nopal.

As the Hohokam discovered 2,300 years ago, this springtime miracle can be augmented by human hands. Having migrated north from northwestern Mexico, they cultivated cotton, corn, and beans in tilled, rowed, and irrigated fields for about 1,700 years. The Hohokam, like northern Puebloans in the 14th and 15th centuries, moved out of the area as a result of the combination of droughts, longer winters, and other causes. They are believed to be ancestors of the present-day Pimans: the Pima and Tohono O'odham.

From the time the Hohokam left until the American Civil War, the once fertile Salt River valley lay forgotten, used only by occasional small bands of Pima and Maricopa peoples. Then, in 1865, the U.S. Army established Fort McDowell in the mountains to the east, where the Verde River flows into the Salt. To feed the men and the horses stationed there, Jack Swilling, a former Confederate army officer, had the idea of reopening the Hohokam canals in 1867. Within a year, fields bright with barley and pumpkins earned the area the name of Punkinsville. But by 1870, when the town site was plotted, the 300 inhabitants had decided that their new city would rise "like a phoenix" from the ashes of a vanished civilization.

Phoenix indeed grew steadily. Within 20 years, it had become large enough—at about 3,000 people—to wrest the title of territorial capital from Prescott. By 1912, when Arizona was admitted as a state, the area, irrigated by the brand-new Roosevelt Dam and Salt River Project, had a burgeoning cotton industry. Copper and cattle were mined and raised elsewhere but were banked and traded in Phoenix, and the cattle were slaughtered and packed here in the largest stockyards outside Chicago.

Meanwhile, the climate, so long a crippling liability, became an asset. Desert air was the prescribed therapy for the respiratory ills rampant in the sooty, factory-filled East; Scottsdale began in 1901 as "30-odd tents and a half dozen adobe houses" put up by health seekers. By 1930, visitors looking for warm winter recreation rather than a cure filled the elegant San Marcos Hotel in Chandler and the new Arizona Biltmore, first of the many luxury resorts for which the area is now known worldwide.

Phoenix and central Arizona are places in which to take it easy, go slowly, and dress informally. As old desert hands say, you don't begin to see the desert until you've looked at it long enough to see its colors; and you aren't ready to get up and move until you've seen the sun go down.

Pleasures and Pastimes

Dining
Phoenix's culinary traditions arise from a unique blend of Old West and New West cultures. In the mid-19th century, the north-Mexican rancho cooking that had been in Arizona for 150 years was joined by the Anglo-European food of American settlers. Arizona Territory was also an outpost of the West's cattle-ranching boom, and the railroads brought a significant early influx of Chinese settlers.

By the mid-20th century, the Valley was rich in Mexican food, mostly in the style of the adjoining Mexican state of Sonora; steak houses (Phoenix was a major stockyard center until the 1970s); and Chinese restaurants, mostly Cantonese. There was plenty of family eating, heartburn, and *agita*. When Phoenicians wanted to get fussy, men put on bola ties and women donned silver-and-turquoise jewelry, and they paid someone to pour "Continental" sauces on their steaks.

Then, during the 1970s, things took off. Southeast Asian refugees introduced spicy Asian dishes that were instantly welcome in a city used to salsa and sweet-and-sour. Immigrants from Central America and the Middle East brought more variations on familiar themes, as well as new approaches. Soon, "southwestern international" was born, and by the late '80s, it had taken hold of America's culinary imagination. Still, Arizona being what it is, Phoenix also has plenty of good old meat-and-potatoes and diner fare.

Golf
Phoenix has become a golf mecca, due to the warm weather, azure skies, and serene vistas of the desert. The explosive growth of the area has brought many new courses to the Valley over the past 15 years. Phoenix and the surrounding environs boast world-class courses designed by Jack Nicklaus, Tom Weiskopf and Jay Morrish, Pete Dye, Arnold Palmer and Ed Seay, and Ted Robinson, to name a few. The city provides an impressive array of courses—golfers may choose lush, manicured fairways with tranquil lakes and fountains or get right out in the wild dunes and scrub brush of the natural desert.

Hot-Air Ballooning
For a bird's-eye view of the spectacular desert landscape, try a hot-air balloon ride. The peaceful silence of life hundreds of feet up is unforgettable; since the balloon is carried on the wind, you'll experience no wind yourself. In addition to this tranquillity, many illusive desert creatures can only be viewed in their natural habitat from balloon.

Mountains
The Valley of the Sun is ringed by mountains, which provide many options for outdoor activities. Squaw Peak is just north of downtown Phoenix and Camelback Mountain and the Papago Peaks are landmarks between Phoenix and Scottsdale. South of the city, not 5 mi from downtown, rise the much less lofty peaks of South Mountain Park. This 12-mi-wide chain of dry mountains divides the Valley from the rest of the Sonoran Desert.

Past Tempe (pronounced tem-*pee*), and Mesa to the east, the barren peaks of the Superstition Mountains—named for their eerie way of seeming just a few miles away and luring unwary prospectors to a dusty death—are the first of a series of mountains that stretch all the way into New Mexico. To the west, past Glendale and Tolleson, the formidable, barren-seeming White Tank Mountains separate the Valley from the empty lands that slope steadily downward toward the Colorado River and the Mojave Desert of California.

But north of Phoenix, behind the dusty Hieroglyphic Mountains (misnamed for Hohokam petroglyphs found there), rises the gigantic Mogollon Rim. This shelf of land, almost as wide as Arizona, was thrust 2,000 to 5,000 ft into the air back in the Mesozoic age; it got its name for posing an overwhelming *mogollon* (obstruction) to Spanish-speaking explorers probing northward. These slopes are green with pine trees, and the alpine meadows are lush with grasses and aspen. Here, after gold was found in the early 1860s, President Lincoln sent the Arizona Territory's first governor to found the capital at Prescott (☞ The Verde Valley, Jerome, and Prescott *in* Chapter 4) and secure mineral riches for the Union.

Today, the northern mountains serve as a cool, green refuge for Valley dwellers. The bumpy wagon roads up the Black Canyon toward Prescott and Flagstaff were key summer escape routes 100 years ago, and their dramatically engineered successor, the four-lane, split-level I–17, leads tens of thousands on exodus every weekend from May to September.

EXPLORING PHOENIX

When low-cost air-conditioning made its summer heat manageable, the Sun Belt boom began. From 1950 to 1990, the Phoenix urban area more than quadrupled in population, catapulting real estate and home-building into two of the state's biggest industries. Cities planted around Phoenix have become its suburbs, and fields that for decades grew cotton and citrus now grow microchips and homes. Glendale and Peoria on the west side, and Tempe, Mesa, Chandler, and Gilbert on the east, make up the nation's third-largest silicon valley.

Numbers in the text correspond to numbers in the margin and on the Exploring Downtown and the Cultural Center, Exploring Scottsdale, and Side Trips Near Phoenix maps.

Great Itineraries

IF YOU HAVE 3 DAYS

See the Heard Museum for its internationally acclaimed collection of Native American artifacts, and swing by the Central Library on your way downtown to the Arizona Science Center and Phoenix Museum of History. On day two, rise early and begin your day at Frank Lloyd Wright's Taliesin West; then head south into Scottsdale for a day of gallery browsing and a walk through Old Town. On your final day, take in Phoenix's stunning natural environs: Visit the Desert Botanical Gardens or spend some time exploring the stark beauty of the surrounding desert on horseback, by Jeep, or even by hot-air balloon.

IF YOU HAVE 5 DAYS

Follow the tour above, and on the fourth day, consider some hiking: Even inexperienced hikers will enjoy the walk up to Papago Park's Hole in the Rock or the 1.2-mi trip to the top of Squaw Peak, whereas the more experienced may choose to ascend Camelback Mountain. South Mountain Park has many trails for hikers of all abilities. Pro-

Greater Phoenix

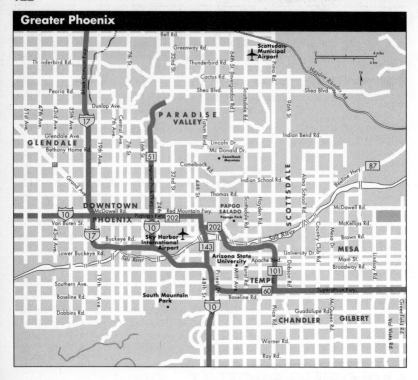

ceed to Tempe, where the rest of the day can be spent strolling on Mill Avenue and checking out the unique architecture of the Arizona State University campus. On your fifth day, drive the loop of the Apache Trail, enjoying breathtaking views of Fish Creek Canyon—or drive north to take a tour of Arcosanti or explore the Old West town of Wickenburg.

IF YOU HAVE 7 DAYS

Expand your drive of the Apache Trail to include an overnight stay in Globe, taking full advantage of such attractions along the way as the view from Weaver's Needle and stroll through Boyce Thompson Arboretum, or check out the ancient Hohokam ruins at Casa Grande to the south of Phoenix.

Downtown Phoenix

The renovated east end of downtown gives you a look at Phoenix's past and present, as well as a peek at its future. Restored homes from the original townsite give visitors an idea of how far the city has come since its inception around the turn of the last century, while several fine museums point to the Valley of the Sun's increasing sophistication in the coming one.

A Good Walk

Park you car in the parking structure on the southeast corner of 5th and Monroe streets (be prepared, it can be cramped), and begin your tour in the blocks known as the Heritage and Science Park; 5th to 7th streets between Monroe and Adams contain **Heritage Square** ①, the **Arizona Science Center** ②, and the **Phoenix Museum of History** ③. From the corner of 5th and Monroe, walk a block north to Van Buren Street. On the northwest corner of the intersection, you'll see two glass-clad office towers with a lane of royal palms between them. Follow the palm trees: They lead to the **Arizona Center** ④. Leaving the Arizona Center, from the corner of 3rd and Van Buren, walk a block west to 2nd Street and two blocks south on 2nd Street, passing the 24-story Hyatt Regency hotel on your right, then another block and a half west on Adams Street to the **Museo Chicano** ⑤. You can walk to Heritage and Science Park from here, catch a DASH shuttle back, or continue on two more blocks west toward the striking facade of the **Orpheum Theatre** ⑥.

If you're really an indefatigable walker, continue south through the plaza on the Orpheum's east side to Washington Street; head east on Washington Street, passing Historic City Hall and the county courthouse on your right. At the intersection of Washington and 1st Avenue, you'll see Patriots Square Park on the southeast corner; cross diagonally (southeast) through the park to the corner of Jefferson Street and Central Avenue. Another block east on Jefferson and then a block south on 1st Street will take you to the site of the **America West Arena** ⑦. From the arena, walk back to Jefferson Street and Central Avenue to catch the DASH shuttle back to your car.

TIMING

In moderate weather, this walk is a pleasant daylong tour; from late May to mid-October, it's best to break it up over two days. Be sure to take advantage of the 35¢ DASH (Downtown Area Shuttle; ☞ By Bus *under* Getting Around *in* Phoenix and Central Arizona A to Z, *below*).

Sights to See

❼ America West Arena. This 20,000-seat, multifacility sports palace is the home of the Phoenix Suns, the Arizona Rattlers arena football team, the Phoenix Coyotes NHL team, and the Arizona Sandsharks professional soccer team. Almost a mall in itself—with cafés and shops, in addition to the team offices—it's interesting to tour even when there's no game on. The lobby entrance has displays of postmodern video art, including "Electro-Symbio Phonics," a neon/video sculpture of three robot figures fashioned out of small televisions. ⊠ *201 E. Jefferson St., at 2nd St.,* ☎ *602/379–2000.*

❹ Arizona Center. Beyond an oasis of dramatic fountains and manicured, sunken gardens stands the curved, two-tiered structure that is downtown's most impressive shopping venue. In addition to several good eateries, you'll find the state's biggest sports bar here—would you believe eight restaurant-size spaces spread over two stories, indoors and out? There is a variety of chain and specialty stores, from men's and women's clothing to southwestern art and '50s collectibles; a 24-screen movie-theater complex should be completed by 1998. Evenings usually find street performers and live music (including top Valley jazz artists) out in the courtyard. ⊠ *Van Buren St. between 3rd and 5th Sts.,* ☎ *602/271–4000 or 602/949–4353.*

NEED A
BREAK?

For some restful refreshment, stop by **Amalfi** (⊠ 455 N. 3rd St., ☎ 602/257–0605), an Italian sidewalk café that serves great sandwiches and desserts, as well as Italian sodas and steamed coffees.

★ ☝ **❷ Arizona Science Center.** This concrete monolith, designed by architect Antoine Predock, opened in April 1997. Lively "please touch" exhibits provide an entertaining educational experience for kids and grown-ups alike—learn about the physics of making gigantic soap bubbles and the technology of satellite weather systems, or listen in to the control tower at Sky Harbor airport. Under the dome of Dorrance Planetarium, dazzling computer graphics simulate orbits and eclipses, as well as three-dimensional space flight. The Irene P. Flinn theater has a 50-ft-high projection screen. ⊠ *600 E. Washington St.,* ☎ *602/716–*

124

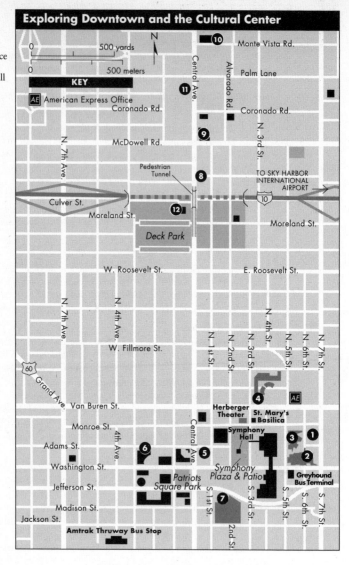

Exploring Downtown and the Cultural Center

2000. ⊠ *Museum $6.50; combination museum, theater, and plane-tarium $11.* ⊙ *Daily 10–5.*

❶ Heritage Square. In a parklike setting from 5th to 7th streets between Monroe and Adams, this city-owned block contains the only remaining homes from the original Phoenix townsite. On the south side of the square, along Adams Street, stand four houses built between 1899 and 1901. The midwestern-style **Stevens House** holds the **Arizona Doll and Toy Museum** (⊠ 602 E. Adams St., ☎ 602/253–9337). Next to it, in the California-style **Stevens-Haustgen House,** is the **Native Ring Project** (⊠ 614 E. Adams St., ☎ 602/534–2243), which rotates exhibits from the Pueblo Grande museum collection and sells handcrafted Native American jewelry and gifts. The **Teeter House,** the third house in the row, is now a Victorian-style tearoom. The fourth dwelling is the **Silva House,** a bungalow from 1900 restored by the Salt River Project (one of the Valley's two major power companies and its largest irrigator), which features presentations about turn-of-the-century life for settlers in the Phoenix township. On the south side of Adams Street, the **Thomas House** and **Baird Machine Shop**—both under restoration in 1997—are slated to become the Italian bakery-and-pizzeria combination of the Valley's favorite maestro-chef, Chris Bianco.

The queen of Heritage Square is the **Rosson House,** an 1895 gingerbread Victorian in the Queen Anne style. Built by a physician who served a brief term as mayor, it is the sole survivor of the fewer than two dozen Victorians erected in Phoenix. It was bought and restored by the city in 1974. A 30-minute tour of this classic is worth the modest admission price. ✉ *6th and Monroe Sts.,* ☎ *602/262–5071.* ☞ *$3.* ☉ *Wed.–Sat. 10–3:30, Sun. noon–3:30.*

NEED A BREAK?

The Victorian-style tearoom in the **Teeter House** (E 622 E. Adams St., ☎ 602/252–4682) serves such authentic tea fare as Devonshire cream, scones with berries, and cucumber sandwiches. Heartier gourmet sandwiches and salads are also available. The staff will happily box any of your choices, should you prefer to enjoy them on the lawn outside.

⑤ Museo Chicano. Artistic works of Hispano-American artists from both the United States and Mexico are showcased here. Exhibits display the broad range of classic and modern Hispanic culture, making this site one of the premier centers for contemporary Latin American art. ✉ *25 E. Adams St.,* ☎ *602/257–5536.* ☞ *$2.* ☉ *Tues.–Sat. 10–4.*

⑥ Orpheum Theatre. The Spanish-colonial-revival architecture and exterior reliefs of this 1929 movie palace have long been admired, and now, after an extensive renovation by artisans and craftsmen (completed in 1997), the eclectic ornamental details of the interior have been meticulously restored. Call for details on guided tours. ✉ *203 W. Adams St.,* ☎ *602/252–9678.*

★ ☾ **③ Phoenix Museum of History.** This striking glass-and-steel museum, which opened in 1996, offers a healthy dose of regional history from the 1860s (when Anglo settlement began) through the 1930s. A counterclockwise tour through interactive exhibits allows guests to appreciate the city's multicultural heritage as well as witness its growth. Visitors are invited to play Sniff That Barrel (to guess its contents) at a replica of Hancock Store (a 1860s Circle-K equivalent) or take a turn at packing a toy wagon with color-coded blocks as if for a cross-country trip. ✉ *105 N. 5th St.,* ☎ *602/253–2734.* ☞ *$5.* ☉ *Mon.–Sat. 10–5, Sun. noon–5.*

The Cultural Center

The heart of Phoenix's downtown cultural center is the rolling greensward of the Margaret T. Hance park, also known as Deck Park. Built atop the I–10 tunnel under Central Avenue, it spreads over 1 mi from 3rd Avenue on the west to 3rd Street on the east, and ¼ mi from Portland Street north to Culver Street. Completed in 1993, it is the city's second-largest downtown park (the largest is half-century-old Encanto Park, 2 mi northwest). Growing at the same rapid rate as the city itself, this neighborhood has received a giant face-lift as of late—efforts to revitalize downtown have included the construction of a new library in 1995 and the expansion or renovation of nearly all the area's museums.

A Good Walk

Park free in the lot of the **Phoenix Central Library** ⑧ at the corner of Central Avenue and East Willetta Street. Two blocks north on Central, on the other side of McDowell Road, is the modern, green-stone structure of the **Phoenix Art Museum** ⑨. North of the museum, enjoy a brief respite from the noise and traffic of Central Avenue by heading one block east on Coronado Road to Alvarado Road. Follow residential Alvarado north for two longish blocks (zigzagging a few feet to the east at Palm La.) to Monte Vista Road; turn left onto Monte Vista and proceed 50 yards west to the entrance of the **Heard Museum** ⑩. From the Heard, head south on Central Avenue toward the red-granite Viad Tower, the lobby of which contains the **Breck Girl Hall of Fame** ⑪. Follow Central Avenue south, and just past the library, on the southwest corner of Central Avenue and Culver Street, lies the **Ellis–Shackelford House** ⑫.

TIMING

Seeing all of the neighborhood's attractions makes a comfortable day tour in moderate weather; in the warm months, it is too much for one day. Bus 0 runs up and down Central Avenue every 10 minutes on weekdays and every 20 minutes on Saturdays.

Sights to See

⑪ **Breck Girl Hall of Fame.** On the ground floor of the red, granite **Viad Corporate Center,** is a campy stop sure to be appreciated by pop-culture enthusiasts. This one-room museum contains more than 150 of the signature pastel portraits from the "Breck Girl" shampoo ads—which date from the 1930s—including pictures of Brooke Shields, Kim Basinger, Cybill Shepherd, and other now-famous former Breck Girls. A guide can detail the life and times of Mr. Edward J. Breck, whose lasting contributions to society include being the first person to differentiate between dry and oily. ⊠ *1850 N. Central Ave.,* ☎ *602/207–4000.* ⊠ *Free.* ☉ *Weekdays 11–3.*

NEED A BREAK?

The grassy park of the Viad Corporate Center is a great place to stop for a rest. A string of tiered fountains snakes through the 2-acre park and sculpture garden, which contains a collection of lifelike works in bronze—some so realistic, you might unwittingly pass right by them. Stop to appreciate their whimsical touches, such as the blue-capped window washer's paperback copy of *Rear Window* tucked in his overalls.

⑫ **Ellis–Shackelford House.** Built in 1917, this two-story, prairie-style building is the lone survivor of the large homes of early civic and business leaders that once lined Central Avenue. It now houses the Phoenix Historic Preservation Office. A restored railcar of the Phoenix Street Railway is kept in back. ⊠ *1242 N. Central Ave.,* ☎ *602/261–8699.*

★ ☾ ⑩ **Heard Museum.** Pioneer Phoenix settlers Dwight and Maie Heard had a Spanish-colonial-revival building erected on their property to house the impressive collection of southwestern art they amassed on their travels; today, the site has developed into the nation's premier showcase of Native American art and culture, with an impeccable collection of more than 32,000 works of art and ethnographic objects. In addition to galleries filled with fine art, basketry, pottery, weavings, and bead work, the Heard has interactive art-making exhibits for children and live demonstrations by artisans. ⊠ *22 E. Monte Vista Rd.,* ☎ *602/252–8848 or 602/252–8840.* ⊠ *$6; free Wed. after 5.* ☉ *Mon.–Sat. 9:30–5, Wed. 9:30–8, Sun. noon–5.*

⑨ **Phoenix Art Museum.** After an extensive three-year expansion and renovation, completed in 1996, the green quartz exterior of this modern museum adds yet another piece of eye-catching architecture to Central Avenue. More than 13,000 objets d'art are on display inside, including 18th- and 19th-century European paintings and drawings and the American West collection, which features painters from Frederic Remington to Georgia O'Keeffe. A clothing-and-costume collection has items that date from 1750, and the Asian art gallery is filled with fine Chinese porcelain and pieces of intricate cloisonné. ⊠ *1625 N. Central Ave.,* ☎ *602/257–1222 or 602/257–1800.* 🎟 *$4; tours free.* ☉ *Tues. and Thurs.–Sat. 10–5, Wed. 10–9, Sun. noon–5.*

⑧ **Phoenix Central Library.** Not often is a library on the must-see list for a city, but architect Will Bruder's magnificent 1995 contribution to Central Avenue is absolutely worth a stop. The curved building's copper-penny exterior evokes images of the region's sunburnt mesas; inside, skylights, glass walls, and computer-controlled mirrors keep the structure bathed in natural light. A five-story glass atrium, known as the Crystal Canyon, is best appreciated from a speedy ride in one of three glass elevators. At the top, from the largest reading room in North America, check out a cable-suspended steel ceiling that appears to float overhead; catch views to the north and south from 32-ft, floor-to-ceiling windows. Free one-hour tours are offered on Fridays; call to arrange in advance. ⊠ *1221 N. Central Ave.,* ☎ *602/262–4636; 602/262–6582 tour reservations.* ☉ *Mon.–Wed. 9–9, Thurs.–Sat. 9–6, Sun. 1–5.*

NEED A BREAK?	Across Willetta Street from the library, the white house with blue shutters is **Mooo Chos Coffees & More** (E 102 E. Willetta St., ☎ 602/528-3936)— a converted residence that turns out sandwiches, desserts, and coffee drinks; grab a cappuccino and relax by the fireplace or wander through the house following the trail of country-themed bric-a-brac, all of which is for sale.

Papago Salado

The word "Papago," meaning "bean eater," was a term given by 16th-century Spanish explorers to a vanished native people of the Phoenix area. Farmers of the desert, the Hohokam (as they are more properly called) grew corn, beans, squash, and cotton. They lived in central Arizona from about AD 1 to 1450, at which point their civilization collapsed and disappeared for reasons unknown—some conjecture drought, floods, or internal strife—abandoning the Salt River (Rio Salado) valley but leaving behind remains of villages and a complex system of irrigation canals. The Papago Salado region is located between Phoenix and Tempe and contains the Pueblo Grande ruins, the Desert Botanical Garden, the Phoenix Zoo, and a variety of potential recreational activities amid the buttes of Papago Park.

A Good Drive

Stop at the **Pueblo Grande Museum and Cultural Park,** on Washington Street between 44th Street and the Hohokam Expressway (AZ 143). Follow Washington Street east 3½ mi to Priest Drive and turn north. Priest Drive becomes Galvin Parkway north of Van Buren Street; follow signs to entrances for the **Phoenix Zoo** and **Papago Park,** or to the **Desert Botanical Garden.** To visit the **Hall of Flame** afterward, drive south on Galvin Parkway to Van Buren Street; turn east on Van Buren and drive ⅛ mi, turning south at Project Drive (at the buff-color stone marker that reads SALT RIVER PROJECT).

TIMING

Seeing all the sights requires the better part of a day. You may want to save the Desert Botanical Garden for the end of your tour, as it stays open until 8 PM October–April and 10 PM May–September and is particularly lovely when lit by the setting sun or by moonlight.

Sights to See

★ ☺ **Desert Botanical Garden.** Opened in 1939 to conserve and showcase the ecology of the desert, these 150 acres contain more than 4,000 different species of cacti, succulents, trees, and flowers. A stroll along the ½-mi-long "Plants and People of the Sonoran Desert" trail is a fascinating lesson in the many adaptations that plants, animals, and people have made to desert living; children will enjoy playing the self-guiding game "Desert Detective." ⊠ *1201 N. Galvin Pkwy.,* ☎ *602/941–1217 or 602/941–1225.* ☞ *$7.* ⊙ *Oct.–Apr., daily 8–8; May–Sept., daily 7 AM–10 PM.*

⟁ **Hall of Flame.** Retired firefighters lead tours through more than 100 restored fire engines and tell harrowing tales of the "world's most dangerous profession." Kids can climb on a 1916 engine, operate alarm systems, and learn lessons of fire safety from the pros. More than 3,000 helmets, badges, and other fire-fighting-related articles are on display, dating from as far back as 1725. ⊠ *6101 E. Van Buren St.,* ☎ *602/ 275–3473.* ☞ *$4.* ⊙ *Mon.–Sat. 9–5, Sun. 12–4; tours at 2.*

Papago Park. A blend of hilly desert terrain, streams, and lagoons, this park has picnic ramadas, a frisbee-golf course, a playground, hiking and biking trails, and even largemouth bass and trout fishing (urban fishing license required for anglers age 15 and over—pick one up at sporting-goods or Circle-K stores). The hike up to landmark **Hole-in-the-Rock** is popular—but remember that it's much easier to climb up to the hole than to get down. **Governor Hunt's Tomb,** the white pyramid at the top of ramada 16, commemorates the former Arizona leader and provides a lovely view. ⊠ *625 N. Galvin Pkwy.,* ☎ *602/256–3220.* ⊙ *Daily 6 AM–midnight.*

⟁ **Phoenix Zoo.** Five designated trails wind through this 125-acre zoo, which has replicas of such habitats as an African savanna and a tropical rain forest. Meerkats, warthogs, desert bighorn sheep, and endangered Arabian oryx are among the unusual sights, as is Ruby the Asian elephant, who puts brush to canvas to rival the best of abstract impressionists. In 1997 the zoo opened yet another habitat—the Forest of Uco, home to the endangered spectacled bear from South America's high-mountain rain forests. The Children's Trail introduces young visitors to small mammals from throughout the world, and a stop at the big red barn provides a chance to help groom goats and sheep. The 30-minute narrated tour on the safari train costs $2 and provides a good overview of the park. In December, the popular "Zoo Lights" exhibit transforms the area into an enchanted forest of more than 600,000 twinkling lights, many in the shape of the zoo's residents. ⊠ *455 N. Galvin Pkwy.,* ☎ *602/273–7771.* ☞ *$8.50.* ⊙ *Daily 9–5; call for special summer hrs May–Labor Day.*

Pueblo Grande Museum and Cultural Park. Phoenix's only national landmark, this park was once the site of a 500-acre Hohokam village. In 1929, the city hired archaeologists to begin excavations of the dusty mounds here, discovering that this large community—the size of a football field and supporting about 1,000 people—contained homes, storage rooms, cemeteries, and several ball courts; the Pueblo Grande was also a primary village at the headgate of canals serving dozens of smaller sites for over 20 mi to the north and west. The small museum has a wall map of the elaborate Hohokam canal system, and houses the site's uncovered relics, including the signature red-on-buff Hohokam pottery. Catch the 10-minute orientation video in the Gallery Theatre Site. ⊠ *4619 E. Washington St.,* ☎ *602/495–0901.* ☞ *$2; free Sun.* ⊙ *Mon.–Sat. 9–4:45, Sun. 1–4:45.*

Scottsdale

Historic sites, nationally known art galleries, and lots of boutiques fill downtown Scottsdale; a quick walking tour can easily turn into an all-day excursion if you browse. Historic Old Town Scottsdale features the look of the Old West, while fashionable 5th Avenue is known for shopping and a concentration of Native American jewelry and crafts stores. Cross onto Main Street and enter a world frequented by the international art set (Scottsdale has the third-largest artist community in the U.S.); discover more galleries and interior-design shops along Marshall Way and Craftsman Court. The walk that follows is an overview of the area; the Shopping section, *below,* has specific recommendations.

A Good Walk

Park in the free public lot on the corner of 2nd Street and Wells Fargo Avenue, east of Scottsdale Road. A portion of the garage is signed for a three-hour limit; go to upper levels that don't carry time restrictions, as enforcement is strict.

Start your walk by exiting the parking structure from its northeast corner, where a short brick-paved sidewalk leads northward to the sculpture- and fountain-filled plaza of Scottsdale Mall. You'll immediately come upon the **Scottsdale Center for the Arts** ⑬. Stroll counterclockwise around the Mall's lovely grounds, passing Scottsdale's library and municipal buildings, and ending up on the plaza's west side by the **Scottsdale Chamber of Commerce** ⑭ and **Scottsdale Historical Museum** ⑮. Continue west to the intersection of Brown Avenue and Main Street to reach the heart of **Old Town Scottsdale** ⑯, occupying four square blocks from Brown Avenue to Scottsdale Road, between Indian School Road and 2nd Street. From Main Street in Old Town, cross Scottsdale Road to the central drag of the **Main Street Arts District** ⑰. Turn north onto Goldwater Boulevard and gallery-stroll for another two blocks. At Indian School Road, head one block east to the **Marshall Way Arts District** ⑱. Continue two blocks north on Marshall Way to the fountain of prancing Arabian horses that marks **Fifth Avenue** ⑲. You can catch the trolley back to Scottsdale Mall here, on the south side of the intersection of 5th Avenue and Stetson Drive, or walk the five blocks south on Scottsdale Road and one block east on Main Street.

Short drives north from downtown Scottsdale are two other worthy attractions: the **Buffalo Museum** and Frank Lloyd Wright's winter home, **Taliesin West.** You may want to check them out prior to your visit to Old Town or tack them on to the end of a day trip.

TIMING

Plan to spend a full day in Scottsdale, as there's a lot to take in between the countless galleries and shops. Although your tour can easily be completed on foot, a trolley runs through the downtown area: Ollie the Trolley tours all of Scottsdale and charges $4 for an all-day pass during high season, $2 during summer months (☎ 602/970–8130 for information). Also look for horse-drawn Wagonmasters (☎ 602/423–1449), providing romantic transportation throughout Old Town Scottsdale, as well as props for souvenir snapshots.

The best option, if you're interested in touring the galleries, is to visit on a Thursday and do the Scottsdale **Art Walk** (☎ 602/990–3939), held from 7 to 9 PM each Thursday year-round (except Thanksgiving). Main Street takes on a party atmosphere during the evening hours when everyone is browsing, as do nearby Marshall Way and Fifth Avenue.

Sights to See

OFF THE
BEATEN PATH

BUFFALO MUSEUM OF AMERICA – Tucked away in a Scottsdale shopping plaza, this eclectic little museum pays homage to the American bison—commonly referred to as the buffalo—and its important role in American history. The museum's contents range from the awesome shaggy beast itself—courtesy of modern taxidermy—to a variety of original commis-

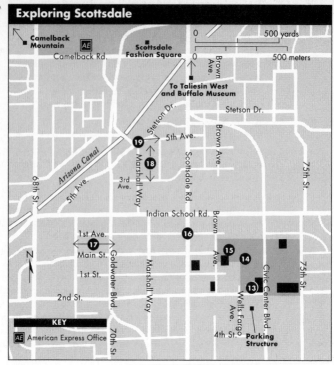

Exploring Scottsdale

sioned works of fine art, to props from the film "Dances with Wolves." The "Buffalo Bill Room" showcases the legendary hunter's personal possessions, including his Sharps rifle; a life-size, hand-carved wood statue of Buffalo Bill is also on site, as are impressive renditions of Billy the Kid, Jesse James, and Daniel Boone. The downstairs gift shop is a mélange of all things buffalo—collectibles for sale include clocks, banks, tins, plates, old stereoscope cards, even a promotional poster from Hunter S. Thompson's novel "Where The Buffalo Roam." ⊠ *10261 N. Scottsdale Rd.,* ☎ *602/951-1022.* ⊡ *$3.* ⊙ *Mon.–Fri. 9–5.*

⑲ **Fifth Avenue.** For more than 40 years, this shopping stretch has been home to a fashionable collection of boutiques and specialty shops. Whether you're seeking fine art or handmade Native American arts and crafts, casual clothing or cacti, you'll find it here—plus colorful storefronts, friendly merchants, even an old "cigar store" Indian. After a full day of paintings, turquoise jewelry, and knickknacks, children especially may enjoy casting their eyes upon the six-story monster screen of the **IMAX Theater** (⊠ 4343 N. Scottsdale Rd., ☎ 602/945–4629), at the east end of the avenue. ⊠ *5th Ave. between Goldwater Blvd. and Scottsdale Rd.*

NEED A
BREAK?

The busy, little fresco-walled **Pickniken Restaurant** (E 7117 E. 6th Ave., at Stetson Dr., ☎ 602/949–1615 or 602/970–3661) serves up snacks and sandwiches—try a Caesar salad sandwich on homemade bread. They'll also gladly pack up a picnic to be enjoyed elsewhere.

★ ⑰ **Main Street Arts District.** Gallery after gallery on Main Street and First Avenue, particularly on the blocks between Scottsdale Road and 69th Street, displays artwork of myriad styles—contemporary, western realism, Native American, and traditional. Several antiques shops are also here; specialties include elegant porcelains and china, fine antique jewelry, and Oriental rugs. With very few exceptions, casual visitors are welcome to browse and ogle.

NEED A
BREAK? For a cool drink or light meal during daytime gallery-hopping, try **Arcadia Farms** (E 7014 E. 1st Ave., ☎ 602/941-5665), where such eclectic sandwiches as rosemary-seasoned focaccia with chicken, roasted eggplant, and feta cheese are brought out to diners on a tree-shaded patio. This spot can get crowded at lunchtime, so call ahead for a reservation.

⑱ Marshall Way Arts District. Another niche of galleries, concerned predominantly with contemporary art, lines the blocks of Marshall Way north of Indian School Road. Upscale gift and jewelry stores can be found here too. Farther north on Marshall Way across 3rd Avenue, the street is filled with more art galleries and creative stores with a southwestern flair.

⑯ Old Town Scottsdale. Billed as "the West's Most Western Town," this area of Scottsdale features rustic storefronts and wooden sidewalks; it's touristy, but it also gives visitors a genuine taste of life here 80 years ago. Many stores carry kitschy souvenirs, but you'll also find high-quality jewelry, pots, and Mexican imports.

NEED A
BREAK? The southeast corner of 1st Avenue and Scottsdale Road marks a landmark of sorts: the pink-and-white **Sugar Bowl Ice Cream Parlor** (E 4005 N. Scottsdale Rd., ☎ 602/946-0051), run by the Huntress family since 1958 and frequented by Paradise Valley cartoonist Bil Keane (his "Family Circus" works with references to the parlor are featured in the menu). Sandwiches and salads are served in addition to gooey sundaes and parfaits.

⑬ Scottsdale Center for the Arts. Galleries within this cultural and entertainment complex rotate exhibits frequently, with an emphasis on contemporary art and artists. The airy and bright **Museum Store** (☎ 602/874-4644) has a great collection of unusual jewelry, as well as stationery, posters, and art books. ⊠ 7380 E. 2nd St., ☎ 602/994-2787. 🎫 Free. ☾ Mon.–Sat. 10–5, Thurs. 10–8, Sun. 12–5.

⑭ Scottsdale Chamber of Commerce. Pop inside to pick from local maps, guidebooks, and brochures in abundance. Ask for a walking-tour map of Old Town Scottsdale's historic sites, which the helpful staff will be pleased to provide. ⊠ 7343 Scottsdale Mall, ☎ 602/945-8481 or 800/877-1117. ☾ Weekdays 8:30–6:30, Sat. 10–5, Sun. 11–5.

⑮ Scottsdale Historical Museum. Scottsdale's first schoolhouse, this redbrick building houses a version of the 1910 schoolroom, as well as photographs, original furniture from the city's founding fathers, and displays of other treasures from Scottsdale's early days. ⊠ 7333 Scottsdale Mall, ☎ 602/945-4499. 🎫 Free. ☾ Wed.–Sat. 10–5, Sun. noon–4. Closed July–Aug. and holidays.

OFF THE
BEATEN PATH **TALIESIN WEST** – Ten years after visiting Arizona in 1927 to consult on designs for the Biltmore hotel, architect Frank Lloyd Wright chose 600 acres of raw, rugged Sonoran Desert at the foothills of the McDowell Mountains, just outside Scottsdale, as the site for his permanent winter residence. Wright and apprentices proceeded to construct a "desert camp" here, using "organic architecture"—designed to integrate the buildings with their surroundings and respect the natural setting of the land. An ingenious harmony of indoor and outdoor space is the result; in addition to the living quarters, drafting studio, and small apartments of the Apprentice Court, Taliesin West also has two theaters, a music

pavilion, and the "Sun Trap"—a charming structure of sleeping spaces surrounding an open patio and fireplace. Two guided tours cover different parts of the interior, and a guided "Desert Walk" winds through the petroglyphs and landscape from which Wright drew his vision, as well as the experimental desert residences designed by his apprentices. Tour times vary, so call ahead; all visitors must be accompanied by a guide. ✉ *12621 Frank Lloyd Wright Blvd.,* ☎ *602/860–8810 or 602/860–2700.* 🎫 *Guided tour (1 hr) $10 winter, $8 summer; Behind the Scenes tour (3 hrs) $25 winter, $20 summer; Desert Walk tour (90 mins) $12.* ☉ *Daily 8:30–5:30, winter; 7:30–4:30, summer.*

Tempe

Charles Trumbell Hayden arrived on the east end of the Salt River in the 1860s. There he built a flour mill and began a ferry service to cross the then-flowing Rio Salado, founding the town then known as Hayden's Ferry in 1871. Other settlers soon arrived, including an Englishman who felt—upon approaching the town from Phoenix and seeing the butte, river, and fields of green mesquite—that the name should be changed to Tempe after the Vale of Tempe in Greek mythology. Hayden took umbrage at the suggested name change but finally relented in 1879.

Today Tempe is Arizona's sixth-largest city and the home of Arizona State University's main campus and a thriving student population. A 20- to 30-minute drive from Phoenix, the tree- and brick-lined Mill Avenue (on which Hayden's mill still stands) is the main drag, rife with student-oriented hangouts, bookstores, boutiques, eateries, and a repertory movie house.

Tempe's banks of the now-dry Rio Salado are the future site of a sprawling commercial and entertainment district, which includes plans to refill the river—inflatable dams are the brainchild—and ply the waters once again with ferry service.

A Good Walk

Parking is available in the public structure just north of University Drive between Ash and Mill avenues. From **La Casa Vieja,** on the southwest corner of Mill Avenue and 1st Street, cross 1st Street and enjoy your stroll through the sculpture garden en route to **Tempe Arts Center.** Stroll north 50 ft toward the Rio Salado and out onto the old Mill Avenue bridge (the new bridge is to the east of the old one), where you can check out the Arts Center's rooftop artwork. Turn around and head south on Mill Avenue, passing the old Hayden flour mill, as well as "A" Mountain (on which spirited ASU students have painted the state's initial) to your left. Continue south along shop-lined Mill Avenue until you reach 5th Street; walk a block east on 5th toward the inverted pyramid of **Tempe City Hall.** Follow the pathway west, through the Plazita de Descanso, to continue browsing on Mill Avenue. Another two blocks south on Mill, crossing through University Drive and then proceeding the longer block south toward Apache Boulevard, will take you to the Grady Gammage Auditorium and ASU art museums and galleries on the southwest corner of the **Arizona State University** campus. At this point you can walk back up Mill Avenue, catch the free FLASH shuttle northward (it stops on the north corner of Gammage Pkwy. and Mill Ave.), or wind your way northward through the university campus up toward San Devil Stadium. Definitely also tour the **Mystery Castle,** a curious sight well worth the short drive from downtown Tempe.

TIMING

If you're planning to shop as well as tour the campus and museums, allow four or five hours for exploring (and taking periodic breaks) in downtown Tempe. Allow 1½–2 hours on either end of your agenda for a tour through the Mystery Castle.

Sights to See

Arizona State University. What was formerly the Tempe Normal School for Teachers—in 1886, a four-room redbrick building and 20-acre cow pasture—is now the sprawling 750-acre campus of ASU, home to the largest student population in the Southwest. Stop by the **ASU Visitor Information Center** (✉ 826 E. Apache Blvd., at Rural Rd., ☎ 602/965–0100) for a copy of a self-guided walking tour. You'll wind past public art and innovative architecture—including a music building that bears a strong resemblance to a wedding cake (designed by Taliesin students to complement Wright's Gammage Auditorium) and a law library shaped like an open book—and end up at the 74,000-seat **ASU Sun Devil Stadium,** home to the school's Sun Devils, headquarters for the NFL's Arizona Cardinals, and the site of 1996's Super Bowl XXX.

Heralded for its superior acoustics, the circular **Grady Gammage Auditorium** (✉ Mill Ave. at Apache Blvd., ☎ 602/965–4050) was the last public structure completed by architect Frank Lloyd Wright, who detached the rear wall from grand tier and balcony sections in an effort to surround every patron with sound. The stage is large enough to accommodate a full symphony orchestra, as well as the Gammage's 2,909-pipe organ. The Gammage displays art exhibits throughout the lobby and in two on-site galleries. During the school year, free half-hour tours are offered weekdays 1–3:30 PM.

While touring the west end of the campus, stop into the gray-purple stucco **Nelson Fine Arts Center** (☎ 602/965–2787), just north of the Gammage Auditorium. The center's museum houses some fine examples of 19th- and 20th-century painting and sculpture, contemporary art, and American crafts, as well as an American and European print collection. ☉ *Tues. 10–9, Wed.–Sat. 10–5, Sun. 1–5.*

A short walk east, just north of the Hayden Library, ASU's experimental gallery and collection of crockery and ceramics are located in the **Matthews Center** (☎ 602/965–2875). ☉ *Wed.–Sat. 10–5, Sun. 1–5. Call for summer hrs.*

In Matthews Hall, the **Northlight Gallery** (☎ 602/965–6517) exhibits works by both renowned and emerging photographers. Admission to all ASU museums is free. ☉ *Mon.–Thurs. 10:30–4:30, Sun. noon–4:30.*

OFF THE BEATEN PATH	**MYSTERY CASTLE** – At the foot of South Mountain lies a curious dwelling hand-built from desert rocks, railroad refuse, and anything else its builder, Boyce Gulley, could get his hands on. The castle is still a private home; Boyce's daughter Mary Lou, for whom the castle was built, lives here and leads every tour. Chock-full of oddities that will fascinate everyone in the family, the castle has 18 rooms with 13 fireplaces, 90 bottle-glass portholes, a downstairs grotto, floating cantilever stairway, and a roll-away bed with a mining railcar as its frame. Be sure to ask how Bing Crosby's golf club became embedded in the ceiling. ✉ 800 E. Mineral Rd., at the end of S. 7th St., ☎ 602/268–1581. ☜ $4. ☉ Tues.–Sun. 11–4.

La Casa Vieja. In 1871, when Tempe was still known as Hayden's Ferry, this "old house" was built as the port for founding father Charles Hayden's ferry across the Salt River. Built of native adobe, the hacienda is modeled after Spanish mansions and was the town's first building. The late Carl Hayden, former U.S. senator from Arizona, was born here. Now a steak house, the structure retains its original dimensions; the lobby and dining rooms contain historical documents and photographic mementos pertaining to the frontier history of the hamlet of Tempe. ⊠ *3 W. 1st St.,* ☎ *602/967–7594.* ⊙ *Sun.–Thurs. 11–11, Fri.– Sat. 11 AM–midnight.*

Tempe City Hall. Local architects Rolf Osland and Michael Goodwin constructed this inverted pyramid not just to win awards for its innovative design (which they have) but also to shield city workers from the desert sun. The pyramid is constructed mainly of bronzed glass and stainless steel; the point is conceptually buried in a sunken courtyard lushly landscaped with jacaranda, ivy, and flowers, out of which the pyramid widens to the sky. Stand underneath and gaze upward to experience a weird sensation akin to the fish's-eye view of a glass-bottomed boat. ⊠ *31 E. 5th St., 1 block east of Mill Ave.,* ☎ *602/ 967–2001.* ☞ *Free.*

NEED A BREAK?	The outdoor patio of the **Coffee Plantation** (E 680 S. Mill Ave., ☎ 602/ 829-7878) is the site of a lively social scene—students cramming, local residents chatting over a cup of joe, and poets and musicians presenting their latest masterpieces. The lively Centerpoint plaza, a block west of Mill Avenue between 6th and 7th streets, has great spots to enjoy your cappuccino or a snack—relax fountainside surrounded by the giant bronze bunny statues, or take a seat on the plaza's scattered concrete rhomboids that resemble cubes of tofu in a strong wind.

Tempe Arts Center. A small indoor gallery and an eclectic outdoor sculpture garden feature works by local, state, and national artists. From the old Mill Avenue bridge, the roof's anamorphic image of Mona Zona, a sunglasses-clad Mona Lisa, comes into focus. ⊠ *Northwest corner of Mill Ave. and 1st St.,* ☎ *602/968–0888.* ☞ *$2 donation requested.* ⊙ *Tues.–Sun. noon–5.*

DINING

By Howard Seftel

Once a sleepy backwater, the ever-growing Phoenix and its surrounding environs draw millions of visitors every year: tourists, conventioneers, and winter snowbirds who roost for months at a time. The population boom has been matched by an astonishing restaurant renaissance. Not only have inventive local chefs turned southwestern cuisine into one of the country's hottest culinary rages, but members of the area's new ethnic communities—Persians, Ethiopians, Salvadorans, Vietnamese—have brought their foods with them. Authentic Thai, Chinese, and Indian restaurants are thriving. Naturally, you get can also get superb south-of-the-border dishes from every region of Mexico here, whether it be the Yucatan or Baja. Well-heeled travelers with sophisticated tastes will be thrilled with Phoenix's gastronomic offerings. In fact, some of the city's restaurants rank among the country's best.

Restaurants are remarkably casual. Except for a handful of high-end spots, slacks and sports shirt are dressy enough for men; pants or a simple skirt are appropriate for women.

Remember that restaurants change hours, locations, chefs, prices, and menus more frequently than Imelda Marcos changes shoes; they can also close down with breathtaking suddenness. Before you go out to eat, do the smart thing: Call. Show up without notice during tourist season, and you may find the fast-food, drive-through window the only place in town without a two-hour wait. All listed restaurants serve dinner and are open for lunch unless otherwise specified.

CATEGORY	COST*
$$$$	over $35
$$$	$25–$35
$$	$15–$25
$	under $15

per person for a three-course dinner, excluding drinks, service, and sales tax (6%–7%)

Scottsdale

American

$$$–$$$$
★
✕ **Rancho Pinot Grill.** The attention to quality paid by the husband-and-wife proprietors here—he manages, she cooks—has made this one of the town's top eating spots. The inventive menu changes daily, depending on what's fresh. If you're lucky, you might come on a day when the kitchen features *posole,* a mouthwatering broth with hominy, salt pork, and cabbage. Creative entrées include quail with soba noodles, rosemary-infused chicken with Italian sausage, and grilled sea bass atop basmati rice. ⊠ *6208 North Scottsdale Rd.,* ☏ *602/468-9463. Reservations essential. AE, D, MC, V. Closed Sun. and Mon. and mid-Aug.–mid-Sept. No lunch.*

$$$
✕ **Don & Charlie's.** A favorite with major-leaguers in town for spring training, this venerable chophouse specializes in prime-grade steak and baseball memorabilia—nearly every square inch of the walls is covered with pictures, autographs, and uniforms. But once the food arrives, even sports nuts ignore the decor. The New York sirloin, prime rib, and double-thick lamb chops are everything you could hope for; sides include au gratin potatoes and creamed spinach. Serious carnivores can confidently step up to the plate here; it's impossible to strike out. ⊠ *7501 E. Camelback Rd.,* ☏ *602/990-0900. AE, D, DC, MC, V. No lunch.*

$$$
✕ **Gregory's Grill.** This charming bistro is tiny, with seating for maybe 20 patrons. The menu is equally small, but outstanding. Look for appetizers like duck prosciutto, salmon seviche, and a lovely tower fashioned from veggies and goat cheese. Entrées include beer-marinated beef tenderloin, apple-crusted salmon, and grilled pork chops with quinoa risotto. Be sure to note: You can save a bundle by bringing your own beer or wine. ⊠ *7049 E. McDowell Rd. (Papago Plaza shopping center),* ☏ *602/946-8700. AE, D, MC, V. Closed Sun. No lunch.*

$–$$
✕ **Bandera.** If you're looking for a quick, tasty dinner before a night out on the town, try this casual, high-volume spot. The menu changes weekly, but you can always count on the wonderfully moist and meaty rotisserie chicken; you'll see the birds spinning in the big window before you even walk through the door. If you're not a poultry fan, salads, fresh fish, prime rib, and meat loaf usually make it on the menu; the mashed potatoes are divine—you'll think Mom is in the kitchen peeling spuds. If you get here at prime eating hours, especially on weekends, be prepared to wait for a table. ⊠ *3821 N. Scottsdale Rd.,* ☏ *602/994-3524. Reservations not accepted. AE, MC, V. No lunch.*

$–$$
✕ **Pinnacle Peak Patio.** This spot is strictly for tourists. Over 1,600 diners can sit down to eat at one time at this western restaurant, the largest in the world; another 1,400 can dine under the stars out on the patio. Founded in 1957, the Peak hasn't altered its menu in the last 15 years—a menu that consists solely of five grilled steaks and hickory-roasted chicken. "Big Marv" Dickson has personally manned the grill since 1961, cooking up over 2 million pounds of beef himself—he credits its delectable porterhouse and T-bones to mesquite smoke's magic, but everyone else knows Marv as a Steak Jedi, with a sixth sense for beef. Live country bands play nightly. Wear a tie you don't mind leaving be-

Al Amir, **16**
Altos, **23**
Arizona Kitchen, **35**
Avanti, **54**
Bandera, **49**
Big Wong, **36**
Blue Burrito Grille, **27**
Brio, **45**
C-Fu Gourmet, **70**
Cafe Patou, **13**
Cafe Terra Cotta, **19**
Carlsbad Tavern, **48**
Centro Cafe & Bakery, **1**
Chaparral Restaurant, **22**
China Village, **7**
Chompie's Deli, **3**
Christopher's Bistro, **28**
Christopher's, **28**
Citrus Cafe, **71**
Coup des Tartes, **39**
Don & Charlie's, **46**
Eddie's Grill, **37**
El Bravo, **9**
El Chorro Lodge, **21**
Eliana's Restaurant, **55**
Euro Cafe, **66**
Franco's Trattoria, **15**
Golden Swan, **14**
Gourmet House of
Hong Kong, **57**
Greekfest, **29**
Gregory's Grill, **52**
Havana Patio Cafe, **4**
Honey Bear's BBQ, **53**
House of Tricks, **64**
L'Ecole, **47**
La Hacienda, **5**
La Fontanella, **42**
Lalibela, **33**
Las Cazuelas, **34**
Lily's Cafe, **32**
Lon's at the Hermosa, **25**
Los Dos Molinos, **62**
Malee's on Main, **51**
Marco Polo Supper
Club, **17**
Maria's When in
Naples, **12**
Marquesa, **5**
Mary Elaine's, **43**
Mrs. White's Golden
Rule Cafe, **58**
Oregano's, **50**
Original Pancake
House, **44**
Oyster Grill, **60**
Pho Bang, **8**
Pinnacle Peak Patio, **6**
Pinon Grill, **18**
Pizzeria Bianco, **59**
Rancho Pinot Grill, **20**
Razz's Restaurant and
Bar, **11**
Richardson's , **31**
Rosa's Mexican Grill, **67**

Phoenix Dining

32nd St.

Bell Rd.

Greenway

Lookout
Mountain
Preserve

Thunderbird Rd.

Cactus Rd.

Peoria   Rd.

Dunlap Ave.

Black Canyon Fwy.

43rd Ave.

35th Ave.

7th Ave.

Central Ave.

7th St.

Squaw Park
Recreational
Area

PARAD
VALL

Glendale Ave.

Bethany Home Rd.

19th Ave.

Grand Ave.

Indian School Rd.

Squaw Peak Pkwy.

32nd St.

Camel

Papago Fwy.

McDowell Rd.

7th St.

16th St.

Red Mountain

Van Buren   St.

Buckeye Rd.

Sky Harbor
International
Airport

Lower Buckeye Rd.

19th Ave.

Salt River

Southern Ave.

Baseline Rd.

Dobbins Rd.

South
Mountain
Park

hind. ✉ *10426 E. Jomax Rd., Scottsdale,* ☎ *602/967–8082. AE, D, DC, MC, V. No lunch Mon–Sat.*

Asian

$$–$$$ ✕ **Sushi on Shea.** You may be in the middle of the desert, but Sushi on Shea's briny, fresh aquatic fare will make you think you're on the ocean's edge. Yellowtail, toro, shrimp, scallops, freshwater eel, and even monkfish liver pâté are among the long list of delights here. Check out the *nabemono* (hot pot or meals-in-a-bowl) prepared at your table. The best dish? Maybe it's the *una-ju* (broiled freshwater eel with a sublime smoky scent), served over sweet rice. The fact that some people believe eel is an aphrodisiac only adds to its charms. ✉ *7000 E. Shea Blvd.,* ☎ *602/483–7799. AE, D, DC, MC, V. No lunch Sun.*

$$ ✕ **Malee's on Main.** This fashionable eatery serves up sophisticated, Thai-inspired fare. Especially recommended is *Ahoi Phannee,* a medley of seafood in a bamboo-leaf bowl moistened with red curry sauce redolent of coconut, lime leaf, and Thai basil. The Thai barbecued chicken, grilled to a sizzle and coated with rum, is outstanding. Beware: Take Malee's heat levels seriously—even the "mild" dishes have a bite. ✉ *7131 E. Main,* ☎ *602/947–6042. AE, DC, MC, V. No lunch Sun.*

Breakfast and Brunch

$$$ ✕ **Golden Swan.** This desert oasis is a great place for a leisurely Sunday champagne brunch. Sit outside under canvas umbrellas or in a covered pavilion that juts into a koi-filled lagoon with palms and hibiscus bushes lining its banks. The Golden Swan has a unique brunch shtick: Everything except dessert is laid out in the kitchen under the watchful eyes of toque-clad chefs. Try the veal tortellini in lobster sauce, giant prawns, or filet mignon. ✉ *7500 E. Doubletree Ranch Rd. (Hyatt Regency at Gainey Ranch),* ☎ *602/991–3388. Reservations essential. AE, D, DC, MC, V.*

$ ✕ **Original Pancake House.** This breakfast landmark does one thing, and does it extremely well—pancakes. These flapjacks inspire worship from local admirers, who wait patiently for a table on weekends. Chief among the griddled glories is the signature apple pancake: Homemade batter is poured over sautéed apples and partially baked. Then the concoction is flipped over, glazed with cinnamon sugar, and baked some more. It's creamy, sweet, bubbly . . . and huge. Other varieties, like the German pancake, are also exceptional. ✉ *6840 E. Camelback Rd.,* ☎ *602/946–4902. Reservations not accepted. No credit cards.*

French

$$$ ✕ **Cafe Patou.** The hearty French cuisine here is prepared with flair and skill. Appetizers range from the rustic charcuterie platter—duck pâté, prosciutto, sausage, cheese, olives, and cornichons—to the scallops and baked semolina in balsamic vinegar sauce. Vigorous appetites will appreciate entrées like the venison Stroganoff, filet mignon served pot-au-feu style, and pork tenderloin stuffed with shrimp and covered with lobster sauce. If you prefer something simpler (and cheaper), try the superb crepes or the flat breads gilded with toppings like escargots, roasted vegetables, or olives and anchovies. ✉ *7000 E. Shea Blvd.,* ☎ *602/951–6868. AE, D, DC, MC, V.*

International

$$$ ✕ **Marco Polo Supper Club.** Named after the 13th-century Italian adventurer, Marco Polo specializes in "East meets West" cuisine. While the poet insists that "East is East and West is West, and never the twain shall meet," Marco Polo proves not only can they meet, they can develop a healthy relationship. Some of the unique dishes: filet mignon broccoli steak, a smashing combination of prime beef, broccoli, and mushrooms stir-fried in a hoisin oyster sauce; Hong Kong chicken, breast of chicken stuffed with cheese, shrimp, bean sprouts, and spinach over noodles; and lobster and shrimp pasta with thick Asian noodles in a spicy marinara sauce. The setting is just as sophisticated as the fare with lots of polished brass and Frank Sinatra music playing softly in the background. ⊠ 8608 E. Shea Blvd., ☎ 602/483–1900. AE, DC, MC, V. No lunch.

$$$ ✕ **Razz's Restaurant and Bar.** There's no telling what part of the globe chef-proprietor Erasmo "Razz" Kamnitzer will use for culinary inspiration. However, you can count on his creations to give dormant taste buds a wake-up call: Black bean paella is a twist on a Spanish theme; South American bouillabaisse is a fragrant fish stew, stocked with veggies; and *bah mie goreng* teams noodles with fish, meat, and vegetables, perked up with dried cranberries and almonds. ⊠ 10321 N. Scottsdale Rd., ☎ 602/905–1308. AE, DC, MC, V. Closed Sun. and Mon. No lunch.

$$ ✕ **L'Ecole.** Not too many folks would entrust their teeth to a student dentist, but you'll have no regrets putting yourself in the talented hands of the student-chefs at the Valley's premier cooking academy. You get a three-course dinner for about $20, a real bargain. Look for inventive appetizers like ginger soy gravlax, and main dishes like fillet Rossini. Since the students also pull server duty, you can count on being pampered, too. ⊠ 8100 E. Camelback Rd. (Scottsdale Culinary Institute), ☎ 602/990–7639. Reservations essential. D, MC, V. Closed weekends.

Italian

$$$ ✕ **Franco's Trattoria.** The Florence-born Franco puts together meals
★ that sing with the flavors of Tuscany. Start with focaccia and hunks of imported Italian cheeses sliced off huge wheels. Next, sample the antipasto or the tasty risotto. Main dishes are hearty and vibrant; naturally, veal is a specialty. One example is the *orecchie d'elefante* (so named because it seems as massive as an elephant's ear), which is veal pounded to millimeter thinness, breaded, fried, and splayed across the plate, coated with tomatoes and shallots, basil, and lemon. ⊠ 8120 N. Hayden Rd., ☎ 602/948–6655. AE, MC, V. Closed Sun. and July. No lunch.

$$–$$$ ✕ **Maria's When in Naples.** In a town teeming with Italian restaurants, this is a standout. The antipasto spread laid out just inside the entrance is sure to grab your attention, and it tastes as good as it looks. The homemade pasta is another winner. Check out the *salsiccia Pugliese* (fettuccine robustly topped with homemade sausage, leeks, porcini mushrooms, and white wine sauce), or the *orecchiette Barese* (ear-shape pasta tossed with cauliflower, pancetta, sun-dried tomato, olive oil, and cheese). ⊠ 7000 E. Shea Blvd., ☎ 602/991–6887. AE, D, DC, MC, V. No lunch weekends.

$ ✕ **Oregano's.** This happening, jam-packed pizza-pasta-sandwich parlor lures customers with two irresistible come-ons: good food and low prices. Oregano's offers two types of Chicago pizza: the stuffed, deep-dish kind and the thin-crust model. Both are great. So are the untraditional lasagnas, in particular, the artichoke lasagna, made with whole wheat pasta (it's worth the 30-minute wait). Sandwich fans will appreciate the baked Italian hoagie, stuffed with lots of pepperoni, capicolla, salami, and provolone, then loaded with tomatoes, onions, peppers, and olives. ⊠ *3622 N. Scottsdale Rd.,* ☎ *602/970–1860. Reservations not accepted. AE, D, MC, V.*

Mexican

$$$ ✕ **La Hacienda.** The food here is nothing like the run-from-the-border
★   fare you find at neighborhood taco stands—it's more like the food of Mexico's colonial grandee. The appetizers, such as a mushroom crepe enlivened with *huitlacoche* (a fungus of almost trufflelike intensity), are stunning. The entrées are heavy with seafood: huge, grilled Gulf shrimp; red snapper in a Veracruzana sauce; lightly seared ahi tuna, encrusted with potatoes. *Cochinillo asado* is La Hacienda's signature dish—roast suckling pig, wheeled up to the table and carved to order. Finish with *cajeta* ice-cream crepes or the mesmerizing pumpkin-chocolate cheesecake. ⊠ *7575 E. Princess Dr. (Scottsdale Princess resort),* ☎ *602/585–4848. AE, D, DC, MC, V. No lunch.*

$–$$ ✕ **Carlsbad Tavern.** This is Mexican food served New Mexican style, which means dishes flavored with lots of hot-chili bite. Get yourself a potent frozen margarita (Carlsbad Tavern has a nice selection of premium tequilas) and wash down starters like red chili potato pancakes and ravioli stuffed with smoked duck and tequila-marinated grilled shrimp. Entrées continue the flavor assault: *Cane adovada* is pork simmered in red chili sauce; the *machaca* tamale duo features two shredded beef tamales, one in green chili sauce, the other coated with spicy red chili. Lamb fans won't want to pass up lamb pierna, a wood-grilled, braised leg of lamb topped with a spoon-licking red wine sauce. ⊠ *3315 North Hayden Rd.,* ☎ *602/970–8156. Reservations not accepted. AE, D, DC, MC, V.*

Middle Eastern

$–$$ ✕ **Al Amir.** Get ready for a genuine taste of the Middle East. Appetizers are a key part of the Middle Eastern dining experience, and Al Amir gives them the respect they deserve. Along with traditional favorites like *baba ghanoush* (mashed eggplant), hummus, falafel, and tabbouleh, this spot serves *ma'anek,* juicy Lebanese sausages zinged with cloves; *safiha,* canape-size pockets of dough stuffed with ground lamb; and *moujadara,* mashed green lentils topped with fried onions. Main dishes feature kabobs, but it pays to explore the less familiar options. The *kebbe bil sanyeh* is sensational with layers of heavily seasoned ground beef baked with bulgur wheat and pine nuts. Don't leave without ordering *knafeh,* a warm cheese pastry smothered in syrup. ⊠ *8989 E. Via Linda,* ☎ *602/661–1137. AE, D, MC, V. Closed Sun.*

Southwestern

$$$–$$$$ ✕ **Pinon Grill.** Delicious southwestern fare is served up in a rustic, woodsy atmosphere. Try not to fill up on the green chili corn bread that greets you when you're seated. You'll need to save room for regional dishes that are bursting with flavors. Every restaurant in town serves grilled ahi tuna, but no one else fires it up with a dreamy red jalapeño basil sauce and cools it down with a melon salsa like this place does. At dessert time, either the rich chocolate taco or intense chocolate pâté ends the meal on a high note. ⊠ *7401 N. Scottsdale Rd. (Inn at Regal McCormick Ranch),* ☎ *602/948–5050. AE, D, DC, MC, V.*

$$$ ✕ **Cafe Terra Cotta.** This Scottsdale branch of the acclaimed Tucson
★   original shows you how the Southwest was won. The kitchen is at the top of its form: inventive creations and sophisticated flavors do the region proud. It's easy to put a meal together. Start off with buffalo carpac-

cio drizzled with chili-infused oil or a quesadilla filled with duck and smoked Gouda cheese. Next, move to lamb chops in an ancho-chili mole or salmon crusted with sunflower seeds and yellow chili sauce. Desserts are just as formidable, especially the orange-curd tart. ✉ *6166 N. Scottsdale Rd. (Borgata Shopping Center),* ☎ *602/948–8100. AE, D, DC, MC, V.*

Spanish

$$$–$$$$ ✕ **Marquesa.** One of the Valley's jewels, this restaurant pays homage ★ to Catalonia, the region around Barcelona. Everything here is right on target, from the setting to the service. Appetizers are extraordinary: *Anec D'Napoleon,* phyllo dough pouches stuffed with a heady blend of duck, foie gras, and mushrooms; and *pebrots del piquillo,* crab and fontina cheese baked into sweet red peppers. Main dishes include a monkfish-veal loin duo; pan-roasted rack of lamb; and a first-class paella crammed with lobster, shrimp, mussels, clams, chicken, and *chistora* (a sharp Spanish sausage). For dessert, the Gran Torres cheesecake and flan are equally wonderful. ✉ *7575 E. Princess Dr. (Scottsdale Princess resort),* ☎ *602/585–4848. Reservations essential. AE, D, DC, MC, V. No lunch.*

North Central Phoenix

American

$$$ ✕ **El Chorro Lodge.** Near the Phoenix Mountains Preserve, El Chorro has been doing business in this picturesque location for 60 years. Sit outside, gaze at the mountains and stars, and try not to make a meal of the famous sticky buns that immediately come to your table. El Chorro's forte is prime-graded meat. Beef Stroganoff, top sirloin, and the chateaubriand for two will get any carnivore's juices flowing. Fresh ocean fare like orange roughy and swordfish are also skillfully prepared. The dense chocolate-chip pecan pie makes the decision to linger over dessert an easy one. ✉ *5550 E. Lincoln Dr.,* ☎ *602/948–5170. AE, D, DC, MC, V.*

$$ ✕ **Coup Des Tartes.** This casual spot serves deftly crafted Mediterannean-themed fare in a homey setting. (It used to be an antiques store.) The menu changes weekly; try to come when lamb shank with dried fruit is featured—it's outstanding, as are the dessert pastries, especially the banana brûlée tart. It's BYOB here, so pick up a bottle before you come. ✉ *4626 N. 16th St.,* ☎ *602/212–1082. AE, D, DC, MC, V. Closed Wed. No lunch weekends.*

$$–$$$ ✕ **Oyster Grill.** Nobody is ever going to mistake downtown Phoenix for Fisherman's Wharf, but at the Oyster Grill, you may think you hear the sounds of seagulls overhead. The daily menu lets you know that fish is fresh that day, and there's only one method of preparation: grilled over alder wood. If you have adventurous tastes, you'll enjoy the Sonoran oyster curry stew (plump bluepoints in a spicy, curry-tinged cream broth with eggplant, onions, and crispy fried leeks). Along with an oyster bar, there's a full-scale dining room. ✉ *455 N. Third St. (Arizona Center),* ☎ *602/252–6767. AE, D, DC, MC, V.*

$$ ✕ **Texaz Grill.** The down-home fare here is served in a cowboy setting that oozes with neighborhood charm. Texaz Grill deals in meat, pardner. The T-bone steak and butter-soft fillet are very satisfying, but it's the he-man-size chicken-fried steak that lures most folks here. The fork-tender beef is encased in crisp batter and moistened with a ladle of thick, peppery country gravy; the mashed potato side—honest-to-goodness spuds with the skin mashed in—is a worthy accompaniment. Order yourself a Lone Star Brew, put some coins in the jukebox, and loosen your belt. ✉ *6003 N. 16th St.,* ☎ *602/248–7827. Reservations not accepted. AE, MC, V. No lunch Sun.*

Asian

$–$$ ✕ **China Village.** This place doesn't pretend to be anything more than it is: a neighborhood spot dishing out traditional Chinese fare. However, the old favorites are prepared better here than just about anyplace else. Favorites include the tangerine beef, lemon chicken, and twice-cooked pork. Vegetable lovers should make sure they order the yui-shan eggplant, which features skin-on, cooked-to-a-pulp eggplant laced with minced pork and heavily seasoned with ginger, garlic, and hot chilies. ✉ *12005 N. 32nd St.,* ☎ *602/953–1961. AE, D, DC, MC, V.*

Breakfast and Brunch

$$$$ ✕ **Terrace Dining Room.** The Phoenician's Terrace Dining Room serves
★ the most lavish (and expensive) Sunday brunch in town. Some say the spread here is as close to brunch perfection you'll find this side of the Pearly Gates. Attention is paid to every detail, from the wheel of costly Reggiano-Parmigiano cheese to the fresh artichoke hearts in the salad. Additionally, the staff is trained to anticipate your every whim. First, wander around the sushi section, the jumbo shrimp table, the homemade pastas, the pâtés, the crepes, and the blintzes and waffles. Then stroll to the main dishes: Salmon and lamb chops are fired up on the grill, while filet mignon and pork tenderloin in port sauce await you in sterno-fired trays. Be sure to save room for desserts like homemade ice cream, elegant chocolate truffles, or pear-rhubarb tart. A constantly replenished champagne glass filled with Mumm's Cuvee Napa keeps the meal bubbling. Don't plan anything more strenuous than a nap for the afternoon. ✉ *6000 E. Camelback Rd. (The Phoenician),* ☎ *602/423–2530. Reservations essential. AE, D, DC, MC, V.*

$–$$ ✕ **Chompie's Deli.** Run by Brooklyn refugees, this bustling deli brings a bite of the Big Apple to Phoenix. All the AM necessities are in perfect working order: smoked fish, blintzes, homemade cream cheeses, and herring in cream sauce. The outstanding bagels will remind New York expats of what they used to get in the old neighborhood; about 20 varieties are baked fresh daily. There's also a top-notch bakery on the premises, with rugulach, pies, and coffee cake. Bring a newspaper, or schmooze with your pals. Sometimes you have to stop and smell the bagels. ✉ *3202 E. Greenway Rd.,* ☎ *602/971–8010. Reservations not accepted. AE, MC, V.*

French/Continental

$$$$ ✕ **Chaparral Restaurant.** Everything about the place is old-fashioned:
★ the tuxedoed staff, the elegant decor, and the timeless menu. Foodies in search of the latest trends won't be happy here, but discerning diners who appreciate classic fare will be delighted. Starters include rich lobster bisque with a puff-pastry cap topped with caviar and crème fraîche. For your main course, all the standards are offered: Beef Wellington, Veal Oscar, Steak Diane, and Sole Meuniere. There aren't too many places left that know their way around these dishes. Dress up, and make believe it's 1958. ✉ *5402 E. Lincoln Dr. (Marriott's Camelback Inn),* ☎ *602/948–6644. Reservations essential. AE, D, DC, MC, V. No lunch.*

$$$$ ✕ **Christopher's.** For high-end gourmet fare, Christopher's is un-
★ matched in the Arizona area. Although you can order à la carte, chef Christopher Gross' "Menu Prestige," a seven-course, $85 gastronomic tour-de-force, is definitely worth serious consideration. A typical dinner might start off with house-smoked Irish salmon followed by sautéed foie gras garnished with figs. Next you might get sweetbreads with asparagus and parsnips. The fish course could be sautéed cod with chanterelle mushrooms, and the meat course might bring a venison chop with roasted artichokes in cognac and red wine sauce. A cheese soufflé could be next, followed by dessert. The wine list is as staggering as

the fare, with dozens of outstanding wines offered by the glass. Come armed with plenty of conversational topics—you'll be here close to three hours. ✉ 2398 E. Camelback Rd., ☎ 602/957–3214. *Reservations essential. Jacket required. AE, D, DC, MC, V. Closed Mon. No lunch*

$$$$ ✕ **Mary Elaine's.** Swanky, formal, and austerely elegant, Mary Elaine's ★ is the Phoenician's showcase restaurant. Look out the big picture windows for a sweeping view of Phoenix, then edge into dinner with roasted langoustines and saffron risotto, veal sweetbreads, or seared foie gras with spiced pineapple and 100-year-old Balsamico. The main dishes such as maple-glazed squab, monkfish medallions, and veal tenderloin should please the most demanding patrons. ✉ 6000 E. Camelback Rd. (The Phoenician), ☎ 602/941–8200. *Reservations essential. Jacket required. AE, D, DC, MC, V. Closed Sun. No lunch.*

$$$ ✕ **Christopher's Bistro.** Less formal than Christopher's next door, the inventive fare here is just as compelling. Starters range from classic onion soup and escargots bourguignonne to vegetable risotto and pasta with essence of white truffle oil. The main dishes furnish hearty bistro satisfaction: duck cassoulet, prime-grade steak and pommes frites, rack of lamb, and grilled salmon. Don't leave without trying the award-winning chocolate tower dessert. ✉ 2398 E. Camelback Rd., ☎ 602/957–3214. *AE, D, DC, MC, V. No lunch weekends.*

Greek

$$–$$$ ✕ **Greekfest.** All the vigorous flavors of the Aegean are brought to life at this pretty place with whitewashed walls that feels like an island taverna. A good way to experience as many of the tastes as possible is to call for the appetizer combo. Look for *taramosalata* (mullet roe blended with lemon and olive oil), *tzatziki* (cucumbers, garlic, and yogurt), and *melintzanosalata* (eggplant with lemon and sesame paste). Another favorite is *saganaki* (*kefalograviera* cheese flamed with brandy and extinguished with a squirt of lemon and a shout of "Opa!" by the staff). Entrées, many featuring lamb and shrimp, are equally hard-hitting. Try *exohiko* (chunks of lamb mixed with eggplant, peppers, zucchini, and mushrooms). For dessert, the *galaktoboureko* (a warm custard pie baked in phyllo dough and scented with cloves and honey) is a triumph of western civilization. ✉ 1940 E. Camelback Rd., ☎ 602/265–2990. *AE, D, DC, MC, V. No lunch Sun.*

Indian

$$ ✕ **Taste of India.** Bread is one of the tests of an Indian kitchen, and the models here—bhatura, naan, paratha, poori—are superb. The kitchen uses just about every spice in the spice rack for dishes like lamb kashmiry and tandoori chicken. Vegetarians rightly complain about the slim vegetarian pickings in this town, but Taste of India's meatless specialties make wonderful alternatives to the usual sprout-ridden platters. Try *benghan bhartha*, fashioned from eggplant, or *bhindi masala*, a tempting okra dish. Indian desserts include fragrant *ras malai*, a Bengali treat of sweet milk and cheese, with bits of pistachio. ✉ 1609 E. Bell Rd., ☎ 602/788–3190. *AE, D, MC, V.*

International

$$$–$$$$ ✕ **Tarbell's.** Sure it's sleek, smart, and glitzy, but Tarbell's distinguishes itself from the trendoid pack with careful attention to its deftly prepared dishes. The menu changes daily, but you can usually count on the vibrant smoked rock shrimp starter to be around. If they're available, order the aromatic mussels, steamed in a heady broth of white wine and shallots. On the pricey end of the entrée scale, there's always a first-rate New York steak with French-style pommes frites. On the low end, there's surprisingly good pizza. Your sweet tooth isn't neglected, either, especially if you opt for the rich Hawaiian chocolate mousse.

✉ *3213 E. Camelback Rd.,* ☎ *602/955–8100. AE, D, DC, MC, V.*
No lunch.

$$$ ✕ **Lon's at the Hermosa.** Set in a beautifully restored 1930s adobe inn,
★   Lon's resonates with Old Arizona charm. Wood-beamed ceilings, bee-
hive fireplaces, and original cowboy art create an authentic, rustic west-
ern feel. The inventive menu gets inspiration from the world over.
Appetizers may include grilled polenta pie with wild mushroom ragout,
ravioli filled with vegetables and goat cheese, or garlic prawns with
pineapple relish. Many of the main dishes are grilled over wood: loin
of pork, filet mignon, rack of lamb, ahi tuna, and salmon. Pasta,
chicken, duck, and veal are other standouts. For dessert, look for the
gingered crème brûlée tart or chocolate truffle pâté. ✉ *5532 N. Palo
Cristi Dr. (Hermosa Inn),* ☎ *602/955–7878. AE, D, DC, MC, V. No
lunch weekends.*

$$$ ✕ **RoxSand.** Quirky, risky, imaginative—it's no wonder that knowl-
★   edgeable foodies flock to RoxSand, perhaps the most interesting restau-
rant in the state. Chef RoxSand Scocos doesn't follow trends; she sets
them. Who else would think to stuff tamales with curried lamb moistened in a Thai-style peanut sauce? The heavenly *b'stilla* is a Moroc-
can-inspired appetizer of braised chicken wrapped in phyllo dough,
covered with almonds and powdered sugar. A recent special, mango
and wild rice soup, taps taste buds you didn't know you had. The main
courses are equally exotic. Air-dried duck is a house specialty, served
with buckwheat crepes and a pistachio-onion marmalade. Feta-stuffed
chicken breast with polenta-fried shrimp is another offbeat success.
Desserts are wicked, especially the B-52 torte, an intoxicating disk of
chocolate laced with Kahlua and Bailey's. ✉ *2594 E. Camelback Rd.
(Biltmore Fashion Park),* ☎ *602/381–0444. AE, DC, MC, V.*

Mexican/Latin American

$$–$$$ ✕ **Havana Patio Cafe.** This Cuban and Latin-American fare says "Yan-
qui, come back." The food is very flavorful, but not hot with chili heat.
Appetizers are marvelous, particularly the shrimp pancakes, potato cro-
quettes, and Cuban tamale. The best options for main dishes are the
ropa vieja, shredded braised beef served with *moros,* a blend of black
beans and rice; *pollo Cubano,* chicken breast marinated in lime, orange, and garlic; and *mariscos con salsa verde,* shellfish simmered in
a traditional green sauce. Vegetarians will adore the *causa azulada,* a
Peruvian platter featuring a blue mashed potato cake layered with car-
rot and served on Swiss chard. ✉ *6245 E. Bell Rd.,* ☎ *602/991–1496.
AE, D, DC, MC, V. Closed Mon.*

$$ ✕ **Richardson's.** This neighborhood haunt can be noisy and crowded,
and the waitstaff incredibly (if not offensively) surly, but the fiery
fugue of flavors known as New Mexican–style still packs 'em in until
midnight. Loose-cushioned, Santa Fe adobe booths surround three
sides of a lively bar, and an open kitchen turns out chilies rellenos, en-
chiladas, and other first-rate standbys. Shrimp, chicken, and chops come
off the pecan wood burning grill with distinctive, savory undertones;
Chimayo chicken is flavorfully stuffed with spinach, dried tomatoes,
poblano chilies, and asiago cheese and served with Richardson's sig-
nature twice-baked green chili potato. Expect a wait on weekends; and
don't expect to linger—they're usually ready to seat the next patrons
at your table the minute you set down your fork. ✉ *1582 E. Bethany
Home Rd.,* ☎ *602/265–5886. AE, MC, V.*

$ ✕ **Blue Burrito Grille.** Healthy Mexican food? That used to mean stub-
bing out your cigarette before you ate an enchilada-taco combo plate.
Not anymore. At Blue Burrito Grille, you can find good-for-you, south-
of the-border fare; this place conclusively demonstrates that just be-
cause the kitchen holds the lard, it doesn't have to hold the taste. Among

the heart-healthy menu items are chicken burritos, fish tacos, tamales Mexicanos, enchiladas rancheras, vegetarian burritos, and outstanding blue corn vegetarian tacos. ⊠ *3118 E. Camelback Rd.,* ☎ *602/ 955–9596. Reservations not accepted. AE, MC, V.*

$ ✕ **El Bravo.** This unprepossessing storefront won't impress anyone with
★ its interior design. The principal decor motif is the collage of bad checks posted by the "Order Here" window. But cognoscenti of Mexican food won't care about the decorating lapses. This place dishes out some of this town's best Sonoran fare. (Sonora is the Mexican state that borders Arizona.) Burros here are edible works of art, like the machaca (shredded beef) burro. The counter help routinely tries to talk gringos out of it (too spicy, they say), but don't be deterred. Enchiladas, chimichangas, and tacos are just as thrilling. If you've got a taste for chili zest, try the red beef popover—it will leave your tongue tingling. Even the sweets, not every Mexican restaurant's strength, are outstanding. Go for the chocolate chimichanga—it's like a creamy Mexican s'more. ⊠ *8338 N. Seventh St.,* ☎ *602/943–9753. Reservations not accepted. No credit cards.*

Southwestern

$$$–$$$$ ✕ **Vincent Guerithault on Camelback.** No one can say for sure whether
★ chef Guerithault prepares French food with a southwestern flair, or southwestern fare with a French touch. But why suffer from a hardening of the categories? Whatever this talented chef prepares will be incredibly tempting. You may want to make a meal of the famous appetizers: The duck tamale, smoked salmon quesadilla, and chipotle lobster ravioli are all ravishing. Main dishes are just as strong. The sautéed veal sweetbreads with blue cornmeal are out-of-this-world. The duck confit, rack of lamb, baked salmon, and grilled wild boar loin make choosing an entrée difficult. Loosen your belt for dessert. The signature crème brûlée arrives in three thin pastry cups filled with vanilla, coffee, and coconut custard. ⊠ *3930 E. Camelback Rd,* ☎ *602/224–0225. Reservations essential. AE, D, DC, MC, V. No lunch weekends.*

$$ ✕ **Sam's Cafe.** This is the southwestern restaurant that locals bring their skittish Midwestern relatives to with perfect confidence. Nothing's too far out, but most everything is interesting and tasty. The fragrant poblano chicken chowder is a fine way to begin. So are the Sedona spring rolls, flour tortillas wrapped around chicken and veggies, with a chipotle barbecue sauce. The hands-down main dish winner is the inventive chicken-fried tuna, a lightly battered slab adorned with a jalapeño cream gravy, served with chili-mashed potatoes. Steaks, chops, tacos, and pastas (try the chicken pasta, flamed with tequila) provide outstanding entrée support. The chilled flan, fashioned from yams, drizzled with caramel sauce and garnished with pecans, is worth a dessert splurge. ⊠ *2566 E. Camelback Rd. (Biltmore Fashion Park),* ☎ *602/954–7100. AE, D, DC, MC, V.*

Spanish

$$–$$$ ✕ **Altos.** This hot spot attracts well-dressed locals who are as sophisticated as the fare. The food here bursts with the scents of Iberia— garlic, sherry, olive oil, saffron. Calamari de Pedro (tender squid dipped in a saffron batter and sizzled in olive oil) is a good appetizer for sharing. *Sombrilla Andaluza* is mesmerizing, a Portobello mushroom marinated in olive oil, garlic, and sherry, then grilled and festooned with red cabbage, parsley, and Serrano ham. Main dishes are also invigorating. The *filete pelon* is a buttery filet mignon topped with cabrales, a creamy Spanish blue cheese. *Lomo en adobo* is pork loin, smothered in a lusty sauce with hints of chili, sesame seeds, sugar, and peanuts providing a 12-tone scale of flavor notes. The sugar-glazed chocolate espresso crème brûlée may be the single best dessert in Arizona. ⊠ *5029 N. 44th St.,* ☎ *602/808–0890. AE, D, DC, MC, V. No lunch weekends.*

Central Phoenix

American

$$$ ✕ **Eddie's Grill.** This is what "New American" cuisine is all about. Chef
★   Eddie Matney's creative imagination livens up traditional dishes in un-
     expected ways. Take the restaurant's signature platter, seared New York
     steak with potatoes. It's not the same old beef and spuds. Instead, you
     get a beautiful sirloin strip encased in a mashed potato crust, dusted
     with Parmesan and Romano cheeses, then lightly fried and topped with
     a cabernet demi-glace. The seafood cioppino pot pie—shellfish in a
     fennel-flavored broth with a puff pastry crust—is irresistible. Mango
     and five-peppercorn-coated chicken breast, served over roasted plan-
     tain and chili mashed potatoes, is hardly your typical poultry snoozer.
     The lively, sophisticated setting is another plus. ⊠ *4747 N. 7th St.,* ☎
     602/241–1188. AE, D, DC, MC, V. No lunch weekends.

$$ ✕ **Steamed Blues.** Crabs in the desert? No, it's not a mirage. This restau-
     rant specializes in blue crabs that are still swimming when you order
     them. Prepare to be serenaded by the sound of pounding mallets as
     diners attack their dinner—you might think you're in the middle of the
     "Anvil Chorus" scene in "Il Trovatore." If you prefer not to hammer
     your meal, there are soft-shell crabs, as well as crab cakes and steamed
     shrimp. The "Boardwalk" fries—fresh-cut, seasoned, sizzling potatoes—
     will make you think you're on a Chesapeake Bay pier. ⊠ *4843 N. 8th
     Pl.,* ☎ *602/966–2722. Reservations not accepted. AE, D, DC, MC,
     V. No lunch weekends.*

$$ ✕ **T-Bone Steak House.** Looking for a cowboy steak-house experi-
     ence, away from the diesel-spewing tourist buses and cars with Wis-
     consin license plates? You won't see staged gunfights or Indian dances
     at T-Bone Steak House. You'll just see seriously good steaks in a ranch-
     house setting. The small menu sticks to the basics: a monstrous 2-pound
     porterhouse, a 1-pound T-bone, and 12-ounce sirloin, all of them juicy
     and flavorful. Another bonus: the view. The restaurant sits about
     halfway up South Mountain. Come at dusk for a great look at the twin-
     kling city lights below. ⊠ *10037 S. 19th Ave.,* ☎ *602/276–0945. AE,
     DC, MC, V. No lunch.*

$ ✕ **Honey Bear's BBQ.** Honey Bear's motto—"You don't need no teeth
     to eat our meat"—may fall short on grammar, but this place isn't
     packed with folks looking to improve their language skills. Barbecue
     lovers are here to pig out. If you've got barbecue fever, the meaty pork
     ribs are the cure. This is Tennessee-style barbecue, which means these
     smoky baby backs are lined with a fantastic barbecue sauce—thick,
     zippy, and slightly sweet with a wonderful orange tang. There are ter-
     rific go-withs, too, like the sausage-enhanced "cowbro" beans and
     scallion-studded potato salad. If a slab of ribs still leaves you hungry,
     finish up with the homemade sweet potato pie. ⊠ *5012 E. Van Buren
     St.,* ☎ *602/273–9148. Reservations not accepted. AE, D, MC, V.*

$ ✕ **Mrs. White's Golden Rule Cafe.** You can get second-hand arte-
     riosclerosis just walking past this landmark soul food parlor, but if your
     arteries can handle it, this is the place to be nutritionally incorrect. Look
     for chicken-fried steak so tender you can dispense with your knife; over-
     size pork chops in a fried crust; heavenly Southern-fried chicken that
     will make you wish you never heard of the government's nutritional
     pyramid; and lovely smothered chicken, battered poultry heaped with
     a thick, country gravy. Why "Golden Rule" Cafe? At the end of the
     meal, just tell the cashier what you had—your conscience and your belly
     will both be happy. ⊠ *808 E. Jefferson,* ☎ *602/262–9256. Reserva-
     tions not accepted. No credit cards. Closed weekends. No dinner.*

Asian

$-$$ ✕ **Gourmet House of Hong Kong.** This popular Chinese restaurant draws customers who aren't interested in the "One from column A, one from column B" fare served up most other places. Instead, they get genuine Chinatown specialties like chow fun (thick rice noodles). Try the assorted meat version, topped with chicken, shrimp, pork, and squid. Lobster with black bean sauce may be the world's messiest platter, but it's also one of the tastiest. Don't wear anything that needs to be dry-cleaned. Along with an extensive seafood list, Gourmet House provides adventurous diners with such delights as five-flavor frogs' legs, duck feet with greens, and beef tripe casserole. ⊠ *1438 E. McDowell Rd.,* ☎ *602/253–4859. AE, D, DC, MC, V.*

Italian

$$$–$$$$ ✕ **Avanti.** More than two decades old, this swanky place with its mirrored black-and-chrome interior still has old-fashioned elegance. So does the food. The proprietors haven't spent the last 20 years redefining Italian gastronomy. They have, however, fine-tuned the standard Italian-Continental repertoire. Homemade pasta makes a wonderful first course, particularly the gnocchi and spinach ravioli. Tried-and-true entrées like veal chops, cioppino, and shrimp in a brandy-garlic sauce still deliver a powerful sensory experience. Give Avanti credit for refusing to keep up with the times and not confusing change for progress. ⊠ *2728 E. Thomas, Rd.,* ☎ *602/956–0900, AE, D, DC, MC, V. No lunch weekends.*

$$–$$$ ✕ **La Fontanella.** This outstanding neighborhood Italian restaurant is
★ a winning combination of quality and value. The mom-and-pop proprietors deliver all the hard-hitting flavors of their native land: *suppli,* a Roman specialty, rice croquettes filled with cheese; and escargots, bubbling in garlic and butter get the meal off to a fast start. All the entrées are first-rate; some are out-of-this-world. Among the latter are lamb *agrassato,* lamb shank braised in wine with raisins, pine nuts, and potatoes; osso buco, gilded with pancetta; seafood *reale,* shrimp and scallops in a sherry cream sauce; and the herb-crusted rack of lamb. For dessert, La Fontanella's homemade gelato puts an exclamation mark on dinner. ⊠ *4231 E. Indian School Rd.,* ☎ *602/955–1213. AE, D, DC, MC, V. No lunch weekends.*

$-$$ ✕ **Pizzeria Bianco.** Stradavarius made violins. Tiffany made lamps.
★ Bronx-native Chris Bianco is another craftsman. He makes pizza. It's good enough to inspire memories of Naples, even if you've never been there. The secret? A wood-fired brick oven and a passion for quality. Bianco's pizza crust is a work of art, not too bready, not too light, and just chewy enough to keep your jaws happy. The toppings include imported cheeses, homemade fennel sausage, wood-roasted cremini mushrooms, and the freshest herbs and spices. The small menu also features antipasto and sandwiches on fresh-baked bread. ⊠ *623 East Adams St.,* ☎ *602/258–8300. MC, V. Closed Mon. No lunch weekends.*

Mexican/Latin American

$$–$$$ ✕ **Such Is Life.** No chips. No mariachis. No servers in swirling Mexi-
★ can skirts. No tacos, enchiladas, or burritos. Such Is Life doesn't rely on gringo touches to attract business. Its authentic, Yucatan-inspired Mexican fare is enough to keep the place packed. For starters, try the *nopal polanco,* a prickly pear cactus pad topped with chihuahua cheese and chorizo. The lusty, lemon-tinged chicken soup is also thick with poultry, avocado, and hard- boiled egg. Entrées include chicken mole and adobo pork, simmered in a fragrant ancho chili, sesame, and orange sauce. If the kitchen has just received a shipment of Gulf shrimp, get them grilled in garlic. ⊠ *3602 N. 24th St.,* ☎ *602/955–7822. Reservations essential. AE, D, DC, MC, V. Closed Sun. No lunch Sat.*

$$ ✕ **San Carlos Bay Seafood Restaurant.** From the street, San Carlos Bay
★ doesn't look like much. Inside, though, it's another story—the best Mexican seafood in town is served here. Start off with a seafood cocktail teeming with octopus or shrimp, in a riveting tomato-based liquid spiked with onions, cilantro, lime, and pepper. Among the main dishes, the Veracruz-style fish features filleted snapper zestily coated with olives, onions, tomatoes, and peppers. The delicious, meaty crustaceans come soaked in a devilishly hot sauce. For seafood that doesn't make your nostrils flare, check out the well-stocked seven seas stew. ⌧ *1901 E. McDowell Rd.,* ☎ *602/340–0892. Reservations not accepted. No credit cards.*

$–$$ ✕ **Los Dos Molinos.** Is this the place that launched a thousand chips?
★ You bet it is. Set in a historic building, this restaurant features New Mexican–style Mexican food. For the uninitiated, that means HOT! After one bite, folks not used to this kind of fiery fare tend to look like they've just swallowed a live hand grenade. On the other hand, legions of heat seekers practically worship the Hatch, New Mexico chilies that form the backbone of the dishes here. Adobada ribs, a specialty, feature fall-off-the-bone meat marinated in red chilies. The green chili enchilada is potentially lethal. So is the innocuous-looking beef taco. But along with fire, the food also packs a real flavor wallop. About the only item that won't burn your lips is the *sopaipilla,* the New Mexican antidote to chili flames. It's a pillow of fried dough, brought steaming to the table, doused with cinnamon, honey, or powdered sugar. Los Dos Molinos doesn't cater to mass bland tastes. If you can't stand the heat, stay out of this kitchen. ⌧ *8646 S. Central Ave.,* ☎ *602/243–9113. Reservations not accepted. AE, D, MC, V. Closed Mon.*

$ ✕ **Eliana's Restaurant.** This family-run restaurant is the place for south-of-south-of-the-border fare. Eliana's is a small ethnic gem featuring the budget-priced specialties of El Salvador. The lack of ambience is offset by the kitchen's culinary skills. You can make a meal of the appetizers: *pupusas* (corn patties stuffed with pork, peppers, and cheese); *pasteles* (meat turnovers); and tamales, filled with chicken and vegetables. Main dishes will wipe out hunger pangs for about the price of a movie ticket. There's *pollo encebollado* (fried chicken with rice and beans), and *mojarra frita,* a whole fried tilapia, an Arizona farm-raised fish popular in Latin America. You can wash your meal down with refreshing homemade fruit drinks, a good way to take your mind off the desert heat. ⌧ *1627 N. 24th St.,* ☎ *602/225–2925. Reservations not accepted. AE, D, MC, V. Closed Mon.*

East Valley: Tempe, Mesa, Chandler

American

$$$–$$$$ ✕ **Top of the Rock.** The iron law of restaurant physics proclaims that
★ food quality declines the higher off the ground you get. (Airline food is the ultimate proof.) But Top of the Rock seems to be the exception to the rule. This beautiful room, set atop a Tempe butte, features a panoramic, 360-degree view of the Valley through its big picture windows. The food will also make your head swivel. The lobster Napoleon appetizer—lobster layered between crispy wontons lined with boursin cheese—is good enough to order for entrée and dessert. Main dishes include sugar-spiced barbecue salmon, roasted veal chop, free-range chicken, and mesquite-grilled Black Angus sirloin steak. The house specialty dessert is black bottom pie, with a chocolate praline center and chocolate mousse topping. This is a great spot for a romantic dinner. ⌧ *2000 Westcourt Way (Buttes resort), Tempe,* ☎ *602/225–9000. Reservations essential. AE, D, DC, MC, V. No lunch.*

Asian

$$–$$$ ✕ **Yamakasa.** Yamakasa, one of the Valley's top Japanese restaurants, and its next-door neighbor, C-Fu Gourmet, order their ocean fare in tandem. So you can be sure the high-quality sushi here is briny fresh. And the skilled sushi masters know what to do with the raw material. There's particular artistry in the hand rolls. Two *nabemono* (hot pot) dishes are also worth investigating. Another specialty is *shabu-shabu,* thin-sliced beef, swished in a boiling, sake-seasoned, vegetable-filled broth. ("Shabu-shabu" is the hissing sound the meat makes when it hits the liquid.) ⊠ *2051 W. Warner, Chandler,* ☎ *602/899–8868. AE, D, DC, MC, V. Closed Mon. No lunch Sun.*

$$ ✕ **C-Fu Gourmet.** This is serious Chinese food, the kind you'd expect to
★ find on Mott Street in New York or Grant Street in San Francisco. C-Fu's specialty is fish—fish so fresh you can see several species doing the backstroke in big holding tanks. If you've ever wondered why shrimp is a delicacy, it will be clear once you bite into these crustaceans. After they're fished out of the tank, they're steamed and bathed in a potent garlic sauce. Clams in black bean sauce and tilapia in a ginger-scallion sauce also hit all the right buttons. There's a daily dim sum brunch, too. ⊠ *2051 W. Warner, Chandler,* ☎ *602/899–3888. AE, D, DC, MC, V.*

French

$$–$$$ ✕ **Citrus Cafe.** A French bistro in Chandler? Skeptics are encouraged to see for themselves. The French proprietors may not boast a fancy Scottsdale address, but they serve some of the best French fare in the Valley. The first encouraging sign is the menu. It's printed on a marker board because it changes daily according to what's fresh in the market. You won't need more encouragement after the food arrives. Try the *feuilleté aux champignons* (mushrooms in puff pastry) or duck pâté studded with pistachios. The main dishes are pure French comfort food: veal kidneys, sweetbreads, leg of lamb, roast pork, and occasionally even rabbit. For dessert, there's *vacherin,* a marvelous mound of baked meringue that you won't see anyplace else in town. ⊠ *2330 N. Alma School Rd., Chandler,* ☎ *602/899–0502. AE, D, DC, MC, V. Closed Sun. and Mon. and Aug. No lunch.*

German

$–$$ ✕ **Zur Kate.** An unpretentious delight with genuine "gemutlichkeit," this restaurant has a homey congeniality that no interior designer can manufacture. The place is crammed with enough Deutschland clues to point even Inspector Clouseau in the right direction: beer steins, flags, travel posters, and, on weekends, live oom-pah-pah music. The menu covers traditional German territory, which means lots of pork. Some of the favorites are smoked pork chop, a ground ham and pork loaf, breaded pork cutlet, and homemade bratwurst. Side dishes are as filling as they are tempting: potato dumplings, home fries, a tart potato salad, and pungent sauerkraut. ⊠ *4815 E. Main St., Mesa,* ☎ *602/ 830–4244. Reservations not accepted. MC, V. Closed Sun. (Sun.–Mon. in summer).*

International

$$ ✕ **House of Tricks.** There's nothing up the sleeves of Robert and Robin Trick, the chef-proprietors of this rustic-looking restaurant. Set just a couple of blocks from the State University and Mill Avenue, Tempe's main thoroughfare, House of Tricks attracts locals who appreciate the always-inventive fare. The imaginative appetizer list is known for its offbeat creations, like cheese and avocado blintzes and stuffed grape leaves in chipotle plum sauce. The main dishes are equally clever. The roast eggplant and goat cheese lasagna is outstanding. Grilled rack of pork with a jalapeño-orange marmalade and scallops in a saffron

Pernod sauce also get high marks. The patio bar is a pleasant place to pass a mild Valley evening. ⊠ *114 E. 7th St., Tempe,* ☎ *602/968–1114. AE, D, DC, MC, V. Closed Sun.*

$–$$ ✕ **Euro Cafe.** If this place had a motto, it would be "Nothing succeeds like excess." When it comes to portion size and hard-hitting flavors, this kitchen doesn't know the meaning of restraint. The southern Mediterranean-themed fare is staggering, in every sense. The Chicken Palm dish, adorned with palm hearts and artichokes heaped over pasta, could be spread over dinner for two or three nights, if you have the willpower to resist finishing it in one sitting. The gyros platter, heaped with capers, sun-dried tomatoes, red peppers, and two kinds of Greek cheeses, puts you to the test as well. And beware the penne carbonara, an unconscionable quantity of pasta tubes fattened with ham and bacon, drenched in a creamy cheese sauce. ⊠ *1111 S. Longmore, Mesa,* ☎ *602/962–4224. AE, D, DC, MC, V.*

Mexican

$ ✕ **Rosa's Mexican Grill.** This festive, family-friendly restaurant summons up images of a Baja beach "taqueria" without the flies. The tacos are Rosa's true glory. Beef, pork, and chicken are marinated in fruit juices and herbs for 12 hours, slowly oven-baked for another 10, then shredded and charbroiled. The fish taco, pepped up with cabbage, radishes, and lime, is also in a class by itself. Spoon on one of Rosa's five fresh homemade salsas. ⊠ *328 E. University, Mesa,* ☎ *602/964–5451. No credit cards. Closed Sun. and Mon.*

Middle Eastern

$ ✕ **Tasty Kabob.** Persian food is heavily seasoned, but never spicy hot.
★ Perfumed basmati rice, for example, is often teamed with several grilled kabobs—skewers of ground beef, lamb, chicken, or beef tenderloin. The stews here, called "khoresht" and "polo," also give you a taste of authentic Persian fare. If "baghali polo" is on the menu, don't hesitate—it's dill-infused rice tossed with lima beans and lamb shank. ⊠ *1250 E. Apache Blvd., Tempe,* ☎ *602/966–0260. AE, D, MC, V. Closed Mon.*

West Valley: West Phoenix, Glendale, Litchfield Park

Asian

$–$$ ✕ **Big Wong.** Forget about Big Wong's hardbound menu, which the staff thrusts in the hands of all non-Chinese customers. Ask for the dog-eared, stapled sheets titled "Authentic Chinese Menu." Here you'll find the specialties that make this place a favorite after-hours hangout for other Chinese restaurant chefs. Tired of wonton soup? Try the crab meat and asparagus soup, or the broth made with shark's fin and shredded chicken. Bored with egg rolls? Try appetizers like smoked pork leg, deep-fried oysters, or cold jellyfish. Big Wong takes you into the mysterious world of clay-pot cooking. Shrimp with vermicelli is one of the more unthreatening versions. Risk takers may prefer the sea cucumber and duck-feet duo, or the pot filled with preserved vegetables and pork fat. ⊠ *616 W. Indian School Rd.,* ☎ *602/277–2870. MC, V. No lunch Sat.*

$–$$ ✕ **Pho Bang.** Tidy and unpretentious, Pho Bang delivers top-notch Vietnamese fare. The catfish soup, for example, features an outstanding broth zipped up with lemon, pineapple, and fennel. Naturally there's pho, meal-size noodle soups stocked with various cuts of beef. Splurge on the shrimp and beef specialty—it's a combination dinner and floor show. The server trundles over three plates: one with transparently thin slices of marinated beef and raw shrimp; one with piles of mint, lettuce, cilantro, pickled leeks, cucumber, and carrot; and one with rice paper. Fire up the portable grill and cook the beef and shrimp. When they're done, combine with the veggies, roll in rice paper, and dip into the national condiment, fish sauce. It's all as good as it sounds. ⌧ *1702 W. Camelback Rd.,* ☎ *602/433–9440. Reservations not accepted. MC, V.*

International

$ ✕ **Centro Cafe & Bakery.** If the word "value" makes you happy, this
★ splendid restaurant will make you light up with pleasure. How the young chef-proprietor can deliver such big portions of powerfully flavored Mediterranean fare at such low prices is a question only his accountant can answer. In the meantime, savvy diners get to enjoy fresh-baked breads, pizzas, hearty pastas, chicken dishes, and homemade desserts. Everything sings with some combination of wine, garlic, lemon, capers, olives, sun-dried tomatoes, and cheese. Almost nothing on the menu goes for more than $8.95. ⌧ *15820 N. 35th Ave.,* ☎ *602/938–3383. AE, D, DC, MC, V. Closed Mon. No lunch weekends.*

$ ✕ **Lalibela.** Looking for something different? Locals are discovering
★ that the Valley's only Ethiopian restaurant makes for a fun night out. Forget about silverware. Ethiopians wrap their food in "injera," a spongy, slightly sour bread that looks like what would result if you mated a tortilla to a crepe. Break off a piece and scoop up *doro wat,* chicken cooked in spiced butter sauce. *Alicha sega wat* brings beef bathed in a rich curry scented with turmeric. Vegetarian dishes are first-rate. True adventurers may opt for *kitfo,* finely ground raw beef mixed with butter and cardamom. ⌧ *8946 N. 19th Ave.,* ☎ *602/870–4555. AE, D, MC, V. No lunch Mon.*

Mexican

$ ✕ **Las Cazuelas.** Set in a somewhat forlorn shopping strip, Las Cazuelas is bright and spiffy once you step in. Cheap, tasty, and family-friendly, it attracts locals yearning for fresh Mexican seafood. The Costa Brava gives you an idea why this place is popular: It's a seafood stew packed with shrimp, octopus, squid, clams, scallops, crab, and red snapper, accompanied by potatoes, carrots, and squash in a lip-smacking broth fired with red chili. You'll get change back from a $10, too. Landlubber dishes like the chili verde plate and carnitas burro are also quite tasty. ⌧ *5150 W. McDowell,* ☎ *602/278–4885. AE, DC, MC, V.*

$ ✕ **Lily's Cafe.** It can be a bit tricky to find, but folks have managed to make their way to this family-run restaurant for almost 50 years. What's the attraction? Friendly mom-and-pop proprietors greeting regulars and newcomers; a jukebox with south-of-the-border hits; low prices; spic-and-span cleanliness; and absolutely fresh Mexican fare. Beef is the featured ingredient. The chimichanga (it's like a deep-fried burro) is world-class, stuffed with tender beef and covered with cheese, guacamole, and sour cream. Fragrant tamales, spunky red chili beef, and chili rellenos right out of the fryer also shine. ⌧ *6706 N. 58th Dr., Glendale,* ☎ *602/937–7757. Reservations not accepted. No credit cards. Closed Mon. and Tues. and Aug.*

Southwestern

$$$–$$$$ ✕ **Arizona Kitchen.** A few years ago, with the help of a researcher who studies Native American foods, management here put together a bold southwestern menu. This is how, centuries ago, Coronado and his staff might have eaten, if they'd brought along some open-minded cooks willing to learn from the natives. Appetizers like blue-corn piki rolls, stuffed with capon and goat cheese, and the wild boar anasazi bean chili give you an indication of what's to come. Entrées include grilled sirloin of buffalo in cabernet-and-vanilla chili negro sauce, and grilled venison medallions in blackberry zinfandel cocoa sauce. For dessert, try the chili-spiked ice cream in the striking turquoise "bowl" of hardened sugar. This spot is about 20 minutes from downtown Phoenix.

✉ *300 E. Indian School Rd. (Wigwam Resort), Litchfield Park,* ☎ *602/ 935–3811. AE, D, DC, MC, V. Closed Sun. and Mon. and July–Aug. No lunch.*

LODGING

Metropolitan Phoenix has a considerable array of lodging options, from world-class resorts and dude ranches to roadside motels, from luxury and executive hotels to no-frills business suites and family-style operations where you can do your own cooking.

Resorts are usually far from the heart of town—too far to be convenient if your interests are in Phoenix proper. The exceptions: the historic Arizona Biltmore, unthinkably far out when it was built and now handily close in; the gigantic Pointe Hilton on South Mountain, less than 3 mi from the airport; and its two sister Pointe resorts, each within 7 mi of downtown. Most of the other resorts are in the neighboring, tourist-friendly city of Scottsdale; a few are scattered 20 to 30 mi to the north in the quickly expanding communities of Carefree and Cave Creek. Dude-ranch territory is 60 mi northwest, in the town of Wickenburg.

Business and family hotels are closer to town—and to the average vacation budget. Many properties cater to corporate travelers during the week, but lower weekend rates to entice leisure travelers; remember to ask about weekend specials when calling a hotel's reservations desk. Until 20 years ago, families simply pulled into any of the dozens of modestly priced downtown courtyard motels. That is no longer a safe option, as the neighborhood has become seedy; aside from the airport area, however, no new downtown hotel district has emerged, so lodging offerings are scattered throughout Phoenix.

Travelers flee snow and ice to bask in the Valley of the Sun. As a result, winter is the high season, peaking in January through March. Summer season—generally considered May 1 through September 30—is giveaway time, when weekend packages at the fanciest resorts cost less than a winter night at a mid-range hotel.

CATEGORY	COST*
$$$$	over $250
$$$	$150–$249
$$	$75–$149
$	under $75

All prices are for a standard double room during high season, excluding taxes and service charges.

Scottsdale

$$$$ 🏨 **Hyatt Regency Scottsdale at Gainey Ranch.** A fun place for families, this resort has a showy theme-park ambience. A huge neoclassic water park includes fountains and waterfalls, 10 pools, a small sand beach, water volleyball, a water slide, and lagoons plied by gondolas. Three golf courses offer a choice of terrains—dunes, arroyo, or lakes— to suit a fancy for sand or water traps. Public areas are grand and lushly appointed; a large attractive piazza, lined with seating and gurgling steams and fountains, spills out from the lobby. Rooms are comfortable, although of average size and rather bland. ✉ *7500 E. Doubletree Ranch Rd., Scottsdale 85258,* ☎ *602/991–3388,* 🖷 *602/483–5550. 493 rooms, 7 casitas. 3 restaurants, 2 lounges, 10 pools, 3 9-hole golf courses, 8 tennis courts, croquet, health club, concierge floor, free parking. AE, D, DC, MC, V.*

$$$$ ⊞ **Marriott's Camelback Inn.** Founded in the mid-'30s, this historic resort is a swank oasis of comfort and relaxation in the gorgeous valley between Camelback and Mummy Mountains. The 125-acre property, much of which maintains a natural desert feel, contains two landscaped pool areas and two 18-hole golf courses. Don't miss the acclaimed full-service spa. Rooms are notably spacious and come in a wide variety of configurations. The luxurious bathrooms are accented with custom tile and glass blocks. ⊠ *5402 E. Lincoln Dr., Scottsdale 85253, ☎ 602/948–1700 or 800/242–2635, ℻ 602/951–8469. 424 rooms, 24 suites. 3 restaurants, 2 lounges, coffee shop, 2 pools, spa, Turkish bath, 2 18-hole golf courses, 8 tennis courts, hiking, horseback riding, business services, meeting rooms, free parking. AE, D, DC, MC, V.*

$$$$ ⊞ **The Phoenician.** Guests enter a bright, airy lobby to find towering
★ fountains, gleaming marble, and smiling faces of a service staff who will do handsprings to satisfy. You may question the suitability of some of the French-provincial decor and authentic Dutch-master paintings for a desert locale, but there's no question that a great deal of attention was paid to details. A 2-acre cactus garden showcases hundreds of varieties of cacti and succulents, the Centre for Well Being spa has an inspiring meditation atrium, and the resort's centerpiece oval pool is lined with mother-of-pearl tiles. Rooms at the Phoenician, the highest-priced resort in town, are spacious with cream walls, tasteful rattan furnishings in muted tones, Italian-marble bathrooms, and private patios. Ask for a room facing south, with views of the resort's pools and the city. Two of the resorts restaurants, **Mary Elaine's** and **The Terrace Dining Room** (☞ Dining, *above*) offer some of the best dining in the city. ⊠ *6000 E. Camelback Rd., Scottsdale 85251, ☎ 602/941–8200 or 800/888–8234. 569 rooms, 107 casitas, 73 suites. 4 restaurants, 7 pools, barbershop, beauty salon, sauna, steam room, golf privileges, 12 tennis courts, archery, badminton, basketball, croquet, health club, jogging, volleyball, pro shop, billiards, children's programs, business services, free parking. AE, D, DC, MC, V.*

$$$$ ⊞ **Scottsdale Princess.** On the 450 beautifully landscaped acres of this resort, Mexican-colonial architecture is set against the splendor of the McDowell Mountains. Rooms in the red-tile-roof main building and the casitas are furnished in muted desert hues, with sand-color rugs and bedspreads contributing to the overall airy effect. All rooms have private terraces and large bathrooms with double sinks, a shower and a bathtub, separate vanity areas, and silk-padded hangers in walk-in closets. The **Marquesa** restaurant (☞ Dining, *above*) has been consistently rated one of the best in the state. ⊠ *7575 E. Princess Dr., Scottsdale 85255, ☎ 602/585–4848 or 800/344–4758, ℻ 602/585–0091. 450 rooms, 125 casitas, 75 villas. 5 restaurants, bar, 3 pools, spa, steam room, 2 18-hole golf courses, 9 tennis courts, health club, racquetball, squash, pro shops, business services, free parking. AE, D, DC, MC, V.*

$$$–$$$$ ⊞ **Scottsdale Plaza Resort.** Arched doorways, soft-beige stucco, and tiered stone fountains lend Old World charm to this hotel's Spanish-Mediterranean feel. Although it lacks the requisite lush golf fairways, this 40-acre independent hotel is out to compete with the five-star big boys. Handsome whitewashed oak furniture and designer window treatments decorate the rooms, which have special-touch amenities such as a petite box of assorted chocolate truffles left on the pillow. **Remington's,** the hotel's main restaurant, features live jazz combos. Business travelers beware: Each phone call—even those ending in busy signals—carries a 75¢ tariff. ⊠ *7200 N. Scottsdale Rd., Scottsdale 85253, ☎ 602/948–5000 or 800/832–2025, ℻ 602/951–5152. 224 rooms, 180 suites, 10 lodges. 2 restaurants, 3 lounges, 5 pools, beauty salon,*

154

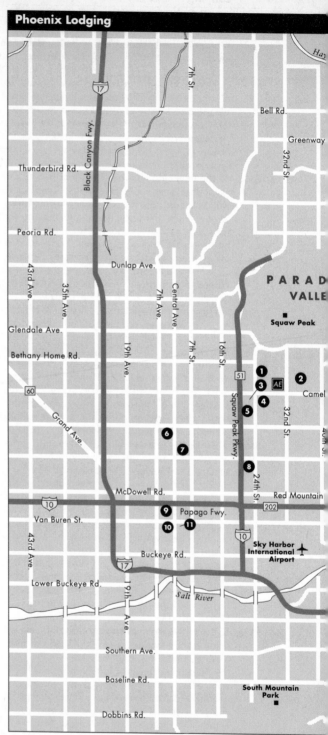

Phoenix Lodging

0
4 miles
0
6 km
KEY
AE American Express Office
N
Hayden Rhodes Aqueduct
TO CAREFREE AND CAVE CREEK
Scottsdale Municipal Airport
SCOTTSDALE
Scottsdale Rd.
Pima Rd.
Thunderbird Rd.
64th St. (Invergordon Rd.)
Cactus Rd.
Shea Blvd.
Shea Blvd.
96th St.
Via De Ventura
Tatum Blvd.
Indian Bend Rd.
Lincoln Dr.
Mc Donald Dr.
Camelback Mountain
Rd.
Indian School Rd.
Beeline Hwy.
87
44th St.
40th St.
Thomas Rd.
Hayden Rd.
Alma School Rd.
McDowell Rd.
Fwy.
Papago Park
McKellips Rd.
202
Salt River
Country Club Rd.
Mesa Dr.
Brown Rd.
143
Priest Dr.
Arizona State University
Rural Rd.
University Dr.
MESA
Main St.
Apache Blvd.
Dobson Rd.
Broadway Rd.
Lindsay Rd.
Mill Ave.
101
10
48th St.
TEMPE
Superstition Fwy.
60
Baseline Rd.
Price Rd.
Guadalupe Rd.
McQueen Rd.
GILBERT
12
13
14
15
16
17
18
19
20
21
22
23
24
25
26
27
28
29
30
31
32

putting green, 5 tennis courts, exercise room, 3 racquetball courts, pro shop, free parking. AE, D, DC, MC, V.

$$$ 🏨 **Radisson Resort Scottsdale.** With tons of sports options, this hotel is the perfect match for active types who desire the facilities of a swank resort in a decidedly more low-key setting. Two-story buildings house guest rooms, accessible via pathways winding through the well-kept grounds. Rooms themselves are traditionally furnished and predominantly unremarkable. Some might say the lobby plaza is overdecorated, but the effect is generally pleasant; a scattershot assortment of green granite sculpture, oversize urns, gilt armchairs upholstered in peach plaid, and grape- and mauve-bordered carpets somehow manage to harmonize. ✉ *7171 N. Scottsdale Rd., Scottsdale 85253,* ☎ *602/991–3800,* ℻ *602/948–1381. 286 rooms, 32 bi-level suites, 2 luxury suites. Restaurant, patisserie, no-smoking rooms, beauty salon, 2 18-hole golf courses, 21 tennis courts, basketball, volleyball. AE, D, DC, MC, V.*

$$$ 🏨 **Sunburst Resort.** This sedate, low-rise hotel may be Scottsdale's best-kept secret. Five two-story structures line attractive grounds dotted with orange trees and Adirondack chairs clustered beneath oversized canvas umbrellas. Roomy accommodations are decorated with patterned bedspreads in vivid, primary colors, benches upholstered in whimsical cow-print material, and intricately carved pine furnishings; each room's private balcony is accessible via handsome French doors. Motorists will appreciate self-parking close to the room. ✉ *4925 N. Scottsdale Rd., Scottsdale 85251,* ☎ *602/945–7666. 206 rooms, 6 suites. Restaurant, bar, pool, refrigerators, exercise room, meeting rooms, free parking. AE, D, DC, MC, V.*

$$–$$$ 🏨 **Regal McCormick Ranch.** Boating is not the only surprise at this property, the only lakeside resort in the town. Besides sweeping views of tranquil, 40-acre Camelback Lake, this hotel includes such amenities as private patios for every room, each furnished with a cunning set of high barstools and café table. Inside bathrooms have gilt-framed mirrors and cushiony, overstuffed easy chairs lure guests to curl up for a relaxing spell. Sailboats, paddle boats, and a canoe are available gratis from the resort's pool director. ✉ *7401 N. Scottsdale Rd., Scottsdale 85253,* ☎ *602/948–5050 or 800/243–1332,* ℻ *602/991–5572. 125 rooms, 49 villas. 2 restaurants, lounge, lake, pool, 2 18-hole golf courses, 4 tennis courts, boating. AE, D, DC, MC, V.*

$–$$ 🏨 **Safari Resort.** Built in the 1940s, the Safari was one of the city's first ★   resorts. Two stories of "Palm-Beach–style" rooms have sliding Arcadia-door entrances and private patios or balconies that overlook verdant lawns flanked with magnolia trees and swaying palms. The Safari's not posh; in fact, as a "resort," it's charmingly downscale—right down to some of the 24-hour coffee shop's waitresses, who have been calling guests "Hon" for well over 40 years. Plentiful amenities at affordable prices, however, make devotees of first-time guests unfussy enough to appreciate this low-key gem. ✉ *4611 N. Scottsdale Rd., Scottsdale 85251,* ☎ *602/945–0721 or 800/845–4356,* ℻ *602/ 946–4703. 177 rooms, 10 suites. Restaurant, bar, coffee shop, no-smoking rooms, refrigerators, 2 pools, beauty salon, putting green, horseshoes, shuffleboard, volleyball, coin laundry, free parking. AE, D, MC, V.*

$–$$ 🏨 **Scottsdale's 5th Avenue Inn.** Location, location, location! The most attractive feature of this three-story, exterior corridor motel is its walking distance to Scottsdale's Old Town and boutique/gallery enclave. Modest rooms have outdated-but-serviceable furnishings that include a sofa, coffee table, and petite writing desk, as well as a generous-size, open-closet dressing area. ✉ *6935 Fifth Ave., Scottsdale 85251,* ☎ *602/ 994–9461 or 800/528–7396,* ℻ *602/947–1695. 92 rooms. Breakfast room, pool, hot tub, free parking. AE, D, DC, MC, V.*

$ ⊞ **Motel 6 Scottsdale.** The best bargain in Scottsdale lodging is easy
to miss, but it's worth hunting for the sign, set back on the north side
of Camelback Road. Just steps away from the Scottsdale Fashion
Square, this motel is also close to the specialty shops of 5th Avenue
and Scottsdale's Civic Plaza. Amenities aren't a priority here, but the
price is remarkable considering the stylish and much more expensive
resorts found close by. Rooms are small and spare with blue carpets
and print bedspreads, but the well-landscaped pool offers a pleasant
outdoor respite under the palms. ⊠ *6848 E. Camelback Rd., Scottsdale 85251,* ☎ *602/946–2280,* ℻ *602/949–7583. 122 rooms. Pool,
hot tub, parking. AE, D, DC, MC, V.*

North of Scottsdale: Carefree and Cave Creek

$$$$ ⊞ **The Boulders.** The Valley's most serene and secluded luxury re-
★   sort hides among the hill-size granite boulders in the foothills town
of Carefree, 30 minutes north of Scottsdale. Golf courses stretch like
emerald carpets between the giant 12-million-year-old granite stones,
and adobe casitas cluster along open paths that wind through the raw
beauty of the natural desert. (Staffers will pick you up and drive you
around the sprawling resort in golf carts.) Casitas are compact but
comfortable, with exposed log-beam ceilings, ceiling fans, and curving, pueblo-style half-walls and shelves; each has a patio with a view,
a miniature kiva fireplace, and a spacious bath and dressing area with
a deep tub and adobe vanity. ⊠ *34631 N. Tom Darlington Dr.,
Carefree 85377,* ☎ *602/488–9009 or 800/553–1717,* ℻ *602/488–
4118. 160 casitas, 33 patio homes. 4 restaurants, 2 pools, spa, 2 18-
hole golf courses, 6 tennis courts, exercise room, hiking, horseback
riding, jogging, business services, meeting rooms, free parking. AE,
D, DC, MC, V.*

North Central Phoenix: Biltmore District and Paradise Valley

$$$$ ⊞ **Arizona Biltmore.** Designed by Frank Lloyd Wright's colleague Al-
bert Chase McArthur, the so-called Jewel of the Desert has been a masterpiece among world-class resorts since it opened in 1929. A vast,
dramatic lobby has stained-glass skylights, wrought-iron pilasters, and
cozy sitting alcoves that invite guests to linger, especially to enjoy live
piano—usually jazz—in the evenings. Impeccably manicured grounds
contain open walkways, fountains, and scores of raised flower beds in
colorful bloom. The Paradise Pool and its twin towers (which enclose
a 92-ft water slide) is truly a sight to behold. Although less impressive
than the rest of the extravagant property, standard rooms are comfortable, featuring natural muted colors, mission-style furnishings,
and large tan and off-white marble baths. ⊠ *24th St. and Missouri Ave.,
Phoenix 85016,* ☎ *602/955–6600 or 800/950–0086,* ℻ *602/381–
7600. 481 rooms, 78 suites, 61 villas. 2 restaurants, lobby lounge, 5
pools, 2 18-hole golf courses, putting green, 8 tennis courts, health club,
jogging, concierge, car rental, free parking. AE, D, DC, MC, V.*

$$$ ⊞ **Hermosa Inn.** The ranch-style lodge at the heart of this small resort
was the home and studio of cowboy artist Ron Megargee in the 1930s;
today the adobe structure houses a favorite local restaurant, Lon's, justly
popular for its New American cuisine. The surrounding 6 acres, which
mix lush lawns with desert landscaping, are dotted with individually
decorated casitas and villas. The serene atmosphere and such ameni-
ties as mini-kitchens, comfortable desk space, and free Continental break-
fast make it an ideal environment for businesspeople and low-key
travelers. ⊠ *5532 N. Palo Christi Rd., Paradise Valley, 85253,* ☎ *602/
955–8614 or 800/241-1210,* ℻ *602/955–8299. 24 rooms, 11 suites.*

Restaurant, bar, kitchenettes, pool, 2 hot tubs, 3 tennis courts, free parking. AE, D, DC, MC, V.

$$$ 🏨 **Ritz-Carlton.** Like an 11-story false front, this sand-color neo-Federal mid-rise facing Biltmore Fashion Square mall hides a graceful, well-appointed luxury hotel. Large public rooms are decorated with 18th- and 19th-century European paintings and a handsome china collection is on display. Rooms are done in shades of mint and celery, with an armoire holding a TV and refrigerator (stocked), a small closet with a safe, and a white-marble bath basin well supplied with amenities. ⊠ *2401 E. Camelback Rd., Phoenix 85016,* ☎ *602/468–0700,* 𝖥𝖠𝖷 *602/ 468–0793. 281 rooms, 4 suites. 2 restaurants, 2 bars, pool, 2 saunas, tennis court, bicycles, exercise room, concierge floor, business services, parking (fee). AE, D, DC, MC, V.*

$$–$$$ 🏨 **Camelback Courtyard by Marriott.** Built in 1990, this four-story hostelry delivers compact elegance in its public areas and reliable, no-frills comfort in its rooms and suites. A medium-size lap pool and whirlpool fill the courtyard, landscaped with granite boulders and palms. Strategically located, over 50 different dining options are within walking distance. Considerable savings are achieved by dropping such "hotel" features as 24-hour room service (it's available from 5 to 10 PM) and relying on the neighboring upscale malls for gift and grooming shops, travel services, and the like. ⊠ *2101 E. Camelback Rd., Phoenix 85016,* ☎ *602/955–5200,* 𝖥𝖠𝖷 *602/955–1101. 144 rooms, 11 suites. Restaurant, bar, pool, hot tub, exercise room, meeting rooms, free parking. AE, D, DC, MC, V.*

$$–$$$ 🏨 **Red Lion's La Posada Resort.** Views are incredible at this sprawling, one-story resort, where Camelback Mountain looms spectacularly over the property's low, terra-cotta–tiled roofs. The vast Lagoon Pool is the resort's centerpiece, replete with cascading waterfalls, passageways under red boulder formations, and the swim-up Grotto Bar. Athletic enthusiasts will enjoy a bevy of options for sports activities. Standard rooms sport verdigris iron furniture and peach-and-slate Navajo-patterned bedspreads. Built in 1978, the property still has common areas and appointments which, though well kept, are sorely in need of aesthetic update, although the lounge's round, sunken disco floor may fulfill your burning, unresolved "Saturday Night Fever" fantasies. ⊠ *4949 E. Lincoln Dr., Paradise Valley 85253,* ☎ *602/952– 0420,* 𝖥𝖠𝖷 *602/840–8576. 252 rooms, 10 suites. Restaurant, lounge, 2 pools, 3 hot tubs, massage, sauna, 2 putting greens, 6 tennis courts, exercise room, horseshoes, racquetball, volleyball, pro shop, nightclub, free parking. AE, D, DC, MC, V.*

$$ 🏨 **Phoenix Inn.** A block off a popular stretch of Camelback Road, this three-story property is a remarkable bargain, considering it has amenities not generally seen in properties of the same price category—leather love seats, refrigerators, and microwaves, for example. Continental breakfast is served daily from 6 to 10 in a pleasant breakfast room with a large television. ⊠ *2310 E. Highland Ave., Phoenix 85016,* ☎ *602/ 956–5221 or 800/956–5221,* 𝖥𝖠𝖷 *602/468–7220. 120 rooms, 6 suites. Breakfast room, pool, hot tub, exercise room, coin laundry. AE, D, DC, MC, V.*

Central Phoenix

$$$–$$$$ 🏨 **Hilton Suites.** A model of excellent design within tight limits, this practical and popular 11-story atrium is likely to become a classic. A more luxurious version of the frequent-traveler suites concept, it sits off Central Avenue, 2 mi north of downtown amid the "Central Corridor" cluster of office towers. The marble-floor, pillared lobby opens into an atrium containing palm trees, trickling natural-boulder fountains, and a lantern-lighted café, where guests enjoy a bite while the gliding, glass elevators slice through the background. Each room has an exercise bike and VCR, and a large bathroom that opens to both a living room and bedroom. ⊠ *10 E. Thomas Rd., 85012,* ☎ *602/222–1111,* ℻ *602/265–4841. 226 suites. Restaurant, bar, kitchenettes, refrigerators, in-room VCRs, indoor lap pool, sauna, hot tub, exercise room, free parking. AE, D, DC, MC, V.*

$$$ 🏨 **Embassy Suites.** Just 5 mi from downtown, this four-story open-courtyard hotel has lush palms and olive trees surrounding bubbling fountains and a sunken pool. Free cooked-to-order breakfasts and an evening "manager's reception" social hour are held in the spacious clubhouse at café tables, by a large sunken fireplace–conversation pit, with a wide-screen TV off in the corner. Each suite has a hair dryer, iron and ironing board, and a wet bar with microwave, sink, and mini-refrigerator. ⊠ *2333 E. Thomas Rd., 85016,* ☎ *602/957–1910,* ℻ *602/955–2861. 183 suites. Restaurant, kitchenettes, refrigerators, pool, hot tub, exercise room, laundry service, airport shuttle, free parking. AE, D, DC, MC, V.*

$$$ 🏨 **Hyatt Regency Phoenix.** This premier hotel, with its disk-shape rotating restaurant atop 24 floors of dark sandstone, is a downtown landmark. The seven stories of spare, all-white atrium design—there's a surreal, tiered space-station–feel here—have suspended giant sculptures in the cavernous core and whooshing glass-windowed elevators. Rooms are spacious and comfortable, with thoughtful appointments ranging from original artwork to down pillows and in-room coffeemakers. Note: the atrium roof blocks east views on floors 8–10. ⊠ *122 N. 2nd St., 85004,* ☎ *602/252–1234,* ℻ *602/254–9472. 667 rooms, 45 suites. 2 restaurants, bar, no-smoking rooms, pool, exercise rooms, concierge, business services, meeting rooms, car rental. AE, D, DC, MC, V.*

$$ 🏨 **Best Western Executive Park.** One of downtown's hidden jewels,
★ this hotel has charm, a great location—and great prices. The Heard Museum, Phoenix Art Museum, and central library are within walking distance. Simple and elegant, the rooms are brightened by peach-and-sand-color walls and prints by southwestern masters. ⊠ *1100 N. Central Ave., 85004,* ☎ *602/252–2100,* ℻ *602/340–1989. 107 rooms. Restaurant, bar, no-smoking rooms, pool, hot tub, sauna, exercise room, meeting rooms, free parking. AE, D, DC, MC, V.*

$$ 🏨 **Hotel San Carlos.** Built in 1927 on the site of the city's first school, this historic seven-story hotel has been a downtown landmark for decades. The lobby echoes back to the '30s and '40s high style of the hotel's heyday, replete with shiny copper elevator doors and vintage Austrian crystal chandeliers. Ceiling fans, moldings, and old-style radiators add to the bygone-era charm. Be forewarned: Accommodations here are markedly snug compared to modern hotels (and if you think the rooms are small, wait until you see the pool). ⊠ *202 N. Central Ave., 85004,* ☎ *602/253–4121 or 800/528–5446,* ℻ *602/253–6668. 135 rooms. Restaurant, café, pool, exercise room, meeting rooms, parking (fee). AE, D, DC, MC, V.*

$$ 🏨 **Lexington Hotel.** Only 3 mi from downtown, this is Phoenix's best bet for fitness enthusiasts and sports-lovers. The Lexington houses a health facility, which includes among other things, a full-size indoor basketball court, a 40-station machine workout center, and a large outdoor waterfall pool. The ambience is bright, modern, and informal. Rooms range in size from moderate (in the cabana wing, first-floor rooms have poolside patios) to very small (tower wing). This is where visiting teams—and fans—like to stay. ⊠ *100 W. Clarendon Ave., 85013,* ☎ *602/279–9811,* ℻ *602/285–2932. 180 rooms. Restaurant, sports bar, pool, beauty salon, hot tub, massage, sauna, steam room, health club, racquetball, free parking. AE, D, DC, MC, V.*

Near Sky Harbor Airport

$$$–$$$$ 🏨 **The Buttes.** Two miles east of Sky Harbor, nestled in desert buttes at I–10 and AZ 60, this hotel joins dramatic architecture (the lobby's back wall is the volcanic rock itself) and classic Southwest design (pine and saguaro-rib furniture, works by major regional artists) with stunning Valley views. "Radial" rooms are largest, with the widest views; inside rooms face the huge free-form pools, with waterfall, hot tubs, and poolside cantina. The elegant Top of the Rock restaurant is a definite plus. ⌧ *2000 Westcourt Way, Tempe 85282,* ☎ *602/225–9000 or 800/843–1986,* 🆕 *602/438–8622. 353 rooms. 2 restaurants, 3 bars, pool, sauna, 4 tennis courts, health club, hiking, jogging, bicycles, concierge floor, business services, meeting rooms, free parking. AE, D, DC, MC, V.*

$$–$$$$ 🏨 **Pointe Hilton on South Mountain.** The Southwest's largest resort, 15 minutes from downtown, sits next to South Mountain Park, a 16,000-acre desert preserve that offers hiking, mountain biking, and horseback riding. Rooms and public areas are unremarkable; the facilities are the draw: On site are a premier four-story sports center and three separate restaurants. Landscaped walkways and roads link everything on the 750-acre property; carts and drivers are on 24-hour call. The Hilton also runs two identically themed resorts in the area: the Pointe Hilton at Squaw Peak (☎ 602/997–2626 North Phoenix) and the Pointe Hilton Tapatio Cliffs (☎ 602/866–7500). ⌧ *7777 S. Pointe Pkwy., Phoenix 85044,* ☎ *602/438–9000 or 800/876–4683,* 🆕 *602/ 431–6535. 636 suites. 3 restaurants, 3 lobby lounges, lake, 6 pools, saunas, 18-hole golf course, 10 tennis courts, health club, hiking, horseback riding, jogging, racquetball, volleyball, coin laundry, meeting rooms, free parking. AE, D, DC, MC, V.*

$$–$$$ 🏨 **DoubleTree Guest Suites.** In the Gateway Center, just 1½ mi north of the airport, this honeycomb of six-story towers is the best of a dozen choices for the traveler who wants to get off the plane and into a comfortable, centrally located property. Rooms have wet bars with microwaves and refrigerators. Vacationers beware: Bedroom furnishings cater to corporate guests traveling light—two-drawer credenzas serve as bureaus and dinky wardrobes function as closets. ⌧ *320 N. 44th St., Phoenix 85008,* ☎ *602/225–0500 or 800/800–3098,* 🆕 *602/225– 0957. 242 suites. Restaurant, bar, pool, sauna, exercise room, meeting rooms, free parking. AE, D, DC, MC, V.*

$$ 🏨 **Hampton Inn Airport.** This four-story, interior-corridor hotel 9 mi from downtown is both affordable and accommodating. Rooms are moderate size, appointed with handsome armoires and bright-colored leaf or fish prints for drapes and bedspreads. Free Continental breakfast is available each morning in the lobby, where a good-size television is tuned to the local wake-up news show. Take advantage of the hotel shuttle running from 5 AM to midnight. ⌧ *4234 S. 48th St., Phoenix 85040,* ☎ *602/438–8688,* 🆕 *602/431–8339. 130 rooms, 4 suites. Refrigerators, in-room VCRs, pool, hot tub, jogging, meeting rooms, airport shuttle, free parking. AE, D, DC, MC, V.*

East Valley: Tempe and Mesa

$$–$$$ 🏨 **Hilton Pavilion.** The ambience of this eight-floor property is defined by its atrium's etched glass and brass, tropical greenery, and art deco–style furniture. Rooms are medium size, with plum and teal carpeting, average-size baths, small closets, and a large lighted table; corner suites and the top two floors have the best views. The hotel is in the heart of the East Valley, just off AZ 60, and the area's largest shopping mall, Fiesta Mall, is across the street; downtown Phoenix is 18 mi away. ⌧ *1011 W. Holmes Ave., Mesa 85210,* ☎ *602/833–5555 or 800/544–*

5866, FAX *602/649–1380. 201 rooms, 62 suites. Restaurant, 2 bars, refrigerators, pool, hot tub, exercise room, business services, free parking. AE, D, DC, MC, V.*

$$–$$$ ⬚ **Tempe Mission Palms Hotel.** Set snugly between the Arizona State
★ University campus and Old Town Tempe, this three-story courtyard hotel is handy to the East Valley and downtown Phoenix. The tone is set by a handsome, casual lobby—Matisse-inspired upholstery on overstuffed chairs—and an energetic, young staff. Many visitors stay here for ASU sports events and the pro-football Cardinals (the stadium is virtually next door). Rooms are bright, simple southwestern, and comfortable; interior hallways are lined with sconces of weathered metal and frosted glass. The hotel's popular "Monster Bar"—adorned with an 8-ft-long Gila monster suspended from the ceiling— becomes a lively sports lounge when a game is on. ✉ *60 E. 5th St., Tempe 85281,* ☎ *602/894–1400 or 800/547–8705,* FAX *602/968–7677. 303 rooms. Restaurant, bar, pool, sauna, 3 tennis courts, exercise room, business services, meeting rooms, airport shuttle, free parking. AE, D, DC, MC, V.*

$$ ⬚ **Twin Palms Hotel.** Across the street from ASU's Gammage Auditorium and minutes from Old Town Tempe, this seven-story high-rise hotel underwent extensive renovations in 1997. The domed-window facade, check-in area, bar and lounge are among recent improvements. As for rooms, faux finishes creatively mask dated, textured walls and corner basins strike strategic blows against cramped bathrooms. Guests receive free admission to facilities at the nearby ASU Recreation Complex with three Olympic-size pools, badminton and squash courts, and aerobics classes. ✉ *225 E. Apache Blvd., Tempe 85281,* ☎ *602/967–9431,* FAX *602/303–6602. 140 rooms. 1 suite. Bar, no-smoking rooms, pool, concierge floor, airport shuttle, free parking. AE, DC, MC, V.*

$ ⬚ **Mesa Travelodge.** This small, plain motel three blocks west of Mesa's downtown center has burgundy carpet, warm muted-tone wallpaper, and bedspreads and art prints in southwestern motifs. The rooms overlook a small pool. The motel's busy corner spot can mean continual street noise, but low prices help compensate. ✉ *22 S. Country Club Dr., Mesa 85210,* ☎ *602/964–5694,* FAX *602/964–5697. 39 rooms. Pool, free parking. AE, D, DC, MC, V.*

NIGHTLIFE AND THE ARTS

The Arts

Phoenix performing-arts groups have grown rapidly in number and sophistication, especially over the past two decades. The permanent home to the Arizona Theatre Company, Actors Theatre, and Ballet Arizona, the **Herberger Theater Center** (✉ 222 E. Monroe St., ☎ 602/ 252–8497) also presents a variety of visiting dance troupes and orchestras.

Facing the Herberger Theater, **Symphony Hall** (✉ 225 E. Adams St., ☎ 602/262–6225) is home to both the Phoenix Symphony and the Arizona Opera, as well as a venue for touring Broadway shows and top-name performers. The **Orpheum Theatre** (✉ 203 W. Adams St., ☎ 602/252–9678) showcases various performing arts, including children's theater, and film festivals. Arizona State University splits an impressive performance schedule between the **Gammage Auditorium** (✉ Mill Ave. at Apache Blvd., Tempe, ☎ 602/965–3434), **Sundome Center** (✉ 19403 R. H. Johnson Blvd., Sun City West, ☎ 602/975–1900), and **Kerr Cultural Center** (✉ 6110 N. Scottsdale Rd., Scottsdale, ☎ 602/ 965–5377).

The most comprehensive ticket agencies are the **Arizona State University Ticket Office** (✉ Gammage Center, Tempe, ☎ 602/965–3434) and **Dillard's ticket line** (☎ 602/503–5555).

Classical Music

Arizona Opera (✉ 4600 N. 12th St., Phoenix, ☎ 602/266–7464), one of the nation's most respected regional companies, stages an opera season, primarily classical, in Tucson and Phoenix.

Phoenix Symphony Orchestra (✉ 455 N. 3rd St., Suite 390, Phoenix, ☎ 602/495–1999), the resident company at Symphony Hall, has reached the first rank of American regional symphonies. Its rich season includes orchestral works from classical and contemporary literature, a chamber series, composer festivals, and outdoor pops concerts.

Dance

A. Ludwig Co. (☎ 602/965–3914), the Valley's foremost modern dance troupe, includes choreography by founder-director Ann Ludwig, an ASU faculty member, in its repertoire of contemporary works.

Ballet Arizona (✉ 3645 E. Indian School Rd., ☎ 602/381–0184), the state's professional ballet company, presents full seasons of classical and contemporary works (including commissioned pieces for the company) in Tucson and in Phoenix, where it performs at the Herberger Theater Center, Symphony Hall, and Gammage Auditorium.

Film

If you're looking for something besides the latest blockbuster, the **Camelview 5** (✉ Goldwater Blvd. and Camelback Rd., Scottsdale, ☎ 602/423–9900) and **Valley Arts Cinema** (✉ 509 S. Mill Ave., Tempe, ☎ 602/829–6668) show major foreign releases and domestic art films. **Cine Capri** (✉ 2323 E. Camelback Rd., ☎ 602/956–4200), a classic wide-screen theater from the '60s, occasionally offers such giant-screen revivals as *Dr. Zhivago* and *Spartacus*.

Galleries

The gallery scene in Phoenix and Scottsdale is so extensive that your best bet is to consult the "art exhibits" listings in the weekly *New Times* or the Friday "Weekend" section of the *Arizona Republic*.

Theater and Shows

Actors Theatre of Phoenix (✉ Box 1924, Phoenix 85001-1924, ☎ 602/253–6701) is the resident theater troupe at the Herberger. The theater presents a full season of drama, comedy, and musical productions.

Arizona Theatre Company (✉ 808 N. 1st St., ☎ 602/256–6995) is the only resident company in the country with a two-city (Tucson and Phoenix) operation. Productions range from classical dramas to musicals and new works by emerging playwrights. The Phoenix season runs October–June at the Herberger.

Black Theater Troupe (✉ 333 E. Portland St., ☎ 602/258–8128) performs at its own house, the Helen K. Mason Center, a half block from the city's Performing Arts Building on Deck Park. It presents original and contemporary dramas and musical revues, as well as adventurous adaptations, such as its recent versions of *Dancers* and *5 Guys Named Moe*.

Childsplay (✉ Box 517, Tempe 85280, ☎ 602/350–8101 or 800/583–7831) is the state's professional theater company for young audiences and families. Rotating through many a venue—Herberger Theater Center, Scottsdale Center for the Arts, and Tempe Performing Arts Center—these players deliver colorful, high-energy performances of works ranging from adaptations of *Charlotte's Web* and *The Vel-*

veteen Rabbit to a theatrical salute to surrealist painter René Magritte and the power of imagination.

Great Arizona Puppet Theatre (⊠ 3302 N. 7th St., ☎ 602/262–2050 or 602/277–1275) mounts a year-long cycle of inventive puppet productions, mostly original, in a converted church; it also offers puppetry classes.

DINNER THEATERS

Copper State Dinner Theatre (⊠ 6727 N. 47th Ave., Glendale, ☎ 602/ 937–1671), the Valley's oldest troupe, stages light comedy at Max's, a West Valley sports bar, Friday and Saturday nights and Sunday afternoons.

Murder Ink Productions (⊠ 1801 S. Jentilly La., Suite C-12, Tempe, ☎ 602/967–6800) presents audience-interactive whodunits at Slim & Curly's Steakhouse (Mesa), Avanti (Scottsdale), Beef Eater's (Phoenix), and Le Rhone's Tropicana Cafe (Phoenix).

WILD WEST SHOWS

At **Rawhide Western Town & Steakhouse** (⊠ 23023 N. Scottsdale Rd., Scottsdale, ☎ 602/502–1880), the false fronts on the dusty Main Street contain a train depot, saloons, gift shops, and craftspeople. City slickers can take a ride on a stagecoach or gentle burro and kids will enjoy the Petting Ranch's barnyard animals. Hayrides travel a short distance into the desert for weekend "Sundown Cookouts" under the stars; dinner in the steak house is served nightly.

Rockin' R Ranch (⊠ 6136 E. Baseline Rd., Mesa, ☎ 602/832–1539) includes a petting zoo, a reenactment of a wild shoot-out, and—the main attraction—a nightly cookout with a western stage show. Pan for gold or take a wagon ride until the "vittles" are served, followed by music and entertainment. Similar to its competitor, Rawhide, Rockin' R is a better deal because the price of entry is all-inclusive.

Nightlife

Downtown Phoenix used to close up at sunset—until the advent of the Arizona Center. The heart of town at last has nightclubs, restaurants, and upscale bars that compete with livelier resorts and clubs in Scottsdale, along Camelback Road in north-central Phoenix, and elsewhere around the Valley.

Among music and dancing styles, country and western has the longest tradition here; jazz, surprisingly, runs a close second. Rock clubs and hotel lounges are also numerous and varied. The Valley attracts a steady stream of pop and rock acts; for concert tickets, try Dillard's (☎ 602/503–5555).

The best listings and reviews are in the *New Times* free weekly newspaper, distributed Wednesday, and the Friday "Weekend Calendar" section of the *Arizona Republic*. *PHX Downtown,* a free monthly available in downtown establishments, has an extensive calendar for the neighborhood's events from art exhibits and poetry readings to professional sporting events.

Bars and Lounges

America's Original Sports Bar (⊠ 455 N. 3rd St., Arizona Center, ☎ 602/252–2112) is big and boisterous, with 57 TVs (seven giant screens), indoor basketball, and an outdoor volleyball court.

AZ88 (⊠ 7353 Scottsdale Mall, Scottsdale, ☎ 602/994–5576) has the cosmopolitan vibe of a big-city bar and an artful design mélange of glass, convex mirrors, and re-bar.

Chez Nous (⊠ 675 W. Indian School Rd., ☎ 602/266–7372), a dark martini lounge, attracts older patrons, as well as retro-chic twentysomething hipsters.

Macayo's Depot Cantina (⊠ 300 S. Ash Ave., Tempe, ☎ 602/966–6677), in a former train station, is a bustling "meet market" popular with students from the nearby ASU campus.

The **Plaza Bar** (⊠ 122 N. 2nd St., ☎ 602/252–1234), on the mezzanine of the Hyatt Regency Phoenix, provides a sparkling downtown view. Tables just outside the bar proper offer a quieter getaway.

Top of the Rock Bar (⊠ 2000 W. Westcourt Way, Tempe, ☎ 602/431–2370), the lounge in Top of the Rock restaurant at the Buttes, attracts an older, professional crowd to drink in cocktails and the city's most spectacular view.

Casinos

Just northeast of Scottsdale, **Fort McDowell Casino** (⊠ 2 mi east of Shea Blvd. on AZ 87, ☎ 602/843–3678 or 800/843-3678) is popular with the Scottsdale-resort crowd. In addition to the cards, slots, and keno games, offtrack greyhound wagering takes place in a classy, mahogany room with 18 giant video screens. Although reservations are required 24 hours in advance for both individuals and groups, definitely take advantage of the casino's Valley-wide shuttle.

Clubs

Downside Risk (⊠ 7419 E. Indian Plaza, ☎ 602/945–3304) is a sure bet for a chic, young crowd in the mood to libate and gyrate.

Empire (⊠ 4824 N. 24th St., ☎ 602/955–5244) is a happening nightclub, with two full bars, 11 pool tables, and dancing Tuesday–Saturday nights.

Jetz (⊠ 7077 E. Camelback Rd., Scottsdale, ☎ 602/970–6001) has three glitzy dance floors, an extensive bar, and a good-looking crowd. The annex, **Stixx**, is filled with billiard tables.

Martini Ranch (⊠ 7295 E. Stetson Dr., Scottsdale, ☎ 602/970–0500) attracts a high number of singles and hosts such bands as Planet Funk and the Boogie Knights on the outdoor stage.

The Works (⊠ 7223 E. 2nd St., ☎ 602/946–4141) has house and techno, as well as rave and tribal music, overflowing from the dance floor out into art gallery and courtyard.

Coffeehouses

Willow House (⊠ 149 W. McDowell Rd., ☎ 620/252–0272) is a self-described "artist's cove" that draws scores of artsy, bohemian-types. A converted residence, the Willow House has a variety of rooms in which java junkies can recline on sofas, people-watch, or set up for all-night backgammon. Thursday-night poetry readings are a big draw. The espresso flows until midnight on weeknights, 1 AM on weekends.

Comedy

The Improv (⊠ 930 E. University Dr., Tempe, ☎ 602/921–9877), part of a national chain, showcases better-known headliners Tuesday–Sunday; shows cost between $10 and $15.

Star Theater (⊠ 7146 E. 6th Ave., Scottsdale, ☎ 602/423–0120) features the "family sensitive" Oxymoron'Z Improvisational Troupe on Friday and Saturday nights; reservations are required.

Country and Western

Handlebar-J (⊠ 7116 E. Becker La., Scottsdale, ☎ 602/948–0110) has a lively, 10-gallon-hat–wearing crowd.

At **Mr. Lucky's** (⌧ 3660 W. Grand Ave., ☎ 602/246–0686), the grand-daddy of Phoenix western clubs, you can dance the two-step all night (or learn it, if you haven't before).

The **Red River Opry** (⌧ 730 N. Mill Ave., Tempe, ☎ 602/829–6779) performs foot-stompin' matinee and evening country and bluegrass shows. Reserve your seat in advance.

The Rockin' Horse (⌧ 7316 E. Stetson Dr., Scottsdale, ☎ 602/949–0992) features country dance lessons Mondays and live country bands Tuesday–Sunday.

Toolies Country Saloon and Dance Hall (⌧ 4231 W. Thomas Rd., ☎ 602/272–3100) has live bands seven nights a week, and often books well-known national acts.

Jazz

For a current schedule of jazz happenings, call the **Jazz in AZ Hotline** (☎ 602/254–4545).

Azz Jazz Cafe (⌧ 1906 E. Camelback Rd., ☎ 602/263–8482) is an intimate spot designed to showcase jazz combos.

Beeloe's Cafe (⌧ 501 S. Mill Ave., Tempe, ☎ 602/894–1230) is a funky subterranean joint with wall murals of famous pieces by Dalí and Botticelli, parlor sofas for tarot-card readings, and live jazz every night of the week.

J. Chew & Co. (⌧ 7320 Scottsdale Mall, Scottsdale, ☎ 602/946–2733) is a cozy, popular spot with indoor and outdoor seating. Nadine Jansen sings, plays piano, and lifts her fluegelhorn here Tuesday–Saturday from 8:30 to 12:30, drawing scores of devotees and many visiting celebrities.

Orbit Cafe (⌧ 40 E. Camelback Rd., ☎ 602/265–2354) has live jazz and blues Thursday–Sunday in a contemporary art-deco setting with a casual ambience.

Timothy's (⌧ 6335 N. 16th St., ☎ 602/277–7634) joins fine French-influenced southwestern cuisine with top jazz performances from 8:30 to 12:30 nightly, and there's no cover charge.

Microbreweries

Bandersnatch Brew Pub (⌧ 125 E. 5th St., Tempe, ☎ 602/966–4438) is a popular, unhurried student hangout that features a large collection of brewed-daily *cervezas*.

Coyote Springs Brewing Co. (⌧ Camelback Rd. at N. 20th St., ☎ 602/468–0403; ⌧ 122 E. Washington St., ☎ 602/256–6645), the oldest brewpub in Phoenix, has delicious handcrafted ales and lagers, and a thriving patio scene at the Camelback location. Try a raspberry brew.

Hops! (⌧ 2584 E. Camelback Rd., Biltmore Fashion Park, ☎ 602/468–0500; ⌧ 7000 E. Camelback Rd., Scottsdale Fashion Square, ☎ 602/945–4677; ⌧ 8668 E. Shea Blvd., Scottsdale, ☎ 602/998–7777) serves up bistro cuisine and fills frothy-headed mugs with amber and wheat drafts from the display brewery.

Rock and Blues

Blue Note (⌧ 8708 E. McDowell Rd., Scottsdale, ☎ 602/946–6227), unlike its famous namesake in New York City, focuses on blues instead of bebop.

Char's Has the Blues (⌧ 4631 N. 7th Ave., ☎ 602/230–0205) is the top Valley blues club, with live bands playing nightly.

Mason Jar (⊠ 2303 E. Indian School Rd., ☎ 602/956–6271) has a nightly schedule of rock bands.

Rhythm Room (⊠ 1019 E. Indian School Rd., ☎ 602/265–4842) hosts a variety of local and touring blues artists.

OUTDOOR ACTIVITIES AND SPORTS

Participant Sports

When participating in outdoor activities in Phoenix, be aware that the desert heat imposes its particular restraints—even in winter, hikers and cyclists should wear lightweight opaque clothing, a hat or visor, and high UV-rated sunglasses and should carry a water supply of one quart per person for each hour of activity. The intensity of the sun makes strong sunscreen (SPF 15 or higher) a must, and don't forget to apply it to hands and feet. From May 1 to October 1, don't jog or hike from one hour after sunrise until a half hour before sunset. During those times, the air is so hot and dry that your body will lose moisture—and burn calories—at a dangerous, potentially lethal rate. Don't head out to desert areas at night, however, to jog or hike in the summer; that's when rattlesnakes and scorpions are out hunting.

Bicycling

Although the terrain is relatively level, the desert climate makes special demands on cyclists; note the advice on hours and clothing, *above.* Be sure to have a helmet and a mirror when riding in the streets: There are few adequate bike lanes in the Valley.

Scottsdale's Indian Bend Wash (⊠ Along Hayden Rd., from Shea Blvd. south to Indian School Rd.) has bikeable paths winding among its golf courses and ponds. **Pinnacle Peak,** about 25 mi northeast of downtown Phoenix, is a popular place to take bikes for the ride north to Carefree and Cave Creek, or east and south over the mountain pass and down to the Verde River, toward Fountain Hills. Mountain bikers will want to check out the **Trail 100,** which runs throughout the Phoenix Mountain preserve (enter at Dreamy Draw park, just east of the intersection of Northern Ave. and 16th St.). **Cave Creek** and **Carefree,** in the foothills about 30 mi northeast of Phoenix, offer pleasant riding with a wide range of stopover options. **South Mountain Park** (☞ Hiking, *below*) is the prime site for mountain bikers, with its 40-plus mi of trails—some of them with challenging ascents and all of them quiet and scenic.

For rentals, contact **Wheels N' Gear** (⊠ 7607 E. McDowell Rd., Scottsdale, ☎ 602/945–2881). For detailed maps of bike paths, contact **Phoenix Parks and Recreation** (☎ 602/262–6861). To get in touch with fellow bike enthusiasts and find out about regular and special-event rides, contact the **Arizona Bicycle Club** (Gene or Sylvia Berlatsky, ☎ 602/264–5478), the state's largest group. Popular Sunday-morning rides start in Phoenix's Granada Park (⊠ 20th St. and Maryland Ave.) and end up at a local breakfast spot.

Arizona Scenic Biking (☎ 602/905–2453) provides hotel pickup, mountain bikes and equipment, and a CPR-certified tour leader for half-day rides on bike paths and canal banks that pass through the Papago Park area and by ASU's Sun Devil Stadium. **Desert Biking Adventures** (⊠ 7119 E. Shea Blvd., #109–247, Scottsdale 85254, ☎ 602/320–4602) offers two- and four-hour mountain-biking excursions through the Sonoran desert.

Four-Wheeling

Taking a Jeep through the backcountry has become a popular way to experience the desert terrain's saguaro-covered mountains and curious rock formations. A number of companies offer four-wheeling packages for $50–$75 for short excursions.

Arizona Awareness (⊠ 835 E. Brown St., ☎ 602/947–7852) ventures down to the Verde River on its own exclusive trail.

Arrowhead Jeep Tours (☎ 602/942–3361) has cowboy and gold-prospector guides who take passengers out for open-air Jeep drives, with stops to pan for gold.

Carefree Jeep Adventures (☎ 602/488–0023 or 800/294–5337) travels into the Tonto National Forest on rugged old stage and mining roads, stopping for botany lessons, an exploration of hilltop Hohokam ruins, and a brief tour of a reconstructed 1880's gold mine; riders also have a chance to try their hand at a six-gun target shoot along the way.

Scottsdale Jeep Rentals (☎ 602/951–2191) rents Jeeps and provides free trail maps to those who prefer to drive themselves and eschew the company of a talkative guide.

Golf

Arizona boasts more golf courses per capita than any other state west of the Mississippi River, an embarrassment of riches that, coupled with its surfeit of sunny days, makes the Grand Canyon State a golfer's paradise. Playing fees tend to be low and waiting times short, even though golf draws visitors from all over the world. In the Valley of the Sun, more than 100 courses, from par-3 to PGA championship links, are available (some lighted at night), and the PGA's Southwest section has its headquarters here. For a detailed listing, contact the **Arizona Golf Association** (⊠ 7226 N. 16th St., Phoenix 85020, ☎ 602/944–3035 or 800/458–8484).

Ahwatukee Country Club (⊠ 12432 S. 48th St., ☎ 602/893–9772), an upscale course just south of South Mountain Park, is semiprivate but also has a public driving range.

Arizona Biltmore (⊠ 24th St. and Missouri Ave., ☎ 602/955–9655), the granddaddy of Phoenix golf courses, offers two 18-hole PGA championship courses, lessons, and clinics.

Encanto Park (⊠ 2705 N. 15th Ave., ☎ 602/253–3963) is an attractive, affordable public course.

Gold Canyon Golf Club (⊠ 6100 S. Kings Ranch Rd., Apache Junction, ☎ 602/982–9449) is a desert course in the Superstition Mountains area.

Grayhawk Golf Club (19600 N. Pima Rd., Scottsdale, ☎ 602/502–1800), a high-end daily-user course, has championship design by Tom Fazio and immaculate conditioning, making it a favorite of Valley visitors.

Hillcrest Golf Club (⊠ 20002 N. Star Ridge, Sun City West, ☎ 602/584–1500) is the best course in the Sun Cities.

Papago Golf Course (⊠ 5595 E. Moreland St., ☎ 602/275–8428) is a low-price public course in a scenic city setting.

Raven Golf Club at South Mountain (⊠ 3636 E. Baseline Rd., Phoenix, ☎ 602/437–3800) follows a traditional design with thousands of drought-resistant Aleppo pines and Lombardy poplars, making it a cool, shady haven for summertime golfers.

Scottsdale Family Golf Center (⊠ 8111 E. McDonald Dr., Scottsdale, ☎ 602/991–0018) combines golf, a driving range, and lessons at all levels; take the kids.

Thunderbird Country Club (⊠ 701 E. Thunderbird Trail, Phoenix, ☎ 602/243–1262) has 18 holes of championship-rated play on the north slopes of South Mountain. Sweeping views of the city are a bonus.

Tournament Players Club of Scottsdale (⊠ 17020 N. Hayden Rd., Scottsdale, ☎ 602/585–3600), a 36-hole course created by Tom Weiskopf and Jay Morrish, is the site of the PGA Phoenix Open.

Troon North (⊠ 10320 E. Dynamite Blvd., Scottsdale, ☎ 602/585–5300) offers a challenging 36-hole course, designed by Weiskopf and Morrish, that makes excellent use of the existing desert.

Health Clubs

The **Arizona Athletic Club** (⊠ 1425 W. 14th St., Tempe, ☎ 602/894–2281), near the airport at the border between Tempe and Scottsdale, is the Valley's largest facility. Nonmembers pay a day rate of $10.

Jazzercise (☎ 602/893–1557 or 800/348–4748) has 27 franchised sites in the Valley.

Naturally Women (⊠ 2827 W. Peoria Ave., ☎ 602/678–4000; ⊠ 3320 S. Price Rd., Tempe, ☎ 602/838–8800; ⊠ 7750 E. McDowell Rd., ☎ 602/947–8300), closed Sunday, focuses on women's needs, from its health profiles to its diet and exercise programs; it offers one free visitor's day, then a day rate of $10 thereafter.

The **YMCA** (☎ 602/528–5540) offers full facilities—including weight rooms, aerobics classes, pool, and racquetball privileges—to nonmembers at seven Valley locations. Rates are $8 per day.

Hiking

Be sure to bring plenty of water with you when hiking and drink often.

The Valley has some of the best desert mountain hiking in the world—the **Phoenix Mountain Preserve System** (☎ 602/495–0022), in the mountains that surround the city, even has its own park rangers who can help you select and plan your hikes. Phoenix's hiking trails are some of the most heavily used in the world—and for good reason.

Camelback Mountain (⊠ North of Camelback Rd. on 48th St., ☎ 602/256–3220), another landmark hike, has no park, and the trails are more difficult. This is for intermediate to experienced hikers.

The **Papago Peaks** (⊠ Van Buren St. and Galvin Pkwy., ☎ 602/256–3110) were sacred sites for the Tohono O'odham tribe and probably the Hohokam before them. The soft sandstone peaks contain accessible caves, some petroglyphs, and splendid views of much of the Valley. This is another good spot for family hikes.

Squaw Peak Summit Trail (⊠ 2701 E. Squaw Peak Dr., just north of Lincoln Dr., ☎ 602/262–7901) ascends the landmark mountain at a steep 19% grade, but this 1.2-mi trail is a local favorite. Children can handle the hike if adults take it slowly—allow about 1½ hours each direction. Call ahead to schedule an easy hike with a ranger who introduces desert geology, flora, and fauna.

South Mountain Park (⊠ 10919 S. Central Ave., ☎ 602/495–0222) is the jewel of the city's Mountain Park Preserves. At 16,500 acres, it is the world's largest city park, and its mountains and arroyos contain more than 40 mi of marked and maintained trails—all open to hikers, horseback riders, and mountain bikers. It also has three auto-accessible lookout points, with 65-mi sight lines. Rangers can help you plan hikes to view some of the 200 petroglyph sites.

Horseback Riding

More than two dozen stables and equestrian tour outfitters in the Valley attest to the saddle's enduring importance in Arizona—even in this auto-dominated metropolis.

All Western Stables (⊠ 10220 S. Central Ave., ☎ 602/276–5862), one of several stables at the entrance to South Mountain Park, offers rentals, guided rides, hayrides, and at the end of the trail, steak fries.

MacDonald's Ranch (⊠ 26540 N. Scottsdale Rd., Scottsdale, ☎ 602/585–0239) offers one- and two-hour trail rides, as well as guided breakfast, lunch, and dinner rides through desert foothills above Scottsdale.

Superstition Stables (⊠ Windsong and Meridian Rds., Apache Junction, ☎ 602/982–6353) is licensed to lead tours throughout the entire Superstition Mountains area for more experienced riders; easier rides are also available.

Hot-Air Ballooning

Want to tour Phoenix from above? Check out the many sunrise and sunset hot-air-balloon ascents, which offer a remarkable desert sight-seeing experience. More than three dozen companies offer this uplifting experience. The average fee is $135 per person and most companies offer hotel pickup. Flight paths and landing sites vary with wind speeds and directions; a roving land crew follows each balloon in flight. Time in the air is generally between 1 and 1½ hours, but allow three hours for the total excursion. Be prepared for changing temperatures as the sun rises or sets, but it's not actually any colder up in the balloon's basket (known as the gondola).

Adventures Out West (☎ 602/996–6100 or 800/755–0935) will send you home with a free video of your flight taped from the balloon.

Hot Air Expeditions (☎ 602/502–6999 or 800/831–7610) offers the best ballooning in Phoenix. Flights are long, the staff is gracious and charming, and the gourmet treats are prepared by one of the Valley's most venerable chefs, Vincent Guerithault.

Unicorn Balloon Company (☎ 602/991–3666 or 800/468–2478) has been in business since 1978 and is operated by the state's ballooning examiner for the FAA.

Jogging

Phoenix's unique 200-mi network of canals provides a naturally cooled (and often landscaped) scenic track throughout the metro area. Two other popular jogging areas are Phoenix's **Encanto Park,** 3 mi northwest of Civic Plaza, and Scottsdale's **Indian Bend Wash,** which runs for more than 5 mi along Hayden Road. Both have lagoons and tree-shaded greens.

Sailplaning

At the Estrella Sailport, **Arizona Soaring Inc.** (⊠ Box 858, Maricopa 85239, ☎ 602/821–2903) gives sailplane rides in a basic trainer or high-performance plane for prices ranging from $48 to $90. The adventuresome can opt for a wild 15-minute acrobatic flight for $100.

Tennis

Hole-in-the-Wall Racquet Club (⊠ 7677 N. 16th St., Pointe Hilton at Squaw Peak Resort, ☎ 602/997–2626) has eight paved courts available for same-day reservation at $15 per hour.

Kiwanis Park Recreation Center (⊠ 6111 S. All America Way, Tempe, ☎ 602/350–5201, ext. 4) has 15 lighted premier-surface courts (all for same-day or one-day-advance reserve). Before 5 PM, courts rent for $4.50, after 5 PM, the rate is $6; $2 drop-in programs are offered for single players weekdays, 10:30–noon.

Mountain View Tennis Center (⊠ 1104 E. Grovers Ave., ☎ 602/788–6088), just north of Bell Road, is a Phoenix city facility with 20 lighted courts that can be reserved for $3 for 90 minutes of singles play during the day; after dark, the light fee is $2.20.

Phoenix Civic Plaza Sports Complex (⊠ 121 E. Adams St., ☎ 602/256–4120) has three lighted rooftop courts available for $4–$6.

Phoenix Tennis Center (⊠ 6330 N. 21st Ave., ☎ 602/249–3712), a city facility with 22 lighted hard courts, charges $1.50 per person for 1½ hours on the courts; if it's after dark, add a $2.20 light fee.

Watering Hole Racquet Club (⊠ 901–C E. Saguaro Dr., ☎ 602/997–7237) has nine hard, lighted courts that rent for $15 per hour.

Tubing

In a region not known for water, one indigenous aquatic sport has developed: Tubing—riding an inner tube down calm water and mild rapids—has become a very popular tradition on the Salt and Verde rivers. Outfitters that rent tubes include **Salt River Recreation** (⊠ Usery Pass and Power Rds., Mesa, ☎ 602/984–3305), conveniently located and offering shuttle-bus service to and from your starting point. Tubes are $8 per day, all day 9–4; tubing season runs May–September.

Spectator Sports

Auto Racing

Phoenix International Raceway (⊠ 7602 S. 115th Ave., Avondale, ☎ 602/252–3833), the Valley's NASCAR track, holds a Winston Cup 500 each October and the IndyCar Slick 50 race each April.

Balloon Racing

The **Thunderbird Hot-Air-Balloon Classic** (☎ 602/978–7208) has grown into a schedule of festivities surrounding the national invitational balloon race, held the first weekend in November.

Baseball

See Pleasures and Pastimes *in* Chapter 1 for information on **Cactus League** spring training. Games start at the end of February; **Dillard's** (☎ 602/503–5555) sells tickets.

Arizona Diamondbacks (⊠ Box 2095, Phoenix 85001, ☎ 602/514–8400) is one of two expansion teams joining the Major League in 1998; they'll be playing at the new Bank One Ballpark, affectionately referred to as "BOB," a 48,500-seat facility currently under construction.

Basketball

Even without bad-boy Charles Barkley, the **Phoenix Suns** (⊠ 1st and Jefferson Sts., ☎ 602/379–7867) continue to fill all 19,000 spectator seats in the America West Arena; tip-off is usually at 7 PM.

Golf

The **Phoenix Open** (☎ 602/585–4334), played each January at the Tournament Players Club of Scottsdale, is a $1 million PGA Tour event. In March, women compete in the **Standard Register PING Tournament** (☎ 602/942–0000), at the Moon Valley Country Club.

Hockey

The **Phoenix Coyotes** (☎ 602/379–7825) face off in the America West Arena; whether you come for the cross-checking, hooking, or to watch the Zamboni, you'll revel in the First-World extravagance that is artificial ice in the desert.

Rodeos

The **Parada del Sol,** held each January by the Scottsdale Jaycees (⊠ Box 292, Scottsdale 85251, ☎ 602/990–3179), includes a rodeo, a lavish parade famed for its silver-studded saddle, and a 200-mi daredevil ride from Holbrook down the Mogollon Rim to Scottsdale by the Hashknife Pony Express. The **Rodeo of Rodeos,** sponsored in March by the Phoenix Jaycees (⊠ 4133 N. 7th St., ☎ 602/263–8671), has one of the Southwest's oldest and best parades. The **World's Oldest Rodeo** (⊠ Box 2037, Prescott 86302, ☎ 800/358–1888), held each July as part of Frontier Days, gives the Phoenix rodeos a run for their money.

SHOPPING

Since its resorts began multiplying in the 1930s and 1940s, Phoenix has acquired a healthy share of high-style clothiers and leisure-wear boutiques. But well before that, western clothes were dominant here—jeans and boots, cotton shirts and dresses, 10-gallon hats and bola ties (the state's official neckwear). They still are.

In the past decade, Sun Belt awareness has brought a tide of interest in southwestern furnishing styles as well, from the pastels of the desert mountains and skies to handmade lodgepole furniture of the pueblo and rancho. These—as well as Mexican tiles and tinware, wrought iron and copper work, courtyard fountains and paper flowers—have never died out here. Always an essential part of the way southwesterners shape their homes, work spaces, and public places, these crafts have flourished in the current revival.

On the scene long before, of course, were the arts of the Southwest's true natives—Navajo weavers, sand painters, and silversmiths; Hopi weavers and kachina-doll carvers, Pima and Tohono O'odham (Papago) basket makers and potters, and many more. Inspired by the region's rich cultural traditions, contemporary artists have flourished here as well, making Phoenix—and in particular Scottsdale, a city with more art galleries than gas stations—one of the Southwest's largest art centers (alongside Santa Fe, New Mexico).

Most of the Valley's power shopping is concentrated in central Phoenix and downtown Scottsdale. But auctions and antiques shops cluster in odd places—and as treasure hunters know, you've always got to have an eye open.

Arts and Crafts

Folklorico (⊠ 7216 E. Main St., Scottsdale, ☎ 602/947–0758) is a purveyor of whimsical Oaxacan Mexican woodcarvings and southwestern folk arts and crafts.

Gilbert Ortega (⊠ 7237 E. Main St., Scottsdale, ☎ 602/481–0788) is the Valley's largest—and most omnipresent—dealer in Native American jewelry and crafts, with nine Scottsdale locations alone. While stores have ample stock in varying price ranges, discriminating Native American–jewelry buyers do best here.

The **Heard Museum Shop** (⊠ 22 E. Monte Vista Rd., ☎ 602/252–8344) sells a fine selection of southwestern Native American arts and crafts—both traditional and modern—including many one-of-a-kind items.

Jewels of the West (⊠ 7132 E. 5th Ave., Scottsdale, ☎ 602/945–4052) features a fine selection of watches and has hard-to-find gold Navajo- and Hopi-overlay jewelry.

Two Gray Hills (⊠ 7146 E. 5th Ave., Scottsdale, ☎ 602/947–1997 or 800/238–0798) is the only Native-American–operated boutique amid the glut of 5th Avenue stores dealing in Native jewelry, crafts, and kachina dolls. This shop is the best place to discover the styles and lore of native jewelry, and they pledge to beat the price of any neighborhood competitor.

Auctions

Barrett-Jackson Classic Car Auction (⊠ WestWorld Showgrounds, Pima Rd., north of Frank Lloyd Wright Blvd., Scottsdale, ☎ 602/273–0791) showcases over 900 rare and antique cars; serious collectors and oglers alike flock from around the world to this annual mega-auction, held Thursday–Sunday every third weekend in January.

Markets

Guadalupe Farmer's Market (⊠ 9210 S. Av. del Yaqui, Guadalupe, ☎ 602/730– 1945) has all the fresh ingredients of Mexican cuisine that you'd find in a rural Mexican market—tomatillos, many varieties of chili peppers (fresh and dried), fresh-ground *masa* (cornmeal) for tortillas, cumin and cilantro, and on and on.

Mercado Mexico (⊠ 8212 S. Av. del Yaqui, Guadalupe, ☎ 602/831–5925) carries shelf after shelf of ceramic, paper, tin, and lacquerware, all at unbeatable prices.

Patriot's Square Marketplace (⊠ Patriot's Square Park, Washington St. and Central Ave., ☎ 602/848–1234) sells arts and crafts, locally grown produce, baked goods, and homemade jams and salsas, livening up downtown every Wednesday from 10 AM to 2 PM, October–April.

Shopping Centers

Biltmore Fashion Park (⊠ 24th St. and Camelback Rd., Phoenix, ☎ 602/955–8400) has posh shops lining its open-air walkways, as well as some of the city's most popular restaurants and cafés. **Macy's** and **Saks Fifth Avenue** are its anchors, and high-end designer boutiques are its stock-in-trade—**Via Veneto, Gucci,** and **Polo by Ralph Lauren** are among them. **Cornelia Park** offers an awe-inspiring collection of MacKenzie-Childs, Ltd., glassware as well as furnishings, tiles, and linens. Biltmore Fashion Park—home to RoxSand, Steamers, Oscar Taylor's, and Christopher's—also has more fine eating in a small radius than anywhere else in Arizona (☞ Dining, *above*).

The Borgata (⊠ 6166 N. Scottsdale Rd., ☎ 602/998–1822), a re-creation of a medieval Italian walled village, may slip into pretentiousness, but it offers a pleasant enough selection of boutiques and galleries. **Dos Cabezas** (☎ 602/991–7004) has won a well-deserved following as a creative source of southwestern interior and apparel design.

Two-tiered **El Pedregal** (⊠ Scottsdale Rd. and Carefree Hwy., ☎ 602/488–1072), 30 minutes north of Scottsdale in the town of Carefree, is a serene, attractive shopping plaza. At the foot of a 250-ft boulder formation, it contains posh boutiques and a satellite of the Heard Museum. In the spring and summer, don't miss Thursday-night concerts in the courtyard amphitheater.

Metrocenter (⊠ I–17 and Peoria Ave., ☎ 602/997–2641), on the west side of Phoenix, is an enclosed double-deck mall; although this is the largest mall in the Southwest, its muzak-filled, disinfected environment might just as easily be in St. Louis or Seattle or Secaucus. Anchor department stores are **Dillard's, JCPenney, Macy's, Robinsons-May,** and **Sears.** Adjacent to the mall, a roller coaster zips through Taj-Mahal–esque minarets at **Castles 'N' Coasters** (⊠ 9445 N. Metro Pkwy. E, ☎ 602/997–7575), where a miniature-golf park and video-game palace round out the fun.

Mill Avenue in Tempe is the main drag for ASU's student population; small, interesting shops and eateries make for great browsing or just hanging out. **Urban Outfitters** (✉ 545 S. Mill Ave., ☎ 602/966–7250) sells rough-edged, trendy gear and affordable housewares. The way-cool **Changing Hands Bookstore** (✉ 414 Mill Ave., ☎ 602/966–0203) has three stories of new and used books and an inviting atmosphere that will tempt you to linger—as many students do.

Paradise Valley Mall (✉ Cactus Rd. and Tatum Blvd., ☎ 602/996–8840), in northeastern Phoenix, is an older mall, anchored by Macy's department store.

At swank **Scottsdale Fashion Square** (✉ Scottsdale and Camelback Rds., Scottsdale, ☎ 602/941–2140), retractable skylights open to reveal sunny skies above. Besides having Robinsons-May and Dillard's, it is anchored by **Neiman Marcus**. The collection of stores runs toward the upscale including **J. Crew, Jessica McClintock,** and **Artafax. FAO Schwarz,** the **Disney Store,** and **Warner Bros. Studio Store** are attractions for kids.

Superstition Springs Center (✉ AZ 60 and Superstition Springs Rd., Mesa, ☎ 602/832–0212), 30 mi east of Phoenix, has the usual complement of shops and eateries, plus a pleasant outdoor cactus garden to stroll in. The handsome indoor carousel and 15-ft Gila-monster slide keep the kids occupied.

SIDE TRIPS NEAR PHOENIX

All the following sites are within a 1½-hour drive of Phoenix. To the north, Arcosanti and Wickenburg make interesting half-day or day trips from Phoenix. Consider stopping along the way to visit the reenactments of life during Arizona's territorial days at the Pioneer Arizona Living History Museum and the petroglyphs of Deer Valley Rock Art Center. You also might consider Arcosanti and Wickenburg as stopovers on the way to or from Flagstaff, Prescott, or Sedona (☞ Chapter 4).

South of Phoenix, an hour's drive takes visitors back to prehistoric times and the site of Arizona's first known civilization, as well as one of its major pioneer western towns. Florence, one of central Arizona's first cities, is rich in examples of territorial architecture. The Casa Grande Ruins National Monument captures vivid reminders of the Hohokam Indians, who began farming this area more than 1,500 years ago.

Deer Valley Rock Art Center

15 mi north of downtown Phoenix on I–17. Exit at W. Deer Valley Rd. and drive 2 mi west.

On the lower slopes of the Hedgepeth Hills, Deer Valley Rock Art Center has the largest concentration of ancient petroglyphs in the metropolitan Phoenix area. Some 1,500 of the cryptic symbols are found here, left behind by various Native American cultures that have lived in the Valley (or passed through) over the past thousand years. Pick up an interpretive trail guide to the ¼-mi path and a viewing tube (a contraption that cuts glare) and head out for an ancient history lesson. ✉ 3711 W. Deer Valley Rd., Phoenix, ☎ 602/582–8007. *$3. ⊙ Tues.–Fri. 9–2, Sat. 9–5, Sun. noon–5; call for summer hrs.*

Pioneer Arizona Living History Museum

☜ ❷⓿ *25 mi north of downtown Phoenix on I–17, just north of the Carefree Highway (AZ 74).*

Side Trips Near Phoenix

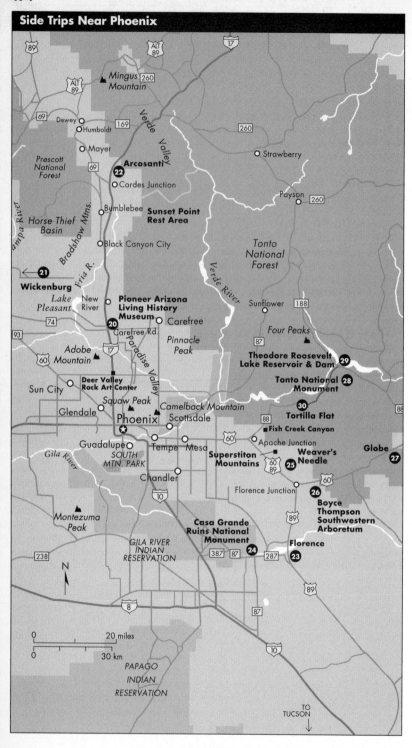

US 89
ALT 89
17
Mingus Mountain 260
ALT 89
169 Verde Valley
260
Dewey
Humboldt
69
Mayer
Strawberry
Prescott National Forest
Arcosanti **22**
Payson 260
Cordes Junction
Bumblebee
Sunset Point Rest Area
Tonto National Forest
Horse Thief Basin
Bradshaw Mtns.
Black Canyon City
Fria R.
Verde River
Hassayampa River
21 ←
Suntlower 188
Wickenburg
Lake Pleasant New River
Pioneer Arizona Living History Museum
20
Carefree
74
Carefree Rd.
Four Peaks
93
Pinnacle Peak
87
Adobe Mountain
60
17 Paradise Valley
Theodore Roosevelt Lake Reservoir & Dam 29
Deer Valley Rock Art Center
Tonto National Monument 28
Sun City
Squaw Peak
Camelback Mountain
Tortilla Flat 30
Glendale
Scottsdale
88
88
Phoenix ✪
■ Fish Creek Canyon
Guadalupe
Tempe Mesa
60
Apache Junction
Weaver's Needle
Superstiton Mountains
Globe
SOUTH MTN. PARK
60 89 **25**
Gila River
Chandler
60 **27**
10
Florence Junction
26
Montezuma Peak
89
Boyce Thompson Southwestern Arboretum
Casa Grande Ruins National Monument
GILA RIVER INDIAN RESERVATION
Florence
238
387 87 **24** 287 **23**
N
89
8
87
0   20 miles
0   30 km
10
PAPAGO INDIAN RESERVATION
TO TUCSON ↓

The Pioneer Arizona Living History Museum contains 28 original and reconstructed buildings from throughout territorial Arizona. Costumed guides filter through the bank, schoolhouse, and print shop, as well as the Pioneer Opera House, where classic melodramas—audiences are encouraged to hiss the villain and cheer the hero—are performed daily. This museum is popular with the grade-school-field-trip set and it's your lucky day if you can tag along for their tour of the site—particularly when John-the-Blacksmith forges, smelts, and answers sixth-graders' questions that adults are too know-it-all to ask. For an extra $5 per adult, tour the grounds via the historically reproduced Conestoga wagon. ⊠ *Pioneer Rd. Exit (Exit 225) off I–17,* ☎ *602/465–1052.* 🖃 *$5.75* ⊙ *Oct.–May, Wed.–Sun. 9–4.*

Wickenburg

㉑ *65 mi from Phoenix. Follow I–17 north for about 25 mins to the Carefree Hwy. (AZ 74) junction. About 30 mi west on AZ 74, take the AZ 89/93 north and go another 10 mi to Wickenburg.*

This city, home of dude ranches and tall tales, is named for Henry Wickenburg, whose nearby Vulture Mine was the richest gold strike in the Arizona Territory. By the late 1800s, these banks of the (now-dry) Hassayampa River hosted a booming mining town with the seemingly endless supply of gold, copper, and silver. Resident miners developed a reputation for waxing overenthusiastic about the area's potential wealth, helping to coin the phrase "Hassayamper" for tellers-of-tales throughout the Old West. Another legend has it that a drink from the Hassayampa River will cause one to fib forevermore—a tough claim to test, since for most of the river's 100-mi course it flows only underground. Nowadays, Wickenburg Old West atmosphere attracts visitors for its wide range of dude-ranch opportunities, quaint downtown, and western museum; antique buffs will enjoy a choice mixture of shops, most of which are found on Tegner and Frontier streets.

Those interested in the lore of the American West will find the 20,000-square-ft **Desert Caballeros Western Museum** (⊠ 21 N. Frontier St., ☎ 520/684–7075 or 520/684–2272) a worthwhile stop; kids enjoy re-creations of a turn-of-the-century general store and local street scene. On the northeast corner of Wickenburg Way and Tegner streets, check out the **Jail Tree** where prisoners were chained, the desert heat sometimes finishing them off before their sentences were served. Maps for self-guided walking tours of Wickenburg's historic buildings are available at the **Wickenburg Chamber of Commerce** (⊠ 216 N. Frontier St., ☎ 520/684–5479), in the city's old Santa Fe Depot.

The self-guided trails of **Hassayampa River Preserve** wind through lush cottonwood-willow forests, dense mesquite bosquets, and around a 4-acre, spring-fed pond and marsh habitat; visitors will spot wildlife aplenty, but it's rare birds that abound here, including waterfowl, herons, and Arizona's rarest raptors. ⊠ *3 mi southeast of Wickenburg on U.S. 60,* ☎ *520/684–2772.* ⊙ *Wed.–Sun.; hrs vary seasonally, call ahead.*

Dining and Lodging

$ ✕ **Anita's Cocina.** Reliable TexMex fare is featured here—fresh, steaming tamales are especially tasty, for either lunch or dinner. Try a fruit burrito for dessert. ⊠ *57 N. Valentine St.,* ☎ *520/684–5777. No credit cards.*

$$$$ ✕🏠 **Rancho de los Caballeros.** This 20,000-acre property combines the dude-ranch experience with first-class amenities. Meals are served in the lodge's bright, festive dining room; guests are asked to dress for

each night's sit-down dinner—jackets or western vests for men. Rooms are spacious, done in low-key southwestern decor. Some contain two queen-size beds and can be creatively configured—through a system of adjoining doors—to annex separate living rooms or sleeping quarters for children. *Daily,* the Pasa Tiempo newsletter, lists such scheduled activities as nature hikes or tennis round-robins, or guests can simply lounge by the mesquite fire, which burns in a copper-hooded fireplace in the lodge's original 1948 *sala* (living room). ⊠ *1551 S. Vulture Mine Rd., 85390,* ☎ *520/684–5484,* ℻ *520/684–2267. 79 rooms. Lounge, pool, driving range, 18-hole golf course, 4 tennis courts, horseback riding, children's programs. Closed mid-May—Sept. No credit cards.*

$$$ ✕▥ **Kay El Bar Ranch.** Tucked into a hollow beside the Hassayampa River just 2½ mi north of town, this is what dude ranches used to be—personable, low-key, and away from it all, with more horses than people, but not too many of either. This National Historic Site, opened as a dude ranch in 1925, was revived in 1980 by congenial sisters Jane Nash and Jan Martin, and accepts only 20 guests at a time. Immense, old salt cedars tower over fat saguaros and some of the biggest mesquite trees in Arizona, all shading the eight-room lodge; a two-bedroom, two-bath cottage with private patio (built in 1914); and charming adobe cookhouse, where family-style meals are served three times a day. While each room in the lodge has its own small, modern bathroom, these quarters are compact and no-frills, designed for sleeping rather than hanging out. During the day, trail rides are led by authentic cowboys. In the evenings, lively conversation and laughter spills out from under the high ceilings of the lodge's living room, where guests snack on homemade hors d'oeuvres by the stone fireplace and enjoy evening cocktails. ⊠ *Box 2480, Wickenburg 85358,* ☎ *520/684–7593. 8 rooms, 1 cottage. Bar, pool, golf privileges, horseback riding, Ping-Pong, volleyball, library. MC, V. Closed May–mid-Oct.*

Nightlife

The **Rancher Bar** (⊠ 910 W. Wickenburg Way, ☎ 520/684–5957) has a modern-day saloon atmosphere, where real live wranglers and cowboys meet up to shoot some pool after a hard day's work; a live country-music combo plays weekend nights, when the two-stepping locals really file in.

Arcosanti

㉒ *65 mi north of Phoenix on I–17, near the exit for Cordes Junction (AZ 69).*

A mile down a partly paved road northeast from the gas stations and cafés, this evolving complex and community of Arcosanti was masterminded by Italian architect Paolo Soleri to be an urban habitat in which architecture and ecology function in symbiosis. Arcosanti is being built by its residents as a totally energy-independent town. It looks almost like a huge playground or contemporary-art theme park, with desert-rock retaining walls and huge solar greenhouses; it's full of inspiring ideas for dramatic design and ecologically sensitive living. It's worth taking the time out for a tour, a bite at the café, and bringing home one of the hand-cast bronze wind-bells made at the site. ⊠ *I–17 at Cordes Junction, near the town of Mayer,* ☎ *520/632–7135.* ▦ *$5 donation.* ☉ *Daily 9–5; tours hourly 10–4.*

En Route   If you're continuing from Arcosanti to Prescott, consider stopping in at **Young's Farm** (⊠ Junction of AZ 69 and AZ 69 169, ☎ 520/632–7272). Family-run since 1947, Young's has hayrides, a nursery, a petting zoo, and a potbellied pig named Clementswine. The store has become a beloved purveyor of fresh vegetables, potpies, cider, honey, and fresh bread.

Florence

㉓ *Take U.S. 60 east (Superstition Freeway) to Florence Junction (U.S. 60 and AZ 79) and head south 16 mi on AZ 79 to Florence.*

This old western town southeast of Phoenix is distinguished by an American Victorian courthouse and more than 150 other sites listed on the National Register of Historic Places. Some visitors may recognize Florence as the location where *Murphy's Romance* was filmed.

The **Pinal County Historical Society** (✉ 715 S. Main St., ☎ 520/868–4382) displays furnishings from 1900s houses and Native American crafts and tools. Open Thursday–Monday, **McFarland Historical State Park** (✉ Main and Ruggles Sts., ☎ 520/868–5216), houses memorabilia of former Governor and U.S. Senator Ernest W. McFarland in 1878-era Pinal County Courthouse. The **Pinal County Visitor's Center** (✉ 135 N. Pinal St., ☎ 520/868–4331) answers questions and provides brochures weekdays 9–4 September through May, 10–2 June through August.

Casa Grande Ruins National Monument

㉔ *9 mi west of Florence on AZ 287 or, from I–10, 14 mi north on AZ 387. When leaving the ruins, take AZ 87 north 35 mi back to U.S. 60.*

Established in 1918, the Casa Grande Ruins National Monument provides a close look at a structure first seen by European explorers in the 17th century. Allow an hour to inspect the site, longer if park rangers are giving a talk at the interpretive ramada or leading a tour.

Start at the visitor center, where a small museum features artifacts and information on the Hohokam, who lived here and farmed irrigated cotton fields until they vanished mysteriously in about AD 1450. Step outside and begin your self-guided tour with an inspection of the 35-ft-tall (that's four stories, folks) Casa Grande (Big House), built around 1350, which is covered by a modern roof for protection from the sun and wind. Neighboring structures are much smaller, and only a bit of the 7-ft wall around the compound is still in evidence. The original purpose of Casa Grande still puzzles archaeologists; some think it was an ancient astronomical observatory—its walls face the four cardinal points of the compass and a circular hole in the upper west wall aligns with the setting sun during summer solstice. Cross the parking lot by the covered picnic grounds and climb the platform for a view of an unexcavated ball court, said to date from the 1100s. Although only a few prehistoric sites can be viewed, more than 60 are included in the monument area. ✉ *1 mi north of Coolidge on AZ 87,* ☎ *520/723–3172.* ✎ *$2, or $4 per carload.* ☉ *Daily 8–5.*

Dining

$ ✕ **Old Pueblo Restaurant.** Of the down-home Mexican and American fare served here, the steak fajita burros, chimichangas, and fish tacos are favorites. The Friday-night all-you-can-eat shrimp and catfish dinner really packs in the locals. ✉ *505 S. Main St., Florence,* ☎ *520/868–4784. AE, D, DC, MC. V. Closed Sat.*

SIDE TRIP AROUND THE APACHE TRAIL

Making a large loop east of Phoenix, this 150-mi drive was called by President Theodore Roosevelt "the most awe-inspiring and most sublimely beautiful panorama nature ever created." A stretch of winding highway, the AZ 88 portion of the Apache Trail follows closely the route forged through wilderness in 1906 to move construction supplies to build Roosevelt Dam, which lies at the northernmost part of the loop. Take a day or two to drive the trail, drink in the marvelous vistas, and stop to explore along the way.

From the town of Apache Junction, you can choose to drive the trail in either direction; there are advantages to both. If you begin the loop in a clockwise direction—heading eastward on AZ 88—your drive may be more relaxing; you'll be on the farthest side of this narrow dirt road some refer to as the "white-knuckle route," with its switchbacks and drop-offs straight down into spectacular Fish Creek Canyon. If you follow the route in the counterclockwise direction—continuing on U.S. 60 past the town of Apache Junction—you'll be passing from at-traction to attraction such that they can be most appreciated.

The tour below follows the route counterclockwise, and assumes that you'll be taking full advantage of the several sites between Phoenix and the city of Globe. Although the drive itself can be completed in one day, we recommend spending a night in Globe, and continuing the loop back to Phoenix the following day.

Superstition Mountains

From Phoenix, take I–10 and then U.S. 60 (the Superstition Freeway) east through the suburbs of Tempe, Mesa, and Apache Junction.

As the Phoenix metro area gives way to cactus- and creosote-dotted desert, the massive escarpment of the Superstition Mountains heaves into view and slides by to the north. The Superstitions are supposedly home to the legendary **Lost Dutchman Mine,** the location—not to mention the existence—of which has been hotly debated since pioneer days.

Weaver's Needle

㉕ *About 11½ mi southeast of Apache Junction, off U.S. 60, take the Per-alta Trail Rd. (just past King's Ranch Rd.). An 8-mi, rough gravel road leads to the start of the Peralta Trail.*

The 4-mi round-trip Peralta Trail winds 1,400 ft up a small valley for a spectacular view of Weaver's Needle, a monolithic rock formation that is one of Arizona's more famous sights. Allow a few hours for this rugged and challenging hike, bring plenty of water and a snack or lunch, and don't hike it in the middle of the day in summer.

Boyce Thompson Southwestern Arboretum

★ **㉖** *12 mi east of Florence Junction (U.S. 60 and AZ 79).*

A "living museum" at the foot of Picketpost Mountain, the **Boyce Thomp-son Southwestern Arboretum** is one of the treasures of the Sonoran Desert. From the visitor center, well-marked, self-guided trails tra-verse 35 acres, winding through all of the desert's varied habitats—from gravelly open desert to lush creekside glades—rich with native flora that coexists alongside imported exotic specimens that have ac-climated to the southwestern desert. The **Smith Interpretive Center,** a National Historic Site, houses displays on such topics as geology and mining plus two greenhouses with cacti and other succulents. Bring a picnic lunch and enjoy the arboretum's lovely picnic grounds. ✉ 37615 Hwy. 60, Superior 85273, ☎ 520/689–2811. ☎ $4. ☉ Daily 8–5.

En Route A few miles farther, **Superior** is the first of several modest mining towns and the launching point for a dramatic winding ascent through the Mescals to a 4,195-ft pass that affords panoramic views of this copper-rich range and its huge, dormant, open-pit mines. Collectors will want to watch for antiques shops through these hills, but be forewarned that quality varies considerably. A gradual descent will take you into **Miami** and **Claypool,** once-thriving boomtowns that have carried on quietly since major-corporation mining ground to a halt in the 1970s. Working-class buildings are dwarfed by the mountainous piles of copper tailings to the north. At a stoplight in Claypool, AZ 88 splits off northward to the Apache Trail, but continue on U.S. 60 another 3 mi to make the stop in the city of Globe.

Globe

🚩 *U.S. 60, 51 mi east of Apache Junction, 25 mi east of Superior, and 3 mi east of Claypool's AZ 88 turnoff.*

On the southern reaches of Tonto National Forest, the city of Globe is the most cosmopolitan of the area's mining towns. Initially, it was gold and silver that brought miners here—the city allegedly got its name from a 50-pound boulder of silver found by prospectors—though the region is now renowned as one of North America's richest copper deposits. Swing by the **Globe Chamber of Commerce** (✉ 1¼ mi north of downtown on U.S. 60., Box 2359, Globe 85502, ☎ 520/425–4495 or 800/804–5623) to pick up brochures detailing the self-guided **Historic Downtown Walking Tour.** Currently in an exciting renaissance, downtown Globe's historic Broad Street offers shopping opportunities and a local artists co-op, with more period buildings slated for renovation into boutiques and eateries. The restored, turn-of-the-century Gila County Courthouse houses the **Cobre Valley Center for the Arts** (✉ 101 N. Broad St., ☎ 520/425–0884), showcasing works by local artists; be sure to visit the ladies and their looms in the basement **Weaver's Studio.**

For a step some 800 years back in time, tour the 2 acres of excavated Salado Indian ruins on the southeastern side of town. The **Besh-Ba-Gowah Ruins and Museum** contains remnants of the more than 200 rooms - occupied here by Salado Indians during the 13th and 14th centuries. Besh Ba Gowah is a name given by the Apaches, who—arriving in the 17th century—found the pueblo abandoned and just moved right on in; loosely translated, the name means "metal camp," as remains left on the site point to it as part of an extensive commerce and trading network. ✉ 150 N. Pine St., ☎ 520/425–0320. ⌨ $2. ☼ Daily 9–5.

If you're driving the Apache Trail loop in one day, stop here to fill up the tank, as Globe is the last chance to gas up until looping all the back to U.S. 60 at Apache Junction.

Dining and Lodging

$ ✕ **Blue Ribbon Cafe.** Beyond the curtained windows of the entry parlor, this charismatic country kitchen is the local favorite, serving up three meals a day on signature bright blue tablecloths. The most unusual menu item is the miner's pasty—pronounced pass-tea—a seasoned meat and potato pie, said to have originated in Cornwall, England and resembling a lumpy calzone. ✉ 474 N. Broad St., ☎ 520/425–4423. AE, D, DC, MC, V. Closed weekends.

$ ✕ **Chalo's.** This casual roadside spot offers some of the best Mexican food you'll find north of the border. Try an order of stuffed *sopaipillas* (puffed Indian bread filled with pork and beef, beans, and red or green chilies). ✉ 902 E. Ash St., ☎ 520/425–0515. No credit cards.

$ ▥ **El Rey Motel.** Hosts Rebecca and Ricardo Bernal lovingly operate this quintessential roadside motel where wagon wheels and potted plants dot the grounds. This nostalgic ranch-style property offers small, immaculate rooms, covered parking spaces, and a shared central picnic and barbecue area. Ask for room number 10 if you want to spend a night where Rebecca—daughter of Arthur—Miller and actor Daniel Day-Lewis honeymooned. ⊠ *1201 E. Ash St.,* ☎ *520/425–4427,* FAX *520/402–9147. 23 rooms. AE, D, MC, V.*

$ 🖳 **Noftsger Hill Inn.** Built in 1907, this bed-and-breakfast was originally the North Globe Schoolhouse; now, former classrooms serve as guest rooms with private baths, filled with mining-era antiques and affording fantastic views of the Pinal mountains and historic Old Dominion mine. Innkeepers Frank and Pam Hulme promise you'll enjoy walking off "miner-size" portions of their Sonoran-style breakfasts with the hike through the scenic Copper Hills behind the old school. ⊠ *425 North St.,* ☎ *520/425–2260. 5 rooms. MC, V.*

Nightlife

Run by the San Carlos Apache tribe, **Apache Gold** (⊠ 5 mi east of Globe on U.S. 70, ☎ 520/425–7692 or 800/272–2433) has over 200 state-of-the-art slots, Keno, and both video and live poker; call about the free shuttle service to most of Globe's hotels and motels.

Shopping

Broad Street, Globe's main drag, is lined with a number of antiques and gift shops. The restored facade of **Simply Sarah** (⊠ 294 N. Broad St., ☎ 520/425–2248) could stop traffic for its artistry and craftsmanship alone; inside, Sarah Anna Day's upscale merchandise consists of ladies clothing in predominantly natural fibers and high-quality accessories. Try **Turquoise Ladies** (⊠ 996 N. Broad St., ☎ 520/425–6288) for owner June Stratton's collection of uniquely Globe souvenirs and stories. On the corner of Ash and Hill streets, **Copper City Rock Shop** (⊠ 566 Ash St., ☎ 520/425–7885) specializes in Arizona minerals and mining antiques.

En Route At the stoplight 3 mi south of Globe on U.S. 60, AZ 88 splits off to the northwest. About 25 mi later on AZ 88, heading toward the Tonto National Monument, you'll see towering quartzite cliffs about 2 mi in the distance; look up and to the left for glimpses of the 40-room **Upper Ruins,** 14th-century condos left behind by the Salado Indians. These particular ruins can't be seen from within the national monument, so pull out those binoculars.

Tonto National Monument

❷❽ *30 mi northwest of U.S. 60 on AZ 88.*

This well-preserved complex of 13th-century Salado Indian cliff dwellings is worth a stop. The self-guided walking tour of the **Lower Ruins** is interesting, but the more adventurous will opt to take a ranger-led tour of the 40-room **Upper Ruins,** offered on selected mornings November–April; tour reservations are required, and should be made as far as a month in advance. ⊠ *HC 02, Box 4602, Roosevelt 85545,* ☎ *520/467–2241.* 🎟 *$4 per carload.* ☼ *Daily 8–5; tours Wed., Sat., and Sun at 9:30 AM.*

Theodore Roosevelt Lake Reservoir and Dam

❷❾ *5 mi northwest of Tonto National Monument on AZ 88.*

Flanked by the desolate Mazatzal and Sierra Anchas mountain ranges, this aquatic recreational area is a favorite with bass anglers, water skiers, and boaters. Not only is this the largest masonry dam on the planet, but the massive bridge—completed for $21 million in 1996—is the longest two-lane, single span, steel-arch bridge in the nation.

En Route   Past the reservoir, AZ 88 turns west and becomes a meandering dirt road, eventually winding its way back to Apache Junction via the magnificent, bronze-hued volcanic cliff walls of **Fish Creek Canyon,** with views of the sparkling lakes, towering saguaros, and a vast array of wildflowers.

Tortilla Flat

③   AZ 88, 38 mi southeast of Roosevelt Dam; 18 mi northeast of Apache Junction

Close to the end of the Apache Trail are the old-time restaurant and country store of authentic stagecoach stop **Tortilla Flat** (⊠ 1 Main St., AZ 88, 85290, ☎ 602/984–1776). This is a fun place to stop for a well-earned rest and refreshment—miner- and cowboy-style grub, of course—before heading back the last 18 mi to civilization. Enjoy a hearty bowl of killer chili and save room for prickly-pear-cactus ice cream.

PHOENIX AND CENTRAL ARIZONA A TO Z

Arriving and Departing

By Bus
Greyhound Lines (⊠ 2115 E. Buckeye Rd., ☎ 602/389–4200 or 800/ 231–2222) has statewide and national routes from its main terminal near Sky Harbor airport.

By Car
If you're coming to Phoenix from the west, you'll probably come in on I–10. This transcontinental superhighway's last link was joined in 1990 in a tunnel under downtown Phoenix. The trip from the Los Angeles basin, via Palm Springs, takes six to eight hours, depending on where you start. From San Diego, I–8 slices across low desert to Yuma and on toward the Valley on what the Spanish called El Camino del Diablo (the Devil's Highway); at Gila Bend, take AZ 85 up to I–10. The trip takes a total of six to seven hours. From the east, I–10 takes you from El Paso, across southern New Mexico, and through Chiricahua Apache country into Tucson, then north to Phoenix (a total of about 9–11 hours).

From the northwest, I–40 crosses over from California and runs along old Route 66 to Flagstaff. East of Kingman, however, U.S. 93 branches off diagonally to the southeast, becoming U.S. 60 at Wickenburg and continuing into Phoenix.

The northeastern route, I–40 from Albuquerque, crosses Hopi and Navajo historic lands to Flagstaff, where I–17 takes you south to Phoenix—an eight-hour journey. For a scenic shortcut, take AZ 377 south at Holbrook to Heber and the pines of the Mogollon Rim; then take AZ 260 down the 2,000-ft drop to Payson and AZ 87 through the forests of saguaro cactus into Phoenix.

By Plane
Most air travelers visiting Arizona fly into **Sky Harbor International Airport** (☎ 602/273–3300). Just 3 mi east of downtown Phoenix, it is surrounded by freeways linking it to almost every part of the metro area.

AIRLINES

Sky Harbor is the home airport of **America West** (☎ 800/235–9292) and a hub for **Southwest** (☎ 800/435–9792). Other airlines with frequent flights to Sky Harbor are **Alaska** (☎ 800/426–0333), **American** (☎ 800/433–7300), **Continental** (☎ 800/525–0280), **Delta** (☎ 800/221–1212), **TWA** (☎ 800/221–2000), **United** (☎ 800/241–6522), and **US Airways** (☎ 800/428–4322).

British Airways (☎ 800/247–9297) has direct service from London's Gatwick airport to Sky Harbor. **LTU International Airways** (☎ 800/888–0200) flies nonstop once a week from Dusseldorf, Germany.

For flights to the Grand Canyon, Page, Lake Havasu, and other Arizona points, try **America West** (☎ 800/235–9292), **Great Lakes Airlines** (☎ 800/274–0662), and commuter **Skywest** (☎ 800/453–9417).

BETWEEN THE AIRPORT AND DOWNTOWN

It's easy to get from Sky Harbor to downtown Phoenix (3 mi west) and Tempe (3 mi east). The airport is also only 20 minutes by freeway from Glendale (to the west) and Mesa (to the east). Scottsdale (to the northeast) is harder to reach, requiring a jaunt on the Squaw Peak Parkway (AZ 51) or a route of all surface streets; both options take 30–45 minutes by car, depending on traffic.

Sky Harbor has limited bus service, ample taxi service, and very good shuttle service to points throughout the metro area. Very few hotels offer a complimentary limo or shuttle, but most resorts do. You should definitely rent a car, either at the airport or wherever you are staying (most rental firms deliver).

By Bus. In about 20 minutes, **Valley Metro buses** (☎ 602/253–5000) will get you directly from Terminal 2, 3, or 4 to the bus terminal downtown (⊠ 1st and Washington Sts.) or to Tempe (⊠ Mill and University Aves.). With free transfers, the bus can take you from the airport to most other Valley cities (Glendale, Sun City, Scottsdale, etc.), but the trip is likely to be slow unless you take an express line. Fare is $1.25.

The **Red Line** runs westbound to Phoenix every half hour from about 6 AM until after 9 PM weekdays. Saturday, you take Bus 13 and transfer at Central Avenue to Bus 0 north; there is no Sunday service. The Red Line runs eastbound to Tempe every half hour from 3:30 AM to 7 PM weekdays (no weekend service); in another 25 minutes, it takes you to downtown Mesa (⊠ Center and Main Sts.).

By Car. Tempe is 10 minutes from the airport by car; Glendale and Mesa are 25 minutes away; and Scottsdale and Sun City, 30–45 minutes. The following companies have airport booths or free pickup from nearby lots: **Alamo** (☎ 800/327–9633), **Avis** (☎ 800/831–2847), **Budget** (☎ 800/527–0700), **Dollar** (☎ 800/800–4000), **Enterprise** (☎ 800/829–1853), **Hertz** (☎ 800/654–3131), **National** (☎ 800/227–7368), **Thrifty** (☎ 800/367–2277), and, if you care more about your wallet than about appearances, **Rent-a-Wreck** (☎ 602/252–4897 or 800/828–5975).

By Limousine. A few limousine firms are allowed to cruise Sky Harbor, and many more provide airport pickups by reservation. All of these are on 24-hour call. **AAA Transportation** (☎ 602/242–3094) charges $15–$50, depending on distance. **Classic Limousine** (☎ 602/252–5166) will take up to six passengers (by reservation only) for $65, depending on how far you're going. **Scottsdale Limousine** (☎ 602/946–8446) also requires reservations but offers a toll-free number (☎ 800/747–8234); it costs from $40 to $70, plus tip.

By Shuttle. The blue vans of **Supershuttle** (☎ 602/244–9000 or 800/258–3826) cruise Sky Harbor, each taking up to seven passengers to their individual destinations, with no luggage fee or airport surcharge. Fares range from competitive with the cheapest taxi for a short run, such as downtown Phoenix or Tempe, to 25% or more below the best taxi fares on longer trips. You can reserve a Supershuttle back to the airport (call ahead to schedule pickup, and allow one hour at the airport before your flight). Wheelchair vans are also available. Drivers accept credit cards and expect tips.

By Taxi. Only three firms are licensed to pick up at Sky Harbor's commercial terminals. All add a $1 surcharge for airport pickups, do not charge for luggage, and are available 24 hours a day. A trip to downtown Phoenix can range from $6.50 to $12. The fare to downtown Scottsdale averages about $15–$16. **AAA Cab** (☎ 602/253–8294), **Checker/Yellow Cab** (☎ 602/252–5252), and **Courier Cab** (☎ 602/232–2222) all charge about $2 for the first mile and $1.30 per mile thereafter. All expect tips.

By Train. Amtrak (☎ 800/872–7245) provides train service in Arizona with bus transfers to Phoenix. Eastbound train passengers will stop in Flagstaff, where Amtrak buses depart daily for Phoenix at 12:45 PM. Westbound train travelers will likely make the transfer in Tucson, where Amtrak-run buses have limited service to Phoenix on Sunday, Tuesday, and Thursday nights at 10:05 PM. What used to be Phoenix's downtown train terminal is now the **Amtrak Thruway Bus Stop** (✉ 4th Ave. and Harrison St., ☎ 602/253–0121).

Getting Around

To get around Phoenix, *you will need a car.* The metro area developed in the automobile era, and only a few downtowns (Phoenix, Scottsdale, Tempe) are pedestrian-friendly. There is no mass transit beyond a bus system that does not even run seven days a week.

By Bus
Valley Metro (☎ 602/253–5000) is a good rudimentary bus system, with 19 express lines and 51 regular routes that reach most of the Valley suburbs. But there are no 24-hour routes; only a skeletal few lines run between sundown and 10:30 PM or on Saturday, and there is no Sunday service. Fares are $1.25, with free transfers. The City of Phoenix also runs a 30¢ **Downtown Area Shuttle (DASH),** with purple minibuses circling the area between the Arizona Center and the state capitol at 10-minute intervals. The system also serves major thoroughfares in several suburbs—Glendale, Scottsdale, Tempe, Mesa, and Chandler. The City of Tempe operates the **Free Local Area Shuttle (FLASH),** which serves the downtown Tempe and Arizona State University area from 7 AM until 8 PM. In addition, **Dial-a-Ride** services (☎ 602/253–4000) are available throughout the Valley on Sundays.

By Car
Driving is easy in the Valley of the Sun: Rain and fog are rare, and snow is even rarer. Most metro-area streets are well marked and well lighted, and the freeway system is making gradual progress in linking Valley areas. Arizona requires seat belts on front-seat passengers and children 16 and under. (For car-rental agencies, ☞ Between the Airport and Downtown, *above.*)

Around downtown Phoenix, AZ 202 (Papago Freeway), AZ 143 (Hohokam Freeway), and I–10 (Maricopa Freeway) make an elongated east–west loop, embracing the state capitol area to the west and Tempe to the east. At mid-loop, AZ 51 (Squaw Peak Freeway) runs north into

Paradise Valley. And from the loop's east end, I–10 runs south to Tucson, 100 mi away; U.S. 60 (Superstition Freeway) branches east to Tempe and Mesa.

Driving in the Valley presents one major challenge: Phoenix and its suburbs are laid out on a single, 800-square-mi grid of horizontal and vertical streets. Even the freeways run predominantly north–south and east–west. (Grand Avenue, running about 20 mi from northwest downtown to Sun City, is the *only* diagonal.) This makes places easy to find, but it also means you must allow a lot of driving time to get from point A to point B, since you have to trace two legs of a right triangle to do it.

Central Avenue is the main north–south grid axis: All roads parallel to and east of Central are numbered *streets*; all roads parallel to and west of Central are numbered *avenues*. The numbering begins at Central and increases in each direction.

Weekdays, 6–9 AM and 4–6 PM, the center or left-turn lanes on the major surface arteries of 7th Street and 7th Avenue become one-way traffic-flow lanes between McDowell Road and Dunlap Avenue. These specially marked lanes are dedicated mornings to north–south traffic (into downtown) and afternoons to south–north traffic (out of downtown).

By Taxi

Taxi fares are unregulated in Phoenix, except at the airport. (For a listing of leading firms and their fares, ☞ Between the Airport and Downtown, *above*.) The 800-square-mi metro area is so large that one-way fares in excess of $50 are not uncommon; you might want to ask what the damages will be before you get in. Except within a compact area, such as central Phoenix, travel by taxi is not recommended.

Contacts and Resources

Emergencies

Police, fire, ambulance, or **highway** emergencies (☎ 911). The **Poison Control Center** (☎ 602/253–3334).

DOCTORS AND DENTISTS

The **Maricopa County Medical Society** (☎ 602/252–2844) and the **Arizona Osteopathic Medical Association** (☎ 602/840–0460) offer referrals during business hours on weekdays. The **American Dental Association Valley chapter** (☎ 602/957–4864) has a 24-hour referral hot line.

HOSPITALS

Samaritan Health Service (☎ 602/230–2273) has four Valley hospitals—Good Samaritan (downtown), Desert Samaritan (east), Maryvale Samaritan (southwest), and Thunderbird Samaritan (northwest)—and a west Valley urgent-care clinic; all share a 24-hour hot line. **Scottsdale Memorial Hospital** (☎ 602/481–4000 or 602/860–3000) has two campuses in the northeastern valley. **Maricopa County Medical Center** (☎ 602/267–5011) has been rated one of the nation's best public hospitals.

LATE-NIGHT PHARMACIES

Walgreen's has fourteen 24-hour locations throughout the Valley. The easiest way to locate the one nearest you is to call ☎ 800/925–4733. **Osco Drug** (☎ 800/881–6726) has 24-hour outlets, including central Phoenix (✉ 3320 N. 7th Ave., ☎ 602/266—5501), west Phoenix (✉ 35th and Glendale Aves., ☎ 602/841–7861), Scottsdale (✉ Scottsdale and Shea Rds., ☎ 602/998–3500), and Mesa (✉ 1836 W. Baseline Rd., ☎ 602/831–0212).

Guided Tours

Reservations for tours are a must all year, with seats often filling up quickly in the busy season, October–April. All tours provide pickup services at area resorts, but some offer lower prices if you drive to the tour's point of origin. For various outdoor excursions, *see* Outdoor Activities and Sports, *above*.

ORIENTATION TOURS

Gray Line Tours (✉ Box 21126, Phoenix 85036, ☎ 602/495–9100 or 800/732–0327) gives seasonal, three-hour narrated tours including downtown Phoenix, the Arizona Biltmore hotel, Camelback Mountain, mansions in Paradise Valley, Arizona State University, Papago Park, and Scottsdale's Old Town; the price is about $27.

Open Road Tours (✉ 748 E. Dunlap, No. 2, Phoenix 85020, ☎ 602/997–6474 or 800/766–7117) offers excursions to Sedona and the Grand Canyon, Phoenix city tours, and Native American–culture trips to the Salt River Pima Indian reservation.

For $35, **Vaughan's Southwest Custom Tours** (✉ Box 31312, Phoenix 85046, ☎ 602/971–1381 or 800/513-1381) gives a 4½-hour city tour for 11 or fewer passengers in custom vans, stopping at the Heard Museum, the Arizona Biltmore, and the state capitol building. Vaughan's will also take visitors east of Phoenix on the Apache Trail. The tour is offered on Tuesdays and Saturdays, September–May; the cost is $60.

SPECIAL-INTEREST TOURS

Arizona Scenic Tours (✉ 2801 E. Victor Hugo Ave., Phoenix 85032, ☎ 602/971–3601) heads past Pinnacle Peak toward the Verde River on dirt desert roads. Two people can expect to pay $50 each (beverages included) for four hours.

Cimarron Adventures and River Co. (✉ 7714 E. Catalina Dr., Scottsdale 85251, ☎ 602/994–1199) arranges half-day float trips down the Salt, Verde, and Gila rivers. Trips cost about $55 per person.

Wagonmasters (✉ 7319 E. Second St., Scottsdale 85251, ☎ 602/423–1449 or 602/501–3239) leads 15-minute to one-hour horse-drawn-carriage tours around Old Scottsdale for $20–$70.

WALKING TOUR

A 45-minute self-guided walking tour of **Old Scottsdale** takes visitors to 14 historic sites in the area. Maps showing the route can be picked up in the Scottsdale Chamber of Commerce (☞ *below*).

Opening and Closing Times

Generally, banks are open Monday–Thursday 9–4, Friday 9–6. Selected banks have Saturday-morning hours, and a few large grocery stores have bank windows that stay open until 9 PM. Most enclosed shopping malls are open weekdays 10–9, Saturday 10–6, and Sunday noon–5; some of the major centers (☞ Shopping, *above*) are open later on weekends. Many grocery stores are open 7 AM–9 PM, but several stores within major chains throughout the Valley are open 24 hours.

Radio Stations

AM

KTAR 620: news, talk, sports. **KIDR 740:** children. **KFYI 910:** news, talk. **KOOL 960:** oldies. **KISO 1230:** adult contemporary. **KOPA 1440:** classic rock. **KPHX 1480:** Spanish-language.

FM
KBAQ 89.5: classical. **KJZZ 91.5:** accoustic jazz, National Public Radio.
KKFR 92.3: Top 40. **KOOL 94.5:** oldies. **KHTC 96.9:** '70s favorites.
KSLX 100.7: classic rock. **KZON 101.5:** alternative rock. **KNIX 102.5:**
country. **KEDJ 106.3:** modern rock. **KVVA 107.1:** Spanish-language.

Visitor Information

Arizona Office of Tourism (✉ 2702 N. 3rd St., Suite 4015, Phoenix
85004, ☏ 602/230–7733 or 800/842–8257). **Native American Tourism
Center** (✉ 4130 N. Goldwater Blvd., Suite 114, ☏ 602/945–0771, FAX
602/945–0264) aids in arranging tourist visits to reservation lands; they
can't afford to send information packets, but visitors are welcome to
call, fax, or stop in Monday–Friday 8–5. **Phoenix Chamber of Commerce** (✉ Bank One Plaza, 201 N. Central Ave., Suite 2700, Phoenix
85073, ☏ 602/254–5521). **Phoenix and Valley of the Sun Convention
and Visitors Bureau** (✉ Arizona Center, 400 E. Van Buren St., Suite
600, Phoenix 85004; ✉ Hyatt Regency Phoenix, 2nd and Adams Sts.;
☏ 602/254–6500 for both). **Scottsdale Chamber of Commerce** (✉ 7343
Scottsdale Mall, ☏ 602/945–8481 or 800/877–1117) is open weekdays 8:30–6:30, Saturday 10–5, and Sunday 11–5.

Weather

The Arizona Republic's **Pressline** (☏ 602/271–5656, then press 1010)
gives tomorrow's forecast and up-to-date Valley conditions. **Weatherline**
(☏ 602/265–5550) provides three-day forecasts. The National Weather
Service (☏ 602/379–4000, then press 4) has a local extended forecast
recording.

6 Eastern Arizona

Northeast of Phoenix, the White Mountains are a cool escape, even when the saguaro-dotted plains are baking mercilessly in sweltering desert heat, these forested peaks contain trout-filled streams and placid lakes. In the winter, the White Mountains have some of the Southwest's best skiing. Farther north, explore Indian Ruins at Casa Malpais and Homolovi Ruins State Park and marvel at the forces of nature at Petrified Forest National Park and Painted Desert.

By Jenner
Bishop

IN A STATE OF DRAMATIC NATURAL WONDERS, Eastern Arizona is often overlooked—truly a tragedy, as it is one of Arizona's great outdoor playgrounds. In the White Mountains, northeast of Phoenix, you can hike amid the largest stand of ponderosa pine in the world while inhaling fresh, clean air; fish for trout in babbling brooks; swim in clear reservoirs fed by unsullied mountain streams; and, at night, camp under the millions of stars twinkling overhead. The region's winter sports are just as varied: You can ski, snowboard, snowshoe, and snowmobile on hundreds of miles of designated trails.

An unparalleled natural beauty, however, is what really makes the region remarkable—the White Mountains are unspoiled high country at its best. Certain areas have been designated as primitive wilderness, removed from the touch of man. In these vast tractless ranges, the air is rent with piercing cries of hawks and eagles and majestic herds of elk graze in verdant, wildflower-dotted meadows. Besides the alpine pleasures of fields and forests, the mountains have a number of unique geological characteristics. Past volcanic activity has left the land strewn with cinder cones and the whole region is bounded by the Mogollon Rim—a 200-mi geologic upthrust that splits the state. Much of the plant life is similarly unique; this is one of the only places in the country where such desert plants as juniper and manzanita grow intermixed with mountain pines and aspen.

The human aspects of the landscape are equally appealing. Historic Western towns are friendly outposts of down-home hospitality and the region's many prehistoric ruins are reminders of the rich native cultures that once flourished here. Native Americans are still a vital presence in the region: Nearly half of the White Mountains is Apache Reservation. Visitors are welcome to explore most Reservation lands. All that's required is a permit—easily obtained from tribal offices.

There's more to eastern Arizona than the White Mountains, however. To the north, along historic Route 66, you'll find the Painted Desert and Petrified Forest National Park and Homolovi Ruins State Park—extraordinary attractions in their own right. The austere mesas of the Painted Desert are world famous for their multihued sedimentary layers. Nature has also worked its wonders on the great fallen logs of the Petrified Forest National Park. In Triassic times, the park was a great steamy swampland; some 225 million years ago, seismic activity forced the swamp's decaying plant matter (and a number of deceased dinosaurs) deep underground, where a series of chemical events replaced the organic matter with stone. Fifty miles west of these unusual geologic remains are remnants of a more recent time: Homolovi Ruins State Park marks the site of five major ancestral Hopi pueblos, one of which contains over 700 rooms. Between these artifacts of times past and the recreational bounty of the White Mountains wilderness, eastern Arizona offers a cultural and outdoor experience that defines the pleasures of Arizona.

Pleasures and Pastimes

Dining

CATEGORY	COST*
$$$$	over $35
$$$	$25–$35
$$	$15–$25
$	under $15

*per person for a three-course dinner, excluding drinks, service, and sales tax (6%–7%)

Lodging

CATEGORY	COST*
$$$$	over $250
$$$	$150–$249
$$	$75–$149
$	under $75

All prices are for a standard double room during high season, excluding taxes and service charges.

Indian Ruins

North of Springerville-Eagar, both Casa Malpais and the Raven Site Ruins are prehistoric pueblo sites with construction characteristics of both the Anasazi peoples to the north and the Mogollon peoples to the south. Today, both the Hopi and Zuni peoples hotly claim individual affiliations with these sacred ruins—particularly Casa Malpais, thought to have been a prominent religious center with an impressive astronomical calendar and the largest kiva (sunken ceremonial chamber) ever discovered in the Unites States. Nearby Lyman Lake State Park has petroglyph trails boasting some of the regions more accessible rock art. West of Holbrook, the Homolovi Ruins State Park is home to a large complex of Hopi ancestral pueblos.

Outdoor Activities and Sports

Although facilities and specific trails are listed under the towns below, some region-wide recreational information is worth noting here.

BIKING

Many White Mountains towns actively promote mountain biking, and there are plenty of rental and service facilities in Pinetop-Lakeside and Show Low. Pedal through the pines on the White Mountains Trail system, with its 200 mi of interconnecting multiuse trails.

Many bike routes follow forest-service roads, which carry heavy traffic during the logging season from April to November; be alert for logging trucks traveling at high rates of speed along these bumpy, narrow paths.

CAMPING

The Apache Sitgreaves National Forest has over 35 different campgrounds, from tent camping to RV hookups. The White Mountain Apache Reservation maintains 32 camping areas throughout its 1.6-million-acre reservation. During busy summer months, secure campground reservations 10 days in advance (☞ Outdoor Activities and Sports *in* Eastern Arizona A to Z, *below*).

FISHING

Anglers flock to the more than 65 lakes and reservoirs in the White Mountains. The White Mountain Apache Reservation alone has more than 300 mi of trout streams and 26 major lakes, and the Apache Sitgreaves National Forest is one of the nation's most visited forests for sportfishing.

The region's catch is predominantly German browns and rainbow and brook trout, but anglers also pull up the occasional arctic grayling; watch, too, for the native Apache trout, the official state fish, with dark spots spaced evenly over its body and no pink coloring on its sides. Early spring is prime trout-fishing season, but even in the winter, devoted anglers can be found ice fishing out on Nelson Reservoir or on Hawley Lake—which commonly posts the state's coldest wintertime temperatures.

High-country warm-water fishing consists of mostly of largemouth bass, walleye, bluegill, and catfish. Lyman Lake and Show Low Lake are good bets for catching walleye, argued by many to be the tastiest fish caught in the region. When lake fishing in the White Mountains, use worms and nightcrawlers for bait—they'll double your chances of catching something, attracting both cold-water and warm-water varieties of fish.

An Arizona fishing license is required at these sites; on tribal land, an additional White Mountain Apache fishing license is required.

GOLF
The High Country's links draw many golf enthusiasts from the Valley of the Sun and Tucson. In addition to cool temperatures and thin, fresh, pine-scented air, these mountain fairways angle through lush, scenic forests of Aspen, blue spruce, and ponderosa pine and wind past lakes, streams, and springs.

HIKING
Hikers of all abilities will enjoy the White Mountains' scenic treks through marvelous vistas of tiered, high-desert terrain. There are also abundant opportunities for wildlife viewing. Pinetop-Lakeside is renowned as the hub for an exceptional multiuse trail system designed in nonrepeating loops and with varying degrees of difficulty. Advanced hikers should stop by individual ranger stations for Geological Survey and Forest Service maps, as well as for local rangers' tips on the myriad trails and day or overnight-camping hikes. When planning your hike through high-desert country, allow one hour for each 2 mi of trail covered, plus an additional hour for every 1,000 ft gained in altitude. Be aware that poison ivy grows in these wilderness areas; learn to recognize the stuff and steer clear!

Farther north, day hikes through the Painted Desert Wilderness's loose clay and sand are one of the best ways to explore the park's backcountry.

SKIING
Famous regionally as a winter skiing destination, the White Mountains offer hilly, wooded landscapes that invite cross-country exploration. Greer is an ideal hub for cross-country skiers: The nearby Pole Knoll Trail System and surrounding forest-service roads make for 33 mi of local cross-country trails. No matter where you stay in the White Mountains, the drive to Sunrise Park Resort—the state's largest ski resort—is never more than an hour away and equipment-rental facilities are located throughout the region.

SNOWMOBILING
Dense forest and expansive meadows comprise a well-known snowmobiler's scenic playground; the adventuresome enjoy long-distance routes connecting Sunrise Ski Area to Williams Valley (near the town of Alpine) or Hannagan Meadow.

Volcanoes
A 1,158 square-mi volcanic field extends from Show Low to Springerville and from Greer to just south of St. Johns. Containing over 405 vents and covers, the Springerville Volcanic Field is a "young" volcanic field—the most recent eruption was 300,000 years ago—and is the third-largest volcanic field of its kind in the continental United States. These extinct cinder-cone volcanoes and eroded lava flows create an especially unusual landscape.

Exploring Eastern Arizona

A tour of eastern Arizona can best be completed by making a loop. The mountain towns of Pinetop-Lakeside, Greer, and Springerville-Eagar are connected by AZ 260. In winter months you'll have to stick to major thoroughfares, as many Forest Service roads are closed. Call the **Road Condition Information Line** (☎ 602/241–3100, ext. 7623) before departing.

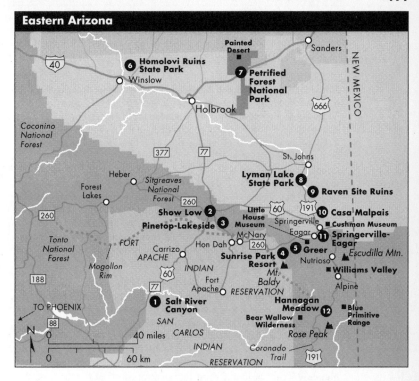

Eastern Arizona

Numbers in the text correspond to numbers in the margin and on the Eastern Arizona map.

Great Itineraries

Your White Mountains experience will depend immensely on what season you visit and what your interests are: If your main intention is recreational activities, you shouldn't have any trouble getting where you need to go in a reasonable amount of time; if, on the other hand, you enjoy long drives through breathtaking mountain scenery, you'll need more time to venture farther afield. It's going to be difficult, however, to combine long drives and exploration with sporting activities without a significant chunk of time.

The itineraries below assume that you're traveling between March and October, when both primary and secondary roads are passable. If you're visiting during the winter, you may have to rearrange your trip to accommodate seasonal road closures and chain requirements.

IF YOU HAVE 3 DAYS

Your options are limited if you only have three days to explore the mountains, given the distance from Phoenix, and the condition of the roads much of the year. Your best bet is to drive up to **Pinetop-Lakeside** ③, **Greer** ⑤, or **Springerville-Eagar** ⑪ and take advantage of a day or two of hiking, fishing, or biking. Snow enthusiasts commonly make the pilgrimage to **Sunrise Park Resort** ④ for just a mere day or two.

On the other hand, if your main priority is visiting the **Petrified Forest** ⑦, spend the first night in 🏨 **Show Low** ② at any one of the ubiquitous chain motels lining the freeway. On day two, continue on and tour the park; spend the night in nearby 🏨 Holbrook, or make the scenic 75-mi drive southeast into **Springerville-Eagar** ⑪, where you'll find several lodging options. Another option is to retrace your route back on

AZ 77 and head east for accommodations in ⊞ **Pinetop-Lakeside** ③.
Spend your third day driving back to Phoenix. You can return via U.S.
60 or opt for the daylong trip down the Coronado Trail, one of the
state's most scenic byways.

IF YOU HAVE 5 DAYS

After exploring the **Painted Desert** and **Petrified Forest National Park** ⑦,
head south to the White Mountains and spend the night in either
⊞ **Springerville-Eagar** ⑪ or **Pinetop-Lakeside** ③, depending on whether
you take AZ 77 or U.S. 180. From either of these twin towns, indulge
a day of local sightseeing and spend the following day working your
way across east–west AZ 260 through the Apache Sitgreaves National Forest and parts of the White Mountain Apache Reservation,
making a stop in tiny ⊞ **Greer** ⑤. On the last day, retrace your route
back to Phoenix via U.S. 60 or, if departing from Springerville-Eagar,
via the Coronado Trail. If you're looking for solitude and remote
beauty, skip poking along AZ 260's towns and head straight from the
Petrified Forest down U.S. 180 to ⊞ **Hannagan Meadow** ⑫, returning on the remainder of the Coronado Trail for day five.

IF YOU HAVE 7 OR MORE DAYS

Spend two nights in Holbrook, devoting a full day to the **Painted
Desert** and **Petrified Forest National Park** ⑥, and the next half day to
touring the **Homolovi Ruins State Park** ⑥ and enjoying the drive south
to **Pinetop-Lakeside** ③ or **Springerville-Eagar** ⑪. From either of these
points, take advantage of the multitude of recreational opportunities
that line east–west AZ 260. Return to Phoenix via the Coronado
Trail, stopping for at least one night in Alpine or ⊞ **Hannagan
Meadow** ⑫; if you don't want to repeat portions of the drive on AZ
260 and you enjoy peaceful, scenic back roads, pick up a map of
Forest Service routes from any ranger station and meander toward
Hannagan Meadow and U.S. 191 on Forest Service roads that sprout
south and east from AZ 373 and AZ 261.

When to Tour Eastern Arizona

If you're a snow enthusiast, winter is definitely the time to tour the
White Mountains; those visiting in the beginning of January who want
to witness some real-life mushing should check out the Alpine Annual
Sled Dog Races.

During warmer months, take advantage of the wide variety of outdoor
activities possible in the area. In the middle of May, the tiny hamlet of
Greer comes alive to celebrate Greer Days with a parade, crafts, dances,
and a fishing derby.

Crowds begin converging on the White Mountains starting in late
June, when school is out and Valley of the Sun temperatures start to
become uncomfortably warm.

Autumn is a splendid time for a drive down the Coronado Trail, with
hairpin turns winding through the yellows and golds of resplendent stands
of Aspen and Oak. The Pinetop-Lakeside Fall Festival is held annually
the last weekend of September, with a parade and impressive assort-
ment of craft booths. White Mountain Apache Tribal Fair is celebrated
each Labor Day weekend with a parade and professional rodeo.

THE WHITE MOUNTAINS

At elevations ranging from 7,000 to more than 9,000 ft, the White Mountains of east-central Arizona are a winter wonderland and a summer
haven. Writing in the 1870s, John Gregory Bourke called the region
"a strange upheaval, a freak of nature, a mountain canted up on one

side; one rides along the edge and looks down two or three thousand feet into . . . a weird scene of grandeur and rugged beauty." It is still grand and rugged, carved by deep river canyons and tall cliffs covered with ponderosa pine. It is also much less remote than it was in Bourke's time, with a full-scale real-estate boom now underway.

Winter travelers through the White Mountains should be aware that weather conditions can change without notice in these higher elevations. Call for weather information before heading out to White Mountains highways (☞ Getting Around By Car *in* Eastern Arizona A to Z, *below*.)

Salt River Canyon

① *40 mi past Globe on U.S. 60 north.*

Exposing a time lapse of 500 million years, these multicolored spires, buttes, mesas, and canyon walls have inspired this canyon's nickname as the "mini–Grand Canyon." Approaching the Salt River Canyon from Phoenix, U.S. 60 climbs through rolling hills and the terrain changes to forests of ponderosa pine. After entering the San Carlos Indian Reservation, the highway drops 2,000 ft—from the Natanes Plateau into the canyon's vast gorge—and makes a series of hairpin turns down to cross the Salt River. Stop before crossing the bridge to stretch your legs and wander along the banks of the Salt, enjoying its rock-strewn rapids (on hot Arizona days you can slip your shoes off and dip your feet into the chilly water for a cool respite).

En Route The road out of the Salt River Canyon climbs along the canyon's northern cliffs, providing views of this truly spectacular chasm, unfairly overlooked in a state full of world-famous gorges. The highway continues some 50 mi northward to the **Mogollon Rim**—a huge geologic ledge that bisects much of Arizona—and its cool upland pine woods.

Show Low

② *60 mi north of the Salt River Canyon on U.S. 60.*

Why yes, Show Low *is* an odd name for a town. Local legend has it that two partners, Clark and Cooley, homesteaded the surrounding 100,000 acres in 1870, but found themselves wanting to dissolve the partnership some years later after an argument. The two decided to play cards, after which the winner would buy out the loser. On the last hand of the night, Cooley was a point behind when Clark allegedly offered "show low and you win." Cooley cut the deck and came up with the Deuce of Clubs, thereby winning the game and the land. Part of the partners' then-ranch is now the town of Show Low, and the main drag through town is called Deuce of Clubs.

Show Low has none of the charm of its neighboring White Mountains communities, but it is the main commercial center for the high country. Additionally, the city is a crossing point for east–west traffic along the Mogollon Rim and traffic headed for Holbrook and points north. If you're heading up to the Painted Desert and Petrified Forest from Phoenix, you might want to spend the night here. No lodging options are listed below, as the extent of Show Low's motels are bland chain properties.

Dining

$ ✕ **High in the Pines.** A block east of Deuce of Clubs, this quaint deli and coffeehouse has tasty specialty sandwiches—the Garlic Pepper Loin sandwich is out of this world. A variety of European-style charcuterie boards include fine selections of pâtés, meats, and cheeses served with a fresh baguette. ⊠ *201 E. Hall,* ☎ *520/537–1453. Closed Sun. No dinner. No credit cards.*

Outdoor Activities and Sports

FISHING

Show Low Lake (⊠ 5 mi south of Show Low, 1 mi off AZ 260 on Show Low Lake Rd., ☎ 520/520/368–5111) has a small bait shop, boat rentals, and a launch on site. **Bill's Lake** (⊠ 7756 White Mountain Lake Rd., ☎ 520/537–8301 or 520/537–9589) is stocked with trout, bass, and catfish, and requires no fishing license; it's a favorite spot for youngsters and nonanglers, who pay by the pound for whatever fish they catch.

GOLF

Silver Creek Golf Club (⊠ 2051 Silver Lake Blvd., Show Low 85901, ☎ 520/537–2326) is an 18-hole championship golf course. **Concho Valley Country Club** (⊠ 7 County Rd., off AZ 61; 28 mi northeast of Show Low, ☎ 520/337–4644) is open year-round and has a sparkling spring-fed stream meandering through its par-72 course.

SKIING

In Show Low's Safeway Plaza, **Play It Again Sports** (⊠ 161 E. Deuce of Clubs, ☎ 520/537–0451) rents skis, snowboards, some bibs and jackets, and stays open until 10 PM during weekend night-skiing season.

Pinetop-Lakeside

❸ *15 mi southeast of Show Low on AZ 260.*

At 7,200 ft, the community of **Pinetop-Lakeside** is known for its proximity to the world's largest strand of ponderosa pine. The modest year-round population is 8,000, but with a recent summer months' count skyrocketing as high as 30,000, the secret of Pinetop-Lakeside as a mountain resort town is now officially out. Once popular only with the retirement- and summer-home–set, the city now lures thousands of "flat-landers" and "desert-rats" up from the Valley of the Sun with its gorgeous scenery, excellent multiuse trails, the White Mountains' three premier golf courses, and temperatures rarely exceeding 85°F.

The community of Pinetop-Lakeside was formed when the two towns incorporated in 1984—although they still retain separate post offices. On weekends, you'll often find fruit and vegetable stands along the slowly curving highway purveying modestly priced, fresh Arizona produce. The main drag is known as both AZ 260 and White Mountain Boulevard.

Dining and Lodging

$–$$ ✕ **Christmas Tree.** Chicken and dumplings "like Grandma's" are the house specialty, but honey duck served with fried apples and lean, char-broiled chicken with steamed zucchini are also highly recommended. A variety of steaks, chops, and seafood is also available, as well as a children's menu. Beloved American humorist Erma Bombeck—who kept a retreat cabin in Pinetop—raved about the fresh baked peach pie; save room for a slice. ⊠ *Woodland Rd. and White Mountain Blvd.,* ☎ *520/ 367–3107. Closed Mon. and Tues. No lunch. D, MC, V.*

$ ✕ **Annie's Gift Shop and Tea Room.** Across the highway from the Lakeside Fire Department, this spot's hearty specialty sandwiches and other delectables make it the local in-spot for lunch. Don't count on a late one—Annie's closes at 2:30 PM. ⊠ *2849 White Mountain Blvd.,* ☎ *520/368–5737. Closed Sun. and Mon. No dinner. AE, MC, V.*

$$–$$$ 🏨 **Coldstream B&B.** This historic 1920s residence was built for lumber executive James McNary, namesake of the neighboring town.

Overflowing with country charm, guests here are encouraged to deposit their troubles in the "Worry Box" at the entrance, so as to have nothing interfere with their relaxing by a roaring fireplace or out on the patio and manicured lawns. Social tea is a favorite ritual here, served daily at 4 PM. ⊠ *3042 Mark Twain Dr., Pinetop, 85935,* ☎ *520/369–0115. 5 rooms with bath. Hot tub, golf privileges, billiards. AE, D, MC, V.*

$$ ⊞ **Northwoods Resort.** Each individual cottage-cabin at this mountain retreat has its own covered porch and barbecue; inside, natural wood paneling, brick fireplaces, and wall-to-wall carpeting add to the homey feel. Full electric kitchens have full-size refrigerators and microwaves; adjacent dinette sets are as perfectly suited for a game of canasta as for a bite to eat. While some of the decor is a far cry from elegant, proprietors here keep their promise to provide "meticulously maintained" accommodations. ⊠ *Box 397R, AZ 260 at milepost marker 352, Pinetop, 85935,* ☎ *520/367–2966 or 800/813–2966,* FAX *520/367–2969. 14 cabins. Refrigerators, outdoor hot tub, coin laundry. D, MC, V.*

Nightlife and the Arts

FILM

Lakeside Cinema (⊠ AZ 260 and Billy Creek Rd., Pinetop, ☎ 520/367–7469) in Safeway Plaza shows first-run movies.

LOUNGES

Charlie Clark's (⊠ 1701 E. White Mountain Blvd., Pinetop, ☎ 520/367–4900) lounge has pool tables and offtrack betting.

Outdoor Activities and Sports

BIKING

The trailhead for **Country Club Trail** is at the junction of Forest Service Roads 182 and 185; these 3½ mi of moderate-difficulty mountain biking can be spiced up by following the spur-trail to the top of Pat Mullen Mountain and back. The 8-mi **Panorama Trail** affords astonishing views from the top of extinct double volcanoes known as the Twin Knolls and passes though a portion of designated wildlife habitat area.

Pick up individual trail brochures or a $2 booklet on the **White Mountains Trailsystem** from the Pinetop-Lakeside Chamber of Commerce, Lakeside Ranger Station, or local sporting goods stores. **White Mountain Cyclery, Ltd.** (⊠ 43 W. White Mountain Blvd., Pinetop, ☎ 520/367–2453 or 800/380–1557) rents mountain bikes for about $15 a day.

FISHING

East of Pinetop-Lakeside and 9 mi south of AZ 260 on AZ 473, 260-acre **Hawley Lake** sits on 8,200-ft Apache territory and yields mostly rainbow trout; rental boats are available in the marina. Open mid-May–October, **Fred's Lake** (☎ 520/367–3474) requires no license—you just pay for whatever you catch by the pound. They also rent poles, and will clean your catch. **Bob's Bang Room & Pawn Shop** (⊠ 3973 AZ 260, Lakeside, ☎ 520/368–5040) stocks supplies and deals in pawned fishing equipment.

GOLF

White Mountain Country Club (⊠ AZ 260 and Country Club Dr., ☎ 520/367–4357), the most challenging of Pinetop-Lakeside's courses, is a par-72 private course with steep fairways through ponderosa forests and several doglegs. **Pinetop Country Club** (⊠ 2 mi east of AZ 260 on Buck Springs Rd., ☎ 520/369–2461) boasts several uphill holes, including a wicked number nine played through a dense grove of ponderosa pine. **Pinetop Lakes Golf & Country Club** (⊠ ¼ mi east of AZ 260 on Buck Springs Rd., ☎ 520/369–4184) has fewer trees, but it offers several water hazards by way of compensation. If you want to spend some time on the driving range, visit the **Triple Tee Golf Center** (⌧ 504 N. Woodland, ☎ 520/368–6625).

HIKING

Named one of the country's "Top Ten Trail Towns" by the American Hiking Society, Pinetop-Lakeside is the primary trailhead for the **White Mountains Trailsystem,** roughly 200 mi of interconnecting multiuse loop trails spanning the White Mountains. Pick up a trail booklet at the Pine-top-Lakeside Chamber of Commerce, Lakeside Ranger Station, or local sporting-goods stores for $2.

☾ Half a mile off AZ 260 on Woodland Rd., **Big Springs Environmental Study Area** is a ½-mi loop trail that wanders by riparian meadows, two streams, and a spring-fed pond; a series of educational signs are devoted to the surrounding flora and fauna.

☾ The well-traveled and very easy **Mogollon Rim Interpretive Trail** follows a small part of the 19th-century **Crook Trail** along the Mogollon Rim; the ¼-mi path, with a trailhead just west of the Pinetop-Lakeside city limits, is well marked with interpretative placards describing local wildlife and geography.

HORSEBACK RIDING

Thunderhorse Ranch (⌧ Box 2065, Lakeside 85929, ☎ 520/368–5593) offers one-hour, two-hour, and half-day rides into the wilderness.

SKIING

Ski Bums, Inc. (⌧ 1624 W. White Mountain Blvd., ☎ 520/368–5155 or 800/774–4754) has snowboards for rent, as well as skis, accessories, and roof racks. The **Skier's Edge** (⌧ 560 W. White Mountain Blvd., ☎ 520/367–6200 or 800/231–3831) has cross-country and downhill ski packages, and rents snowshoes for $12 a day.

Shopping

Orchard Antiques (⌧ 1664 White Mountain Blvd., Lakeside, ☎ 520/368–6563) is a reliable purveyor of high-quality furniture, glass, sterling, and deals in some quilts and vintage clothing. **Pinecrest Lane Antiques** (⌧ 50 Pinecrest Lane, Pinetop, ☎ 520/367–0943) has "a house and barn full" of furniture, including iron and brass beds. In a historical log cabin, **Harvest Moon Antiques** (⌧ 392 White Mountain Blvd., Pinetop, ☎ 520/367–6973) specializes in Old West relics, ranging from buckskins and Apache wares to old guns and U.S. Cavalry items; look for the tepees set up outside.

Hon-dah

8 mi south of Pinetop-Lakeside.

The name of this small town comes from the Apache phrase "welcome to my house." In this case, the house is White Mountain Apache–owned and –operated **Hon-Dah Casino** (⌧ Junction of AZ 73 and AZ 260, ☎ 520/369–0299 or 800/929–8744) with a small poker room, video poker and blackjack, and hundreds of slot machines, even for nickel and penny wielders. The **Timbers Lounge & Showroom** has live entertainment five nights a week, ranging from musicians—mostly country bands—to magicians and stand-up comics. Besides gambling and entertainment options, there's a truly remarkable dining deal. **Indian Pine Restaurant** serves the cheapest bite in town; the hearty $2.75 Casino Breakfast Special consists of two eggs, three pancakes, a choice of bacon or sausage, and really does cost only $2.75—plus gratuity, of course!

En Route Named after the McNary Lumber Company, **McNary** was once a thriving company town, supporting over 2,000 residents. The sawmill was destroyed by fire in 1979, mill owners moved their operation eastward to Eagar, and now McNary is little more than a ramshackle community among the pines of the White Mountain Apache Reservation. During summer months, however, slow down if you see a tent and a sign advertising Indian fry bread. It's worth a stop to try this doughy fried dish with honey or other fillings for a taste of Native American cuisine.

Sunrise Park Resort

❹ *17 mi southeast of McNary; 7 mi south of AZ 260 on AZ 273.*

In winter and early spring, ski-lovers and snow-lovers alike will want to visit this ski area. There's plenty more than downhill and cross-country skiing here, including snowboarding, snowmobiling, and snowshoeing. The resort has 11 lifts and 65 trails on three mountains rising to 11,000 ft. Eighty percent of the downhill runs are for beginning or intermediate skiers, but novices aren't relegated to a bunny slope—many less-intense trails begin at the top of the mountains, so skiers of varying skill levels can enjoy riding the chairlifts together. One-day lift tickets are about $32.

New in 1997, Sunrise's **Snowboard Park** features implanted wood and metal rails, jumps of all difficulty levels, and its own sound system. Restricted to snowboarders only, the area—between the Pump House and Fairway runs—can support enthusiasts' quests to "get a great ollie, hit the kicker and go big," while simultaneously lessening tension on the hill between boarders and skiers.

For cross-country skiers, eight interconnecting cross-country trails total 13½ mi in length and snowmobilers enjoy their own 25 mi of separate, designated trail. ⊠ *Box 217, McNary 85930,* ☎ *800/554–6835 or 520/735–7669; 800/772–7669 or 602/735–7676 for snow reports at Sunrise Park. AE, D, MC, V.*

For rentals, the **Sunrise Sports Center** (⊠ 7 mi south of AZ 260 on AZ 273, ☎ 602/735–7669) has a variety of equipment, from skis, snowboards, and snowshoes in the winter to mountain bikes in the summer. **Action Ski Rental** (⊠ Base of Apache and Cyclone Peaks, ☎ 520/735–7240) offers high-quality downhill and snowboard equipment and offers free hot waxes any time of the day.

Greer

★ ❺ *35 mi southeast of Pinetop-Lakeside and 15 mi southwest of Eagar on AZ 260; 8 mi east of the AZ 273 turnoff, take AZ 373 south.*

The charming community of Greer sits just south of AZ 260 among pine, spruce, and aspens on the banks of the Little Colorado River. This portion of gently sloping National Forest land is covered with meadows and reservoirs and dominated by 11,590-ft Baldy Peak. Much of the surrounding area remains under the control of the Apache nation, so visitors must take care to respect the land and Apache law. AZ 374 is also Greer's "Main Street"; it winds through the village and crosses the Little Colorado River; eventually coming to a dead end, it's affectionately called "The Road to Nowhere."

Dining and Lodging

$ ✕ **Cattle Kate's Restaurant and Lodge.** The inviting interior of this log-construction dining room is accented by red bandanna napkins and a stuffed Alaskan brown bear peering down from the mezzanine. Specialties here include the catch of the day, chicken fritters, and rocky mountain oysters—the specialty of the house. Call ahead, the dining room keeps seasonal hours. ⊠ *80 N. Main St., Greer 85927,* ☎ *520/735–7744. MC, V.*

$$–$$$ 🏨 **Peaks at Greer.** For those who prefer greater privacy or amenities than Greer's cabin or B&B options, this is the only hotel-style accommodation in town. In addition to a bar and restaurant off the lobby, there's a basement game room. During summer months, the deck and patio are lovely spots to enjoy a bite from the restaurant or a good book. Cabin accommodations have rustic interiors and full-size kitchens. ⊠ *Box 132, Greer 85927,* ☎ *520/735–7777,* FAX *520/735–7204. 11 rooms, 3 suites, 2 cabins. Restaurant, bar, no-smoking rooms. AE, D, MC, V.*

$$–$$$ 🏨 **Red Setter Inn.** From the vaulted ceilings over the breakfast area and
★   the antique toy collection to the player piano in the Gathering Room, owners Jim Sankey and Ken Conant haven't overlooked a single detail in designing their 7,000 square ft, hand-hewn log inn. Rooms are individually accoutered—many have fireplaces and French doors opening onto private decks or balconies. All accommodations have private bathrooms, many with whirlpool bathtubs and hand-painted ceramic-tile accents. From the "Angler's Room," one can fish the river literally steps from a private deck. Guests who set out to hike or fish during the day are sent off with custom-packed gourmet sack lunches. If it's less-strenuous repose you're seeking, grab an Adirondack chair on the great expanse of redwood deck that overlooks the Little Colorado River's west fork, or venture downstairs into the game room— with several antique arcade games, a wide variety of board games, and a video library of over 300 titles, including every *I Love Lucy* ever shot. ⊠ *8 Main St., Box 133, Greer 85927,* ☎ *520/735–7441,* FAX *520/735– 7425. 9 rooms. No-smoking rooms, fishing, cross-country skiing, recreation room. AE, MC, V.*

$$–$$$ 🏨 **White Mountain Lodge.** Built in 1892, the Lodge is the oldest original building still standing in Greer. Authenticity's unmistakable charm radiates from this B&B, where innkeepers Charlie and Mary Bast are both gracious hosts and well-versed local historians to those smart enough to inquire about the house's past—ask about the fabled night Greer's rogues and rocket scientists had a few too many and decided it was just as good a time as any to raise the roof. Rooms in the lodge are appointed in different themes, most of which settle into the cozy, country-decor arena—upstairs, however, the Navajo room features more traditional southwestern decor. Don't miss Mary's homemade cookies or hot spiced cider. ⊠ *Box 143 or 140 Main St., Greer 85927,* ☎ *520/735–7568,* FAX *520/735–7498. 7 rooms, 3 cabins. No-smoking rooms, fishing, cross-country skiing. D, DC, MC, V.*

⛺ **Rolfe C. Hoyer Campgrounds.** These choice 100 campground units have showers, flush toilets, and the other nearby amenities offered by the town of Greer. Firewood is available for $4 per bag, sold between camp's Squirrel Loop and Turkey Loop. The campsite fee is $12 a night per vehicle. Local wildlife is abundant—remember to secure campsites from foraging four-legged friends. ⊠ *AZ 373, directly south of AZ 260,* ☎ *520/333–4372. Closed Oct.–Apr.*

Nightlife and the Arts

Tiny Greer's nightlife can be found in the bar and lounge of the **Mollie Butler Lodge** (⊠ 109 Main St., ☎ 520/735–7226), where tourists and locals congregate to play a game of pool or sink into cozy seats surrounding a sunken fireplace.

Outdoor Activities and Sports

The **Circle B Market** (✉ 38940 AZ 373, ☎ 520/735–7540) rents cross-country skis and toboggan sleds in winter, and fishing boats, mountain bikes, and inner tubes the rest of the year; fishing licenses and reservation permits are also for sale.

FISHING

The three **Greer Lakes** are actually the **Bunch, River,** and **Tunnel** reservoirs. Bait and fly-fishing options are scenic and plentiful; boat launches are available for those partial to trolling. Winding through Greer, the **Little Colorado River**'s **West Fork** is also well stocked with trout.

HIKING

The difficult but still accessible **Mt. Baldy Trail** begins at **Sheeps Crossing,** southwest of Greer on Forest Service Road 87. In just under 8 mi (one way), the trail climbs the northern flank of 11,590-ft Mt. Baldy, the second-highest peak in Arizona and from the heights of which spectacular views of the Salt River Canyon and Mogollon Rim can be seen. Note that the very summit of Baldy is on the White Mountain Apache Reservation; considered sacred land, this final ¼ mi to the summit is off-limits to non-Apaches. The boundary is clearly marked; please respect it, regardless of how much you might wish to continue on to the peak.

SKIING

Cross-country skiers find Greer an ideally situated hub for some of the mountains best trails. About 2½ mi south of AZ 260 on AZ 373, a trailhead marks the starting point for the **Pole Knoll Trail System,** over 30 mi of well-marked cross-country trails interlacing through the Apache Sitgreaves National Forest and color-coded by experience level. Trail maps are available from the Springerville Ranger District Office (✉ 165 S. Mountain Dr. or Box 760, Springerville 85938, ☎ 520/333–4372.)

OFF THE BEATEN PATH

LITTLE HOUSE MUSEUM – This museum's collection of local pioneer and ranching memorabilia is interesting, but it's the mesmerizing tones from a rare collection of automatic musical instruments that you'll come away remembering—that, and the museum's colorful curator, Wink Crigler, with her lore of this region's lively past. The museum is open for 90-minute tours from Memorial Day to Labor Day; arrange winter tours by advance reservation. ✉ 5 mi east of Greer Junction (AZ 260 and AZ 373), turn south on South Fork Rd. and go 3 mi, ☎ 520/333–2286. ✉ $4. ☉ Tours Thurs.–Sat. at 11 and 1:30, Sun. and Mon. at 1:30.

Lyman Lake State Park

❽ *18 mi north of Springerville on U.S. 180/191; 55 mi southeast of Petrified Forest National Park on U.S. 180.*

Created in 1915 by damming the Little Colorado River for irrigation purposes, the 3-mi-long **Lyman Lake** reservoir is popular for its wide variety of water-sport activities. In addition to the boating, waterskiing, wind surfing, and sailing options, the lake has designated swimming beaches for those who prefer to stick closer to shore.

Anglers will appreciate a buoyed-off "no-wake" area at the lake's west end, where fishing efforts won't be disturbed by passing speedboats and water-skiers. Contributions to the creel here will include largemouth bass and crappie, as well as the "good size" (6–8 lbs.) channel catfish that can be pulled up from May to August. Locals recommend early spring as prime season for walleye—the tastiest catch of all; Lyman Lake also has lots of crawdads, a.k.a. "poor man's shrimp."

Between Memorial Day and Labor Day, rangers operate twice-daily pontoon boat rides across the lake to the **Petroglyph Trail**—where some of the state's most wondrous and accessible rock art lies chiseled in basalt.

Other attractions in the 118-acre park include a volleyball court, horseshoe pits, rockhounding opportunities, and the rare chance to observe the park's resident small herd of buffalo. Camping facilities are also available. ⊠ *Box 1428, St. Johns 85936,* ☎ *520/337–4441.*

Raven Site Ruins

❾ *12 mi north of Springerville on U.S. 180/191; 60 mi southeast of Petrified Forest State Park on U.S. 180.*

Overlooking the banks of the Little Colorado River, these prehistoric pueblos contain two kivas, over 800 rooms, and exhibit cultural features of both the Mogollon peoples to the south and the Anasazi people to the north. While not as steeped in mysticism as neighboring Casa Malpais, these ruins provide opportunities for hands-on excavation lessons and ruins-sifting in the site's field lab. At Raven Site Ruins' **White Mountain Archaeological Center,** James and Carol Cunkle lead amateurs, students, and professionals in unearthing the evidence of the pottery-making Native American cultures that flourished here from about AD 1000 to 1450. The tiny museum is a marvel. ⊠ *HC 30, St. Johns 85936,* ☎ *520/333–5857.* ⊠ *$3.50, including 1-hr guided tour.* ☉ *May–mid-Oct., daily 10–5.*

Casa Malpais Archaeological Project

❿ *2 mi north of downtown Springerville on U.S. 60.*

This 16-acre pueblo complex is piquing the interest of a growing number of world-class anthropologists and astronomers. "House of the Badlands" (a sobriquet for the rough-textured ground's effect on bare feet) has a series of narrow terraces lining eroded edges of basalt (hardened lava flow) cliff, as well as an extensive system of subterranean rooms nestled within the earth's fissures underneath. Strategically designed gateways in the walls of the complex allow for streams of sunlight to precisely illuminate significant petroglyphs prior to the setting equinox or solstice sun. Perhaps most importantly, Casa Malpais is home to the 55-ft-diameter Great Kiva—the largest Native American ceremonial chamber known to exist in North America. Strong evidence suggests that these sacred ruins were once inhabited solely by a class of scholars and holy men among the ancient Mogollon peoples. Ask about the ruins' conspicuous lack of excavated cooking apparati—these lucky guys probably ordered their room service from up the block (☞ Raven Site Ruins, *above*). ⊠ *Box 390, Springerville 85938,* ☎ *602/333–5375.* ☉ *Guided tours depart daily from the Casa Malpais Museum (*⊠ *318 Main St., Springerville,* ☎ *520/333–5375) at 9 AM, 11 AM, and 2:30 PM. The cost is $3. Closed June–Sept.*

En Route　The junction of U.S. 180/191 and U.S. 60, just north of Springerville, is the perfect jumping-off spot for a driving tour of the **Springerville Volcanic Field.** If you travel 6 mi north on U.S. 180/191, it leads to westward views of the **Twin Knolls**—double volcanoes that erupted twice here about 700,000 years ago. Traveling west on U.S. 60, Green's Peak Rd. and various south-winding Forest Service roads make for a leisurely, hour-long drive past **St. Peter's Dome** and a stop for impressive views from **Green's Peak,** the topographic high point of the Springerville Field. A detailed driving tour brochure is available gratis from the Round Valley Chamber of Commerce (⊠ *318 Main St., Springerville 85938,* ☎ *520/333–2123).*

Springerville-Eagar

⑪ *37 mi east of Pinetop-Lakeside on AZ 260; 75 mi southeast of Petri-fied Forest National Park on U.S. 180.*

Christened "Valle Redondo," or Round Valley, by early Basque set-tlers of the late 1800s, sister cities Springerville and Eagar are tucked into a circular, high mountain basin. Nestled on the back side of mas-sive 11,000-ft Escudilla Mountain, this self-proclaimed "Gateway to the White Mountains" sits in a different climate belt from nearby Greer and Sunrise Resort; insulated by its unique geography, temper-atures and snowfall in Springerville-Eagar are markedly less severe than in neighboring mountain towns. Geographically, the Round Valley also served as a unique Old West haven for the lawless—a great place to conceal stolen cattle and hide out for a while; Butch Cassidy, the Clantons, and the Smith gang all spent time here.

The **Reneé Cushman Art Collection Museum** is only open to the public by special appointment, but a visit here is worth the extra effort. Reneé Cushman, the only child of European artist Victor Scharf, was born in Paris, France, and her travels took her all over the globe—includ-ing Springerville, where she and her second husband purchased a ranch after World War II and Reneé fulfilled her lifelong dream of ranching and riding (a dream acquired during her Argentina-spent youth.) Years later, well into the stint with husband number three and living out of state, she made frequent visits back to her Springerville ranch.

Now, Mrs. Cushman's extensive collection of objets d'art—some ac-quired on her travels, some collected with the accumulated resources of three wealthy husbands, some willed to her by her artistic father—is administered by the Church of Latter-Day Saints. Although not a member of the LDS herself, Renné Cushman always nurtured a soft spot for the Mormons after they rescued her herd from a blizzard one year and the bishop later took in an abandoned child she brought back from France. Confused? You won't be after your visit. With a story this wild, just imagine her treasure of goods: a Rembrandt engraving, Tiepolo pen-and-inks, as well as an impressive collection of European antiques, some of which date back to the 15th century. Call the Round Valley Chamber of Commerce (☎ 520/333–2123) to arrange your visit.

Dining and Lodging

$–$$ ✕ **Booga Reds.** Despite a profusion of hanging plastic plants in the knotty-pine–paneled dining room, the delicious home-style cooking here is worth a stop. Fish-and-chips and roast-beef dinners with home-made mashed potatoes and gravy top the menu; should your palette demand something spicier, however, try one of the many Mexican dishes. Save room for an unforgettable piece of the daily fruit or cream pie. Booga Reds opens at 5:30 for an early breakfast, but closes at 9 PM—so make your dinner an early one, too. ⊠ *521 E. Main St., Springerville,* ☎ *520/333–2640. MC, V.*

$–$$ ▦ **Reed's Lodge.** The moderate-size rooms of this mostly single-story, exterior-hallway motor lodge are accented with such Western touches as knotty-pine paneling or Navajo-print bedspreads. Proprietress Rox-anne Knight's knowledge of the city and surrounding environs is not to be surpassed. ⊠ *514 E. Main St., Springerville 85938,* ☎ *520/333–4323 or 800/814–6451,* 𝖥𝖠𝖷 *520/333–5191. 50 rooms. Outdoor hot tub. AE, D, DC, MC, V.*

⚠ **Big Lake.** Four campgrounds scattered along the southeast shore of this lake, 30 mi southwest of Round Valley, are the White Mountains' most popular summer spots. The civilized **Rainbow** site offers paved loops to its 150-plus units, replete with hookups and access to deluxe rest rooms and a store. The lake's smaller sites, **Grayling, Cutthroat,** and **Brookchar,** are less swank, but are within easy walking distance of Rainbow's amenities and share the picturesque tableau of looming 11,590-ft Mt. Baldy. The lake has a marina and boats and motors are available for rent. ⊠ *24 mi south of AZ 260 on AZ 261,* ☎ *520/333–4372. Closed in winter.*

Nightlife

Out on the edge of town where U.S. Highways 60 and 180 enter Springerville, the bright yellow **Little River Lounge** (⊠ 262 W. Main St., ☎ 520/333–5790) has pool tables and darts.

Outdoor Activities and Sports

For all your mountain-sport needs, stop in the **Sweat Shop** (⊠ 74 N. Main St., Eagar, ☎ 520/333–2950); they rent a variety of skies, snowboards, and mountain bikes.

FISHING

Just off U.S. 191, **Nelson Reservoir** is well stocked with rainbow, brown, and brook trout; the lake is between Springerville-Eagar and the town of Alpine, just outside the hamlet of Nutrioso. **Troutback** (⊠ Box 344, Springerville, ☎ 520/333–2371) will tailor guided half- or full-day fishing trips to novices and seasoned anglers alike; fly rod and reels can be rented for $10 a day.

Sport Shack (⊠ 329 E. Main St., Springerville, ☎ 520/333–2222) sells fishing tackle, licenses, and reservation permits. **Western Drug** (⊠ 105 E. Main St., Springerville, ☎ 520/333–4321) stays open 365 days a year and has a well-stocked sporting-goods section.

Coronado Trail

★ *123 mi from Springerville to Clifton.*

Surely one of the world's curviest roads, this steep winding portion of U.S. 191 was referred to as the "Devil's Highway" in its prior incarnation as U.S. Route 666. More significantly, the route parallels the one allegedly followed over 450 years ago by Spanish explorer Francisco Vásquez de Coronado on his search for the legendary Seven Cities of Cíbola with streets paved of gold and jewels.

This 123-mi stretch of highway is renowned for its spectacular scenery's transition over a dramatic 5,000-ft elevation change—from rolling meadows to spruce- and ponderosa-pine–covered mountains, down into the Sonoran Desert's piñon pine, grassland savannas, juniper stands, and cacti. A trip down the Coronado Trail crosses through Apache Sitgreaves National Forest, as well as the White Mountain Apache and San Carlos Indian Reservations.

Cautious switchback-navigating will result in stretches on which motorists barely exceeding 10 mph; allow a good four hours to make the drive, more if you plan to stop and leisurely explore—which you should.

Perched on the edge of the Mogollon Rim, pause at **Blue Vista** to take in views of the Blue Range Mountains to the east, and the succession of tiered valleys dropping some 4,000 ft back down into the Sonoran Desert. Still above the rim, this is one of your last opportunities to enjoy the blue spruce, ponderosa pine, and high-country mountain meadows.

South of Blue Vista, the Coronado Trail continues twisting and turn-ing, crossing under 8,786-ft **Rose Peak.** Named for the wild roses growing on its mountainside, Rose Peak is also home to a fire look-out tower—staffed during the May-through-July dry-lightning sea-son—from which peaks over 100 mi away can be seen on a clear day. This is a great picnic-lunch stop!

After Rose Peak, enjoy the remaining scenery some 70 more miles to the mining towns of Clifton and Morenci. U.S. 191 then swings back west, links up with U.S. 70, and provides a fairly straight shot through Safford and across rather uninteresting desert toward Globe.

Alpine

27 mi south of Springerville-Eagar on U.S. 191.

Known as the "Alps of Arizona," the tiny, scenic village of Alpine pro-motes its variety of winter recreation opportunities, but warmer-month outdoor enthusiasts will find that Alpine, sitting on the lush plains of the San Francisco River, is centrally located to many excellent hiking, fishing, and mountain-biking excursions.

Lodging

⚠ **Luna Lake Campgrounds.** These 50 units offer pristine primitive camp-ing. There are no showers, and rest rooms are vault-toilets. Bring your own campfire wood. Fees are $6 per vehicle per night. ⊠ *5 mi east of U.S. 191 on U.S. 180,* ☎ *520/339–4384. Open May–Oct.*

Outdoor Activities and Sports

BIKING

The 8-mi **Luna Lake Trail** (⊠ 5 mi east of U.S. 191 on U.S. 180) is a good two-hour cruise for beginning and intermediate cyclists. The trailhead is on the north side of the lake, just before the campground entrance.

FISHING

From May to October, try **Fite's Fishery** (⊠ Box 156, 85920, ☎ 520/339–4421). A divergence of the San Francisco River's headwaters, **Luna Lake** (⊠ 5 mi east of U.S. 191 on U.S. 180) is well stocked.

GOLF

Alpine Country Club (⊠ 2½ mi east of the AZ 180 and U.S. 191 junc-tion, Box 526, 85920, ☎ 520/339–4944), at 8,500 ft above sea level, is the highest golf course in the Southwest.

HIKING

The 3-mi hike on the **Escudilla National Recreation Trail** journeys to the top of towering 10,912-ft **Escudilla Mountain,** Arizona's third-tallest peak.

SKIING

Williams Valley Winter Sports Area (⊠ 4½ mi west of Alpine on For-est Service Rd. 249, ☎ 520/339–4384) has 12½ mi of varying-diffi-culty cross-country trails maintained by the Alpine Ranger district. **Toboggan Hill** is a favorite place for families with sleds, toboggans, and tubes.

SNOWMOBILING

Trails begin just off Forest Service Road 249, on the west side of Williams Valley Winter Sports Area, and the snowmobile staging area and network of snow-covered Forest Service roads extends for miles; snowmobilers are asked to respect marked boundaries to the adjacent Bear Wallow Wilderness area, in which all motorized equipment is pro-hibited. Pick up an Apache Sitgreaves National Forest map from the Alpine Ranger District (⊠ U.S. 191 at U.S. 180 or Box 469, Alpine

85920, ☎ 520/339–4384) and call for conditions prior to heading out, as weak links in longer routes sometimes "burn out."

Hannagan Meadow

★ ⑫   *52 mi south of Springerville-Eagar on U.S. 191; 22 mi south of Alpine on U.S. 191.*

Surely one of the state's most remote locations, Hannagan Meadow is pastorally mesmerizing, home to splendid camping areas and the site of a former famous face-off between the region's sheep and cattle ranchers. Lush and isolated at a 9,000-ft-plus elevation, the meadow is home to elk, deer, and range cattle, as well as blue grouse, wild turkey, and the occasional eagle. Adjacent to the meadow, the Blue Range Primitive Area gives access to miles of untouched wilderness and some beautiful rugged terrain.

OFF THE BEATEN PATH   **BLUE RANGE PRIMITIVE AREA –** Directly east of Hannagan Meadow, this area remains the last designated primitive area in the United States. "The Blue"—as its lovingly referred to by locals—is home to the 170,000 unspoiled acres of diverse terrain surrounding the Blue River. The Blue is all about the deep quiet and solitude of the area's forests and canyon; no motorized or mechanized equipment is allowed—including mountain bikes—and passage is restricted to foot or horseback. A large number of trails interlace through The Blue: prehistoric paths of the ancient native peoples, cowboy trails to move livestock between pastures and water sources, access routes to lookout towers, and fire trails. Most trails on The Blue run between the rim of the canyon and its floor, with dozens of connector trails linking main routes and making a variety of daylong loop hikes possible, although avid backpackers and campers will definitely want to spend a few days. There are many trailheads; contact the Alpine Ranger District (✉ Junction of U.S. 180 and U.S. 191, Box 469, Alpine, ☎ 520/339–4384) for trail maps and information.

Dining and Lodging

$–$$ ✕🏨 **Hannagan Meadow Lodge.** No kidding—the owners of this remote lodge are living-their-dream lottery jackpot winners. They bought the property in 1996 and transformed it into a paragon of casual mountain elegance. Antique bureaus and floral prints in gilded frames round out a genteel, Victorian vibe upstairs in the main lodge, where every room promises a great night's sleep with ornate brass and enamel beds and 100% down pillows. Cabins—with their log construction and wood floors—are more rustic, most with either fireplaces or wood-burning stoves for heat. The lodge's dining room is truly the pièce de résistance with hewn log beams and ceilings, and an all-windows wall that overlooks the pristine meadow. A general store sells sundries as well as fishing supplies, and rents snowmobiles, cross-country skis, and mountain bikes. ✉ HC 61, Box 335, Alpine 85920, ☎ 520/339–4370 or 800/547–1416. 8 rooms, 13 cabins. Restaurant, bar, hiking, horseback riding, fishing, mountain bikes, cross-country skiing, snowmobiling. AE, D, MC, V.

▲ **Hannagan Meadow.** This intimate collection of eight campsites sits under a canopy of trees surrounded by tall, mature forest. There's no fresh water supply at Hannagan, but the meadow's lodge, where you can shower for $5, is within walking distance. ✉ U.S. 191 and FS Rd. 576, ☎ 520/339–4384. Open May–Oct.

▲ **KP Cienega.** These five single-unit campsites in a lush meadow are a prime site for viewing the local wildlife and livestock. ✉ U.S. 191 and FS Rd. 54, ☎ 520/339–4384. Open May–Oct.

book profits from the Visitor Center fund the continued research and interpretive activities for the park.

Picnicking is allowed inside the park. You may hike into the nearby wilderness areas to camp, but you must obtain a park permit for an overnight stay. Free permits are issued at both visitor centers (☞ *above*) and at the Painted Desert Inn.

Visitors can begin the 28-mi-long drive through the park either from the northern I–40 entrance or the southern entrance off U.S. 180. Those continuing on to New Mexico will want to enter from the park's south entrance, ending up with I–40's straight shot over the border toward Albuquerque. Visitors with accommodations in Holbrook will probably want to tour the park from south end to north end, saving dramatic vistas of the Painted Desert and a setting sun for last. ✉ *North entrance: off I–40, 30 mi east of Holbrook. South entrance: off U.S. 180, 19 mi southeast of Holbrook. Box 2217, Petrified Forest 86028,* ☎ *520/524–6228.* ▤ *$10 per vehicle; receipt is valid for reentry within the next 7 days.* ☉ *Daily 7:30–5.*

Dining and Lodging

$–$$ ✕ **Butterfield Stage Co.** Predictable but reliable steak-house fare, including a salad bar and a kid's menu, is offered in an atmosphere made indisputably Western by rows of authentic pairs of longhorns—disembodied, of course— aligned atop each and every booth. A landmark from old Route 66 days, just look for the stagecoach on the roof. ✉ *609 West Hopi Dr., Holbrook 86025,* ☎ *520/524–3447. No lunch. AE, MC, V.*

$–$$ ✕ **Mesa Italiana Restaurant.** Fresh pastas, homemade sauces, and virgin olive oil can be a welcome break from menu after menu of either tacos or T-bones. ✉ *2318 N. Navajo Blvd., Holbrook 86025,* ☎ *520/ 524–6696. Closed Mon. MC, V.*

$ ▥ **Best Western Arizonian Inn.** The large, handsome rooms are furnished with a suite of formal, ersatz-cherrywood furniture. Some rooms have microwaves. ✉ *2508 E. Navajo Blvd., Holbrook 86025,* ☎ FAX *520/ 524–2611. 70 rooms. Refrigerators, pool. AE, D, DC, MC V.*

$ ▥ **Wigwam Motel.** Classic Route 66 kitsch, the Wigwam consists of 15 bright white, roadside cement wigwams where you can sleep inexpensively in a surreal environment. As you might expect, wigwams are phoneless, but—ode to Mother Progress—these wigwams have cable. ✉ *811 W. Hopi Dr., Holbrook 86025,* ☎ *520/524–3048. 15 wigwams. MC, V.*

Shopping

McGees Beyond Native Tradition (✉ 2114 E. Navajo Blvd., Holbrook 86025, ☎ 520/524–1977) is the area's premier source of high-quality, Native American jewelry, rugs, Hopi baskets, and kachina dolls; owner Bruce McGee has long-standing, personal relationships with Reservation artisans and a knowledgeable staff that adroitly assists first-time buyer and seasoned collector alike.

EASTERN ARIZONA A TO Z

Arriving and Departing

By Bus

White Mountain Passenger Lines (✉ 319 S. 24th St., Phoenix 85034, ☎ 520/537–4539 or 602/275–4245) has service between Phoenix and Show Low; one-way fares are around $40. **Greyhound Lines** (☎ 800/ 231–2222) travels from Phoenix to Winslow, 50 mi west of Petrified Forest National Park.

By Car

If arriving from points west via Flagstaff, I–40 leads directly to Holbrook, where drivers can take AZ 77 south into Show Low or U.S. 180 southeast to Springerville-Eagar. Those departing from the metropolitan Phoenix area will want to take scenic drive northeast on U.S. 60, or the only-slightly-faster AZ 87 North to AZ 260 East, both of which lead to Show Low. From Tucson, AZ 77 North connects with U.S. 60 at Globe and continues through Show Low up to Holbrook. From New Mexico, drivers can enter the state on I–40 and take U.S. 191 south into Springerville-Eagar, or continue on to Holbrook and reach the White Mountains via AZ 77. Lastly, for those who want to drive the Coronado Trail south-to-north, U.S. 70 and AZ 78 link up with the U.S. 191 from Globe to the west and New Mexico cities to the east, respectively.

By Plane

Show Low Municipal Airport (✉ Junction of U.S. 60 and AZ 77, ☎ 520/537–5629) has two runways. **Great Lakes Airlines** (☎ 800/274–0662) offers three daily flights from Phoenix to Show Low during the week and two daily flights on Saturday and Sunday.

By Train

Amtrak (✉ 800/872–7245) trains depart daily at 6:45 AM from Flagstaff to Winslow. Those traveling from Phoenix will need to take the Amtrak bus—which departs Phoenix-area stations three times daily bound for Flagstaff—and stay overnight in Flagstaff to catch the early-morning train to Winslow. From Albuquerque, Winslow is only a three-hour ride, leaving daily at 5:18 PM.

Getting Around

By Car

You'll absolutely need a car to tour Eastern Arizona, especially since most of the region's top scenic attractions are between towns. Rental facilities are few and far between in these parts, so you'll do well to rent a car from your departure point, whether it's Phoenix, Flagstaff, or Albuquerque.

Motorists should travel prepared, with jumper cables, a shovel, tire chains, and—for tire traction—a bag of kitty litter. Chain requirements apply to all vehicles, including those with four-wheel drive. Bridges and overpasses freeze first and are often slicker than normal road surfaces; never assume sufficient traction simply because a road appears to be sanded. If you must travel in poor visibility conditions, drivers should turn on the headlights and always keep the highway's white reflectors to their right. For road conditions through the region, contact the Department of Public Safety's **Road Condition Information Line** (☎ 602/241–3100, ext. 7623).

CAR RENTALS

Enterprise Rent-A-Car (✉ 1001 Navajo Blvd., inside Tate's Automotive dealership, Holbrook 86025, ☎ 520/524–9143 or 800/736–8222). **Enterprise Rent-A-Car** (✉ 651 W. Deuce of Clubs, Show Low 85901, ☎ 520/537–5144). **White Mountain Car Rental** (✉ Show Low Airport, Show Low 85901, ☎ 520/532–0576 or 800/532–0576).

Contacts and Resources

Emergencies

Halfway between Show Low and Pinetop-Lakeside, **Navapache Regional Medical Center** (✉ 2200 Show Low Lake Rd., Show Low 85901, ☎ 520/537–4375) has a trauma center and 24-hour acute care. **White**

Mountain Communities Hospital (⊠ 118 S. Mountain Ave., Springerville 85938, ☎ 520/333–4368) has 24-hour emergency room facilities and services the Round Valley area, as well as Sunrise Park Resort.

Guided Tours

Whether your preference is lakes or streams, **Troutback** (⊠ Box 344, Springerville 85938, ☎ 520/333–2371) specializes in fly-fishing excursions and llama pack trips through some of the White Mountains' most spectacular scenery.

Outdoor Activities and Sports

The office of **Arizona State Parks** (⊠ 1300 W. Washington St., Phoenix 85007, ☎ 602/542–4174) can provide detailed information about any of the state-run parks and their recreational facilities.

Stop by any White Mountains ranger station and pick up a copy of the 20-page Forest Service brochure entitled "Recreational Opportunities in the Apache Sitgreaves National Forest" for further descriptions of the hiking, horseback riding, camping, bicycling, fishing, and boating options in the area. A similar booklet is available from the White Mountain Apaches detailing opportunities on Reservation land.

CAMPING

Call or write the **U.S. Forest Service** (⊠ 2022 White Mountain Blvd., Pinetop-Lakeside 85935, ☎ 520/368–5111) for a brochure listing all public camping facilities in the Apache–Sitgreaves National Forest, most of which operate April through November. To assure a campsite, you must make reservations in advance for any fee campground; **National Forest Service Campground Reservations** (☎ 800/280–2267) is open January through mid-September, weekdays 9–9 and weekends 11 AM– 7 PM.

Book your campground site well in advance with the **White Mountain Apache Tribe** (⊠ Box 220, Whiteriver 85941, ☎ 520/338–4385) and you needn't have any reservations about your reservation on the Reservation.

Visitor Information

CHAMBERS OF COMMERCE

Alpine Chamber of Commerce (⊠ Box 410, Alpine 85920, ☎ 520/339– 4330). **Holbrook Chamber of Commerce** (⊠ 100 E. Arizona Ave., Holbrook 86025, ☎ 520/524–6558 or 800/524–2459). **Pinetop-Lakeside Chamber of Commerce** (⊠ 592 W. White Mountain Blvd., Lakeside 85929, ☎ 520/367–4290).

For the Springerville-Eagar area, contact the **Round Valley Chamber of Commerce** (⊠ 318 Main St., Box 31, Springerville 85938, ☎ 520/ 333–2123). **Show-Low Chamber of Commerce** (⊠ 951 W. Deuce of Clubs or Box 1083, Show Low 85901, ☎ 520/537–2326 or 888/746– 9569). **White Mountain Apache Office of Tourism** (⊠ Box 26, Whiteriver 85941, ☎ 520/338–1230).

LAND-MANAGEMENT AGENCIES

Alpine Ranger District (⊠ U.S. 191 at U.S. 180 or Box 469, Alpine 85920, ☎ 520/339–4384). **Apache Sitgreaves National Forest** (⊠ Box 640, Springerville 85938, ☎ 520/333–4301). **Arizona Game & Fish Department** (⊠ 2878 E. White Mountain Dr., Pinetop 85935, ☎ 520/367–4281). **Lakeside Ranger District** (⊠ R.R. 3, Box B-50, Lakeside 85929, ☎ 520/368–5111). **Petrified Forest Ranger Office** (⊠ Box 2217, Petrified Forest 86028, ☎ 520/524–6228). **San Carlos Apache Nation** (⊠ Box 97, San Carlos 85550, ☎ 520/475–2343 or 888/275–2653). **Springerville Ranger District** (⊠ Box 760, 165 S.

Mountain Ave., Springerville 85938, ☎ 520/333–4372). **White Mountain Apache Wildlife & Recreation** (✉ Box 220, Whiteriver 85941, ☎ 520/338–4385) is the contact for all Reservation fishing, camping, and hiking.

Weather

Arizona Weather Information (☎ 602/861–9400, ext. 7623) includes current and forecasted information for the White Mountains area.

7 Tucson

Tucson may have buried many of its Spanish roots, but you'll find remnants of this heritage in the El Presidio neighborhood; in the Mission San Xavier del Bac, an architectural masterpiece set in the midst of the Tohono O'odham Reservation; and in the city's myriad Mexican restaurants. Nature-lovers will like the many outdoor options, including Saguaro National Park, which sandwiches the city on its east and west sides, and the Arizona–Sonora Desert Museum, a beautifully landscaped zoo.

By Edie Jarolim

ALTHOUGH IT IS ARIZONA'S second-largest city, Tucson feels like a small town—one enriched by its deep Native American, Spanish, Mexican, and Old West roots. It is at once a bustling center of business and a kicked-back university and resort town. Metropolitan Tucson has more than 700,000 year-round residents, increased by "snowbirds," who come to the area in winter to enjoy the warm sun that shines on the city more than 320 days a year. Winter temperatures hover around 65°F during the day and 38°F at night. Summers are unquestionably hot—with July averaging 104°F during the day and 75°F at night—but, as Tucsonans are fond of saying, "it's a dry heat" (Tucson averages only 11 inches of rain a year). There are plenty of places to escape from the sun, including Sabino Canyon and Mt. Lemmon.

In a part of the world where everything seems new and buildings more than 50 years old are viewed as historic places, Tucson is an exception. Historians have dated Tucson's earliest citizens to AD 100, when the Hohokam Indians made their home in the fertile farming valley. During the 1500s, Spanish explorers arrived to find Pima Indians enjoying the mild weather and growing crops.

The name Tucson came from the Indian word *stjukshon* (pronounced "*stook*-shahn"), meaning "spring at the foot of a black mountain." (The springs at the foot of Sentinel Peak, made of black volcanic rock, are now dry.) The name became Tucson (originally pronounced "*tuk*-son") in the mouths of the Spanish explorers who built the *presidio* (walled city) of San Augustin del Tuguison in 1776 to keep Native Americans from reclaiming the city. Replacing the presidio that had previously been established to the south in Tubac, this new walled city was affectionately called the Old Pueblo by early settlers, and the nickname has stuck till this day.

Father Eusebio Francisco Kino, a Jesuit missionary, first visited the village in 1687 and returned a few years later to build missions in the area. His influence is still strongly felt throughout the region, especially at the noteworthy Mission San Xavier del Bac south of Tucson on the Tohono O'odham Reservation.

Four flags have flown over Tucson—those of Spain, Mexico, the U.S. Confederacy, and the Union. In fact, a strong Spanish and Mexican influence is still visible in the city's architecture and culture. Arizona didn't become a state until 1912, and its colorful days as a territory are still very much a part of the area's lore. In the 1850s the Butterfield stage line was extended to Tucson, bringing adventurers, a few settlers, and more than a handful of outlaws. The arrival of the railroad in 1880 marked another spurt of growth, as did the opening of the University of Arizona in 1891.

Tucson's growth really took off during World War II, thanks to Davis-Monthan Air Force Base. It was also around this time that air-conditioning made the desert hospitable to visitors and residents alike. Today many of Tucson's refugees come from California because a lower cost of operating businesses (Arizona is a right-to-work, or nonunion, state) has lured many aerospace and high-tech industries. The economy also relies heavily on tourism and the university, although, come summer, you'd never guess. When the snowbirds and students depart, Tucson has a sleepy feel that reminds you just how much the desert still determines the city's pace.

Pleasures and Pastimes

Astronomy

Stargazers can peer through the telescope at the Flandrau Space and Science Center or take part in one of the University of Arizona's astronomy camps. City ordinances against "light pollution" allow viewing of the usually clear desert skies at night, even in the city center.

Dining

Tucson's culinary reputation is growing, and there are restaurants in town to satisfy every appetite. Southwestern cuisine, in its element here, ranges from barbecue and cowboy steaks to light nouvelle recipes that use such innovative ingredients as cactus and blue corn.

Tucson's residents have long boasted about their city's Mexican food, some rather grandly proclaiming their town "Mexican Food Capital of the U.S." (a title regularly challenged by San Antonians and Phoenicians). Most of the Mexican food in Tucson is Sonoran style—that is, derived from the cooking native to the adjoining Mexican state of Sonora. It's the type that's familiar to most Americans, featuring cheese, mild peppers, corn tortillas, and beef or chicken. Although Sonoran Mexican food has a well-earned reputation for being high in calories and saturated fats, many restaurants in Tucson now feature otherwise authentically prepared dishes cooked without lard. (Note that the salsa served with baskets of tortilla chips may be spicier than what you are used to. Proceed with caution. Similarly, when you ask the staff whether a dish is "hot," remember that their definition may be quite different from yours.) If you can take the heat, you've come to the right place.

CATEGORY	COST*
$$$$	over $35
$$$	$25–$35
$$	$15–$25
$	under $15

per person, excluding drinks, service, and 7% sales tax (5% state plus 2% city)

Golf

You can easily dedicate a vacation to golf in Tucson, which has some of the best desert courses in the country and plenty of sunshine in which to play them. Options range from spreads in posh resorts to very reasonably priced but excellent municipal courses.

Hiking

Tucson abounds with desert trails to explore in the winter and, in summer, there are lots of cooler trekking options in nearby mountain ranges. Among the places to hike are Saguaro (pronounced "suh-*war*-oh") National Park, Mt. Lemmon, Sabino Canyon, "A" Mountain, and Catalina State Park.

Horseback Riding

It wouldn't be a trip to the Southwest without at least one day on the back of a horse. Tucson has plenty of stables and lots of scenic places to trot around.

Lodging

In Tucson you can enjoy the luxury of a desert resort or the more basic accommodations offered by small motels. A number of guest ranches—some of them from the 1800s when they were real working cattle ranches—can be found on the outskirts of town. There is also a variety of bed-and-breakfasts in the area, ranging from bedrooms in modest homes to private cottages nestled on wildlife preserves.

CATEGORY	COST*
$$$$	over $180
$$$	$125–$180
$$	$75–$125
$	under $75

All prices are for a standard double room, excluding room tax (9.5% in Tucson and 6.5% in Pima County). Prices given here are winter, or high-season, rates.

Mexican Culture

You can see Tucson's south-of-the-border soul in everything from the city's tile-roof architecture to its mariachi festivals and abundance of Mexican restaurants.

Native American Culture

The reservations of the Pascua Yaqui and the Tohono O'odham peoples border Tucson; many events in town celebrate the culture of these tribes as well as that of other Native Americans in Arizona. Native American crafts range from exquisite jewelry and basketry to the more pedestrian (but still authentic) tourist items.

Western Lore

The west was never lost in Tucson, where city slickers mingle with cowboys at guest ranches, country-and-western dance clubs, steak houses, and western-wear stores.

EXPLORING TUCSON

Tucson covers more than 500 square mi in a valley ringed by mountains (the main surrounding ranges are the Santa Catalinas to the north, the Santa Ritas to the south, the Rincons to the east, and the Tucson Mountains to the west). For the most part, touring the area requires having a car. The central portion of town, where most shops, restaurants, and businesses are located, is roughly bounded by Wilmot Road on the east, Oracle Road on the west, River Road to the north, and 22nd Street to the south. The older downtown section, accessible just east of I–10 off the Broadway-Congress exit, is much smaller and easy to navigate on foot. (Streets there don't run true to any sort of grid, however, and many of them are one way, so it's best to get a good, detailed map.) Those accustomed to living in humid areas may find themselves unprepared for Tucson's dry climate: If you're out walking in the hot weather, stop for frequent fluid breaks.

Numbers in the text correspond to numbers in the margin and on the Downtown Tucson, University of Arizona, Tucson, and Side Trips Near Tucson maps.

Great Itineraries

IF YOU HAVE 1 DAY

Some of Tucson's most characteristic sights lie on the west side of town. You'll get a good feel for this city if you drive out to Saguaro National Park West and the Arizona–Sonora Desert Museum, with a stop at Old Tucson Studios if you're traveling with kids.

IF YOU HAVE 3 DAYS

Follow the first day's itinerary. The next morning, drive out to the Mission San Xavier del Bac and enjoy Indian fry bread for lunch in the plaza. Military buffs should continue south to the Titan Missile Museum; shoppers will enjoy trips in the same direction to Tubac and Nogales, Mexico. On the third day, head downtown to the El Presidio district to explore Tucson's early history and, in the afternoon, visit one of the several museums at the University of Arizona.

What you do on the fourth day depends on the weather: If it's hot, visit Sabino Canyon or Mt. Lemmon to cool off; if it's not, you might enjoy breakfast at Tohono Chul Park, followed by a visit to Biosphere 2. On the fifth day, head east, where a hike in Saguaro National Park East can be followed by an underground tour of Colossal Cave.

Downtown

The area flanked by Franklin and Pennington streets on the north and south and by Church and Main avenues on the east and west encompasses more than 130 years of the city's architectural history, dating from the original walled El Presidio del Tucson, a Spanish fortress built in 1776, when Arizona was still part of New Spain. A good deal of Tucson's history was destroyed in the 1960s, when large sections of downtown were bulldozed to make way for high-rises and parking lots, but it's still possible to explore parts of the original Spanish settlement and to see a number of the posh residences that accompanied the arrival of the railroad.

A Good Tour

If you drive up to **"A" Mountain (Sentinel Peak)** ①, you'll get a great perspective of downtown Tucson. Come down from on high and head east along Congress Street; at the Santa Cruz river you'll come to the **Garden of Gethsemane**, a grouping of religious figures sculpted by Felix Lucero to fulfill a religious vow made when his life was spared in World War I. Continue east along Congress and then go south on Granada to the historical society's **Sosa-Carillo-Fremont House** ② (you needn't worry about parking here; the huge convention center lot is at your feet). Farther south (take Granada again and then go east on Cushing Street) is the shrine of **El Tiradito (The Castaway)** ③. Now circle back north to the **St. Augustine Cathedral** ④; Stone Street, where the cathedral is located, runs one way to the south in this part of town, so you'll need to take Convent Avenue north to Ochoa Street and backtrack on Stone. Those traveling with kids will want to go east on McCormick to 6th Avenue and the **Tuscon Children's Museum** ⑤. In either case, head north on Church Avenue to Alameda, then east to Main, where you'll find parking for the **Tucson Museum of Art and Historic Block** ⑥; this complex includes the **La Casa Cordova** ⑦, the **J. Knox Corbett House** ⑧, and the **Stevens Home** ⑨. Walk east on Alameda and then south on Church to reach the **Pima County Courthouse** ⑩, downtown's great architectural jewel.

TIMING

If you're in town from late November through late March, don't miss the Naciemento, a traditional Mexican Christmas display in La Casa Cordova. The entire room is filled with folk-art miniatures arranged in elaborate scenes from the Old and New Testaments and from Mexican rural life. For the eight nights from December 15 through Christmas Eve, you can witness Las Posadas, a traditional procession started in Mexico in 1587 to introduce Christmas to the Aztecs. On the final night, the procession ends up at St. Augustine Cathedral. Take note that the Tucson Museum of Art's free guided tours of its historic complex are given Wednesdays and Thursdays at 11.

Sights to See

① **"A" Mountain (Sentinel Peak).** The original name of this mountain, just west of downtown, was derived from its function as a lookout point for the Spanish. In 1915, fans of the University of Arizona football team whitewashed a large "A" on its side to celebrate a victory, and the tradition has been kept up ever since. The Pima Indian village and the

"A"
Mountain, **1**

El Tiradito, **3**

J. Knox
Corbett
House, **8**

La Casa
Cordova, **7**

Pima County
Courthouse, **10**

Sosa-Carillo-
Fremont
House, **2**

St. Augustine
Cathedral, **4**

Stevens
Home, **9**

Tucson
Children's
Museum, **5**

Tucson
Museum of Art
and Historic
Block, **6**

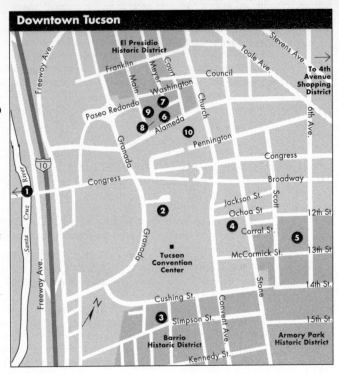

Downtown Tucson

cultivated fields that once flanked the peak are long gone, but you can still see the ruins of an early (1870–80) adobe residence and flour mill at its base. During the day, it's a great place for visitors to get an overview of the town's layout; at night, it's generally crowded with amorous teenagers. ⊠ *Congress St. on Sentinel Peak Rd.*

❸ El Tiradito (The Castaway). No one seems to know the details of the story behind this little shrine, but everyone agrees a tragic love triangle was involved. A bronze plaque indicates only that it is dedicated to a sinner who is buried here on unconsecrated ground. The many candles that line the cactus-shrouded spot attest to its continuing importance in local Catholic lore. A modern-day miracle: The shrine's inclusion on the National Register of Historic Places helped prevent a freeway from plowing through the Barrio Historico District. ⊠ *Main Ave., just south of Cushing St.*

❽ J. Knox Corbett House. Built in 1906–7, this house was occupied by members of the Corbett family until 1963. Tucson's Hi Corbett field (the major league Colorado Rockies use this field for spring training) is named for the grand nephew of the original occupants, J. Knox Corbett, a businessman, and Elizabeth Hughes Corbett, daughter of Tucson pioneer Sam Hughes. The two-story, Mission Revival–style residence has been furnished with American Arts and Crafts pieces; the Stickley brothers, Roycroft, Tiffany, and Morris are among the more famous names represented. ⊠ *180 N. Main Ave.,* ☎ *520/624-2333.* ▨ *Free.* ☉ *Mon.–Sat. 10–4, Sun. noon–4.*

❼ La Casa Cordova. One of the best examples of the simple but elegant Sonoran row house, a Spanish style adapted to adobe construction, La Casa Cordova is also one of the oldest buildings in Tucson: The original part was constructed in about 1848. It's now home to the Mexican Heritage Museum; when you enter through the double doors on Meyer

Avenue, the room on your right has an exhibit of the history of the presidio, while three rooms off the patio display furnishings of the Indian and pioneer settlers of the period. After visiting the museum, you'll understand why adobe—brick made of mud and straw, cured in the hot sun—was so widely used in early Tucson. It provides a natural insulation from the heat and cold, and it is durable in Tucson's dry climate. In some cases, the woody cactus ribs built into the walls and ceilings for extra support poke through the hard-packed adobe. ⊠ *175 N. Meyer Ave.,* ☏ *520/624–2333.* ☑ *Free.* ⊗ *Mon.–Sat. 10–4, Sun. noon–4.*

NEED A BREAK?
On the patio of Old Town Artisans, a multiroom marketplace set in a 19th-century adobe building, the pretty **Cocina** (E 186 N. Meyer Ave., ☎ 520/622–0351) restaurant is a nice spot for a salad or sandwich.

★ ⑩ **Pima County Courthouse.** This Spanish colonial–style building with its landmark mosaic-tile dome is among Tucson's most beautiful historic structures. It was built in 1927 on the site of the original single-story adobe court of 1869; a portion of the old presidio wall can be seen in the south wing of the courthouse's second floor. To the side of the building, the County Assessor's office hosts a diorama depicting the area's early days (if the location seems odd, remember that the Spanish were big on taxation, too). The courthouse, which is still being used today, is on the eastern side of **El Presidio Park**, a modern square once occupied by the Plaza de las Armas, the largest plaza in the El Presidio area. ⊠ *115 N. Church St., between Alameda and Pennington Sts.*

➋ **Sosa-Carillo-Fremont House.** One of Tucson's oldest adobe residences, this was the only building spared when the surrounding barrio was torn down to build the Tucson Convention Center. Originally purchased by José Maria Sosa in 1860, it was owned by the Carillo family for 80 years. The restored house, now a branch of the Arizona Historical Society, is furnished in 1880s fashion and has changing displays of territorial life. ⊠ *Convention Center Complex, between the Music Hall and the Arena (parking at 151 S. Granada Ave.),* ☏ *520/622–0956.* ☑ *Free; walking tours of the Presidio and Tucson Historic District $4.50.* ⊗ *Wed.–Sat. 10–4; walking tours Nov.–Mar., Sat. at 10.*

➍ **St. Augustine Cathedral.** Construction began in 1896 on one of downtown's most striking structures, set in what had earlier been the Plaza de Mesilla. Although the imposing pink building was modeled after the Cathedral of Queretaro in Mexico, a number of its details reflect the desert setting: Above the entryway, next to a bronze statue of St. Augustine, are carvings of a saguaro cactus, yucca, and horned toad. Compared with the magnificent facade, the modernized interior is a bit disappointing. ⊠ *192 South Stone Ave.*

➒ **Stevens Home.** It was here that wealthy politician and cattle rancher Hiram Stevens and his Mexican wife, Petra Santa Cruz, entertained many of Tucson's leaders—including Edward and Maria Fish—during the 1800s. A drought brought the Stevenses' cattle ranching to a halt in 1893, and Stevens killed himself in despair, after unsuccessfully attempting to kill his wife (the bullet was deflected by the comb she wore in her hair). The 1865 house, just north of the Edward Nye Fish House (☞ Tucson Museum of Art and Historic Block, *below*) and architecturally similar, was restored in 1980 and is now home to one of Tucson's most elegant restaurants, Janos (☞ Dining, *below*). After summer 1998, when Janos's lease is up, it will be used by the museum for exhibition space. ⊠ *150 N. Main Ave.*

☾ ➎ **Tucson Children's Museum.** Kids are encouraged to touch and explore the exhibits here, which are oriented toward science, language, and history: They can crawl inside a giant model of the heart and lungs or turn on the electricity in the streets of a model town. Art supplies and musical instruments add to the fun (and din). The "Take A Hike" program lets girls and boys pretend to take part in a variety of professions, encouraging them to consider careers that have traditionally been restricted by gender. ⊠ *200 S. 6th Ave.,* ☎ *520/792–9985.* ☞ *$5.* ◷ *Sat. 10–5, Sun. noon–5; call for weekday hrs.*

★ ❻ **Tucson Museum of Art and Historic Block.** Tucson's past is interpreted for visitors in downtown's main cultural center. The five historic buildings on this block are listed in the National Register of Historic Places; you can enter **La Casa Cordova** (☞ *above*), the **Stevens Home** (☞ *above*), the **J. Knox Corbett House** (☞ *above*), and the **Edward Nye Fish House** (☞ *below*). The **Romero House,** believed to incorporate a section of the presidio wall, is not open to the public. In the center of the museum complex is the **Plaza of the Pioneers,** honoring Tucson's early citizens.

The modern **Tucson Museum of Art** building houses a permanent collection of pre-Columbian art and hosts some interesting traveling shows, most of them contemporary. The highlight here may well be the gift shop, featuring a colorful array of work by local artisans. The museum's permanent and changing exhibitions of western art fill an 1868 adobe, the **Edward Nye Fish House,** which belonged to an early merchant, entrepreneur, and politician, and his wife, Maria Wakefield Fish, a prominent educator. The building is notable for its 15-ft beamed ceilings and saguaro-cactus-rib supports. Nearby, the J. Knox Corbett House is furnished in the Arts and Crafts style. Additions to the contemporary central building and, eventually, expansion into the Stevens house, are in the works. To get a feel for the entire complex and how it fits together historically, try to arrange your visit to coincide with one of the free docent tours. Those interested in exploring the El Presidio District further can also get a self-guided tour map from the museum. ⊠ *140 N. Main Ave.,* ☎ *520/624–2333.* ☞ *$2; Tues. free. Free guided tours Wed. and Thurs. at 11 AM. ◷ Mon.–Sat. 10–4, Sun. noon–4. Closed Mon. Memorial Day through Labor Day (no guided tours during that period).*

The University of Arizona

A university might not seem to be the most likely spot for a vacation visit, but this one is unusual. Not only is the institution itself of historical importance, but it also supports several museums with exhibitions ranging from astronomy to photography. It's best to call ahead and verify opening and closing hours for the university's museums; budget cuts have caused schedule changes in a number of cases. If you drive, you're best off leaving your car in a university garage or lot. Central ones include those on Second Street between Highland and Mountain avenues; at the junction of Speedway Boulevard and Park Avenue; and on Second Street at Euclid Avenue. Rates are $1.25 per hour, except during university holidays, when parking is free.

The U of A, as the University of Arizona is known locally (versus ASU, its rival state university in Phoenix), covers 325 acres and is a major economic influence on the city. Approximately 33,500 students attend graduate and undergraduate classes here. The original land for the university was "donated" by a couple of gamblers and a saloon owner in 1891 (their benevolence was reputed to have been inspired by a bad hand of cards), and $25,000 of territorial money was used to build Old Main (the original building) and hire six faculty members. Money ran out before Old Main's roof was placed, but a few enlightened local

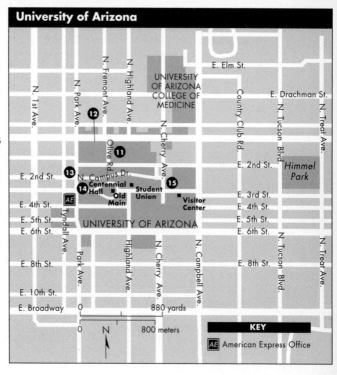

University of Arizona

citizens pitched in funds to finish it. Most of the city's populace was less enthusiastic about the institution: They were disgruntled when the 13th Territorial Legislature granted the University of Arizona to Tucson and awarded rival Phoenix with what they considered to be the real prize—an insane asylum and a prison.

A Good Tour

Start your tour on the northwestern corner of campus, at the junction of Speedway Boulevard and Park Avenue, where you'll find a large parking garage. A pedestrian underpass leads to the **Center for Creative Photography** ⑪, located in a gray concrete building on the left. Catercorner from the center on the right-hand side is the small **University of Arizona Museum of Art** ⑫. Head directly south two blocks on Park Avenue and then go east on Second Street to reach the **Arizona Historical Society's Museum** ⑬. One block to the south on University Boulevard, just inside the main gate of the university, is the **Arizona State Museum** ⑭. As you head east, University Boulevard turns into the grassy University Mall; continue on to Cherry Avenue to reach the **Grace H. Flandrau Science Center and Planetarium** ⑮.

TIMING

It's hard to see everything there is to see on the huge university campus in a single day—allot your time accordingly. During the school semesters, you're better off visiting on the weekend, when there's no fee for parking and it's less of a hassle to find a legal spot; there's no problem in summer, when most of the students leave campus.

Sights to See

✋ ⑬ **Arizona Historical Society's Museum.** Well-displayed exhibits transport visitors through the history of Southern Arizona, the Southwest United States, and Northern Mexico, starting with the Hohokam Indians and Spanish explorers and highlighting important influences. Children will especially enjoy the dark (and slightly spooky) replica of a mine shaft and the old cars and wagons in the transportation section. The library houses an extensive collection of historical Arizona photographs and sells reprints of most of them for a small fee. (If you're driving and this is your first stop, park your car in the garage at the corner of Second and Euclid streets and then inquire at the museum about the token system.) ⊠ *949 E. 2nd St.,* ☎ *520/628–5774.* ☜ *Suggested donation $3.* ☉ *Mon.–Sat. 10–4, Sun. noon–4; library Mon–Fri. 10–4, Sat. 10–1. Closed Sun.*

⓮ **Arizona State Museum.** Just inside the main gate of the university is the oldest museum in the state, dating from territorial days (1893). Exhibits in the original (south) building focus on the state's ancient history, including fossils and a fascinating sample of tree-ring dating. The cultural traditions, origins, and contemporary lives of native tribes of Arizona and of Sonora, Mexico, are explored through a variety of displays and video programs. ⊠ *Park Ave. at University Ave.,* ☎ *520/621–6302.* ☜ *Free.* ☉ *Mon.–Sat. 10–5, Sun. noon–5.*

NEED A BREAK?   Just outside the campus gate, University Boulevard is lined with student-oriented eateries. **Geronimoz** (⊠ 800 E. University Blvd., at Euclid, ☎ 520/623–1711) stands out with its good burgers and salads. Beer aficionados should head over to the upscale **Gentle Ben's** (⊠ 865 E. University Blvd., ☎ 520/624–4177), one of Tucson's few brewpubs.

★ ⓫ **Center for Creative Photography.** Ansel Adams conceived the idea of this museum, which houses a superb collection of his work and that of many other major 20th-century photographers, including Paul Strand, W. Eugene Smith, Edward Weston, and Louise Dahl-Wolfe. Changing exhibits in the main gallery highlight various holdings of the collection, but if you'd like to spend an hour looking at the pictures of a particular photographer in the center's archives, call to arrange an appointment. ⊠ *1030 N. Olive Rd. (north of 2nd St.),* ☎ *520/621–7968.* ☜ *$2 suggested donation.* ☉ *Weekdays 11–5, Sun. noon–5.*

☞ ⓯ **Grace H. Flandrau Science Center and Planetarium.** Attractions here include a 16-inch public telescope; the impressive Star Theatre, where a multimedia show brings astronomy to life; an interactive meteor exhibit; and, in the basement, a Mineral Museum, which exhibits more than 2,000 rock and gem samples, some rather rare. Laser light shows are held at night. Bring a camera—special adapters allow you to take pictures through the telescopes. ⊠ *Cherry Ave. and University Blvd.,* ☎ *520/621–4515; 621–7827 recorded message.* ☜ *Exhibits $3, laser light show $6, exhibits plus theater $6.* ☉ *Mon.–Tues. 9–5, Wed.–Thurs. 9–5 and 7–9, Fri. 9–5 and 7–midnight, Sat. 1–5 and 7–midnight, Sun. 1–5. Show times vary. Telescope hrs: in summer, Tues.–Sat. 8–10 PM; in winter, Wed.–Sat. 7:30–10 PM.*

⓬ **University of Arizona Museum of Art.** This small museum houses a wide-ranging collection of European paintings from the Renaissance through the 17th century. Two of the museum's highlights are the 26 astounding panels of Fernando Gallego's 1488 Ciudad Rodrigo altarpiece and the second largest collection in the world of bronze, plaster, and ceramic sculpture by Jacques Lipschitz. ⊠ *Fine Arts Complex, Bldg. 2 (southeast corner of Speedway Blvd. and Park Ave.),* ☎ *520/621–7567.* ☜ *Free.* ☉ *Sept.–mid-May, weekdays 9–5, Sun. noon–4; mid-May–Aug., weekdays 10–3:30, Sun. noon–4.*

East of I–10 including Central Tucson

The University of Arizona, built in 1891, determined the direction that the city would grow: A good many of the city's major attractions are east of its only major freeway, I–10. Sights worth seeing in central Tucson, as the area near the university is called, include a city park, a zoo, and botanical gardens. Nature has provided a lot of touring options farther to the north, where the imposing Santa Catalina Mountains lie, and to the far east, where you can view an abundance of cacti and caverns. Those interested in World War II should take a detour south to see a huge repository of old military aircraft.

A Good Tour

Start your drive at the **Tucson Botanical Gardens** ⑯. Two kiddie options are close by: The **Reid Park Zoo** ⑰ is less than 10 minutes to the southeast; if you head northwest, it'll take you about the same time to get to **Playmaxx/The Yozeum** ⑱. From here, distances get a bit greater (remember, Tucson spreads out over 500 square mi), so some decisions need to be made. You can head northeast, stopping off at **Fort Lowell Park and Museum** ㉑ and **De Grazia's Gallery in the Sun** ㉒ en route to **Sabino Canyon** ㉓ or **Mt. Lemmon** ㉔ (it's unlikely you'll have time to do both); or go all the way east to **Saguaro National Park East** ㉕ and **Colossal Cave** ㉖.

TIMING

If it's warm when you visit, outdoor attractions such as the Tucson Botanical Gardens and Saguaro National Park East are best visited in the morning. Sabino Canyon and Mt. Lemmon, on the other hand, are cooler than the rest of the city, the former because of shade provided by Coconino National Forest, the latter because of its elevation. Colossal Cave stays at a constant, comfortable temperature, making it a nice year-round adjunct to a Saguaro National Park East tour.

Sights to See

⊙ ㉖ **Colossal Cave.** The limestone grotto that lies 20 mi east of Tucson (take Broadway Blvd. or E. 22nd St. to Colossal Cave Rd.) is the largest dry cavern in the world. Indeed, parts of it have yet to be explored. Informed guides discuss the fascinating crystal formations and relate the many romantic tales surrounding the cave, including the legend that an enormous sum of money stolen in a stagecoach robbery is hidden here and has never been recovered. ⊠ *Intersection of Colossal Cave Rd. and Old Spanish Trail Rd.,* ☎ *520/647–7275.* ⊠ *$6.50.* ⊙ *Oct.–mid-Mar., Mon.–Sat. 9–5, Sun. and holidays 9–6; mid-Mar.–Sept., Mon.–Sat. 8–6, Sun. and holidays 8–7.*

㉒ **De Grazia's Gallery in the Sun.** Arizonan artist Ted De Grazia, who depicted Southwest Indian and Mexican life, built this sprawling, spacious single-story museum with the assistance of Native American friends using only natural material from the surrounding desert. You can visit De Grazia's workshop, former home, and grave site as well. Although none of the artist's original works are for sale, the museum's gift shop has a wide selection of prints, ceramics, and books by and about the colorful artist. ⊠ *6300 N. Swan Rd.,* ☎ *520/299–9191.* ⊠ *Free.* ⊙ *Daily 10–4.*

㉑ **Fort Lowell Park and Museum.** This restful city park was once the site of a Hohokam Indian village and, many centuries later, a fort built to protect the fledgling city against the Apaches (1873–91). The former commanding officer's quarters, reconstructed and turned into a museum, gives a glimpse of military life in territorial days with archaeological and military artifacts on display. Some of the descendants of the inhabitants of El Fuerte, a Mexican village that arose among the abandoned fort buildings in the 1890s, still live in a narrow alley near the museum called El Callejón. ⊠ *2900 N. Craycroft Rd.,* ☎ *520/885–3832.* ⊠ *Free.* ⊙ *Wed.–Sat. 10–4.*

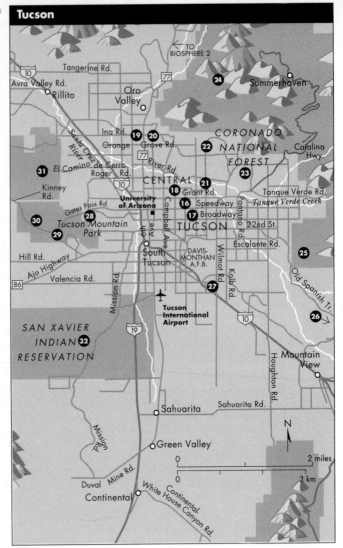

Tucson

🖐 ⑲ **Gadsden-Pacific Toy Train Museum, Ltd.** Children of all ages will enjoy this museum in the northern sector of the Foothills Mall, across from the administrative offices. Visitors can make the 11 little locomotives run around the room by pushing various buttons; miniature cranes, milk cars, and fork loaders add to the action. ✉ *7401 N. La Cholla Blvd., at Ina Rd.,* ☎ *520/790–0337.* 🎟 *Free.* ⏱ *Wed. 4–8, Sat. 10–6, Sun. noon–5.*

⑳ **Mt. Lemmon.** One of the Santa Catalina Mountains, Mt. Lemmon is the southernmost ski slope of the continental United States, but you don't have to be a skier to visit. In spring and fall you can enjoy picnicking and hiking in this lovely area, which has some 150 mi of well-marked and well-maintained trails; in summer the mountain's 9,157-ft elevation brings welcome relief from the heat. If you're making the trip in winter, check road conditions by calling 520/749–3329. And be sure to fill up the tank before you leave town any time of year, because there are no gas stations on Mt. Lemmon Highway, the road that winds and twists its way for 28 mi up the mountainside.

The journey up the mountain is interesting in itself: Every 1,000 ft of elevation is equivalent to traveling 300 mi north, so you'll move from typical Sonoran Desert plants in the foothills to vegetation similar to that found in southern Canada at the top. Along the way, you'll see rock formations that look as though they were carefully balanced against each other by architects from another planet.

At milepost 18, on the left-hand side of the road when you're ascending, the **Palisades Ranger Station** can give you current information on the mountain's campgrounds, hiking trails, and picnic spots; it's also a good place to buy maps and books. It's open Friday through Sunday 9 to 5 in winter, daily 9 to 6 in summer. The station does not have a published telephone number, but you can call the Coronado National Forest (☎ 520/749–8700) if you have any questions.

Just before you reach the ski resort, you'll pass through the tiny alpine-style village of **Summerhaven,** which has a couple of casual restaurants, lots of gift shops, and a few pleasant lodges.

Mt. Lemmon Highway ends at **Mt. Lemmon Ski Valley** (☎ 520/576–1321; 520/576–1400 for a recorded snow report). Skiing here depends on natural conditions—there's no artificial snow—so call ahead. There are 16 runs, open daily, ranging from beginner to advanced. Lift tickets cost $27 for an all-day pass and $22 for a half day (starting at 1 PM). Ski equipment can be rented, and instruction is available. Even in off-season, you can take a ride on the double chairlift that whisks you to the top of the slope—some 9,100 ft. The cost is $6. Many ride the lift and then head out on one of several trails that crisscross the summit. ⊠ *Take Tanque Verde Rd. to the Catalina Hwy., which becomes Mt. Lemmon Hwy. as you head north.*

NEED A BREAK?

The **Iron Door** (☎ 520/576–1321) in Mt. Lemmon Ski Valley is open weekends 10–5:30, weekdays 10:30–5:30 (give or take half an hour, depending on the weather). In winter, the focus is on burgers, chili, corn bread, and soups; in warmer weather, lots of salads turn up on the menu. This place is popular on the weekends—parking can be tough.

㉗ Pima Air and Space Museum. This huge facility ranks among the largest private collections of historic aircraft in the world. More than 200 flight machines are on display. You'll see a full-scale replica of the Wright brothers' 1903 Wright Flyer and a mock-up of the X-15, the world's fastest aircraft. You can tour the surprisingly low-key presidential plane used on official business by both John F. Kennedy and Lyndon B. Johnson. World War II veterans find the museum particularly moving, but all ages should enjoy this walk through U.S. aviation history. ⊠ *6000 E. Valencia Rd. (I–10 exit 267),* ☎ *520/574–9658.* ☜ *$6, tram ticket $2.* ☉ *Daily 9–5 (last admission at 4).*

㉘ Playmaxx/The Yozeum. A member of the Duncan (of yo-yo fame) family has put together a delightful historical exhibit of the wood-and-string toys, dating from 1929 through the 1980s. The guided tours include films of old yo-yo contests and demonstrations of yo-yo assembly. Anyone with a yo-yo can come in the first Saturday of the month for complimentary instruction classes. ⊠ *2900 N. Country Club Rd.,* ☎ *520/ 322–0100.* ☜ *Free.* ☉ *Tues.–Fri. 9–5, Sat. 9–1.*

㉗ Reid Park Zoo. This small but well-designed zoo won't tax the children's—or your—patience. Ask who's new when you arrive; the many baby animals born here each year are adorable. The zoo has a South

American enclosure, which includes a rain forest and exotic birds. If you're visiting in the summertime, go early in the day when the animals are active. ⊠ *Reid Park, Lake Shore La., off 22nd St. between Alvernon Way and Country Club Rd.,* ☎ *520/791–4022 recorded hrs; 520/791–3204 administration.* ⊠ *$3.50.* ⊙ *Daily 9–4.*

★ ㉓ **Sabino Canyon.** Year-round, but especially during summer, locals flock to this oasis in the northeast corner of town. Part of the Coronado National Forest but filled with saguaros and other desert flora and fauna, this is a good spot for hiking, picnicking, or enjoying the waterfalls, streams, natural swimming holes, and shade trees that provide a respite from the heat. No cars are allowed, but a narrated tram ride (about 45 minutes round-trip) takes you to the top of the canyon. You can hop off and on at any of the nine stops. There's also a tram ride to adjacent Bear Canyon, where you can hike to the popular Seven Falls (it'll take about 1½ hours each way from the drop-off point). ⊠ *Sabino Canyon Rd. in the Santa Catalina foothills,* ☎ *520/749–2861 recorded tram information; 520/749–8700 visitor center.* ⊠ *Tram $5, Bear Canyon tram $3. Call for daily schedules.* ⊙ *Visitor center weekdays 8–4:30, weekends 8:30–4:30.*

㉕ **Saguaro National Park East.** About 16 mi from the town center, the eastern portion of the national park that sandwiches Tucson covers more than 67,000 acres and climbs through five climate zones, which makes for some dramatic hikes through the foothills of the Rincon Mountains. An 8-mi paved Cactus Forest Drive leads to a variety of trailheads and picnic areas. Ask for a detailed map at the visitor center (☞ Saguaro National Park West, *below,* for more information about the unique cacti that are concentrated here). ⊠ *Old Spanish Trail (take Speedway Blvd. or 22nd St. E),* ☎ *520/733–5153.* ⊠ *$4 per vehicle, $2 individuals entering by bicycle or on foot.* ⊙ *Visitor center daily 8:30–5; park roads 7 AM–sunset.*

★ ⑳ **Tohono Chul Park.** A 48-acre retreat designed to promote the conservation of arid regions, Tohono Chul—the name means "desert corner" in the language of the Tohono O'odham Indians—uses a demonstration garden, greenhouse, and geology wall to educate visitors about this unique desert area. Shady nooks and nature trails allow for leisurely sitting or strolling. A small art gallery and tearoom (☞ Dining, *below*) are additional reasons to visit this peaceful landscaped setting. ⊠ *7366 N. Paseo del Norte,* ☎ *520/742–6455.* ⊠ *$2 suggested donation.* ⊙ *Park daily 7 AM–sunset; building Mon.–Sat. 9:30–5, Sun. 11–5.*

⑯ **Tucson Botanical Gardens.** This 5-acre oasis in the center of town includes a tropical greenhouse; a sensory garden, where visitors are encouraged to touch, smell, or listen to various plants; historical gardens, which display the Mediterranean landscaping that the property's original owners planted in the 1930s; a garden designed to attract birds; and a cactus garden. The grounds are also home to Native Seeds/SEARCH, an organization that helps farmers throughout the Southwest and northern Mexico by collecting, growing, and selling seeds of crops that thrive in arid areas. ⊠ *2150 N. Alvernon Way,* ☎ *520/ 326–9686.* ⊠ *$4.* ⊙ *Daily 8:30–4:30.*

OFF THE
BEATEN PATH

BIOSPHERE 2 – You may have heard some of the publicity surrounding the once-controversial project taking place in the little town of Oracle, some 45 minutes north of central Tucson. The least flattering accounts described it as eight cultists locked up together in a terrarium for two years in preparation for colonizing Mars. But not long after the original "crew" left the enclosure in 1994, Biosphere 2 went legit: The bank-roller of the project, Texas oil billionaire Edward P. Bass, ejected the original directors and hired a group of distinguished scientists to do research on the sealed ecosystem. In November 1995, Columbia University and Biosphere 2 signed a five-year agreement for Columbia's Lamont–Doherty Earth Observatory to manage and direct all of Biosphere's scientific, educational, and visitor-center operations. Still, although the original Biospherians have gone and an array of serious educational programs are underway, vestiges of the commercialism that characterized the project remain: Biosphere logo merchandise is still sold in gift shops all around the complex, and Alan Alda narrates an introductory film.

The miniature world created within Biosphere includes tropical rain forest, savanna, desert, thorn scrub, marsh, ocean, and agricultural areas, including almost 4,000 plant and animal species. A film and cutaway model explain the project. Guided walking tours, which last about two hours, don't enter most of the sealed sphere, but the living quarters of the Biospherians have recently been opened to the public, and indoor and outdoor observation areas let you peer in at the rest. The Canyon del Oro restaurant, overlooking the Santa Catalina Mountains, has a full menu of sandwiches and hearty entrées; there are also a variety of snack bars. Reasonably priced hotel suites with excellent views are available on Biosphere's premises. ⊠ *AZ 77, mile marker 96.5,* ☎ *520/896-6200 or 800/828-2462.* ☜ *$12.95. C Daily 8:30–5; guided tours every ½ hr, 9–4.*

West of I–10

If you're interested in the flora and fauna of the Sonoran Desert—as well as some of its appearances in the cinema—west is an ideal direction for you to take.

A Good Tour

From central Tucson, take Speedway Boulevard west; when the houses begin to thin and stands of cacti begin to thicken, you'll see the **International Wildlife Museum** ㉘. Continue west on Speedway to where it joins Anklam Road and becomes Gates Pass Road; at the juncture of Gates Pass and Kinney roads, you'll see signs directing you to **Old Tucson Studios** ㉙. Return to this juncture and continue on Kinney Road for about 10 mi until you come to the **Arizona–Sonora Desert Museum** ㉚. It's a short drive along the same road to the Red Hills Information Center, which will introduce you to **Saguaro National Park West** ㉛. If you don't want to backtrack, drive northeast through the park on Golden Gate Road until you reach Picture Rocks Road; it'll turn into Ina Road, which leads to I–10. Take I–10 south (the sign will read EAST–TO EL PASO) to I–19, which only goes in one direction from here. You'll soon come to the turnoff for **Mission San Xavier del Bac** ㉜.

TIMING

Although the distances between the attractions in this area are not negligible, it's easy to tour all the sights in a single day since they're on a fairly direct route to one another. The best plan is to set out in the cooler early morning to Saguaro National Park, which has no shaded areas (it's also the best time to see the wildlife at its liveliest). Spend the rest of the morning at the Desert Museum, where you can have lunch at the Ironwood Terrace (in any case, allow at least two hours for your visit). The hottest time of the afternoon can be spent ducking in and out of attractions at Old Tucson, visiting the air-conditioned International Wildlife Museum, or enjoying the indoor sanctuary of San Xavier Mission.

Sights to See

★ ㉚ **Arizona–Sonora Desert Museum.** The name "museum" is misleading; this delightful site is more like a beautifully planned zoo. In this microcosm of a desert environment, hummingbirds, cactus wrens, rattlesnakes, scorpions, bighorn sheep, and prairie dogs all busy themselves in natural habitats ingeniously planned to allow the visitor to look on without disturbing them. An Earth Sciences Center features a damp limestone cave and meteor and mineral displays that encourage visitors to feel the texture of the stones and inspect them under magnifying glasses. ⊠ *2021 N. Kinney Rd.,* ☎ *520/883–2702.* 🎫 *$8.95.* ☉ *Mar.–Sept., daily 7:30–6; Oct.–Feb., daily 8:30–5. Last ticket sales 1 hr before closing. MC, V.*

㉘ **International Wildlife Museum.** A Petting Menagerie at this facility allows kids to touch a variety of animal skins; they can also learn about more than 200 species of birds and mammals from all over the world via interactive computers. ⊠ *4800 W. Gates Pass Rd.,* ☎ *520/617–1439.* 🎫 *$5.* ☉ *Daily 9–5.*

★ ㉜ **Mission San Xavier del Bac.** The oldest Catholic church in the United States still serving the community for which it was built, San Xavier was founded in 1692 by Father Eusebio Francisco Kino, who established 22 missions in northern Mexico and southern Arizona. It was constructed out of native materials by Franciscan missionaries between 1777 and 1797. Today it is owned by the Tohono O'odham Indian tribe (the name means "desert people who have come from the earth").

The beauty of the mission, with elements of Spanish, Baroque, and *mudejar* (Spanish Islamic) architectural styles, is highlighted by the stark landscape against which it is set, inspiring an early-20th-century poet to dub it "White Dove of the Desert." Inside, there's a wealth of painted statues, carvings, and frescoes. The mission has more recently been called the Sistine Chapel of the United States by Paul Schwartzbaum, who worked on restoring Michelangelo's masterwork in Rome and helped supervise the restoration of the mission's artwork. Begun in 1992, the project was completed in 1997. Mass is celebrated daily at San Xavier, four times on Sunday morning. Call ahead for information about special celebrations.

Across the parking lot from the mission, **San Xavier Plaza** has a number of shops that sell fine Native American crafts. Look especially for crafts made by the Tohono O'odham tribe, including jewelry, pottery, and baskets featuring man-in-the-maze designs and friendship bowls. ⊠ *San Xavier Rd., 9 mi southwest of Tucson on I–19,* ☎ *520/294–2624.*

NEED A BREAK?   For wonderful Indian fry bread—large, round pieces of dough taken fresh from the hot oil and topped with all sorts of delicious possibilities— stop in the **Wa:k Snack Shop** (☎ no phone) at the back of San Xavier Plaza. You can also have breakfast or a Mexican lunch here.

㉙ **Old Tucson Studios.** This film set–cum–theme park, seriously damaged by fire in 1995, reopened after some $13 million of renovations in early 1997. Many of the adobe structures that were used as movie backdrops (the studio was built for the 1940 motion picture *Arizona*) still stand, but the complex was redesigned with wider streets, larger buildings, and a more logical layout. Actors in Western garb sing and dance in the Town Square and roam the streets talking to visitors, especially children. Kids also enjoy the simulated gun fights, carousel ride, stunt shows, petting farm, stagecoach rides, log rides, mine tour, and more, while adults gravitate towards the screenings of the old Westerns and the little-bit-bawdy Grand Palace Hotel's Dance Hall Revue. There are plenty of places to chow down and to buy souvenirs. ⊠ *201 S. Kinney Rd. (inside Tucson Mountain Park),* ☎ *520/883–0100.* ☒ *$14.95.* ☉ *Late Dec.–mid Apr. daily 9–7; rest of the yr 10–6.*

★ ❸ **Saguaro National Park West.** This is the smaller (24,000 acres) and most visited section of the national park that flanks Tucson—its eastern and western portions are divided by the city. Together the sections are home to the world's largest concentration of the huge saguaro cactus, which is native to the Sonoran Desert and known for its towering height (often 50 ft) and arms that reach out in weird configurations. The cactus is ribbed vertically with accordion-like pleats that expand to store water gathered through its shallow roots during the infrequent desert rain showers. In the springtime (usually April or May), the giant succulent sports a tiny party hat of white blooms. At any time of year, the sight of these kings of the desert ruling over their quiet domain is awe-inspiring.

The slow-growing cacti (they can take up to 15 years to grow 1 ft) are protected by state and federal laws, so enjoy but don't disturb them. In recent years, they have suffered a decline because a decrease in the coyote population has led to an abundant rabbit population. Rabbits and other small animals nibble at the base of the young saguaro, gathering nutrients and water for survival and thereby hindering or halting the cactus's slow growth.

Before you venture into the desert, it's worth stopping in at the impressive visitor center. A slide show (given every half hour from 8:30 to 4:30) offers a Native American perspective of the saguaro cactus. An extremely lifelike display simulates the flora and fauna of the region. Walkways from the side of the center lead out onto short nature trails; you can obtain information about longer hiking trails that wind through the park. Ask how to get to Signal Hill, where you can inspect petroglyphs (rock drawings) left by the Hohokam Indians centuries ago. Keep in mind that desert critters such as snakes and scorpions aren't necessarily hostile unless you crowd them, so just watch your step and respect their habitat. ⊠ *Kinney Rd.,* ☎ *520/733–5158.* ☒ *Free.* ☉ *Visitor center daily 8:30–5; park roads 6 AM–sunset.*

DINING

While Tucson's variety of restaurants is impressive, the city doesn't offer much in the way of late-night dining. Most restaurants in town are shuttered by 10 PM. Some spots that keep later hours are noted below. In addition, two locations of **Coffee, Etc.** (⊠ 2830 N. Campbell Ave., ☎ 520/881–8070; ⊠ 6091 N. Oracle Rd., ☎ 520/544–8588), with good coffee and a varied menu, are open 24 hours.

Northwest Tucson

Continental

$$$$ ✕ **Anthony's.** This is *the* special-occasion restaurant for many Tucsonans. Pink linen, stemmed crystal, pink-rim china, and—on the glassed-in terrace—lighting that precludes your seeing your dining companion very well, add to the romantic atmosphere here. Service is uncharacteristically formal for Tucson. Such dishes as the seafood relleno (an Anaheim chili stuffed with Jack cheese, shrimp, and scallops) or the veal Sonoita (sliced veal tenderloin with roasted garlic, sun-dried tomatoes, and goat cheese) put a contemporary spin on the otherwise Continental menu. A pianist who plays from 7 nightly draws locals to the

cocktail lounge. ⊠ *6440 N. Campbell Ave.,* ☎ *520/299–1771. AE, DC, MC, V. No lunch weekends.*

French

$$–$$$ ✕ **Café Beaujolais.** Tapestry chairs with wrought-iron ivy designs, pink walls, and the sounds of Mozart or Bach provide a nice backdrop for the short, classic bistro menu. Mushrooms baked in a puff pastry shell with a touch of Stilton are a delicious but rich starter; you won't be settling if you opt for the house salad, crunchy with walnuts and fresh greens. The lamb chops with garlic mashed potatoes are the ultimate in comfort food; the lighter mussels in a white wine and shallot sauce won't disappoint, either. Crème brûlée aficionados will be very happy with the almond-redolent version made in house, as all the desserts are. ⊠ *5931 N. Oracle Rd.,* ☎ *520/887–7359. AE, D, MC, V. Closed Mon. No lunch weekends.*

Southwest

$$–$$$ ✕ **Café Terra Cotta.** Everything about this restaurant says Southwest—from the decor, with its bright pastels and bleached woods, to the food, including such contemporary Southwest specialties as prawns stuffed with herbed goat cheese, pork tenderloin with black beans, and pizza with artichokes and herbed mozzarella. The garlic-custard appetizer is superb. This is the place for native yupsters and their out-of-town guests. ⊠ *St. Philip's Plaza, 4310 N. Campbell Ave.,* ☎ *520/577–8100. AE, D, DC, MC, V.*

$$ ✕ **Tohono Chul Tea Room.** The food is fine, though it's not the reason to make the drive to the northwest part of town. What's unique here is the setting. The tearoom is nestled in a wildlife sanctuary and surrounded by a cactus garden. Although the tearoom is typically southwestern, with lots of Mexican tile and light wood and a cobblestone patio, the menu covers southwestern, Mexican, and American dishes. House favorites include chicken enchiladas made with Monterey Jack cheese, corn, and green chilies, and a sliced-tomato-and-basil sandwich served on French sourdough bread. Sunday brunch is especially good—which can mean long waits in high season. ⊠ *7366 N. Paseo del Norte,* ☎ *520/797–1222. AE, D, MC, V.* ☉ *Mid-Sept.–mid-Apr. 8–5, mid-Apr.–mid-Sept. 8–8.*

Downtown Tucson and 4th Avenue

Greek

$$ ✕ **Athens.** A Greek oasis of tranquillity off bustling 4th Avenue, Athens creates a serene Mediterranean atmosphere with its lace curtains, wooden wainscoting, white stucco walls, and potted plants. Order a dish of creamy *taramasalata* (Greek caviar). Follow it with *kotopoulo stin pita* (grilled chicken breast with a yogurt-cucumber sauce on fresh-baked pita). If it's Greek comfort food you're after, order the moussaka or the *pastitsio* (a pasta-, meat-, and bechamel-filled lasagna). ⊠ *500 N. 4th Ave., No. 6,* ☎ *520/624–6886. AE, D, DC, MC, V. Closed Sun. No lunch.*

Guatemalan

$ ✕ **Maya Quetzal.** This friendly, family-owned restaurant on trendy 4th Avenue is inexpensive enough to allow those unfamiliar with Guatemalan food—and who isn't?—to sample lots of different dishes. Try the *tortitas de espinaca* (lightly fried spinach patties with walnuts, tomato, and garlic) or the *pollo en jocón* (chicken with cilantro-flavor green sauce). All dishes come in vegetarian versions, and all the meat is free-range. A large, brightly colored mural and Guatemalan crafts add to the congenial atmosphere. The food may be a bit bland for palates expecting Mexican fire, but you'll be eating for a good cause. A portion

of all profits go to help Guatemalan refugees. ✉ *429 N. 4th Ave.,* ☎
520/622–8207. Reservations not accepted. MC, V. Closed Sun.

Mexican

$–$$ ✕ **Café Poca Cosa.** Eschewing the cheese-saturated Sonoran standbys,
★   chef-owner Susana Davila creates exciting recipes inspired by different regions of her native Mexico, here at Café Poca Cosa, arguably
Tucson's best restaurant. The innovative menu, which changes daily,
might include *pollo à mole* (chicken in a spicy chocolate-based sauce)
or pork *pìbil* (made with a tangy Yucatan barbecue seasoning). Locals
were happy for Susana's success after she got a huge write-up in
Gourmet magazine, but are grumpy because it's so much harder to get
a table these days. The tiny original restaurant across the street (✉ 20
S. Scott Ave.), also a lively treat, is open for breakfast and lunch during the week. ✉ *88 E. Broadway, beside the Clarion Hotel* ☎ *520/
622–6400. MC, V. Closed Sun.*

$–$$ ✕ **El Charro Café.** Started by Monica Flin in 1922 and run by her grand-
niece and her grandniece's husband today, El Charro still serves excellent versions of the American-Mexican staples Flin claims to have
originated—chimichangas (flour tortillas rolled around seasoned beef
or chicken and deep-fried) and cheese crisps, most notably. Daily "fit-
ness-fare" specials such as seafood enchiladas are delicious as well as
healthful. A lounge serves appetizers and drinks. ✉ *311 N. Court Ave.,*
☎ *520/622–1922. AE, D, DC, MC, V.*

$–$$ ✕ **El Minuto Café.** This brightly decorated, bustling restaurant in Tuc-
son's historic barrio is a good bet for those seeking a late meal downtown. It's open until midnight Friday and Saturday, until 10 PM the
rest of the week. In business for more than 50 years, El Minuto serves
up topopo salads (a variety of goodies, including guacamole, heaped
into a crispy tortilla shell); huge burritos; and green corn tamales (in
season) made just right. The spicy menudo is a great hangover rem-
edy (just don't ask what's in it). ✉ *354 S. Main Ave.,* ☎ *520/882–
4145. AE, D, DC, MC, V.*

Southwestern

$$$–$$$$ ✕ **Janos.** This downtown restaurant is so revered that when the Tuc-
★   son Museum of Art did not renew the lease of the 1855 adobe home
that Janos has long occupied, the city council voted to allot funds for
the museum to expand elsewhere. The offer was refused, however, and
the restaurant is looking for a new home (although it should remain
in its current location through August 1998)—not that location mat-
ters: It's the innovative and superlative Southwest menus created by
chef-owner Janos Wilder that the crowds come for anyway. Typical of-
ferings include a mushroom-and-Brie-stuffed chili appetizer and pan-
seared salmon with a smoky maple syrup glaze; the baklava with
apricots and macadamia nuts is outstanding. Combinations are usu-
ally very successful, but the high prices make the occasional failure all
the more disappointing. The summer and fall dinner specials allow the
less well-heeled to indulge in a meal here. ✉ *150 N. Main Ave.,* ☎
*520/884–9426. AE, DC, MC, V. Closed Sun. Nov.–mid-May; Sun. and
Mon. late May–Nov. No lunch.*

South Tucson

Mexican

$–$$ **South 4th Avenue.** Every Tucsonan you meet will argue the merits of
a favorite "real" Mexican restaurant, but invariably it's on or near 4th
Avenue in South Tucson. Technically a separate city, South Tucson has
a large Mexican-American population and thus many authentic and
inexpensive places to find good south-of-the-border cuisine. Among

Tucson Dining and Lodging

Dining

Anthony's, **9**

Arizona Inn
Restaurant, **22**

Athens, **27**

Le Bistro, **17**

Boccata, **43**

Café Beaujolais, **4**

Café Poca Cosa, **33**

Café Terra Cotta, **10**

Cottonwood Cafe, **37**

The Dish, **24**

El Charro Café, **29**

El Minuto Café, **31**

Gavi, **56**

Govinda, **15**

Janos, **32**

The Kingfisher
Grill, **18**

Maya Quetzal, **30**

Le Mediterranean, **44**

New Delhi Palace, **54**

Olive Tree, **48**

Pinnacle Peak
Steakhouse, **49**

Presidio Grill, **25**

Rancher's Club, **50**

Le Rendez-Vous, **41**

Sachiko Sushi, **53**

Seri Melaka, **52**

South Tucson/
4th Avenue, **35**

The Tack Room, **46**

Tohono Chul Tea
Room, **1**

Ventana Room, **39**

Vivace, **42**

Yoeme, **16**

Zemam, **36**

KEY

AE American Express Office

Lodging

Adobe Rose Inn, **23**

Arizona Inn, **22**

Best Western Ghost Ranch Lodge, **14**

Canyon Ranch, **45**

Casa Alegre, **20**

Casa Tierra, **19**

Catalina Park Inn, **26**

Clarion Santa Rita, **33**

Doubletree Hotel, **38**

Embassy Suites Tucson-Broadway, **51**

Hacienda del Sol, **14**

Hotel Congress, **34**

Lazy K Bar Guest Ranch, **40**

Loews Ventana Canyon Resort, **39**

Marriott University Park, **21**

Miraral, **8**

Omni Tucson National Spa, **3**

Peppertrees, **28**

Ramada Inn Foothills, **47**

Sheraton Tucson El Conquistador, **6**

Tanque Verde Ranch, **57**

Triangle L Ranch Bed & Breakfast, **7**

Tucson Hilton East, **55**

Westin La Paloma, **13**

Westward Look Resort, **5**

White Stallion Ranch, **2**

The Windmill Inn at St. Phillip's Plaza, **11**

the most popular are **Crossroads** (⊠ 2602 S. 4th Ave., ☎ 520/624–0395), **Gran Guadalajara** (⊠ 2527 S. 4th Ave., ☎ 520/620–1321), **Guillermo's Double L** (⊠ 1830 S. 4th Ave., ☎ 520/792–1585), **Micha's** (⊠ 2908 S. 4th Ave., ☎ 520/623–5307), and **Mi Nidito** (⊠ 1813 S. 4th Ave., ☎ 520/622–5081), all open for both lunch and dinner. You'd be hard-pressed to have a bad meal—or a bad time—at any of these friendly, informal places. Many have mariachi bands on the weekends. MasterCard and Visa are accepted at most.

Central Tucson

American

$$–$$$ ✕ **Kingfisher Grill.** Kingfisher has drawn critical kudos and a loyal local following, but it may be becoming a victim of its quick success. Prices are creeping up without a commensurate return in consistency. That said, the restaurant's regional American cuisine continues to dazzle much of the time. The chic setting—low lighting, bright turquoise and neon contrasting with warm brick walls and comfy black banquettes—is matched by the innovative menu, which changes seasonally. You might find mesquite-grilled pork loin chops or crayfish étouffée on the menu. From 10 to midnight, choose from a menu of soups, salads, burgers, and selections from the oyster bar. ⊠ 2564 E. Grant Rd., ☎ 520/323–7739. AE, D, DC, MC, V. No lunch weekends.

Continental

$$$ ✕ **Arizona Inn Restaurant.** Sit out on the patio overlooking the grounds of this classic historic inn, or enjoy the view through huge windows in the dining room, a light, airy place with many 1930s southwestern details. A fire warms the room on chilly evenings. Steamed fish of the day served with ginger and leeks is a specialty, and the mesquite-smoked quail is also popular. Locals love to come in for Sunday brunch or a civilized afternoon high tea in the library (Thanksgiving through Easter only). There is no longer a dress code, but men will likely feel most comfortable wearing a jacket. ⊠ 2200 E. Elm St., ☎ 520/325–1541. AE, MC, V.

$$ **The Dish.** The descriptions on the Mediterranean-kissed menu here may
★ be whimsical—salads are categorized as "green dishes" and labeled "simple," "fancy," and "big," for example—but the food is really good. Even the butter, embedded with toasted onions, is yummy. Try the mussels steamed in saffron or the aforementioned "fancy salad," which includes goat cheese and tiny yellow tomatoes, for starters. Entrées include citrus-glazed salmon and anise-crusted pork tenderloin. ⊠ 3200 Speedway Blvd., ☎ 520/326–1714. AE, MC, V. Closed Sun. and Mon. No lunch.

Ethiopian

$ ✕ **Zemam.** It can be hard to get a table in this tiny eatery, a favorite
★ with locals. The sampler plate, which includes any three items on the small menu, is your best bet, allowing you to try such dishes as *yesimir wat* (a spicy lentil-based dish), and *zigni* (a milder beef dish with a tomato sauce). Most of the food has a stewlike consistency; don't come if you feel the need to crunch. Everything is served on a communal platter topped with *injera*, a spongy bread, and eaten with the hands. Prices are ridiculously low, considering the food quality and quantity, and alcohol is bring your own. ⊠ 2731 E. Broadway, ☎ 520/323–9928. Reservations not accepted. MC, V. Closed Mon.

French

$$$–$$$$ ✕ **Le Rendez-vous.** The clientele is a bit blue-haired and the service a tad hovering, but you'll hardly notice as you concentrate on the tasty cuisine. The most expensive French restaurant in town prepares duck

à l'orange that is as crispy as it should be and veal medallions with calvados as tender. A spa menu and bistro menu are available for those watching their weights or their wallets. The lunch menu is wide-ranging and rather moderately priced. ✉ *3844 E. Fort Lowell Rd.,* ☎ *520/323–7373. AE, D, DC, MC, V. Closed Mon. No lunch weekends.*

$$$ ✕ **Le Bistro.** A new impressionist-style mural on a formerly nondescript
★ building now beckons you into Le Bistro, one of the prettiest restaurants in town. Potted palms tower over tables covered with chic burgundy-and-black cloths splashed with pink flowers, and Art Nouveau–style etched mirrors grace the walls. The setting is matched by the creations of young chef-owner Laurent Reux. Born in Brittany, many of his fish and shellfish dishes are inspired by the seascape of his native region. Two of his specialties include salmon in a ginger crust with lime butter and Long Island duck in a raspberry vinaigrette. Lunch prices are very reasonable. ✉ *2574 N. Campbell Ave.,* ☎ *502/327–3086. AE, D, MC, V. No lunch weekends.*

Greek

$$ ✕ **Olive Tree.** In an appealing Santa Fe–style building, the Olive Tree serves up fine versions of such Greek standards as moussaka, shish kebab, and stuffed grape leaves, but also includes more unusual dishes on its menu. The Lamb Bandit is baked in foil with two types of cheese, potatoes, and vegetables. Daily fresh-fish specials are broiled or sautéed in garlic, oregano, and olive oil and served with a well-prepared orzo. This is not light cuisine. If you don't have room for supersweet baklava, a cup of strong Greek coffee makes for a satisfying finish. ✉ *7000 E. Tanque Verde Rd.,* ☎ *520/298–1845. AE, DC, MC, V. No lunch Sun.*

Indian

$–$$ ✕ **New Delhi Palace.** Vegetarians, carnivores, and seafood lovers will all find something to enjoy at this elegant Indian restaurant. The congenial staff is helpful in explaining the menu, which features a wide variety of tandoori dishes, curries, rice, and breads. The "heat" of each dish can be adjusted to individual preference by the chef. ✉ *6751 E. Broadway,* ☎ *520/296–8585. AE, DC, MC, V.*

Italian

$$–$$$ ✕ **Vivace.** Daniel Scordato has had his hand in some of the best Italian
★ restaurants in town, and his latest venture continues to be a big hit. During high season, Vivace fills up even on weekday nights, mostly with a well-heeled, well-turned-out crowd. It's all very industrial chic—gray columns, black iron chairs, open kitchen—but this is still Arizona, which means the black-and-white–clad servers are not SoHo frosty to match. Appetizers are a little pricey compared with the rest of the menu, though the grilled shrimp in a phyllo cup with tomato, basil, and garlic sauce is hard to resist. For a lighter alternative to such dishes as rich osso buco, try the linguine with grilled salmon. One caveat: The room can get very noisy. ✉ *4811 E. Grant Rd., Ste. 155,* ☎ *520/795–7221. MC, V. No lunch Sun.*

Japanese

$$ ✕ **Sachiko Sushi.** You can get good versions of teriyaki, udon noodles, and even some Korean dishes at this low-key Japanese restaurant in an east-central strip mall, but as its name suggests, the main reason to come is sushi. The super-fresh fish is well priced, especially when you consider the quality. Lunch specials are even more of a bargain. Come Friday or Saturday night and see a predominantly Japanese crowd chow down before crooning "I Left My Heart in San Francisco" and other karaoke standards. ✉ *1101 N. Wilmot St., Suite 109,* ☎ *520/886–7000. AE, D, MC, V. No lunch Sun.*

Malaysian

$ ✕ **Seri Melaka.** Malaysian food, like Thai, uses plenty of curry, coconut, and other tasty condiments in its sauces. This popular restaurant on the east side of town is the place to indulge in good versions of such dishes as *satay* (grilled meat on a skewer with peanut sauce) and *lemak* (shrimp or chicken with vegetables in a sweet curry sauce). An extensive selection of well-prepared Chinese dishes is also on the menu. There's a buffet at lunchtime seven days a week, and early-bird dinner specials Monday through Friday 4:30–6. ⊠ *6133 E. Broadway,* ☎ *520/747–7811. AE, D, DC, MC, V.*

Native American

$ ✕ **Yoeme.** Proceeds of this tiny restaurant, owned and run by the Pasqua Yaquis who have two small reservations in the area, are funneled back into the community. But the worthy cause you're really contributing to is your taste buds. Specialties include Native American fry bread (deep-fried puffed dough) topped with spicy red chili or honey. The rest of the dishes are similar to the Mexican ones of the same name—not surprising, as the Yaqui tribe migrated from south of the border—though the tortillas are crispier and the enchiladas are topped, not stuffed. Nothing here costs more than $5; the combination plates and huge breakfast burritos are a steal. ⊠ *1545 N. Stone Ave.,* ☎ *520/623–2046. No reservations. No credit cards. Closed Sun.*

Southwest

$$–$$$ ✕ **Cottonwood Cafe.** Almost every evening, even in summer, the dimly lit Cottonwood Cafe bustles with folks wanting to check out its hip Southwest scene (which, atypically for Tucson, continues until the witching hour). Every room in this sprawling hacienda-style complex, a farm in the 1920s, is decorated to the tee, with subtle earth tones, distressed-metal sconces, and smooth leather-backed chairs. The grilled calamari appetizer, served with a tangy tapenade, might be followed by lime ancho chicken, accompanied by grilled peppers and flour tortillas. And the margaritas are really as good as the servers claim. ⊠ *60 N. Alvernon Way,* ☎ *520/326-6000. AE, D, DC, MC, V.*

$$–$$$ ✕ **Presidio Grill.** If it weren't for the organ pipe cacti flanking the window, you might think you were in one of New York's chic downtown haunts, with stylish black booths, art deco–style room dividers, and brightly painted girders. The menu, however, has definite southwestern flair. Dinner entrées include chicken Santa Fe, served with black beans, flour tortillas, grilled scallions, and two types of salsa; and prickly pear marinated pork tenderloin with sesame noodles. Across the street from the city's main art cinema in the University of Arizona area, this place is open unusually late (for Tucson) on weekends. The bar sees a lot of singles action. ⊠ *3352 E. Speedway Blvd.,* ☎ *520/327–4667. AE, MC, V.*

Steak Houses

$$$ ✕ **Rancher's Club.** The four wood grills on which most of the foods are prepared are the key to the success of this upscale western-style restaurant, with its dark wood, mounted animal heads, and sidesaddles. As the friendly staff explains, different woods impart different flavors to foods, so diners must be ready to make a choice from two grills: Mesquite wood is offered every day, and hickory, sassafras, and wild cherry alternate during the week. The lobster is especially good, and the steaks are excellent, too (a note on the menu advises "Our steaks are copious and we encourage you to share"). An array of sauces, butters, and condiments provides diners with interesting ways to flavor their food. ⊠ *5151 E. Grant Rd.,* ☎ *520/321–7621. AE, D, DC, MC, V. Closed Sun. No lunch Sat.*

$$ ✕ **Pinnacle Peak Steakhouse.** No nouvelle-cuisine fans welcome here: Anybody caught eating fish tacos or cactus jelly would probably be hanged from the rafters—along with all the ties snipped from loco city slickers. This is a cowboy steak house that the tourists love. It's fun, it's Tucson, and the food ain't half bad, either, partner. Excellent mesquite-broiled steak comes with salad and pinto beans. If you can handle more after all that, try the hot apple cobbler with vanilla ice cream. The restaurant is part of Trail Dust Town, a re-creation of a turn-of-the-century town, complete with an "opera" house featuring cancan girls and a barbershop quartet, souvenir shops, and an old-time photographer's studio. ✉ 6541 E. Tanque Verde Rd., ☎ 520/296–0911. Reservations not accepted. AE, D, DC, MC, V. No lunch.

Vegetarian

$ ✕ **Govinda.** One of the few places in town with a strictly nonmeat menu, this Hare Krishna–run restaurant has reasonably priced all-you-can-eat lunch and dinner buffets that include vegan options. Selections of hot and cold dishes vary daily, but ingredients are consistently fresh and the food is tasty, if not particularly spicy. There are three areas to eat: one with low tables and cushions (diners must remove their shoes to eat in here); an adjoining light-wood dining room; and an outdoor patio with a snack bar from which you can hear the squawks of the resident peacocks. No alcohol is served or permitted. ✉ 711 E. Blacklidge Dr., ☎ 520/792–0630. Reservations not accepted. MC, V. Closed Sun. and Mon. No lunch Tues.

Northeast Tucson

Continental

$$$$ ✕ **Ventana Room.** This dining room in the Loews Ventana Canyon Re-
★ sort is a triumph of understated elegance: muted colors, low ceilings, and spectacular views—either of the lights of Tucson or the towering waterfall on the property. The contemporary Continental menu, which changes seasonally, has a California-inspired emphasis on lower-fat, lower-cholesterol preparation. Popular à la carte entrées include a buffalo tenderloin and seared ahi tuna; in addition, there's a five-course chef's tasting menu ($55). Jackets are no longer required, but men may feel a bit out of place without one. ✉ 7000 N. Resort Dr., ☎ 520/299–2020. AE, D, DC, MC, V. No lunch.

Italian

$$$ ✕ **Boccata.** In a tasteful mall in the foothills of the Santa Catalina Moun-
★ tains, this pretty restaurant has flowered tablecloths that match the delicate aubergine and Tuscan-yellow walls, and the artwork ranges from contemporary to Victorian whimsy. The menu is mostly northern Italian cuisine, with some southern French dishes for good measure. Try the polenta lasagna with delicately thin layers of eggplant and Gorgonzola or fettucine with shrimp, scallops, and mussels in basil pesto. Go Gallic for dessert: The profiteroles with homemade vanilla ice cream and warm chocolate sauce are superb. ✉ 5605 E. River Rd., ☎ 520/577–9309. AE, DC, MC, V. No lunch.

Mediterranean

$–$$ ✕ **Le Mediterranean.** A generally nondescript dining room, pleasant enough in a pastel contemporary mode, gives little hint of the exotic fare on the menu. In addition to Greek dishes such as moussaka and lamb kebab, there are also good versions of Middle Eastern specialties, such as *shawarma* (beef marinated with tahini sauce) and falafel. When ordering, keep in mind that the portions are hefty. The *baba ghanoush* (mashed eggplant) appetizer, for example, comes with huge amounts of olives, carrots, and radishes. On weekends, a belly dancer winds her way through the tables. ⌧ *4955 N. Sabino Canyon Rd.,* ☎ *520/529–1330. AE, D, DC, MC, V. Closed Mon. No lunch.*

Southwest

$$$–$$$$ ✕ **Tack Room.** This restaurant has won many awards for its food, and the setting—in a rustic but elegant old adobe on the grounds of a former resort—is romantic, but the service is a tad overfussy and the menu has rested on its laurels for too long. It's also irritating to pay extra for such standard accompaniments to expensive entrées as potatoes and vegetables. That said, it's still worth coming here for a dress-up splurge. Dark-wood beams and furnishings and a blue-and-maroon color scheme are complemented by the lighter dusty-rose linen and southwestern landscapes by local artists hang on the walls. Arizona four-pepper steak flavored with different chilies is a favorite, as is the rack of lamb for two, prepared with mesquite honey, cilantro, and southwestern limes. ⌧ *7300 E. Vactor RanchTrail,* ☎ *520/722–2800. AE, D, DC, MC, V. Closed Mon., mid-May–mid-Dec., and 1st 2 wks of July. No lunch.*

Eastside

Italian

$–$$ ✕ **Gavi.** Tucson has its share of good Italian restaurants, but this is one of the few that really feel . . . well, ethnic, even though it's in a strip mall on a major road on the far east side of town. There's almost always a line to get into the small dining room, decorated with pictures of the Milan championship soccer team. An open kitchen lets you watch while specials such as scallops and shrimp Serenata (spaghettini with a creamy sauce of mushrooms, spinach, garlic butter, and wine) or staples like rich fettuccine carbonara are being prepared. ⌧ *7865 E. Broadway Blvd.,* ☎ *520/290–8380. AE, D, DC, MC, V. No lunch.*

LODGING

You'll find a dazzling array of lodging options in Tucson, everything from glitzy resorts and modern hotels to low-key dude ranches, historic inns, and bed-and-breakfasts; there are even some cozy Victorian homes in the latter category.

The **Arizona Association of Bed and Breakfast Inns** (⌧ Box 7186, Phoenix 85012, ☎ 800/284–2589) can provide referrals to member inns in the area. Seven of the larger, more professionally run inns in town have formed **Premier Bed & Breakfast Inns of Tucson** (⌧ 316 E. Speedway Blvd., 85705, ☎ 520/628–1800 or 800/628–5654, ℻ 520/792–1880). Write or call for a brochure. **Old Pueblo HomeStays RSO** (⌧ Box 13603, Tucson 85732, ☎ ℻ 520/790–2399 or 800/333–9776) specializes in smaller, more casual bed-and-breakfasts in Arizona and northern Mexico but also lists a number of the larger inns.

Prices vary widely between seasons. Room rates in summer—generally defined as April 15 through October 1—are sometimes as much as 60% lower than those in the winter, and visitors who don't mind warmer weather can get real deals at resorts that are quite pricey during the busy time. Note: Unless you book months in advance, you'll be hard-pressed to find a hotel room at any price in Tucson the week before and during the huge gem and mineral show (usually in February).

Unless otherwise indicated, price categories for guest ranches include all meals and most activities.

Northwest Tucson

$$$$ 🏨 **Lazy K Bar Guest Ranch.** In the Tucson Mountains, 16 mi north-west of town at an altitude of 2,300 ft, this family-oriented guest ranch will please children as well as adults. As you might expect, horseback riding is a focus, with mounts available for greenhorns as well as those with experience. Guest rooms are in eight *casitas*, or cottages. Those in the older structures, made of Mexican Indian stucco, have fireplaces and wood-beam ceilings, whereas rooms in the newer, adobe-brick buildings are larger and more modern. The daily fare in the community dining room is hearty and good. ⊠ *8401 N. Scenic Dr., 85743,* ☎ *520/744–3050 or 800/321–7018,* ℻ *520/744–7628. 23 rooms. Pool, library. AE, D, MC, V. 3-night minimum stay.*

$$$$ 🏨 **Miraval.** This newcomer some 20 mi north of Tucson is giving
★   Canyon Ranch (☞ *Northeast Tucson, below*) a run for its money with its even more secluded desert setting, beautiful southwestern rooms, and myriad health-oriented programs, many of them incorporating Eastern ideas. Some of the "mindfulness" choices may strike you as a bit odd—especially the "Equine Experience" or horse therapy (for you, not the horse)—but you're likely to come away with lots of useful relaxation techniques and things to contemplate. Meals, including tasty all-you-can-eat buffets (calories and fat content noted, of course), and tips are all part of a set fee. ⊠ *5000 East Via Estancia Miraval, Catalina 85739,* ☎ *520/825–4000 or 800/825–4000,* ℻ *520/792–5870. 106 rooms. 2 restaurants, bar, 3 pools, 2 tennis courts, spa, croquet, exercise room, horseback riding, bicycles. AE, D, DC, MC, V.*

$$$$ 🏨 **Omni Tucson National Golf & Spa Resort.** Perfect for couples with separate sybaritic interests, Tucson National has an excellent golf course (it hosts the PGA's Tucson Chrysler Classic tournament annually) *and* a full-service spa, where you can be coiffed, waxed, wrapped, worked over, and scrubbed to your heart's content. Smaller than most of Tucson's major resorts, it's also closer to town and thus to sight-seeing and shopping. Oddly, of the six levels of accommodations available, the most expensive (hacienda) are the least attractive. ⊠ *2727 W. Club Dr., 85741,* ☎ *520/297–2271 or 800/528–4856,* ℻ *520/297–7544. 167 rooms. 3 restaurants, 3 bars, 2 pools, beauty salon, spa, 27-hole golf course, 4 lighted tennis courts, basketball, exercise room, volleyball. AE, D, DC, MC, V.*

$$$$ 🏨 **Sheraton Tucson El Conquistador.** You'll know you're in the South-
★   west when you step into the cathedral-ceiling lobby of this golf and tennis resort: It has a huge copper mural filled with cowboys and cacti, as well as a wide-window view of one of the pools set against a backdrop of the rugged Santa Catalina Mountains. This friendly, relaxing place draws families and out-of-town conventioneers as well as locals, who take advantage of summer rates for the Sheraton's excellent sports facilities. Rooms, either in private casitas or the main hotel building, have stylish light-wood furniture with tinwork and pastel-tone spreads and curtains, as well as balconies or patios (some suites have kiva-shape fireplaces). ⊠ *10000 N. Oracle Rd., 85737,* ☎ *520/ 544–5000 or 800/325–3525,* ℻ *520/544–1224. 428 rooms. 4 restaurants, piano bar, 4 pools, sauna, 1 9-hole and 2 18-hole golf courses, 31 tennis courts, basketball, 2 exercise rooms, horseback riding, racquetball, volleyball, bicycles. AE, D, DC, MC, V.*

$$$$ 🏨 **Westin La Paloma.** Vying with the Sheraton and Loews Ventana for
★   convention business, this sprawling pink resort has lots of options for individual and family relaxation: Golf, fitness, and beauty centers are top-notch; a huge pool has Arizona's longest resort water slide; and reasonably priced child care at a special play lounge as well as the addition of an adults-only and kids-only pool help both parents and kids

enjoy their stay. Service is excellent all around. ⊠ *3800 E. Sunrise Dr., 85718,* ☎ *520/742–6000,* FAX *520/577–5878. 487 rooms. 5 restaurants, 2 bars, 3 pools, beauty salon, 3 hot tubs, 27-hole golf course, 12 tennis courts, aerobics, croquet, exercise room, jogging, racquetball, volleyball, business services. AE, D, DC, MC, V.*

$$$$ 🏨 **Westward Look Resort.** Built as a residence by William and Mary Watson in 1912, this property was converted to a guest ranch in the 1920s and then to a resort in 1943. The lobby is now in what was once the Watsons' traditionally Southwest-style living room; the couple probably couldn't have envisioned the property's new wellness center, offering all kinds of New Age treatments. Guest rooms have been redone in earthy olive, terra-cotta, and rust tones, with comfy leather chairs, wrought-iron bed frames, and mission-style furniture; all offer coffeemakers. The hotel's fine dining room serves innovative American fare, including ostrich. ⊠ *245 E. Ina Rd., 85704,* ☎ *520/297–1151 or 800/722–2500,* FAX *520/297–9023. 236 rooms, 8 suites. 2 restaurants, 3 pools, 3 spas, 8 tennis courts, exercise room, horseback riding, mountain bikes, shops. AE, D, DC, MC, V.*

$$$$ 🏨 **White Stallion Ranch.** If you feel as if this place is right out of the
★   film *High Chaparral,* you won't be imagining things. Many scenes from the movie were shot on the ranch, which sits on 3,000 acres of desert mountain land. The True family—Cynthia, Russell, and Michael—has run the White Stallion for almost 30 years, and it feels very homey. Children are welcome and large groups are easily accommodated. Horseback rides, a weekend rodeo, cookouts, and hikes along mountain trails are just a few of the activities offered. A herd of longhorn cattle and a wide variety of birds, desert cottontail rabbits, and peacocks make their home on the grounds. Children will enjoy the petting zoo, where llamas, potbellied pigs, and miniature horses are among the residents. There are no telephones or TVs in the spare but comfortable rooms. ⊠ *9251 W. Twin Peaks Rd., 85743,* ☎ *520/297–0252 or 888/977–2624,* FAX *520/744–2786. 32 rooms. Bar, pool, hot tub, 2 tennis courts, basketball, horseback riding, Ping-Pong, shuffleboard, volleyball, billiards. No credit cards. Closed May–Sept.*

$$$ 🏨 **Hacienda del Sol.** It's hard to categorize this place, which sits on
★   32 acres in the Santa Catalina foothills: It's part guest ranch, part resort, and entirely gracious. Built in Santa Fe style in 1929, it was originally a posh finishing school for girls and attracted stars—among them Katharine Hepburn and Spencer Tracy—when it was converted to a guest ranch during World War II. Some of the one- and two-bedroom casitas have fireplaces and private porches looking out on the Tucson Mountains. Relaxing activities here include yoga, massage, and naturalist-led walks. This is a nice, lower-priced alternative to the larger resorts. ⊠ *5601 N. Hacienda del Sol Rd., 85718,* ☎ *520/299–1501,* FAX *520/299–5554. 23 units, 9 suites. Restaurant, pool, tennis court, horseback riding, library. AE, D, MC, V.*

$$–$$$ 🏨 **Windmill Inn at St. Phillip's Plaza.** This all-suite hotel is in a chic
★   shopping plaza filled with glitzy boutiques and good restaurants (☞ Café Terra Cotta *in* Dining, *above*). Each suite has a separate sitting area, microwave, wet bar, two TVs, and three telephones (local calls are free). A few dollars extra will buy you a view of the pool rather than the parking lot. Complimentary coffee, muffins, and a newspaper are delivered to your door. All in all, it's a good deal for the price. ⊠ *4250 N. Campbell Ave., 85718,* ☎ *520/577–0007 or 800/547–4747,* FAX *520/ 577–0045. 122 suites. Minibars, pool, bicycles, library, laundry. AE, D, DC, MC, V.*

$$ 🏨 **Triangle L Ranch Bed & Breakfast.** Buffalo Bill was among the regular visitors to Triangle L, which was built in the 1880s. Cottages are scattered about the property's 80 acres. Co-owner Tom Beeston repairs stringed instruments (there's an amazing collection of historic ones on the premises) and will take you out to see his studio. The ranch, out near Biosphere 2 and Catalina State Park, is a bird-watcher's paradise: Songbirds, hawks, ravens, and quail abound in the area. ⊠ *2805 N. Triangle L Ranch Rd., Box 900, Oracle 85623, (about a 45-min drive north of Tucson),* ☎ *520/896–2804,* ℻ *520/623–6732. 4 private cottages. D, MC, V.*

West of Tucson

$$ 🏠 **Casa Tierra.** For a real desert experience, head out to this bed-and-
★   breakfast on 5 acres of land near the Arizona–Sonora Desert Museum and Saguaro National Monument West. For the last 1½ mi you'll be driving along a dirt road. This adobe house was built by Lyle Hymer-Thompson in 1989 expressly to serve as a bed-and-breakfast. Rooms have private entrances from individual back patios; all look out onto a lovely central courtyard with a paloverde tree and other desert foliage. The southwestern-style furnishings include Mexican *equipales* (chairs with pigskin seats), tiled floors, and viga-beam ceilings. ⊠ *11155 W. Calle Pima, 85743,* ☎ ℻ *520/578–3058. 3 rooms. Kitchenettes, hot tub. No credit cards. 2-night minimum stay. Closed June–mid-Sept.*

Downtown Tucson and University of Arizona

$$$ 🏠 **Marriott University Park.** The bubbling brook and lush greenery of the atrium lobby make this modern structure, which rose up at the edge of the University of Arizona campus in 1996, a bit incongruous in the desert, but nevertheless a convenient, comfortable, and reasonably priced addition to the local lodging scene. ⊠ *880 E. 2nd St., Tucson 85719,* ☎ *520/792–4100,* ℻ *882–4100. 250 rooms. Restaurant, lounge, pool, hot tub, sauna, exercise room, video games, concierge floor, business services. AE, D, DE, MC, V.*

$$ 🏠 **Clarion Santa Rita.** The lobby of this historic hotel gleams with marble flooring and comfortable couches. The rooms are standard but have coffeemakers, irons, microwaves, and hair dryers. Ask for a room with a view of the outdoor pool, a lovely remnant of the original hotel. It's also home to the excellent Café Poca Cosa (☞ Dining, *above*). Continental breakfast, newspapers, and local phone calls are all on the house. ⊠ *88 E. Broadway, 85701,* ☎ *520/622–4000 or 800/ 622–1120,* ℻ *520/620–0376. 152 rooms. Restaurant, refrigerators, pool, exercise room, library. AE, D, DC, MC, V.*

$ 🏠 **Hotel Congress.** Loved by many for its idiosyncratic charm, this downtown hotel was built in 1919 and restored to its original western version of art deco style. The rooms, which vary in size, are individually furnished: All have black-and-white tiled baths and the original iron beds, and some have desks and tables. Near the main Sun Tran terminal, and close to downtown art galleries and restaurants, this is an excellent choice for those who don't have a car. However, the downside of this convenient location is that it can be noisy. ⊠ *311 E. Congress St., 85701,* ☎ *520/622–8848 or 800/722–8848,* ℻ *520/792– 6366. 40 rooms. Restaurant, bar, beauty salon, nightclub, shop. AE, MC, V.*

Central Tucson

$$$$ 🏠 **Arizona Inn.** This sprawling lodging, which has remained in the same
★   family since it opened in 1930, is an oasis in the center of town: Although close to the university and many sights, the inn's beautifully landscaped 14 acres seem far away from it all. The spacious rooms are

spread out in pink stucco houses; all have patios and some have fire-places. Rent a guest house—reasonably priced when shared by three or more—if you really want to luxuriate. The unobtrusively friendly service sets a standard for hotel hospitality. Locals as well as guests frequent the hotel's restaurant (☞ Dining, *above*) and its cocktail lounge, which often has a piano player. ⊠ *2200 E. Elm St., 85719,* ☎ *520/325–1541 or 800/933–1093,* ℻ *520/881–5830. 86 rooms. 2 restaurants, bar, tea shop, pool, 2 tennis courts, croquet, Ping-Pong, library. AE, MC, V.*

\$\$\$ 🏨 **Doubletree Hotel.** Convenient to the airport and to the center of town, this comfortable, contemporary-style property is also across the road from the municipal golf course at Randolph Park, which hosts the LPGA tournament every year. Most of the participants stay here. ⊠ *445 S. Alvernon Way, 85711,* ☎ *520/881–4200,* ℻ *520/323–5225. 295 rooms. 2 restaurants, pool, beauty salon, hot tub, 3 tennis courts, exercise room. AE, D, DC, MC, V.*

\$\$\$ 🏨 **Embassy Suites Tucson–Broadway.** This centrally located hotel is 10 mi from Tucson International Airport, 5 mi from downtown, and a bit less than 5 mi from the University of Arizona. Accommodations are two-room suites opening onto an atrium full of plants. Among the extras are a free cooked-to-order breakfast every morning and com-plimentary happy hour every evening. ⊠ *5335 E. Broadway, 85711,* ☎ *520/745–2700,* ℻ *520/790–9232. 142 suites. Kitchenettes, pool, coin laundry, free parking. AE, D, DC, MC, V.*

\$\$ 🏨 **Adobe Rose Inn.** With its thick adobe walls, lodgepole pine furnishings, and kiva fireplaces, this welcoming inn incorporates the best of south-western style. The clean, unfussy lines of the 1933 house make it a per-fect setting for the latest in Santa Fe designs. Each room has its own color TV, coffeemaker, robe, iron, and hair dryer; two also have fire-places. A central but quiet location, an inviting pool, and no-holds-barred breakfasts—amaretto French toast with macadamia nuts, say—make this a most appealing place to stay. ⊠ *940 N. Olsen Ave., 85719,* ☎ *520/318-4644 or 800/328–4122,* ℻ *520/325–0055. 3 rooms, 1 cottage. Pool, hot tub. AE, D, MC, V.*

\$\$ 🏨 **Casa Alegre.** You'll enjoy poking around the knickknacks and an-
★ tiques—everything from a hand-hewn Mexican mine shovel to an or-nate 19th-century French clock—in friendly Phyllis Florek's "Happy House," as comfortable as it is fascinating. The 1916 Craftsman-style bungalow is near the university, 4th Avenue, and downtown, and it's a straight shot west from here to the desert museum and other west-side attractions. A plunge into the pool and hot tub in the ramada-shaded backyard are an ideal end to a day of sightseeing. Breakfasts are co-pious and delicious. ⊠ *316 E. Speedway Blvd., 85705,* ☎ *520/628-1800 or 800/628–5654,* ℻ *520/792–1880. 5 rooms. Pool, hot tub, free parking. D, MC, V.*

\$\$ 🏨 **Catalina Park Inn.** Classical music plays softly in the living room of this beautifully restored 1927 neoclassical house, still a bastion of civilization, though Tucson is no longer the rough-and-tumble desert town it was when this home was built. The original art nouveau tile work and butler's pantry are among the many architectural details you're likely to ogle. All rooms have phones, TVs, robes, irons, and hair dryers. Full gourmet breakfasts are included. ⊠ *309 E. 1st St., 85705,* ☎ *520/792–4541 or 800/792–4885,* ℻ *520/792–0838. 6 rooms. MC, V.*

\$\$ 🏨 **Peppertrees.** This restored Victorian just off the University of Ari-zona campus allows guests their privacy along with the usual bed-and-breakfast camaraderie. Two appealing classic contemporary-style guest houses at the rear of the tree-shaded main house have full kitchens, washers and dryers, and individual patios. Rooms are also available in the antiques-filled main house (furnished with pieces from innkeeper Marjorie Martin's family in England) and in a separate studio apartment. Martin, a gourmet cook who has published a book of her recipes, prepares elaborate morning repasts for her visitors. ⊠ *724 E. University Blvd., 85719,* ☎ ⅡⅩ *520/622–7167 or 800/348–5763. 4 rooms, 2 2-bedroom guest houses. D, MC, V.*

$–$$ 🏨 **Best Western Ghost Ranch Lodge.** The bleached-out cow skulls pop-
★ ularized by Georgia O'Keeffe are now a Southwest cliché, but they weren't in 1936 when the New Mexico artist gave the then-unusual logo to conservationist Arthur Pack as a wedding gift. The neon sign he made with this design still lights up the entrance to the former hotel Pack, opened in 1941 on what was then the main road into Tucson. The Spanish tile–roof units are spread out over 8 acres that encompass an orange grove and garden with 400 varieties of cacti. Rooms are all decorated with modern motel furnishings, but still retain such original features as brick walls and sloped wood-beam ceilings. The cottages, with a separate kitchen, sitting area, and carport, are a bargain. Continental breakfast is complimentary. ⊠ *801 W. Miracle Mile, 85705,* ☎ *520/791–7565 or 800/456–7565,* ⅡⅩ *520/791–3898. 83 units. Restaurant, bar, pool, hot tub, shuffleboard. AE, D, DC, MC, V.*

Northeast Tucson

$$$$ 🏨 **Canyon Ranch.** Opened in 1979 on the site of the old Double U Guest
★ Ranch, Canyon Ranch draws an international crowd of glitterati to its superb spa facilities (it's been voted World's Best Spa by the readers of *Condé Nast Traveler* five times since 1990). Set on 70 acres in the desert foothills northeast of Tucson, two activity centers include a 62,000-square-ft spa complex and an 8,000-square-ft Health and Healing Center, where dietitians, exercise physiologists, behavioral-health professionals, and medical staff attend to body and soul (you can have your astrological chart done, your handwriting analyzed, and your tarot cards read). This is a wonderful place to be pampered, but beware: Unless you've got loads of cash to burn, the benefits of the stress-reduction programs may be wiped out when you get the bill. ⊠ *8600 E. Rockcliff Rd., 85750,* ☎ *520/749–9000 or 800/742–9000,* ⅡⅩ *520/ 749–1646. 153 rooms and suites. Indoor pool, 3 outdoor pools, beauty salon, spa, 8 tennis courts, aerobics, health club, basketball, racquetball, squash. AE, D, MC, V. 4-night minimum stay.*

$$$$ 🏨 **Loews Ventana Canyon Resort.** One of the newer desert resorts, Ventana Canyon is unquestionably luxurious, but also snootier than most other Tucson properties. The setting is spectacular: Expect to see desert cottontails around the 93-acre grounds, along with hummingbirds, quail, and other birds. Rooms are modern and chic, furnished in soft pastels and light woods; each bath has a miniature TV and an oversize tub with a nice supply of bubble bath. The center of this open, airy property is an 80-ft waterfall that cascades down the Catalina Mountains into a little lake. Guests can enjoy everything from poolside snacks to fine Continental cuisine at the Ventana Room (☞ Dining, *above*). ⊠ *7000 N. Resort Dr., 85750,* ☎ *520/299–2020 or 800/234–5117,* ⅡⅩ *520/299–6832. 398 rooms. 4 restaurants, bar, lobby lounge, 2 pools, beauty salon, spa, 2 18-hole golf courses, 8 tennis courts, exercise room, hiking. AE, D, DC, MC, V.*

$$ 🏨 **Ramada Inn Foothills.** Families as well as business travelers stay in this upscale link in the Ramada Inn chain on the northeastern side of town, close to lots of restaurants and to Sabino Canyon. An attractive light stucco building with rounded corners, this property has the expected generic rooms, but are more than serviceable. A Continental breakfast is complimentary, as are beer and wine in the afternoon. Free passes to a local health club are available, and golf and tennis facilities are nearby. ⊠ *6944 E. Tanque Verde Rd., 85715,* ☎ *520/886–9595 or 800/228–2828,* ⅣX *520/721–8466. 113 rooms. Restaurant, lounge, pool, sauna. AE, D, DC, MC, V.*

Eastside

$$$$ ☷ **Tanque Verde Ranch.** The most upscale of Tucson's guest ranches and one of the oldest in the country, Tanque Verde sits on more than 600 beautiful acres in the Rincon Mountains between Coronado National Forest and Saguaro National Monument. Rooms in the main ranch house or in private casitas are all furnished in tasteful southwestern style; most have patios and some have fireplaces. Service is relaxed but very attentive. Cookouts and indoor meals are delicious. Many of the guests have been coming here for years. Everything runs smoothly in high season, but we've had reports of spotty room maintenance in summer. ⊠ *14301 E. Speedway Blvd., 85748,* ☎ *520/296–6275 or 800/234–3833,* ⅣX *520/721–9426. 70 rooms, 4 houses. 1 indoor and outdoor pool, spa, 5 tennis courts, basketball, exercise room, horseback riding, horseshoes, volleyball, fishing. AE, D, MC, V.*

$$$ ☷ **Tucson Hilton East.** This east-side property is convenient to Sabino Canyon and Saguaro National Monument East as well as to Davis-Monthan Air Force Base. An airy glass-atrium lobby takes full advantage of the view of the Santa Catalina Mountains. ⊠ *7600 E. Broadway, 85710,* ☎ *520/721–5600 or 800/648–7177,* ⅣX *520/721–5696. 232 rooms. Restaurant, bar, pool, spa, concierge floor. AE, D, DC, MC, V.*

NIGHTLIFE AND THE ARTS

The Arts

Tucson, known as the most cultured of Arizona's cities, is one of only 14 cities in the United States that are home to a symphony as well as to opera, theater, and ballet companies. Winter is the high season for most of Tucson's cultural activities because that's when most of the visitors come, but there's something going on all the time.

Summer is when **Downtown Saturday Night,** a year-round event, really comes alive. On the first and third Saturday nights of each month (about 7–10 PM), Tucson's downtown arts district opens up its galleries, studios, and cafés. There's often dancing in the street—everything from calypso to square dancing—and musical performances ranging from jazz to gospel. Most of the activity takes place along Congress Street and Broadway (from 4th Ave. to Stone St.) and along 5th and 6th avenues. You can also explore this area via a free, docent-led Thursday Night Artwalk. For more information contact the **Tucson Arts District Partnership, Inc.** (☎ 520/624–9977), which also has material on self-guided gallery and historic district walking tours.

The cost of attending any cultural event in Tucson will be a pleasant surprise to anyone who's accustomed to paying East or West Coast prices: Symphony tickets can be purchased for as little as $5 for some concerts, and tickets to a touring Broadway musical can often be had for $22. Parking is frequently free. Most of the city's cultural activity takes place either downtown in the arts district, where the **Tucson Convention Center** (⊠ 260 S. Church St., ☎ 520/791–4101; 520/791–4266 box office) complex and the El Presidio neighborhood are, or at the University of Arizona, where the UA Presents Series is held at **Centennial Hall** (⊠ 1020 E. University Blvd., ☎ 520/621–3341). The 1997 season includes everything from the New York City Opera's *La*

Bohème to *Kiss of the Spider Woman*. Tickets to Tucson arts and entertainment events can often be purchased through **Dillard's Box Office** (☎ 800/638–4253).

The free *Tucson Weekly,* published every Wednesday and found in most convenience stores, and the Friday edition of *The Arizona Daily Star* both have complete listings of what's going on in town.

Dance

Tucson shares its professional ballet company, **Ballet Arizona** (☎ 888/322–5538) with Phoenix. Performances, which range from classical to contemporary, are held at the Music Hall in the Tucson Convention Center (☞ *above*). The most established of the modern dance companies, **Orts Theatre of Dance** (⊠ 930 N. Stone Ave., ☎ 520/624–3799), schedules a variety of outdoor and indoor performances.

Music

The **Tucson Symphony Orchestra** (⊠ 443 S. Stone Ave., ☎ 520/882–8585 box office; 520/792–9155 main office), part of Tucson's cultural scene since 1929, holds concerts in the music hall in the Tucson Convention Center complex and at the Pima Community College Center for the Arts). A variety of concerts and recitals, many of them free, are offered by the **University of Arizona's School of Music and Dance** (☎ 520/621–2998 for a recorded listing of events in the upcoming week). A chamber-music series is hosted by the **Arizona Friends of Chamber Music** (☎ 520/298–5806) at the Leo Rich Theater in the Tucson Convention Center from October through April. The **Arizona Opera Company** (☎ 520/293–4336), centered in Tucson, puts on five major productions each year at the Tucson Convention Center's Music Hall.

Tucson's jazz scene encompasses everything from afternoon jam sessions in the park to Sunday jazz brunches at resorts in the foothills. Call the **Tucson Jazz Society Hot Line** (☎ 520/743–3399) for information about the many events around town.

From late February through late June, the Tucson Parks and Recreation Department hosts a **series of free concerts** on the weekends. The Tucson Pops Orchestra plays at the De Meester Outdoor Performance Center in Reid Park, while the Arizona Symphonic Winds performs at Morris T. Udall Park (Tanque Verde and Sabino Canyon Rds.). It's smart to arrive at least an hour before the music starts (usually at 7:30) so that you can position your blanket exactly where you want it. A series of lunchtime concerts take place at the main library, downtown, on Wednesdays from late February to early May. Call 520/791–4079 for schedules and directions.

Poetry

The **Tucson Poetry Festival** (☎ 520/620–2045 for details) is held in early spring. A large range of poets, some internationally acclaimed—Allen Ginsberg and Amiri Baraka have been participants—come to town for three days of readings and related events.

The **University of Arizona Poetry Center** (⊠ 1216 N. Cherry Ave., ☎ 520/321–7760) runs a free series open to the public. Phone during fall and spring semesters for information on scheduled readers.

Theater

Theater groups in town include Arizona's state theater, the **Arizona Theatre Company** (☎ 520/884–8210), which performs everything from classical to contemporary drama at the Temple of Music and Art (⊠ 330 S. Scott Ave., ☎ 520/622–2823) from September through May. It's worth coming just to see the beautifully restored Spanish colonial/Moorish–style theater, and dinners served at the adjoining B&B

Cafe (☎ 520/792–2623 for reservations), coordinated to show times, are tasty preludes to a performance. The **a.k.a. theatre** (✉ 125 E. Congress St., ☎ 520/623–7852) specializes in avant-garde productions. **Invisible Theatre** (✉ 1400 N. 1st Ave., ☎ 520/882–9721) presents contemporary plays and musicals.

Children love the old-fashioned melodramas at the **Gaslight Theatre** (✉ 7010 E. Broadway, ☎ 520/886–9428), where hissing the villain and cheering the hero are part of the audience's duty. There is free popcorn, and beer, wine, soft drinks, and pizza are sold.

Nightlife

Bars and Clubs

Although Tucson doesn't have the huge selection of bars and clubs available in some major cities, there's something here to suit nearly every taste. In addition to the places listed below, most of the major resorts have nightspots with late-night drinks and sometimes dancing.

COUNTRY AND WESTERN

An excellent house band gets the crowd two-stepping every night except Sunday and Monday at the **Maverick** (✉ 4702 E. 22nd St., ☎ 520/748–0456). On Sunday night the **Cactus Moon Cafe** (✉ 5470 E. Broadway Blvd., ☎ 520/748–0049) has a terrific all-you-can-eat buffet for $3 and free dance lessons. It's worth a drive to **The Stampede** (✉ 4385 W. Ina Rd., ☎ 520/744–7744), the Southwest's largest country-and-western nightclub, with two dance floors, pool tables, free dance lessons (call for a schedule), and a western clothing boutique.

JAZZ

Of the various clubs around town, **Cafe Sweetwater** (✉ 340 E. 6th St., ☎ 520/622–6464) is the most consistent in the quality of its jazz acts—and the food's pretty good, too. There's usually a lively jazz pianist at the **Arizona Inn** (☞ Lodging, *above*).

ROCK, BLUES, AND MORE

Berky's (✉ 5769 E. Speedway Blvd., ☎ 520/296–1981) has live music—R&B and rock and roll—every night; there's a newer location on lively 4th Avenue (✉ 424 N. 4th Ave., ☎ 520/622–0376). The **Chicago Bar** (✉ 5954 E. Speedway Blvd., ☎ 520/748–8169) is a good place to catch Tucson blues legend Sam Taylor; other nightly acts often include reggae and rock. **Club Congress** (✉ 311 E. Congress St., ☎ 520/622–8848) is the main venue in town for cutting-edge rock bands who play on Friday and sometimes Sunday and Tuesday. Downtown's **Empire Cafe and Lounge** (✉ 61 E. Congress St., ☎ 520/885–9779) tends to book bands with an '80s inclination. **The Outback** (✉ 296 N. Stone Ave., ☎ 520/622–4700) hosts performers like Los Lobos, Starship, and Cameo, who wouldn't fill the convention center but draw a good crowd. Go totally retro at the **Shelter** (✉ 4155 E. Grant Rd., ☎ 520/326–1345), a former bomb shelter where the early '60s still reign.

Casinos

After a long struggle with the state of Arizona, two Native American tribes now operate casinos on their Tucson-area reservations. The Pascua Yaqui tribe runs the **Casino of the Sun** (✉ 7406 S. Camino de Oeste, ☎ 520/883–1700 or 800/344–9435), which has lots of slot and video-gambling machines, as well as keno, high-stakes bingo, and live poker. The Tohono O'odham tribe's **Desert Diamond Bingo and Casino** (✉ 7350 S. Old Nogales Hwy., ☎ 520/294–7777) has 500 one-arm bandits and video poker in addition to live keno, bingo, and poker. Both are open daily, 24 hours a day. No alcohol is sold or permitted at either casino.

OUTDOOR ACTIVITIES AND SPORTS

Participant Sports

Ballooning

Balloon America (⊠ Box 31255, Tucson 85751, ☎ 520/299–7744) and **Southern Arizona Balloon Excursions** (⊠ Box 5265, 530 W. Saguaro St., Tucson 85703, ☎ 520/624–3599) offer champagne celebrations and daily flights (in season; usually September or October to May or June) by FAA-certified pilots.

Bicycling

Tucson, ranked among America's top-five bicycling cities by *Bicycling* magazine, has designated bikeways, routes, lanes, and paths for bikers all over the city—through rugged terrain, up and down winding roads, and along frequently used byways in the Tucson area. The **Tucson Transportation Department** (☎ 520/791–4372) will mail you city bike maps. You can pick up maps at the office of the **Pima Association of Governments** (⊠ 177 N. Church St., Suite 405, 520/792–1093).

Most bike stores in Tucson carry the monthly newsletter put out by the Tucson chapter of **GABA** (Greater Arizona Bicycling Association, ⊠ Box 43273, Tucson 85733), which lists rated group rides. Visitors are welcome. Reliable bike renters include the **Bike Shack** (⊠ 940 E. University Ave., ☎ 520/624–3663) and **Full Cycle** (⊠ 3232 E. Speedway Blvd., ☎ 520/327–3232).

Bird-Watching

Birds can be seen in the city in such places as Sabino Canyon and Mt. Lemmon. In the nearby Santa Rita Mountains, Madera Canyon (☞ Side Trips Near Tucson, *below*) is a bird-lovers' haven.

You can find out what's flying by phoning the **Tucson Audubon Society**'s 24-hour line (☎ 520/798–1005); the latest sightings of rare or interesting avians in the area are recorded regularly. The society's **Audubon Nature Shop** (⊠ 300 E. University Blvd., Suite 120, ☎ 520/629–0510) carries field guides, bird feeders, and binoculars, along with a wide range of natural history books. The **Wild Bird Store** (⊠ 3522 E. Grant Rd., ☎ 520/322–9466) is an excellent resource for bird-watching books, maps, and trail guides. Tours are offered by **Wings, Inc.** (⊠ 1643 N. Alvernon Way, Suite 105, Tucson 85712, ☎ 520/320–9868) and **Borderlands** (⊠ 2550 W. Calle Padilla, Tucson 85745, ☎ 520/882–7650). The Tucson office of the **Nature Conservancy** (⊠ 300 E. University Blvd., Suite 230, ☎ 520/622–3861) arranges seasonal bird-watching tours ranging in length from a few hours to several days; call or write for information.

Camping

The closest public campground to Tucson is probably at **Catalina State Park** (⊠ 11570 N. Oracle Rd., ☎ 520/628–5798), about 9 mi north of town on AZ 77. In the desert foothills of the Santa Catalinas, the campground accommodates tents as well as RVs. It fills up quickly in good weather because it's close to town. Unfortunately, there is no reservation system.

Recreational vehicles can park in any number of facilities around town. The **Metropolitan Tucson Convention and Visitors Bureau** (☞ Visitor Information *in* Tucson A to Z, *below*) can provide information about specific locations.

Golf

The Tucson & Southern Arizona Golf Guide, published by Madden Publishing, Inc. (⊠ Box 42915, Tucson 85733, ☎ 520/322–0895), describes and rates all the local courses; send $5 for a copy. For a golf package based on your budget, interests, and experience, you might contact **Tee Time Arrangers** (⊠ 6286 E. Grant Rd., ☎ 520/296–4800 or 800/742–9939). If you're planning to stay a week or more, **Tucson's Resort Golf Card** (⊠ 6286 E. Grant Rd., Tucson 85712, ☎ 520/886–8800), offering year-round discounts at 10 of the area's best courses, is a good deal. The **Golf Stop Inc.** (⊠ 1830 S. Alvernon Way, ☎ 520/790–0941), owned and run by two LPGA pros, can fit you with custom clubs, repair your old irons, or give you video lessons.

MUNICIPAL COURSES

One of Tucson's best-kept secrets is that the city's five municipal courses are maintained to standards that in most parts of the country can be found only at the best country clubs. The flagship of these low-priced municipal golf courses within the city of Tucson (Randolph North, Dell Urich, El Rio, Fred Enke, and Silverbell) is Randolph North, which hosted the PGA and LPGA Tour for many years. To make reservations at these city-operated courses, contact the **Tucson Parks and Recreation Department** (☎ 520/791–4336) at least a week in advance.

PUBLIC COURSES

Dorado Golf Course (⊠ 6601 E. Speedway Blvd., ☎ 520/885–6751), on the east side of town, has an executive 18-hole course that's good for those who just want to play a few short rounds.

Raven Golf Club at Sabino Springs (⊠ 9777 E. Sabino Greens Dr., ☎ 520/760–1253) is an 18-hole, par-71 course in a gorgeous setting.

Rio Rico Resort & Country Club (⊠ 1069 Camino Carampi, ☎ 520/281–8567), south of Tucson, near Nogales, was designed by Robert Trent Jones Jr.; it's one of Arizona's lesser-known gems.

San Ignacio Golf Club (⊠ 4201 S. Camino del Sol, ☎ 520/648–3468), in Green Valley, was designed by Arthur Hills and is a challenging 18-hole desert course.

Tubac Golf Resort (⊠ 1 Otera Rd., ☎ 520/398–2211 or 520/398–2021), some 45 minutes south of Tucson, will look familiar to you if you've seen the film *Tin Cup*.

RESORTS

Many avid golfers check into one of the tony local resorts (most are described in more detail *in* Lodging, *above*) and do nothing but tee off for a week. Golf vacation specialists include **Tucson National Golf & Conference Resort,** cohost of an annual PGA winter open, with 27 holes and beautiful, long par 4s, designed by the great Robert Bruce Harris; **Westin La Paloma,** which has a 27-hole layout designed by Jack Nicklaus (rated among the top 75 resort courses by *Golf Digest*); **Sheraton Tucson El Conquistador,** its 45 holes in the Santa Catalina foothills affording 360-degree views of the city; the 36-hole Tom Fazio–designed course at **Lodge at Ventana Canyon** (⊠ 6200 N. Clubhouse La., 85750, ☎ 520/577–1400 or 800/828–5701); and **Starr PassGolf Resort** (⊠ 3645 W. Starr Pass Blvd., 85745, ☎ 520/670–0500 or 800/503–2898), which now has guest casitas for those who want to devote as much time as possible to playing its 18 magnificent holes in the Tucson Mountains. The Arnold Palmer–managed club was developed as a Tournament Player's Course and has become a favorite of visiting pros; playing its Number 15 signature hole has been likened to threading a moving needle. Those who don't mind getting up early to beat the heat will find some excellent golf packages at these places in the summer.

Health Clubs

5th Street Fitness (⊠ 5555 E. 5th St., ☎ 520/571–7000) has an indoor swimming pool, sauna, hot tub, and aerobics classes. Nonmembers receive a free one-day pass; additional days cost $15 for all facilities.

FIT (Fitness & Health Institute of Tucson) (⊠ 11 S. Church Ave., Suite 5030, ☎ 520/623–6300) charges $5 for visitors to use their indoor swimming pool, Nautilus equipment and free weights, racquetball, basketball, sauna, and steam room.

Tucson Racquet & Fitness Club (⊠ 4001 N. Country Club Rd., ☎ 520/795–6960) has extensive facilities, including 11 racquetball courts, two Olympic-size lap pools, and martial arts classes; it's open 24-hours a day. Visitors pay $10.

Hiking

For hiking inside Tucson city limits, you might test your skills climbing trails up Sentinel Peak ("A" Mountain). There are also many hiking possibilities in the area's state and city parks: There are literally hundreds of trails in the immediate Tucson area. **Catalina State Park** (☞ Camping, *above*) is crisscrossed by hiking trails. One of them, an easy two-hour walk, leads to the Romero Pools, a series of natural *tinajas,* or stone tanks, that are full of water for much of the year.

The local chapter of the **Sierra Club** (⊠ 738 N. 5th Ave., Suite 214, Tucson 85705, ☎ 520/620–6401) welcomes out-of-town visitors on their weekend hikes around the area. There's a $2 suggested donation per person for nonmembers. For hiking on your own, a good source of information is **Summit Hut** (⊠ 5045 E. Speedway Blvd., ☎ 520/325–1554), which has a collection of hiking reference materials and a friendly staff who will help you plan and outfit your trip. Packs, tents, bags, and climbing shoes can be rented here.

Horseback Riding

Desert-High Country Stables (⊠ 6501 W. Ina Rd., ☎ 520/744–3789), in the northwest part of town, has trail rides, hayrides, and cookouts.

Pusch Ridge Stables (⊠ 13700 N. Oracle Rd., ☎ 520/825–1664), adjacent to Catalina State Park, serves up a cowboy-style breakfast at the end of your trail ride; gentle children's walks are also available.

Rockhounding

Be sure to check in advance that you're not removing anything from protected areas such as national parks or Indian reservations. Amateur traders and buyers might consider joining the thousands of professionals who come to town in February for the huge **Tucson Gem and Mineral Show** (⊠ Box 42543, Tucson 85733, ☎ 520/322–5773), the largest of its kind in the world. Many precious stones as well as affordable samples are displayed and sold here.

Tennis

A number of the hotels and resorts in town have tennis facilities. Many courts are at Loews Ventana Canyon, Sheraton Tucson El Conquistador, Westin La Paloma, Westward Look, and Canyon Ranch resorts (☞ Lodging, *above*). The **Randolph Tennis Center** (⊠ 50 S. Alvernon Way, ☎ 520/791–4896) has 25 courts, 11 lighted, at very reasonable rates. **Fort Lowell Park** (⊠ 2900 N. Craycroft Rd., 520/791–2584) and **Himmel Park** (⊠ 1000 N. Tucson Blvd., ☎ 520/791–3276) each have eight lighted courts and similarly low prices. **Catalina High School** (⊠ 3645 E. Pima), singer Linda Ronstadt's alma mater and a favorite among local tennis enthusiasts, has good, well-lighted courts at no charge (they're open to the public when school's out).

Spectator Sports

Baseball

In 1993 Tucson welcomed the **Colorado Rockies** to their inaugural season of Cactus League practice games; since then the city has taken to the fledgling major-league team. Call 520/327–9467 for schedule and ticket information (tickets can be hard to come by during the exhibition season, especially when the Rockies face the locally popular Chicago Cubs and San Francisco Giants). The Rockies share Hi-Corbett Field (⊠ 3400 E. Camino Campestre) with the **Tucson Toros** (☎ 520/325–2621), a minor-league team. Picnickers and squirrels sit side by side in adjacent Randolph Park to enjoy the games of both teams. Inside the stadium, during training games, beer is sold behind first and third bases. Parking isn't easy to come by in the area, so park in any of the Randolph Park lots west of Hi-Corbett Field and take a short, pleasant walk through the park to get to the stadium.

Rodeo

In the last full week of February, Tucson hosts **Fiesta de Los Vaqueros,** the largest annual winter rodeo in the United States, a five-day extravaganza with more than 600 events and a crowd of more than 44,000 spectators per day, at the **Tucson Rodeo Grounds** (⊠ 4823 S. 6th Ave., ☎ 520/294–8896). The rodeo kicks off with a 2-mi-long parade through downtown Tucson. Daily seats at the rodeo range from $8 to $14.

SHOPPING

San Xavier Plaza, across from San Xavier mission, carries the work of a variety of native peoples, including the Tohono O'odham, upon whose reservation the church is located (☞ West of I–10, *in* Exploring, *above*). Those looking for work by other regional artists might drive down to Tubac, a community 45 mi south of Tucson. Hard-core bargain hunters usually continue south to the Mexican border and Nogales (☞ Side Trips Near Tucson, *below*).

In Tucson itself, much of the retail activity is focused around malls, but you'll find shops with more character in two areas: downtown and 4th Avenue. You'll find a number of art galleries, antiques shops, and crafts stores in the downtown district. Congress Street is a particularly good block to browse, and the **Old Town Artisans complex** (⊠ 186 N. Meyer Ave., ☎ 520/623–6024), across from the Tucson Museum of Art, has a large selection of southwestern wares. The adjoining 4th Avenue neighborhood, near the University of Arizona, is also fertile ground for unusual items. Artsy boutiques and second-hand stores line 4th Avenue between Second and Ninth streets.

Specialty Shops

ART GALLERIES

Art Life in Southern Arizona (⊠ Box 36777, Tucson 85740, ☎ 520/797–1271), published annually, lists local galleries and artists.

Philabaum Contemporary Glass (⊠ 711 S. 6th Ave., ☎ 520/884–7404) sells beautiful designs in a difficult medium, mastered by Tom Philabaum. The more cutting-edge downtown galleries include **Etherton Gallery** (⊠ 135 S. 6th Ave., ☎ 520/624–7370) and **Dinnerware Artists Cooperative** (⊠ 135 E. Congress St., ☎ 520/792–4503).

BOOKS

In central Tucson, the **Book Mark** (⊠ 5001 E. Speedway Blvd., ☎ 520/881–6350) has very well stocked shelves, covering a wide range of topics; local writers often give readings here. Pick up your topographical maps and specialty guides to Arizona at **Tucson's Map and Flag Center** (✉ 3239 N. 1st Ave., ☎ 520/887–4234). Seekers of books by and about women should stop in at **Antigone** (✉ 411 N. 4th Ave., ☎ 520/792–3715), which also sells creative feminist cards and T-shirts.

CACTI

You won't need to stick a cactus in your suitcase if you want to take back a spiny souvenir (it's illegal anyway): **B&B Cactus Farm** (✉ 11550 E. Speedway Blvd., ☎ 520/721–4687), on the far eastern side of town (you'll pass it en route to Saguaro National Park East) has a huge selection of desert plants and will ship all over the country.

GIFTS

Del Sol (✉ 435 N. 4th Ave., ☎ 520/628–8765) specializes in folk art, jewelry, and southwestern-style clothing. Reasonably priced ethnic jewelry, apparel, and crafts can be purchased at the **United Nations Center** (✉ 2911 E. Grant Rd., ☎ 520/881–7060).

JEWELRY

For a splurge, consider buying something by **Beth Friedman** (✉ Old Town Artisans, 186 S. Meyer Ave., ☎ 520/622–5013); her designs in silver and semiprecious stones are unsurpassed.

NATIVE AMERICAN ARTS AND CRAFTS

Bahti Indian Arts (✉ St. Philip's Plaza, 4300 N. Campbell Ave., ☎ 520/577–0290) specializes in Native American art, including high-quality jewelry, pottery, rugs, and more. **Huntington Trading Co.** (✉ 111 E. Congress, ☎ 520/628–8578) carries masks and pottery made by the Yaqui and Tarahumara Indians and beadwork by the Huichols. The **Kaibab Shops** (✉ 2841 N. Campbell Ave., ☎ 520/795–6905) have been selling a wide variety of Native American crafts for more than 50 years.

WESTERN WEAR

Arizona Hatters (✉ 3600 N. First Ave., ☎ 520/292–1320) can fit you for that Stetson you've always wanted. **Corral Western Wear** (✉ 4525 E. Broadway Blvd., ☎ 520/322–6001), with a large array of shirts, hats, belts, jewelry, and boots, caters to both urban and authentic cowboys and cowgirls. **Stewart Boot Manufacturing** (✉ 30 W. 28th St., South Tucson, ☎ 520/622–2706) has been making handmade leather boots for more than 50 years. Factory imperfects are available.

Malls and Shopping Centers

El Con Mall (✉ 3601 E. Broadway at Alvernon Way, ☎ 520/795–9958) is Tucson's oldest mall and has more than 135 stores, including JCPenney, Robinsons-May, Dillard's, and Montgomery Ward. It also is home to a popular discount movie theater.

Foothills Mall (✉ 7401 N. La Cholla Blvd., at Ina Rd., ☎ 520/742–7191), the most upscale of the malls, hadn't been very crowded since its two anchor department stores departed, but a Barnes and Nobles superstore and Saks outlet store are beginning to draw other retailers in. Right now the mall features a variety of tony boutiques, a 16-plex cinema, and the Gadsden-Pacific Toy Train Museum, Ltd. (☞ Exploring, *above*).

Park Mall (✉ 5870 E. Broadway, at Wilmot Rd., ☎ 520/747–7575) has more than 120 stores, including Sears, Dillard's, and Macy's.

St. Philip's Plaza (✉ 4280 N. Campbell Ave., at River Rd., ☎ 502/886–7485) arranges its chic shops around a series of Spanish-style outdoor patios. After shopping such boutiques as Nicole Miller, El Presidio, and Turquoise Door galleries, you can enjoy a meal at Café Terra

Cotta (☞ Dining, above), Ovens, or Daniel's, all among Tucson's chic eateries.

Tucson Mall (⊠ 4500 N. Oracle Rd., at Wetmore Rd., ☎ 520/293–7330) is probably the most heavily shopped mall in town, with Robinsons-May, Dillard's, Macy's, Mervyn's, Sears, JCPenney, and more than 200 specialty shops. For tasteful southwestern T-shirts, belts, jewelry, and posters, try Señor Coyote, on Arizona Avenue, a section of the first floor devoted to regional items.

SIDE TRIPS NEAR TUCSON

There's something for everyone—history buffs, bird-watchers, hikers, Mexican-food lovers, and folks whose idea of heaven is to shop until they drop—en route from Tucson to Nogales along I–19. The road roughly follows the Camino Real (King's Road), which the conquistadors and missionaries traveled from Mexico up to what was once the northernmost portion of New Spain.

The Asarco Mineral Discovery Center

15 miles south of Tuscon off I-19

Opened in February 1997 by the American Smelting and Refining Co. (ASARCO), which has been digging for copper in this area since 1961, this facility is designed to elucidate the importance of mining to our everyday lives. Exhibits in two connected buildings include a walk-through model of an ore crusher, videos that explain various refining processes, and a theater that shows a half-hour film on extraction of minerals form the earth. The big draw, however, is the yawning open pit of the Mission Mine, some 2 mi long and 1¾ mi wide—impressive, though it doesn't exactly bolster the case that the center tries to make about how environmentally conscious mining has become. ⊠ *1421 W. Pima Mine Rd.,* ☎ *520/625-0879.* ☞ *$6.* ☉ *Wed–Sun. 10–6. Tours of the Mission Mine open pit, which take about 1 hour, leave the center on the half-hour; the last one starts at 4:30.*

Titan Missile Museum

🜧 *25 mi south of Tucson.*

During the Cold War, Tucson was ringed by 18 Titan II missiles. Of the total 54 such missiles that existed in the United States, the only one that was left intact when the Salt II treaty with the Soviet Union was signed has been turned into this rather sobering museum. Guided tours take visitors down 55 steps into the command post where a ground crew of four lived. Among the fascinating sights is a 114-ft, 165-ton, two-stage liquid-fuel rocket. Now empty, it originally held a nuclear payload with 214 times the explosive power of the bomb that destroyed Hiroshima. ⊠ *1580 W. Duval Mine Rd. (I–19 exit 69),* ☎ *520/791-2929.* ☞ *$6.* ☉ *Nov.–Apr., daily 9–5; May–Oct., Wed.–Sun. 9–5 (last tour at 4).*

Madera Canyon

🜨 *61½ mi southeast of Tucson; exit 63 off I–19, then east on White House Canyon Rd. for 12.5 mi (it turns into Madera Canyon Rd.).*

At Madera Canyon, the Coronado National Forest meets the Santa Rita Mountains—among them Mt. Wrightson, the highest peak in southern Arizona at 9,453 ft. With approximately 200 mi of scenic trails, the **Madera Canyon Recreation Area** (☎ 520/670–5464 in Tucson) is

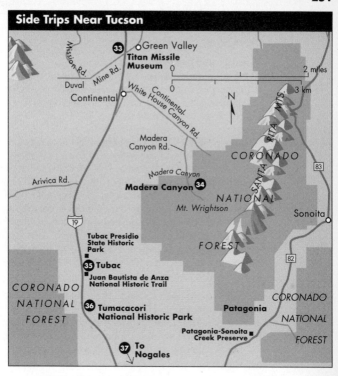

Side Trips Near Tucson

a favorite destination for hikers. Higher elevations and thick pine cover make it especially popular in summer with Tucsonans looking to escape the heat. Birders flock here year-round; about 400 avian species have been spotted in the area. As you enter the recreation area, you'll see a small visitor center, open only on weekends and operated by the volunteer Friends of Madera Canyon. Nearby, the **Bog Springs campground** has 13 sites with toilets, potable water, and grills, available on a first-come, first-served basis. The cost is $5 per vehicle per night.

Tubac

★ ㉟ *45 mi south of Tucson.*

Tubac is the site of the first European settlement in Arizona in 1726. A year after the Pima Indian uprising in 1851, a military garrison was established here to protect early Spanish settlers, missionaries, and peaceful Indian converts of the nearby Tumacacori Mission from further attack. It was from here that Juan Bautista de Anza led the expedition of 240 colonists across the desert that resulted in the founding of San Francisco in 1776. Arizona's first newspaper, the *Weekly Arizonian,* was printed here in 1859, and in 1860 Tubac was the largest town in Arizona. Today, the quiet little town is a popular art colony. Crafts sold in the more than 80 shops—mostly staffed by the artists who make the goods sold in them—range from carved wooden furniture and hand-thrown pottery to delicately painted tiles and silk-screen fabrics. The annual **Tubac Festival of the Arts** has been held in February for more than 30 years. For dates or other information about the town, contact the **Tubac Chamber of Commerce** (☎ 520/398–2704).

There's an archaeological display of portions of the original 1752 fort at the **Tubac Presidio State Historic Park and Museum** in the center of town. In addition to the visitor center and the adjoining museum, which has detailed the history of the early colony, the park includes Tubac's 1885 schoolhouse and a pleasant picnic area. ⊠ *Box 1296 Presidio Dr.*, ☏ *520/398–2252.* ⌨ *$2.* ☾ *Daily 8–5.*

Dining and Lodging

$ ✕ **Tubac Country Market.** Just north of Tubac on the road paralleling I–19, this combination gift shop, deli, and grocery also has a patio restaurant that's open every day for breakfast and lunch. ⊠ *2261 E. Frontage Rd.*, ☏ *520/398–9532 or 398–9870. MC, V.*

$$–$$$ ☷ **Amado Territory Inn.** Although this bed-and-breakfast is directly off the frontage road of busy I-19 in the town of Amado, it feels worlds away from the noisy highway. The inn is part of a complex that includes a plant nursery, a naturopathic healer, and a silversmith. The inn, built in 1996, resembles a late 19th-century ranch house, but a soaring ceiling and contemporary Southwestern art give it a distinctly modern feel. Rooms are furnished with pieces handcrafted in Mexico; some have balconies overlooking the Santa Rita Mountains. A full gourmet breakfast is included. ⊠ *Box 81, 3001 E. Frontage Road, Amado, AZ 85645,* ☏ *520/398-8684 or 888/398-8684,* ℻ *520/398-8186. 9 rooms. MC, V.*

En Route   You can tread the same road as the conquistadors: The first 4½ mi of the de Anza National Historic Trail from Tumacacori to Tubac were dedicated in 1992. You'll have to cross the Santa Cruz River (which is usually pretty low) three times in order to complete the hike, and the path is rather sandy, but it's a pleasant journey along the tree-shaded banks of the river.

Tumacacori National Historic Park

36   *3 mi south of Tubac; exit 29 off I–19.*

The site where Tumacacori National Historic Park now stands was visited by missionary Father Eusebio Francisco Kino in 1691, but the Jesuits didn't build a church here until 1751. You can still see some ruins of this simple structure, but the main attraction is the mission of San José de Tumacacori, built by the Franciscans around 1799–1803. A combination of circumstances—Apache attacks, a bad winter, and Mexico's withdrawal of funds and priests—caused the friars to flee in 1848, and persistent rumors of wealth left behind by both the Franciscans and the Jesuits led treasure seekers to pillage the site unsuccessfully. It was finally protected in 1908, when it became a national monument.

Information about the mission and the de Anza trail is available at the visitor center. Guided tours are also offered daily (more in winter than in summer). A small museum displays some of the mission's original artifacts. In addition to a Christmas Eve service, costumed historical high masses are held at Tumacacori in spring and fall. An annual fiesta held here the first weekend of December features arts and crafts and food booths. ☏ *520/398-2341.* ⌨ *$2.* ☾ *Daily 8–5.*

Nogales

37   *15 mi south of Tumacacori, 63 mi south of Tucson.*

A bustling border town, Nogales can get fairly rowdy on weekends, when underage Tucsonans head south to drink. In addition to the usual border schlock, however, there are some good restaurants and fine-quality crafts and furnishings. If you're just coming for the day, it's best to park on the Arizona side of the border (you'll see many guarded lots that cost about $4 or $5 for the day) and walk across. Practically all the good shopping is within easy strolling distance of the border.

Dining

$$ ✕ **El Balcon de la Roca.** East of the railroad tracks and off the beaten tourist path, La Roca (as everyone calls it) is a favorite of Tucsonans. The setting—a series of tiled rooms on the sprawling second floor of a stately old stone house, with a balcony overlooking a charming patio—is lovely and the food is very good. Among the variety of meat or seafood dishes is *carne tampiqueña*, an assortment of grilled meats that comes with a chili relleno and an enchilada. ⊠ *Calle Elias 91,* ☎ *631/2–07–60 or 631/2–08–91. AE, DC, MC, V.*

$ ✕ **Elvira.** The free shot of tequila that comes with each meal will whet your appetite for Elvira's fine fish dishes, chicken mole, or chili rellenos. This large, friendly restaurant (divided into more intimate dining areas) is at the very end of Avenida Obregón next to the border and popular with frequent visitors to Nogales. ⊠ *Av. Obregón 1,* ☎ *631/2–47–73. Reservations not accepted. DC, MC, V.*

Shopping

The shopping area centers mainly on Avenida Obregón, which begins a few blocks west of the border entrance and runs north–south; just follow the crowds. You'll find a wide selection of handicrafts, furnishings, and jewelry here, though if you go off on some of the side streets, you might come across more interesting things at better prices. Except at shops that indicate otherwise, bargaining is not only acceptable but expected. The following shops, however, tend to have fixed prices:

Casa Bonita (⊠ Av. Obregón 134, ☎ 631/2–30–59) sells jewelry, tinwork mirrors, carved wooden chests, and other interesting household items.

El Changarro (⊠ Calle Elias 93, ☎ 613/2–05–45) carries high-quality (and high-priced) furniture, antiques, pottery, and handwoven rugs. It's just next door to El Balcon de la Roca (☞ Dining, *above*).

El Sarape (⊠ Av. Obregón 161, ☎ 631/2–03–09) specializes in sterling silver jewelry from Taxco and designer clothing for women.

Maya de México (⊠ Av. Obregón 150) is the place to come for smaller folk art items, including Day of the Dead displays, blue glass, painted dishes, colorful clothing—you name it—on two levels.

TUCSON A TO Z

Arriving and Departing

By Bus

Buses to Los Angeles, El Paso, Phoenix, Flagstaff, Douglas, and Nogales (Arizona) depart and arrive regularly from Tucson's **Greyhound Lines terminal** (⊠ 2 S. 4th Ave., at E. Broadway, ☎ 520/792–3475). For travel to Phoenix, **Arizona Shuttle Service, Inc.** (☎ 520/795–6771) runs express service from three locations in Tucson every hour on the hour, 4 AM–10 PM every day; the trip takes approximately 2½ hours. One-way fare is $19. Call 24 hours in advance for reservations. **Arizona Flying Coach** (☎ 520/887–8788) offers similar service; it has a few less vans scheduled but there are four pickup points and prices are slightly lower ($15).

By Car

From Phoenix, 111 mi northwest, I–10 east is the road that will take you to Tucson. Also a major north–south traffic artery through town,

I–10 has well-marked exits all along the route. At Casa Grande, 70 mi north of Tucson, I–8 connects with I–10, bringing travelers into the area from Yuma and San Diego. From Nogales, 63 mi south on the Mexican border, take I–19 into Tucson.

By Plane

Check plane fares carefully when you're planning your trip. Though you may not want to spend time in Phoenix, sometimes it's cheaper to fly into that city and then take a scenic 2½-hour drive down the Pinal Pioneer Parkway (U.S. 79), or a speedier (½-hour) trip on I–10, to Tucson.

Tucson International Airport (☎ 520/573–8000) is 8½ mi south of downtown, west of I–10 off the Valencia exit. Carriers include **Aerocalifornia** (☎ 800/237–6225); **Aeromexico** and its subsidiary, **Aerolitoral** (☎ 520/573–8315); **American** (☎ 800/433–7300); **America West** (☎ 800/235–9292); **Continental** (☎ 520/623–3700); **Delta** (☎ 800/221–1212); **Great Lakes Aviation** (☎ 800/274–0662); **Northwest** (☎ 800/225–2525); **Reno Air** (☎ 800/736–6247); **Southwest** (☎ 800/435–9792); and **United** (☎ 800/241–6522).

BETWEEN THE AIRPORT AND DOWNTOWN

In addition to the modes of transportation listed below, many hotels provide courtesy airport shuttle service; inquire when making reservations.

By Car. It makes sense to rent at the airport; all the major rental-car agencies—Avis, Budget, Hertz, and National Interrent—are represented, along with Alamo, Dollar, and Value. The driving time from the airport to the center of town varies, but it's usually less than half an hour; add 15 minutes during rush hours (7:30–9 AM and 4:30–6 PM). Parking is not a problem in most parts of town.

By Taxi. Taxi rates vary widely; they are unregulated in Arizona. It's always wise to inquire about the cost of a trip before getting into a cab. You shouldn't pay much more than $18 from the airport to central Tucson. A few of the more reliable cab companies are **ABC** (☎ 520/623–7979), **Airline Taxi** (☎ 520/887–6933), and **Fiesta Taxi** (☎ 520/622–7777), whose drivers speak both English and Spanish.

By Van or Bus. For $8.50–$26, depending on the location, **Arizona Stagecoach** (✉ Office at airport, ☎ 520/889–1000), takes groups and individuals to all parts of Tucson. If you're traveling light and aren't in a hurry, you can take a city **Sun Tran** (☎ 520/792–9222) bus to central Tucson. Bus 11, which leaves every half hour from a stop at the left of the lower level as you come out of the terminal, goes north on Alvernon Way, and you can transfer to most of the east–west bus lines from this main north–south road; ask the bus driver which one would take you closest to the location you need. You can also transfer to a variety of lines from Bus 25, which leaves less frequently from the same airport location and heads to the Roy Laos center at the south of town (☞ Getting Around, *below*).

By Train

Amtrak (✉ Station: 400 E. Toole St., ☎ 520/623–4442) serves the city with westbound and eastbound trains three times a week.

Getting Around

A car is almost a requirement if you're really going to explore Tucson and southern Arizona. You can get around the small downtown area on foot and by bus or taxi, but Tucson is generally very spread out and public transportation is somewhat limited when it comes to sightseeing.

By Bus and Trolley

Within the city limits, public transportation is available through **Sun Tran** (☎ 520/792–9222), Tucson's bus system. On weekdays, buses start running at around 5 AM; some lines operate until 10 PM, but most only go until 7 or 8 PM. Service is more limited on weekends. A one-way ride costs 85¢; transfers are free, but be sure to request them when you pay your fare, for which exact change is required. Those with valid Medicare cards can ride for 35¢. Call for information on Sun Tran bus routes.

The city-run **Van Tran** (☎ 520/620–1234) has specially outfitted vans for riders with disabilities. Call for information and reservations.

By Car

Much of the year, traffic in Tucson isn't especially heavy, but during the busiest winter months (December through March), streets in the central area of town can get congested. There's a seat-belt law in the state, as well as one that requires children under the age of four to ride in a secure child-restraint seat. Don't even think of drinking and driving; if you do, you'll spend your vacation in jail. Arizona's strict laws against driving under the influence are strongly enforced.

Contacts and Resources

Car Rentals

If you haven't rented a car at the airport (☞ Between the Airport and Downtown, *above*), you might try **U-Save Auto Rental** (☎ 520/790–8847), **Enterprise** (☎ 520/881–9400), or **Rent-a-Ride** (☎ 520/750–1900 or 520/622–0162), all in the city center. In addition, **Carefree Rent-a-Car** (☎ 520/790–2655) rents reliable used cars at good rates. If you think you might be interested in driving farther into Mexico than Nogales, where you can park on the U.S. side of the border, check in advance to make sure that the rental company will allow this.

Emergencies

For the **police, ambulance, fire department,** dial 911, a free call from public pay phones.

DOCTORS AND DENTISTS

From Monday through Friday, the **Pima County Medical Society** (☎ 520/795–7985) will refer visitors to Tucson physicians. The **Arizona State Dental Association** (☎ 520/881–7237) can recommend a dentist in the area.

HOSPITALS

Columbia El Dorado Hospital (⊠ 1400 N. Wilmot Rd., ☎ 520/886–6361). **Columbia Northwest Medical Center** (⊠ 6200 N. La Cholla Blvd., ☎ 520/742–9000). **St. Joseph's Hospital** (⊠ 350 N. Wilmot Rd., ☎ 520/296–3211). **Tucson General Hospital** (⊠ 3838 N. Campbell Ave., ☎ 520/318–6300). **Tucson Medical Center** (⊠ 5301 E. Grant Rd., ☎ 520/327–5461). **University Medical Center** (⊠ 1501 N. Campbell Ave., ☎ 520/694–0111).

LATE-NIGHT PHARMACIES

Several **Walgreen's** (☎ 800/925–4733) and **Osco Drug stores** (☎ 800/654–6726) are open for 24-hour service. In order to be referred to these chains' closest all-night pharmacies, you'll need to enter the area code and the first three digits of the number from which you are phoning.

Guided Tours

ADVENTURE AND ECO-TOURS

Sunshine Jeep Tours (☎ 520/742–1943) and **High Desert Convoys** (☎ 520/323–3386) arrange trips to the Sonoran Desert in open-air four-wheel-drive vehicles. **Baja's Frontier Tours** (☎ 520/887–2340 or 800/726–7231) and **Desert Path Tours** (☎ 520/327–7235) explore the natural history of the area. **Arizona Offroad Adventures** (☎ 520/882–6567 or 800/689–2453) run an array of mountain-bike excursions, ranging from gentle half-day sessions in Tucson to "extreme" tours through rough terrain and weeklong trips through Arizona. In winter, the Colorado-based **Rocky Mountain Cattle Moo-vers** (☎ 520/682–2088 or 800/826–9666) leads city slickers on a cattle drive from the northwest part of town to the foothills of the Tortolita Mountains.

ORIENTATION TOURS

Great Western Tours (☎ 520/721–0980) and **Tucson Tours & Entertainment** (☎ 520/297–2911) take individuals and groups to such popular sights as Old Tucson, Sabino Canyon, and the Arizona–Sonora Desert Museum. In-depth tours of the city and its neighborhoods are also available. **Old Pueblo Tours** (☎ 520/575–1175), with a slightly different itinerary—including "A" Mountain and San Xavier del Bac Mission—provides a fine historical overview of the area. Many tour operators are on limited schedules (or close altogether) during the summer, but **Off the Beaten Path Tours** (☎ 502/529–6090) has excellent customized excursions year-round.

SPECIAL-INTEREST TOURS

In the spring and fall, those interested in visiting the area's historic missions can contact **Kino Mission Tours** (☎ 520/628–1269), which has professional historians and bilingual guides on staff.

WALKING TOURS

Tucson's historic districts make for great walks. For one easy-to-follow self-guided tour, head for the **Convention & Visitors Bureau** (☞ Visitor Information, *below*). The friendly, knowledgeable docents of the **Arizona Historical Society** (☎ 520/622–0956) conduct walking tours of El Presidio neighborhood (departing from the Sosa-Carillo-Fremont House) every Saturday at 10 from November through March; the cost is $4.50.

Radio Stations
The following are a few of the many popular stations in Tucson.

AM

KNST 790: News, talk; **KTKT 990:** Sports Entertainment Network; **KJYK 1490:** Top 40; **KUAT 1550:** National Public Radio, jazz.

FM

KUAT 89.1: National Public Radio, jazz; **KUAZ 90.5:** Classical; **KXCI 91.3:** Alternative rock, folk, blues; **KLPX 96.1:** Rock; **KIIM 99.5:** Country.

Visitor Information
The **Metropolitan Tucson Convention and Visitors Bureau** (✉ 130 S. Scott Ave., 85701, ☎ 520/624–1817 or 800/638–8350) is open weekdays 8–5 and weekends 9–4.

OTHER USEFUL NUMBERS

Chamber of Commerce (☎ 520/792–1212). **Local and state road conditions** (☎ 520/573–7623). **Tucson Parks and Recreation Department** (☎ 520/791–4873). **Weather** (☎ 520/881–3333).

8 Southern Arizona

Southern Arizona is a wonderful assemblage of mountains, deserts, canyons, and dusty cowboy towns— and it still remains largely undiscovered by travelers. Here you can explore historic sights from old mining enclaves to a territorial prison. Natural lures include the ominous, towering rock formations of Chiricahua National Monument, the myriad underground chambers of Kartchner Caverns, the many-armed cacti in Organ Pipe National Monument, and a variety of pristine Nature Conservancy preserves.

FOR MANY PEOPLE, the question, "Why visit Southern Arizona?" can be answered in two words: Cochise
County. The name alone evokes every dime-novel
By Edie Jarolim   image of the Wild West—ferocious Indian wars, vast land grants, huge
mineral stakes, and savage shoot-'em ups, which all took place in a
setting not so different from the one visitors see today. Abandoned mining towns and sleepy Western hamlets dot a lonely landscape of rugged
rock formations, deep pine forests, dense mountain ranges, and scrubby
grasslands.

South of Sierra Vista, just above the Mexican border, a stone marker
commemorates the spot where the first Europeans set foot in what is
now the United States. In 1540, 80 years before the Pilgrims landed at
Plymouth Rock, Spanish conquistador Don Francisco Vásquez de
Coronado led one of Spain's largest expeditions from Mexico along
the fertile San Pedro River valley, where the little towns of Benson and
St. David are found today. They had come north to seek the legendary
Seven Cities of Cibola where Indian pueblos were rumored to have doors
of polished turquoise and streets of solid gold.

The real wealth of the region, however, lay in its rich veins of copper
and silver, not tapped until more than 300 years after the Spanish
marched on in disappointment. Then all hell broke loose. Fortune
seekers who rushed to the region to get in on a sure thing were met by
the Chiricahua Apaches, led by Cochise and Geronimo. From rugged
mountain hideaways, the Indian warriors fought off encroaching settlers and the U.S. cavalry sent to protect them.

Although the search for mineral booty in Southeastern Arizona is much
more notorious, the western side of the state wasn't entirely untouched
by the rage to plunder the earth. The leaching plant built by the New
Cornelia Copper Company in 1917 transformed the sleepy desert community of Ajo into one of the most important mining districts in the
state. It was interest in going for the gold in California that gave rise
to the town of Yuma: The Colorado River had to be crossed to get to
the west coast, and Fort Yuma was established in part to protect the
Anglo ferry business at a good fording point of the river from Indian
competitors. The Yuma tribe lost that battle, but another group of Native Americans, the Tohono O'odham, fared better in this part of the
state. Known for a long time as the Papago—or "bean eaters," a name
given them by the Spanish—they were deeded a large portion of their
ancestral homeland by the Bureau of Indian Affairs. The largest of
their three reservations, stretching across an almost completely unde-
veloped section of southwestern Arizona, encompasses 2,774,370 acres.

Pleasures and Pastimes

Bird-Watching

Southern Arizona has been ranked as one of the five best areas for bird-
watching in the United States; nearly 500 species have been spotted in
the area. To the east, birders flock to the Patagonia-Sonoita Creek and
Ramsey Canyon preserves, the San Pedro Riparian National Conservation Area, the ponds and dry lake beds south of Willcox, and the Por-
tal-Cave Creek area in the Chiricahua Mountains near the New Mexico
border. To the west, the Buenos Aires and Imperial national wildlife refuges
are among the many places famed for their abundance of avian visitors.

Camping

There are at least 100 camping areas scattered throughout the southern region of Arizona. Though it can get very chilly at night in the desert,

the weather's usually good enough year-round to make sleeping out under the vast, starry night sky an appealing option. Summertime is the time to camp in the state's cooler higher-altitude campgrounds.

Dining

In Southern Arizona, cowboy fare is more common than haute cuisine. But there are exceptions to the rule, especially in the wine-growing area and in Bisbee, both popular with Tucson yuppies for weekend outings. And of course, a region that shares its border with Mexico is bound to have a fair number of good tacquerias.

CATEGORY	COST*
$$$$	over $25
$$$	$17–$25
$$	$10–$17
$	under $10

per person, excluding drinks, service, and sales tax

Ghost Towns

A number of the smaller mining communities of Cochise County died when their veins of ore ran out, and their adobe buildings gradually melted back into the desert under the summer monsoons. Some of what are termed ghost towns in the area are only heaps of rubble, but others give strong evidence of better days. In addition to Gleeson, and Fairbank, a few holdouts remain—enough to keep the post office open—in Dos Cabezas, 15 mi southeast of Willcox, where you'll see the 1885 Wells Fargo station still standing. A tunnel through the mountaintop connects the eastern and western halves of the abandoned town of Hilltop, farther southeast of Willcox. Six miles northwest of Portal in the Chiricahua Mountains, Paradise was active in the 1900s, and a few old-timers still live here. Look for the old town jail among the ruined buildings.

Hiking

You can trek around Nature Conservancy preserves such as Ramsey Canyon, Arivaipa Canyon, the Patagonia-Sonoita Creek Sanctuary, and Muleshoe Ranch; Organ Pipe and Chiricahua national monuments; and dramatic mountain ranges such as the Huachucas, the Patagonias, the Rincons, the Whetstones, and the Dragoons.

Lodging

There are a number of lodgings with character in Southern Arizona: Two historic hotels, some guest ranches, a couple of Nature Conservancy properties, and an increasing array of bed-and-breakfasts (including a converted jail and an astronomical observatory) that let you lay down your head surrounded by nature and history. Still, the bulk of the places to stay in the area are of the park-your-car-outside-the-room chain variety.

CATEGORY	COST*
$$$$	over $125
$$$	$95–$125
$$	$65–$95
$	under $65

All prices are for a standard double room in high (summer) season, excluding room tax.

Stargazing

The telescopes at Kitt Peak, a world-famous observatory, are open to the public, and stargazing dinners have recently been initiated there. It's hard to find a more beautiful and remote spot to set an eye to the sky.

Wineries

Connoisseurs debate the merits of the various wineries that have sprung up in the region southeast of Tucson since 1974, but if you want to decide for yourself, you might want to tour some of the region's wineries.

Exploring Southern Arizona

Numbers in the text correspond to numbers in the margin and on the Southeast Arizona and Southwest Arizona maps.

Great Itineraries

IF YOU HAVE 2 DAYS

If you are headed east from Tucson, poke around the town of **Patagonia** ② and the Patagonia-Sonoita Creek preserve in the morning, and then continue on to **Tombstone** ④ in the afternoon. After strolling the shoot'em-up capital, move along to ⊞ **Bisbee** ⑤, a good place to spend the night. Take the mine tour the next morning and devote the afternoon to exploring the shops on Main Street.

If you're going west, take a leisurely drive to **Kitt Peak National Observatory** ⑭. Stop at the Tohono O'odham Reservation capital, **Sells** ⑮, en route to ⊞ **Ajo** ⑯, where you'll sleep. Plan to spend most of the next day hiking or driving around **Organ Pipe Cactus National Monument** ⑰, but set aside a little time to explore the pleasant mining town.

IF YOU HAVE 4 DAYS

Begin your tour in Arizona Wine Country. First, head to **Patagonia** ② where you can visit the vineyards around **Sonoita** ① and Elgin. Overnight in the ⊞ **Sierra Vista** ③ area; if you've stayed in or near Ramsey Canyon, you're likely to be greeted by hummingbirds in the morning. Head out early for **Tombstone** ④ so you can spend the morning exploring the town; plan to see the sights of ⊞ **Bisbee** ⑤ in the afternoon. Devote the next day to **Chiricahua National Monument** ⑧ and overnight in **Willcox** ⑩. It won't take you long to see that little town's sights; on your way back west, stop at **Benson** ⑫, where you can take a train ride, visit Kartchner Caverns (if they're open by the time you visit), or go down to the Amerind Foundation.

When to Tour Southern Arizona

As you might expect, the desert areas are popular in winter, and the cooler mountain areas are more heavily visited in summer months. For the most part, prices don't change seasonally, however, so your body's comfort level rather than your purse should be the determining factor in timing a stay.

SOUTHEAST ARIZONA

From the rugged forests of its mountains to the desert grasslands of Sierra Vista, many consider the southeast corner of Arizona to be the state's most scenic region. Much of this area is part of Cochise County, named in 1881 in honor of the chief of the Chiricahua Apache. Cochise waged war against troops and settlers for 11 years, but he was respected by Indian and non-Indian alike for his integrity and leadership skills. Today Cochise County is dotted by small towns, many of them much smaller—and all much tamer—than they were in their heyday. Cochise County is home to six and part of the seventh of the 12 mountain ranges—including the Huachucas, Mustangs, Whetstones, and Rincons—that compose the 1.7-million-acre Coronado National Forest.

Southeast Arizona

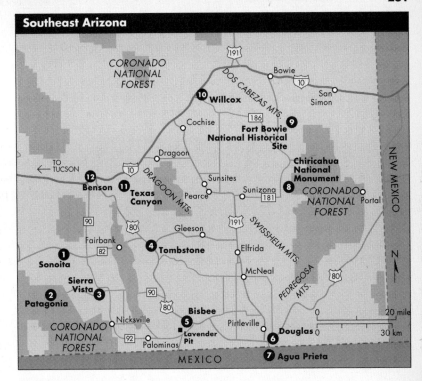

Sonoita

1 *34 mi southeast of Tucson on I-10 to AZ 83; 57 mi west of Tombstone.*

There's not much to see in Sonoita, once little more than a truck stop at the junction of AZ 83 and AZ 82, but the establishment of a number of wineries and upscale restaurants here is a sign that the traditional ranching region around the town is changing.

OFF THE BEATEN PATH

WINE COUNTRY – If you'd like to sample some local product and learn more about wine making, stop at **R. W. Webb** (⊠ 13605 E. Benson Hwy., ☎ 520/762-5777). Take I-10 east about 12 mi, and get off at Vail, Exit 279. Most of the other growers are in the area where Routes 82 and 83 intersect: Get back on I-10 for two more exits, and then drive south on Route 83 for 24 mi to Sonoita. Growers in the scenic ranching region nearby include **Callaghan** (⊠ 3 mi south of Elgin, ☎ 520/455-5650), **Sonoita Vineyards** (⊠ 3 mi southeast of Elgin, ☎ 520/455-5893), **The Village of Elgin Winery** (⊠ Elgin, ☎ 520/455-9309), and **Arizona Vineyards** (⊠ 1830 Patagonia Hwy., 4 mi northeast of Nogales on Rte. 82, ☎ 520/287-7972).

Dining and Lodging

$$ ✕ **Er Pastaro.** The last thing you'd expect to find in the middle of Marlboro Country is this Italian restaurant, established by a Rome-born former manager of Regine's in New York. The specialty is pasta, with a variety of fresh sauces. There's a good choice of Italian wines. ⊠ 3084 Hwy. 82, ☎ 520/455-5821. No credit cards. Closed Mon. and Tues. and July–Aug. No lunch.

$$ ✕ **Karen's Cafe.** The country French menu, which changes nightly, offers an array of salads, a pasta of the day, and two meat or fish entrées—say, a grilled French-cut pork chop in a Calvados cream sauce. Lots of local wines are available, a number of them by the glass. One annoyance: The fresh-baked bread, good though it is, costs extra. ⊠ *471 Upper Elgin Rd., Elgin,* ☎ *520/455–5282. MC, V. Closed Mon. and Tues. No dinner Wed. and Sun.*

$$ ☒ **Vineyard Bed-and-Breakfast.** A friendly burro, a couple of dogs, and a parrot named Fred all welcome guests to this B&B, which sits on a 20-acre, high-country (5,100-ft) spread just outside Sonoita. Three of the country-style guest rooms occupy a 1916 adobe ranch house. Whether you're lying in a live oak-shaded hammock or swimming in the pool surrounded by plum and peach trees, you'll find this a supremely relaxing setting. Breakfasts, served on a closed-in sunporch, are generous—sourdough pecan waffles, apple fritters, and puff pancakes are all possibilities. Fresh eggs come courtesy of the B&B's hens. ⊠ *92 Los Encinos Rd., Sonoita 85637,* ☎ *520/455–4749. 3 rooms, 1 casita. Pool. No credit cards.*

Patagonia

➋ *12 mi south of Sonoita via AZ 83.*

Served by a spur of the Atchison, Topeka, and Santa Fe railroad, Patagonia was a shipping center for cattle and ore. The town declined after the railroad departed in 1962, and the old depot is now the town hall. Today, art galleries and boutiques coexist with real Western saloons in this tiny, tree-lined village in the Patagonia Mountains. The **Patagonia visitor's center** (⊠ 315 McKoewn Ave., ☎ 520/394–0060) shares quarters with the only kosher winery in Arizona, the **Santa Cruz Winery** (⊠ 154 McKoewn Ave., Patagonia, ☎ 520/394–2888). The **Mesquite Grove Gallery** (⊠ 371 McKoewn Ave., ☎ 520/394–2358) carries an appealing array of local crafts.

At the Nature Conservancy's **Patagonia–Sonoita Creek Preserve,** 1,400 acres of riparian habitat are protected along the Patagonia–Sonoita Creek. More than 275 bird species have been sighted here, along with deer, javelina, coatimundi, desert tortoise, snakes, and more. There is a self-guided nature trail; guided walks are given every Saturday at 9 AM. Three concrete structures near an elevated berm of the Railroad Trail serve as reminders of the land's former use. ⊠ *Make a right on 4th Ave., which comes to a dead end, and then make a left. This paved road soon becomes dirt and leads to the preserve in about ¼ mi;* ☎ *520/394–2400.* ⊡ *$5 suggested donation for nonmembers.* ⊙ *Wed.– Sun. 7:30–3:30.*

Eleven miles south of town, **Patagonia Lake State Park** is popular for water sports, picnicking, and camping. Formed by the damming of Sonoita Creek, the 265-acre reservoir lures fishers with its largemouth bass, crappie, bluegill, and catfish; it's stocked with trout in the wintertime. You can rent rowboats, paddleboats, and canoes at the marina as well as camping and fishing supplies. Most swimmers head for Boulder Beach. ⊠ *400 Lake Patagonia Rd.,* ☎ *520/287–6965.* ⊡ *$5 for day use, $15 camping (partial hookups).* ⊙ *Visitor center daily 9– 4:30, gates closed 10 PM–4 AM.*

Dining and Lodging

$$–$$$ ✕ **Marie's.** Marie's has endeared itself to Patagonia's residents, not only because it's open for dinner most of the week (a rarity here), but also because of the sophisticated Mediterranean fare. Try the freshly made chicken pâté with pistachios, spinach pie, or roast pork loin in white wine and mustard sauce. A good finish is the chocolate hazelnut torte, a house specialty. ✉ *340 Naugle Ave.,* ☎ *520/394–2812. MC, V. Closed Mon. and Tues. No lunch Wed.–Sat.*

$–$$ ✕ **Ovens of Patagonia.** Known for it's great quiches and salads, this
★ spot also serves dishes with a Cuban-Mexican influence: burritos, pan rellenos, and bread stuffed with fillings such as cinnamon chipotle chicken or chorizo and onions. Don't pass up the key lime pie. ✉ *Corner 3rd Ave. and AZ 82,* ☎ *520/394–2483. No credit cards.*

$ ✕ **McGraw's Wagon Wheel Cantina.** The adjoining patio restaurant, serving ribs, chicken, and burgers, is a recent development, but the cowboy bar, with its neon beer signs and mounted moose head, has been around since the early 1900s. This is where every Stetson-wearing ranch hand in the area comes to listen to the country jukebox and down a long neck, maybe accompanied by some poppers (deep-fried hot peppers stuffed with cream cheese). ✉ *400 W. Naugle St.,* ☎ *520/394–2433. AE, MC, V.*

$$ 🏠 **Duquesne House.** The rooms of this corrugated tin-roof adobe B&B, built as a miner's boardinghouse at the turn of the century, were decorated with a wonderfully whimsical hand by owner Regina Medley, an artist who also has a gift gallery in town. The three two-room suites that the miners used to occupy as apartments have private entrances; by the time you read this, there should be an additional guest suite in the main house, where breakfast is served. ✉ *357 Dusquesne Ave., Box 772, Patagonia 85624. 4 suites. No credit cards.*

$ 🏠 **Stage Stop Inn.** Old Territorial appearance notwithstanding, the building isn't historic and the rooms are standard motel issue, but this is still a good place to lay your hat for the night. The public areas have character, the center-of-town location is prime, and the price is right. ✉ *303 W. McKeown Ave., Patagonia 85624,* ☎ *520/394–2211; 800/ 923–2211 in AZ. 43 rooms with bath. Restaurant, pool. AE, D, DC, MC, V.*

Sierra Vista

❸ *42 mi northeast of Patagonia via AZ 82 to AZ 90.*

A temperate climate year-round has attracted retirees to this town, which is 4,620 ft above sea level. But although Sierra Vista itself is fairly characterless, with lots of tract housing, RV parks, chain motels, and fast-food restaurants, it's a good base from which to explore some of the area's most interesting sights.

Historic Fort Huachuca, currently the headquarters of the army's Global Information Systems Command, is the last of the great Western forts still in operation. It dates back to 1877, when the Buffalo Soldiers, the first all-black regiment in the U.S. forces, came to aid settlers battling invaders from Mexico, Indian tribes reluctant to give up their homelands, and assorted American desperadoes hiding out from crimes committed back east. Three miles from the fort's main gate is the **Fort Huachuca Museum,** housed in a late 19th-century frame building that originally served as bachelor officers' quarters. The museum and its annex across the street provide a fascinating record of military life on the frontier. ✉ *AZ 90, west of Sierra Vista,* ☎ *520/533–5736.* 🎟 *Free.* ☉ *Weekdays 9–4, weekends 1–4.*

It's fitting that the **Coronado National Memorial** should lie at a remote outpost near the Mexican border. Those driving to this park dedicated to Francisco Vásquez de Coronado, who trod this route in 1540 seeking the mythical Seven Cities of Cibola, will see much the same stunning vista of Arizona and Mexico as the conquistador saw. It's a little more than 3 mi via a dirt road from the visitor center to Montezuma

Pass, and another ½ mi on foot to the top of the nearly 7,000-ft Coronado Peak, where the views are best. Other trails include Joe's Canyon Trail, a steep 3-mi route (one-way) down to the visitor center, and Miller Peak Trail, 12-mi round-trip to the highest point in the Huachuca Mountains (Miller Peak is 9,466 ft). The turnoff for the monument is 16 mi south of Sierra Vista on AZ 92; the visitor center is 5 mi in. ⊠ *4101 E. Montezuma Canyon Rd., Hereford,* ☎ *520/366–5515.* 🖃 *Free.* ⊙ *Visitor center daily 8–5.*

Hikers and bird-watchers alike flock to the **Ramsey Canyon Preserve,** managed by the Nature Conservancy. The convergence of two mountain and desert systems—this spot marks the northernmost limit of the Sierra Madre, the southernmost limit of the Rockies, and it's at the edge of the Chihuahuan and Sonoran deserts—as well as the presence of the fresh water of the San Pedro River, makes it a mecca for bird life. Rare species such as the Elegant trogon nest here and between April and October, 14 species of hummingbird come to the area—more than get together anywhere else in the United States. There are only 13 parking spots, which fill up quickly in the busiest months of April, May, and August; advance reservations are required at all times. You'll need to reserve even further in advance for one of the Conservancy's fully equipped cabins in the preserve (consider booking a year ahead of time). Register at the visitor center, where maps and books on the area's natural history, flora, and fauna are available. ⊠ *27 Ramsey Canyon Rd., Hereford (about 6 mi from Sierra Vista; go south on AZ 92 and take a right on Ramsey Canyon Rd.),* ☎ *520/378–2785.* 🖃 *$5 suggested donation.* ⊙ *Daily 8–5.*

OFF THE
BEATEN PATH

SAN PEDRO RIPARIAN NATIONAL CONSERVATION AREA – Many people view this conservation area from the window of the San Pedro and Southwestern Railroad (☞ Benson, *below*). With the exception of the excursion line, no motorized vehicles are permitted to enter the preserve, but you can walk into the wilderness from parking areas at three bridges on AZ 92, AZ 90, and AZ 82. The latter, AZ 82, is in the town of Fairbank, the site for the preserve's headquarters, run by the Bureau of Land Management.

The San Pedro River, partially hurled below ground by an 1887 earthquake, may not look like much for most of the year but it sustains an impressive array of flora and fauna. In order to maintain this fragile desert ecosystem, some 56,000 acres were set aside in 1988 as a protected riparian area. (Approximately 70%–80% of the state's wildlife depends on riparian habitats, which now comprise only .5% of Arizona's land.) More than 250 types of avian species come here, and you can occasionally spot javelinas, bobcats, and mountain lions. Some 40,000 years ago, this was the domain of woolly mammoths and mastodons: Many of the huge skeletons you may have gawked at in Washington's Smithsonian Institute or New York's Museum of Natural History came from the massive fossil pits in the area. As evidenced by a number of small, unexcavated ruins, the various migratory Indian tribes who passed through centuries later also found this valley hospitable, in part because of its many useful plants. ⊠ *Bureau of Land Management headquarters, Fairbank (8 mi northeast of Sierra Vista),* ☎ *520/458–3559.* 🖃 *Free.* ⊙ *7:45 AM–4:15 PM, conservation area open 24 hrs.*

Lodging

$$–$$$ 🛏 **Ramsey Canyon Inn Bed & Breakfast.** Bird-watchers find paradise
★   at this country Victorian–style B&B, just down the road from Ramsey Canyon; you'll find them gathered around the hummingbird feeders before breakfast, excitedly checking off the different species on their

bird lists. Others will be equally impressed by the cooking skills of innkeeper Shirlene DeSantis, who bakes two pies a day while she's preparing elaborate breakfasts, and by her wonderful wood-and-stone inn, which incorporates local Arizona history with planks from the old post office at Fort Huachuca, the train station at Fairbank, and the Lavender Pit Mine in Bisbee. ⊠ *31 Ramsey Canyon Rd., Hereford 85615,* ☎ *520/378–3010,* ⅋ *520/378–0487. 6 rooms, 2 1-bedroom cottages. No credit cards.*

$$ 🏠 **Casa de San Pedro.** An interest in avians draws visitors to this contemporary hacienda-style bed-and-breakfast abutting the San Pedro Riparian National Conservation Area, and the hosts do everything they can to nourish it—they even provide a computer with Robert Tory Peterson software on it, so guests can identify what they spot from the picture windows in the high-ceiling common room.There are a number of hiking trails just beyond the back of the house, and regular weekend birding courses and tours are offered. Guest quarters are bright and modern, and handcrafted wooden furnishings from northern Mexico lend local character. Breakfasts, which always include fresh-baked goods, are designed to be as healthy or indulgent as you like; they're light on cheese and eggs, and meat is served on the side. ⊠ *8933 S. Yell La., Hereford, 85615,* ☎ *520/366–1300,* ⅋ *520/366–9701. 10 rooms. Library. MC, V.*

Tombstone

❹ *28 mi northeast of Sierra Vista via AZ 90; 24 mi south of Benson via AZ 80.*

It's hard to imagine now, but Tombstone, headquarters for most of the area's gamblers and gunfighters, was once bigger than San Francisco. These days it derives most of its revenue from tourism. The legendary headquarters of Wild West rowdies, Tombstone was part of an area called Goose Flats in the late 1800s and was prone to attack by nearby Apache tribesmen. The intrepid prospector, Ed Schieffelin, wasn't discouraged by those who cautioned that "all you'll find there is your tombstone." In 1877 he struck one of the West's richest veins of silver in the tough old hills and gave the town its name as an ironic "I told you so." He called the silver mine Lucky Cuss, figuring that he fit the description himself.

The promise of riches attracted all types of folks, including outlaws. Soon gambling halls, saloons, and houses of prostitution sprang up all along Allen Street. In 1881 the Earp family and Doc Holliday battled to the death with the Clanton boys at the famous shoot-out at the OK Corral. Over the past 100 years or so, scriptwriters and storytellers have done much to rewrite the exact details of the confrontation, but it's a fact that the town was the scene of several gunfights in the 1880s. On Sundays, you can witness replays of some of these on Allen Street.

Tombstone's rough-and-ready heyday was popularized by Hollywood in the 1930s and capitalized on by the local tourist industry in the decades that followed, but there's more to the town than the OK Corral, the souvenir shops on Allen Street, and the staged shoot-outs. "The town too tough to die" (it survived two major fires, an earthquake, the closing of the mines, and the moving of the county seat to Bisbee) was also a cultural center, and many of its original buildings remain intact. Check with the **Tombstone Chamber of Commerce and Visitor Center** (⊠ 4th and Allen St., ☎ 520/457–3929), which is open daily 9 to 5, for a walking tour that includes several of the town's currently unmarked sights.

Boot Hill Graveyard, where the victims of the OK Corral shoot-out are buried, is on the northwestern corner of town, facing U.S. 80. If you're put off by the commercialism of the place—you enter through a gift shop that sells novelty items in the shape of tombstones—remember that Tombstone itself is the result of crass acquisition, a trait that tends to be decried in the present while its manifestations in the past are romanticized. Chinese names in one section bear testament to the laundry and restaurant workers who came from San Francisco during the height of Tombstone's mining fever. About a third of the more than 350 graves dug here from 1879 to 1974 are unmarked.

For an introduction to the town's—and the area's—past, visit the **Tombstone Courthouse State Historic Park.** Displays include a reconstruction of the original 1882 courtroom, area artifacts, and numerous photographs of prominent—and notorious—town figures. ⊠ *Toughnut and 3rd Sts.,* ☎ *520/457–3311.* ⌑ *$2.50.* ☉ *Daily 8–5.*

Originally a boardinghouse for the Vizina Mining Company and later a popular hotel, the **Rose Tree Inn Museum,** with its 1880s period rooms and huge rose bush on the patio, displays the gentler side of life in Tombstone. ⊠ *Toughnut and 4th Sts.,* ☎ *520/457–3326.* ⌑ *$2.* ☉ *Daily 9–5.*

You'll get a dramatic version of the town's past, narrated by Vincent Price, in the **Historama**—a 26-minute multimedia presentation on Tombstone's history. At the adjoining **OK Corral,** a recorded voice-over details the town's most famous event, while life-size figures of the gunfight's participants stand poised to shoot. Photographer C. S. Fly, whose studio was next door to the corral, didn't record this bit of history, but Geronimo and his pursuers were among the historical figures he did capture with his camera. Many of his fascinating Old West images may be viewed at the **Fly Exhibition Gallery.** ⊠ *Allen St., between 3rd and 4th Sts.,* ☎ *520/457–3456.* ⌑ *Historama $2.50, OK Corral and Fly Exhibition Gallery $2.50, combination ticket $5.* ☉ *Daily 8:30–5; Historama shows every hr on the hr 9–4.*

Allen Street, the town's main drag, is lined with restaurants and curio shops. Many of the street's buildings still bear bullet holes from their livelier days, and some of the remaining artifacts are interesting—including the original printing presses for the town's newspaper, the **Tombstone Epitaph** (⊠ *9 S. 5th St.,* ☎ *520/457–2211*), founded in 1880 and still publishing. If you're looking to wet your whistle, stop by the **Crystal Palace** (⊠ *Allen and 5th Sts.,* ☎ *520/457–3611*), where a beautiful mirrored mahogany bar, wrought-iron chandeliers, and tinwork ceilings date back to Tombstone's heyday. Locals come here on weekends to dance to live country-and-western music.

Another Tombstone institution, the **Bird Cage Theater** is a former music hall where Caruso, Sarah Bernhardt, and Lillian Russell—among others—performed. It was also the site of the longest continuous poker game recorded, started when the Bird Cage opened in 1881 and lasting eight years, five months, and three days. Some of the better-known players included Diamond Jim Brady, Adolphus Busch (of brewery fame), and William Randolph Hearst's father. The cards were dealt round the clock; players had to give a 20-minute notice when they were planning to vacate their seats, because there was always a waiting list of at least 10 people ready to shell out $1,000 (the equivalent of about $30,000 today) to get in. In all, some $10 million dollars changed hands.

When the mines closed in 1889, the Bird Cage was abandoned and locked up, but the building has remained in the hands of the same family, who threw nothing out, through five generations. The displays are dusty and chaotic, but if you poke around, you can find such treasures as the 1881 Black Maria hearse that brought all the victims of the OK Corral shoot-out—and everyone else who died in Tombstone—to the Boot Hill cemetery. The basement, which served as a bordello, was opened in 1995 to the public for the first time since 1889. All the original furnishings and fixtures are intact, and you can still see the personal belongings left behind by the ladies of the night when the mines closed because they didn't want to drag them to their next destination, California. ⊠ *6th and Allen Sts.,* ☎ *520/457–3421.* ⊡ *$4.* ⊙ *Daily 8–6.*

Dining and Lodging

$$ ✕ **Nellie Cashman's.** You can order up anything from a burger to a hearty dinner platter of juicy pork chops or chicken-fried steak in this homey spot, named for the original owner, a Tombstone pioneer who opened a hotel and restaurant in 1882. Old photographs and postcards decorate the walls. Nellie's is also a great place for a country breakfast complete with biscuits and gravy. ⊠ *5th and Toughnut Sts.,* ☎ *520/457–2212. AE, D, MC, V.*

$–$$ ☷ **Best Western Look-Out Lodge.** Touches like western-print bedspreads, Victorian-style lamps, and locally made wood-hewn clocks give the rooms here a lot of character. All have views of the Dragoon Mountains and desert valley. A Continental breakfast is included. The front desk and switchboard of the motel close at 10 PM, so you'll need to check in and receive any phone calls before then. ⊠ *U.S. 80 West, Box 787, 85638,* ☎ *520/457–2223 or 800/652–6772,* ℻ *520/457–3870. 40 rooms. Pool. AE, D, DC, MC, V.*

$–$$ ☷ **Tombstone Boarding House.** Two meticulously restored 1880s adobes sit side by side in a quiet residential neighborhood. Guests of this friendly bed-and-breakfast sleep in one house and go next door to have a hearty country breakfast. ⊠ *108 N. 4th St., Box 906, 85638,* ☎ *520/457–3716,* ℻ *520/457–3038. 8 rooms. No credit cards.*

Bisbee

❺ *24 mi south of Tombstone.*

Like Tombstone, Bisbee was a mining boomtown, but its wealth was in copper, not silver, and its success much longer lived. It wasn't until 1975 that the Phelps Dodge Company closed its last mine and the city went into decline. However, it was rediscovered in the early 1980s by burned-out city dwellers and revived as a kind of Woodstock West. The permanent population is a mix of retired miners and their families, aging hippie jewelry makers, and enterprising young restaurateurs and boutique owners. The latter two groups are currently ascendant, and the town is getting a bit touristy, but its complexion is likely to shift again soon: The Phelps Dodge Company has plans to reopen the area's old copper mines.

If you want to head straight into town from U.S. 80, get off at Brewery Gulch interchange. You can park here and cross under the highway, taking Main or Commerce or Brewery Gulch Street, all of which meet here.

Another option is to continue driving on U.S. 80 about ¼ mi to where it intersects with AZ 92. Pull off the highway on the right into a gravel parking lot, where a short, typewritten history of the **Lavender Pit Mine** can be found attached to the hurricane fence surrounding the area (Bisbee isn't big on formal exhibits). The hole left by the copper miners is huge, with piles of lavender-hue "tailings," or waste, creating mountains around it. Arizona's largest pit mine yielded some 94 million tons of copper ore out of more than 280 million tons of raw materials before the town's mining activity came to a halt.

For a real lesson in mining history, take the **Copper Queen mine tour.** The mine is less than a half mile to the east of the Lavender Pit, across U.S. 80 from downtown at the Brewery Gulch interchange. Tours are led by one of Bisbee's several retired copper miners, who are wont to embellish their official spiel with tales from their mining days. They're also very capable, safety-minded people (any miner who survives to lead tours in his older years would have to be), so don't be concerned about the precautionary dog tags (literally—they're donated by a local veterinarian) issued to each person on the tour.

The tours, which depart daily at 9, 10:30, noon, 2, and 3:30 (you can't enter the mine at any other time), last anywhere from 1 to 1½ hours, and visitors go into the shaft via a little open train, like those the miners rode when the mine was active. Before you climb aboard, you're outfitted in miner's garb—a yellow slicker and a hard hat with a light that runs off a battery pack strapped to your waist. You may want to wear a sweater or light coat under your slicker because the temperature in the mine is a brisk 47°F on average. You'll travel by train thousands of feet into the mine, up a grade of 30 ft (not down, as many visitors expect). Those who are a bit claustrophobic might consider taking one of the surface tours that depart from the building at the same times as the mine tours (excluding 9 AM). They cover Old Bisbee and the perimeter of the Lavender Pit mine, as well as the old leaching plant. ⊠ *478 N. Dart Rd.,* ☎ *520/432–2071.* ⊠ *Mine tour $8, surface tour $7.* ☉ *Daily.*

The **Mining and Historical Museum** is housed in the old redbrick Phelps Dodge general office, right across the street from the Copper Queen mine. The museum is filled with old photographs and artifacts from the town's mining days and explores other aspects of the first 40 years of Bisbee's history, from 1887 to 1920. ⊠ *No. 5 Copper Queen Plaza,* ☎ *520/432–7071.* ⊠ *$3.* ☉ *Daily 10–4.*

The venerable old **Copper Queen Hotel** (☞ Dining and Lodging, *below*), built a century ago, is behind the Mining and Historical Museum. It has housed the famous as well as the infamous: "Black Jack" Pershing, John Wayne, Teddy Roosevelt, and mining executives from all over the world made this their home away from home.

Brewery Gulch, a short street running north and south, is adjacent to the Copper Queen Hotel (walk out the front door of the Copper Queen, make a left, and you'll be there in about 20 paces). Largely abandoned, it's lined with boarded-up storefronts. In the old days, the brewery housed there allowed the dregs of the beer that was being brewed to flow down the street and into the gutter.

Bisbee's **Main Street** is very much alive and retailing. This hilly commercial thoroughfare is lined with appealing crafts shops, boutiques, and restaurants, many of them in well-preserved turn-of-the-century brick buildings.

Dining and Lodging

$$–$$$ ✕ **Stenzel's.** Although this intimate restaurant, set in a white clapboard cottage off the side of the road, is touted by locals for its seafood specialties, the succulent barbecued ribs and well-seasoned grilled chicken breast are equally fine. ⊠ *207 Tombstone Canyon,* ☎ *520/432–7611. MC, V. Closed Wed. No lunch weekends.*

$$ ✕ **Café Roka.** Roka is the deserved darling of the hip Bisbee crowd.
★   The constantly changing northern Italian–style evening menu is small, but you can count on whatever you order—chicken with ricotta and

basil cannelloni, sea scallops with spinach pasta—to be wonderful. Portions are generous, and the entrée price ($9–$16) includes soup, salad, and a pasta-based main course preceded by a sorbet. The dining room, with exposed brick walls and the original 1906 tinwork ceiling, looks onto a central bar that offers a nice selection of wines and cognacs. ⊠ *35 Main St.,* ☎ *520/432–5153. MC, V. Closed Sun.–Tues. No lunch.*

$–$$ ✕⊞ **High Desert Inn.** In the heart of downtown Bisbee, the High Desert
★ Inn is housed in the old (1901) Cochise County Jail building, though you'd never know it. Behind a classical facade highlighted by four monumental Doric columns, this sophisticated but friendly hostelry offers lovely contemporary-design rooms that include color TV and private telephones (a rarity in Bisbee accommodations). Decor includes wrought-iron beds from France, wicker and wrought-iron tables, and art moderne lamps. The inn has a small bar and a dining room, which doubles as an art gallery. Open for dinner Thursday through Sunday, the restaurant is run by a Cordon Bleu–trained chef. ⊠ *8 Naco Rd., Box 145, 85603,* ☎ *520/432–1442 or 800/281–0510. 5 rooms. Restaurant. D, MC, V.*

$$ ⊞ **Copper Queen Hotel.** Built by the Copper Queen Mining Company
★ (which later became the Phelps Dodge Corporation) at a time when Bisbee was the biggest copper-mining town in the world, this hotel in the heart of downtown Bisbee has been operating since 1902. Some of the accommodations are small or oddly laid out and the walls between them are thin, but all have a Victorian charm. Ask for a room that's been renovated. Guests over the years have included a host of wild and crazy prospectors as well as more respectable types. Today's visitors are also a varied lot, as likely to include a film producer scouting locations as a retired snowbird from Minnesota. ⊠ *11 Howell Ave., Drawer CQ, 85603,* ☎ *520/432–2216 or 800/247–5829,* ℻ *520/432–4298. 45 rooms. Dining room, bar, pool. AE, D, DC, MC, V.*

$–$$ ⊞ **Clawson House.** Terrific views of the town from the sunporch, a light-filled kitchen, and generous but health-conscious breakfasts are among the reasons to seek out this bed-and-breakfast on Old Bisbee's Castle Rock. The owners' art and antiques collections grace a beautifully restored former residence, built in 1895 for the superintendent of the Copper Queen Mine. If the Clawson House is full, you'll be offered alternate accommodations in the same owners' **Main Street Inn** (⊠ 26 Main St., ☎ 520/432–5237), two 1888 buildings with one suite and eight guest rooms furnished in handsome southwestern style. ⊠ *116 Clawson Ave., Box 454, 85603,* ☎ *520/432–5237 or 800/467–5237. 3 rooms, 2 with shared bath. AE, D, MC, V.*

$–$$ ⊞ **School House Inn.** You'll flash back to your classroom days at this former schoolhouse, built in 1918 at the height of Bisbee's mining days and now transformed into a spacious bed-and-breakfast inn. Perched on the side of a hill, the two-story brick building has a pleasant outdoor patio shaded by an oak tree. In keeping with its educational past, the inn's rooms all have a theme—music, history, geography, arithmetic—reflected in the decor (though, surprisingly, there is no writing desk in the writing room). Twelve-foot-high ceilings contribute to an overall airy effect, but the old floors can be creaky at night. ⊠ *818 Tombstone Canyon Rd., Box 32, 85603,* ☎ *520/432–2996 or 800/537–4333. 9 rooms. AE, D, DC, MC, V.*

Douglas

❻ *23 mi southeast of Bisbee.*

This town on the U.S.–Mexico border is rather depressed these days, perhaps because of Mexico's recent economic woes. It was founded in

1902 by James Douglas to serve as the copper-smelting center for the mines in Bisbee. Douglas's house, now owned by the Arizona Historical Society, is open to the public as the **Douglas/Williams House Museum** (⊠ 1001 D Ave., ☎ 520/364–2687 or 520/364–2636). There's not much to see here and hours are limited, but there are some interesting old photographs and mementos.

The must-see historic landmark in town and still the center of much of Douglas's activity is the **Gadsden Hotel** (☞ Dining and Lodging, below), built in 1907. The lobby contains a solid white Italian-marble staircase, two authentic Tiffany vaulted skylights, and a 42-ft stained-glass mural. One thousand ounces of 14-karat gold leaf were used to decorate the capitals. When you leave the hotel and walk out onto G Avenue, Douglas's main thoroughfare, you'll be taking a stroll back through time. A film company shooting here had to do very little to make the restaurants and shop fronts fit its 1940s plot line.

Before Douglas became the smelter for Bisbee, the site was the annual roundup ground for local ranchers, Mexican and American—among them John Slaughter, who was the sheriff of Cochise County after Wyatt Earp. The 140-acre **John Slaughter Ranch/San Bernardino Land Grant** gives a glimpse of life near the border in the late 19th and early 20th centuries. This National Historic Landmark includes the Slaughter family ranch house as well as a number of the ranch's original outbuildings. A car shed holds a 1915 Model T Ford identical to the one owned by John Slaughter. You can also visit ruins of a military outpost established here in 1911 during the Mexican civil unrest and maintained by the U.S. Army until 1923. Much of the ride out to the ranch is via a graded dirt road that traverses a strikingly western landscape of rolling hills and desert scrub. ⊠ *15 mi east of Douglas (from town, go east on 15th St., which turns into Geronimo Trail and leads to the ranch),* ☎ *520/558–2474.* ☞ *$3.* ☉ *Wed.–Sun. 10–3.*

Dining and Lodging

$–$$ ✕ **Grand Cafe.** The Marilyn Monroe tribute wall and red velvet–draped dining niche in the back may be a bit kitschy, but the Mexican cooking is taken very seriously. Soups range from a soothing *caldo de queso,* laced with cheese and chunks of fresh potato, to a bracing, nicely spiced *menudo.* The refried beans served on the side of such well-prepared Sonoran specialties as chilies relleno are wonderfully flavorful—and not blended into mushy oblivion, as they are at too many restaurants. ⊠ *1119 G Ave.,* ☎ *520/364–2344. MC, V.*

$ ☷ **Gadsden Hotel.** Unfortunately, this hotel promises more than it delivers. The public areas are comfortable, but the rooms' old plumbing and fixtures aren't always well maintained. And, although the hotel underwent a major renovation in the 1990s, most of the rugs, drapes, and shower curtains look as though they were installed in the 1970s. Still, the prices are low—and you won't do better in Douglas. Suites and apartments with kitchenettes are available. ⊠ *1046 G Ave., 85607,* ☎ *520/364–4481,* ℻ *520/364–4005. 160 rooms. Restaurant, bar, coffee shop, beauty salon. AE, DC, MC, V.*

Agua Prieta

➐ *10 blocks from the center of Douglas, which extends to the Mexican border.*

Agua Prieta doesn't fit the stereotype of a Mexican border town. It's easy to imagine you're far from the States when you sit in the leafy plaza in the center of town. Agua Prieta's prime attraction for U.S. visitors is its assorted array of stores, offering inexpensive Mexican glassware, onyx and silver jewelry, pottery, cowboy boots, and ironwood carvings done by the Seri Indians. Since Agua Prieta is a free port, you can buy liquor at very reasonable prices. **Las Novedades Curios** (✉ Calle 3, 304, ☎ 633/8–07–30) is among the shops you'll find near the border crossing on Avenida Panamericana (the continuation of Douglas's Pan American Ave.). Note that most shops close for afternoon siesta and all day Sunday. You can have a decent Mexican lunch at **La Hacienda** (✉ Corner of Calle 6 and 1st St., turn left from Av. Panamericana at the border crossing, ☎ 633/8–06–74). Tacos, burritos, enchiladas, and such are served in a pleasant setting sparked by colorful jugs of artificial flowers, pottery, and hanging plants. You can leave your car at the free (though unsupervised) parking lot at the corner of 3rd Street and Pan American Avenue in Douglas and walk across the border.

En Route   As you drive from Douglas to Chiricahua National Monument, just past the town of Elfrida on U.S. 191, you'll see a turnoff for the ghost towns of Gleeson and Courtland. There's little to see here now except a few adobe ruins, but it's an interesting side trip if you've got time—and good shocks. As you approach Gleeson, the paved road becomes rutted dirt and marked by a turnoff just east of Tombstone on AZ 80; some building ruins and an old cemetery can still be seen.

Chiricahua National Monument

❽ *58 mi northeast of Douglas on AZ 191 to AZ 181.*

The vast fields of desert grass that characterize most of the immediate area are suddenly transformed into a landscape of forest, mountains, and striking rock formations as you enter the 12,000-acre Chiricahua National Monument. Dubbed the Land of the Standing-Up Rocks by the Chiricahua Apache—who lived in the mountains for centuries and, led by Cochise and Geronimo, tried for 25 years to prevent white pioneers from settling here—this is an unusual site for a variety of reasons. The vast outcroppings of volcanic rock worn by erosion into strange pinnacles and spires are set in a forest where autumn and spring occur at the same time. Because of the particular balance of sunshine and rain in the area, in April and May visitors will see brown, yellow, and red leaves coexisting with new green foliage. Summer in Chiricahua National Monument is exceptionally wet: From July through September there are thunderstorms nearly every afternoon. In addition, few other areas in the United States have such a variety of plant, bird, and animal life. Along with the plants and animals of the Southwest, the Chiricahua Mountains also host a number of Mexican species. Deer, coatimundis, peccaries, and lizards live among the aspen, ponderosa pine, Douglas fir, oak, and cypress trees—to name just a few. This is a natural mecca for bird-watchers, and hikers have more than 17 mi of scenic trails, ranging from half a mile to 13 mi long. At the visitor center, you can purchase a brochure describing the trails for 25¢. Lists of the mammals, snakes, and birds in the region are also available, and in spring and summer rangers give interpretive talks at the visitor center or at the campground amphitheater. ✉ *Visitor center on AZ 181,* ☎ *520/824–3560.* 🎟 *$4 per car.* 🕐 *Daily 8–5.*

OFF THE
BEATEN PATH

PEARCE – The gold camp of Pearce, 1 mi off Route 191, 29 mi south of Willcox, has a post office and one viable store; the ruins of the mill, the mine, and many old adobes are very much in evidence. Gold was discovered here in 1894, and the town maintained a thriving population of 1,500 for some time. People began to drift away in the 1930s, when the mine closed, turning Pearce into a ghost town.

Dining and Lodging

$ ✕ **Frontier Pizza and Cafe.** This is one of those middle-of-nowhere shanties that restores your faith in roadside cooking. Huge veggie breakfast burritos wrap a tortilla around the real green stuff, not canned or frozen versions, and the daily baked cinnamon rolls and apple fritters are super. Decent pizza as well as all-you-can-eat spaghetti specials and fish fries draw locals from all around this untouristed area; nothing costs more than $7.95. ⊠ *Hwy. 191, ¼ mi north of Hwy. 181, Sunizona,* ☎ *520/824–3202. D, MC, V.*

$$$$ 🏨 **Grapevine Canyon Ranch.** This guest ranch in the Dragoon Mountains adjoins a working cattle ranch. Visitors get the chance to
★   watch—and, in some cases, participate in—real day-to-day cowboy activities. Horses for all levels of experience are on hand, and there are lots of trails for hiking this quintessentially western terrain. Accommodations vary—some are rather plain, whereas others have striking southwestern-style furnishings—but all have spacious decks and porches. Rates include meals and all activities. ⊠ *Box 302, Pearce 85625,* ☎ *520/826–3185 or 800/245–9202,* 🖷 *520/826–3636. 12 rooms. Pool, hot tub, horseback riding, coin laundry. AE, D, MC, V. 4-night minimum in peak season, 2-night minimum off-season.*

$$ 🏨 **Portal Peak Lodge.** This barracks-style structure, just east of Chiricahua National Monument and almost on Arizona's border with New Mexico, is notable less for its rooms (clean and pleasant, but nondescript) than for its winged visitors: The Elegant trogon, 14 types of hummingbird, and 10 species of owl are among the 330 varieties of birds that flock to nearby Cave Creek Canyon. ⊠ *Box 364, Portal 85632,* ☎ *520/558–2223,* 🖷 *520/558–2473. 16 rooms. Restaurant, grocery. AE, D, MC, V.*

Fort Bowie National Historical Site

❾ *8 mi northwest of Chiricahua National Monument. To reach the site, take AZ 186 east from Chiricahua National Monument; some 5 mi north of the junction with AZ 181, you'll see signs directing you to the road leading to the fort.*

It's a bit of an outing to this site of Arizona's last battle between Native Americans and U.S. troops in the Dos Cabezas (Two-Headed) Mountains. After driving down a graded but winding gravel road, you'll come to a parking lot where a reasonably well-maintained trail leads 1½ mi to the historic site. The fort itself is virtually in ruins, but there's a small ranger-staffed visitor center with a book-sale area, some historical displays, and rest rooms.

The various points of interest along the way, all indicated by historic markers, include the **Butterfield stage stop,** a crucial link in the journey from east to west in the mid-19th century that happened to be located in the heart of Chiricahua Apache land. Chief Cochise and the stagecoach operators ignored one another until sometime in 1861, when hostilities broke out between U.S. Cavalry troops and the Apache. After an ambush by the chief's warriors at Apache Pass in 1862, U.S. troops decided a fort was desperately needed in the area, and Fort Bowie was built within weeks. There were skirmishes for the next 10 years, followed by a peaceful decade. Renewed fighting broke out in 1881. Geronimo, the new leader of the Indian warriors, finally surrendered in 1886. The fort was abandoned eight years later and fell into disrepair. ⊠ *Visitor Center,* ☎ *520/847–2500.* 🎟 *Free.* ☉ *Daily 8–5.*

Willcox

 26 mi northwest of Fort Bowie National Historical Site on AZ 186.

Willcox, a major cattle-shipping center, has fewer than 4,000 residents. Its downtown looks like an Old West movie set. An elevation of 4,167 ft renders the climate here moderate in summer and chilly in winter. Apple-pie fans from as far away as Phoenix know this little town as Arizona's apple-growing headquarters and come here to get baked goods. If you visit in winter, you can see some of the more than 10,000 sandhill cranes that roost at the **Willcox Playa,** a 37,000-acre area resembling a dry lake bed some 12 mi south of Willcox. They migrate in late fall and head north to various nesting sites in February. Just outside Willcox you'll find the headquarters for the **Muleshoe Ranch Cooperative Management Area** (⊠ Exit 340 off I-10, turn right on Bisbee Ave., take it to Airport Road, turn right again, after 15 miles take the right fork at a junction just past a group of mailboxes, and continue to end of the road, ☎ 520/586–7072), nearly 49,000 acres of riparian desert land in the foothills of the Galiuro Mountains that are jointly owned and managed by the Nature Conservancy, the U.S. Forest Service, and the U.S. Bureau of Land Management. It's a 30-mi drive on a dirt road to the ranch—it takes about an hour to get there—but the scenery, wildlife, and hiking are well worth the bumps. Backcountry hiking and mountain-biking trips can be arranged by the ranch, and a variety of overnight accommodations are also available (☞ Lodging, *below*).

The **Rex Allen Arizona Cowboy Museum,** in Willcox's historic district, was set up as a tribute to Willcox's most famous native son, cowboy singer Rex Allen, who now lives in Tucson (he comes back to his hometown the second week of every October for Rex Allen Days, which include an annual rodeo and other Western events). He starred in several rather average cowboy movies during the '40s and '50s for Republic Pictures, but he's probably most famous as the friendly voice that narrated Walt Disney nature films. Even if you're not a Rex Allen fan, you're likely to be interested by the old-timers who volunteer at the museum—a number of them knew Allen as a child—as well as by things like the glittery suits the star wore on tour (they'd do Liberace proud). In the back room, the Willcox Cowboy Hall of Fame, dedicated to the town's cattle drivers and rodeo riders, salutes the women as well as the men who worked the local circuit. ⊠ *155 N. Railroad Ave.,* ☎ *520/384–4583.* ☎ *$2.* ☉ *Daily 10–4.*

The **Willcox Commercial Store** (⊠ 180 N. Railroad Ave., ☎ 520/384–2448), less than a block down the street from the Rex Allen Cowboy Museum, was established in 1881; it's the oldest retail establishment in Arizona that's still operating in its original location. Locals like to boast that Geronimo used to shop here. Today it's a clothing store, with a large selection of western wear.

The Chamber of Commerce is home to the one-room **Museum of the Southwest,** which focuses on the Native American and military history of the area. You can see a rifle and sword belonging to relatives of Civil War general Orlando Willcox, for whom the town was named, though his only contact with it was a single ride-through on the train (his memoirs don't even mention a visit to Arizona). Across the parking lot, you'll see Stout's Cider Mill (on the frontage road to I–10), where everyone comes to pick up a high-rise apple pie. ⊠ *1500 N. Circle I Rd.,* ☎ *520/384–2272 or 800/200–2272.* ☎ *Free.* ☉ *Mon.–Sat. 9–5, Sun. 1–5.*

Lodging

$$ 🏨 **Muleshoe Ranch.** This former late-19th-century health spa is now run by the Arizona chapter of the Nature Conservancy. Accommodations vary—five furnished housekeeping casitas have kitchens or kitchenettes, baths, and linens, whereas one ($10) is more rustic—but all are in a beautiful natural setting on a dirt road. There's a visitor center, a nature trail, natural hot springs (for use by casita guests only), and a common room. ✉ *30 mi northwest of Willcox, R.R. 1, Box 1542, 85643,* ☎ *520/586–7072. 6 cabins. 2-night minimum Sept.–May and holiday weekends. No credit cards.*

Texas Canyon

⓫ *16 miles west of Willcox off I-10.*

A dramatic change of scenery along I-10 will signal that you're entering Texas Canyon. The rock formations here are exceptional—huge boulders appear to be delicately balanced against each other.

Texas Canyon is the home of the **Amerind Foundation** (a contraction of "American" and "Indian"), founded by amateur archaeologist William Fulton in 1937 to foster understanding about Native American cultures. The research facility and museum, built between 1930 and 1959, are housed in a Spanish colonial revival–style structure designed by noted Tucson architect H. M. Starkweather (the landmark Arizona Inn in Tucson is another example of his work).

The museum's rotating displays of archaeological materials, crafts, and photographs give an overview of Native American cultures of the Southwest and Mexico. The adjacent Fulton–Hayden Memorial Art Gallery displays an assortment of art collected by William Fulton. ✉ *Dragoon Rd., 1 mi southeast of I–10 (Exit 318),* ☎ *520/586–3666.* 🎟 *$3.* ☉ *Sept.–May, daily 10–4; June–Aug., Wed.–Sun. 10–4.*

Benson

⓬ *12 mi of west of Texas Canyon; 50 mi east of Tucson.*

Once the hub of the Southern Pacific Railroad and a stop on the Butterfield Stagecoach route, Benson has for many years been a fairly sleepy little town. If you walk up and down central 4th Street, you'll get a flavor for Benson's earlier days in such buildings as the **Hi Wo Company Grocery** (✉ 398 E. 4th St.), still owned by the descendants of the Chinese railroad worker–turned–entrepreneur who gave the store its name in 1896. One block south of 4th Street, the little **San Pedro Valley Arts and Historical Society Museum** (✉ Corner S. San Pedro Ave. and E. 5th St., ☎ 520/586–3070) has permanent and rotating displays relating to Benson's past.

With the start-up of the **San Pedro and Southwestern Railroad** in early 1995, Benson began to draw a few more visitors. The San Pedro and Southwestern Railroad's *Grey Hawk* began chugging out of Benson in the spring of 1994 and has since been making its way through the San Pedro Riparian National Conservation Area (☞ Sierra Vista, *above*) on a regular basis. It's the only motorized vehicle permitted to ride through the preserve; the outdoor panoramic car is a favorite with bird-watchers. The lively narration broadcast over the train's PA system helps flesh out the San Pedro Valley's colorful cast of boom-time characters, including the inhabitants of the ghost town of Charleston. **Charleston,** where the San Pedro train turns around, once saw more action than Tombstone, some 9 mi away. Outlaws Johnny Ringo and the Clanton brothers used to hang around the town's four 24-hour saloons, and Curley Bill Brocius, shot dead by Wyatt Earp, is said to be buried there, though no grave site was ever found. The *Grey Hawk* stops for an hour in the ghost town of **Fairbank,** during which time a three-piece western troupe entertains passengers while they eat lunch. You can order a barbecue meal, prepared by a nearby ranch, in advance, or bring your own food. The Bureau of Land Management is restoring Fairbank, the onetime rail and stagecoach stop; you can wander around a number of ramshackle buildings that date back to 1882, including a post office and a general store established by the Goldwater brothers, or hike to the ruins of a mill used to crush ore for the Tombstone mines. The four-hour round-trip departs from Benson's new depot. ⊠ *796 E. Country Club Dr.,* ☎ *520/586–2266 or 800/269–6314.* ✍ *$24. Trains run Thurs.–Sun. Call ahead for schedules.*

Recently, the town has begun annexing property along Highway 90 and building additional chain hotels in anticipation of the long-awaited opening of **Kartchner Caverns State Park,** delayed at least a year from the originally announced date of November 1997. Great precautions have been taken to protect this wet cave system, which includes two 100-ft-high chambers connected by 2½ mi of passageway, from destructive dryness and light. Very few people have been granted advance previews of the place, discovered by two Tucson cavers in 1974 and kept secret for years in order to protect it, but on the basis of the pictures published in the September 1995 issue of *Arizona Highways,* it promises to be spectacular. ⊠ *Take AZ 90 (exit 305 off I–10), 9 mi south to the cave entrance. For information about the opening date, contact the Benson–San Pedro Valley Chamber of Commerce (☞ Visitor Information in Southern Arizona A to Z, below).*

OFF THE
BEATEN PATH

SINGING WIND BOOKSHOP – As you pass through Benson on I-10, watch for Ocotillo Avenue, Exit 304. Take a left and drive about 2¼ mi, where a mailbox with a backward SW signals that you've come to the turnoff for Singing Wind Bookshop. Make a right at the mailbox and drive ¼ mi until you see a green gate. Let yourself in, close the gate, and go another ¼ mi to the store. If you don't see the proprietor, who also runs the ranch, ring the large gong out front and she's sure to come out and welcome you. This unique bookshop-on-a-ranch has a good selection of books on Arizona wildlife, history, and geology. ⊠ *Ocotillo Ave.,* ☎ *520/586-2425.*

Dining and Lodging

$ ✗ **Horseshoe Cafe.** For a good green-chili burrito or a patty melt, stop in at this funky café, which has occupied the same place on Benson's main street for more than 50 years. You know you're in cowboy country when you see the neon horseshoe on the ceiling, the macramés of local cattle brands, and the large Wurlitzer jukebox with its selection of sad C&W sounds. ⊠ *154 E. 4th St.,* ☎ *520/586–3303. MC, V.*

$$ ⊡ **Skywatcher's Inn.** You don't have to be an astronomer to enjoy stay-
★   ing at this bed-and-breakfast on the grounds of the private Vega-Bray Observatory. Even with the unaided eye, you'll marvel at the night sky that spreads out from this hilltop property near Benson; six powerful telescopes here, however, bring the universe even closer. The B&B, built in 1995 to accommodate the demands of sleepy stargazers, reflects the owners' delight in science: The comfortable rooms have gadgets like lightening lamps, and one has the constellations painted on the ceiling, visible in black light. During the day, you can peruse books, fossils, and minerals in a classroom, or gaze out at ducks swimming in one of three nearby ponds through a telescope in the breakfast room.

✉ *Astronomers Rd., 2 mi southeast of I–10 (Exit 306). Reservations:* ✉ *420 S. Essex La., Tucson 85711,* ☎ ℻ *520/745–2390. 1 room with shared bath (with daytime observatory guests), 2 suites. MC, V.*

SOUTHWEST ARIZONA

Many people just speed through southwest Arizona on their way to California, but the area has much to offer travelers willing to slow down for a closer look. The turbulent history of the West is writ large in this now-sleepy part of the state. It's home to the Tohono O'odham Indian Reservation (the largest in the country after the Navajo Nation's) and site of such towns as Ajo, created—and almost undone—by the copper-mining industry. Yuma, abutting the California border, was a major crossing point of the Colorado River as far back as the time of the conquistadors.

Natural history is also a lure in this starkly scenic region: Organ Pipe Cactus National Monument provides a number of trails for desert hikers, while birders and other nature watchers will revel in the many unusual species to be observed at two little-visited wildlife refuges: Buenos Aires abutting the Tohono O'odham Reservation and Imperial on the lower Colorado.

On warm weekends and especially during semester breaks, the 130-mi route from Tucson to Ajo is well traveled by cars headed southwest to Puerto Penasco (Rocky Point), Mexico, the closest outlet to the sea for Arizonans. Much of the time, however, one can go for long stretches west on AZ 86 without seeing another vehicle. A great part of the way the landscape is flat, abundant with low-lying scrub and cactus as well as mesquite, ironwood, paloverde, and other desert trees.

Buenos Aires Wildlife Refuge

⑬ *66 mi southwest of Tucson; from Tucson, take AZ 86 west 22 mi to AZ 286; go south 40 mi to milepost 8, and it's another 3 mi east to the preserve headquarters.*

This remote nature preserve, in the Altar Valley and encircled by seven mountain ranges, is the only place in the United States where a remnant of the vast Sonoran/savannah grasslands that once spread over the entire region can still be seen. The fragile ecosystem was almost completely destroyed by overgrazing, and a program to restore native grasses is currently in progress. But it was in order to save the masked bobwhite quail, formerly common here but thought to have become extinct, that the U.S. Fish and Wildlife Service purchased the Buenos Aires Ranch and its surrounding property in 1985; the ranch now serves as headquarters for the 115,000-acre preserve. Bird-watchers consider Buenos Aires unique because nowhere else in this country can you see a "grand slam" (four species) of quail: Montezuma, Gambel's, scalies, and masked bobwhite. If it rains, the 100-acre Aguirre Lake, 1½ mi north of the headquarters, attracts wading birds, shore birds, and waterfowl—in all, more than 250 avian species have been spotted here. They share the turf with deer, antelope, coatimundi, badgers, bobcats, and mountain lions. Treks to Brown Canyon, accessible only by guided tour, are held the second and fourth Saturday of every month ($3 per person). ✉ *Box 109, Sasabe, 85633,* ☎ *520/823–4251.* ✎ *Free.* ☉ *Preserve headquarters, Mon.–Fri. 7–3:30; visitor information office (in Arivaca, on the eastern side of the preserve) daily 8–2.*

Dining and Lodging

$$$$ ✕▥ **Rancho de la Osa.** This guest ranch, set on 250 eucalyptus-shaded acres five minutes from the Mexican border and abutting the Buenos Aires preserve, has—and has been visited by—a lot of history. The land

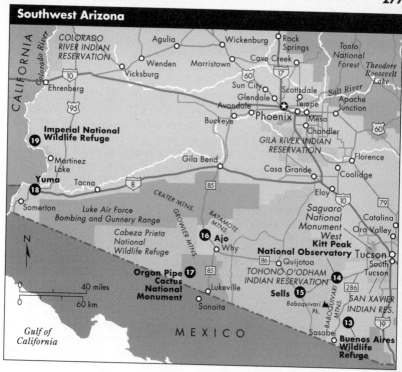

Southwest Arizona

was originally part of an 1812 grant made to the Ortiz brothers by the King of Spain; the central hacienda was built in 1889; and those who have stayed here since the 1920s, when two adobe structures were built to accommodate guests, have included Lyndon Johnson and Adlai Stevenson. The Undersecretary of State for International Affairs, while here recuperating from bronchitis, worked on the document that became known as the Marshall Plan. All rooms have wood-burning fireplaces, private entrances, and porches with Adirondack chairs. Bread baked on the premises, salads made with ingredients grown in the ranch's garden, and water drawn from the well on the property all contribute to the back-to-basics serenity of a stay here. Rates include all meals. ⊠ *1 La Osa Ranch Rd., Sasabe 85633,* ☎ *520/823–4257 or 800/872–6240,* ⅀⅀ *520/823–4238. 16 rooms. Restaurant, lounge, pool, spa, hiking, horseback riding, bicycles, billiards, library. D, MC, V.*

Kitt Peak National Observatory

⑭ *56 mi southwest of Tucson; to reach Kitt Peak from Tucson, take I–10 to I–19 south, and then AZ 86. After 44 mi on AZ 86, turn left at the AZ 386 junction and follow the winding mountain road 12 mi up to the observatory. (In inclement weather, contact the highway department to confirm that the road is open.)*

Funded by the National Science Foundation and managed by a group of more than 20 universities, Kitt Peak National Observatory is part of the Tohono O'odham Reservation. After much discussion back in the late 1950s, tribal leaders agreed to share a small section of their 4,400 square mi with the observatory's telescopes. Among these is the McMath, the world's largest solar telescope, which is cooled by piped-in coolant. From a visitors' gallery, you can see into the telescope's light-path tunnel, which goes down hundreds of feet into the mountain. In addition to the vital research into aspects of the sun carried out here, Kitt Peak scientists have also observed distant galaxies. The newest scope, Skywatch, installed in 1997, is likely to attract the most attention as the world's largest asteroid-hunting telescope: Someone here will know in advance if there's a giant piece of space debris hurtling towards Earth to demolish us. The scientists and staff are friendly and knowledge-able and keen to share their enthusiasm for astronomy.

The museum's visitor center has exhibits on astronomy and informa-tion about the telescopes at the facility. Free guided tours, which take about an hour, depart from the center daily at 10, 11:30, 1, and 2:30. Complimentary brochures enable you to take self-guided tours. There's a picnic area about 1½ mi below the observatory. Aside from vending machines in the observatory buildings, there's no place to get food or gas within 20 mi of Kitt Peak. In late 1996, the observatory began of-fering nightly stargazing dinner tours ($35 per adult) for up to 20 peo-ple; reservations should be booked as far in advance as possible. ⊠ *Kitt Peak National Observatory,* ☎ 520/318–8726; 520/318–7200 *for recorded message.* 🖃 *Suggested donation $2 per person.* ⊗ *Visi-tor center daily 9–3:45.*

Sells

🕔 *32 mi southwest of Kitt Peak via AZ 386 to AZ 86.*

The Tohono O'odham Reservation, the second largest in the United States, covers some 4,400 square mi between Tucson and Ajo, stretch-ing south to the Mexican border and north almost to the city of Casa Grande. To the south of Kitt Peak, the 7,730-ft Baboquivari Peak is considered sacred by the Tohono O'odham as the home of their deity, I'itoi ("elder brother"). A little less than halfway between Tucson and Ajo, Sells, the tribal capital of the Tohono O'odham, is a good place to stop for gas or a soft drink. If you want something more substan-tial, head for the Sells Shopping Center where you'll see **Basha's Deli & Bakery** (⊠ Topawa Rd., ☎ 520/383–2546). It's a good-size mar-ket and can supply all the makings for a picnic, including a picnic table near the store's entrance. Across the road from Basha's, **Margaret's Arts and Crafts** (⊠ Topawa Rd., ☎ 520/383–2800) sells baskets and other wares made on the reservation. You can also buy crafts at the **Turquoise Turtle** (⊠ AZ 86, near the Chevron Station, ☎ 520/383–2411). Much of the time there's little to see or do in Sells, but in winter an annual rodeo and fair attract thousands of visitors. For details about activi-ties on the reservation, contact the **Tohono O'odham Nation office** (☎ 520/383–2221).

En Route At Why, approximately 60 mi from Sells, AZ 86 forks off into the north and south sections of AZ 85. Originally the name of the community at this Y-shape intersection was spelled, simply and descriptively, "Y," but in 1950 the town was told that it had to have a three-letter name in order to be assigned a postal code. Hence the querulous appellation that has kept travelers wondering ever since.

Ajo

🕕 *90 mi northwest of Sells.*

"Ajo" (pronounced "*ah*-ho") is Spanish for garlic, and some say the town got its name from the wild garlic that grows in the area. Others claim the word is a bastardization of the Indian word "au-auho," re-ferring to red paint derived from a local pigment.

For many years Ajo, like Bisbee to the east, was a thriving Phelps Dodge Company town. Copper mining had been attempted in the area in the late 19th century, but it wasn't until the 1911 arrival of John Greenway, general manager of the Calumet & Arizona Mining Company, that the region began to be developed profitably. Calumet and Phelps Dodge merged in 1935, and the huge New Cornelia pit mine produced millions of tons of copper until the mine finally closed in 1985. With the town's main source of revenue gone, Ajo looked for a time as though it might shut down, but many retirees are now being lured here by the warm climate and low-cost housing.

At the center of town is a sparkling white Spanish-style plaza, designed in 1917 by Isabella Greenway, wife of the Calumet mine manager and an important figure in her own right: In the 1930s she opened the Arizona Inn in Tucson, and she was friends with such dignitaries as Eleanor Roosevelt. The shops and restaurants that line the plaza's covered arcade today are rather modest. Unlike Bisbee, Ajo hasn't yet drawn an artistic crowd—or the upscale boutiques and eateries that tend to follow.

You get a panoramic view of the town's huge open pit mine, almost 2 mi wide, from the **New Cornelia Open Pit Mine Lookout Point.** Some of the abandoned equipment remains in the pit, and various stages of mining operations are diagrammed at the visitors' ramada, where there's also a separate viewing area for a 30-minute film about Phelps Dodge's mining operations. ⊠ *Indian Village Rd.,* ☎ *520/387–7746.* ▨ *$1 suggested donation.* ☉ *Generally 10–4 in high season. Closed Sun. and May–Oct.*

The **Ajo Historical Society Museum** has collected a mélange of articles related to Ajo's past from local townspeople. The displays are rather disorganized, but some of the historical photographs and artifacts are fascinating, and the museum is inside the Territory-style St. Catherine's Indian Mission, built around 1916. ⊠ *160 Mission St.,* ☎ *520/387–7105.* ▨ *Free.* ☉ *Generally 10–4 Mon.–Sat., Sun. noon–4 in high season; call ahead to confirm. Closed May–Oct.*

The 860,000-acre **Cabeza Prieta National Wildlife Refuge,** about 10 minutes from Ajo, was established in 1939 as a preserve for endangered bighorn sheep and other Sonoran Desert wildlife. A permit is required to enter, and only those with four-wheel-drive vehicles, needed to traverse the rugged terrain, can obtain one. For additional information or for an entry permit, contact the **refuge office** (⊠ 1611 N. 2nd Ave., Ajo 85321, ☎ 520/387–6483).

Dining and Lodging

$ ✕ **Señor Sancho.** Just about everybody in Ajo comes to this unprepossessing roadhouse at the north end of town for generous portions of Mexican food, well prepared and very reasonably priced. This friendly spot has light-wood booths and colorful murals with a Mexican motif. All the standard favorites are on the menu—hearty combination platters, tacos, enchiladas, chili rellenos, flautas, and even a good chicken mole. ⊠ *663 N. 2nd Ave.,* ☎ *520/387–6226. No credit cards.*

$$–$$$ 🏨 **Mine Manager's House Inn.** Another remnant of the town's Phelps Dodge heyday, this 5,000-square-ft, 1919 mansion overlooks the entire town from its site atop the highest hill in Ajo. Full breakfasts are served on linens and fine china in the former mine superintendent's light-filled formal dining room. ⊠ *601 W. Greenway Dr., 85321,* ☎ *520/387–6505,* FAX *520/387–6508. 5 rooms. Hot tub, coin laundry. MC, V.*

$$ 🏨 **Guest House Inn.** Built in 1925 to accommodate visiting Phelps Dodge VIPs, this lodging is one of six Southwest "Bird 'n' Breakfast Fly-Inns": Guests can head out early to nearby Organ Pipe National Mon-

ument or just sit on the patio and watch the quail, cactus wrens, and other warblers that visit the Sonoran Desert. Rooms are furnished in a range of southwestern styles, from light Santa Fe to rich Spanish colonial. ✉ *3 Guest House Rd., 85321,* ☎ *520/387–6133. 4 rooms. AE, DC, MC, V.*

Organ Pipe Cactus National Monument

⓱   *32 mi southwest of Ajo; from Ajo, backtrack to Why and take AZ 85 south for 22 mi to reach the visitor center.*

Anyone interested in exploring the flora and fauna of the Sonoran Desert should head for Organ Pipe Cactus National Monument, abutting Cabeza Prieta National Wildlife Refuge (☞ Ajo, *above*) but much more accessible to visitors. The monument is the largest gathering spot north of the border for organ pipe cacti. These multiarmed cousins of the saguaro are fairly common in Mexico but rare in the States. Because they tend to grow on south-facing slopes, you won't be able to see many of them unless you take one of the two scenic loop drives, the 21-mi **Ajo Mountain Drive** or the 53-mi **Puerto Blanco Drive**, both on winding, graded dirt roads. The latter trail, which takes half a day to traverse, brings you to Quitobaquito, a desert oasis with a flowing spring. ✉ *Rte. 1,* ☎ *520/387–6849.* ✐ *$4 per vehicle.* ☉ *Visitor center daily 8–5.*

Yuma

⓲   *170 mi northwest of Ajo.*

Many people tend to think of Yuma as a convenient en route stop—these days, between San Diego and Phoenix or Tucson—and this was equally true in the past. It's difficult to imagine the lower Colorado River, now dammed and bridged, as either a barrier or a means of transportation, but up until the early part of the century, this section of the great waterway was a force to contend with. Records show that since at least 1540 the Spanish were using Yuma (then the site of a Quechan Indian village) as a ford across a relatively shallow juncture of the Colorado.

Some three centuries later, the advent of the shallow-draft steamboat made the settlement a point of entry for fortune seekers heading up through the Gulf of California for mining sites in eastern Arizona. Fort Yuma was established in 1850 to guard against Indian attacks, and by 1873 the town was a county seat, a U.S. port of entry, and an army quartermaster depot. The building of the Yuma Territorial Prison in 1876 helped stabilize the economy.

The steamboat shipping business, undermined by the completion of the Southern Pacific Railroad line in 1877, was finished off by the building of Laguna Dam in 1909, which controlled the overflow of the Colorado River and made agricultural development in the area possible. In World War II, Yuma Proving Ground was used to train bomber pilots, and General Patton readied some of his desert war forces for battle at a number of classified areas near the city. Many people who served here during the war returned to Yuma to retire, and the city's economy now relies largely on tourism. According to weather statistics, the sun shines more on Yuma than on any other U.S. city.

Most of the interesting sights in Yuma are at the north end of town. Stop in at the **Convention and Visitors Bureau** (✉ 377 S. Main St., ☎ 520/783–0071) and pick up a walking-tour guide to the historic downtown area. Stop by the **Arizona Historical Society Museum,** housed in the Century House. This adobe structure, built around 1870 and once owned by prominent businessman E. F. Sanguinetti, exhibits artifacts from Yuma's territorial days and details the military presence in the area. ⊠ *240 S. Madison Ave.,* ☎ *520/782–1841.* ☞ *Free.* ☉ *Tues.– Sat. 10–4.*

If you cross the railroad tracks at the northernmost part of town, you'll come to **Yuma Crossing National Historic Landmark,** which consists of the Quartermaster Depot, the Territorial Prison, and Fort Yuma. The mess hall of Fort Yuma, later used as a school for Indian children, now serves as the small **Fort Yuma Quechan Indian Museum.** Historical photographs, archaeological items, and Quechan arts and crafts are on display. ⊠ *On CA 24, 1 mi north of town,* ☎ *619/572– 0661.* ☞ *$1.* ☉ *Weekdays 8–5, Sat. 10–4.*

On the other side of the river from Fort Yuma, the quartermaster depot, created toward the end of the Civil War period, was responsible for resupplying army posts to the north and east. Freight brought upriver by steamboat was unloaded here and distributed by wagon overland to Arizona forts. The depot's earliest building (1853), which originally served as the home of riverboat captain G. A. Johnson, is the centerpiece of the **Yuma Crossing State Historic Park.** The various other roles the residence served—including a weather bureau and home for customs agents—are also detailed on the guided tour through the house. The entire quartermaster complex was closed until the fall of 1997, when it reopened as a state park. Full details of the project were not available at press time, but the surrounding warehouses will display the various types of transportation that had their impact on Yuma, including a replica of the first biplane that flew into the area. ⊠ *4th Ave. between 1st St. and the Colorado River Bridge,* ☎ *520/ 329–0471.* ☞ *$3.* ☉ *Daily 8–5.*

The most notorious tourist sight in town, **Yuma Territorial Prison** was built largely by the convicts who were incarcerated here from 1876 until 1909, when the prison outgrew its usefulness. The hilly site on the Colorado River, chosen for security purposes, precluded further expansion.

Visitors gazing today at the tiny cells that held six inmates each, often in 115°F heat, are likely to be appalled, but the prison was once considered a model of enlightenment: In an era when beatings were common, the only punishments meted out were solitary confinement and assignment to a dark cell. The complex housed a hospital as well as the only library in Yuma, open to the public. The 25¢ fee charged townspeople for a prison tour financed the acquisition of new books. The inmates' food was sufficiently varied and plentiful to inspire locals to dub the place the Country Club of the Colorado.

The 3,069 people who served time at this penal institution, the only one in the Arizona Territory during its tenure, included men and women from 21 different countries. They came from all social classes and were sent up for everything from armed robbery and murder to violation of the Mexican Neutrality Act and polygamy. R. L. McDonald, incarcerated for forgery, had been the superintendent of the Phoenix public school system. Chosen as the prison bookkeeper, he absconded with $130 of the inmates' money when he left. Pearl Hart, convicted of stagecoach robbery, gained such notoriety for her crime that she attempted a career in vaudeville after her release.

The site of the former mess hall opened as a museum in 1940, and the entire prison complex was designated a State Historic Park in 1961. ⊠ *Near Exit 1 off I–8,* ☎ *520/783–4771.* ☞ *$3. Free interpretive programs at 11, 2, and 3:30.* ☉ *Daily 8–5.*

The 40-acre **Saihati Camel Farm** is at the far southern end of town. The landscape near Yuma inspired Saudi Arabia native Abdul-Wahed Saihati to raise and breed his favorite animals here along with more exotic desert-loving breeds, such as oryx (antelope) and wildcats. It's fun to help feed the well-groomed, friendly dromedaries—not a biter or spitter among 'em—and to see some rare animal species, many of them purchased from the San Diego Zoo. ⊠ *15672 S. Ave. 1 E (between County 15th and County 16th Sts.),* ☎ *520/627–2553.* ☒ *Guided tours $3.* ⊙ *Guided tours Mon.–Sat. at 10 and 2, Sun. at 2. Reservations advised.*

Dining and Lodging

$ ✕ **Chretin's Mexican Food.** A Yuma institution, Chretin's opened as a dance hall in the 1930s before it became one of the first Mexican restaurants in town in 1946. Don't be put off by the nondescript exterior or the entryway, which leads back past the kitchen and cashier's stand into three large dining areas. The food is all made on the premises, right down to the chips and tortillas. Try anything that features *machaca* (shredded spiced beef or chicken). ⊠ *485 S. 15th Ave.,* ☎ *520/782–1291. D, MC, V. Closed Sun.*

$ ✕ **Lutes Casino.** Almost always packed with locals at lunchtime, this large, funky restaurant and bar claims to be the oldest pool hall and domino parlor in Arizona. It's a great place for a burger and a brew. ⊠ *221 S. Main St.,* ☎ *520/782–2192. Reservations not accepted. No credit cards.*

$$–$$$ ☒ **Radisson Suites Inn.** One wing of this sprawling hostelry surrounds a well-manicured courtyard with a fountain and several orange trees; another faces the pool and Cabana Club, where the complimentary Continental breakfast and happy-hour drinks are served. This is an all-suites property, and each accommodation has a separate sitting area with a desk, and such amenities as an in-room coffeemaker and microwave. ⊠ *2600 S. 4th Ave., 85364,* ☎ *520/726–4830 or 800/333–3333,* ᡃᴬˣ *520/341–1152. 164 suites. Lobby lounge, refrigerators, pool, hot tub, coin laundry, airport shuttle. AE, D, DC, MC, V.*

$$ ☒ **Best Western Coronado Motor Hotel.** This Spanish tile–roof lodg-
★   ing, convenient to both the freeway and downtown historical sights, was built in 1938 and is run by the son of the original owner. Bob Hope used to stay here during World War II, when he entertained the gunnery troops training in Yuma. The rooms have such extras as irons and ironing board, microwaves, hair dryers, and modem phone jacks. Breakfast is included. ⊠ *233 4th Ave., 85364,* ☎ *520/783–4453 or 800/528–1234,* ᡃᴬˣ *520/782–7487. 86 rooms. Restaurant, lobby lounge, refrigerators, in-room VCRs, pool, coin laundry. AE, D, DC, MC, V.*

Imperial National Wildlife Refuge

⑲   *40 mi north of Yuma; from Yuma, take U.S. 95 north past the Proving Ground and follow the signs to the refuge.*

Guided tours (☞ Southern Arizona A to Z, *below*) are the best way to visit the 25,765-acre Imperial National Wildlife Refuge, created by backwaters formed when the Imperial Dam was built. Something of an anomaly, the refuge is home both to species indigenous to marshy rivers and to creatures that inhabit the Sonoran Desert, which lines its banks here—desert tortoises, coyotes, bobcats, and bighorn sheep. Most of all, though, this is bird-lovers' heaven. Thousands of waterfowl and shorebirds live here year-round, and migrating flocks of swallows pass through in the spring and fall. During those seasons, expect to see everything from pelicans and cormorants to Canada geese, snowy egrets, and a variety of rarer species. Canoes can be rented at Martinez Lake Marina, 3½ mi southeast of the refuge headquarters. It's best to visit from mid-October through May, when temperatures are lowest and the ever-present mosquitoes are least active. The well-marked Painted Desert Nature Trail, about a mile long, takes you through the different levels of the Sonoran Desert. As we went to press, the trail leading to the water was not yet completed, but from an observation tower at the visitor center you can see the river, as well as the fields being planted with rye and millet, on which the migrating birds like to feed. ⊠ *Red Cloud Mine Rd., Box 72217, 85365,* ☎ *520/783–3371.* 🎟 *Free.* ☉ *Visitor center mid-Apr.–mid-Oct., weekdays 8–4:30; rest of yr, weekdays 8–4:30, weekends 9–4.*

SOUTHERN ARIZONA A TO Z

Arriving and Departing

By Air

You'll need to rent a car to tour most of Southern Arizona. The best plan is to fly into Tucson, which is the hub of the area, or Phoenix, which has the most flights, and pick up a car at the airport.

SIERRA VISTA

America West (☎ 800/235–9292) has regular flights from Phoenix to the Libby Army Airfield at Fort Huachuca (⊠ 2100 Airport Ave., ☎ 520/459–8575).

YUMA

America West Express (☎ 800/235–9292) has direct flights to Yuma International Airport (⊠ 2191 32nd St., ☎ 520/726–5882) from Phoenix. **Sky West** (☎ 800/453–9417), a Delta subsidiary, flies nonstop from Los Angeles.

By Bus

SOUTHEASTERN ARIZONA

Greyhound Lines (☎ 800/231–2222) has service from Tucson (⊠ 2 S. 4th Ave., ☎ 520/792–3475) to the stations in Benson (⊠ 242 E. 4th St., ☎ 520/586–3141) and Willcox (⊠ 622 N. Haskell Ave., ☎ 520/384–2183). The line uses **Bridgewater Transport** (⊠ 445 W. 2nd St., ☎ 520/628–8909) in Tucson for its runs to Bisbee (⊠ 7 Okay St., ☎ 520/432–5359), Douglas (⊠ 538 14th St., ☎ 520/364–2233), and Sierra Vista (⊠ 28 Fab Ave., ☎ 520/458–3471). You'll need to book a tour if you want to take the bus to Tombstone.

SOUTHWESTERN ARIZONA

The **Ajo Stage Line** (☎ 800/242–9483) runs buses three times a week from Tucson and four times a week from Phoenix to Ajo. You can get to the bus station in Yuma (⊠ 170 E. 17th Pl., ☎ 520/783–4403) from a variety of directions via **Greyhound Lines** (☎ 800/231–2222).

By Car

SOUTHEASTERN ARIZONA

From Tucson, take I–10 east. When you come to Benson, take U.S. 80 south to reach Tombstone, Bisbee, and Douglas. If you want to go to Sonoita and Patagonia, or just take a pretty drive, turn off I–10 earlier, at the exit for AZ 83 south; you'll come to Sonoita where this road intersects AZ 82 and from there you can either continue on south to Patagonia or head west to Tombstone.

SOUTHWESTERN ARIZONA

Ajo lies on AZ 85 (north–south), Yuma at the junction of I–8 and U.S. 95. For a scenic route to Ajo from Tucson (126 mi), take AZ 86 west to Why and turn north on AZ 85. Yuma is 170 mi from San Diego on I–8, and it is 300 mi from Las Vegas on U.S. 95.

By Train

Amtrak (☎ 800/872–7245) trains run three times a week from Tucson east to the Benson depot (✉ 4th St. at San Pedro Ave.) and west to Yuma (✉ 281 Gila St.). Both are unstaffed stations with no phones.

Getting Around

You can see much of what you'd want to see in Bisbee, Tombstone, Ajo, and Patagonia by strolling around, but wheels are still an advantage in almost all of Southern Arizona's towns.

By Bus

The **Bisbee Bus** (☎ 520/432–2285) line, operated by Catholic Community Services, has a 1½-hour-long route in and around Bisbee. Buses, which cost 60¢, run Monday through Friday from 6:50 AM to 6:10 PM; there's wheelchair lift equipment.

Sierra Vista Public Transit (☎ 520/459–0595), also under the aegis of the Catholic Community services, charges $1 for the general public. Buses operate Monday through Friday 6:30–6:30, Saturday 8:30–4:30.

By Taxi

SOUTHEASTERN ARIZONA

You can phone **Benson Taxi** (☎ 520/586–7688) to get around. For a cab in Bisbee, call **Sun Arizona Taxi** (☎ 520/432–7899). In Sierra Vista, **Angel Transport** (520/458–0027) is reliable.

SOUTHWESTERN ARIZONA

Ajo Stage Lines (☎ 520/387–6467) operates as a taxi service in town.

Friendly Taxi Service (☎ 520/783–1000) and **Yuma City Cab** (☎ 520/782–0111) have the newest, cleanest taxis in Yuma.

Contacts and Resources

Camping and Hiking

Destinet (☎ 800/280–CAMP) handles reservations for many of the local campgrounds, but unless you know which one you want in advance, phoning is an exercise in frustration: There's no way to get through to a real person on the automated phone system.

SOUTHEASTERN ARIZONA

Douglas Ranger District (✉ R.R. 1, Box 228-R, Douglas 85607, ☎ 520/364–3468) and the **Sierra Vista Ranger Station** (✉ 5990 S. Hwy. 92, Hereford, 85615, ☎ 520/378–0311) can give you information about camping and hiking in the Coronado National Forest, which covers most of the mountain ranges in southeastern Arizona.

SOUTHWESTERN ARIZONA

Contact the Bureau of Land Management's **Yuma District Office** (✉ 3150 Winsor Ave., Yuma 85365, ☎ 520/726–6300) for details about outdoor recreational activities.

Car Rentals

The following car-rental companies are represented at Yuma International Airport: **Avis** (☎ 520/726–5737); **Budget** (☎ 520/344–1822); and **Hertz** (☎ 520/726–5160).

Emergencies

Call 911 to reach the **fire department, police,** and **emergency medical services.**

Bisbee Copper Queen Hospital (✉ 101 Cole St., ☎ 520/432–5383). **Benson Hospital** (✉ 450 S. Octollo St., ☎ 520/586–2261). **Sierra Vista Community Hospital** (✉ 300 El Camino Real, ☎ 520/458–4641). In Willcox, **Northern Cochise Community Hospital** (✉ 901 Rex Allen Dr., ☎ 520/384–2720).

For medical problems go to **Ajo Community Health Center** (✉ 410 Malacate St., ☎ 520/387–5651) or **Yuma Regional Medical Center** (✉ 2400 S. Avenue A, ☎ 520/344–2000). The drugstores in most southern Arizona towns shut down at around 5 PM. Yuma, where the following pharmacies stay open until at least 9 on the weekdays, is an exception: **Super Kmart** (✉ 2375 W. 32nd St., ☎ 520/344–0856); **Smith's** (✉ 500 W. 24th St., ☎ 520/782–2529); **Payless** (✉ 600 W. Catalina Dr., ☎ 520/726–7810); **Walgreen's** (✉ 1150 W. 8th St., ☎ 520/783-6834; ✉ 3121 S. 4th Ave., ☎ 520/344–0453).

Guided Tours

BIRD-WATCHING

The **Southeastern Arizona Bird Observatory** (✉ Box 5521, Bisbee 85603, ☎ 520/432–1388) offers a wide array of avian-oriented activities year-round.

RIVER TOURS

You can take a boat ride up the Colorado with **Yuma River Tours** (✉ 1920 Arizona Ave., Yuma 85364, ☎ 520/783–4400). Twelve- to 45-person jet-boat excursions are run by Smokey Knowlton, who has been exploring the area for more than 36 years.

TRAIN EXCURSIONS

The **San Pedro and Southwestern Railroad's** *Grey Hawk* (☎ 520/586–2266 or 800/269–6314) travels through the San Pedro National Riparian Conservation Area (☞ Benson, *above*).

On Saturdays and Sundays from October through June, you can take a two-hour round-trip jaunt on the **Yuma Valley Railway** (☎ 520/783–3466). The 1922 coach, pulled by one of two historic diesel engines, departs at 1 PM from the 8th Street station in Yuma and runs south alongside the Colorado River for about 11 mi. Tickets cost $10.

Visitor Information

SOUTHEASTERN ARIZONA

Benson–San Pedro Valley Chamber of Commerce (✉ 226 E. 4th St., Box 2255, Benson 85602, ☎ 520/586–2842), open Monday–Friday 9–6, Saturday 9–5. **Bisbee Chamber of Commerce** (✉ 7 Main St., Box BA, Bisbee 85603, ☎ 520/432–5421), open Monday–Friday 9–5, Saturday–Sunday 10–4. **Douglas Chamber of Commerce** (✉ 1125 Pan American, Douglas 85607, ☎ 520/364–2477), open Monday–Friday 9–5, Saturday 10–2. **Patagonia Visitors Center** (✉ Box 241, 315 McKoewn Ave., 85625, ☎ 520/394–0060), open Wednesday–Monday 10–5. **Sierra Vista Chamber of Commerce** (✉ 21 E. Willcox, Sierra Vista 85635, ☎ 520/458–6940 or 800/288–3861), open Monday–Friday 8–5, Saturday 9–1. **Tombstone Office of Tourism** (✉ Box 917, Tombstone 85638, ☎ 520/457–3421 or 800/457–3423). **Tombstone Chamber of Commerce and Visitor Center** (✉ 4th and Allen St., ☎ 520/457–3929), open daily 9–5. **Willcox Chamber of Commerce & Agri-**

culture (⊠ 1500 N. Circle I Rd., Willcox 85643, ☎ 520/384–2272 or 800/200–2272), open Monday–Saturday 9–5, Sunday 1–5.

SOUTHWESTERN ARIZONA

The **Ajo Chamber of Commerce** (⊠ AZ 85, just south of the plaza, 321 Taladro, Ajo 85321, ☎ 520/387–7742), open Monday–Saturday 9–4 most of the year but closes down for part of the summer. The **Yuma Convention and Visitors Bureau** (⊠ 377 S. Main St., Box 11059, Yuma 85366, ☎ 520/783–0071), open Monday–Friday 9–5.

9 Portraits of Arizona

*The What and the Why
of Desert Country*

The Native Southwest

Books and Videos

THE WHAT AND THE WHY
OF DESERT COUNTRY

ON THE BRIGHTEST and warmest days my desert is most itself because sunshine and warmth are the very essence of its character. The air is lambent. A caressing warmth envelops everything in its ardent embrace. Even when outlanders complain that the sun is too dazzling and too hot, we desert lovers are prone to reply, "At worst that is only too much of a good thing."

Unfortunately, this is the time when the tourist is least likely to see it. Even the winter visitor who comes for a month or more is likely to choose January or February because he is thinking about what he is escaping at home rather than of what he is coming to here. True, the still-warm sun and typically bright skies make a dramatic contrast with what he has left behind. In the gardens of his hotel or guest ranch, flowers still bloom and some of the more obstreperous birds make cheerful sounds, even though they do not exactly sing at this season. The more enthusiastic visitors talk about "perpetual summer" and sometimes ask if we do not find the lack of seasons monotonous. But this is nonsense. Winter is winter, even in the desert.

At Tucson's elevation of 2,300 feet it often gets quite cold at night, even when shade temperatures during the day rise to 75°F or higher. Most vegetation is pausing, though few animals hibernate. This is a sort of neutral time when the desert environment is least characteristic of itself. It is almost like late September or early October, just after the first frost, in southern New England. For those who are thinking of nothing except getting away, rather than learning to know a new world, this is all very well. But you can't become acquainted with the desert itself at that time of year.

By April the desert is just beginning to come into its own. The air and the skies are summery without being hot; roadsides and many of the desert flats are thickly carpeted with a profusion of wildflowers such as only California can rival. The desert is smiling before it begins to laugh, and October and November are much the same. But June is the month for those who want to know the true desert. That is the time to decide once and for all if it is, as for many it turns out to be, "your country."

It so happens that I am writing this not long after the 21st of June, and I took special note of that astronomically significant date. This year, summer began at precisely 10 hours and no minutes, mountain standard time. That means that the sun rose higher and stayed longer in the sky than on any other day of the year. In the north there is often a considerable lag in the seasons as the earth warms up, but here, where it is never very cold, the longest day and the hottest are likely to coincide pretty closely. So it was this year. On June 21 the sun rose almost to the zenith so that at noon it cast almost no shadow. And it was showing what it is capable of.

Even in this dry air, 109°F in the shade is pretty warm. Under the open sky the sun's rays strike with an almost physical force, pouring down from a blue dome unmarked by the faintest suspicion of even a fleck of cloud. The year has been unusually dry (even for the desert). During the four months just past, no rain—not even a light shower—has fallen. The surface of the ground is as dry as powder. And yet, when I look out of the window, the dominant color of the landscape is an incredible green.

On the low foothills surrounding the steep rocky slopes of the mountains, which are in fact 10 to 12 miles away but in the clear air seem much closer, this greenness ends in a curving line following the contour of the mountains' base, inevitably suggesting the waves of a green sea lapping the irregular shoreline of some island rising abruptly from the ocean. Between me and that shoreline the desert is sprinkled with hundreds, probably thousands, of evenly placed shrubs, interrupted now and then by a small tree—usually mesquite or what locals call a cat's-claw acacia.

More than a month ago all the little perennial flowers and weeds, which spring up after winter rains and rush from seed to flower and to seed again in six weeks, gave up the ghost at the end of their short lives. Their hope of posterity lies now invisible, either upon the surface of the bare ground or just below it. Yet even when summer thunderstorms come in late July or August, these seeds will not make the mistake of germinating. They are triggered to explode into life only when they are both moist and cool—which they will be February or March when their season comes again. Neither the shrubs nor the trees seem to know that no rain has fallen during these long months. The leathery, somewhat resinous leaves of the dominant shrub—the attractive plant unattractively dubbed creosote bush—are not at all parched or wilted. Nor are the deciduous leaves of the mesquite.

Earlier in the year the creosote was covered with bright yellow pealike flowers, the mesquite with pale yellow catkins. Now the former is heavy with gray seed and on the mesquite are forming long pods that Indians once ate and that cattle now find an unusually rich food.

It looks almost as though the shrubs and trees could live without water. But of course they cannot. Every desert plant has its secret, though not always the same one. In the case of mesquite and creosote it is that their roots go deep and that, below 6 feet, there is no wet or dry season in the desert. What little moisture is there is pretty constant throughout the year, in dry years as well as wet. Like the temperature in some caves, it never varies. The mesquite and creosote are not compelled to care whether it has rained for four months or not. And unlike many other plants, they flourish whether there has been less or more rain than usual.

Plants with substantial root systems that do not reach very deep are more exuberant some years than others. Thus the Encelia, the brittlebush, which in normal years literally covers many slopes with thousands of yellow, daisylike flowers, demands a normal year. Though I have never seen it fail, I am told that in very dry years it comes into leaf but does not flower, whereas in really catastrophic droughts it does not come up at all, as the roots lie dormant and hope for better times. Even the creosote bush, which never fails, profits from surface water, and when it gets the benefit of a few thunderstorms in late July or August, it will flower and fruit a second time, sprinkling the desert expanse once again with yellow. . . .

On such a day as this, even the lizards, so I have noticed, hug the thin shade of the bushes. If I venture out, the zebratails scurry indignantly away, the boldly banded appendages that give them their name curved high over their backs. But I don't venture out very often during the middle of the day. It is more pleasant to sit inside where a cooler keeps the house at a pleasant 80°F. And if you think that an advocate of the simple life should not succumb to a cooler, it is you rather than I who is inconsistent. Even Thoreau had a fire in his cottage at Walden, and it is no more effete to cool oneself in a hot climate than it is to get warm before a stove in a cold one. The gadget involved is newer, but that is all.

In this country "inclemency" means heat. One is "sunbound" instead of snowbound, and I have often noticed that the psychological effect is similar. It is cozy to be shut in, to have a good excuse for looking out of the window or into oneself. A really blazing day slows down the restless activity of a community very much as a blizzard does in regions that have them. Where there is either, a sort of meteorological sabbath is usually observed even by those who keep no other.

OBVIOUSLY the animals and plants that share this country with me take it for granted. To them it is just "the way things are." By now I am beginning to take it for granted myself. But being a man, I must ask what they cannot: What *is* a desert, and why is it what it is? At 32° latitude one expects the climate to be warm. But the desert is much more than merely warm. It is a consistent world with a special landscape, a special geography, and, to go with them, special flora and fauna adapted to that geography and that climate.

Nearly every striking feature of this world, be it the shape of the mountains or the habits of its plant and animal inhabitants, goes back ultimately to the grand fact of dryness—the dryness of the ground, of the air, of the whole sum total. And the most inclusive cause of dryness is the simple lack of rain.

Some comparisons with wetter regions may bring that into sharper focus. Take, for example, southern New England. By world standards it gets a lot—namely some 40 inches—of rain per year. Certain southern states get even more: about 50 inches for east Tennessee, nearly 60 for New Orleans. Some areas on the West Coast get fantastic amounts, like the 75 inches at Crescent City, California, and the unbelievable 153 inches—nearly four times what New York City gets—recorded one year in Del Norde County, California.

Nevertheless, New England's 40 is a lot of water, either comparatively or absolutely. The region around Paris, for instance, gets little more than half that amount. Forty inches is, in absolute terms, more than most people imagine. One inch of rain falling on an acre of ground means more than 27,000 gallons of water. No wonder irrigation in dry regions is a formidable task even for modern technology.

In terms of vegetation, 40 inches is ample for the kind of agriculture and natural growth that we tend to think of as "normal." It means luxuriant grass, rapid development of second-growth woodland, a veritable jungle of weeds and bushes in midsummer. In inland America, rainfall tends to be less than in coastal regions. Moving west from the Mississippi, it declines sharply and begins to drop below 20 inches a year at about the 100th meridian or, very roughly, at a line drawn from Sioux Falls, South Dakota, through Oklahoma City. This means too little water for most broad-leafed trees and explains why the southern Great Plains were as treeless when the white man first saw them as they are today.

OUR TRUE DESERTS lie farther west still: the Great Basin Desert in Utah and Nevada, the Chihuahuan in New Mexico, the Sonoran in Arizona, and the Mohave in California. The four differ among themselves but they are all arid, and they all fulfill what is probably the most satisfactory definition of "desert": namely, a region where the ground cover is not continuous—where the earth remains bare of vegetation between the plants that manage to grow. Over these American deserts rainfall varies considerably, and with it the character and extent of vegetation. In southern Arizona, for instance, there are about 4 inches of rain at Yuma, nearly 11 around Tuc-

son. Four inches means sand dunes that look like pictures of the Sahara that the word "desert" calls to most people's minds. Eleven means that where soil is suitable, well-separated individuals of such desert plants as cacti and paloverde trees will flourish.

But if scant rainfall makes for deserts, what makes for scant rainfall? To that there are two important answers. One is simply that most nonmountainous regions tend to be dry if they lie in that belt of permanently high atmospheric pressure extending some 30 or 35 degrees on each side of the equator where calms are frequent and winds erratic. Old sailors used to call this region "the horse latitudes," though nobody knows exactly why. (You can take your choice of three equally unconvincing explanations. One is that horses tended to die on ships lying long in the hot calms. Another: The boisterous changeableness of winds when they do come suggests unruly horses. A third is that they were originally named after an English explorer, Ross, whose name Germans mistook for their old word for "horse.") In any event, Tucson falls within the "horse latitudes." Most of the important deserts of the world, including the Sahara and the Gobi, lie within this belt.

Mountains lying across the path of moist winds also make for scant rainfall. In our case, the Coast Ranges of California lie between us and the Pacific. From my front porch, which looks directly across the desert to some of the southernmost Rockies, I can see, on a small scale, what happens. So many times a moisture-laden mass of air reaches as far as these mountains. Dark clouds form, and sometimes the whole range is blotted out. Torrential rain is falling—but not a drop on me. Either the sky is blue overhead or the high clouds that have blown my way dissolve before my eyes as they reach warm air rising from the sun-drenched flats. I live in what geographers call a "rain shadow" cast by the mountains. At their summit rainfall is nearly twice as much as it is down here, and as a result they are clothed with pines from 6,000 or 7,000 feet right up to the 9,000-foot peak. When I do get rain in midwinter and midsummer, it is usually because winds have brought moisture up from the Gulf of Mexico by an unobstructed southern route, or because in summer a purely local thundershower has formed out of hot air rising from the sun-beaten desert floor. Most of the time the sun is hot, even in winter, and the air is usually fantastically dry, the relative humidity being often less than 10.

NATURALLY the plants and animals living in such a region must be specially adapted to survive under such conditions, but the casual visitor usually notices the strangeness of the landscape before he is aware of flora or fauna. Peculiar features of the landscape are also the result of dryness, even in ways that are not immediately obvious.

The nude mountains reveal their contours, or veil them as lightly as late Greek sculptors veiled their nudes, because only near the mountaintops can anything grow tall enough to obscure the outlines. A little less obvious is the fact that the beautiful "monuments" of northern Arizona and southern Utah owe their unusual forms to the sculpting of windblown sand—or that sheer cliffs often rise from a sloping cone of rocks and boulders because there is not enough draining water to break them down and distribute them over the surrounding plain as they would be distributed in regions with heavier rainfall. But the most striking example of all is the greatest single scenic wonder of the region, the Grand Canyon itself. This narrow gash, cut a mile deep through so many strata that the river now flows over some of the oldest rock exposed anywhere on earth, could have been formed only in a very dry climate. As recently as 200 years ago the best-informed observer would have taken it for granted that the river was running between those sheer walls at the bottom of the gorge simply because it had found them out. Today few visitors are not aware that the truth is the other way around, that the river cut its own course through the rock. But most laymen do not ask the next questions: Why is the Grand Canyon unique, or why are such canyons, even on a smaller scale, rare? The answer to those questions is that a set of very special conditions was necessary.

First, there must have been a thick series of rock strata slowly rising during a period when a considerable river flowed over it. Second, that considerable river must have carried an unusual amount of hard sand or stone fragments in suspension so that it could cut downward at least as rapidly as the rock over which it flows rose. Third, that considerable river must have coursed through very arid country. Otherwise rain, washing over the edges of the cut, would widen it at the top as the cut went deeper. That is why broad valleys are characteristic of regions with normal rainfall and canyons require arid country.

And the Grand Canyon is the grandest of all canyons because at that particular place all the necessary conditions were fulfilled more exactly than at any other place. The Colorado River carries water from a relatively wet country through a dry one, it bears with it a fantastic amount of abrasive material, the rock over which it flows has been slowly rising during several millions of years, and too little rain falls to rapidly (in geological time) widen the gash that it cuts. Thus in desert country everything from the color of a mouse or the shape of a leaf to the largest features of mountains is more likely than not to have the same explanation: dryness.

So far as living things go, all this adds up to what even an ecologist may call, forgetting himself for a moment, an "unfavorable environment." But like all such pronouncements, this one doesn't mean much unless we ask "unfavorable for what and for whom?" For many plants, for many animals, and for some people it is very favorable indeed. Many of the first two would languish and die if transferred to some region where conditions were "more favorable." It is here, and here only, that they flourish. Likewise, many people feel healthier and happier in the bright dry air than they do anywhere else. And since I happen to be one of them, I not unnaturally have a special interest in the plants and animals that share my liking for just these conditions. For many years now I have been amusing myself by inquiring of them directly what habits and what adjustments they have found most satisfactory. Many of them are delightfully ingenious and eminently sensible. . . .

IHAVE LIVED in this house and been lord of these few acres for nearly five years, and the creatures who share the desert with me have already summed me up as a softy and have grown contemptuously familiar. It is not only that the cactus wrens sit on the backs of my porch chairs. The round-tailed ground squirrels—plain, sand-colored, chipmunk-like animals—are digging rather too many burrows rather too close about the house. The jackrabbits—normally the most timid as well as the fleetest of creatures—take nibbles at the few plants I have set out and refuse to leave off until I arrive shouting and waving my arms a few feet from where they are. Sooner or later something may have to be done to discourage this impudent familiarity, but for the present I am getting some good looks at creatures who usually don't wait to be looked at. Yesterday, for instance, I saw what at first I thought was a bird eating seeds from the upper branches of a creosote bush. It turned out to be a ground squirrel belying his name by climbing several feet above ground among the slender swaying branches of the creosote to eat the small fuzzy seeds. This is doubtless no addition to Knowledge with a capital K. But it is an addition to my knowledge, and that is the next best thing. I like to investigate such matters for myself when I can. "What on earth do they live on?" is a common question from those newcomers not too egotistical to notice that creatures other than those of their own kind do live here somehow. Obviously "creosote seeds" is one answer so far as the ground squirrel is concerned.

People of many races have been known to speak with scorn of those who live where nature makes things easy. In their inclement weather, the stoniness of their soil, or their rigorous winters, they find secret virtues to make even a thing like London fog praiseworthy. Making a virtue out of necessity is not itself a virtue. But there may be something of value in that process. We grow strong against the pressure of a difficulty and test our ingenuity by solving problems. Individuality and character are developed by challenge. We tend to admire trees, as well as people, who bear the stamp of success from struggles with adversity. People who have not had too easy a time of it develop character. And there is no doubt about the fact that desert life has character. Plants and animals are so clearly what they are because of the problems they have solved. They are part of some whole. They belong. Animals and plants, as well as people, become especially interesting when they fit their environment, when to some extent they reveal what their response to it has been. And nowhere more than in the desert do they reveal it.

–Joseph Wood Krutch

Joseph Wood Krutch (1898—1970), one of America's noted natural-history writers, contributed to *The Nation* for many years as a drama and literary critic and lived his last 18 years outside Tucson. *The Voice of the Desert*, from which this essay was excerpted, *Grand Canyon*, and *Henry David Thoreau* are among Krutch's 21 books.

THE NATIVE SOUTHWEST

CONSIDERING THE ARIDITY of the Southwest, the tremendous cultural productivity of its native civilizations is a fascinating case of people turning the challenges of nature into a meaningful existence. Within the compass of the state of Arizona, Native American pottery and cliff dwellings are the most apparent evidence of this. In fact, they are isolated phenomena on a vast trade route that spanned from the Pacific coast all the way to Mesoamerica, an area in which not only goods, but pottery-making techniques, agricultural technologies, and spiritual beliefs were transmitted.

Some 4,000 years ago—at least 8,000 years after humans crossed the Bering Strait land bridge that once allowed passage on foot between Asia and North America—a major transition in cultures around the world saw people shifting from nomadic hunting-and-gathering lifestyles to more settled agricultural existence. In the southwest, ancient pioneers brought the practice of cultivating corn, squash, and beans north from Mesoamerica. One group in particular, the Hohokam, is believed to have fostered this. In an area straddling the Arizona-New Mexico border, the Hohokam developed a highly productive system. Some archaeologists believe that they migrated from northwestern Mexico with knowledge of planting, growing, and irrigating. Others picture an evolution of Archaic peoples who gradually took on Mesoamerican practices. Either way, they had great success and in turn influenced their northern and eastern neighbors for more than a thousand years. Their artisans produced ritual objects, jewelry, and stone and ceramic wares with great skill. They regularly traded with Mesoamerican tribes, and Pacific-coast exchange brought in raw materials for their own and other regional artisans.

The flowering of Hohokam culture began around 2,300 years ago. The period of their growth, expansion, and eventual decline, when they began to take new ideas in from the north, lasted about 1,500 years— twice as long as the Roman Empire. During that time, they cultivated corn, beans, squash, agave, and cotton, using remarkable irrigation methods. Some of their networks of canals stretched three miles from the Salt and Gila rivers to planted fields. Their contact with Mesoamerican cultures periodically brought new strains of corn to the Southwest along with religious beliefs, ritual practices, and the ball game and ball courts well known from the Maya. The Hohokam culturally fertilized the region, providing a base for the Pueblo culture that has survived into the modern era.

The Mogollon (pronounced mo-go-*yone*) were another group, occupying an area stretching from eastern-central Arizona into New Mexico from 2,000 to 500 years ago. They took on Hohokam and so-called Anasazi cultural patterns, but they never fully embraced an agricultural lifestyle. They became skillful potters, especially those living near the Mimbres River. Their contact with the Anasazi resulted in the production of some of the Southwest's most outstanding pottery. The principle Mimbres Mogollon site is now the Gila Cliff Dwellings National Monument in New Mexico.

Romanticized, mythicized, and perhaps misunderstood, the so-called Anasazi left wondrous architectural remains, most notably at Mesa Verde in Colorado, Chaco Canyon in New Mexico, and Canyon de Chelly, Betatakin, and Keet Seel in Arizona. Composed of various groups living around the Four Corners area, they have generated the most intense interest. For centuries they lived seminomadically, hunting, gathering, and marginally cultivating corn, squash, and beans. They eventually settled into villages and adopted much of the Hohokam culture, more than their Mogollon neighbors did.

These various Ancestral Pueblo peoples were not pueblo dwellers yet, however. They were slow to establish year-round communities. Perhaps they weren't convinced that the Hohokam model would work in their rugged, dry canyonlands. With fewer and smaller rivers, they couldn't irrigate on the Hohokam scale. About 1,500 years ago the Pueblo cultural pattern called Anasazi began to take shape, owing, perhaps, to the introduction of a new, more productive strain of corn.

Ancestral Pueblo peoples made a significant contribution to southwestern culture with their architecture. Their remarkable stone masonry evolved out of a pithouse style used by Archaic peoples. A precursor of the kiva, the pithouse was constructed around a shallow, circular dugout with mud walls packed around vertical pole supports. The new stone-and-mortar houses, on the other hand, were very often rectangular in plan. In small communities they were built on a scale to house groups of a few families. These groups would have individual clan *kivas* (the Hopi word for underground ceremonial chambers) or single great kivas.

The soaring cliff dwellings of Canyon de Chelly, Betatakin, Keet Seel, and Mesa Verde represented another type of settlement, more protected from the elements and, perhaps, raiders. Villagers cultivated the land around them. All of these communities had kivas, ritual spaces central to the lives of deeply spiritual people.

Ancestral Pueblo culture reached its height about 1,000 years ago. Hitherto Puebloans had continued to refine their use of water, not actually irrigating, but using sporadic rainfall to the greatest advantage. They would line stones across slopes and cut ditches to distribute rainfall and limit erosion. Occasionally they dug canals in order to channel rainwater into planted fields. Unquestionably, they were expert dry farmers, coaxing abundance out of a harsh environment.

At the time of this climax, some people began moving from smaller, widespread communities into larger, denser settlements—perhaps like today's migrations to cities. The volume of trade in nearly all directions was tremendous, and Pueblo artisans were making superb pottery. Decorative techniques varied from region to region: black-on-white, black-on-red, black-on-orange, red-on-orange, and expressive combinations of these. People also etched petroglyphs into, and painted pictograms onto, rock faces. Rock art is found at almost all Anasazi and Sinagua sites. The quantity of artifacts that they left behind—utility and ceremonial items alike—is unparalleled among Native North American groups.

Around 850 years ago, a cultural decline began. Drought and climatic change put pressure on the Pueblos' settled, agricultural lifestyles. Longer winters shortened growing seasons in which less rain fell. Villagers continued to move to more productive areas. By the late 1200s, Canyon de Chelly was unoccupied. Chaco Canyon had been vacant for 100 years. Settlements at Wupatki continued a little longer, into the 1300s. The Hopi Mesas, on the other hand, first built in the 1100s, were growing. They absorbed some of their migrating neighbors, and their traditions testify to their assimilation of ancient Pueblo culture.

There are also a great number of transitional settlements, many yet to be excavated, that accommodated groups leaving the immediate Four Corners area. Some of them are quite substantial. Considering these transitional settlements, what used to be a question of a culture simply disappearing can now take a more human shape. The Anasazi didn't vanish—they chose to move. Over a couple of centuries they gradually migrated to new locations, slightly altering their lifestyles. (For some of them, that may have been part of a centuries-old practice.) In the process they passed on their knowledge to the people they joined: the Hopi, the New Mexican Zuñi, the Acoma, and other Pueblos. The Zuñi perspective on this migration is telling. As opposed to archaeologists' causes—drought, climatic change, deforestation, disease, warfare—they see it as a process of searching for "the center place," a place of spiritual rightness. And that center place is where present-day Pueblos are living.*

THE SINAGUA, their name meaning "without water" in Spanish, belonged to a diverse group called the Hakataya, spread out across central Arizona. Wupatki, Walnut Canyon, Tuzigoot, and the inappropriately named Montezuma Castle are all Sinagua sites. These people absorbed Hohokam, Mogollon, and Anasazi cultural patterns: agriculture, village life, and the Mesoamerican ball game; stone masonry and cliff-dwelling architecture; and pottery.** Situated in the middle of these three groups, they became a composite but separate culture.

As the so-called Anasazi waned, Hopi and Navajo cultures grew. The Navajo, an Apachean group from the north, gradually migrated southward along the Rocky Mountains about 5,000 years ago and settled in unoccupied places around Pueblo villages. Hunting and gathering were just about all that the land would support for them. Over time they learned farming techniques from the Pueblos and traded with them and as a result took on a character distinct from other Apachean groups, such as the 19th-century Chiracahua and Mescalero Apache. Living in small, dispersed groups, Navajos also raided Pueblo farms and villages—a practice in retrospect notoriously Apachean.

Soon after the Navajo came the Spanish, invading the Southwest early in the 16th century. Unlike Anglo-European conquerors, they allowed elements of native cultures to survive, provided that they accept a transfusion of Catholicism and alien governance. Of course, their intrusion into southwestern life was far from cordial. Their first contact was with New Mexican Pueblos, whose understandable lack of interest in accepting Spanish rule met with the sword. Pueblo retaliation brought further hostility from the invaders, who murdered hundreds of natives and destroyed villages.

The Spanish didn't have the chance to overrun the Apacheans, whose scattered settlements were more difficult to locate than were pueblos. After the Pueblo Revolt of 1680, which drove the Spanish away, only to have them return 12 years later, the Navajo periodically housed Pueblos seeking refuge from reprisals. In return, the Pueblos taught them rituals, customs, agricultural techniques, and arts—in some of which, like weaving, they eventually surpassed their teachers. In the 1700s, drought led many Hopis to seek refuge among the Navajo in the formerly vacated Canyon de Chelly—a poignant example of the long-standing cooperative relationship of the two groups.

The Navajo also picked up European skills, some of them from the Pueblos. Directly from the Spanish they learned about silversmithing, raising cattle, and riding horses—and they became superior horsemen. Horses extended their gathering range and gave them greater mobility for trading and raiding. The Navajo were not nomadic, however. Many of them had different seasonal residences, log-and-earth hogans, as they continue to do today. These are maintained as permanent dwellings.

After independent Mexico ceded New Mexico to the United States in 1848, the Southwest's new proprietors decided to put an end to Indian raids. Over the next 16 years U.S. troops and the Navajo clashed repeatedly. The United States set up army posts within Navajo territory. They attempted to impose treaties, but U.S. agents often arranged treaties with individual headmen who had no authority that the Navajo as a whole could accept.

This misunderstanding of Navajo organization had tragic results. When raids continued, the U.S. territorial governor believed he had been betrayed. In order to safeguard the so-called frontier, he called in Colonel Kit Carson to destroy Navajo crops and livestock. Over the next few months, the People, as the Navajo call themselves, began to give themselves up. In 1864, as many as 8,000 Navajo made the forced Long Walk to captivity in Fort Sumner, 300 miles to the southeast.***

The People were allowed to return to their land after four years of concentration-camp life. Fewer in number and greatly demoralized, they had to reconstruct their lives from scratch, rebuilding customs and lifestyles that had been impossible, if not forbidden, in the camps. Since then, Navajo ingenuity and an impressive ability to seize opportunities have gained them a measure of success in modern America. Their democratically governed community—Navajo Nation—numbers more than 250,000.

THE HOPI didn't suffer such brutality. After conflicts with the Spanish—at the end of which they destroyed their own Christianized village of Awatovi in order to maintain the purity of Hopi ritual—their largely noncombative stance with the U.S. government afforded the Hopi more or less hands-off treatment.

In their proper observance of tradition and ritual the Hopi are unique even among traditional Native Americans. In fact it was to Hopi spiritual leaders that many Native American traditionalists turned in the 1950s in what eventually became the Indian Unity Movement. Hopi beliefs focus on the relationship between the people, the land, and the Creator. In this strict moral order, prayer and ritual—which include the kachina rain power being dances—are necessary to keep the natural cycle in motion and to ensure the flow of life-sustaining forces. The earth is sacred, and they are its keepers.

The Hopi may well be the best dry farmers on the planet, successfully harvesting crops on a precarious 8 to 15 inches of rain per year—and no irrigation. Doubtless they manage this because they have perfected ancient Ancestral Pueblo techniques. The mesas on which they chose to live contain precious aquifers, particularly essential to life in such an arid territory. These vast water sources no doubt sustained them and their migrant guests when Pueblo peoples left places like Wupatki and Walnut Canyon and Canyon de Chelly 700 years ago. Unfortunately, the Hopi Tribal Council, which represents the progressive Christianized members of the Hopi, has sold sacred land to strip miners who in turn have destroyed parts of Black Mesa and depleted the aquifer. This is one indication of the rift at Hopi between modernizers and those who continue to practice traditional ways. The traditionalists reside in the villages of Oraibi, Hotevilla, and Shun-gapovi. They are, understandably, intolerant of whites. They follow the Hopi Way even as contemporary life and the Tribal Council pose ever greater threats to it.

The present-day Tohono O'odham (called Papago by the Spanish) and the Pima, in central-southern Arizona, are descendants of the Hohokam. The Spanish first encountered them in the 17th century cultivating former Hohokam territory, using some of the ancient irrigation canals. Both tribes are Pimans, and both continue some Hohokam practices: living in rancherías along canals and performing costume dances and other rituals that link them to Uto-Aztecan language groups nearby in Mexico. The Pima live on the Salt River Reservation south of Phoenix, and the Tohono O'odham reservation stretches north from the Mexican border.

Like the Southwest's history, perspectives on Native American cultures are complex and fascinating—and have become confused in the clash of Euro-American and Native American ways. Take, for example, the enchanting and mysterious word *Anasazi,* which enters into almost any discussion of native Arizonans. This Navajo word, meaning both "ancient ones" and "enemy ancestors," automatically implies a Navajo perspective. Another of equal value is that of the Hopi, whose name for the ancient culture, *Hisatsinom,* means "people of long ago." Yet another perspective is that of the New Mexican Zuñi, who prefer the word *Enote:que,* "our ancient ones, our ancestors." *

To scientifically trained Euro-American archaeologists, the term *Anasazi* conveniently groups together a variety of ancient Pueblo peoples who had similar lifestyles but often divergent adaptations to southwestern conditions. In past decades researchers encouraged the myth of a lost Anasazi civilization and posed virtually unanswerable questions about who the people were and how and why they "vanished" from the scene. Had they taken the beliefs and statements of the Hopi and of New Mexican Pueblos seriously—acting as both archaeologists and anthropologists—the *Hisatsinom- Enote:que-Anasazi* would have fit seamlessly into the continuity of Native American life.

The perspective we can never know is that of the Ancestral Pueblos themselves—we don't even know what language they spoke. Yet we can try to get a sense of their worldview by listening to contemporary Pueblos. If we project their uniquely American customs into the past, aspects of their ancestral culture come to life. And while Western tradition has its own ancient echoes, such as "know yourself" or "love your neighbor," traditional Pueblo ways speak of a life balanced in its relationship with the earth.

Sources

Ancient Ruins of the Southwest: An Archaeological Guide. David Grant Noble. Flagstaff: Northland Publishing Co., 1981.

Indian Country. Peter Mathiessen. New York: The Viking Press, 1984.

***The Navaho.* Clyde Kluckhon and Dorothea Leighton. Cambridge, Mass.: Harvard University Press, 1974.

**Those Who Came Before: Southwestern Archaeology in the National Park Sys-*

tem. Robert H. Lister and Florence C. Lister. Flagstaff, Ariz.: Southwestern Parks and Monuments, 1983.

* What Happened to the Anasazi? Why Did They Leave? Where Did They Go? A Panel Discussion at the Anasazi Heritage

Center. Jerold G. Widdison, ed. Albuquerque: Southwest Natural and Cultural Heritage Association, 1990.

–Stephen Wolf

Stephen Wolf is a staff editor at Fodor's.

BOOKS AND VIDEOS

Books

Essays and Fiction

Going Back to Bisbee, by Richard Shelton, *Frog Mountain Blues,* by Charles Bowden, and *The Mountains Next Day,* by Janice Emily Bowers, are all fine personal accounts of life in southern Arizona. The hipster fiction classic *The Monkey Wrench Gang,* by Edward Abbey, details an ecoanarchist plot to blow up Glen Canyon Dam. *Stolen Gods,* a thriller by Jake Page, is set largely on Arizona's Hopi reservation and in Tucson. Three novels by Tucson-based writers skillfully evoke the interplay between Native American culture and contemporary Southwest life: *Pigs in Heaven,* by Barbara Kingsolver, *Almanac of the Dead,* by Leslie Marmon Silko, and *Yes Is Better Than No,* by Byrd Baylor. Wild West adventure, with all of the mythological glory that Hollywood has tried to capture, abounds in Zane Grey's novels—buy a new copy or look for any of the charming illustrated hardcover editions in used- or out-of-print bookstores. Tony Hillerman's mysteries will put you in an equally southwestern mood.

General History

Arizona Cowboys, by Dane Coolidge, is an illustrated account of the cowboys, Indians, settlers, and explorers of the early 1900s. Buried-treasure hunters will be inspired by *Lost Mines of the Great Southwest,* by John D. Mitchell, which is just enough of a nibble to start you sketching maps and planning strategy. First printed back in 1891, *Some Strange Corners of Our Country,* by Charles F. Lummis, takes readers on a century-old journey to the Grand Canyon, Montezuma Castle, the Petrified Forest, and other Arizonan "strange corners." For a dip into the backroads of the past, try *Arizona Good Roads Association Illustrated Road Maps and Tour Book,* a 1913 volume, replete with hotel ads, reprinted by Arizona Highways magazine. *Roadside History of Arizona,* by Marshall Trimble, will bring you up to date on many of the same thoroughfares. *Ghost Towns of Arizona,* by James E. and Barbara H. Sherman, gives historical details on the abandoned mining towns that dot

the state and provides maps to find them. For an anthology that covers the entire state's literature, consult *Named in Stone and Sky: An Arizona Anthology,* edited by Gregory McNamee.

Native American History

Two books provide excellent surveys of the ancient and more recent Native American past and cover in more depth sites mentioned in this guidebook. *Those Who Came Before: Southwestern Archaeology in the National Park System,* by Robert Lister and Florence Lister, provides a well-researched and completely accessible summary of centuries of life in the region informed by both contemporary Indian and archaeological perspectives. David G. Noble's *Ancient Ruins of the Southwest* covers similar territory more briefly and portably and includes directions for driving to sites. *Hohokam Indians of the Tucson Basin,* by Linda Gregonis, offers an in-depth look at this prehistoric tribe. In *Hopi,* by Susanne Page and Jake Page, the daily, ceremonial, and spiritual life of the tribe is explored in detail. Study up on the history of Hopi silversmithing techniques in *Hopi Silver,* by Margaret Wright. The beautifully illustrated *Hopi Indian Kachina Dolls,* by Oscar T. Branson, details the different ceremonial roles of the colorful Native American figurines. Navajo homes, ceremonies, crafts, and tribal traditions are kept alive in *The Enduring Navajo,* by Laura Gilpin. Navajo legends and trends from early days to the present are collected in *The Book of the Navajo,* by Raymond F. Locke.

A superb collection of Native American stories, songs, and poems, *Coming to Light,* edited by Brian Swann, includes material from all over the country, not only the Southwest.

Natural History

A Guide to Exploring Oak Creek and the Sedona Area, by Stewart Aitchison, provides natural-history driving tours of this very scenic district. In *100 Desert Wildflowers in Natural Color,* by Natt N. Dodge, you'll find a color photo and brief description of each of the flowers included. Also written by Natt N. Dodge, *Poisonous Dwellers of the Desert* gives precise information on both venomous and non-venomous creatures of the Southwest. *Cacti of the Southwest,* by W. Hubert Earle, depicts some of the best-known species of the region with color photos and descriptive material. For comprehensive information on Grand Canyon geology, history, flora and fauna, plus hiking suggestions, pick up *A Field Guide to the Grand Canyon,* by Steve Whitney. *Common Edible and Useful Plants of the West,* by Muriel Sweet, gives the layperson descriptions of medicinal and other plants and shrubs, most of which were first discovered by Native Americans. *Roadside Geology of Arizona,* by Halka Chronic, is a good resource for finding the causes of the striking natural formations you'll see throughout the state.

Crafts

The Traveler's Guide to American Crafts: West of the Mississippi, by Suzanne Carmichael, gives browsers and buyers alike a useful overview of Arizona's traditional and contemporary handiwork.

General Interest

Arizona Highways, a monthly magazine, features exquisite color photography of this versatile state. Useful general travel information, fine pictures, and well-written historical essays all make *Arizona,* by Larry Cheek, a good pretrip resource.

Videos

The Arizona landscape has starred in a slew of films either as itself or as a stand-in for similar terrain—the Sahara Desert, for instance—around the world. Parts of the Kevin Costner comedy *Tin Cup* (1996) were shot in Tubac. Much of director John Woo's bombastic *Broken Arrow* (1995), starring John Travolta and Christian Slater, was shot around Marble Canyon, which was also used, along with the Page/Lake Powell area, in the Mel Gibson–Jodie Foster vehicle *Maverick* (1994). Tom Hanks trotted through Monument Valley and Flagstaff in *Forrest Gump* (1994). The Tucson area served as the backdrop for much of *Boys on the Side* (1994), starring Whoopi Goldberg, Drew Barrymore, and Mary-Louise Parker. The nouveau westerns *Tombstone* (1993), starring Val Kilmer and Kurt Russell, and Sharon Stone's *The Quick and the Dead* (1995) both made use of various sites in Mescal. Woody Harrelson and Juliet Lewis raged

through Holbrook, Winslow, and other towns in *Natural Born Killers* (1994), and the Yuma area was used to otherworldly effect in the science-fiction film *Stargate* (1994). Yuma stands in for a lot of places, including Morocco in the Joseph von Sternberg's *Morocco* (1930), starring the sultry Marlene Dietrich, and the Bob Hope comedy *Road to Morocco* (1942).

The famous canyon loomed large in *Grand Canyon* (1991), starring Kevin Kline, Steve Martin, and Danny Glover. The independent cult hit *Red Rock West* (1991), directed by John Dahl and starring Nicolas Cage, was filmed in Willcox and other southeastern Arizona locales. Cage also starred, with Holly Hunter, in *Raising Arizona* (1987). Footage for the Joel Coen–directed film was shot in Scottsdale, Phoenix, and other locations. Chevy Chase frolicked through the Grand Canyon, Monument Valley, and Flagstaff in *National Lampoon's Vacation* (1983). Clint Eastwood stared down all comers in *The Outlaw Josey Wales* (1976), which showcases Patagonia and Mescal. Italian director Michelangelo Antonioni's *Zabriskie Point* (1968) includes scenes of Carefree and Phoenix. Marilyn Monroe dropped in on Phoenix in *Bus Stop* (1956). Gerd Oswald's noirish *A Kiss Before Dying* (1955), starring Robert Wagner and Joanne Woodward, filmed in Tucson. Parts of *The Bells of St. Mary's* (1954) take place in Old Tucson. Some Arizona locations worked better than the real thing in Fred Zinnemann's *Oklahoma!* (1954). Jean Harlow whooped it up as a harried movie superstar in Victor Fleming's very funny *Bombshell* (1933), which has scenes shot in Tucson proper.

Among the many classic westerns shot in Arizona are *The Searchers* (1956), *She Wore a Yellow Ribbon* (1949), *Fort Apache* (1948), and *Stagecoach* (1939), all directed by John Ford and starring John Wayne, both of whom spent a lot of time filming in the state over the years; *Gunfight at the OK Corral* (1957), starring Burt Lancaster and Kirk Douglas; *Johnny Guitar* (1954), director Nicholas Ray's Freudian take on the Old West that features Joan Crawford in a gender-bending performance as a tough-gal gunslinger; director Howard Hawks's moody *Red River* (1948), which stars John Wayne and Montgomery Clift; and Ford's *My Darling Clementine* (1946), in which Henry Fonda plays a reluctant sheriff.

INDEX

WHEREVER YOU TRAVEL, *H*ELP IS NEVER FAR AWAY.

From planning your trip to

providing travel assistance along

the way, American Express®

Travel Service Offices are

always there to help

you do more.

http://www.americanexpress.com/travel

American Express Travel Service Offices are located throughout
Arizona. For the office nearest you, call 1-800-AXP-3429.

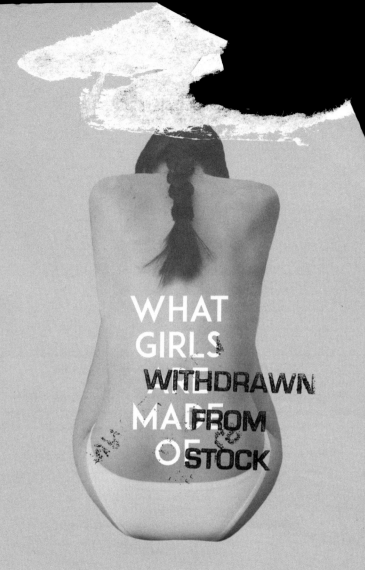

WHAT GIRLS ARE MADE OF

WITHDRAWN FROM STOCK

ELANA K. ARNOLD

ANDERSEN PRESS

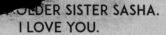

...LDER SISTER SASHA.
I LOVE YOU.

This edition first published in 2018 by
Andersen Press Limited
20 Vauxhall Bridge Road
London SW1V 2SA
www.andersenpress.co.uk

2 4 6 8 10 9 7 5 3 1

First published in 2017 in the USA by Carolrhoda Lab
This edition published by arrangement with Carolrhoda Books, a division of Lerner Publishing
Group, Inc, 241 First Avenue North, Minneapolis 55401, USA.

British Library Cataloguing in Publication Data available.

ISBN 978 1 78344 771 8

MIX
Paper from
responsible sources
FSC® C012700

Printed and bound in Great Britain
by Clays Limited, Bungay, Suffolk, NR35 1ED